WomenSaints
365 Daily Readings

Madonna Sophia Compton

with Maria Compton Hernandez
and Patricia Campbell

A Crossroad Book
The Crossroad Publishing Company
New York

The Crossroad Publishing Company
16 Penn Plaza—481 Eighth Avenue
New York, NY 10001

This book is set in 12/14 Perpetual
The display type is Lilith

Printed in the United States of America

Library of Congress Cataloging-in-Publication data is available.

ISBN 10: 0-8245-2413-6
ISBN 13: 978-0-8245-2413-5

1 2 3 4 5 6 7 8 9 10   12 11 10 09 08 07 06

Contents

Acknowledgments

I want to thank Bishop Kallistos Ware for his encouragement and support in undertaking this project. Maria and I want to thank our mother, Trudy, for her dedicated, awesome love and support. I want to offer my deep gratitude to Mother Susanna and all of the dear sisters at Our Lady of Kazan monastery; I learned so much from you. Thanks to Cheryl Beaver-Peterson and Fr. Leo Joseph for their proofing and suggestions. Thanks also to Sister Nonna Harrison and Brother Seraphim for their valuable input. Thanks to all of the many wonderful women at Lydia's House for holding the vision of a truly ecumenical Church, and for living out that vision. During the early stages of this project, Patricia lost her husband, Bill, to cancer. We offer this as a testimony of love to him and to all the saints who go before us and continue to support us in our journey home.

"Here is the patience and faith of the saints." *Rev. 13:10*

Introduction

Part One: On Women Saints from Various Traditions

Women have been a source of inspiration since time immemorial. Jung said that the feminine element is the "anima" or "soul of the world." Although many inspiring books have been written in honor of great women heroines, reformers, poets, authors, teachers, politicians, and philosophers, this book attempts to focus on women whom the Christian world recognizes as "saints," that is, women whose lives were not only monumental but holy. Although St. Paul called all who belong to Jesus Christ saints (Rom. 1:7), the term *saints* has come to designate a particular holiness. These are women whose lives were sacred, that is, set apart from the profane. The sacred life is set apart because it represents a state that strives to be more than human, and in its imitation of Christ this life is thus always in exile in a world that has turned from God. Women saints participate in God's grace and divine life while still striving in a human body. In the early monastic tradition, those who embraced an ascetic lifestyle were called angels.

Lives of women saints are quite popular today—both in academic circles, which attempt to understand the history of how women saints cultivated and experienced their relationship with the sacred; and with aspirants, who strive to see in these women a model for developing their own sanctity. Why do these women's holy lives—

especially those women living in an era so different from our own—continue to hold so much power and meaning for us? Although they may have led lives very different from our own, they are not merely legends left over from a prior era, ghosts of a time when women seemed to find meaning in self-denigrating and mortifying rituals that we struggle to understand today. Rather, they seem to generate interest because of some unifying principle that we ourselves experience as women, one that reflects a timeless need to encounter a deeper experience with God's love in Christ. They remind us that although they endured their own private agonies, they also managed to become living embodiments of God's grace and to function as heralds in the society in which they lived. We find strength in their stories as we realize that we too are on the same path to freedom through intimacy with our God and through a deeper understanding of our own personal mission in the world.

Such women were in the religious life as well as married, although historically the Church has raised up far more women religious to the official status of canonization. This trend is changing in all the churches and reflects a healthy and holistic movement of inclusivity. It is important to note, however, that in earlier generations, choosing cloister did not eliminate most of the basic freedoms for women, as it did for men. A woman often found that, while family life kept her disempowered from connecting with her inner creativity (because of the prevalent traditions of those times), monastic life opened an opportunity for her to become educated, to write, to study the arts, to learn calligraphy, and so on. More than this, since (until recently) there was seldom a role for female theologians and scholars in the Church—and in particular, in married life—it was often the only avenue for a woman to *speak*: whether it was a prophetic or mystic voice, a call for reform of church or state, or a call to counsel. If we see a prevailing theme (so frequently, one tends to think of it as almost archetypal) in these stories of the woman who would do almost anything to avoid an early marriage, this is clearly one reason why. Surrounded by their sisters in monastic life, these women could find a haven wherein they could transcend the limitations of their gender and more readily assert the validity of their own experience. Many realized their visions by starting their own orders or establishing their own monastic rules.

In researching women's lives during more than a decade of teaching graduate school, I nurtured a growing desire to investigate these women's lives in an attempt to understand them better, and eventually, to reclaim and compile a women's history of holiness. I began the work assisted by a graduate student, Patricia Campbell, and then I asked my sister Maria to join the project. Among the three of us, we represent the Roman, Orthodox, and Anglican traditions. Although we have different approaches to our material, and represent different sides of the Church's political dimensions, we were all enthusiastic about the format outlined here, which includes daily Bible readings, reflections, and prayers.

As Fr. McBrien has noted, in his excellent ecumenical book *Lives of Saints*, "The task of reconstruction and reclamation is not only historical and theological, but also liturgical. . . . The stories of women saints need to be recognized, proclaimed and then appropriately celebrated." In the past, the Church's saints and major feast days were celebrated through reading the Divine Office, or Breviary, which was a Christian journey through the "wheel of the year." Adding prayers and an antiphon (a short scriptural reflection that can be memorized and recalled throughout the day) is our attempt to bring sacred time into profane time, that is, to make an abbreviated liturgical breviary of women saints for each day of the year. This provides an opportunity for a woman to take a few minutes out of each busy day and reflect, in a prayerful way, on the path another woman before us has taken in her journey home to God. Through the saints, bonds of charity are forged that find expression in liturgical praise.

All Christian churches seek to invoke God's divine presence through a variety of practices, including prayer, sacraments, singing, and ritualized posture or performance. The Roman and Orthodox traditions, as well as some parts of the Anglican communion (sometimes called Anglo-Catholic), include artistic representations of Christ, Mary, and the saints through the ritualized use of icons and statues. Unlike many post-Reformation churches, these churches utilize the power of images, particularly icons and beautiful paintings, to transform our experience and deepen our spiritual understanding. In honoring this practice, we have included the many Marian feast days that address her through different iconographic cults. All three major sacramental churches have a Divine Liturgy and a Divine Office which celebrate their churches' saints, and we have used saints from all traditions in compiling our women's history of holiness.

Nonetheless, when undertaking the task of writing a book of daily readings dedicated to women saints, I was initially concerned about whether it would be possible to find 365 women to include. Even if my colleagues and I represented more than one religious tradition, it seemed a daunting task. As many others have noted in writing women saints' biographies over the past two decades, male saints are represented far more than female saints in all liturgical calendars. In the Roman, Orthodox, and Episcopal church calendars, males outnumber females more than four to one. In the Roman church, in optional memorials that bracket women who were once traditionally celebrated in the Canon of the Mass (such as Agatha, Lucy, and Perpetua, to name but a few), the numbers shrink even further, although these women continue to be celebrated in the Orthodox liturgies.

The non–Roman Catholic churches, while filling in the gaps, are still woefully gender-imbalanced. Women comprise 18 percent of the Episcopal, 15 percent of the Lutheran, and about 25 percent of the Russian Orthodox liturgical calendars. However, the Anglican church has recently included a liturgical book often used in Divine Office services called *Celebrating the Saints*, which supplements their sanctoral *Lesser Feasts and Fasts* in many places, and these readings include a number of more modern women now recognized as saints. *Celebrating the Saints* also includes numerous women of other Protestant denominations, which I found to be a truly ecumenical approach to shaping a liturgical calendar. We gathered all the traditional women saints in the modern Roman calendar, as well as saints celebrated in the Franciscan calendars (which honor numerous Franciscan women not celebrated elsewhere), and combined them with a number of more modern religious figures, some of whom have not yet been canonized. As we added the many major and minor feasts of women celebrated in the daily Divine Offices of all the Orthodox churches combined, we saw the numbers begin to build. We decided to retell the biographies of women who had been dropped from the calendar after Vatican II, as well as the group of saintly women known as the Beguines (women in the Middle Ages who formed communities that produced many mystics who were never officially canonized). Finally, by including a list of little-known Celtic saints and other saints celebrated in small local cults around the world, we one day discovered that we had a full list.

Next came an even more daunting task: arranging the women to correspond with the proper dates. I feel confident that some of our date placements will puzzle some of our readers, especially those who wonder why we did not stick to one calendar. Because there are so many women with dates that coincided, however, leaving many other days empty, we finally had to settle on using the "old calendar dates" (Roman, Celtic, Byzantine, and Russian) in some cases, in other cases preserving the new calendar dates. The decision was at times rather arbitrary. In a few cases we assigned a date to a woman because the date was empty, but most of the time—especially in the case of Protestant women—we tried to celebrate her life on the date of her birth or death. We apologize in advance if some of these date placements, especially the feast days of Mary, are confusing or disappointing to some of our readers.

One of the most tragic aspects of our Christian history is that battles have been fought over altering liturgical calendars. Wars were waged and councils were called and still there remained splits and gaping wounds in all of the churches. And in some places (such as Russia), these wounds still fester. Perhaps the reason is that sacred time, like sacred space, produces an archetypal form of consciousness which coalesces into structures that we find meaningful. Throughout history, we have sought to create some order out of the chaos of time, sometimes even attempting to "dogmatize" time.

Christ has broken into history and therefore has pierced the historical continuum, but he has not abolished time. We need to observe the cyclical movements of the seasons because to contemplate spatial infinity produces, in most people, deep anxiety. Time reminds us that everything passes away.

The calendar of feast days offers new meaning and value to time because, in the liturgical dimension, moments open up to each other and merge into eternity—the promise of Christ. The lives of the saints are stretched through time in such a way that the events of their personal histories are deposited in the memory of God. The saints are witnesses to the glorious knowledge that God has "renewed your youth like an eagle's" (Psalm 103:5). And because of this, they have taught us that time is also a sacrament.

Part Two: On Asceticism, Mary, and Revelation

"The unity of your hearts is my Feast."

Our Lady to a modern mystic, Myrna of Damascus

As a result of the different theologies which emerged in the East and the West concerning the nature of our common salvation history, there have emerged different ways of interpreting the meaning of suffering, the purpose of cloister, and the role of Mary and her revelations. These are topics we will briefly examine in this section. In the next section, we will look at the definitions of sainthood in the various churches.

One of the challenges of a post-modern sensibility is to engage in dialogue with women (most often, women of a different historical epoch) who seem to tell us that the path to God leads through much suffering. In collecting information about many of these women, we found ourselves asking: why did they so often engage in voluntary mortifications? In recounting these stories, we felt the need to address the issue of asceticism because many modern people are drawn to study the saints but are perplexed at the role of suffering and mortification in so many of their lives. It is now believed, for example, that both Catherine of Siena and Catherine of Genoa brought an early end to their lives through excessive fasting. As many women writers point out today, such a model is not healthy for the modern woman who strives to overcome the disorder of anorexia. We live in a time of fewer dualistic assumptions about the world than was common in the Middle Ages and Renaissance, and we are often appalled that some saints—women in particular—would subject their bodies to the voluntary asceticism common in past eras. Few of us are willing to practice the austerity of many of these women ascetics. We don't live in caves or seclude ourselves in one-room cells for a lifetime. Unlike most cloistered women, we don't practice daily silence. Yet this spiritual concentration and physical isolation must have some appeal to the modern woman who perhaps feels the need for withdrawal from a world beset by its appalling social and spiritual ills. If we have a spiritual search, we almost always come to the realization that in the presence of the sacred, we fall silent. The asceticism of these women's lives calls us to examine ways in which our culture has become enslaved to addictions, to noise, to a ceaseless "doing," and we are called to restore some kind of balance in our own lives.

In attempting to understand the nature of suffering in many of the saints' lives, it is also important to examine how the topic is treated in the various churches. All traditions assert that to follow in the Master's footsteps, we must be willing to take up our own cross (Luke 9:23). Likewise all three of the sacramental churches would no doubt agree that identifying with the suffering Christ is not an end in itself, but a way to enter into greater intimacy with God. But there the resemblance ends. The Latin church tends to stress the atonement nature of Christ's suffering and death (this was especially true prior to the Reformation), whereas the Eastern churches stress the theology of divinization. Saint Athanasius wrote, "God became [man] in order that [man] may become God." In other words, *through grace* the saint becomes what God is *by nature*. This is also at the heart of the mystical tradition in the West, but in a more disguised manner— especially if church authority considered a woman's mysticism suspect. Teresa of Avila, who suffered considerable anxiety when the Inquisition was investigating her writings, was able to sidestep a number of issues by working through the medium of her confessor. Other mystical writers, like Marguerite Porete (who could not defend her mystical writings), were executed.

The understanding of mystical suffering also takes on different interpretations in the different church traditions. The Roman Catholic tradition asserts that suffering is never meaningless because it is redemptive. The saint, by participating in Christ's suffering, may assume the debts of those for whom she prays or for whom she offers up her private pain. When we pick up the cross, we also participate in atonement. Many medieval saints (for example, Catherine of Siena, who authored a spiritual theology called the *Dialogue*) felt compelled to ask for suffering in order to satisfy God's uncompromising justice. In a time of great confusion over the papacy, Catherine asked, in prayer, that her life be sacrificed for the good of the Church. Often saints felt that their prayers and sacrifices would shorten suffering sinners' time in Purgatory. The saints' visions and prophetic voices reinforced this teaching, especially after the Councils of Florence and Trent, when the theology of Purgatory became an established Church teaching. God gave a saint all of her experiences, whether prophetic or painful, in order that she might participate in humankind's salvation.

Post-Reformation churches sought to rectify a theology that made meaning of suffering in this way because they stressed faith over works; they were appalled by the idea that saints or anyone else could have a role in salvation because Christ was the only mediator who could take upon himself the punishment for humanity's sin and injustice. There is only one sacrificial atonement. Yet we find that one of the great saints honored today in the Anglican tradition, Julian of Norwich (herself a pre-Reformation saint in England), also asked for suffering so that she could enter into a deeper understanding of the mystery of Christ. For her, suffering was a means of purification so that she might understand the nature of God; and she was rewarded with a series of visions (called her *Showings*), which she spent the next twenty years contemplating and expanding. In general, however, the Protestant churches were not interested in mortifications or miracles, but rather in the charity and compassion with which great souls lived out their lives. Because Protestant churches stress that we are all saints now by virtue of our redemption in Christ, they tend not to make special exemptions. For most of the post-Reformation churches, suffering is not sought, but neither is it meaningless. If acknowledged, suffering may serve as a learning place where one can encounter Christ, and often Christ's healing power.

In the Orthodox tradition, ascetic purification—which often involved much suffering—was seen as a prerequisite that frequently led to a deep personal experience of God, wherein the saint was totally absorbed in God's presence. Through a process of austerity and repetitive prayer and chanting, the saint strove to become aligned with the place where God's divine nature unfolds; this is called the process of deification. The divisions between the divine and human realms blur, as a saint is invited to become what God is. Many saints in the East became hermits or anchorites, thereby excluding themselves from the world so they could spend their time solely on this task. Solitude was seen as the primary ingredient for becoming a saint.

In fact, a common theme with early Orthodox women saints is their need to don male clothing and become "males" so they could live their lives in a cell on the side of a mountain, instead of within the confines of a convent or family, which was considered a more suitable (and safe) place for a woman to pursue a life of holiness. Or sometimes, as in the case of Matrona of Perge, playing the part of a male served as an escape from an unhappy marriage (in her case, an abusive husband) and fulfilled her deepest desire to live a life of solitude, where she underwent austerities that she herself chose for

Christ. Although fasting and mortification are certainly a part of the ascetic tradition in both the East and West, suffering for atonement for others is generally not a theme found in Orthodoxy. The Orthodox understanding of suffering is that it is a mystery; we live always in the hope of transformation—from suffering into the pure joy of God's life. Through suffering, a saint may be personally transfigured in the process of divinization and thus become a channel of God's spirit to the world.

The precaution that most modern women adopt when reading stories of many of the early women saints is to not internalize a saint's suffering. It is not necessary to take on their suffering at the expense of our own spiritual development. The psychology of our time tells us that in a culture marred by violence and broken relationships, we must beware that we do not practice self-inflicted pain nor endure violence as passive victims in dysfunctional relationships. Yet it is equally important to acknowledge that suffering is a part of every spiritual journey. We live in a world of suffering and oppression; we suffer in our yearning for God; we experience pain when we resist transformation that is calling to us; we witness symptoms of suffering in a culture enslaved to food, drugs, work, and a hundred other opiates, and it affects our own lives. And it is the blood of Christ that nourishes our souls and serves as the model of suffering. Because our God is a God who suffers, it is in the passion of Christ that we identify with the passion of suffering people everywhere.

Mary and the Churches

In developing a book that seeks to be truly ecumenical, we nonetheless still strive to faithfully interpret the individual churches' teachings. This is a delicate task, given the fact that we live in an era where tension between Rome and some of the Orthodox churches has escalated. Both churches have believed, for more than a millennium, that they are descended from the "original faith": Orthodoxy considers Rome to be in heresy, and Rome considers Orthodoxy to be in schism. It is only since Vatican II that theologians and scripture scholars from the two major sister religions have been able to remove their own pejorative lens and meet eye to eye at an ecumenical table to discuss what we hold in common, and not only our differences. Christians from both traditions, especially living in America and Russia, have much to learn from one another.

Many Roman Catholics have been praying for Russia's "conversion" since the Fatima messages, which began around the period of the Bolshevik revolution. Yet, despite the puppet successors the Communist government put into place after Patriarch Tikhon was arrested and removed, Russian religion only went underground. Both the Russian Orthodox and the Ukranian Catholic faithful suffered greatly during these years. Many bishops, more than twelve hundred priests, and twenty million people died during the ghastly years of Stalin's rule; the majority of the faithful kept their faith, however. Throughout that reign of terror, more than half of the children born in Russia were still baptized. Many monasteries continued to function and minister as best they could (see Daily Readings, July 18, Duchess Elizabeth). Millions of thankful Russians rebuilt their cathedrals at an exceedingly rapid rate after the fall of the Soviet Union, especially to Our Lady of Kazan and to Our Lady of Vladimir, who is often called "The Lady Who Saves Russia." Whatever was meant by the "conversion of Russia" in the Fatima messages, it is clearly not a country lacking in faith, Marian devotion, or miracles. I have heard it said by Russian Orthodox who are "elders" in their tradition that they remember when nearly every diocese in Russia had a miracle-working icon.

Ecumenical dialogue has been growing (albeit in fits and starts) between Orthodoxy and the Anglican Church since before the organization of the World Council of Churches (1944). Although the Orthodox and Episcopal churches have grown further apart recently (based, in part, on some modern Episcopal theologians' understanding of the doctrines of the Virgin birth and Resurrection), the Orthodox Church is the oldest dialogue partner with the Anglican Church. This ecumenical partnership was particularly enriched during the period of the Oxford movement and through the Fellowship of St. Alban and St. Sergios. In 1930, Anglican dialogues with several Orthodox churches resulted in several Orthodox patriarchs (Greece, Jerusalem, Antioch, and Alexandria) acknowledging the Anglican Communion's sacraments and holy orders. In the 1978–1988 Lambeth Conferences, all agreed on the misplacement of the *filioque* (the Roman addition to the creedal formula defining Trinitarian doctrine), with an option (now in place in Anglican churches worldwide) to remove it. If the creedal understanding of the early Church remains unchanged, the two churches will continue to move toward full agreement on the major doctrinal formulas defined by the first seven

Ecumenical Councils. As a result of these dialogues, icons of Mary and many of the saints can now be found in many Anglican churches, as the richness of the Orthodox tradition becomes more enmeshed in the Eucharistic and other liturgical celebrations.

We have discovered that an ecumenical book that includes most of the major feast days of Mary, both from the East and from the West, has also been a sensitive task, especially since Marian theology has, in the past century, been a source of division, separating the Roman Catholic Church and all other churches worldwide. Indeed, many theologians have woefully acknowledged that Mariology is the greatest stumbling block to ecumenism because nowhere else is the discrepancy between Church teaching and the New Testament so great. In particular, the declaration of the two recent Marian dogmas caused a great rift in the ecumenical dialogue between Rome and England. The Orthodox churches, which affirmed the Marian teachings of the Assumption and the purity of Mary in its liturgy, never made them dogmatic, instead referring to them as mysteries. The Immaculate Conception is problematic to many Orthodox theologians, not because of Mary's sinlessness, but because it refers to a Western (Augustinian) understanding of inherited original sin. Nonetheless, more recently, Pope John Paul II struggled to restore some balance to the growing rift in his encyclical *Redemptoris Mater* (1987), which expresses hope that in her absolute Fiat to God, Mary does offer potential for ecumenical progress. It also appears that many Protestant churches are reclaiming Mary as the universal Mother, especially in women's circles devoted to a deeper exploration of the sacred feminine mysteries that she embodies.

In many ways, and despite its obstacles, the Anglican and Roman Catholic dialogue has also been particularly enriched since the Oxford movement, when many Anglicans worldwide reclaimed their Catholic roots, that is, the Anglo-Catholic dimension of their faith. In the second half of the nineteenth century, the effects of the Oxford movement were present in many Anglican and Episcopal parishes, where the altar again became the focus of worship and preaching took second place to the Liturgy. Some parishes even today clearly define themselves as Anglo-Catholic, and their churches reflect this through their elaborate redecorations, many of which include images of Mary. The Anglo-Catholic now functions as a full sacramental church with a growing interest in making new saints and in fostering new religious orders, besides the traditional ones it inherited from the Roman Catholic Church, such as the Franciscans and the Benedictines.

Wherever such religious communities exist, Mary is visibly present, complete with her rosaries and holy images. It has been noted many times, especially by Jungians, that the abolition of the cult of the Virgin in the churches (which emerged after the Reformation) has all but suffocated the feminine element, and with it the feminine images of our Mother of mercy and compassion; but that current is changing. The paradox, of course, is that the Anglican Church is the first sacramental church to ordain women. Only in the decades to come will the full ramification unfold of what has begun in our lifetimes.

Apparitions, Revelations, Pilgrimage

Mary's role is central to all churches that celebrate a Liturgy and Divine Office. The Anglican and some Protestant churches tend to limit her feasts to those celebrated in the early Church, such as the Annunciation, the celebration of Theotokos as Mother of God. The Roman church, which celebrates many more feasts in honor of Mary, makes a distinction between *dulia*, which refers to the honor and respect given to the saints, and *hyperdulia*, a higher form of veneration given to Mary. God alone is worthy of actual worship or *latreia*. These distinctions are not as clearly defined in the East, where honor, veneration, and devotion are accorded to the Mother of God, especially in prayers to her such as the Akathists. However, although outsiders may perceive the Orthodox as engaging in worship when they bow before icons of Mary, there is a clear distinction, theologically, between *proskynesis*, the devotion shown to Mary and the saints, and *latreia*, which, again, is reserved for God alone. The Orthodox custom of engaging icons with reverence rests on the principle that icons are windows to eternity, and therefore all icons of the saints are used for us to "gaze through" to God.

In both the East and the West, Marian feast days link pious tradition to events of salvation history related in scripture (e.g., the Annunciation) or by tradition (the Presentation of Mary in the Temple or the Dormition) to geography or local cults (e.g., Lourdes or Blancherea), dogmatic or theological titles (e.g., Immaculate Conception or Theotokos), or the emergence of popular devotions (e.g., the Akathist to the Protective Veil, or the Rosary to the Queen of Peace).

In a book in which so many saints are visionaries and so many feasts of Mary celebrate her apparitions, we again found it necessary to distinguish—albeit briefly—how the churches perceive the role of revelation, at least those churches in which miracles and apparitions play a role. In both the Orthodox and Roman traditions, the piety surrounding Marian apparitions remains anchored in public devotion. Salvation history is full of appearances from the supernatural, in both the Old and the New Testaments. Mary and Joseph themselves had angelic visions and messages. From the Middle Ages, however, when apparitional phenomena in the Roman Catholic Church began to increase, until the current era, when it is again on the rise, theologians and pastors exercised restraint when investigating alleged appearances of Mary. A piety with its sole concentration on Marian visions and "locutions" (the channeled messages she gives to the vision's recipient) can easily become unbalanced and thus distract from the gospel message. The Roman Church only gives private revelations the stamp of approval after much time and investigation, and even then, they never form part of the sacred deposit of faith; Catholics may accept them with human faith if they so desire.

After its formal investigative process, the Catholic Church may officially grant its "negative" approval, which means that it does not forbid Catholics from venerating or even promoting a particular apparition or visionary, but neither does it officially promote it. When the Church approves a saint's revelations—which often have already gone into writing and become available to the public—it assures that the message's content is good and does not contradict dogmatic teaching. Often these saints' revelations become classics and very important parts of Church tradition, such as the works of Catherine of Siena or Teresa of Avila.

While thoroughly gathering the facts about the cause of any apparition or the messages that the alleged vision seeks to impart to the faithful, a number of criteria come into play. There must first be a spiritual and mental assessment of the visionary herself. Secondly, a judgment is made as to whether the messages contradict Church teaching; there is also an analysis of its spiritual fruitfulness. Extravagant claims and apocalyptical messages are treated with reservation. If the Church accepts a message as worthy of belief, it is generally because the message is congruent with the gospel's basic message. While investigating a Marian appearance, the Vatican also uses miracles to attest to an apparition's authenticity, but this is only after good fruits have confirmed that the pilgrimage site is contributing to building up the Church. Without any miracles worked through Mary's intercession, Church approval is less likely. Numerous of the major pilgrimage sites—such as Lourdes, Fatima, and Guadalupe—have, over time, confirmed the sacredness of their location and the propagation of sanctity that occurs there. Even when a pilgrimage site has been recognized and a private revelation spread throughout the world, the Church does not make the acceptance of a vision or its devotion mandatory.

The Catholic Church recognizes three types of visions: corporeal, imaginative, and intellectual. A corporeal vision is one that is seen by the eyes, e.g., the glorious body of Christ or Mary, or the corporeal vision of one who has died. An imaginative vision does not rely on the aid of the visual organ of the eye, and it happens most often in dreams. This type of vision is considered miraculous if a supernatural agent causes it, and if it imparts grace and sanctity to the visionary. An intellectual vision, which Teresa of Avila explained in great detail, takes place in pure understanding, not in the reasoning faculty. It is a miraculous infusion into the mind by a superior order, and its reality is often more pronounced than a corporeal or imaginative vision.

It is this intellectual realm that often gives rise to the pure experience of knowing God in an unmediated state. Mystics since Pseudo-Dionysius (in the fifth century) have often designated the profundity of Divine realities experienced here in negative terms, calling it apophatic mysticism. This is because human speech falls short or the human soul cannot adequately relate it; St. Paul's mystical experience on the road to Damascus is an example of this (1 Cor. 2:9). Although the levels of mysticism may sometimes merge or combine, there are no locutions or messages to be communicated in the highest stage; rather, there is only mystic union. (St. Theresa and others have outlined the stages as seven in number). Indeed, the apophatic tradition has always asserted that all words and images must be stripped away to be open to God's sheer transcendence. Classic works that detail the Western Church's position on apophatic mysticism include those of Meister Eckhart and John of the Cross. This kind of mystical understanding is common to both the East and West; in the East it is taught within the mystical practice of hesychasm or "silence."

In the Orthodox tradition, a saint is rarely a channel for a vision of Christ or the Mother of God, because the Church does not recognize locutions unless they are part of the saint's personal devotions.

Messages are never revealed through a mystic or prophet to establish devotional cults, unless that devotion is to a new icon. The saint's voice, however, may serve as a mouthpiece for the divine in other ways, especially if the saint is a spiritual elder or abbess. In the many "appearances" of the Theotokos through her icons, attention is rarely given to the ascetic or holy person who originally receives the appearance; and often after the revelation the recipient of such a vision recedes into obscurity. The icon is what remains.

The East is fond of speaking of the "apparition" of the icon itself. This generally refers to a mysterious event by which the icon becomes known and then gains renown as a new source of the manifestation of graces. Generally after a revelation wherein the Virgin miraculously appears to a monk, peasant, or holy person, an icon is made in her honor; a cult then develops, especially if the icon turns out to be a miracle worker, such as a myrrh-streaming icon, the most frequent type. The other most common story concerning an icon's appearance usually comes about through a dream; for example, a child has a dream in which the Theotokos tells her to go and dig under a tree or under a church, where there will appear a new type of icon. Often the icon will then gain renown for its healings, and if popular enough, it will expand from a small local cult to one of the more famous iconic types, with many thousands of representations, which are meticulously made to reproduce the original.

There is little freedom of expression in painting icons, which always follows a precise tradition in style and reproduction. The genesis of a famous icon is always mysterious, and its presence is considered sacramental: a means wherein divine grace is infused into the contemplating soul. The icon painter (or "writer") knows that icons are windows to heaven. It is the icon, rather than the holy person who receives the vision, which serves as mediator between the soul and God. The saints honored liturgically in Orthodoxy, on the other hand, do serve as mediators, much as they do in the West. They represent the Word through certain titles, for example, apostle, patriarch, or wonder worker. When spiritual elders (or *staritsi*) speak, they are acknowledged and listened to. Levitation and miracles are found in both the Roman and Orthodox traditions. Although mystics in the Orthodox Church do not generally have visions that are channeled for the world, it is sometimes considered a gift for the aspirant herself or himself to receive a vision (see Daily Readings, January 2, Abbess

Taisiia). Generally a woman's confessor or *staritsa* will advise a deeper prayer life to balance the impact of visions on the visionary's emotional life, and ultimately, one is called to rest in the imageless state of God's presence.

The pilgrimage tradition, both to holy sites and to tombs, is also common to both the East and the West, where pilgrimage serves as a locus of veneration, purification, and rejuvenation. Earlier we spoke about the meaning of the word *sacred*, a term that Jung found very attractive; he saw in the pilgrimage a deep source of archetypal meaning, for it is not only the saint who is sacred. In the Christian tradition, a pilgrimage is sacred precisely because the earthly city becomes, for a time, the city of God, where everything is renewed in joy and seen through the prism of liturgical celebration. Pilgrimage sites are places where miracles often happen, especially miracles of healing. Sometimes the healing is spiritual, as the pilgrim feels strengthened in faith or receives a mystical experience. In both the East and the West, pilgrims frequently gather at gravesites for prayer and liturgical celebration, as many saints have left behind sanctified or incorruptible bodies. In Russia, a long-standing tradition classifies those who make pilgrimage a way of life as *stranniki,* or holy wanderers, journeying from one sacred site to another, seeing life itself as an earthly pilgrimage.

As we journey through our year with these women saints, we are reminded that, as we constantly readjust our lives to attune them to the Divine harmony of God's will, we too are life's pilgrims. The saints model pilgrimage for us, having been to the valley and emerged victorious, and they foreshadow heaven, prefiguring the unity we all seek. Humanity is drawn toward sanctity and the time when all of God's people will at last be gathered around Christ, the source of our unity. The saints help inaugurate on earth the new state of things that will be established at the end of time. Thus, these women are, for us, a promise and a hope.

Part Three: Definitions of Sainthood

> "The 'golden crown' of the saints, known and unknown to the world, will continue to the end of time."
>
> —Sergius Bulgakov

Our definition of saints spans a diverse range of women's lives, with focus on women who were notable in four particular areas:

❧ The martyrs and ascetics, whom the Church first set aside as saints, and whose cults early on were defined by relics, miracles, and pilgrimages

❧ Women who taught wisdom, especially women writers whose work has survived and speaks to us today about the nature of their theology or mysticism

❧ Church leaders, including missionaries; and where the church allows it, deacons, or other ministers, including foundresses

❧ Women, married or religious, who nurtured the poor and sick

Since we have included a number of women in this collection who were never officially canonized, it might be useful, at this point, to also explain what official canonization is, as it is defined today in the various churches.

The canonical procedure for the cause of beatification and canonization in the Roman Catholic Church is clearly the most legalistic of the three traditions, and often the most lengthy (although Pope John Paul II did much to hasten the process). To begin a canonization process, it is usually necessary to wait five years after the candidate's death, whereupon the bishop of the diocese where the person's beatification is being requested initiates the investigation. This initial investigation gathers concrete facts on the person's exercise of Christian virtues that are considered heroic. Heroic virtue—which has always been a principal concern for elevating a person to the category of sainthood—includes both the theological virtues of faith, hope, and charity, as well as the cardinal virtues, such as prudence, justice, temperance, and fortitude. After the initial process, the documentation is passed to the Congregation for the Cause of Saints in Rome, where a panel of nine or more theologians votes on it.

The cause is then passed on to a body of cardinals and bishops, and finally to the Pope, who may then authorize the Congregation to draft the degree for beatification. If the person under consideration is not a martyr (a martyr's cause being considerably easier), a miracle attributed to the servant of God and verifiable after her death is necessary. The canonical investigation proceeds in the same way as that which determined heroic virtue. After the two decrees are in place, the Pope decides on beatification, whereupon the candidate receives the title of Blessed. For canonization, another miracle is needed, which is attributed to the Blessed's intercession. At this time, she receives the title of saint at a Bull of Canonization, and the local cult becomes a part of public worship.

The process of beatification for a martyr is different in that the miracles are not discussed in separate meetings but proceed together. From the time of the early Church, the types of saints have fallen broadly into two categories: the martyrs and the confessors (which includes virgins), that is, those who confessed or suffered for (but did not die for) their faith. Women saints are given numerous other titles, including widow, doctor, foundress, religious, anchoress, abbess, and empress. Despite misunderstanding from some Protestant quarters, the Church does not attempt to make them gods; the saints are servants and friends of God, a point stressed again in an announcement concerning the present procedures for canonization (Holy See Press Office, Sept. 12, 1997, *Present Canonical Procedure in Causes for Beatification and Canonization*).

Although the word *canonization* is frequently used when referring to the public declaration of a saint in the Orthodox Church, technically the term should be "glorification." Less juridical, this process is based more on a perception of whether divinizing grace has occurred, or is occurring, through the vessel of the person under consideration. Although righteous deeds are important, there is no rationalistic analysis of sanctity. Indeed, in some cases, the events of a saint's life may not even be known, as is the case with St. Euphemia, whose life was cloaked in anonymity. Only when miracles were manifested at her tomb, one and a half centuries later, was she glorified as a saint. Or the life may appear very ordinary, as in the case of Theodora of Thessoloniki, who was glorified and recognized as a saint when oil ran from her relics.

In Orthodoxy, if the Holy Spirit's grace and presence are understood to be mystically active, especially through miracles or incorruption of relics, then the saint must, of necessity, be glorified. The Church believes that a saint is a vessel upon whom God is pleased to pour the oil of grace and divinization, and since miracles point to this action having been accomplished in heaven, the Church follows in glorifying God's servant on earth. Sanctity is an important element; a person's mental stability is of much less importance, however. Thus, a category of sainthood has emerged called "Fool for Christ," which generally refers to a person whose life may be characterized by prophecy or miracles, but whose actions appear to make no sense to the society around them. Other designations, or titles, of women saints in the Orthodox Church, besides virgin, martyr, and fool, include: ascetics (hermits or nuns, especially abbesses), *staritsa* (wise elder), deaconess, equal to the apostles (a title generally given to missionaries), wonder-worker, prophet (usually an Old Testament saint), myrrh bearer, or simply righteous.

As in the Roman tradition, the saint's cult is usually acknowledged first, which is then adapted at the regional or national level. Churches of other countries or rites may or may not place the saint's names on their own calendar. A saint's glorification is formalized through a liturgy said in the saint's honor and blessing her or his icon. A feast day is designated in their blessed memory. Icons are of prime importance in the glorification process and in the spread of the cult to other countries or churches. No saint is glorified without an icon.

The non–Roman Catholic churches that are liturgical continue the practice of recognizing heroic virtue and generally proclaim saints both by popular acclamation and by declaration of bishops. The Anglican Church continues in the tradition of adding witnesses to the faith to their liturgical calendar. Unlike the Roman and Orthodox traditions, however, which incorporate prayers to the saint in their liturgy or divine office prayers, the Anglican, Lutheran, and all Protestant churches refrain from praying to the saint formally. The prayers said in their honor are the "collects," which are addressed to God. The post-Reformation churches attempt to focus on sanctity as a virtue to be imitated, rather than saintly phenomena or miracles, which may serve to distance us from the saint. A number of modern people in both the Eastern and Western sacramental churches would tend to agree. Some would suggest that we must reconsider whether our heavenly patrons and miracle workers would not actually prefer to be imitated rather than venerated, for the latter is a much easier thing to do. Founder of the Catholic Worker Movement, Dorothy Day, staunchly refused to be put on such a pedestal when she repeatedly said she did not want to be called a saint. Evelyn Underhill, who has authored many books on saints and mysticism, once said that we recognize spiritual reality most easily when it is perceived as transfiguring human character.

We have included both of these women in our collection, and numerous others, because they fulfill a prophetic role in modern society. We learn from the witnesses of prophetic women who challenged the unjust world in which they found themselves, but who may never make the category of sainthood in either the Roman or Orthodox canons because they did not leave behind a trail of miracles. We must listen to the wisdom of women who, in the ordinariness of their lives, encountered a still small voice that gave their lives meaning. We need women who stand as role models in solidarity with the oppressed. We must attend to the struggles of Christian missionaries who never had a supernatural experience in their lives. We learn from all of them, for they, like the more extraordinary saints, are also sacred. And they teach us that sacredness is a touchstone that we ourselves can reach out and feel with our own hands.

Finally, we learn most, perhaps, from those women who, despite the obstacles in their paths, maintained a sense of balance and radiated the joy of the Spirit while following their heartfelt mission in life. In the lives of all these women, there emerges a striving for perfection coupled with a sincere desire to continually turn their lives over to God. Their need to find and fulfill their vocation or mission in life is often juxtaposed with the equally difficult task of submitting to what they perceive to be God's will, especially in the midst of a spiritual wilderness. However, these were women who did common things uncommonly well, with great joy; their search to serve God in the most perfect way possible has made them unforgettable examples for all of us.

We have tried, in our selection for this collection of women's lives, to choose women who represent sanctity as understood and embodied by their various traditions. In keeping with the way the major churches address prayers, the prayers in this book vary from the "collect" type, where the saint's life is cast into a prayer addressed solely to God or Jesus, to the type addressed directly to the saint for intercession. In the Orthodox Church, this prayer is called a "Tropar" and is incorporated into the canon of liturgical celebrations. We have simply called them prayers (addressed to God) and intercessory prayers (addressed to the saint).

Saints—Alphabetically

	Date	Area of Sainthood
Abbess Taisiia	2-Jan	Abbess, mystic
Adelaide	17-Dec	Queen
Adrienne von Speyr	6-Nov	Mystic, writer
Agatha	5-Feb	Martyr
Agnes	21-Jan	Martyr
Agnes of Montepulciano	20-Apr	Abbess
Agnes of Prague	2-Mar	Religious
Agneta Chang	31-Oct	Korean martyr
Alfred Moes, Mother	18-Dec	Missionary, foundress
Alicia Domon	10-Dec	Missionary
Amelia Bloomer	29-Oct	Activist
Amy Carmichael	16-Dec	Missionary, foundress
Anastasia and the Nativity of Our Lord	25-Dec	Healer, martyr
Anastasia Logacheva	14-Feb	Modern visionary
Anastasia the Patrician	10-Mar	Monk
Angela of Foligno	7-Jan	Visionary
Angela of the Cross	2-May	Tertiary
Angela Salawa	12-Mar	Virgin
Angeli Merci	27-Jan	Tertiary
Angelina, Mother	26-Oct	Foundress

Ann Lee, Mother	4-Aug	Founder (Shakers)
Ann Worchester Robertson	7-Nov	Missionary
Anna Dengal	17-Apr	Foundress
Anna Nitschmann	18-Oct	Missionary
Anne Frank	30-Jun	Visionary
Anne Line	27-Feb	Martyr
Anne-Marie Javouhey	15-Jul	Foundress
Anne Marie Taigi	9-Jun	Prophet
Anne, Mother of Mary	26-Jul	Mother
Anne of St. Bartholomew	7-Jun	Religious
Annunciation, Blessed		
Virgin at the	25-Mar	Mary feast
Anthousa of Constantinople	30-Jul	Ascetic, abbess
Antoinette Blackwell	20-May	First female pastor
Aquilina	13-Jun	Martyr
Assuage My Sorrows Icon	25-Jan	Theotokos icon
Assumption/Dormition	15-Aug	Mary feast
Athanasia of Aegina	12-Apr	Abbess
Athenas-Eudokia	13-Aug	Empress
Attracta	12-Aug	Anchoress, miracle worker
Austreberta	20-Aug	Abbess
Balbina	31-Mar	Martyr
Barbara	4-Dec	Martyr
Barbara Heck	13-Jun	Methodist organizer
Bathild	30-Jan	Anglo-Saxon queen
Beatrice da Silva	1-Sep	Religious
Beatrice of Nazareth	19-Mar	Beguine
Benedicta Cambiagio		
Frassinello	21-Mar	Mystic
Bernadette of Lourdes	16-Apr	Visionary/Mary feast
Bertilla Boscardin	19-Oct	Holy fool
Birgitta of Sweden	23-Jul	Visionary
Boleslawa Maria Lament	29-Jan	Foundress
Brigid of Kildare	1-Feb	Foundress, abbess
Burgundofara (Fare/Fara)	2-Apr	Abbess
Carmelita Manning, Mother	28-Mar	Sister of Mercy
Catherine del Ricci	13-Feb	Mystic, nun
Catherine Doherty	15-Dec	Foundress, reformer
Catherine Laboure	27-Nov	Visionary

Catherine McAuley	11-Nov	Foundress
Catherine of Alexandria	25-Nov	Martyr, philosopher
Catherine of Bologna	9-Mar	Tertiary
Catherine of Genoa	15-Sep	Mystic
Catherine of Siena	29-Apr	Mystic, reformer
Catherine of Sweden	24-Mar	Abbess
Cecile Isherwood	20-Feb	Foundress, missionary
Cecilia	22-Nov	Martyr
Christina Ebner	27-Dec	Mystic
Christina of Brusthem	31-Dec	Holy fool
Christina of Markyate	20-Sep	Anchoress
Clare of Assisi	11-Aug	Foundress, reformer
Clothilde of France	3-Jun	Queen
Colette	6-Mar	Tertiary, reformer
Columba Kim	21-Sep	Martyr of Korea
Concepcion Cabrera de Armida	6-Dec	Writer, foundress
Constance and Her Companions	9-Sep	Missionary
Constance of Aragon	24-Dec	Queen, nun
Cornelia Connelly	19-Apr	Foundress
Corrie ten Boom	15-Apr	Missionary
Cresentia	15-Jun	Martyr
Cumania	21-Dec	Foundress
Cunegund	3-May	Empress
Cuthburga	31-Aug	Foundress
Daria	25-Oct	Martyr
Dolores Rodriguez Sopena	10-Jan	Reformer
Domnica of Carthage	8-Jan	Hermit
Dorothy	6-Feb	Martyr
Dorothy Day	29-Nov	Reformer, activist
Dorothy of Montau	30-Oct	Visionary, anchoress
Dwyn, Saint	25-Jan	Virgin
Dymphna	15-May	Virgin martyr
Ebbe	2-Nov	Abbess
Edburga of Bicester	14-Jun	Foundress, abbess
Edith Cavell	13-Oct	Activist
Edith of Wilton	16-Sep	Religious
Edith Stein	9-Aug	Mystic, martyr

Elfleda	8-Feb	Abbess
Elizabeth	5-Nov	New Testament saint
Elizabeth Ann Seton	4-Jan	Missionary
Elizabeth Cady Stanton	12-Nov	Activist, preacher
Elizabeth Feodorovna	18-Jul	Martyr
Elizabeth Fry	12-Oct	Quaker reformer
Elizabeth Lange	1-Jul	Foundress
Elizabeth of Austria	22-Dec	Tertiary
Elizabeth of Hungary	17-Nov	Tertiary
Elizabeth of Portugal	4-Jul	Queen, tertiary
Elizabeth of Schonau	18-Jun	Visionary
Elizabeth of the Trinity	8-Nov	Mystic
Elizabeth the Good	9-Dec	Mystic
Elizabeth the Wonder-worker	24-Apr	Wonder-worker
Emily de Vialar	17-Jun	Visionary
Enfleda	28-Nov	Religious
Ethelburga of Barking	11-Oct	Abbess
Ethelburga of Faremoutier	7-Jul	Abbess
Ethelburga of Kent	13-Dec	Queen, foundress
Etheldreda Ely (Audrey)	24-Jun	Princess, foundress
Etheldritha	7-Aug	Hermit
Etty Hillesum	30-Nov	Mystic
Eudokia of Heliopolis	1-Mar	Wonder-worker, martyr
Eugenia	24-Dec	Martyr
Euphemia	12-Jul	Martyr, wonder-worker
Euphrasia	13-Mar	Virgin, miracle worker
Euphrosyne of Alexandria	25-Sep	Monk
Eustochia Calafato	20-Jan	Poor Clare, mystic
Evelyn Underhill	16-Jun	Mystic, scholar
Fannie Lou Hamer	14-Mar	Reformer
Fanny Crosby	3-Nov	Hymn writer
Faustina Kowalska	5-Oct	Visionary
Feast of the *Sophia* Icon	8-Sep	Sophia feast
Febronia of Nisbis	25-Jun	Wonder-worker
Felicia Meda	6-Sep	Abbess
Felicitas	7-Mar	Martyr
Florence Allshorn	20-Dec	Missionary
Florence Nightingale	18-May	Foundress

Frances Cabrini, Mother	13-Nov	Missionary
Frances of Rome	8-Mar	Religious
Frances of the Redemption	1-Nov	Mystic
Frideswide	28-Oct	Foundress
Gemma Galgani	11-Apr	Visionary
Genevieve	3-Jan	Contemplative
Germaine Cousin	15-Jun	Virgin
Gertrude of Nivelles	16-Mar	Abbess
Gertrude the Great	16-Nov	Mystic
Gladys May Aylward	29-Feb	Missionary
Glodesind	25-Aug	Abbess
Hadewijch of Brabant	28-Apr	Beguine
Hagar	22-Jan	Old Testament heroine
Hannah	10-Nov	Old Testament heroine
Harriet Monsell	26-Mar	Foundress
Harriet Tubman	20-Jul	Activist
Hedwig of Poland	16-Oct	Queen
Helen and the Holy Cross	21-May	Empress
Heloise	16-May	Abbess, writer
Henrietta Mears	11-Dec	Educator
Hermione	2-Sep	Prophet, martyr
Hilda of Whitby	19-Nov	Abbess
Hildegard of Bingen	17-Sep	Mystic, abbess
Hildegund	21-Apr	Monk
Hildelith	21-Dec	Abbess
Ignatius Hayes, Mother	11-Nov	Foundress
Imelda Lambertini	12-May	Virgin
Immaculate Conception/		
Conception of Mary	8-Dec	Mary feast
Immaculate Heart of Mary	22-Aug	Mary feast
Irene of Cappadocia	29-Jul	Deaconess, prophet
Irene of Thessalonika	5-May	Martyr
Isabella Gilmore	17-Apr	Deaconess
Isabella of Spain	25-Apr	Queen
Isadora	1-May	Fool for Christ
Ita (Ide)	15-Jan	Ascetic
Iveron Mother of God		
Portaitissa Icon	24-Nov	Theotokos icon
Jane Antide Thouret	23-May	Foundress

Jane Frances de Chantal	18-Aug	Religious
Jane of Signa	15-Nov	Anchoress
Jane of Toulouse	31-Mar	Foundress
Jane of Valois	4-Feb	Visionary
Jean Donovan	28-Aug	Modern martyr
Jeanne Delanou	17-Aug	Foundress
Jeanne Fontbonne	23-Nov	Missionary, foundress
Jeanne Jugan	30-Aug	Foundress
Jeanne Marie Guyon	18-Mar	Contemplative
Joan de Lestonnac	28-Jan	Foundress
Joan of Arc	30-May	Visionary, martyr
Joanna the Myrrh Bearer	24-May	Myrrh bearer
Josephina Bakhita	17-May	African missionary
Josephine Leroux	21-Oct	Religious, martyr
Joy of All Who Sorrow Icon	24-Oct	Theotokos icon
Juana Ines de la Cruz	18-Feb	Religious
Judith of Prussia	24-May	Hermit
Julia Emery	9-Jan	Leader in ministry
Julian of Norwich	8-May	Anchoress
Juliana Falconieri	19-Jun	Foundress
Juliana of Cornillon	6-Apr	Visionary
Julie Billiart	8-Apr	Foundress
Junia	3-Dec	Apostle
Kassia	1-Aug	Hymn writer
Kateri Tekawitha	14-Jul	Virgin
Katherine Drexel	3-Mar	Missionary
Kazan Icon of the Mother of God	8-Jul	Theotokos icon
Kentigerna	16-Jan	Anchoress
Kozelschansk Icon of the Theotokos	21-Feb	Theotokos icon
Kursk Root Icon of the Mother of God	26-Nov	Theotokos icon
Kykkos Icon of the Theotokos	26-Dec	Theotokos icon
Life-Giving Spring Icon	3-Apr	Theotokos icon
Lioba (Liobe)	28-Sep	Abbess
Louisa Jacques	27-Mar	Modern mystic
Louise de Marillac	15-Mar	Foundress
Lucia Filippini	10-May	Educator

Lucretia Mott	13-Sep	Preacher, activist
Lucy	13-Dec	Martyr
Lucy of Caltagirone	22-Sep	Religious
Lydda Icon Not Made		
by Hands	25-Feb	Theotokos icon
Lydia	3-Aug	NT, Paul supporter
Lydia Sellon	20-Nov	Religious
Macrina	19-Jul	Holy mother
Macrina the Elder	14-Jan	Holy mother
Madeleine Fontaine	28-Jun	Martyr
Madeleine Sophie Barat	25-May	Foundress
Magdalene of Canossa	10-Apr	Foundress
Marcella	31-Jan	Teacher with Jerome
Margaret Colonna	29-Dec	Religious
Margaret Cusack	6-May	Reformer
Margaret Ebner	20-Jun	Mystic
Margaret Fell	29-Sep	Mother of Quakerism
Margaret of Antioch	21-Jul	Martyr
Margaret of Castello	13-Apr	Tertiary
Margaret of Cortona	22-Feb	Tertiary
Margaret of England	3-Feb	Pilgrim, religious
Margaret of Hungary	18-Jan	Virgin, miracle worker
Margaret of Scotland,		
Queen	11-Jun	Queen, reformer
Margaret Stadler	28-Dec	Religious
Margaret-Mary Alacoque	17-Oct	Visionary
Margarita Tuchkova	10-Sep	Abbess, deaconess
Margarite Bourgeoys	12-Jan	Foundress
Marguerite d'Youville	23-Dec	Foundress
Marguerite of Porete	1-Jun	Beguine
Maria Angela Astorch	2-Dec	Mystic, abbess
Maria Clementine		
Anuarite Nengapete	1-Dec	Martyr
Maria Crescentia Hoss	4-Apr	Tertiary
Maria Francesca Rubatto	6-Aug	Religious
Maria Gabriella of Unity	22-Apr	Victim soul
Maria Goretti	6-Jul	Martyr
Maria Maddalena Bentivoglio,		
Mother	19-Aug	Missionary

Maria Mazzarello	14-May	Foundress, educator
Maria of Olonets	9-Feb	Desert dweller
Maria Solares	5-Mar	Native American leader
Mariam Bouardy	26-Aug	Religious
Marianne of Molokai	10-Jun	Missionary
Marie d'Oignies	22-Jun	Hermit
Marie of the Incarnation (Barbe Acarie)	18-Apr	Mystic
Marie of the Incarnation (Marie Guyart Martin)	30-Apr	Religious
Marie Rose Durocher	6-Oct	Foundress
Marie Victoire Therese Couderc	26-Sep	Religious, writer
Marjory Kempe	19-Sep	Mystic
Martha and Mary	4-Jun	New Testament apostles
Martina	31-Jan	Martyr
Mary Angela Truszkowska	10-Oct	Tertiary, educator
Mary Ann of Jesus of Pardes	28-May	Tertiary, mystic
Mary Assunta	7-Apr	Missionary
Mary Bosanquet	26-Apr	Preacher
Mary Clotilde and Her Companions	23-Oct	Martyrs
Mary Crucifixa	17-Dec	Religious
Mary di Rosa	14-Dec	Foundress
Mary Euphrasia Pelletier	23-Apr	Foundress
Mary Fontanella	28-Dec	Visionary
Mary Frances of the Five Wounds	4-Oct	Tertiary
Mary Frances Schervier	9-Dec	Missionary
Mary Francis Bachmann	29-Jun	Foundress
Mary Hermina Grivot	14-Nov	Missionary
Mary Joseph Rossello	7-Dec	Foundress, educator
Mary Magdalen Postel	17-Jul	Educator
Mary Magdalene	22-Jul	Apostle
Mary Magdelene Pazzi	26-May	Mystic
Mary Martinengo	27-Jul	Contemplative
Mary McKillop	8-Aug	Foundress
Mary of Agreda	11-Sep	Visionary, writer

Mary of Cleophas	9-Apr	Myrrh bearer
Mary of Egypt	1-Apr	Desert dweller
Mary of Providence, Mother	7-Feb	Foundress
Mary of the Passion, Mother	15-Nov	Missionary, foundress
Mary Pandita Ramabai	5-Apr	Indian missionary
Mary Skobtsova, Mother	29-Mar	Reformer, modern martyr
Mary Slessor	11-Jan	Missionary
Mary Sumner	10-Aug	Founder (Mother's Union)
Mary Teresa Bonzel	6-Feb	Tertiary
Mary the Younger	16-Feb	Wonder-worker
Mary Ward	23-Jan	Foundress
Mathilda	17-Mar	Queen
Matrona of Chios	20-Oct	Miracle worker
Matrona of Perge	9-Nov	Monk
Matrona Popova	16-Aug	Holy fool, foundress
Mechthild of Hackeborn	24-Feb	Visionary
Mechthild of Magdeburg	20-Nov	Mystic
Mechtildis of Edelstetten	29-May	Abbess
Melangell (Monacella)	27-May	Hermit
Melania the Elder	8-Jun	Holy mother
Milburga	23-Feb	Abbess, miracle worker
Miriam	6-Jun	Old Testament heroine
Mirozh Sign Icon of the Mother of God	23-Sep	Theotokos icon
Mollie Rogers, Mother	9-Oct	Missionary
Monegund (Monegundis)	2-Jul	Anchoress, foundress
Monesan of Britain (Monessa)	19-May	Virgin
Monica	27-Aug	Mother of St. Augustine
Morwenna	5-Jul	Religious
Mother Joseph of the Sacred Heart	19-Jan	Missionary, foundress
Mother of God: Theotokos, Birth Giver	1-Jan	Mary feast
Myrope	2-Dec	Martyr
Nativity of Mary	8-Sep	Mary feast
Nina of Georgia	14-Jan	Missionary
Non of Wales	3-Jul	Mother, foundress
Nonna	5-Aug	Deaconess, mother

Nympha	29-Feb	Apostle, missionary
Olga of Russia	11-Jul	Evangelizer of Russia
Olympia	25-Jul	Deaconess
Osanna of Mantua	21-Jun	Mystic
Our Lady of Fatima	13-May	Mary feast
Our Lady of Guadalupe	12-Dec	Mary feast
Our Lady of Knock	21-Aug	Mary feast
Our Lady of Mt. Carmel	16-Jul	Mary feast
Our Lady of Perpetual Help	27-Jun	Mary feast
Our Lady of the Angels at Portiuncula	2-Aug	Mary feast
Our Lady of the Rosary	7-Oct	Mary feast
Our Lady of Vladimir, Icon	23-Jun	Theotokos icon
Paraskeva of Serbia	14-Oct	Ascetic
Paula Frassinetti	12-Jun	Foundress
Paula of Rome	26-Jan	Religious scholar
Pega	8-Jan	Miracle worker
Pelagia	8-Oct	Monk
Pelagia of Tarsus	4-May	Martyr
Perpetua	7-Mar	Prophet, martyr
Petronilla	30-May	Martyr
Philippine Duchesne	18-Nov	Missionary, foundress
Philothea the Athenian	19-Feb	Holy Mother, martyr
Phoebe	3-Sep	Deaconess
Photini, the Woman at the Well	20-Mar	NT, Samaritan woman
Pica, Mother of St. Francis	14-Apr	Mother of St. Francis
Placide Viel	4-Mar	Abbess
Potamia	6-Aug	Martyr
Presentation of Mary	21-Nov	Mary feast
Prisca	16-Jan	Apostle
Protection of the Mother of God and the Holy Angels	2-Oct	Mary feast
Pulcheria of Constantinople, Empress	17-Feb	Empress, reformer
Purification of Mary and the Presentation in the Temple	2-Feb	Mary feast
Queenship of Mary	31-May	Mary feast

Radegund	14-Aug	Queen, deaconess
Rafka al Rayes	23-Mar	Religious
Raissa Maritain	12-Sep	Contemplative
Raphaela of the Sacred Heart	6-Jan	Religious
Rictrude	11-May	Abbess
Rita of Cascia	22-May	Religious
Rosalina of Villeneuve	17-Jan	Visionary
Rose of Lima	23-Aug	Mystic
Rose of Viterbo	4-Sep	Prophet
Rose Venerini	7-May	Foundress
Ruth	27-Oct	Old Testament heroine
Samthann	19-Dec	Abbess
Sancia	28-Jul	Queen
Sarah	22-Jan	Old Testament heroine
Scholastica	10-Feb	Foundress, abbess
Secunda and Rufina	10-Jul	Martyrs
Seven Sorrows/Seven Arrows of Mary	14-Sep	Mary feast
Simone Weil	24-Aug	Mystic
Sojourner Truth	2-Jun	Liberator
Solange	10-May	Virgin
Sophia and Her Three Daughters	18-Sep	Martyrs
Sophia of Ainos	5-Jun	Holy mother
Sophia of Kiev	22-Mar	New martyr
Susanna Wesley	24-Jul	Mother of the Wesleys
Susanna	5-Dec	Monk, deacon
Syncletike, Àmma	5-Jan	Desert mother
Tabitha	25-Oct	Disciple
Tatiana of Rome	13-Jan	Deaconess
Tenderness Icon of the Pskov-Caves	7-Oct	Theotokos icon
Teresa, Mother	5-Sep	Missionary
Teresa of Avila	15-Oct	Mystic
Terese of the Andes	13-Jul	Religious, writer
Thea Bowman	30-Mar	Reformer
Thecla of England	27-Sep	Religious
Thekla	24-Sep	Companion to Paul

Theodora, Empress,		
Restorer of Icons	11-Feb	Empress, restorer of icons
Theodora of Arta	11-Mar	Queen
Theodora of Thessaloniki	29-Aug	Religious
Theodore Guerin, Mother	3-Oct	Missionary
Theodosia of Constantinople	29-May	Martyr
Theotokos of Pochaev Icon	7-Sep	Theotokos icon
Theresa Hackelmeier	27-Sep	Missionary
Theresa of Jesus		
Gerhardinger	9-May	Foundress
Theresa of Lisieux	1-Oct	Mystic
Thomias of Lesbos	30-Dec	Martyr, miracle worker
Tikhvin Icon of the		
Mother of God	26-Jun	Theotokos feast
Ursula and Her		
Companions	22-Oct	Martyrs
Ursula Ledochowska	6-Jul	Foundress
Ursulina of Palma	7-Apr	Visionary
Veridiana	15-Feb	Anchoress
Veronica Giuliani	10-Jul	Mystic
Veronica (Veraniki)	12-Feb	NT saint
Victoria Rasoamanarivo	21-Aug	Religious
Villana de'Botti	28-Feb	Tertiary, mystic
Virgin Blachernitissa:		
Dedication of the		
Temple at Blachernae	31-Jul	Theotokos feast
Virgin of Solitude Statue	18-Dec	Mary feast
Walburga	26-Feb	Abbess
Waldetrude	30-Sep	Abbess
Winefride	4-Nov	Foundress
Withburga	9-Jul	Solitary, nun
Xenia	24-Jan	Fool for Christ
Zita	27-Apr	Tertiary

---

*As mentioned elsewhere, the variety of liturgical calendars means that in some cases different days are set aside to honor the same woman. See Evelyn Underhill and Florence Nightingale as two examples.

Saints—Chronologically

Saint	Date
Mother of God: Theotokos, Birth Giver	1-January
Abbess Taisiia	2-January
Genevieve	3-January
Elizabeth Ann Seton	4-January
Àmma Syncletike	5-January
Raphaela of the Sacred Heart	6-January
Angela of Foligno	7-January
Domnica of Carthage and Pega	8-January
Julia Emery	9-January
Dolores Rodriguez Sopena	10-January
Mary Slessor	11-January
Margarite Bourgeoys	12-January
Tatiana of Rome	13-January
Nina of Georgia and Macrina the Elder	14-January
Ita (Ide)	15-January
Prisca and Kentigerna	16-January
Rosalina of Villeneuve	17-January
Margaret of Hungary	18-January
Mother Joseph of the Sacred Heart	19-January
Eustochia Calafato	20-January
Agnes	21-January

Sarah and Hagar	22-January
Mary Ward	23-January
Xenia	24-January
Assuage My Sorrows Icon and St. Dwyn	25-January
Paula of Rome	26-January
Angeli Merci	27-January
Joan de Lestonnac	28-January
Boleslawa Maria Lament	29-January
Bathild	30-January
Martina and Marcella	31-January
Brigid of Kildare	1-February
The Purification of Mary and the Presentation in the Temple	2-February
Margaret of England	3-February
Jane of Valois	4-February
Agatha	5-February
Mary Teresa Bonzel and Dorothy	6-February
Mother Mary of Providence	7-February
Elfleda	8-February
Maria of Olonets	9-February
Scholastica	10-February
Empress Theodora, Restorer of Icons	11-February
Veronica (Veraniki)	12-February
Catherine del Ricci	13-February
Anastasia Logacheva	14-February
Veridiana	15-February
Mary the Younger	16-February
Empress Pulcheria of Constantinople	17-February
Juana Ines de la Cruz	18-February
Philothei the Athenian	19-February
Cecile Isherwood	20-February
Kozelschansk Icon of the Theotokos	21-February
Margaret of Cortona	22-February
Milburga	23-February
Mechthild of Hackeborn	24-February
Lydda Icon Not Made by Hands	25-February
Walburga	26-February
Anne Line	27-February
Villana de'Botti	28-February

Gladys May Aylward and Nympha	29-February
Eudokia of Heliopolis	1-March
Agnes of Prague	2-March
Katherine Drexel	3-March
Placide Viel	4-March
Maria Solares	5-March
Colette	6-March
Perpetua and Felicitas	7-March
Frances of Rome	8-March
Catherine of Bologna	9-March
Anastasia the Patrician	10-March
Theodora of Arta	11-March
Angela Salawa	12-March
Euphrasia	13-March
Fannie Lou Hamer	14-March
Louise de Marillac	15-March
Gertrude of Nivelles	16-March
Mathilda	17-March
Jeanne Marie Guyon	18-March
Beatrice of Nazareth	19-March
Photini, the Woman at the Well	20-March
Benedicta Cambiagio Frassinello	21-March
Sophia of Kiev	22-March
Rafka al Rayes	23-March
Catherine of Sweden	24-March
Blessed Virgin at the Annunciation	25-March
Harriet Monsell	26-March
Louisa Jacques	27-March
Carmelita Manning	28-March
Mother Mary Skobtsova	29-March
Thea Bowman	30-March
Balbina and Jane of Toulouse	31-March
Mary of Egypt	1-April
Burgundofara (Fare / Fara)	2-April
Life-Giving Spring Icon	3-April
Maria Crescentia Hoss	4-April
Mary Pandita Ramabai	5-April
Juliana of Cornillon	6-April
Mary Assunta and Ursulina of Palma	7-April

Julie Billiart	8-April
Mary of Cleophas	9-April
Magdalene of Canossa	10-April
Gemma Galgani	11-April
Athanasia of Aegina	12-April
Margaret of Castello	13-April
Pica, Mother of St. Francis	14-April
Corrie ten Boom	15-April
Bernadette of Lourdes	16-April
Anna Dengal and Isabella Gilmore	17-April
Marie of the Incarnation (Barbe Acarie)	18-April
Cornelia Connelly	19-April
Agnes of Montepulciano	20-April
Hildegund	21-April
Maria Gabriella of Unity	22-April
Mary Euphrasia Pelletier	23-April
Elizabeth the Wonder-worker	24-April
Isabella of Spain	25-April
Mary Bosanquet	26-April
Zita	27-April
Hadewijch of Brabant	28-April
Catherine of Siena	29-April
Marie of the Incarnation (Marie Guyart Martin)	30-April
Isadora	1-May
Angela of the Cross	2-May
Cunegund	3-May
Pelagia of Tarsus	4-May
Irene of Thessalonika	5-May
Margaret Cusack	6-May
Rose Venerini	7-May
Julian of Norwich	8-May
Theresa of Jesus Gerhardinger	9-May
Solange and Lucia Filippini	10-May
Rictrude	11-May
Imelda Lambertini	12-May
Our Lady of Fatima	13-May
Maria Mazzarello	14-May
Dymphna	15-May
Heloise	16-May

Josephina Bakhita	17-May
Florence Nightingale	18-May
Monesan of Britain (Monessa)	19-May
Antoinette Blackwell	20-May
Helen and the Holy Cross	21-May
Rita of Cascia	22-May
Jane Antide Thouret	23-May
Joanna the Myrrh Bearer and Judith of Prussia	24-May
Madeleine Sophie Barat	25-May
Mary Magdelene Pazzi	26-May
Melangell (Monacella)	27-May
Mary Ann of Jesus of Pardes	28-May
Mechtildis of Edelstetten and Theodosia of Constantinople	29-May
Joan of Arc and Petronilla	30-May
Queenship of Mary	31-May
Marguerite of Porete	1-June
Sojourner Truth	2-June
Clothilde of France	3-June
Martha and Mary	4-June
Sophia of Ainos	5-June
Miriam	6-June
Anne of St. Bartholomew	7-June
Melania the Elder	8-June
Anne Marie Taigi	9-June
Marianne of Molokai	10-June
Queen Margaret of Scotland	11-June
Paula Frassinetti	12-June
Barbara Heck and Aquilina	13-June
Edburga of Bicester	14-June
Germaine Cousin and Cresentia	15-June
Evelyn Underhill	16-June
Emily de Vialar	17-June
Elizabeth of Schonau	18-June
Juliana Falconieri	19-June
Margaret Ebner	20-June
Osanna of Mantua	21-June
Marie d'Oignies	22-June
Our Lady of Vladimir Icon	23-June

Etheldreda Ely (Audrey)	24-June
Febronia of Nisbis	25-June
Tikhvin Icon of the Mother of God	26-June
Our Lady of Perpetual Help	27-June
Madeleine Fontaine	28-June
Mary Francis Bachmann	29-June
Anne Frank	30-June
Elizabeth Lange	1-July
Monegund (Monegundis)	2-July
Non of Wales	3-July
Elizabeth of Portugal	4-July
Morwenna	5-July
Maria Goretti and Ursula Ledochowska	6-July
Ethelburga of Faremoutier	7-July
Kazan Icon of the Mother of God	8-July
Withburga	9-July
Secunda and Rufina, and Veronica Giuliani	10-July
Olga of Russia	11-July
Euphemia	12-July
Terese of the Andes	13-July
Kateri Tekawitha	14-July
Anne-Marie Javouhey	15-July
Our Lady of Mt. Carmel	16-July
Mary Magdalen Postel	17-July
Elizabeth Feodorovna	18-July
Macrina	19-July
Harriet Tubman	20-July
Margaret of Antioch	21-July
Mary Magdalene	22-July
Birgitta of Sweden	23-July
Susanna Wesley	24-July
Olympia	25-July
Anne, Mother of Mary	26-July
Mary Martinengo	27-July
Sancia	28-July
Irene of Cappadocia	29-July
Anthousa of Constantinople	30-July
Virgin Blachernitissa: Dedication of the Temple at Blachernae	31-July

Nun Kassia	1-August
Our Lady of the Angels at Portiuncula	2-August
Lydia	3-August
Mother Ann Lee	4-August
Nonna	5-August
Maria Francesca Rubatto and Potamia	6-August
Etheldritha	7-August
Mary McKillop	8-August
Edith Stein	9-August
Mary Sumner	10-August
Clare of Assisi	11-August
Attracta	12-August
Athenas-Eudokia	13-August
Radegund	14-August
Assumption/Dormition	15-August
Matrona Popova	16-August
Jeanne Delanou	17-August
Jane Frances de Chantal	18-August
Mother Maria Maddalena Bentivoglio	19-August
Austreberta	20-August
Victoria Rasoamanarivo and Our Lady of Knock	21-August
Immaculate Heart of Mary	22-August
Rose of Lima	23-August
Simone Weil	24-August
Glodesind	25-August
Mariam Bouardy	26-August
Monica	27-August
Jean Donovan	28-August
Theodora of Thessaloniki	29-August
Jeanne Jugan	30-August
Cuthburga	31-August
Beatrice da Silva	1-September
Hermione	2-September
Phoebe	3-September
Rose of Viterbo	4-September
Mother Teresa	5-September
Felicia Meda	6-September
The *Theotokos of Pochaev* Icon	7-September
Nativity of Mary and Feast of the *Sophia* Icon	8-September

Constance and Her Companions	9-September
Margarita Tuchkova	10-September
Mary of Agreda	11-September
Raissa Maritain	12-September
Lucretia Mott	13-September
Seven Sorrows/Seven Arrows of Mary	14-September
Catherine of Genoa	15-September
Edith of Wilton	16-September
Hildegard of Bingen	17-September
Sophia and Her Three Daughters	18-September
Marjory Kempe	19-September
Christina of Markyate	20-September
Columba Kim	21-September
Lucy of Caltagirone	22-September
Mirozh Sign Icon of the Mother of God	23-September
Thekla	24-September
Euphrosyne of Alexandria	25-September
Marie Victoire Therese Couderc	26-September
Theresa Hackelmeier and Thecla of England	27-September
Lioba (Liobe)	28-September
Margaret Fell	29-September
Waldetrude	30-September
Theresa of Lisieux	1-October
Protection of the Mother of God and the Holy Angels	2-October
Mother Theodore Guerin	3-October
Mary Frances of the Five Wounds	4-October
Faustina Kowalska	5-October
Marie Rose Durocher	6-October
Our Lady of the Rosary and *Tenderness* Icon of the Pskov-Caves	7-October
Pelagia	8-October
Mother Mollie Rogers	9-October
Mary Angela Truszkowska	10-October
Ethelburga of Barking	11-October
Elizabeth Fry	12-October
Edith Cavell	13-October
Paraskeva of Serbia	14-October
Teresa of Avila	15-October

Hedwig of Poland	16-October
Margaret-Mary Alacoque	17-October
Anna Nitschmann	18-October
Bertilla Boscardin	19-October
Matrona of Chios	20-October
Josephine Leroux	21-October
Ursula and Her Companions	22-October
Mary Clotilde and Her Companions	23-October
Joy of All Who Sorrow Icon	24-October
Tabitha and Daria	25-October
Mother Angelina	26-October
Ruth	27-October
Frideswide	28-October
Amelia Bloomer	29-October
Dorothy of Montau	30-October
Agneta Chang	31-October
Frances of the Redemption	1-November
Ebbe	2-November
Fanny Crosby	3-November
Winefride	4-November
Elizabeth	5-November
Adrienne von Speyr	6-November
Ann Worchester Robertson	7-November
Elizabeth of the Trinity	8-November
Matrona of Perge	9-November
Hannah	10-November
Mother Ignatius Hayes and Catherine McAuley	11-November
Elizabeth Cady Stanton	12-November
Mother Frances Cabrini	13-November
Mary Hermina Grivot	14-November
Mother Mary of the Passion and Jane of Signa	15-November
Gertrude the Great	16-November
Elizabeth of Hungary	17-November
Philippine Duchesne	18-November
Hilda of Whitby	19-November
Mechthild of Magdeburg and Lydia Sellon	20-November
Presentation of Mary	21-November
Cecilia	22-November
Jeanne Fontbonne	23-November

Iveron Mother of God Portaitissa Icon	24-November
Catherine of Alexandria	25-November
Kursk Root Icon of the Mother of God	26-November
Catherine Laboure	27-November
Enfleda	28-November
Dorothy Day	29-November
Etty Hillesum	30-November
Maria Clementine Anuarite Nengapete	1-December
Maria Angela Astorch and Myrope	2-December
Junia	3-December
Barbara	4-December
Susanna	5-December
Concepcion Cabrera de Armida	6-December
Mary Joseph Rossello	7-December
Immaculate Conception/Conception of Mary	8-December
Elizabeth the Good and Mary Frances Schervier	9-December
Alicia Domon	10-December
Henrietta Mears	11-December
Our Lady of Guadalupe	12-December
Ethelburga of Kent and Lucy	13-December
Mary di Rosa	14-December
Catherine Doherty	15-December
Amy Carmichael	16-December
Adelaide and Mary Crucifixa	17-December
Mother Alfred Moes and *Virgin of Solitude* Statue	18-December
Samthann	19-December
Florence Allshorn	20-December
Hildelith and Cumania	21-December
Elizabeth of Austria	22-December
Marguerite d'Youville	23-December
Constance of Aragon and Eugenia	24-December
Anastasia and the Nativity of Our Lord	25-December
Kykkos Icon of the Theotokos	26-December
Christina Ebner	27-December
Margaret Stadler and Mary Fontanella	28-December
Margaret Colonna	29-December
Thomias of Lesbos	30-December
Christina of Brusthem	31-December

Daily Readings

JANUARY 1 Mother of God:
Theotokos, Birth Giver

Mary's motherhood is celebrated on the first day of the year in the Roman calendar, and she is celebrated as the Theotokos, or *Birth Giver* on January 8 in the East. In the Anglican Church, January 1 is the feast of the Holy Name of Jesus. The Greek Church also celebrates this day as the feast of the Circumcision of Jesus. On the day of her Son's circumcision and naming, the Holy Mother witnessed the Name "which is above every other name" as it was given to Our Lord, marking our eternal Covenant with both of them for all time. One of the oldest and most important of the major feasts of Mary, the Theotokos, it reminds us that, from the moment the angel first foretold that her Son's name would be Jesus ("God saves") until she stood with him at the foot of the cross, Mary was the model disciple and pilgrim on the path to the fullness of the Kingdom. The Byzantine *Birth Giver* icon shows that, as she fitted a body to Jesus, so she works on our behalf to fit his grace to us so we may more closely resemble him. The title "Mother of God" was ascribed to Mary for Christological reasons at the Council of Ephesus in 431. After Ephesus, churches sprung up in her honor throughout the ancient world. Mary, given to us as our Mother also, cares for humanity and our needs "without interruption until the eternal fulfillment of all the elect" (Lumen Gentium, 62).

Intercessory Prayer:

O Most Blessed Theotokos, Mother of God and our Mother, you are the intercessor for all those who suffer and the tender Mother of compassion for all of our needs. When we look at you, we are reminded what it means to be a true "Christ bearer" and to channel your Son's infinite compassion to others. You were a mother who, like so many mothers, pondered deeply on the meaning of your Son's life and deeds. In your mother's awesome, uniquely mysterious relationship with Christ, you came to know him as no one else could. Intercede for us, that we may bear the Lord as you did, and allow the Holy Name of Jesus to shine forever in our hearts. Through Christ our Lord. Amen.

Antiphon:

Antiphon:

"Rejoice! fervent helper of the Christian race!" (Akathist)

Readings:

"Your realm is an everlasting realm, and your dominion endures through all generations. . . . You are faithful in all your words, and gracious in all your deeds. You uphold all who are falling, and raise up all who are bowed down. The eyes of all creatures look to you, to give them food in due season. You open wide your hand, to satisfy the desires of every living thing." *Psalm 145:13–15 (PCB)*

"And at the end of eight days, when he was circumcised, he was called Jesus, the name given by the angel before he was conceived in the womb." *Luke 2:21 (RSV)*

"I am the mother of fair love, of fear, of knowledge and of holy hope. In me is all grace of the way and of the truth; in me is all hope of life and of virtues." *Roman Missal, 314*

JANUARY 2   Abbess Taisiia

Born in 1840, Abbess Taisiia became a renowned educator, visionary, and Mother of her community. Born Mariia to a mother who had already lost two children in childbirth, mother and daughter became inseparable. After suffering an eye disease at an early age, Taisiaa never fully regained her vision, but she wrote in her autobiography that the Lord sharpened her wisdom and memory. Nicknamed the Blind Wise One by her classmates, by the time she graduated from high school, she had memorized the Gospels. During her First Communion, Maria experienced a vision of heaven, after which she decided to renounce the world. To her great anguish, she cut her tight bond with her mother in order to pursue her mission with the Lord. She joined the Lenshino community, which was struggling and did not yet have the status of a monastery. While there, she suffered a bout with paralysis, which was cured by a vision of St. Michael the Archangel. After many trials, the community was made official and named St. John the Forerunner. Appointed head of the community, Taisiaa served as abbess for thirty years. Abbess Taisiaa once wrote that angels are bodiless, but an individual can become like an angel in her interior life. Her book, *Letters to Beginning Nuns,* has become an Orthodox classic and is found in nearly every women's monastery.

Prayer:

> *Beloved Lord Jesus, Mother Taisiia was a dearly loved spiritual elder who desired only to bring souls closer to you. She advised all who are on a spiritual walk with God to begin everything with love, for without love, righteous acts are meaningless. Help us to follow her example whether in family or in community life; and practice forbearance with one another, so that like her, we may imitate the angel's calm in all we do. Amen.*

Antiphon:

Be still and know that I am God.

Readings:

"Your angel, O God, is encamped around those who revere you." *Psalm 34:7 (PCB)*

"There is a river, the streams whereof shall make glad the city of God; the holy place of the tabernacles of the Most High. God is in the midst of her; and she shall not be moved; God shall help her right early." *Psalm 46:4–5 (NASB)*

"If then you have been raised in Christ, seek the things that are above, where Christ is, seated at the right hand of God. Set your mind on things that are above, not on things that are on the earth; for you are dead, and your life is hid with Christ our God." *Col. 3:1–3 (NASB)*

JANUARY 3 Genevieve

Also known as Genovefa, St. Genevieve of Paris has had a rich cult of civic and natural pride in France since the early sixth century. It is believed that, after losing her parents at age fifteen, she moved to Paris to become a nun. Her life was marked by visions and prophecies, and she was credited with averting the coming of Attila the Hun by advising her countrymen to fast and pray. During the Franks' occupation, she worked to feed a starving people and to secure the release of many prisoners. She was deeply devoted to

Dionysius of Paris, the city's principal apostle and the patron saint of France, and she had a church built in his honor. After her own death, she was enshrined in the Church of Saints Peter and Paul, where subsequent miracles ensured that her cult continued to flourish. Throughout the Middle Ages, her banner was carried in procession in times of epidemic or national crisis. In art she is pictured with a candle and sometimes a demon trying unsuccessfully to blow it out. She is the patron of France and prisoners.

Prayer:

> *O Holy Spirit of God, You are the Voice of prophecy and the ever-present Source which seeks to bestow freedom on all peoples. St. Genevieve was a valiant woman holding high the banner of hope for her fellow citizens and a beacon in times of peril. Inspire us to be a light in times of darkness for those whose lives have lost hope. Be thou our guide and our counselor, our hope and our comfort; and lead all of your creation to the blessed freedom won for us through the merits of Christ our Lord. Amen.*

Antiphon:

In your light may we see light.

Readings:

"God is our refuge and strength, a helper in time of trouble. We shall not fear though the earth should rock, though the mountains fall into the depths of the sea, though its waters rage and foam, though the mountains tremble with its tumult." *Psalm 46:1–3 (NASB)*

" '[A]nd go . . . to them of captivity, unto the children of thy people, and speak unto them' . . . Then the spirit took me up, and I heard behind me a voice of great rushing, saying, 'Blessed be the glory of the Lord.'" *EZ. 3:11–12 (KJV)*

"But the righteous live for ever,
and their reward is with the Lord;
the Most High takes care of them." *Wisdom 5:15 (RSV)*

JANUARY 4 Elizabeth Ann Seton

Elizabeth Ann Seton was born Elizabeth Bailey in New York in 1774. She was raised a devout Episcopalian. She married William Seton when she was nineteen years old, and they had had five children before encountering personal tragedy. William's business failed, and he contracted tuberculosis. William and Elizabeth made the journey to Italy, a warm southern climate, and they stayed with Italian colleagues of his who were devout Roman Catholics. Unfortunately, William died and Elizabeth's only solace came from the compassionate Catholics who surrounded her. When she returned to her children in America, she converted to Catholicism. At the age of thirty-nine, the Bishop of Baltimore commissioned her to begin a new religious order that would focus on educating Catholic youth. The Sisters of St. Joseph eventually became known as The American Daughters of Charity, and Mother Seton was their Superior. Her own children attended the schools she helped to found, and she was in the process of setting up yet another school when she died at age forty-seven. When she was canonized by Pope Paul VI in 1975, over a thousand nuns from her order were present.

Prayer:

Dear Heavenly Father, you gave us Elizabeth Ann Seton as a model for converts, mothers, wives, educators, religious, and widows. She truly was a living example for many women today from all walks of life because of the tremendous range of her life experiences. Through all the sorrows she experienced, she never lost her faith or her desire to understand and act upon your Will in all things. May her example inspire and encourage us to fulfill what you ask of us in our daily lives. Amen.

Antiphon:

And every day, in the temple and at home, they ceased not to teach and to preach Jesus the Christ.

Readings:

"Show me your ways, O Lord; teach me your paths.
Lead me in the way of your truth, and teach me;
For you are the God of my salvation; on you do I wait all day long.
Remember, O Lord, your tender mercies and your loving-kindness;
For they have been ever of old." *Psalm 25:4–6 (KJV)*

"Learn to do well; seek judgment, relieve the oppressed, judge the fatherless, plead for the widow. Come now, and let us reason together, says the Lord." *Isa. 1:17–18 (KJV)*

"Now therefore go, and I will be with you, and teach you what you shall say." *Ex. 4:12 (KJV)*

JANUARY 5 Amma Syncletike

Holy Mother Syncletike was one of the earliest of the Desert Mothers, who left a body of teachings, much like the Desert Fathers of the East. She was born in Alexandria to a wealthy family, and refusing marriage, she cared for her parents until they died. She then distributed her inheritance to the poor and devoted herself to a life of contemplation, following the ascetic model of monastics which was developed in what has often been referred to as the golden age of Egyptian monasticism. After withdrawing to the desert, she gained renown as an Àmma, or spiritual mother and teacher. She taught that poverty is the most powerful weapon against the devil's wiles and that humility is a virtue he can never imitate. Her discourses include both an analysis of the virtues and vices, particularly for those living in community; and an interpretation of the soul's higher states, which the monastic may experience after much ascetic practice. It is believed that she was influenced by the teachings of Pseudo-Dionysus. Polycarp wrote her *vita* and the most famous of her sayings. Toward the end of her life, she had visions of paradise. She died at nearly eighty years old, after predicting the day and hour of her death.

Intercessory Prayer:

O holy Mother and friend of those who forsake the world, dear Amma Syncletike, you loved the women disciples who sat at your feet, and you fed them the bread of your holy wisdom in the desert. Help those of us in the modern world who strive to separate ourselves from all the trappings that lure us from our true desire of finding God, and intercede for each of us that we may take our calling seriously. Pray for those who struggle in the monastic life

*that they might find the fruit of their labor in the sweetness of the
Holy Name of Jesus. Amen.*

Antiphon:
You search the mind and probe the heart, giving each what
we deserve.

Readings:
"Two things have I required of you; deny them not to me before I
die: Remove far from me vanity and lies; Give me neither poverty
nor riches; feed me with food convenient for me, Lest I be full and
deny you, and say: 'Who is the Lord?' Or lest I be poor and steal,
and take the name of my God in vain." *Prov. 30:7–9 (KJV)*

"Rest in the Lord and wait patiently for him; Do not fret because of
him who prospers in his way. . . . Do not fret; it leads only to evil-
doing." *Psalm 37:7–8 (NASB)*

"And the devil, taking him up to a high mountain, showed to him
all the kingdoms of the world in a moment of time; and said to
him: 'To you will I give all this authority and their glory, for it has
been delivered to me, and I give it to whom I will. If you, then, will
worship me, it will all be yours.' And Jesus answered him, 'It is
written, You shall worship the Lord your God, and only him shall
you serve.'" *Luke 4:5–8 (RSV)*

JANUARY 6 Raphaela of the Sacred Heart

Raphaela of the Sacred Heart was born in 1850, one of two
daughters, to a wealthy family in Cordova, Spain. A pious priest
gave her and her sister, Delores, instruction and planted the
seeds that inspired the girls to pursue a religious vocation. Raphaela
and her sister joined the Sisters of Marie Reparatrice in 1873. The
local bishop asked Raphaela and several other nuns to resettle in
Madrid and form a new order, The Handmaids of the Sacred Heart.
Taking her vows and the name Raphaela of the Sacred Heart of Jesus,
she was made Superior of this order in 1877. The congregation was
devoted to teaching and conducting retreats. Unfortunately, sisterly
conflict between Raphaela and Delores caused friction within the
congregation, as Delores continually undermined Raphaela's authority. In 1893, Raphaela resigned as Superior and spent the rest of her

life carrying out menial duties and tasks, living in obscurity in the congregation's house in Rome. Though she spent the last few years of her life in a bedridden state, Raphaela never complained of her illness to the other sisters, many of whom did not know that the pious, old woman was actually the foundress of their order. Raphaela was eventually recognized for her holiness and canonized in 1977. She is a patron of those involved in family conflicts.

Intercessory Prayer:

Dear St. Raphaela, your entire life was spent in loving service and in total submission to the Will of God. You answered God's call to evangelize by offering the gift of your own vocation as an act of complete service to others. When your life brought you into conflict with your sister, you turned away from conflict and surrendered everything to God. Help us as we also strive for reconciliation in family conflicts. May we also adopt a spirit of understanding and generosity in all aspects of life. Amen.

Antiphon:

The humble shall see this, and be glad: you who seek God, let your hearts revive.

Readings:

"I said, 'I will guard my ways, so as to not sin with my tongue; I will guard my mouth. . . .' I kept dumb and silent; And my sorrow grew worse, while I was musing, the fire burned. Then I spoke . . . 'Lord, make me to know my end, and what is the extent of my days. Let me know how transient I am.'" *Psalm 39:1–5 (NASB)*

"In everything . . . treat people the same way you want them to treat you, for this is the Law and the Prophets." *Mt. 7:12 (NASB)*

"Each one of us will have to give an account of himself to God. Therefore let us not judge one another anymore, but rather determine this—not to put an obstacle or a stumbling block in a [brother's] way." *Rom. 14:12–13 (NASB)*

JANUARY 7 Angela of Foligno

The early part of Angela's life in Foligno was spent obsessed with accumulating money, fame, and social power. She hungrily climbed the ladder of success. Born thirty years after Francis of Assisi's death, she had a conversion at Assisi when she made a pilgrimage there. Since she was married, she became a Secular Franciscan. Later, when Angela lost her entire family to the plague, she cloistered herself in a church near the Franciscan friars, and she began to write. Her Franciscan confessor became her scribe and eventually, with many others, her disciple. Her *Book of Visions and Instructions* earned her the title Teacher of Theologians. She was a profound mystic of the early Franciscan tradition, and her works are rich with images that emerged during her conversations with Christ. Once when the Lord told her his love for her was so immense she could not bear it if it were revealed, she begged him to make her able to bear it. He refused. Her recorded conversations have become a classic that has inspired many souls since her peaceful death in 1309. She was beatified in 1693. She is one of the early patrons of Secular Franciscans.

Intercessory Prayer:

Blessed Angela, your revelations of Christ brought light to the darkest depths of your soul, as you left everything and lost everything most dear to you on your way to his Glory. You once wrote that poverty, suffering, and contempt are the elect of your Jesus. Pray for us, that we may be willing to be stripped of anything that stands in the way of a greater reconciliation with our God, and help us to always remember that our self-worth can never be increased through attachments to this world. Amen.

Antiphon:

Blessed are you who are poor, for yours is the kingdom of heaven.

Readings:

"I am passing like a shadow when it lengthens; I am shaken off like the locust. My knees are weak from fasting, And my flesh has grown lean, without fatness. I also have become a reproach to them; When they see me, they wag their head. Help me, O LORD my God; Save me according to Your lovingkindness." *Psalm 109:23–26 (NASB)*

"Therefore repent and return, so that your sins may be wiped away, in order that times of refreshing may come from the presence of the Lord." *Acts 3:19 (NASB)*

"So he got up and came to his father. But while he was still a long way off, his father saw him and felt compassion for him, and ran and embraced him and kissed him. . . . But the father said . . . 'Quickly bring out the best robe and put it on him, and put a ring on his hand and sandals on his feet.'" *Luke 15:20, 22 (NASB)*

JANUARY 8 Domnica of Carthage and Pega

St. Domnica is considered a Holy Mother in Orthodoxy, one of the early virgins who organized an ascetic group of women in the fourth century. Born around 384 during the reign of Theodosios I, she completed her education in Carthage and traveled to Constantinople with four other women; there she met the great patriarch, St. Nectarios. Inspired to become Christian, all five women were baptized and decided to live together and practice the monastic rule. The group grew, and Domnica gained renown as a miracle worker and loving Mother of her congregation. She was also gifted with clairvoyance. After her death, her fame grew among sailors, who believed that her intercession could calm storms.

Pega was a virgin who lived during the eighth century as an anchoress in Northamptonshire. The sister of St. Guthlac, she inherited his Psalter. Pega was noted for curing the blind during her life and for other miracles after her death. Pega's Church, in Peakirk, was named after her.

Prayer:

Graciously hear us, O God, that rejoicing in the feast of Blessed Domnica and Pega, your holy women, we may follow their fervent aspirations to find you in the silence of our souls. With the fruit of their hands, they planted a spiritual vineyard for you in the lands where they lived, and it has brought forth rich mercy in the lives of many who lived after them. By their intercession, may we have the grace to discern your call and find our way home to you through all of life's storm-tossed seas. Amen.

Antiphon:

Peace be with you: as the Father has sent me, so I also send you.

Readings:

"I said, O, that I had the wings of a dove! I would fly away and be at rest.
Behold, I would wander far away, I would lodge in the wilderness.
I would hasten to my place of refuge
From the stormy wind and tempest." *Psalm 55:6–8 (NASB)*

"For You have been a defense for the helpless, . . . a refuge from the storm, a shade from the heat. . . . And on this mountain He will swallow up the covering which is over all peoples, Even the veil which is stretched over all nations. He will swallow up death for all time, And the Lord GOD will wipe tears away from all faces." *Isa. 25:4, 6, 8 (NASB)*

"One thing I do know, that though I was blind, now I see." *Jn. 9:25 (NASB)*

JANUARY 9 Julia Emery

Julia Emery is a beloved daughter of the Episcopal Church, re-membered on this day as one of the early pioneers of its leader-ship. Born in 1852, she was instrumental in helping to establish a Woman's Auxiliary in every diocese and missionary district in the church, traveling worldwide for forty years. Implemented in 1871, the Woman's Auxiliary was an important arm of the General Convention of the Church, and it was particularly active in missionary work, especially with the poor and sick. Julia organized a Church Periodical Club to provide literature for missionaries and worked energetically to secure financial funding for her missions. She balanced her organizational skills with a love of the Church: its sacraments, its people, and spreading the gospel message were the heartbeat of her life. Julia's friends remember her as a person who never criticized a coworker. In her life of service, she was quick to put the Lord first, her colleagues and the ones she served next, and herself last. Under her benevolent eye, many women came to discover leadership positions for themselves in a church that continued to honor women's contributions in every aspect of its work over the next hundred years.

Prayer:

Gracious and Almighty God, you raised up holy woman Julia to love the work of serving you in every member of the church. So engrossed was she in your service that everywhere she went she left behind precious pearls, seeds of your growing kingdom. Keep us also constant in faith and zealous in witnessing to your Word. Knit us together in one mystical body through the fire of the Spirit and for the sake of Jesus Christ our Lord. Amen.

Antiphon:

When he had found one pearl of great price, he went and sold all he had and bought it.

Readings:

"Sing for joy to God our strength, shout aloud to the God of Jacob! Begin the music, strike the tambourine, play the melodious harp and lyre. Sound the ram's horn at the New Moon, and when the moon is full, on the day of our Feast." *Psalm 81:1–3 (NIV)*

"Turn and set your journey and go to the hill country. . . . See I have placed the land before you, go in and possess the land which the Lord swore to give . . . to Abraham, to Isaac, to Jacob, to them and their descendants after them." *Deut. 1:7–8 (NAS)*

"Then I heard the voice of the Lord, saying, 'Whom shall I send, and who will go for Us?' Then I said, 'Here I am, Lord, Send me!'" *Isa. 6:8 (NAS)*

"And he said to me, 'Go! For I will send you far away to the Gentiles.'" *Acts 22:21 (NASB)*

Maria Dolores
Rodriguez Sopena

Maria Dolores Rodriguez Sopena, often called Dolores, felt, from early childhood, that the sick and the poor were part of her family. Born in 1848 in Spain, she lived part of her life in Puerto Rico, where she founded several Centers for Instruction for catechizing and educating the poor and needy. When her mother died, Dolores returned to Madrid and attempted to join a convent; however, she quickly realized that her work was in the world and left it. Dolores found a spiritual director and was led to organize the association of Apostolic Laymen (now called the Sopena Lay Movement) to work in Madrid's overpopulated poor neighborhoods. She opened one of Madrid's first halfway houses, which helped to integrate prisoners back into society. One of her great contributions was the Sopena Social and Cultural Work; since her death it has spread to South America and the Caribbean. Because of an unsuccessful eye operation at age eight, Dolores lived the rest of her life with limited eyesight, yet this disability did not deter her from her vigorous contribution toward making the world a better place for others. She made 199 trips throughout Spain to consolidate her apostolic missions, and she was particularly devoted to workers and worker rights. Maria Dolores died of natural causes in 1918, and she was beatified in March 2003 for her exemplary contribution to Catholic social action. She is the patron of those with eye diseases.

Prayer:

> Beloved Jesus, Maria Dolores expressed her love for you throughout her life by nurturing those whom you called us to minister to in the Beatitudes. Her life with you was expressed in a filial attitude filled with tenderness. Her motto was that any obstacle could be overcome by daily affirming that she was only an instrument in your hands. Through her intercession, give us the fortitude and selflessness to devote ourselves to the compassionate face of God that seeks to bring all of humanity to wholeness in your holy Name. Amen.

Antiphon:

Let your light so shine before others, that they may see your good works.

Readings:

"The Spirit of the Lord GOD is upon me,
Because the LORD has anointed me
To bring good news to the afflicted;
He has sent me to bind up the brokenhearted,
To proclaim liberty to captives
And freedom to prisoners;
To proclaim the favorable year of the LORD
And the day of vengeance of our God;
To comfort all who mourn." *Isa. 61:1–3 (NASB)*

"God has chosen the foolish things of the world to shame the wise, and God has chosen the weak things of the world to shame the things which are strong, and the base things of the world and the despised God has chosen. . . . But by his doing you are in Christ Jesus, who became to us wisdom from God, and righteousness and sanctification, and redemption." *1 Cor. 1:28–30 (NASB)*

JANUARY 11 Mary Slessor

Mary Slessor was a woman of contrasts: fearful when it came to public speaking, she was nonetheless called to a life of evangelical fervor. Born in Scotland in 1848, Mary's alcoholic father died young, and Mary became her family's main provider. She taught Bible classes at her childhood church, yet shunned a social life of her own. At age twenty-seven, she longed to become a missionary in the United Presbyterian Church, and she left for Nigeria, where she spent the next thirty-nine years. Her mission home in Calabar became a school, meditation center, and refuge for the tribal peoples, who grew to love her dearly. She also served as a judge over several tribal districts. In 1914 she was awarded the Silver Cross as a sign of her fervent missionary activities. She died the next year. Mary is remembered on this day in the Anglican calendar along with the Holy Innocents.

Prayer:

Beloved Holy Spirit of God, Mary Slessor was able to discern your call to evangelize in a foreign land, and despite setbacks, she saw her vision to completion. Through her example, help us to stay committed to our ideals and our vocation in life. Keep us from discouragement or despair, and make us willing instruments of your work in the world. Through your gracious love, give us the grace to discern your call. Amen.

Antiphon:

You lead the humble in a straight path.

Readings:

"Tremble, thou earth, at the presence of the God of Jacob, which turned the rock into a standing water, and flint into a mountain of waters." *Psalm 114:7–8 (KJV)*

"When He had finished speaking, He said to Simon, 'Put out into the deep water and let down your nets for a catch.' Simon answered and said, 'Master, we worked hard all night and caught nothing, but I will do as You say and let down the nets.' When they had done this, they enclosed a great quantity of fish, and their nets began to break; so they signaled to their partners in the other boat for them to come and help them. And they came and filled both of the boats, so that they began to sink. But when Simon Peter saw that, he fell down at Jesus' feet, saying, 'Go away from me Lord, for I am a sinful man!' . . . And Jesus said to Simon, 'Do not fear, from now on you will be catching [men.]'" *Lk. 5:4–10 (NASB)*

JANUARY 12 Margarite Bourgeoys

St. Margarite, born Margarite Bourgeouys in the late seventeenth century, was the first Canadian woman to be canonized. She was the foundress of the Congregation of Notre Dame, an order of nontraditional nuns who took vows of poverty, chastity, and obedience, but did not wear habits. Marguerite preferred that her order remain uncloistered, and her congregation was the first of its kind in a foreign country. Her sisters preferred to dress in the garb of the poor, those most insignificant members of society whom they chose to serve. The order was particularly successful in evangelizing the Huron Indians in the Ontario region. Margarite's main interest was in education, and despite many trials on the frontier, she founded numerous schools there. She was canonized in 1988 by Pope John Paul II as an outstanding pioneer in the history of Canada.

Prayer:

Dear Lord Jesus, St. Margarite served you through her vocation and brought many souls to the knowledge of the Christian faith. She endured poverty, cold, and severe tribulations in her attempts to bring the word of truth to the Indians whom she served. She once said that it would be impossible to find a more perfect guardian than your Mother, who sheltered you in her womb. Let the strength of her witness and trust inspire us to find ways each day to bring our faith to life. Amen.

Antiphon:

The integrity of the upright will guide them.

Readings:

"So He declared to you His covenant which He commanded you to perform, that is, the Ten Commandments; and He wrote them on two tablets of stone. The LORD commanded me at that time to teach you statutes and judgments, that you might perform them in the land where you are going." *Deut.4:13–14 (NASB)*

"And many peoples will come and say, "Come, let us go up to the mountain of the LORD, To the house of the God of Jacob; That He may teach us concerning His ways, And that we may walk in His paths." *Isa. 2:3 (NASB)*

"Does not wisdom call, And understanding lift up her voice? On top of the heights beside the way, Where the paths meet, she takes her stand; Beside the gates, at the opening to the city, At the entrance of the doors, she cries out: . . . O naive ones, understand prudence; And, O fools, understand wisdom. Listen, for I will speak noble things; And the opening of my lips will reveal right things. For my mouth will utter truth." *Prov. 8:1–5 (NASB)*

JANUARY 13 Tatiana of Rome

St. Tatiana was part of the early developing Church. Born in the third century to a prominent Roman family, she was an outspoken Christian in a position of influence. The Byzantine churches honored her as a deaconess because her duties included instructing women who wanted to be baptized. Her ministry was so successful that the Emperor Alexander—although he had some tolerance for Christians—insisted that her numerous converts meet only in small groups. However, Alexander resented her charismatic fervor and eventually arrested her. When Tatiana prayed to God to make angels surround her that would be visible to her executioners, eight of the executioners were converted on the spot. They were eventually martyred for this. Tatiana was tortured in an endless array of horrors, but each day she awoke in her prison cell miraculously healed. Another early legend concerning her life was that, while standing before the statues of Alexander's gods, she made the sign of the cross over them and all his precious statues fell to the ground. She was finally beheaded along with her saintly father around the year 225. She is a patron of evangelists and martyrs.

Prayer:

Beloved Lord, you have blessed the Church with many holy women throughout history. St. Tatiana served as a martyr and witness of the early Church, and her holy example brought numerous souls to know the Christian faith. She was a valiant spokeswoman and clung fast to her belief in one God. She died with your beloved name on her lips, Lord. Sustain us when we forsake the idols we have created that separate us from you, and keep us true to our highest ideals. Amen.

Antiphon:

Whoever lives and believes in Me shall never die.

Readings:

"For great is the Lord, and greatly to be praised, revered above all the gods. For all the gods of the people are idols, but the Lord made the heavens. Glory and honour are in his presence, strength and gladness are in his place. Give to the Lord, Oh families of the peoples, ascribe to the Lord glory and strength! Give to the Lord the glory due to his Name . . . worship the Lord in the beauty of holiness." *Chron. 16:25–29 (KJV)*

"Behold the Lord is riding on a swift cloud and is about to come to Egypt; and the idols of Egypt will tremble at his presence, and the heart of the Egyptians will melt within them." *Isa. 19:1 (NASB)*

"And we know that the Son of God has come, and has given us understanding so that we may know Him who is true; and we are in him who is true, in his Son Jesus Christ. This is the true God and eternal life. Little children, guard yourselves from idols." *1 Jn. 5:20–21 (NASB)*

JANUARY 14 Nina of Georgia and Macrina the Elder

St. Nina is honored in the Orthodox Church as Equal to the Apostles and as Enlightener of Georgia. She was born in Cappadocia around the year 280 of noble and illustrious lineage. Her mother, a deaconess, was the sister of the Jerusalem Patriarch Juvenal. From childhood, Nina was devoted to reading Scripture, and for many years she was consumed with the whereabouts of the Lord's Chiton (tunic) (Jn. 19:23–24). She learned that, according to tradition, the tunic had been taken to a place named Gruzia, or Georgia, which had not yet been Christianized. Nina prayed fervently to the Theotokos that she might find the tunic, and the Mother of God appeared to her in a dream, entrusting to her a cross made of vineyard sprigs. Nina took such a cross with her to Georgia and was an avid evangelizer there, healing many people with her simple cross. It is believed that Nina found the incorruptible tunic in Gruzia, and a temple was built there later. She spent thirty-five years of apostolic service in Gruzia, and she is honored as the patron of the Georgian Orthodox Church, one of the oldest Orthodox churches in the world.

January 14 is also the feast of St. Macrina the Elder, a disciple of St. Gregory the Wonder-worker, and grandmother to Sts. Basil, Mother Macrina (see Daily Readings, July 19, Macrina), and Gregory of Nyssa.

Prayer:

Beloved Holy Spirit of God, St. Nina was inspired by you to evangelize in a foreign country which she learned to call her home. She was a faithful instrument of your holy work in apostolic preaching and in miracles of healing. By her faithful intercession and example, lead us toward our true vocations, so that in finding our own work in the world, we will serve you in the most perfect way possible. Amen.

Antiphon:

All things work together for good for those who love God and are called according to his purpose.

Readings:

"You have loved righteousness and hated wickedness; Therefore God, Your God, has anointed you with the oil of joy." *Psalm 45:7 (NASB)*

"Behold, I am bringing them from the north country, And I will gather them from the remote parts of the earth, Among them the blind and the lame, the woman with child and she who is in labor with child, together. . . . And by supplication I will lead them; I will make them walk by streams of waters, On a straight path in which they will not stumble" *Jer. 31:8–9 (NASB)*

"Then the soldiers, when they had crucified Jesus, took his garments, and made four parts, to every soldier a part. . . . Now the coat was without seam, woven from top to bottom, They said therefore among themselves, 'Let us not tear it, but cast lots for it. . . .'" *John 19:23–24 (KJV)*

JANUARY 15 Ita (Ide)

Ita was an Irish nun who, along with Brigid, is among the most sainted women in Ireland. She was born to a royal family near Waterford. Her birth name was Deirdre, but she was nicknamed Itha (or Ita), meaning thirst, because of her thirst for God. Ita moved from Waterford to Killeedy (Limerick) and founded a small nunnery there. She was an ascetic and spent much time praying in solitude and fasting. Devotion to the indwelling Holy Trinity was the core of her life. An old Irish poem, "Isucan," or "Lullaby for the

Infant Jesus," included in a nineteenth-century manuscript, is attributed to Ita. She ran a school for boys and became known as the foster mother of Ireland's early saints. In particular, she was said to have fostered St. Brendan of Ireland, a seafarer and navigator. When St. Brendan asked Ita what three things were most pleasing to God, she responded: a faithful heart, simplicity of life, and open-handedness inspired by charity. According to the Annals of Ulster, she died in the 570s "a tolerant and humorous old woman." She is a patron of seafarers.

Prayer:

Beloved Jesus, Ita was a cherished jewel in your crown whose thirst for you spilled over into a holy love for the souls whom she nurtured. Through her intercession and example, help us to remember that all that we have and all that we are belongs entirely to you. Keep us in your life-giving gaze and bring us, like Ita's foster children, closer to you through lives of faithfulness and simplicity. Amen.

Antiphon:

Fill our days with peace that we may sing your praise.

Readings:

"We sing to you a new song, for you have done wonderful things!
Your saving hand and your holy arm have given the victory.
You have made known your salvation; and revealed your justice to the nations.
You have remembered your love and your faithfulness. . . ." *Psalm 98:1–3 (PCB)*

"She makes linen garments and sells them,
And supplies belts to the tradesmen.
Strength and dignity are her clothing,
And she smiles at the future.
She opens her mouth in wisdom,
And the teaching of kindness is on her tongue.
She looks well to the ways of her household,
And does not eat the bread of idleness.
Her children rise up and bless her." *Prov. 31:24–28 (NASB)*

"When it was evening, the boat was in the middle of the sea, and He was alone on the land. Seeing them straining at the oars, for the wind was against them, at about the fourth watch of the night He came to them, walking on the sea; and He intended to pass by them. But when they saw Him walking on the sea, they supposed that it was a ghost, and cried out; for they all saw Him and were terrified. But immediately He spoke with them and said to them, 'Take courage; it is I, do not be afraid.'" *Mk. 6:47–50 (NASB)*

JANUARY 16 Prisca and Kentigerna

There are a number of Priscas (Priscilla) in the early Church. (The Prisca mentioned in Acts with Aquilah is celebrated on February 13, the Orthodox date.) This Prisca was the wife of Mancius Glabrio, also a martyr. She was the mother of a senator, who also became an early saint, St. Pudens. Their house, which served as a church, was apparently a large headquarters for missionary activity in the early Church, and a catacomb under her home was named after her. She is sometimes represented in art with two lions who refused to harm her, although this image may be a confluence of one or more of the other Priscas. Prisca and her husband were executed, most probably in the reign of Domitian.

Kentigerna, an anchoress, was born in Ireland in the eighth century. The daughter of a prince, she married a neighboring prince and had one son, who also became a saint (St. Fillan). After her husband's death, Kentigerna left Ireland and lived as a hermit nun in Scotland. A church on a small island on Loch Lomond was dedicated to her.

Prayer:

> *Gracious Holy Spirit of God, you have mothered us with your comfort and inspiration; and many mothers in the Church gave birth to saints because of your holy wisdom. Through the intercession of Blessed Prisca and Kentigerna, help all mothers to nourish the souls of their children, so what they eventually grow to hold dear is also dear to God's honor, justice, and righteousness. May they be filled with your blessed grace and strengthened in their inner being, through the merits of Jesus, our Lord and Savior. Amen.*

Antiphon:

O how I love your law; all day long it is in my mind.

Readings:

"If God does not build the house, its builders labor in vain. If God does not watch over the city, in vain is the vigil kept. It is vain to rise up early and go late to rest, eating the bread of anxious toil: for you, O God, give sleep to your beloved. Truly children are a gift from the Most High, the fruit of the womb, a blessing. Like arrows in the hand of a warrior are the children of one's youth. . . ." *Psalm 127:1–4 (PCB)*

"Do not let your heart be troubled; believe in God, believe also in Me. . . . For I go to prepare a place for you." *Jn 14:1 (NASB)*

JANUARY 17 Rosalina of Villeneuve

Rosalina of Villeneuve was born to a prominent French family during the thirteenth century. Her father was a count, and the family was considerably wealthy. Rosalina was an extremely devout and pious child, and from a young age she exhibited a deep passion to nurture the poor. She would sneak food out of her home to share with beggars on the street. When her father caught her smuggling out meals within her cloak, he demanded that she open her hidden stash and admit her wrongdoing. She opened her cloak, and out fell a cascade of brilliant roses, miraculously replacing the food she had been hiding. Her father immediately accepted this sign from God, and instructed the castle's cooks to feed all the hungry townsfolk lined up at their door. Rosalina eventually became a Carthusian nun in the monastery at Bertrand; her mother followed her into the order. Rosalina later became the prioress. It was said that she possessed the gift of reading hearts, and miraculous phenomenon abounded in her presence. She died in 1329 at her monastery, where her incorrupt body remains, and she was beatified in 1851. The site of her tomb has become a place of countless miracles through the centuries. She is the patron of Draguignan, France.

Intercessory Prayer:

Dear Blessed Rosalina, your love for the poor and your unbounded charity toward the disadvantaged were an inspiration to the people of your village. Your example of kindness to the most destitute continues to inspire us even today. May we always attempt to live out the virtue of Gospel charity by helping others whom God may place in our path, remembering that through each individual we assist, we are actually serving Christ. Amen.

Antiphon:

For he satisfies the longing soul, and fills the hungry soul with goodness.

Readings:

"The anointed one delivers the needy when they call,
The poor and those who are helpless,
Having pity on the weak and the needy,
Saving the lives of the poor." *Psalm 72:12–13 (PCB)*

"And like a shepherd he will tend his flock, in his arm he will gather the lambs, and carry them in his bosom; He will gently lead the nursing ewes." *Isa. 40:11 (NAS)*

"I tell you the truth, anyone who has faith in me will do what I have been doing, and even greater things than these, because I am going to the Father. And I will do whatever you ask in my Name, . . . you may ask for anything in my Name, and I will do it." *Jn. 14:12–14 (NIV)*

JANUARY 18 Margaret of Hungary

Princess Margaret was born in 1242 to royal parents who promised God they would dedicate a child to him if Hungary could be liberated from the Tartars. This did occur, and Margaret was invested into a Dominican convent at the age of three as a child oblate. When she was eighteen, her father wished her to be relieved of this promise so she could marry King Ottokar II of Bohemia. But the beautiful Margaret was so intent on living out her religious vocation that she threatened to cut off her nose and lips if she was forced to break her vow of virginity and wed. Her father acquiesced, and she was allowed to make her formal vows as a Dominican. Margaret lived a life of unusual austerity, tending to the poorest of the poor and to the most menial tasks in the convent. Her intense acts of mortification were probably a major cause of her eventual death at age twenty-eight. Soon after, steps were taken to initiate her canonization, due to the large number of witnesses who testified to her sanctity. Numerous miracles and healings were attributed to her intercession.

Prayer:

Dear Heavenly Father, throughout history you have given the world great witnesses who testify to the truth by their austere and courageous lifestyles. Blessed Margaret of Hungary was a shining light of sanctity to all those around her, and her intercession for others remains a testament to her faith. Help us to see the eternal value of even the smallest acts performed for you, and to believe that each tiny sacrifice helps to pave our way to Heaven. Amen.

Antiphon:

Offer the sacrifices of righteousness and put your trust in the Lord.

Readings:

"He summons the heavens above, And the earth, to judge His people: Gather My godly ones to Me, Those who have made a covenant with Me by sacrifice. And the heavens declare His righteousness." He shall call to the heavens from above, and to the earth, that he may judge his people [saying], 'Gather my saints together with me: those who have made a covenant with me through sacrifice.' And the heavens shall declare his righteousness." *Psalm 50:4–5 (NASB)*

"Then Joshua built an altar to the LORD, the God of Israel, in Mount Ebal, just as Moses the servant of the LORD had commanded the sons of Israel, as it is written in the book of the law of Moses, an altar of uncut stones on which no man had wielded an iron tool; and they offered burnt offerings on it to the LORD, and sacrificed peace offerings." *Josh. 8:31 (NASB)*

"Oh Lord, open my lips, That my mouth may declare Your praise. For You do not delight in sacrifice, otherwise I would give it; You are not pleased with burnt offering. The sacrifices of God are a broken spirit; A broken and a contrite heart, O God, You will not despise." *Psalm 51:15–17 (NASB)*

JANUARY 19 Mother Joseph of the Sacred Heart

Mother Joseph of the Sacred Heart was born Esther Pariseau in Montreal in 1823. When she was twenty years old, her father brought her to the Sisters of Charity of Providence so she could fulfill her dream of entering a convent. She was remembered for her seemingly endless array of skills—from carpenter to watchmaker, from architect to mechanic. She used all of her gifts for God's greater honor by becoming a missionary in the Pacific Northwest Territories in the United States. Through her dedicated work, she opened numerous hospitals, academies, Indian schools, and orphanages. She used her architectual and artistic skills to carry out every phase of these efforts, including building design, construction, and even fund-raising. She worked tirelessly in her missionary efforts for nearly sixty years before she died of a brain tumor in 1902. She is most fondly remembered by the Sisters of Charity of Providence in Montreal, where she is honored as a woman who embodied trustful surrender to divine providence.

Prayer:

Beloved Lord, you inspired Mother Joseph to live out her life in joyful service to others. You blessed her with numerous artistic gifts, and she made use of all of them for the glorification of your Kingdom. Through her schools, hospitals, and orphanages, she was able to reach out and touch the world in which she lived by bringing the good news to countless souls. May she inspire us to offer our lives to further your Kingdom here on earth by using the gifts you give us in ways that will bring greater honor and glory to you. Amen.

Antiphon:

Let all things be done with charity.

Readings:

"For you, O God, have not despised nor scorned the affliction of the poor;
You have not hid your face from them, but heard them when they cried to you.

To you comes praise from the great assembly; My vows I will pay
  before those who fear you.
The poor shall eat and be satisfied; those who seek you will sing
  your praise forever!
May their hearts live forever!" *Psalm 22:25–27 (PCB)*

"If any one thinks he is religious, and does not bridle his tongue
but deceives his heart, his religion is in vain. Religion that is pure
and undefiled before God is this: to visit orphans and widows in
their affliction, and to keep oneself unstained from the world."
James 1:27 (RSV)

"To what shall we liken the kingdom of God? Or to what comparison shall we compare it? It is like a grain of mustard seed, which,
when it is sown in the earth, is less than all the seeds that be in
the earth; But when it is sown, it grows up and becomes greater
than all the herbs, and shoots out great branches, so that the
fowls of the air may lodge under the shadow of it." *Mk. 4:30–32
(KJV)*

JANUARY 20 Eustochia Calafato

Eustochia Calafato was baptized Smeralda, which means
"emerald" in Sicilian. The daughter of pious Catholic parents,
she had a vision early in life of the crucified Christ and wanted
only to become his bride. She entered a Poor Clare convent in Santa
Maria di Sascio and took the name Eustochia in 1446. During her
eleven years at that monastery, she ministered to the sick, especially
those affected by the plague. Inspired to found a community based on
a stricter Franciscan poverty, Pope Callistus III granted her permission to move to Montevergine in the city of Messina and enact re-
forms. She was abbess there until her death at age thirty, and her
incorrupt body remains at Messina. The people of Messina consider
her their patron, especially from earthquake. She was canonized in
1988. In art, she is often pictured with the Blessed Sacrament, to
which she was deeply devoted.

Intercessory Prayer:

*Dear St. Eustochia, the spontaneous outpouring of your love,
especially to those suffering from diseases that frighten most
people away, remind us of all that is good in human nature. You*

desired only to walk ever more closely in Christ's footsteps, as did your model, beloved St. Clare. Pray for us that we may recognize the face of Jesus in those suffering around us and that we may constantly strive to imitate the Franciscan spirit of poverty, which alone leads to true freedom. Amen.

Antiphon:

Free us, O God, from what still binds us.

Readings:

"Rulers are not saved by their armies, nor leaders preserved by their strength. A vain hope for safety are our weapons; despite their power, they cannot save. Look on those who reverence you, on those who hope in your love, To deliver their souls from death, and keep them alive in famine. Our souls are waiting for you. You are our help and our shield. In you do our hearts find joy; we trust in your holy name." *Psalm 33:16–22 (PCB)*

"By wisdom a house is built, and by understanding it is established. And by knowledge the rooms are filled with all precious and pleasant riches." *Prov. 24:3–4 (NASB)*

"Then the righteous will answer him, Lord when did we see you hungry and feed you, or thirsty and give you drink? And when did we see you a stranger, and welcome you, or naked and clothe you? And when did we see you sick, or in prison and visit you? And the King will answer them, Truly, I say to you, as you did it to one of the least of these, my brethren, you did it to me." *Mt. 25:37–40 (RSV)*

JANUARY 21 Agnes

Agnes was one of the most famous of the early Roman martyrs. Ambrose, who wrote sermons and hymns to her, reports that she dedicated herself to Christ at age thirteen. She was captured and made to dwell in a house of prostitution as punishment for not renouncing her faith, but an angel of God protected her. Legends concerning this imprisonment include the blinding of a man who gazed upon her naked. She was condemned and initially thrown into a fire, but it would not burn her. She died by the sword after repeatedly affirming Christ as her only master. A basilica was built over her grave in the Via Nomentana. She is most frequently pictured in art with a lamb, a reference to her name (*agnus*). On her feast day in Rome, two lambs were blessed; their wool was used to weave palliums for archbishops. She is patron of rape victims.

Intercessory Prayer:

O holy St. Agnes, when you were taken into the place of shame, you found the angel of the Lord waiting there, ready to console you. Your soul has been glorified and made beautiful with the jewels of grace and virtue. In the midst of the fire, you stretched out your hands to Christ and said, "Behold now I come to You, whom I have loved, whom I have sought, whom I have always desired." Pray for us, holy virgin and martyr, that we may also belong eternally to the one whom the angels serve. Amen.

Antiphon:

I will make the one who is victorious a pillar in my temple, says the Lord.

Readings:

"O send out Your light and Your truth, let them lead me; Let them bring me to Your holy hill And to Your dwelling places. Then I will go to (J)the altar of God, To God my exceeding joy; And upon the lyre I shall praise You, O God, my God." *Psalm 43:3–5 (NASB)*

"[but] to the degree that you share the sufferings of Christ, keep on rejoicing, so that also at the revelation of His glory you may rejoice with exultation. If you are reviled for the name of Christ, you are blessed, because the Spirit of glory and of God rests on you." *1 Pet. 4:13–14 (NASB)*

"For just as the sufferings of Christ are ours in abundance, so also our comfort is abundant through Christ. But if we are afflicted, it is for your comfort and salvation; or if we are comforted, it is for your comfort, which is effective in the patient enduring of the same sufferings which we also suffer; and our hope for you is firmly grounded, knowing that as you are sharers of our sufferings, so also you are sharers of our comfort." *2 Cor 1:5–7 (NASB)*

JANUARY 22 Sarah and Hagar

Sarah and Hagar are the mothers of the Jewish and Islamic nations. In the Orthodox tradition, Sarah is honored as one of the Old Testament saints. Numerous male saints praised their mothers by comparing them to Sarah. Sarah (originally called Sarai in the Bible story) was Abraham's wife, and—in fear for his life—he identified her as his sister so she could be given over as Pharoah's wife while they were in captivity in Egypt. Sarah's feelings during this ordeal are not recorded; she is largely silent in the Genesis text until she struggles with her barrenness and asks Abraham to take Hagar, an Egyptian, as a concubine so that he may have a son. Hagar and Abraham do have a son—Ishmael. After waiting patiently for many years, Sarah finally gives birth to a son also—Isaac—which brings her great joy. Throughout history, Sarah is portrayed as an honored matriarch. God renames her when he blesses her with a child (Gen. 17:15). Abraham's soul mate, it is Sarah's son who leads the great nation that God promised to Abraham. But God also spoke with Hagar, the only woman in the Bible who gives God a name (Èl-roi, or *the God who sees me*). Because she is a foreigner, Hagar is eventually banished from Abraham's clan, perhaps over religious disagreements on how to raise their sons. But God again appears to Hagar to bless her, reassuring her that Ishmael will also lead a great nation. After God comforts Hagar, a spring of life-giving water appears to strengthen her and her son, saving them from death in the wilderness. Sarah and Hagar's stories are complementary, each blessed and sustained by God in different ways.

Prayer:

Almighty and everlasting God, you have many names in the Old Testament texts that honor and praise your power and your mercy. For Sarah, you were a God who brought joy, and her offspring fulfilled a mighty promise to Israel, which was also the seed of Sarah and her husband. For Hagar, you were a God who witnessed her pain and rejection and who saw her as she was. In naming you, she acknowledged that you are the liberator and life-giver of the downtrodden, of all the oppressed peoples of the world. In your intimate relationship with both Sarah and Hagar, you remind us that your Spirit resides in the resilient and trusting heart, and

that, despite everything, your care and love for us are unending.
Amen.

Antiphon:

We praise you for your steadfast love.

Readings:

"Now Lord, You are releasing Your bond-servant to depart in peace, according to Your word; For my eyes have seen Your salvation, Which You have prepared in the presence of all peoples." *Lk. 2:29–31 (NASB)*

"Abraham was 100 years old when his son Isaac was born to him. And Sarah said, 'God has made me to laugh, so that all that hear will laugh with me.'" *Gen. 21:5–6 (KJV)*

"As for Ishmael, I have heard you: Behold I will bless him, and will make him fruitful, and will multiply him exceedingly . . . and I will make him a great nation." "And he will be a wild donkey of a man, and everyone's hand will be against him." *(Gen 17:20 and Gen 16:12) (NASB)*

JANUARY 23 Mary Ward

Mary Ward founded the Institute of the Blessed Virgin Mary, later known as the Loretto Sisters, in 1609. Her intention was to found an order of the religious life that allowed her sisters to live outside the mainstream contemplative tradition and educate young women—an endeavor unheard of during her age and which met with great resistance. She believed that, like the Jesuits, religious women should be free to govern themselves and work an active apostolic ministry in the world. After much oppression, she died in 1645, uncertain whether her mission would succeed. The Loretto Sisters continue to educate girls in boarding schools and academies in Europe, Ireland, and Canada. Mary is remembered in the Carmelite Breviary of the Hours (997 edition) on January 23.

Prayer:

Beloved Lord, you raised up your faithful servant Mary Ward to initiate active service in the world through her ministry of uncloistered nuns. Through her intercession, give us faith to

*continue in our chosen vocation, despite failure or judgment by
those who do not understand us. As she strove to honor the Blessed
Mother Mary by word and deed, help us to bring your holy
wisdom into a world destitute of the spiritual riches of God.
Amen.*

Antiphon:

Unless You, O God, build the house, in vain do the builders
labor.

Readings:

"O God, you are my God, earnestly I seek you: my soul thirsts for
you, my body longs for you, in a dry and weary land where there
is no water. . . . On my bed I remember you, I think of you
through the watches of the night. Because you are my help, I sing
in the shadow of your wings." *Psalm 63:1, 6 (NIV)*

"Do not be dismayed before them, or I will dismay you before
them. Now behold, I have made you today as a fortified city and
as a pillar of iron and as walls of bronze against the whole land."
Jer. 1:17–18 (NASB)

"And he made known to us the mystery of his will according to his
good pleasure, which he purposed in Christ to be put into effect
when the times will have reached their fulfillment—to bring all
things in heaven and on earth together under one head, even
Christ." *Eph. 1:9–10 (NIV)*

JANUARY 24 Xenia

Xenia is a saint in the Russian Church who was named after
the earlier virgin martyr of the fifth century. ("Xeni," the root
of her name, means "stranger.") The Holy Mother Xenia of St.
Petersburg lived in the eighteenth century. She was married to a
wealthy military man and then widowed several years later at age
twenty-six. She sold all of her possessions and adopted her husband's
persona, wearing his military clothes and frequently using his name.
She lived on the street for the next forty-five years. Xenia made predictions, many of which came true. Because of her unusual behavior,
many people she met thought she was a bit insane. Those in Xenia's
orbit of influence felt she was a street saint, as she always reminded

those with whom she came into contact of God's silent, powerful love. She was a Fool for Christ, a category of saints that became very popular in Russian Orthodoxy and was characterized by people who consciously chose to appear foolish to the world so that they might enter into a total renunciation for Christ.

Prayer:

Grant, O Lord, that we who celebrate the feast of Blessed Xenia may find strength in adversity and hope in times of despair. As wisdom and honor were her only clothing, help us, like her, to know that all things of the world pass away and only the love of Christ Jesus remains. Through her intercession, help us to hold up the candle that never goes out in the midst of the darkness. Through Christ our Lord. Amen.

Antiphon:

Full of grace are your lips because God has blessed you forever.

Readings:

"She is clothed with strength and dignity, she can laugh at the days to come. She speaks with wisdom, and faithful instruction is on her tongue. . . . Charm is deceptive and beauty is fleeting, but a woman who fears the Lord is to be praised. Give her the reward she has earned, and let her works bring praise at the city gate." *Prov. 31:25, 26, 30, 31 (NIV)*

"Do not neglect your gift, which was given to you through a prophetic message when the body of elders laid their hands on you." *1 Tim. 4:14 (NIV)*

"You still lack one thing. Sell everything you have and give to the poor, and you will have treasure in heaven. Then come and follow me." *Lk. 18:22 (NIV)*

"But we preach Christ crucified, a stumbling block to the Jews, and an absurdity to Gentiles; but to those who are called, Jews and Greeks alike, Christ the power of God and the wisdom of God. Because the fool of God is wiser than men, and his weakness more powerful." *1 Cor. 1:23–25 (KJV)*

JANUARY 25 *Assuage My Sorrows* Icon
and St. Dwyn

This is the feast day of an icon named *Assuage My Sorrows* (see also, Daily Readings, October 24, *Joy of All Who Sorrow*). This ancient icon of the Mother of God, believed to have originally resided at holy Mt. Athos, has worked miracles for the sick since its rediscovery in the eighteenth century. In a dream, the Theotokos spoke to a noblewoman who had problems with movement in her arms and legs. The Theotokos told the woman to go to Moscow and find the icon of *Assuage My Sorrows* in a church bell tower, to pray before it, and be cured. The woman found the church, begged the priest to bring down all of the icons stored in the tower, and recognized *Assuage My Sorrows* immediately. Following her cure, the icon gained renown, as the faithful and suffering came from many miles to bring their afflictions to the Holy Mother, especially during the plague of 1771. The highly venerated image pictures the Virgin Mother with her Son, and in a beseechingly touching gesture, she looks down at him with tears in her eyes.

January 25 is also the feast of Dwyn, a fifth-century virgin whom the Welsh celebrated as the patron of lovers. The legend says she rejected her admirer, Maelon. Dwyn soon had a dream in which she was given a drink that cured her of her passion and turned Maelon to ice. She then made three wishes: one, that he might be unfrozen; two, that all lovers who were true to each other succeed in their quest for union; and three, that she herself would never have the desire for marriage. St. Dwyn's cult was popular in Portddwyn, where her church was a famous pilgrimage for the sick.

Prayer:

> Beloved Lord Jesus, in every iconographic image of your mother, your redeemed people come from all over the world to pray for their spiritual and temporal needs. She intercedes with you on our behalf as a most tender mother to whom your own heart is always turned in love. Through the intercession of the Blessed Theotokos, who loves us so much, and of blessed Dwyn, who also prayed for the sick and suffering, have mercy on us in our time of need. Amen.

Antiphon:

Hail! Our manifest refuge amid all sorrowful circumstances! (Akathist)

Readings:

"And I said, this is my infirmity, but I will remember the years of the right hand of the Most High. I will meditate on the works of the Lord." *Psalm 77:10–11 (KJV)*

"For as the heaven is high above the earth, so great is his mercy toward them that fear him." *Psalm 103:11 (KJV)*

"The fear of the LORD is the beginning of wisdom, And the knowledge of the Holy One is understanding. For by me your days will be multiplied, And years of life will be added to you." *Prov. 9:10–11 (NASB)*

JANUARY 26 Paula of Rome

St. Paula was a lifelong companion and collaborator with St. Jerome and, according to his praise of her, a brilliant scholar and translator. Born into Roman wealth in the fourth century, she was widowed at thirty-two. She renounced her family (who thought she had gone quite mad) and, taking one of her daughters, followed Jerome to the Holy Land. In Bethlehem, imitating the monastic model of the East, they founded a double monastery, which became the ascetic model for the West. Paula's money supported Jerome during much of his life, so he could pursue his scholarly work. Since Jerome struggled to translate his masterpiece, the Latin Vulgate, it is highly probable that Paula, proficient in Greek, was instrumental in helping him. Jerome was one of the few Western writers of the era who believed that women—at least monastic women—could be egalitarian partners with men. Indeed, Paula seems to have been his soul mate. When she died at fifty-seven, Jerome was inconsolable, and he wrote her a final epitaph, wherein we learn (together with his letters to her) much about her life. Although she was an exceptional Scripture scholar, none of her work or correspondence has survived. When she died, her daughter Eustochium took over supervision of the monasteries. St. Paula is considered one of the first Spiritual Mothers in the West.

Prayer:

Beloved Lord and Savior, your daughter, Paula, was a model of perfection in the ascetic life and a Mother to many daughters who chose to become your early brides. Jerome said that, in embracing poverty for your sake, Paula so excelled in virtue that if all of his limbs were gifted with a human voice, he still could not describe her holiness. You graced her to be buried in the Church of the Nativity, so she might lie close to the birthplace of her eternal king. Through her intercession, may all who struggle in the ascetic life today find the peace and solace that she found in you, Lord. Reveal to each of us the proper path to follow to glorify you most perfectly, using the gifts you have given us.

Antiphon:

Arise, shine out, for your light has come.

Readings:

"For your love is better than wine, Your oils have a pleasing fragrance; Your name is like purified oil; Therefore the maidens love you. Draw me after you and let us run together! The King has brought me into his chambers." *Song of Songs 1:2–4 (NASB)*

"Attend to the sound of my cry, O God, Most High. For it is you to whom I pray. In the morning, you hear my voice: I prepare a sacrifice for you, watching and waiting." *Psalm 5:2–3 (PCB)*

"Therefore brethren, be all the more diligent to make certain about his calling and choosing you; for as long as you practice these things, you will never stumble; for in this way the entrance into the eternal kingdom of our Lord and Savior Jesus Christ will be abundantly supplied to you." *2 Pet. 1:10–11 (NASB)*

JANUARY 27 Angeli Merci

Orphaned at age ten, Angeli Merci was raised by an uncle but learned about the spiritual life on her own. She was deeply wounded when she lost her sister, and she feared for her sister's soul, having died without the sacraments. A vision reassured Angeli that her sister was safe in God's care; it also began her lifelong dedication to God. She became a Third Order Franciscan at age fifteen and, following another vision in which she was told to gather around her a company of women to promote the welfare of souls, she founded the Ursulines at Brescia. They took no vows and wore lay clothes. She envisioned an order that would teach young girls by going into their homes, since it was the only form of teaching available in Italy at the time for young women, and it was her belief that disorder in society was a result of disorder in the family. On a journey to the Holy Land she lost her sight, but she regained it while praying before a crucifix on her return voyage. Angeli Merci died in Brescia in 1540, leaving behind an incorrupt body.

Intercessory Prayer:

> O blessed St. Angeli, you who said, "God has given every person free will, and desires to constrain none," help us to overcome our fear of change that we may better serve the needs of Christ in our world. You went into families' homes to teach their children and thus raise them out of poverty of soul and body. Intercede for us that we may open our eyes to the call of the Spirit, and help us to minister to the needs of the poor and destitute around us. Amen.

Antiphon:

Come, O Bride of Christ and receive the crown that the Lord has prepared for you.

Readings:

"Happy are they who fear the Most High, who greatly delight in God's commands. Their children will be mighty in the land; the offspring of the upright will be blessed. Wealth and riches are in their homes; their justice endures forever.

"Light rises in the darkness for the upright: God is gracious, merciful and just. It is well for those who are generous and lend, who conduct their affairs with justice. The upright will never be moved; they will be remembered forever." *Psalm 112:1–6 (PCB)*

"For it is for this we labor and strive, because we have fixed our hope on the living God, who is the Savior of all . . . , especially of believers. Prescribe and teach these things. Let no one look down on your youthfulness, but rather in speech, conduct, love, faith and purity, show yourself an example of those who believe." *1 Tim. 4:10–13 (NASB)*

"If you abide in my word, then you are truly disciples of mine; and you shall know the truth, and the truth shall make you free." *Jn. 8:31–32 (NASB)*

JANUARY 28 Joan de Lestonnac

Joan (or Jeanne) de Lestonnac was born into a Roman Catholic family in Bordeaux in the sixteenth century. During this time, Calvinism was gaining a foothold in Bordeaux, and her mother came under its influence. Rejecting Catholicism, her mother used Joan as a pawn and tried, unsuccessfully, to convert her. Joan extricated herself from her unhappy home life at seventeen when she married. Widowed in 1597, she was left with four small children, whom she was devoted to. However, when they were old enough, she decided to join the Cistercians at Toulouse. Her youngest son was radically opposed to this decision, which caused her much grief. Joan only remained in the convent for six months, due to ill health, but she recovered after returning to Bordeaux. She then gathered around her a number of young girls and began educating them. Thus began the humble origins of the Order of Notre Dame of Bordeaux. The order grew, with a strong concentration on preserving Catholic education in the midst of a growing Reformation. Mother de Lestonnac, for a time, achieved a period of peace, but her convent life was disrupted when one of her nuns, who aspired to be director of the order, succeeded in slandering and deposing her. Eventually, the nun repented, but Sr. Joan did not wish to be reinstated, as she was nearing retirement. She died in the odor of sanctity on the feast of the Purification in 1640 and was canonized in 1949. She is a principal patron of Catholic education.

Prayer:

Gracious Lord Jesus, you inspired St. Joan de Lestonnac to be a teacher and leader during a period when education for young women was a vital necessity. All the sorrows in her early life were stepping stones to prepare her for this great work. As you were stripped of your garments, Lord, so she was stripped of her rank and made to wear garments of an ordinary nun rather than a

*superior, a cross she bore humbly for your sake. Through her
intercession, help us to strip ourselves of all that we have relied
upon, but which is unnecessary in our journey home to you.
Remind us ever of our own mission, so when trials seem to oppose
us, we view them as only another step in our closer walk with you.
Amen.*

Antiphon:

I have given you as a light to the people.

Readings:

"I will give thanks to you among the peoples, I will sing praises to you among the nations." *Psalm 108:3 (PCB)*

"He has stripped me of my glory and taken the crown from my head . . . and my hope has he removed like a tree. . . . (But) I know that my redeemer lives, and that he shall stand at the latter day upon the earth, and though my skin has been destroyed, then from my flesh, I shall see God. . . ." *Job 19:9–10, 25–27 (RSV)*

"But the Lord stood with me, and strengthened me, in order that through me the proclamation might be fully accomplished." *2 Tim. 4:17 (NASB)*

JANUARY 29 Boleslawa Maria Lament

Throughout history our faith has been sustained by holy women who step forward during difficult times to take necessary leadership roles. Boleslawa Maria Lament is a modern-day saintly leader. She was born in Poland in 1862 and lived by the motto of St. Ignatius, "All for the greater glory of God." As an adult, Maria witnessed firsthand the need for organizations to tend to the suffering and ill, especially during times of war and political unrest. She single-handedly began Catholic ministries to assist those most abandoned and neglected. As other saintly women responded and joined her, Boleslawa Maria soon organized and founded the Missionary Sisters of the Holy Family. She also devoted a great deal of time and effort to achieving unity between Catholics and those of the Orthodox faith in her native Poland. When she died in 1946, people from many faiths mourned her passing. Pope John Paul II honored her in 1991 when he beatified her in Poland, emphasizing that she "set herself apart by showing sensitivity to human misfortune." The Pope commended the holy foundress for her outstanding witness to the faith through her many fruitful apostolates, which continue to flourish throughout Poland today.

Prayer:

Dear Heavenly Father, thank you for blessing our faith throughout history with strong and holy women like Blessed Boleslawa Maria Lament. Through her shining example, many apostolates were established and continue to this day to minister to the poor and most needy. Strengthen us through her example, as her good works continue to be an inspiration to us. May we, too, remember to reach out to those most in need around us. Amen.

Antiphon:

Come to Me, all who labor and are heavy laden, and I will give you rest.

Readings:

"Though father and mother forsake me, You, O God, will receive me. Teach me your way, O God; lead me on a level path. . . . I believe I shall see your goodness in the land of the living. Hope in God, be strong and take heart. Hope in God, the Most High!" *Psalm 27:10–14 (PCB)*

"And when he looked on [the angel] he was afraid and said, 'What is it Lord?' And he said to him, 'Your prayers and your alms have come up for a memorial before the Lord.'" *Acts 10:4 (KJV)*

"Just as all that belongs to me is yours, so all that belongs to you is mine; It is in them that I have been glorified. I am in the world no more but these are in the world as I come to you. O Father most holy, protect them with your Name which you have given me. . . . and all things that are mine are thine, and thine are mine; and I have been glorified in them. And I am no more in the world; and yet they themselves are in the world, . . . keep them in thy name, the name which thou has given me, that they may be one, even as we are." *Jn.17:10–12 (NASB)*

JANUARY 30 Bathild

Born in England, Bathild was kidnapped as a child and sold into slavery. She was sold into the household of the French imperial palace, where she eventually married Clovis II. They had three sons, but her husband was a foolish and selfish man who did little for the good of the people. When he died, her oldest son was only five, so she acted as regent and effected great changes in France. She struggled against the slave traffic and against the buying and selling of ecclesiastical offices. After appointing her friend, Leger, as bishop of Autun, she helped to promote his writings. Leger introduced the Order of Benedictines and established houses for the poor. Bathild and Leger also organized synods and founded a number of monasteries. In her old age, Bathild retired to a nunnery.

Prayer:

> *O Lord Jesus, who has shown us that if we speak but do not act we are only as clanging symbols, teach us, through the intercession of blessed Bathild, to act fearlessly in the world for the cause of your justice. May her merits and example help us to overcome our difficulties and understand in the depths of our souls that you are the source and substance of all our good. May she who fought for the freedom of all, seeing everyone as equal in you, Christ Jesus, help us to open our hearts and minds to the presence of your Spirit among us. Amen.*

Antiphon:

For he has clothed me with a robe of salvation and wrapped me in a mantle of justice, like a bride bedecked with jewels.

Readings:

"Then they will rebuild the ancient ruins, they will raise up the former devastations. . . . But you will be called the priests of the Lord, you will be spoken of as ministers of our God. . . . For I, the Lord, love justice, I hate robbery in the burnt offering, I will faithfully give them their recompense; And I will make an everlasting covenant with them. . . . All who see them will recognize them, because they are the offspring whom the Lord has blessed." Isa. 61:4–9 (NAS)

"When the Lord brought back the captive ones at Zion, then we were like those who dream. Then our mouth was filled with laughter, and our tongue with joyful shouting, Then they said among the nations, 'The Lord has done great things for them.'" *Psalm 126:1–2 (NAS)*

"And I saw a new heaven and a new earth; for the first heaven and the first earth passed away, and there is no longer any sea. And I saw the holy city, new Jerusalem, coming down out of heaven from God, made ready as a bride adorned for her husband." *Rev. 21:1–2 (NASB)*

JANUARY 31 Martina and Marcella

Through the centuries, the Church has been strengthened by the blood of many virgin martyrs who have given witness to the love of Christ by paying the ultimate price of their lives. St. Martina is one of the early Church's brave women martyrs. Her story dates to early in the third century. Martina lived in Rome, and after her parents died she converted to Christianity, denounced paganism, and gave all of her belongings to the poor. Emperor Alexander Severus arrested her and commanded that she return to her pagan roots. She refused, was put through numerous and horrible tortures, and was finally beheaded for her faith. Tradition relates her last words as "I love my Lord Jesus Christ, who strengthens me." Her relics were discovered many centuries later in 1634 in a crypt within a chapel that was dedicated to her. Pope Urban VIII built a new church in her honor and composed hymns to St. Martina, which became part of the Roman Breviary.

This is also the feast day of Marcella, who lived in the latter part of the fourth century. She worked closely with saints Paula and Jerome, establishing the first ascetic houses in Rome, based on the monastic tradition Jerome inherited from the East. Jerome, who dedicated his commentary on Paul's Letter to the Galatians to her, describes his time with her and her sisters as a highlight of his life in Rome. Marcella died when barbarians plundered and burned Rome. Martina and Marcella are patrons of Rome.

Prayer:

Beloved Lord Jesus, saints Martina and Marcella, through their bravery and strength, as witnesses for the early Church, served to convert countless souls through their lives and sacrifices. Help us to remember Martina's simple prayer, "I love my Lord Jesus Christ, who strengthens me," when we are in need of God's strength and renewal. Let us follow their holy example and give witness to our faith through living our daily lives in ways that reflect the Gospel. Amen.

Antiphon:

Gather my saints together unto me; those that have made a covenant with me by sacrifice.

Readings:

"Stretch forth your hand from on high, rescue me from the mighty waters, from the hands of alien foes, whose mouths are filled with lies, and whose hands are raised in perjury. To you will I sing a new song." *Psalm 144:7–9 (PCB)*

"If possible, so far as it depends on you, be at peace will all. . . . Never take your own revenge, beloved. . . . But if your enemy is hungry, feed him, and if he is thirsty, give him drink; for in so doing you will be heaping burning coals upon his head. Do not be overcome by evil, but overcome evil with good." *Rom. 12:18–21 (NASB)*

"I am the true vine, and my Father is the vine grower. Every branch in me that does not bear fruit, He takes away; and every branch that bears fruit, He prunes it, that it may bear more fruit." *Jn. 15:1–2 (NASB)*

FEBRUARY 1 Brigid of Kildare

Also known as Mary of the Gael, Brigid of Kildare was the daughter of a pagan Scottish king and a Christian mother who had been baptized by St. Patrick. As a child Brigid tried to give away as much milk from the dairy to the poor as she was able, against her father's protestations. With seven other girls, she dedicated her young life to God. Her life is colored with miracles, particularly associated with her propensity to manifest food, change water to milk, or supply beer at paschal time. Legend has it that when Patrick heard her take her vows, he mistakenly used the form for ordaining priests. She founded a double monastery at Kildare and instituted a famous center for art and illuminated manuscripts. She is associated with the sacred fire at Kildare, which she and her sisters never allowed to go out. Brigid is the patron of dairy workers.

Prayer:

O Christ Jesus, through the intercession of your beloved Brigid, who once said, "Christ dwells in every creature," manifest your bountiful love for us in community. As she laid the foundation for a golden age of learning, inspire us with new zeal for an ever-deepening understanding of you and your miraculous creation. Help us to follow her example, and kindle in us the Eternal Flame of your everlasting love. Amen.

Antiphon:

You are a chosen race, a royal priesthood, a holy nation, God's own people.

Readings:

"God's revelation to the Anointed One: 'Sit at my side: till I put injustice beneath your feet.' God will send forth from Zion your scepter of power: rule in the midst of your foes. Your people will give themselves freely on the day you lead your host upon the holy mountains.

"From the womb of the morning your youth will come like dew. God has sworn an oath that will not be changed, 'You are a priest forever, after the order of Melchizedek.'" *Psalm 110:1–5 (PCB)*

"I urge you therefore, brethren, by the mercies of God, to present your bodies a living and holy sacrifice, acceptable to God, which is your spiritual service of worship. And do not be conformed to this world, but be transformed by the renewing of your mind, that you may prove what the will of God is, that which is good and acceptable and perfect." *Rom. 12:1–2 (NASB)*

"And he said, 'How shall we picture the kingdom of God, or by what parable shall we present it? It is like a mustard seed, which, when it is sown upon the soil, though it is smaller than all the seeds that are upon the soil, yet when it is sown, grows up and becomes larger than all the garden plants and forms large branches; so that the birds of the air can nest under its shade.'" *Mk. 4:30–32 (NASB)*

FEBRUARY 2 The Purification of Mary and the Presentation in the Temple

The Presentation of Christ (or Presentation in the Temple), also called the Purification of Mary, is celebrated on February 2. The West stresses the day as a celebration of Mary; the East celebrates it primarily as a feast of Jesus. In the East, it is called "Meeting in the Temple" because Mary brings Our Lord to the temple to "meet" his chosen people in the persons of Simeon the elder and Anna the prophetess. The reading from Isaiah on this day reminds us of the purification of the prophet's lips by the burning coal from one of the angelic seraphim (Isa. 6:1–12). Indeed, when Simeon, the prophet, and Anna, the prophetess, come upon Joseph and Mary, they both recognize Christ, which announces that the time of our salvation has come. Simeon's words to Mary ("yea, a sword shall pierce your heart also" [Luke 21:35]) prefigure the mystery of the Virgin's part in her Son's Passion. She presents him as the light of the world. The Roman custom of blessing candles on this day (Candlemas) dates from the eleventh century. During the Candlemas procession, candles were blessed with incense while the antiphon of the Ave Maria was sung. The candles were then distributed to the laity.

Prayer:

Eternal Word, who rides on the cherubim and is presented today in the holy temple according to the law, accept the symbols of love that we bring to you: our doves and candles, our cakes and our children, our incense and songs of praise, our words of consolation and smiles to strangers. Like Simeon the prophet, we have waited all of our lives for you. Like Anna the prophetess, we knew you were coming. You are the fulfillment of our hope and the sign of our redemption. O prophet, priest, and king, let us put away our insecurities and fears, and with open arms boldly cry out: "I took hold of him and I would not let him go." Amen.

Antiphon:

Grace is poured out upon your lips: the Lord has blessed you forever.

Readings:

"How shall I make a return to the Lord for all the good he has done for me?
The cup of salvation I will take up and I will call upon the name of the Lord.
My vows to the Lord I will pay in the presence of all his people.
Precious in the eyes of the Lord is the death of his faithful ones.
O Lord, I am your servant, the son of your handmaid; you have loosed my bonds.
To you will I offer sacrifice of thanksgiving." *Psalm 116:12–18 (PCB)*

"But when Christ appeared as high priest of the good things to come, he entered through the greater and more perfect tabernacle, not made with hands, that is to say, not of this creation; and not through the blood of goats and calves, but through his own blood, he entered the holy place once for all, having obtained eternal redemption." *Heb. 9:11–13 (NASB)*

"And when the days for their purification according to the law of Moses were completed, they brought him up to Jerusalem to present him to the Lord. . . . And behold, there was a man in Jerusalem whose name was Simeon; and this man was righteous and devout, looking for the consolation of Israel, and the Holy Spirit was upon him. And it had been revealed to him by the Holy Spirit that he would not see death before he had seen the Anointed of the Lord." *Lk. 2:22–27 (NASB)*

FEBRUARY 3 Margaret of England

Also called Margarita, St. Margaret was born in Hungary in the twelfth century. Her mother was an English noblewoman, and it is believed that her father was Hungarian. She was related to St. Thomas of Canterbury. Margaret and her mother, who were very close, journeyed together, making numerous pilgrimages to various holy sites, especially Jerusalem and Bethlehem. They remained for several years in the Holy Land, leading a life of prayer and austerity. After her mother died there, Margaret made a pilgrimage to Montserrat in Spain and from there to France. She finally settled at a Cistercian monastery in Puy-en-Velay, where she died of natural causes. Her tomb became famous for miracles and healings, and soon her legend began to circulate. Many Christians made pilgrimages to the shrine at her gravesite to invoke her prayers, where she became known as Margaret the Englishwoman.

Prayer:

O loving God and Savior, Margaret was a pilgrim in search of you during her life, drawing many other pilgrims to you because of her powerful intercession after her death. Empower us to become strong in prayer so that our supplication on behalf of others finds favor in your sight. Help us to remember that praying for those in need is the most precious gift we can give.We ask your special blessing on those whom no one remembers to pray for. May all of your saints on earth find their way to the glorious throne room where the saints in heaven offer unceasing praise and glory to your name. Amen.

Antiphon:

Blessed are they who trust in God; whose hope is in the most high.

Readings:

"If I forget you, Jerusalem, let my right hand wither!
Let my tongue cleave to the roof of my mouth, if I do not remember you,
If I do not set Jerusalem above all my joys!." *Psalm 137:5–6 (PCB)*

"But the Lord is in his holy temple; let all the earth keep silent before him." *Hab. 2:20 (NASB)*

". . . just as [God] chose us in him before the foundation of the world, that we should be holy and blameless before him. In love he predestined us to adoption as [sons] through Jesus Christ . . . to the praise of the glory of his grace, which he freely bestowed on us in the Beloved." *Eph. 1:4–6 (NASB)*

FEBRUARY 4 Jane of Valois

Jane of Valois was the daughter of King Louis XI of France, and although she was a princess, her parents banished her from the court because of a physical deformity. She was raised by guardians miles away from the palace in a country cottage.

At a young age and for political reasons, Jane was betrothed to Louis, Duke of Orleans. He despised her and resented being forced to marry her, never ceasing to humiliate his young bride whenever he had the opportunity. When he became King Louis XII years later, he annulled the marriage and made her Duchess of Berry, a province that the benevolent queen ruled for many years. Eventually she was allowed to accomplish her life's dream: to found an order of nuns whose lives would be based on the Blessed Mother and the virtues she exemplified in the Annunciation. Jane founded the Order of the Annonciades in 1501, and she built and financed the first convent for the order in 1502. She died just three years later in the odor of sanctity, and those who prayed for her intercession reported many miracles of healing.

Prayer:

> *Dear Heavenly Father, you gave us good Jane of Valois as an example of charity and love amidst humiliating and trying circumstances. She strove to live a life based on the virtues of the Virgin Mary, especially silence and humility. She accepted the rejection of her father and husband, carrying only love in her heart, praying for those who persecuted her. May we emulate her virtues and the virtues exemplified by the Blessed Virgin Mary in our daily lives and strive to attain personal sanctity through praying for our enemies and loving those who persecute us. Amen.*

Antiphon:

Blessed are you when they shall reproach you.

Readings:

"Your will is wonderful indeed; therefore will I obey it. The unfolding of your words gives light; it imparts wisdom to the simple. I open my mouth and I sigh as I yearn for your commandments. Turn to me and be gracious, treat me as one who loves your name." *Psalm 119:129–132 (PCB)*

"For bodily exercise profits little; but godliness is profitable unto all things, having promise of the life that now is, and of that which is yet to come. This is a faithful saying and worthy of all acceptation. For therefore, we both labor under the law and suffer reproach, because we trust in the Living God." *Heb. 4:8–10 (KJV)*

"O clement, O loving, O sweet Virgin Mary, pray for us." *(Traditional)*

FEBRUARY 5 Agatha

The ancient Church placed four female pillars of light and purity in the midst of winter's darkness on the calendar: Cecilia (November 22), Lucy (December 13), Agnes (January 21), and Agatha. Both the Eastern and Western churches still celebrate their feasts on the original days. The final light of winter, Agatha died in the early persecution, around 250. Like Agnes, Agatha was sentenced to imprisonment in a house of prostitution, and then she was tortured for her faith. It is said that when her breasts were cut off, she reminded her assailant that he too had a nursing mother. The ancient image of Agatha with her breasts on a plate is a horrific one to visualize, yet it is no less frightening for a modern women to lose her breasts to cancer; thus, Agatha is the patron of this disease.

Prayer:

O God, who among your manifold almighty works has deigned to bestow on women the courage and victory equal to any man, have mercy on us who call out to you for strength, and preserve our bodies from destruction. Through St. Agatha's intercession, heal those who are survivors of sexual assault, and protect all women from danger. Amen.

Antiphon:

I will call upon God who has vouchsafed to heal all my wounds.

Readings:

"Incline your ear, and give answer, for I am poor and needy.
Preserve my life for I am faithful; save the servant who trusts in you.
You are my God, have mercy on me, for to you I cry all the day.
Gladden the soul of your servant, for to you I lift up my soul.
O God, you are good and forgiving, abounding in love to all who call
Give ear to my prayer; hearken to my supplication. In the day of my trouble
I call on you, for you will answer me." *Psalm 86:1–6 (PCB)*

"So then, about this matter of eating meats that have been offered to idols: we know that an idol is really nothing, and that there is no God but one . . . and one Lord Jesus Christ, by whom are all things, and we exist through him." *1 Cor. 8:4–6 (KJV)*

"And it came about while he said these things, one of the women in the crowd . . . said to him, 'Blessed is the womb that bore you, and the breasts at which you nursed.' But he said, 'On the contrary, blessed are those who hear the word of God, and observe it." *Lk. 11:27–28 (NASB)*

FEBRUARY 6 Mary Teresa Bonzel and Dorothy

Mary Teresa Bonzel was born in Germany in 1830 and decided to dedicate her life to God when she reached twenty. She became a Franciscan tertiary, and with nine other sisters she founded a new community called the Poor Franciscans of Perpetual Adoration. Devoted to the Holy Eucharist, she simultaneously desired to dedicate her life to works of mercy and to her order, which focused on children's health and education. In 1875 she and other sisters moved to the United States, founding their first motherhouse in Lafayette, Indiana. Today the sisters still minister in Germany, the U.S., the Phillippines, and Brazil.

St. Dorothy was a virgin martyr who lived in Rome in the second century during the Christian persecution by the emperor Diocletian. On the way to her execution, a prominent lawyer named Theophilus challenged her a last time by mockingly asking her to send him a basket of flowers and apples when she arrived at the heavenly garden. After she died, an angel appeared to Theophilus and presented him with a basket of apples and roses, causing his immediate conversion.

Prayer:

Dear Lord, you have given us Mary and Dorothy as living examples of purity and purpose. You have raised up your servant Mary Teresa to be a soul who has always blessed the Lord of good counsel and believed that because you were at her right hand, she would never fail. Dorothy knew that her life was meant to be solely dedicated to you and that the times in which she lived required brave martyrs to be living witnesses and examples. Let their lives inspire us to accept the daily sacrifices of life as lovingly and joyfully as we can. Amen.

Antiphon:

We rejoice and exult in God. Alleluia.

Readings:

"Set me on the rock that is higher than I; for you are my refuge, my stronghold against evil. Let me dwell in your tent forever! Hide me in the shelter of your wings!
For you, O God, have heard my vows, you have given me the heritage
Of those who love your name." *Psalm 61:3–6 (PCB)*

"For this reason also, since the day we heard of it, we have not ceased to pray for you and to ask that you may be filled with the knowledge of his will in all spiritual wisdom and understanding, so that you may walk in a manner worthy of the Lord, to please him in all respects, bearing fruit in every good work and increasing in the knowledge of God." *Col. 1:9–11 (NASB)*

"These things I have spoken to you, while abiding with you. But the Helper, the Holy Spirit, whom the Father will send in my name . . . will teach you all things, and bring to your remembrance all that I said to you." *Jn. 14:25–26 (NASB)*

FEBRUARY 7 Mother Mary of Providence

Eugenie Smet lived in nineteenth-century France and was a friend of St. John Vianney. From a young age, she felt a calling to religious life. She felt that her particular mission, inspired in the depths of her heart by the Holy Spirit, was to pray for the poor souls in Purgatory. In 1865 she founded the Society for the Helpers of the Holy Souls and took the name Mary of Providence. She became Mother Superior of the new order, whose purpose was to dedicate lives of active apostolic service, offered to God for the souls in Purgatory. The Society for the Helpers of the Holy Souls cared for the poor, the sick, the aged, and the Church's most destitute members. The Society continues to thrive in twenty-two countries across the globe. Mother Mary died in 1871, but her indomitable spirit of love and self-giving continues to inspire members of her order. Pope Pius XII beatified her in 1957.

Prayer:

> Heavenly Father, thank you for blessing your Church with so many
> good women through the centuries who have used their charisms
> for spreading the Gospel. Mother Mary of Providence was a
> shining example of a woman who responded to the Holy Spirit's
> promptings and devoted her life to the charitable act of praying
> and interceding for the poor souls in Purgatory and the Church's
> suffering. Let us remember her witness and pray for the poor souls
> in Purgatory every day, especially those souls most forgotten and
> for whom no one else on earth has remembered to pray. Grant
> eternal rest unto them, O Lord, and let perpetual light shine upon
> them. May they rest in peace. Amen.

Antiphon:

> By your wounds, O Lord, we are healed.

Readings:

> I long for your saving help and your law is my delight. Let me live,
> that I may praise you, and let your precepts help me." *Psalm
> 119:174–175 (PCB)*

> "Create in me a clean heart, put a steadfast spirit within me."
> *Psalm 51:10 (PCB)*

> "'I have placed you as a light for the Gentiles, that you should
> bring salvation to the end of the earth.'" *Acts 13:47 (NASB)*

> "With all prayer and petition pray at all times in the Spirit, and with
> this view in mind, be on the alert with all perseverance and peti-
> tion for all the saints." *Eph. 6:18 (NASB)*

FEBRUARY 8 Elfleda

Elfleda's life was offered up to God at a very early age. The
king and queen of Northumbria (Oswy and Enfleda) left
the young Elfleda at a convent as an offering for their victory over the pagan king, Pendra. Her mother was St. Enfleda (see
Daily Readings, November 28, Enfleda). Elfleda was a child oblate
and novice of the great Hilda of Whitby (see Daily Readings, November 19, Hilda of Whitby), whom she succeeded as abbess after Hilda's
death in 680. During the period she was abbess, Elfleda mediated a

dispute between saints Wilfred and Theodore at the synod at Nidd. She also oversaw the writing of Gregory the Great's biography. Legend tells us a magic girdle given to her by St. Cuthbert cured her of a long-standing paralysis. Elfleda is the patron of calligraphers.

Prayer:

Merciful God, you gave grace to your holy woman, Mother Elfleda, by enabling her to serve the Church with singleness of heart and mind. Grant us the grace to serve you as she did, in simplicity and truth. Through her intercession, grant healing and strength to all those suffering from paralysis, that they may be made whole in mind and body. Through Christ our Lord. Amen.

Antiphon:

It is a good thing to give thanks to the Lord.

Readings:

"My soul, give praise to my God!
I will praise the Most High as long as I live;
I will sing praises to my God while I have my being.
Put no trust in sovereigns, in mortal flesh in whom there is no help.
When their breath departs they return to the earth,
On that day their plans perish.
Happy are they whose help is in God
Whose hope is in the Creator of all, who alone made heaven and earth." *Psalm 146:1–6 (PCB)*

"Blessed be the God and Father of our Lord Jesus Christ, who has blessed us with every spiritual blessing in the heavenly places with Christ." *Eph. 1:3 (NASB)*

FEBRUARY 9 Maria of Olonets

Maria of Olonets was born the eldest child of peasant workers in Novgorod. She was a withdrawn little girl who shunned play; instead her parents often found her memorizing the Psalter in her spare time. She visited several monasteries as a young woman, but was disillusioned with them, feeling that they were also too noisy and crowded. She journeyed to the northern wilderness to live as a hermit with her close friend Anna, who was a runaway serf. They prayed most of the day and only ate porridge, but were blissfully happy. However, the girls were eventually discovered and commanded to enter a monastery. Anna, who was in hiding, fled. Maria went deeper into the wilderness and settled near a men's monastery, which did not want her. They burned her small hut, and in grief and bewilderment, Maria journeyed south, where arrangements were made for her to stay in a monastery with two hundred other nuns. Again, she could not bear the confinement and preferred to live in a cave nearby. Here she prayed unceasingly. After some time, she became ill from fasting and from the cold, and some benefactors transferred her back north. Crippled in body but not in spirit, Maria died shortly afterward, and her body immediately began emitting an unearthly light. Pilgrims came from far and near to attend the funeral of this young girl who had wanted only to become a desert hermit in the Russian forests. She left behind an incorruptible body as her soul flew to the home of her Beloved. After her death in 1860, her original hut in Olonets became a hermitage for other ascetic women who wanted to imitate her bold model of silence and solitude.

Intercessory Prayer:

O holy Maria, you were a simple soul with a deep mystic quest, a pilgrim struggling only to find solitude to commune with your God. You wanted to be completely free to focus all of your time on Christ, and you were clothed in his brilliant image and likeness in death as a blessing. You, whose only friends were the birds and animals, understand the longing of those who want to remove themselves from the world and its cares. Pray for those who are misfits in society, and who long for the peace and serenity of hermetic life. Amen.

Antiphon:

Turn to me with all your heart, says our God.

Readings:

"The eye is not satisfied with seeing, nor is the ear filled with hearing." *Eccl. 1:8 (NASB)*

"O my dove, that are in the clefts of the rock, in the secret places of the stairs, let me see your countenance, let me hear your voice; for sweet is your voice, and your countenance is comely." *Song of Sol. 2:14 (KJV)*

"The women said to him, 'Sir, give me this water, so I will not be thirsty, nor come all the way here to draw water.'" *Jn. 4:15 (NASB)*

"And let the one who is thirsty come; let the one who wishes take the water of life without cost." *Rev. 22:17 (NASB)*

FEBRUARY 10 Scholastica

Scholastica was the twin sister of the famous St. Benedict, and together they founded a double monastery at Mount Cassino in the sixth century. The Benedictines have spread to all parts of the world in the past fourteen hundred years. Gregory the Great wrote about her in his *Dialogues* and tells the famous story about how, toward the end of her life, Scholastica and Benedict met in a farmhouse between the two monasteries for a day of spiritual conference and prayer, as was their yearly custom. However, perhaps knowing she was close to death, she begged her brother to remain with her throughout the night. Fearful of breaking his own monastic rules, he rose to leave, but she, beseeching God, caused a thunderstorm to gather over the place, and they spent their last night together in holy conversation. Scholastica died three days later, and Benedict saw her soul ascend to heaven in the form of a dove. She is the patron of Benedictine nunneries and is invoked for protection from storms.

Intercessory Prayer:

O holy St. Scholastica, you were not content until you had the pearl of great price in the palm of your hand. You pondered God's word with your brother and harvested the riches of the kingdom for all the sisters who followed in your path. Help us to live by the law of love and to discern when real love is stronger than adherence to earthly rules. Blessed sister, God showed forth a testimony of innocence in your soul by beckoning you to soar to heaven like a dove. Intercede for us that we may always aspire to do more because we love more. Amen.

Antiphon:

She opens her mouth with wisdom, and the teaching of kindness is on her tongue.

Readings:

"Is this not the fast that I choose: To loosen the bonds of wickedness, To undo the bands of the yoke, and to let the oppressed go free . . . Is it not to divide your bread with the hungry, and bring the homeless poor into the house? . . . Then your light will break out like the dawn . . . and your righteousness will go before you; the glory of the Lord will be your rear guard." *Isa. 58:6–8 (NASB)*

"O that I had wings like a dove! I would fly away and be at rest. Indeed, I would wander afar, I would take refuge in the wilderness. I would hasten to find me a shelter from the raging wind and tempest." *Psalm 55:7–9 (PCB)*

"You are the light of the world. A city set on a hill cannot be hidden. Neither do [men] light a candle and put it under a bushel, but on a candlestick; and it gives light to all who are in the house." *Mt. 5:14–15 (NASB)*

FEBRUARY 11 Empress Theodora, Restorer of Icons

Empress Theodora is one of the great women saints in the Eastern Church. (This is also the feast day of Our Lady of Lourdes in the West; see Daily Reading, April 16, Bernadette of Lourdes.) She was married to the iconoclast, Emperor Theophilus (iconoclast means "destroyer of images"). It is said that she hid her icons in her palace rooms until his death, when she took power, acting as regent on behalf of her young son, Michael. Many martyrs died during the time of icon persecution, and much valuable Byzantine artwork was destroyed. Theodora called a Church Council to restore the dignity of icon veneration, which had been suppressed for nearly a hundred years. She ruled the Byzantine Empire for fourteen years and retired to a convent in her old age, where she spent the rest of her life in veneration of the holy icons she so dearly loved. She is a patron of icon painters.

Prayer:

O Almighty God, through the intercession of St. Theodora, guide us always toward our highest good, and let your Spirit breathe life into our most heartfelt desires. She was an unwavering light and a strong pillar of orthodoxy, seeking to remain loyal to the Church's ancient traditions by glorifying your Son's incarnation. By the grace that comes through every holy image of him, pour out your wonder on our souls, that we may likewise take your light into the world and reflect your image there. Through Christ our Lord. Amen.

Antiphon:

Eternal Word, for our salvation you emptied yourself and became one of us.

Readings:

"In the image of God he created [him]; male and female he created them." Gen. 1:27 (NASB)

"Give ear, O Shepherd of Israel, you who led Joseph like a flock!
You who are enthroned upon the cherubim,
Shine before Ephraim, Benjamin, and Manasseh!
Stir up your might and come to save us!; Restore us, God of hosts,
Let your face shine, that we may be saved." Psalm 80:1–3 (PCB)

"He is the image of the invisible God, the firstborn of all creation. For by him all things were created, both in the heavens and on earth, visible and invisible." Col. 1:14–15 (NASB)

"Who, although he existed in the form of God, did not regard equality with God a thing to be grasped, but emptied himself, taking the form of a bond-servant." Phil. 2:6–7 (NASB)

FEBRUARY 12 Veronica (Veraniki)

Relegated to the realm of myth by much of the Western Church, Veronica (from "vera," meaning true, and "iconi," meaning image) was believed to be the compassionate woman at the sixth station of the cross who wiped Jesus' face (the story from the apocryphal *Gospel of Nicodemus* also called the *Acts of Pilate*). The cloth, which miraculously captured his image, was widely venerated throughout the Middle Ages, then lost for four centuries. It drew much attention when it was again discovered in a small village monastery at Manoppelo in 1999. The Christ-like image on the cloth matches exactly the shroud of Turin and lacks any characteristics of paint or woven fibers. Yet the image is identical on both sides of the veil, which is now so thin that one can see through it. Whether the story in the apocryphal *Acts* is legend or not will always remain a mystery. However, the belief in icons not made by human hands, such as the shroud, is central to the traditions of both the Eastern and Western churches. In an early story from the Byzantine East, Abgar of Edessa was said to have received Christ's image on a shroud; in the Russian Church, Veraniki is honored as the hemorrhaging woman who only wanted to touch Christ's garment. The Greek Church recognizes both traditions of the shroud and celebrates the woman as Veronica. Most Byzantine churches celebrate this feast on July 12.

Intercessory Prayer:

O holy Veronica, you came to Christ with a heart empty of everything but trust and love. Abandoning the criticism of the crowds, you pressed through all obstacles to behold the bridegroom of your soul for one instant, and in your faith, you were made whole. Fixed steadfastly on the rays of the Lord, O holy one, teach us to likewise beseech with tears our heart's only desire and thus attain a glimpse of the radiance of his face. Amen.

Antiphon:

Give her the reward of her deeds; they will proclaim her as she enters the gates.

Readings:

"Then he [Jacob] said, 'I will not let you go unless you bless me.' So he said to him, 'What is your name?' And he said, 'Jacob.' And he said, 'Your name shall no longer be Jacob, but Israel; for you have striven with God . . . and have prevailed. . . .' So Jacob named the place Peniel, for he said, 'I have seen God face to face, yet my life has been preserved.'" *Gen. 32:27, 28, 30 (NASB)*

"You, O God, build up Jerusalem; you gather the outcasts . . . you heal the broken-hearted, and bind up their wounds." *Psalm 147: 2–3 (PCB)*

"And a woman who had had a hemorrhage for twelve years, and had endured much at the hands of many physicians, and had spent all that she had and was not helped at all . . . after hearing about Jesus, came up in the crowd behind him, and touched his cloak. For she thought, 'If I just touch his garments, I shall get well.' And immediately the flow of her blood was dried up; and she felt in her body that she was healed of her affliction." *Mk. 5:25–29 (NASB)*

FEBRUARY 13 Catherine del Ricci

Catherine del Ricci lived in Italy in the latter part of the sixteenth century. Her mother died when she was an infant. From early childhood she had conversations with her guardian angel. She entered a convent as a child oblate at age six, and later in her life became prioress. She developed a devotion to the Passion and became a stigmatist at age twenty. Every week, from noon on Thursday until 4:00 p.m. on Friday, she manifested Christ's wounds. She had numerous bodily sicknesses, although many who flocked to see her in her ecstasies were cured of theirs. St. Philip Neri declared that she appeared to him while still living (that is, she bilocated), and she was a correspondent with three popes, who sought her prayers.

Prayer:

O beloved God, who poured out your Spirit on your beloved visionary Catherine de Ricci, animate us so that we too may think, speak, and act by the same Spirit. By setting us free from every form of prejudice and fear, help us to know that in you all things are possible, through Christ our Lord. Amen.

Antiphon:

In stillness and silence, my heart waits for you.

Readings:

"My God, I call for help by day; I cry out in the night before you.
Let my prayer come into your presence,
Incline your ear to my cry!
For my soul is full of troubles, and my life draws near to the grave.
I am reckoned as one in the tomb,
I have reached the end of my strength." *Psalm 88:1–5 (PCB)*

"Be merciful to me, O God; be merciful to me.
For my soul trust in you; yea, in the shadow of your wings will I
    make my refuge,
Until these calamities be over.
I will cry to God Most High, unto God that performs all things for
    me." *Psalm 57:1–2 (KJV)*

"For he himself is our peace, who made both groups into one, and broke down the barrier of the dividing wall by abolishing in his flesh the enmity, which is the Law of commandments contained in ordinances, that in himself he might make the two into one new [man], thus establishing peace." *Eph. 2:14–15 (NASB)*

FEBRUARY 14 Anastasia Logacheva

Like many mystics, Anastasia Logacheva lived only partially in this world. From her childhood, she yearned to be in the quietest corner of the house so she could commune with her Lord. For twenty-five years, her parents were in another part of Russia doing military service. She then spent seventeen years of her adult life caring for them in their old age. She supported them by reading the Psalter for the Dead for families, an Orthodox custom that lasts for the first forty days after a person dies. She sought the spiritual direction of the great St. Seraphim of Sarov (1759–1833) who, when her parents were deceased, finally gave her a blessing to fulfill her dream and live the life of a hermit. She built a hut in the deep forest and lived there in total silence for eight years. Once, someone from the village came upon her in the woods and discovered her sitting on top of a huge anthill nearly naked and covered with ants, meditating in unmoved concentration on God. She read one Gospel in its entirety every day, and she had visions of the Mother of God. She was known for her ability to commune with animals so they would not disturb her garden. Other women began to gather around her, and eventually she was placed in charge of a monastic community, where she gained renown as a *staritsa*, or spiritual elder. She died in 1875.

Prayer:

O Lord, your beloved staritsa *Anastasia longed to surrender her entire life to you, and sing only to the one who was her light and her salvation. All that she desired was to gaze upon your beauty and give you praise with all of creation. Even the animals obeyed her because she was so in tune with your natural order. Give us the grace to set aside a part of our lives for you alone, so that we may enter more deeply into the silence of your presence. Amen.*

Antiphon:

For thy loving-kindness is better than life itself.

Readings:

"My soul shall be satisfied as with marrow and fatness
And my mouth shall praise you with joyful lips
When I remember you upon my bed, and meditate on you in the
night watches.
Because you have been my help, therefore in the shadow of your
wings will I rejoice.
My soul follows hard after you; and your right hand upholds me."
Psalm 64:5–8 (KJV)

"Therefore, my beloved brethren, be steadfast, immovable, always abounding in the work of the Lord, knowing that your toil is
not in vain." *Cor. 15:58 (NASB)*

"And after he had sent the multitudes away, he went up to the
mountain by himself to pray; and when it was evening, he was
there alone." *Mt. 14:23 (NASB)*

FEBRUARY 15 Veridiana

St. Veridiana was born in Florence in 1182, during the period when St. Francis was seeking approval for his mendicant order. She was born into nobility, but because her
family was impoverished, she went to live with an aunt, where she
helped to run the household. A favorite tale is told about Veridiana's
ability to mysteriously replenish food: during a famine, she gave away
the beans from her uncle's store, which made him angry, but the next
day, the bean bins were again full. Veridiana wanted to dedicate her
life to God and received a blessing from Francis to become a Third
Order Franciscan and an anchoress. This lifestyle is unusual for a secular third order, since an anchorite life is spent enclosed in a small
cell. She lived there for thirty-four years, taking food and Holy Communion through a tiny window. Known throughout her life for her
generosity, she died while in prayer with her Lord.

Intercessory Prayer:

*O holy Veridiana, your pursuit of the contemplative life led you to
abandon the world for the sake of the serenity of your cell. Pray*

for all those living in the world who yearn to find the Lord in silence, but are called to the duties of family life. Intercede for those who choose the hermetic life, who need to live alone, in a life set apart for God. In all of our journeys, help us to recognize that Christ is always present if we take the time to be present to him. Amen.

Antiphon:

And he said to them: "Take nothing for your journey."

Readings:

"With my whole heart, I seek you;
let me not wander from your commandments.
I have hidden your word in my heart, that I might not sin against you. . . .
I will meditate on your precepts and fix my eyes on your ways.
I will delight in your statutes: I will not forget your word." *Psalm 119:10–11, 15–16 (Beth) (RSV)*

"Do not neglect the gift within you, which was bestowed upon you by prophetic utterance with the laying on of hands by the presbytery. Take pains with these things; be absorbed in them, so that your progress may be evident to all." *1 Tim. 4:14–15 (NASB)*

"And when he had taken the five loaves and two fishes, he looked up to heaven and blessed, and broke the loaves, and gave them to his disciples to set before them; and the two fishes he divided among them all. And they all did eat, and were filled." *Mk. 6:41–42 (KJV)*

FEBRUARY 16 Mary the Younger

Mary called "the younger" was born in Armenia around 875 but lived most of her childhood in Constantinople. She married a military man and moved to Thrace to have a family: four sons, two of whom died early. Her *vita* describes her as being a simple but pious woman who participated in the sacraments frequently. She was known for her philanthropy, which proved to be excessive. Unfortunately, her husband's brother accused her, not only of squandering her husband's property, but also of adultery with a slave. She was imprisoned in her bedroom, and later, when her husband was incensed with madness, beaten. While trying to escape, she fell and hit her head and died several days later. The cult that developed immediately after her death proved her innocence. Miracles began occurring at her tomb. Perhaps the most famous was when a foreigner, who had never met her, was instructed by her in a dream to paint her image, which he executed in great detail. This became the cult's first icon. She is known especially for her intercession for possession.

Prayer:

Lord Jesus, Blessed Mary the Younger was a woman slandered and beaten, suffering blows to her head in the same way you did during your sacred passion. Yet you vindicated her when she went to her death, without bitterness, and praying for those who punished her. Sustain us, Lord, during the times of our darkest trials. Like Mary, O Jesus, we are waiting for you to deliver us into your loving arms; we believe that even when we walk through the valley's deepest shadows, you are a God who never lets us down. Amen.

Antiphon:

Make haste to help me, O Lord.

Readings:

"Hear my voice, O God, in my prayer; preserve my life from dread of the enemy, Hide me from the secret plots of the wicked; from the scheming of evildoers, Who wet their tongues like swords, who aim bitter words like arrows, Shooting from ambush at the blameless." *Psalm 64:1–4 (RSV)*

"He who conceals hatred has lying lips, and he who spreads slander is a fool. When there are many words, transgression is unavoidable, but he who restrains his lips is wise." *Prov. 10:18–19 (NASB)*

"And some began to spit on him, and to cover his face, and to buffet him, and to say to him: Prophesy. And the servants did strike him with the palms of their hands." *Lk. 14:65 (KJV)*

"For it is God's will that by doing right you should put to silence the ignorance of foolish men." *1 Pet. 2:15 (RSV)*

FEBRUARY 17 Empress Pulcheria of Constantinople

The calendars of the Eastern churches honor St. Pulcheria twice, once alone (September 10) and once with her husband, Marcion (February 17). She was also a saint in the old Roman calendar. Acting as regent on behalf of her younger brother Theodocius, she took a vow of chastity as a girl, but she married Marcion later in life to continue her reign after Theodocius died. She organized the Council of Ephesus, and together they were instrumental in convening the Council of Chalcedon twenty years later (451). Pulcheria bitterly fought against Nestorianism (which denied that Mary should be called "Theotokos," or Mother of God) and had three churches built in Constantinople in Mary's honor under this title. She also labored to retrieve the bones of St. John Chrysostom, who had died in exile, to be brought back to the imperial city. She was particularly devoted to St. Euphemia (see Daily Readings, July 12, Euphemia) who was said to work miracles at her tomb at the time of the Chalcedon Council.

Intercessory Prayer:

O Blessed Pulcheria, you toiled under the heavenly direction of your beloved Euphemia to secure the success of the holy councils that sought to dutifully honor Christ and his Holy Mother. You studied the philosophy and theology of your age and made decisions that helped shape the early Church through your unfailing openness to the Holy Spirit's inspiration. You gained the favor of our Lord and the community of Christians in heaven and on earth; intercede for us who labor to understand the changes of the churches in our modern times. Amen.

Antiphon:

With outstretched arms you lead us out of darkness.

Readings:

"Give justice to your Anointed, O God, and righteousness to those Chosen!

That your people may be judged in righteousness, and your poor with justice.

Let the mountains bring forth peace for all the people, and the
hills, justice!
May your Anointed defend the cause of the poor,
Give deliverance to the needy, and punish the oppressor!
May your Anointed endure like the sun, and as long as the moon
through all ages,
like rain that falls on the mown grass,
Like showers that water the earth." *Psalm 72:1–6 (PCB)*

"So also we, while we were children, were held in bondage under
the elemental things of the world. But when the fullness of the
time came, God sent forth his Son, born of a woman, born under
the Law, in order that he might redeem those who were under the
Law." *Gal. 4:3–4 (NASB)*

FEBRUARY 18 Juana Ines de la Cruz

Sor (sister) Juana Ines de la Cruz gained notoriety as the
first great female Baroque literary figure of Latin America.
She was also one of the earliest advocates for women's
rights in the Latin Church to write and publish. She was born in
1651, illegitimate, and raised by her mother's family. Astonishing all
those around her, she began reading at age three, and she was insatiable in her quest for learning throughout the rest of her life. She entered the Convent of St. Jerome in Mexico City, where she had the
privilege of collecting books; she soon amassed the largest library in
her country. She wrote volumes of poems, religious allegories, and
historical commentaries. When she began writing about theology,
however, she entered into a dispute with the Bishop of Puebla, who
censored her. She defended women's rights to engage in theological
commentary. In 1691, she was instructed to turn from her worldly
intellectualism; she replied that science and knowledge would
strengthen faith in God rather than weaken it. The struggle with authority eventually turned into an impasse from which she could not
escape, however, without leaving the convent. To Sister Juana Ines, it
was the ultimate test. In 1693, she stopped writing and sold her four
thousand books to raise money for the poor. She died two years later
of the plague, while caring for her sick sisters.

Prayer:

Lord Jesus, you were a friend of women and encouraged them during your time on earth to break the molds that they found themselves in while living in a pagan environment. In a later era, many, like your beloved Sor Juana Ines, became great teachers, writers, and thinkers. Thank you for the gift of the holy Mothers of the Church, both those who were embraced during their lifetime and those whose time did not permit them to bring forth all their gifts. We learn from all of them. Help all women who struggle with the trials of not having their voices heard. Although the world may not hear, we know that you hear all of our voices. Amen.

Antiphon:

Did not our hearts burn within us, as he talked to us on the road?

Readings:

"For Thou has tried us, O God; Thou has refined us as silver is refined." *Psalm 66:10 (NASB)*

"No temptation has overtaken you but such as is common to [all men]; and God is faithful, who will not allow you to be tempted beyond what you are able, but with the temptation will provide the way of escape also, that you may be able to endure it." *1 Cor. 10:13 (NASB)*

"The woman said to him, 'I know that a Messiah is coming. . . . When that one comes, he will declare all things to us.' Jesus said to her, 'I who speak to you am he.' And at this point his disciples came, and they marveled that he had been speaking with a woman; yet no one said, 'What do you seek?' or 'Why do you speak with her?' *Jn. 4:25–27 (NASB)*

FEBRUARY 19 Philothei the Athenian

Holy Mother Philothei is a well-loved saint in the Greek culture, and her relics are venerated in the Cathedral of Athens. She was born into a wealthy aristocratic family in the mid-sixteenth century, when the Turks were ruling her city. After her parents' death when she was twenty-seven, she changed her name from

Regoula to Philothei ("God-loving") and used her inheritance to found a convent, a hospital, an orphanage, and a homeless shelter. At a time when education was the privilege of boys, she founded a school for girls and called it the Parthenon. She also took in women who were unmarried mothers or victims of rape or abuse, particularly slaves. Turkish soldiers seized her in 1588 while she was attending an all-night vigil in honor of St. Dionysius, first Bishop of Athens; she was severely beaten and left for dead. She died four months later at age sixty-seven and is honored as a martyr in the Greek Church.

Intercessory Prayer:

O holy Mother Philothei, you were the triumphant heroine of Athens who exchanged your riches for the sake of your less fortunate brethren. You encouraged the hopeless and taught the ignorant. O brilliant sun radiating light to those whose lives had been darkened by slavery, in honoring your memory, we ask for your intercession: Pray that we may have the courage to hold nothing back for God, the true lover of our souls. Amen.

Antiphon:

You will cover us with your pinions, and under your wings we will find refuge.

Readings:

"When God restored the fortunes of Zion, it seemed like a dream.
Then our mouth was filled with laughter
And our tongue with shouts of joy.
Then they said among the nations, 'God has done great things for them.'
You have done great things for us! Indeed we are glad.
Restore our fortunes, O God, like the streams in the desert!
May those who sow in tears reap with shouts of joy.
They that go forth weeping, bearing seed for the sowing,
Shall come home with shouts of joy, bringing their sheaves with them." *Psalm 126 (PCB)*

"For you were called to freedom, brethren; only do not turn your freedom into an opportunity for the flesh, but through love, serve one another." *Gal. 5:13 (NASB)*

"But rather, seek ye first the kingdom of heaven; and all these things shall be added unto you. Fear not, little flock, for it is your Father's good pleasure to give you the kingdom. Sell all that you have, and give alms; provide yourself bags which are not old, a treasure in the heavens that does not fail, where no thief approaches, neither moths corrupt. For where your treasure is, there will your heart be also." *Lk. 12:31–37 (KJV)*

FEBRUARY 20 Cecile Isherwood

Cecile Isherwood was born in England, and she served as an Anglican deaconess in South Africa in the Diocese of Grahamstown. She was living a normal, happy life when, at age twenty-one, she heard a sermon given by a visiting bishop from South Africa, requesting workers there. She left everything and went. At the bishop's request, she founded a sisterhood, the Community of The Resurrection of Our Lord, which grew under her direction. The sisters opened an industrial school for girls in Grahamstown, followed by several elementary schools. Cecile worked tirelessly for the oppressed in the face of many obstacles. She was active in helping to change the wretched relations between whites and blacks in South Africa. She once wrote that the Church can never do enough to make up for the great wrong her society had brought to South Africans. She rose every morning for Morning Prayer and Holy Communion, joking that it was good for the sisters to go to work on their knees. She died February 20, 1906, in England at the early age of forty-four, following an operation.

Prayer:

Lord, you made Cecile an instrument of contagious love and joy in a land filled with injustice and sorrow. Through her, many came to your table with a new understanding of your justice and mercy. She understood that what you did for humanity is a great treasure to be shared by all. Help us to understand that living the Christian faith is not just a personal experience; it is a divine gift, and we have a holy right to share it with all we meet. Bless those today who still suffer injustice based on their skin color. Amen.

Antiphon:

May we serve you in holiness all the days of our lives.

Readings:

"But he saves . . . the poor from the hand of the mighty. So the helpless have hope, and unrighteousness must shut its mouth." *Job. 5:15–16 (NASB)*

"I am black but lovely, O daughters of Jerusalem, like the tents of Kedar, Like the curtains of Solomon. Do not stare at me because I am swarthy, for the sun has burned me." *Song of Songs 1:5–6 (NASB)*

"Where there is neither Greek nor Jew, circumcision nor uncircumcision, Barbarian, Scythian, bond nor free: but Christ is all, and in all." *Col. 3:11 (KJV)*

"For I came down from heaven, not to do my own will, but the will of him who sent me. And this is the Father's will which has sent me, that of all which he has given me I should lose nothing, but should raise it up again on the last day." *Jn. 6:38–39 (KJV)*

FEBRUARY 21 *Kozelschansk Icon of the Theotokos*

The glorification of the *Kozelschansk* icon of the Holy Mother is an interesting and typical example of an iconic cult's development at the local level. In 1880, a Count Kapnist resided in the village of Kozelschina, Russia. He had a daughter with a condition that affected the feeling in and use of her arms and legs (possibly multiple sclerosis). The family tried both local and international physicians and were on the verge of contacting the famed Charcot, when the girl was suddenly and instantly cured while praying before her icon. The family took the icon with them on a trip to Moscow, where they met a young blind woman, who told them that the Mother of God had appeared to her in a dream, instructing her where to meet the family carrying the holy image that would cure her. They brought out the Kapnist family icon, and while praying with it, the woman was cured of her blindness. Thus began the spread of the *Kozelschansk* devotion. A chapel, and later a church, was built to honor the Theotokos, and many who came were cured of their illnesses. In 1885, a women's monastery, with a hospital, school, and home for the crippled, was opened in Kozelshchina.

Intercessory Prayer:

Beloved Mother of God, you are well known for wishing to manifest the visible strength and healing power of your Son on behalf of those who honor you. Through your holy icon, you raised from their bed of sickness those crippled in body but not in spirit. Strengthen our own faith, for you are the mighty fortress whom we invoke in our time of need. Intercede for us, preserve our families, and bestow grace on those in distress. Hail, our Joy; protect us from every ill by your precious icon. Amen.

Antiphon:

Your spirit, O God, moves upon the face of the earth.

Readings:

"Though I walk in the midst of trouble, you preserve my life; You stretch out your hand and save me. You will fulfill your purpose for me; Your steadfast love endures forever. Do not forsake the work of your hands." *Psalm 138:7–8 (PCB)*

"Like a terebinth I spread out my branches, laden with honor and grace. I put forth lovely shoots like the vine, and my blossoms were a harvest of wealth and honor. Come to me, you who desire me, and eat your fill of my fruit." *Eccl. 21:16–17 (NEB)*

"And he took the blind man by the hand, and led him out of the village; and when he had spit on his eyes and laid his hands upon him, he asked him: 'Do you see anything?' And he looked up and said, 'I see men as trees, walking.' Then again he laid his hands upon his eyes, and he looked intently and was restored, and saw everything clearly." *Mk. 8:23–25 (RSV)*

"And the angel answered and said to her, 'The Holy Spirit shall come upon you, and the power of the Most High will overshadow you.'" *Lk. 1:35 (NASB)*

FEBRUARY 22 Margaret of Cortona

Margaret of Cortona was born in Tuscany in the mid-thirteenth century, a beautiful girl who lost her mother very young. She did not get along well with her stepmother and left home at seventeen to become a knight's mistress for nine years. After bearing a son, she begged the man to marry her, but he refused. The relationship was severed when she discovered her lover's dead body in the woods and, seeing it as a sign from God, she turned to a life of penitence. Franciscans took in Margaret and her son, and she became a tertiary. Her son also went on to become a Franciscan. She then began conversing with Jesus, who called her his *poverella*. At the direction of her inner voice, she eventually founded her own chapter to work with the sick, calling it Poverelle (Poor Ones). Although Margaret continued to be a victim of slander in her local community because of her prior life, she nonetheless gained notoriety as a famous healer. Throughout a life of condemnation she worked steadily toward her sainthood. When she died, she left a perfectly incorruptible body at Cortona, which can still be viewed after seven hundred years.

Intercessory Prayer:

O holy Margaret of God, you are often called the third great light granted to the Order of the Franciscans. Bless all tertiaries who labor for the love of Jesus as you did. Help us to recognize and welcome the mysterious plan of divine providence in all aspects of our everyday lives. By your example, may we unflinchingly look forward to Christ, heeding not the bitter words of the world. Intercede for us that we may be instruments of God's peace and reconciliation. Amen.

Antiphon:

Every day I will bless you and praise your name forever.

Readings:

"Cast your shadow like night at high noon; Hide the outcasts, do not betray the fugitive. Let the outcasts of Moab stay with you; Be a hiding place to them from the destroyer. . . . [For] oppressors have completely disappeared from the land. A throne will even be established in loving-kindness." *Isa. 16:3–5 (NASB)*

"I am small and despised, yet do not forget your precepts.
Your righteousness is an everlasting righteousness, and your law is the truth.
Trouble and anguish have taken hold on me; yet your commandments are my delight.
The righteousness of your testimony is everlasting; give me understanding and I shall live." *Psalm 119:141–144 (Tzaddi) (KJV)*

"And departing from there, Jesus went along by the Sea of Galilee, and having gone up to the mountain, He was sitting there.

And great multitudes came to him, bringing with them those who were lame, crippled, blind, dumb, and many others, and they laid them down at his feet; and he healed them." *Mt. 15:29–30 (NASB)*

FEBRUARY 23 Milburga

Milburga, born in England in the seventh century, was Mildred of Thanet's elder sister. Milburga founded a nunnery in Wenlock, which her father and her uncle, Wulfhere, king of Mercia, endowed. The Archbishop Theodore consecrated the monastery, which flourished under Milburga's rule. She was well known for her humility and was favored with wonderful graces from God. She had the gift of healing and the spiritual power to bring numerous sinners to repentance. Many miraculous feats were attributed to her. Milburga was also known to have mysterious powers over birds, who listened to her command not to disturb new crops. She died in 722, after a long and painful disease that she bore with serenity. Her last words were: "Blessed are the pure in heart; blessed are the peacemakers." Her tomb was venerated until the Danes destroyed the abbey when they ravaged England. The shrine at her gravesite was forgotten until the Norman Conquest in 1066. When Cluniac monks built a monastery on the same spot as her tomb, it began to sink into the ground and they discovered St. Milburga's bones. Milburga was venerated as a saint in English calendars as early as 950, and she is invoked for protection of crops.

Prayer:

Precious Spirit of God, help us to follow in the footsteps of Milburga. Let us humble ourselves before you so we may open ourselves to the gifts of spirit that you endow each of us with. Help us to be pure in heart and peacemakers in our families and communities. Let the serenity that comes from following and loving you infuse our hearts. Thank you for your blessings in our lives. Amen.

Antiphon:

Love bears all things and believes all things.

Readings:

"I have called upon you, for you will hear me, O God:
Incline your ear to me and hear my speech.
Show your marvelous loving-kindness, You who saves by your
 right hand
all that put their trust in you. . . . Keep me as the apple of your
 eye.
Hide me under the shadow of your wings." *Psalm 17:6–8 (KJV)*

'Who is among you that fears the Lord, that obeys the voice of his
servant, that walks in darkness and has no light? . . . [Yet] trust in
the name of the Lord and rely on God." *Isa. 50:10 (NASB)*

"All the birds of the heavens nested in its boughs, and under its
branches all the beasts of the field gave birth, and all the nations
lived under its shade." *Ez. 31:6 (NASB)*

FEBRUARY 24 Mechthild of Hackeborn

Mechthild of Hackeborn, sometimes confused with Mechthild of Magdeburg (both were nuns who spent time at Helfta), was Abbess Gertrude's sister and Gertrude the Great's friend. Mechthild was in charge of the choir at Helfta, in Germany, and was known as "God's nightingale." Her principal work, called the *Book of Special Grace,* documents her visionary encounters with Christ's life, passion, and death. She belonged to the school of mysticism, common in the Middle Ages, which stressed the love affair of Christ and the soul. Her work is rich with the symbolism of numbers, colors, and the use of plants and animals. After a life of prayer, penance, and much physical suffering, she died in 1299. After her death, Mechthild appeared to her dear friend St. Gertrude in a vision, wearing a robe of shining crystal, set with rubies, emeralds, and other precious stones, and sparkling like the stars in the heavens. The *Book of Special Grace,* which Gertrude transcribed, became quite famous in Europe and England.

Intercessory Prayer:

O, Mechthild, you saw the King of glory appear in the fullness of his splendor, with his golden garment open on both sides to indicate that the soul has free access to the Lord, who always is ready to meet us. Intercede for those of us who struggle to foster a closer relationship with our beloved Jesus that we might some day be blessed with the intimacy you shared with him. As you were graced with sharing the blessed Lord's golden robes of glory, spending your whole life in adoration before him, pray that we too may someday become part of the glorious communion of saints who share in his divinity. Amen.

Antiphon:

As a deer longs for the running stream, so does my soul long for you, my God.

Readings:

"With my whole being, I thirst for God, the living God,
When shall I come to God and appear in his presence?
Day and night, tears are my food;
'Where is your God?' they ask me all day long.
As I pour out my soul in distress, I call to mind how I marched in ranks
Of the great to the house of God, among exultant shouts of praise,
The clamour of pilgrims." *Psalm 42:2–4 (NEB)*

"For you know the grace of our Lord Jesus Christ, that, though he was rich, yet for your sakes he became poor, that through his poverty, you might be rich." *2 Cor. 8:9 (KJV)*

"And there appeared to them tongues as of fire distributing themselves, and they rested on each of them. And they were all filled with the Holy Spirit." *Acts 2:3–4 (NASB)*

"And blessed is she who believed that there would be a fulfillment of what had been spoken to her by the Lord." *Lk. 1:45 (NASB)*

FEBRUARY 25 Lydda Icon Not Made by Hands (Old Calendar)

Lydda was a town not far from Jerusalem where, it is believed in the early Byzantine tradition, the Mother of God consecrated one of the early churches where the apostles were preaching. In the legend of the *Lydda Icon Not Made By Hands*, the image of the Theotokos miraculously appeared on one of the church's columns. During the reign of Julian the Apostate in the fourth century, an attempt was made to remove the icon, but it could not be erased from the stone. Copies of the icon were made, and one was sent to Rome, which was also a miracle worker. The patriarchs of Rome, Jerusalem, Antioch, and Alexandria, who wrote to the iconoclast Emperor Theophilus, all mentioned an icon of the Theotokos not made by human hands. Emperor Constantine VII Porphyrogenitus (912–959) mentions it in his historic sermon about a similar image of Christ, the Edessa Image of the *Savior Not Made By Hands*, also called *The Mandylion*. Copies of the miracle-working icons were great healers. The feast of the *Lydda* icon is celebrated twice, on this date and on June 26, in honor of the copy sent to Rome.

Intercessory Prayer:

O Holy Mother of God, we thank you for all the signs and symbols of your loving presence among us. We know that living the Christian life is about encountering Jesus and coming to know who he is. Although we will never be able to understand all the mysteries of this life, we know that he gave us his own Mother to help make sense of our troubled lives and to intercede for us when we ask. Look down on us from your holy height and entreat your Beloved Son to enlighten our darkened souls and bestow upon us a serene and peaceful life and a good death. May we be granted the great joy of someday seeing you face to face in heaven. Amen.

Antiphon:

Hail! Our hope and defense on the day of judgment! (Akathist)

Readings:

"Keep me as the apple of your eye;
Hide me in the shadow of your wings,
From the wicked who destroy.
As for me, in my justice, I shall see your face;
when I awake, I shall be filled with the sight of your glory."
Psalm 17:8–9, 15 (PCB)

"Wisdom has built her house, she has set up her seven pillars.
She has slaughtered her beasts, she has mixed her wine. She has also set her table.
She has sent out her maids to call from the highest places in the town:
'Whoever is simple, let them turn in here!' *Prov. 9,1–4 (RSV)*

"O most holy Virgin, Mother of the Lord of the hosts on high, Queen of Heaven and earth, almighty intercessor: receive this hymn of praise and thanksgiving from us, thine unworthy servants, and bear our prayers to the throne of God, thy Son, that He may be merciful toward our unrighteousness and extend His grace to them that honor thine honorable name and bow down before thy wonder-working icon with faith and love." *Akathist to Most Sovereign Lady, the Theotokos, concluding prayer 3*

"I have no greater joy than this, to hear of my children walking in the truth." *3 Jn. 4 (NASB)*

FEBRUARY 26 Walburga

St. Walburga was born in 710 in Wimborne, Dorset, England, the niece of St. Boniface, whom she assisted in his missionary work. She studied in Dorset under St. Tatta at the Wimborne monastery before she was sent to organize her own monastery in Germany. On her way to Germany, a fierce storm arose and Walburga calmed it with her prayers. Walburga became the abbess of a double monastery in Heidenheim, Germany, in the eighth century. She was said to be skilled in medicine, and because of her great learning and proficiency in Latin, she is often regarded as Germany's first female author. Walburga is frequently pictured in iconography with three ears of corn, most likely associating her with an earlier fertility cult. Medicinal oil flowed from the rock around her tomb, and her relics were distributed throughout the Rhineland, being associated with many healings. Walburga is patron of sailors.

Intercessory Prayer:

O holy Mother Walburga, from you a beacon of light spread throughout the Rhineland. You became a watchtower of faith and learning for many, and your sweetness and virtue endeared you to all who knew you. You were so attuned to your bridegroom that you had command of the terrifying elements, never lacking in faith. We honor you in songs of praise, O holy healer, and ask for the fortitude to follow your straight path to salvation in Christ our Lord. Amen.

Antiphon:

He hushed the storm to a gentle breeze, and the billows of the sea were stilled.

Readings:

"He sent his word and healed them, and delivered them from their destructions.

Oh, that all would praise the Lord for his goodness, and for his wonderful works . . .

They that go down to the sea in ships, that do business in great waters;

These see the works of the Lord, and his wonders in the deep.

For he commands, and raises the stormy wind, which lifts up there waves therein,

They mount up to the heaven, they go down again to the depths,

Their soul is melted because of trouble. They reel to and fro, and stagger like drunks,

And they are at their wits end.

Then they cry to the Lord in their trouble, and he brings them out of their distress.

He makes the storm to calm, so that the waves therein are still."
Psalm *107:20–29 (KJV)*

"Let the elders that rule well be considered worthy of double honor, especially those who work hard at preaching and teaching. For the Scripture says . . . 'the laborer is worthy of [his] wages.'"
1 Tim. 5:17–18 (NASB)

FEBRUARY 27 Anne Line

Anne Line was born into an ardent Calvinist family in England in the latter part of the sixteenth century. As a teenager she converted to Roman Catholicism, and her family disinherited her. She married Roger Line, also a convert; he was imprisoned shortly afterward and died in exile. Destitute, she became a priest's housekeeper and later took charge of a house of refuge for priests. Despite ill health, she dedicated herself to offering safe haven for persecuted Roman Catholics. On Candlemas Day in 1601, she was setting up the altar for Mass when she was discovered, sentenced to death for harboring priests, and executed the next day. Before she died, she joyfully announced that if she were able, she would have harbored thousands. She was canonized with the forty martyrs of England and Wales in 1970. She is patron of sacristy keepers.

Prayer:

> *O Almighty God, you sent your Son to reveal that the kingdom of heaven is within us. The holy martyr Anne Line lived a simple life of service and heroism, yet she was a shining example of your kingdom. Through her intercession, teach us to live in the world and not be of the world, that we may have the strength to always discern the voice of your presence in the midst of our darkest trials. Through Christ our Lord. Amen.*

Antiphon:

Blessed are the pure of heart, for they shall see God.

Readings:

"I will love thee, O Lord, my strength.
The Lord is my rock, and my fortress, and my deliverer,
My God, my strength, in whom I will trust,
My buckler and the horn of my salvation, and my high tower.
I will call upon the Lord, who is worthy to be praised,
So I shall be saved from my enemies.
The sorrows of death encompassed me and the floods of ungodly men made me afraid.
In my distress, I called upon the Lord, and I cried to my God,
He heard my voice out of his temple, and my cry came before him
Even unto his ears." *Psalm 18:1–6 (KJV)*

"As the Father knows me, even so do I know the Father. And I lay down my life for these sheep. And other sheep I have, which are not of this fold, them also I must bring, and they shall hear my voice, and there shall be one fold and one shepherd. Therefore does my Father love me, because I lay down my life, that I might take it up again." *Jn. 10:15–17 (KJV)*

FEBRUARY 28 Villana de'Botti

Villana de'Botti was born in 1332, the daughter of a Florentine merchant. At age thirteen, she ran away to join a convent but was turned away and sent home. Her parents soon married her to Rosso di Piero, which caused a great change to overtake her. She became infatuated with worldly life and entertainment. Her conversion happened on an occasion when she was inspecting a new dress and her pearls in the mirror and saw, not herself, but a demon staring back at her. Alarmed, she sought a Dominican confessor and shortly afterward became a Dominican tertiary. She became attached to the poor and saw them as an extension of her own growing family. Soon she began having other visions, of Mary and the saints. She frequently went into ecstasy at Mass. She would often pray late at night, and her room was suffused with a supernatural light. On her deathbed, she asked that the Passion be read to her, and at the moment when the words of John were read, "He bowed his head and gave up his spirit," she crossed herself and died. Her body became such a strong object of veneration that it could not be moved for over a month after her funeral. The city's many poor came to bid her goodbye, and she was honored as a saint immediately. Pope Leo XII beatified her in 1824.

Prayer:

Almighty God, when Blessed Villana saw the emptiness of her worldly life, she turned immediately to you and dedicated the rest of her life to serving your poor. Help us to remember that no matter how far we have fallen from you, you await eagerly to lift us up to where you are. You, whose mercies cannot be numbered, grant us also the grace to use our time on earth wisely, that we may be granted entrance into the land of light and joy. Amen.

Antiphon:

We give thanks to you, for you are good; your love endures forever.

Readings:

"We thank you, O God of gods, for your love endures forever.
We thank you, Creator of the universe, for your love endures forever.
You alone have done great wonders, for your love endures forever.
Your wisdom made the heavens, for your love endures forever.
You spread out the earth upon the waters, for your love endures forever.
It was you who made the great lights, for your love endures forever." *Psalm 136:1–7 (PCB)*

"Like newborn babes, long for the pure milk of the word, that by it you may grow in respect to salvation. . . . And coming to him as

WomenSaints

to a living stone rejected by men, but choice and precious in the sight of God, you also, as living stones, are being built up as a spiritual house for a holy priesthood." *1 Pet. 2:2–5 (NASB)*

"Do not love the world, nor the things in the world." *1 Jn. 2:15 (NASB)*

FEBRUARY 29 Gladys May Aylward and Nympha

Born centuries apart, Gladys May Aylward and Nympha both had a fervent calling to evangelize. Gladys Aylward, born in 1902 in England, did very poorly in school, but nonetheless had a deep desire to do missionary work in China. She struggled to learn Chinese and to save the fare to go to China, praying that the Lord would give her the means to do both. Once there, she exchanged her European clothes for Chinese ones and joyfully gave up her citizenship to become more fully identified with her new people. She opened orphanages and was active in the refugee movement during Mao Tse Tung's rule. Her heroic journey to take over a hundred refugee children to freedom across the rugged mountainous country to Siam was recorded in Alan Burgess's book, *The Small Woman*. All who knew Gladys spoke of her great courage and faith in God.

St. Nympha was an evangelist and martyr of the early Church. The Roman Church celebrates her feast with saints Tryphon and Respicius on November 10, and the East celebrates her feast February 29. In Orthodoxy, she was given the title "Apostle to the Seventy."

Prayer:

Beloved Lord, we know that, despite whatever obstacle lies in our path, if we are living in your will and supported by your wisdom and understanding, nothing in the world can hold us back from our true calling. The holy women Gladys and Nympha were both called to spread your word in foreign lands, and therefore became the work of your hands. Make us instruments of your gospel message in our modern world. Help us to be attuned to your

*calling, so that, following the inner desire of our hearts, we may
find ourselves embodying your kingdom on earth. Amen.*

Antiphon:

We praise you, O God, and speak of your marvelous works.

Readings:

"We sing praise to you, sing praise, sing praise to you, Most High.
For your realm is all the earth. We sing to you our hymns of
praise!
Your reign is over all the nations, Over all the peoples of this
earth." *Psalm 47:6–8 (PCB)*

"And he sent them to preach the Kingdom of God, and to heal the
sick. And he said to them, 'Take nothing for your journey, no staff,
nor bag, nor bread, nor money . . . and whatever house you enter,
stay there, and from there depart.'" *Lk. 9:2–4 (RSV)*

"But watch in all things, endure afflictions, do the work of an evangelist, make full proof of your ministry." *2 Tim. 4:5 (KJV)*

MARCH 1 Eudokia of Heliopolis

Eudokia of Heliopolis was a beautiful girl who spent her
early adult life as a courtesan in ancient Damascus. One of
the wealthiest women of her city, she never felt satisfied
until she happened to meet a Christian monk named Germanos. She
overheard him reading Scripture at a neighbor's home and thus began
her thirst for true wealth. Germanos advised her to withdraw alone
to her bedroom for one week to seek God's counsel. During this
time, she had a vision of Michael the Archangel, who led her to the
gate of heaven. Upon returning, Eudokia converted to the Christian
life, dispensed her estate, freed her slaves, and joined a community of
solitary women. A story is told that, during a period of persecution of
the early Church, soldiers were approaching the convent where Eudokia lived to arrest and imprison her. Frightened, she approached
the holy Bema, and the tabernacle that housed the Holy Eucharist.
She removed a piece of the Blessed Sacrament for strength before
being sent to jail for several years. Before she died, she reputedly

raised someone from the dead, causing many conversions. She was eventually beheaded.

Prayer:

> *O master Jesus, you are the skillful potter who refashions all broken vessels, and the shepherd who never loses a sheep. You brought your holy servant Eudokia into your temple wherein lies eternal wealth and unending satisfaction. Once she had discovered you, she knew that your presence in her life was all that mattered. Plant your faith firmly in us, that we may find ourselves rooted in you alone, for only in you can we find the pearl of great price. Amen.*

Antiphon:

For if you love [only] those who love you, what reward do you have?

Readings:

"God be merciful to us and bless us,
And cause His face to shine upon us." *Psalm 67:1 (NKJV)*

"Or what woman, having ten silver coins, when she loses one coin, does not light a lamp and sweep the house and seek diligently until she finds it? And when she has found it, she calls together her friends and neighbors, saying, 'Rejoice with me, for I have found the coin which I had lost.' Even so, I tell you, there is joy before the angels of God over one sinner who repents." *Lk. 15:8–11 (RSV)*

"For this *is* good and acceptable in the sight of God our Savior, who desires all . . . to be saved and to come to the knowledge of the truth." *1 Tim. 2:3–4 (NKJV)*

"Again, the kingdom of heaven is like a merchant seeking goodly pearls; who, when he had found one pearl of great price, went and sold all that he had, and bought it." *Mt. 13:45–46 (KJV)*

MARCH 2 Agnes of Prague

St. Agnes of Prague, sometimes called Agnes of Bohemia, was one of the foremost disciples of St. Clare of Assisi. The daughter of King Ottokar of Bohemia, Agnes was betrothed to the Duke of Silesia at age three, who died three years later. As she aged,

Agnes declined several offers of marriage and decided she wanted to enter the religious life. She was struck with Clare's charisma and sanctity. Clare sent five of her sisters from San Damiano to help Agnes form a community in Prague. Agnes built a monastery, a hospital, and a home for Franciscan friars. Clare's correspondence to her is a beautiful record of her devotion to Agnes and Agnes's community. Like Clare, Agnes preferred a democratic form of community life, and when the Pope pressured her to accept the title of abbess, she preferred to use the term "senior sister." She lived for forty-five years in the humble poverty of the early Franciscan tradition, cooking for the other sisters and mending the clothes of lepers. She died in 1282, but she was not canonized until 1989. Agnes is the patron of Prague.

Intercessory Prayer:

O holy Agnes, you exchanged the fleeting pleasures of this life for contemplation on the eternal. Through self-mastery and service, you followed the direction of your beloved Clare so that you could receive the glorious rays of the Spirit and became a mouthpiece for God in your new life. Intercede on our behalf to the lover of your soul and ours, and entreat the Lord Jesus to save and enlighten us. Amen.

Antiphon:

The women and men who believed in Jesus rejoiced.

Readings:

"Sing a new song to our God.
Give praise in the assembly of the faithful.
Let Israel be glad in its Maker; let Zion's heirs exult in the Most High. Let them praise God's name with dancing, and make music with timbrel and harp." *Psalm 149:1–2 (PCB)*

"Therefore I ask that you do not lose heart at my tribulations for you, which is your glory. For this reason I bow my knees to the Father of our Lord Jesus Christ, from whom the whole family in heaven and earth is named, that He would grant you, according to the riches of His glory, to be strengthened with might through His Spirit in the inner [man]." *Eph. 3:13–16 (NKJV)*

"And at midnight a cry was heard: 'Behold, the bridegroom is coming; go out to meet him!'" *Mt. 25:6 (NJKV)*

"When the crowds found out about it, they followed him; and he welcomed them, and spoke to them about the kingdom of God, and healed those who needed to be cured." *Lk. 9:11 (NRSV)*

MARCH 3 Katherine Drexel

Katherine Drexel was born into an extremely wealthy family of philanthropists in Philadelphia in 1858. At an early age, she tended to the poor who came to the family's open door. She had an excellent early education, and after her mother's death, she asked the Pope to send someone to do missionary work in the "wild west" of Wyoming and New Mexico. The Pope sent her. Using her great wealth to help American Indians, she founded many boarding schools for both Native Americans and African-Americans. Harassed by segregationists, she was undaunted in her efforts to complete her mission, and she started the Sisters of the Blessed Sacrament in Sante Fe, New Mexico, which eventually spread as far as Louisiana, where the first catholic university for African-Americans, Xavier, was established in 1917.

Prayer:

O Christ our God, through the prayers of St. Katherine Drexel, teach us to live simply in solidarity with the ones whom you spoke of so fondly in your beatitudes. Convinced that we are all people of God, Katherine honored the culture of those whom she sought to introduce to you, and she defended them staunchly, as a mother hen guards her brood. Through her intercession, may we honor you in harmony, responsibility, and a spirit of cooperation with all peoples. Amen.

Antiphon:

He has cast down the mighty from their thrones and exalted the lowly.

Readings:

"O come, let us sing to the Lord; let us make a joyful noise to the rock of our salvation.

Let us come before his presence with thanksgiving, and make a joyful noise to him with psalms. For the Lord is a great God, and a great King above all gods.

In his hand are the deep places of the earth; the strength of the hills is his also.

The sea is his, and he made it; and his hands formed the dry land.

O come let us worship and bow down; let us kneel before the Lord our maker.

For he is our God, and we are the people of his pasture, and the
    sheep of his hand.
Today if you will, hear his voice." *Psalm 95:1–7 (NKJV)*

"Do not lie to one another, since you laid aside the old self with its
evil practices, and have put on the new self who is being renewed
to a true knowledge according to the image of the One who created [him], a renewal in which there is no distinction between
Greek and Jew, circumcised and uncircumcised, barbarian,
Scythian, slave and freeman, but Christ is all, and in all." *Col. 3:
9–11 (NASB)*

"And just as you want people to treat you, treat them in the same
way." *Lk. 6:31 (NASB)*

MARCH 4 Placide Viel

Eulalie Victoire Jacqueline Viel was born to a large farming
family in Normandy, France, and lived much of her life during the Franco-Prussian War. When she was eighteen, she
joined the Sisters of the Christian Schools and took the name Placide.
Although she had little education, she was eventually elected Mistress
of Novices and Assistant Mother General. Placide was the niece of another great saint, Marie Madeleine Postel, who was Mother General
at her convent. When her aunt died, Placide took over the leadership
role of Mother General at age thirty-one. This caused a firestorm of
resentment from many of the other sisters, which Placide accepted
humbly, as she strove to understand and carry out God's will. She
worked tirelessly during the turbulent times of the Franco-Prussian
War to organize various war relief efforts and to establish educational
institutions and orphanages throughout Normandy. In 1859 she
gained official approval of her order from Pope Pius IX. Placide died
in 1877, and Pope Pius XII beatified her in 1951.

Prayer:

*Heavenly Father, through the tireless efforts of good and holy
saints like Placide Viel, the Gospel's mission was spread to
countless souls throughout Europe. Help us to be inspired by St.
Placide's example of surrendering all to you for the sake of the
kingdom. May our lives be conformed to you in all things. Help us*

to be detached from the criticism from others, living secure in the knowledge that we are striving to fulfill your wishes above the desires of human hearts. Amen.

Antiphon:

My grace is sufficient for you, for my power is made perfect in weakness.

Readings:

"I delight to do your will, O my God, and your law *is* within my heart. I have proclaimed the good news of righteousness in the great assembly; Indeed, I do not restrain my lips, O LORD. . . . I have not hidden your righteousness within my heart; I have declared your faithfulness and Your salvation; I have not concealed your lovingkindness and your truth from the great assembly." *Psalm 40:8–10 (NKJV)*

"And a servant of the Lord must not quarrel but be gentle to all, able to teach, patient, in humility correcting those who are in opposition, if God perhaps will grant them repentance, so that they may know the truth." *2 Tim. 2:24–25 (NKJV)*

"[Neither] height nor depth, nor any other created thing, shall be able to separate us from the love of God which is in Christ Jesus our Lord" *Rom. 8:39 (NKJV)*

MARCH 5 Maria Solares

Born in 1842 in a Chumash village in southern California, Maria Solares grew up learning two Indian languages, one from each of her parents, as well as English, taught in the Roman Catholic mission near her home. She married and bore three children, and she also pursued the career of doctor and midwife on her reservation. Maria balanced her Catholic faith while still preserving her Native American Indian religion, and she was instrumental in documenting much of her Chumash culture for the Smithsonian Institute. Undaunted, Maria worked for her people when the mission was secularized and the Native Americans were pushed out from their own lands, soon suffering from great poverty and a lack of medical care. Maria died in 1923, and her tribe remembers her as a saintly soul who ministered to them through all their trials and deprivations. They call her "Maria of the Refugees."

Prayer:

> *Beloved God, you are both mother and father to all peoples. Let Jesus' promises give your people freedom to remove all that hinders us from the full realization of your kingdom. Through the good works of your servant Maria Solares, make us ever mindful of the gospel message that calls us to serve your poor, so that all may experience your reign of justice and peace on earth. Amen.*

Antiphon:

Heal our wounds and grant us new life.

Readings:

"For the oppression of the poor, for the sighing of the needy, Now I will arise," says the LORD;
"I will set [them] in safety . . ." The words of the LORD are pure words,
Like silver tried in a furnace of earth, purified seven times.
You shall keep them, O LORD,
You shall preserve them from this generation forever." *Psalm 12: 5–7 (NKJV)*

"Learn to do good; seek justice, rebuke the oppressor; defend the fatherless, plead for the widow." *Isa. 1:17 (NKJV)*

"It is a joy for the just to do justice,
But destruction will come to the workers of iniquity.
[He] who wanders from the way of understanding
Will rest in the assembly of the dead." *Prov. 21:15–16 (NKJV)*

MARCH 6 Colette

Nicolette was born to parents late in age (some say past sixty), who died when she was a teenager. She gave away what she had to the poor and, after being refused entrance into the Benedictine Order, became a Franciscan tertiary and anchoress, never leaving her cell. After receiving a vision of St. Francis that instructed her to reform the Franciscan Order, she hesitated and was struck mute and blind for three days. She left her cell in 1406 to make a pilgrimage on foot to the then schismatic Pope Benedict XIII, and she was granted a blessing to pursue her work. Although she met with resistance, her holiness and miracles drew her much acclaim. She founded seventeen convents and reformed many more; a branch of the Poor Clares is still known as the Collettines. She experienced many ecstasies and predicted her own death on March 6, 1447. Colette was canonized in 1807.

Intercessory Prayer:

> *Dear holy St. Colette, you carried your love for St. Francis into the world to renew his order in France and to inspire a deeper devotion to God through renewal of vows. You who said, "We must faithfully keep what we have promised," please pray for us in our attempts to stay committed to our deepest resolutions, whether public or private. You were a lover of animals and took great care for God's creation; open our eyes to the necessity of caring for our environment and protecting the beauty of the world the Lord has given us. Amen.*

Antiphon:

At the work of your hands, I shout for joy.

Readings:

"Let them praise the name of the LORD, for His name alone is exalted; His glory is above the earth and heaven. And He has exalted the horn of His people, The praise of all His saints—of the children of Israel, a people near to Him. Praise the LORD." *Psalm 148:13–14 (NKJV)*

"So shall my word which goes forth from my mouth, it shall not return to me empty, without . . . succeeding in the matter for which I sent it." *Is. 55:11 (NASB)*

"Now as Jesus passed by, He saw a man who was blind from birth. And His disciples asked Him, saying, "Rabbi, who sinned, this man or his parents, that he was born blind?" Jesus answered, "Neither this man nor his parents sinned, but that the works of God should be revealed in him." *Jn. 9:1–3 (NKJV)*

MARCH 7 Perpetua and Felicitas

Of great significance in the life of the early Church, the moving story of the martyrdom of Perpetua and her companions in the third century still stands as a source of strength and encouragement for Christians today. Perpetua and Felicitas were arrested with other African catechumens under the reign of Septimius Serverus. Perpetua was a young mother, and Felicitas, her servant, was pregnant. Perpetua's visions while in prison—which she documented—became a testimony that circulated throughout the Christian world after their deaths. Leaving her baby with her father, Perpetua went joyfully to her death, exchanging a final kiss of peace with Felicitas before they died and then singing in ecstasy as wild animals mauled her body. Perpetua's prophetic writings remain one of the few accounts of Christian imprisonment and anticipated martyrdom in the early Church recorded by a woman. Perpetua and Felicitas are patrons of mothers separated from their children.

Prayer:

Beloved Lord Jesus, it is your blood that nourished the souls of the martyrs Perpetua and her companions at Carthage and made them models of suffering sainthood for your early Church. Help us to understand that suffering endured for your glory is the seed that also feeds our spirit and makes it grow. Sustain all those who suffer torture and persecution throughout the world this day. Amen.

Antiphon:

And I will raise them up on the last day.

Readings:

"But I am poor and sorrowful; Let Your salvation, O God, set me up on high.
I will praise the name of God with a song, And will magnify him with thanksgiving. . . .
Let heaven and earth praise him, The seas and everything that moves in them." *Psalm 69:30, 31, 34 (NKJV)*

"I persecuted this Way to the death, binding and delivering into prisons both men and women. . . . Now it happened, as I journeyed and came near Damascus at about noon, suddenly a great light from heaven shone around me. And I fell to the ground and heard a voice saying to me, 'Saul, Saul, why are you persecuting Me?'" *Acts 22:4, 6–7 (NKJV)*

"And you, child, will be called the prophet of the Highest; for you will go before the face of the Lord to prepare his ways." *Lk. 1:76 (NKJV)*

"If they persecuted Me, they will also persecute you. . . . But all these things they will do to you for My name's sake, because they do not know the One who sent Me." *Jn. 15:20–21 (NASB)*

MARCH 8 (vigil) Frances of Rome

Frances was born to a prominent Roman family in the fifteenth century. Although she wished to become a nun, she was betrothed to Lorenzo de Ponziani and then married him when she was thirteen years old. They had several children together, and they lived through the Plague, which claimed the lives of two of their children. During this time Frances continued to reach out to those most in need, and many miracles were attributed to her, including the miraculous appearance of food. Frances was graced with many spiritual gifts, including the ability to see her guardian angel. After her husband's death, Frances helped to start the Oblates of Mary, a community of women whose mission was to serve the poor and most destitute. She died in the odor of sanctity at age forty-six, and miracles began manifesting around her body. A young Oblate woman who suffered from a withered hand was cured when she was preparing St. Frances's body for viewing. Soon many other miracles were attributed to her, so much so that her funeral was postponed for several days. Frances's relics reside in a chapel in Rome named in her honor.

Intercessory Prayer:

Dear St. Frances of Rome, you were graced with many wonderful spiritual gifts that you used to continually serve others. As you were graced with the special ability to see your own loving guardian angel, help us to remember to acknowledge our special heavenly companion chosen by God to minister to us. In praying to our own guardian angels, may we better experience their loving intercessions on our behalf throughout our lives. Amen.

Antiphon:

For he shall give his angels charge over thee, to keep thee in all thy ways.

Readings:

"In God is my salvation and my glory: the rock of my strength and my refuge is my God. Trust in him at all times; you people, pour out your heart before him: God is a refuge for us." *Psalm 62:7–8 (KJV)*

"Behold, I send an Angel before you to keep you in the way and to bring you into the place which I have prepared." *Ex. 23:20 (NKJV)*

"About the ninth hour of the day he saw clearly in a vision an angel of God coming in and saying to him, 'Cornelius!' And when he observed him, he was afraid, and said, 'What is it, lord?' So he said to him, 'Your prayers and your alms have come up for a memorial before God.'" *Acts 10:3–4 (NKJV)*

"Now John answered Him, saying, "Teacher, we saw someone who does not follow us casting out demons in Your name, and we forbade him because he does not follow us." But Jesus said, "Do not forbid him, for no one who works a miracle in My name can soon afterward speak evil of Me." *Mk. 9:38–39 (NKJV)*

MARCH 9 Catherine of Bologna

Born in Bologna in 1413, Catherine, whose name means "pure one," was the daughter of a diplomat. He sent her to court as a companion to Princess Margarita, where she studied literature and fine arts. When her father died, Catherine left court to become a Franciscan tertiary. Women gathered around her, and eventually they joined the Poor Clares, with Catherine as their abbess. She had many visions of Christ and authored *On the Seven Spiritual Weapons* and *Revelations*. She was told that the Eucharist was not diminished by one's doubts, which greatly appeased her, as she was often tormented by doubts as to the nature of Christ in the Eucharist. Catherine was an excellent manuscript illuminator, and one of her books remains a treasure at Oxford. When she died, miracles occurred at her grave and her body was exhumed, although it had not even been in a coffin. Catherine's body was found to be incorrupt and remains so today in the convent of the Poor Clares in Bologna.

Intercessory Prayer:

O, St. Catherine, you were a woman of letters, yet you knew that no language could describe the way God loves the soul. You became the holy city arrayed in purest white, so that the one who is throned in glory could take habitation in you. Pray for us that we may also be alive with a divine ardor and discern the voice of God's spirit guiding us from within. Amen.

Antiphon:

The glory of God is the light of the city, and its lamp is the lamb.

Readings:

"Thy word is a lamp unto my feet, and a light unto my path.
I have sworn an oath, and I will perform it: that I will keep thy righteous judgments.
I am afflicted very much: quicken me, Oh Lord, according to thy word.
Accept, I beseech thee, the freewill offerings of my mouth, Oh Lord, and teach me thy judgments.
My soul is continually in my head; yet I do not forget thy law.
The wicked have laid a snare for me; yet I erred not from thy precepts.
Thy testimonies have I taken in as an heritage forever, for they are the rejoicing of my heart.
I have inclined my heart to perform thy statutes always, even unto the end." *Psalm 119:105–112 (Nun) (KJV)*

"The light of the eyes rejoices the heart; and a good report makes the bones fat. The ear that hears the reproof of life abides among the wise. He that refuses instruction despises his own soul; but he that hears reproof gets understanding. The fear of the Lord is the instruction of wisdom; and before honor is humility." *Prov. 15:30–33 (KJV)*

"This is the message which we have heard from Him and declare to you, that God is light and in Him is no darkness at all." *1 Jn. 1:5 (NKJV)*

MARCH 10 Anastasia the Patrician

Relegated to the realm of myth by many scholars, Anastasia remains an honored saint in the Eastern Church. She belongs in the genre of famous women transvestites, that is, women who disguised themselves as monks. In Anastasia's case, having been born into the highest aristocracy of Byzantium, Emperor Justinian pursued her, wanting to make her his bride after the death of his wife, Theodora. Anastasia fled to the desert, where she cut her hair and donned male clothing to live the life of a hermit. She remained enclosed in her cave for twenty-eight years. It is believed that even the other monks in the vicinity who brought her food and water did not know her gender until after her death. One monk, Daniel, who was with her when she died said that she uttered, at the last, Christ's words, "Into your hands I commend my spirit."

Prayer:

Almighty God of righteousness, you called your holy woman Anastasia to dwell with you in the desert, lost to the world but known by you. It was there that she found you, her angel of peace and her faithful guide. She unflinchingly led the ascetic life and with sobriety of mind attained to the beauties of heavenly things. Through her intercession, assist us O God, when we aspire to self-mastery for the sake of your divine knowledge. Jesus taught us that we must go to our closet and shut the door in order to find you (Mt. 6:6). Give us the grace, O good one, to make time in our busy days to remember to talk to you in the silence of our souls. Amen.

Antiphon:

Commune with your own heart upon your bed and be still.

Readings:

"Hear me when I call, O God of my righteousness! You have relieved me in my distress;
Have mercy on me, and hear my prayer.
How long, O you sons of men, will you turn my glory to shame?
How long will you love worthlessness, and seek falsehood?
But know that the LORD has set apart for himself him who is godly;
The LORD will hear when I call to him. . . . Meditate within your heart on your bed, and be still." *Psalm 1:1–4 (NKJV)*

"Shepherd your people with your staff, the flock of Your heritage, Who dwell solitarily in a woodland, in the midst of Carmel." *Mic. 7:14 (NKJV)*

"Let the lowly . . . glory in his exaltation, but the rich in his humiliation, because as a flower of the field he will pass away. For no sooner has the sun risen with a burning heat than it withers the grass; its flower falls, and its beautiful appearance perishes." *James 1:9–11 (NKJV)*

MARCH 11 Theodora of Arta

Theodora of Arta was born in the thirteenth century during a time of tumult between the Eastern and Western churches. The West had attacked Constantinople during the Crusades and placed a Latin bishop on the patriarch's throne. It was the fervent desire of Theodora's father and later her husband, King Michael II, to win back the capital and restore the Orthodox Church in the East. Theodora became a famous historical figure, both for her sanctity as queen and for her peacemaking efforts. Her *vita* describes her as an unpretentious queen, extremely compassionate and always venerating God with her entire soul. As queen, she initially suffered from an abusive marriage. Michael took a consort, and he drove Theodora into exile with their infant son for five years. Michael eventually repented and brought them home, hung his mistress, and began to prepare his son for kingship. Through Theodora's prayers, Michael later converted to a more Christian life and founded several monasteries. Theodora founded a convent to which she retired after her husband's death. She was known for her many all-night vigils and her service to the other nuns. Her biographer explains that she was everything to everyone. She also established an orphanage that can still be found today, with children weaving rugs for sale. During the reign of her son, Nicephorus (who became king of Arta), the Orthodox Empire was reestablished in Constantinople. Theodora predicted the date of her death, and many healings were reported at her tomb.

Intercessory Prayer:

O Blessed Theodora, you were a channel through which God's spirit was poured to all who were placed under your care. You were

serene in the midst of both luxury and poverty, and your sweet
disposition was a beacon of peace to all around you. Intercede
with those who work for the cause of peace on earth, and pray
with us for the unity of Christ's church everywhere. Amen.

Antiphon:
O God, grant peace to all your peoples.

Readings:
"Behold! My Servant whom I uphold, my Elect One in whom My soul delights! . . . I, the LORD, have called you in righteousness, And will hold your hand; I will keep you and give you as a covenant to the people." *Isa. 42:1–6 (NKJV)*

"For then I will restore to the peoples a pure language, that they all may call on the name of the LORD, to serve Him with one accord." *Zeph. 3:9 (NKJV)*

"But you are a chosen generation, a royal priesthood, a holy nation, [God's] own special people, that you may proclaim the praises of Him who called you out of darkness into His marvelous light; who once were not a people but are now the people of God, who had not obtained mercy but now have obtained mercy." *1 Pet. 2:9–10 (NKJV)*

"Jesus came and stood in the midst, and said to them, 'Peace be with you.'" *Jn. 20:19 (NKJV)*

MARCH 12 Angela Salawa

Angela Salawa was born in 1881 in Krakow, Poland, to a large, poor family. When she was eighteen, she made it her personal mission to instruct young women in the city, and she took a private vow of chastity, dedicating her life to the Lord. During World War I, she made every effort to reach out to anyone in need, with no regard to nationality or political agendas. Angela was greatly inspired by the writings of St. Teresa of Avila and St. John of the Cross. In 1918, Angela's health deteriorated and made it difficult for her to minister to wounded soldiers in the war. She made notes in her diary during her bedridden days speaking to Jesus, her savior, "I want you to be adored as much as you were destroyed." She offered up her sufferings to expiate the sins of the world, for the conversion of sinners, and for the growth of the Church throughout the world. After five years of painful struggles, she died at age forty-two, and word of her amazing sanctity and personal suffering soon spread throughout the region. Pope John Paul II proudly beatified her in 1991, as a shining example of a modern saint who lived her life within the world as a living testament to the Gospel.

Prayer:

Heavenly Father, you have blessed our Church with countless holy women through the ages. Blessed Angela was a modern example of how we can respond to the Holy Spirit's call and inspiration and live our lives in union with Christ. Even when she could not physically work to help others, Angela offered her sufferings for countless souls. May she be an inspiration to us to offer up even the smallest sacrifices of daily life in reparation for our own sins and the sins of the whole world. Amen.

Antiphon:

Cast your burden upon the Lord, and he shall sustain you.

Readings:

"I have not hidden Your righteousness within my heart; I have declared Your faithfulness and Your salvation; I have not concealed Your loving-kindness and Your truth from the great assembly. Do not withhold Your tender mercies from me, O LORD; Let Your loving-kindness and Your truth continually preserve me." *Psalm 40:10–11 (NKJV)*

"By loving-kindness and truth, iniquity is atoned for." *Prov. 16:6 (NASB)*

"Though He was a Son, yet He learned obedience by the things which He suffered. And having been perfected, He became the author of eternal salvation to all who obey Him." *Heb. 5:8 (NKJV)*

MARCH 13 Euphrasia

The story of Euphrasia and her convent sisters is an odd one to our ears, yet it harks back to the stories of the early martyrs, who yearned above all else to leave this world to be with their beloved. Euphrasia's father died at an early age, and she and her mother settled close to a convent, which Euphrasia wanted to join at age seven. Her mother left her in the care of the abbess, who soon developed a keen affection for her. When Euphrasia's mother died, she remained at the monastery and took the habit. She was a model of sanctity, and miracles were associated with her presence. She took ill, and she lay dying at age thirty. Her cell mate, Julie, begged her to intercede with God to take her also, and three days after Euphrasia died, Julie died as well. The abbess, deeply grieved in her desire to join two daughters whom she had so deeply loved, prayed earnestly that she might also depart to God's heavenly kingdom. Soon afterward, her lifeless body was found in her cell. The three souls were thus united in heaven, singing praises as they had done together on earth. The tale of their lives dates to the fourth century. March 13 is also the feast of St. Christina of Persia, who died a martyr in the late fourth century.

Prayer:

Beloved Lord, only you know the moment of our passing over into the fullness of eternity, and only you know the reasons why. Give us the hope, strength, and perseverance to accept whatever death you have destined for us, and likewise sustain us when we lose the ones we love. In your light, may we see light and reside serenely in that light. Amen.

Antiphon:

Whoever lives and believes in me shall never die.

Readings

"This I know, that God is with me. In God, whose word I praise, in the Holy One, whose word I praise, in God I trust without fear. What can mortal flesh do against me? My vows to you I will make, O God . . . For you delivered my soul from death." *Psalm 56:11–14 (PCB)*

"Therefore you now have sorrow; but I will see you again and your heart will rejoice, and your joy no one will take from you. And in that day you will ask me nothing. Most assuredly, I say to you, whatever you ask the Father in my name he will give you." *Jn. 16:22–23 (NKJV)*

"According to my earnest expectation and my hope, that in nothing I shall be ashamed, but that with all boldness, as always, so now also Christ shall be magnified in my body, whether it be by life, or by death. For to me to live is Christ, and to die is gain." *Phil. 1:20–22 (KJV)*

MARCH 14 Fannie Lou Hamer

Fannie Lou Hamer is considered a prophet of freedom for her people: poor, black, Southern sharecroppers. Evicted from her plantation home in Mississippi in 1962 for registering to vote, she then committed herself to the nonviolent freedom movement for the rest of her life. She was jailed and beaten, and she suffered permanent eye damage, but throughout, she was sustained by her deep religious faith and her conviction that the Bible was God's Word, delivered for the oppressed. She once wrote, "Christ was a revolutionary person, out there where it was happening." Chapter six in Ephesians was the touchstone of her activism, and she wore well her full armor for Christ. Fannie Lou died March 14, 1977, of breast cancer.

Prayer:

O God, fill us with your grace, so that, called into your service, we may respond like Fannie Lou Hamer's prayer: "I hunger for the work you deign for me Lord: to minister to your poor and oppressed." Help us to hear your call in all the endeavors of our life, great or small, so the world may be a better place because we passed through it with your name on our lips. Amen.

Antiphon:

The Lord is my rock and my salvation.

Readings:

He sent from above, He took me;
He drew me out of many waters . . . [and] delivered me from my
   strong enemy,
From those who hated me, for they were too strong for me.
They confronted me in the day of my calamity, but the LORD was
   my support. . . .
He delivered me because He delighted in me." *Psalm 18:16–20
(NKJV)*

"[God] delivers and rescues, and he works signs and wonders
In heaven and on earth, who has delivered Daniel from the power
   of the lions." *Dan. 6:27 (NKJV)*

"So I have come down to deliver them out of the hand of the
Egyptians, and to bring them up from that land to a good and
large land, to a land flowing with milk and honey." *Ex. 3:8 (NKJV)*

"Finally, my brethren, be strong in the Lord and in the power of His might. Put on the whole armor of God . . . that you may be able to withstand in the evil day. . . . Stand therefore, having girded your waist with truth, having put on the breastplate of righteousness, and having shod your feet with the preparation of the gospel of peace." *Eph. 6:10–14 (NKJV)*

MARCH 15 Louise de Marillac

Louise de Marillac was born in 1591 to a prominent family in France. Her mother died not long after her birth, and her father raised her until she was thirteen. When her father passed away, she lived with her uncle until she was old enough for marriage. Although Louise always desired to live a cloistered lifestyle, she was refused due to her frail health. Eventually, she was wed to a court official named Antoine Le Gras, but her husband died twelve years later, leaving her with a son, Michael. After a period of deep grief, Louise became friends with St. Vincent de Paul. Motivated by her love for the poor and sick, she organized a local charity group that later became the Daughters of Charity. Although they engaged in corporeal and spiritual works of mercy, initially the women did not wear habits; they were active in ministering directly in people's homes. Vincent, the community's spiritual father, did not want the sisters to lose their original charisma by secluding themselves in a cloister. They were the first religious group to open up soup kitchens, a great need in Paris at the time. Together, Louise and Vincent changed the shape of religious ministry in the Church. Louise died in 1660—only a few months before her dearest friend, St. Vincent—leaving behind numerous Daughters of Charity establishments that continue to minister to the poorest of the poor, directly where they are. Louise is patron of those rejected from religious vocations.

Intercessory Prayer:

Dear St. Louise de Marillac, you believed it was your mission to reach out to the poor—not only for their physical needs, but especially for their spiritual well-being. You said it was your goal to give them some knowledge of God's grandeur, beauty, and love, and you hoped that they would have the joy of possessing God eternally. Help us to reach out to all those individuals God may place into our paths this day so that we may also work to bring souls to Christ. Amen.

Antiphon:

They that trust in him shall understand the truth, and they that are faithful in love shall rest in him.

Readings

"I will say of the LORD, '[God] is my refuge and my fortress; my God, in him I will trust.'
Surely he shall deliver you from the snare of the fowler . . . from the perilous pestilence.
He shall cover you with his feathers, And under his wings you shall take refuge." *Psalm 91:2–4 (NKJV)*

"For he shall grow up before him as a tender plant, and as a root out of dry ground: he has no form nor comeliness; and when we shall see him there is no beauty that we should desire him. He is despised and rejected of men: a man of sorrows, and acquainted with grief . . . surely he has borne our griefs and carried our sorrows." *Isa. 53:2–4 (KJV)*

"And let our *people* also learn to maintain good works, to *meet* urgent needs, that they may not be unfruitful." *Titus 3:14 (NKJV)*

MARCH 16 Gertrude of Nivelles

Gertrude of Nivelles was born in 626 to very saintly parents, Blessed Pepin I and Blessed Ida, and from an early age she felt a calling to the religious life. At the age of twenty, Gertrude's saintly father died and her mother built a double monastery at Nivelles, Belgium, making the young Gertrude the abbess. Gertrude lived a very austere life, and eventually she preferred to hand over authority to her niece, St. Wilfetrudis, so she could spend her time studying Scripture and performing acts of personal mortification. She died at age thirty-three, and soon after a cult in her honor developed in the region. Agnes, the third Abbess of Nivelles, dedicated a church to her. Because Gertrude had a great personal devotion to praying for the dead, she is often invoked in prayer for the recently deceased.

Gertrude was also known to intercede with prayer and blessings for travelers, a practice that continued after her death.

Prayer:

Dear Father in Heaven, you gave us St. Gertrude as an example of a truly saintly life lived only for Christ. Through her personal sacrifices, she lived a life of austere love and charity for others, especially those who had died. Help us to follow her example and pray for the poor souls in Purgatory, our brothers and sisters in Christ who are members of the church suffering. Together with St. Gertrude we pray, "Eternal rest grant unto them, O Lord, and let your perpetual light shine upon them, may they rest in peace." Amen.

Antiphon:

Let all things be done with charity.

Readings:

"It was before the LORD, who chose me instead of your father and all his house, to appoint me ruler over the people of the LORD. . . . Therefore I will play music before the LORD. And I will be even more undignified than this, and will be humble in my own sight." *2 Sam 6:21 (NKJV)*

"Call upon me in the day of trouble; I will deliver you, and you shall glorify me." *Psalm 50:15 (NKJV)*

"Therefore did my heart rejoice, and my tongue was glad; moreover also, my flesh shall rest in hope; Because you will not leave my soul in hell, neither will you suffer your holy one to see corruption. You have made known to me the ways of life; you shall make me full of joy with your countenance." *Acts: 2:26–28 (KJV)*

MARCH 17 Mathilda

Mathilda, the daughter of a Saxon count, lived in the tenth century. Her earliest spiritual formation was influenced by life in a monastery under the care of her grandmother and abbess, Maud. She stayed in the convent until her marriage to Duke Henry, who eventually became king of Germany. Although a queen, Mathilda lived a life of deep piety and charity. The people of her country loved her because of her many virtues and acts of kindness to the poor, prisoners, and those ignorant of the Christian faith. After her husband's death, she spent a great deal of time trying to keep peace among her warring sons. One son, Bruno, became a saint and an archbishop. Mathilda spent her latter years in a convent that she helped to found, and she was honored as a saint almost immediately after she died in 968.

Prayer:

Compassionate God, you are our provider and we thank you for the gift of generous souls like Mathilda. They remind us that your love is ever before us and that your grace is ever-present in the poor. Help us to remember that when we give, we tap the fountain of charity that you placed in our hearts and we see the body of Christ in the world. Amen.

Antiphon:

You feed us with the finest wheat.

Readings:

"For those blessed by the Lord shall inherit the land, but those cursed by him shall be cut off. I have been young and now I am old; yet I have not seen the righteous forsaken,
Or his children begging bread. He is ever giving liberally and lending,
And his children becoming a blessing." *Psalm 37:22, 25, 26 (RSV)*

"As the Father loved me, I also have loved you; abide in my love. If you keep my commandments, you will abide in my love, just as I have kept my Father's commandments and abide in his love. These things I have spoken to you, that my joy may remain in you, and that your joy may be full." *Jn. 15:9–11 (NKJV)*

"Masters, give to your servants that which is just and equal; knowing that you also have a Master in heaven." *1 Thess. 4:1 (KJV)*

MARCH 18 Jeanne Marie Guyon

Jeanne Marie Guyon is a favorite saint of many Protestant students of mysticism. The father of Methodism, John Wesley, once said that we would search for many centuries before finding another woman who possessed such holiness. Born in 1648, Jeanne spent most of her childhood in convents, and then married at sixteen. She was widowed twelve years later. By this time, she had become a student of quietism, a contemplative spiritual practice. Together with her spiritual director, Fr. Francois la Comb, and her daughter, she toured widely in France and Switzerland, lecturing on the meditative practice she believed was so transforming. The Roman Church censured her work, and la Comb was imprisoned for life. Jeanne was placed in a convent under interdict, but she continued to write and to draw disciples, the most famous of whom was Bishop Francois de la Mothe Fenelon, who attempted to defend her theories, but failed. While her method differed little from Teresa of Avila's higher levels in the *Interior Castle* or the practice known as *Prayer of the Heart* in the East, authorities misunderstood it, believing that it raised questions about grace and free will. Very charismatic and enormously popular in the early period of the Enlightenment, Jeanne was sentenced to the infamous Bastille in Paris, where her mystical poetry continued to affirm that in the quiet of the soul, no place can separate one from God's love.

Prayer:

Beloved Lord, Jeanne Guyon was a mystic soul whose love for you never faltered. Her form of spiritual practice taught that perfection lay in abandoning every desire in order to contemplate your divine nature, for you are the sole and eternal reality. Her experience of you was like a stream of water lost in the ocean, so lost was her soul when it was absorbed in you. Help us to achieve that place of utter abandonment to your will, which possessed her when she wrote, "Oh, tis enough, whatever befall, To know that God is all in all." Amen.

Antiphon:

But nothing can separate me from the love of Christ.

Readings:

"They almost made an end of me on earth, but I did not forsake your precepts.
Revive me according to Your loving-kindness,
So that I may keep the testimony of Your mouth. Forever, O LORD, Your word is settled in heaven. Your faithfulness endures to all generations;
You established the earth, and it abides." *Psalm 119:87–90 (NKJV)*

"For God alone my soul waits in silence; for my hope is in the Most High." *Psalm 62:5 (PCB)*

"Pray without ceasing." *1 Thes. 5:17 (NASB)*

"[that] in him all the fullness should dwell, and . . . to reconcile all things to himself . . . whether things on earth or things in heaven, having made peace through the blood of his cross. And you, who once were alienated and enemies in your mind . . . yet now he has reconciled in the body of his flesh through death, to present you holy, and blameless, and above reproach in [God's] sight." *Col 1:19–22 (NKJV)*

MARCH 19 Beatrice of Nazareth

The Dutch-born Beatrice of Nazareth is famous for her work *The Seven Manners of Love*, a mystical treatise detailing her visions. After her mother's death, Beatrice's father placed his three daughters in convents. Beatrice, then seven, was left to the school of Beguines at Leau, and her work reflects classical medieval Beguine mysticism. She later learned calligraphy and manuscript illumination. She eventually became a Benedictine prioress, and during her time in that office she had three profound visions—separated by periods of dark nights of the soul—which sent her into ecstasy. During one vision, she was seized with a comprehension of the essence of the Trinity. After her visions, her ascetic lifestyle did not seem as important to her as ministering and caring for the sick and poor, as well as for plants and animals.

Intercessory Prayer:

O holy Beatrice, you lived an exemplary life consecrating yourself to the indwelling God in the Trinity and in the needy, whom you sought for as Christ sought for his lost little sheep. In this way, your hope "to become all to all" was realized, as you opened your hands and heart to all who came to you in need. Assist us also, that our minds and hearts may be transformed, and we may see the face of God in every living creature. Amen.

Antiphon:

Your love is round about me; in you I find my life.

Readings:

"O you simple, understand wisdom; and you fools, be of an under-standing heart. Hear, for I will speak of excellent things; and the opening of my lips shall be right things. . . . All the words of my mouth are in righteousness; there is nothing crooked or perverse in them. They are all plain to them who understand, and right to them that find knowledge." *Prov. 8:5–9 (KJV)*

"And Elijah appeared to them with Moses, and they were talking with Jesus. Then Peter answered and said to Jesus, "Rabbi, it is good for us to be here; and let us make three tabernacles: one for You, one for Moses, and one for Elijah"—because he did not know what to say, for they were greatly afraid. And a cloud came and overshadowed them; and a voice came out of the cloud, saying, 'This is My beloved Son. Hear Him!'" *Mk. 9:4–7 (NKJV)*

MARCH 20 Photini, the Woman at the Well

In the Eastern church, Photini, the Samaritan woman at the well who gave Jesus a drink (Jn. 4:5–42), is honored as a saint and an apostle (the "first evangelist"), and she is given a name. An oral tradition sprang up about Photini, perhaps because she was the first to recognize Christ: first as prophet, then as priest and king (messiah). She immediately went out and shared her revelations with everyone she met. Tradition tells us that she continued to evangelize the rest of her life. The first Apostles sent Photini to work in Carthage after Jesus' death, and her son, Victor, converted St. Sebastian. She had a vision of Jesus telling her to go to Rome, where she converted many and died a martyr. Her name, Photini, means "light" or "enlightened."

Intercessory Prayer:

O holy Photini, you opened your hands to a stranger and gave him a drink, and you found him to be the Lord of your life and of everlasting life. Great martyr, the Church honors you as Equal to the Apostles and as a great evangelizer of the eternal Word, which is Christ. You who recognized that Jesus was the one who was to be the great redeemer and slayer of death, pray to him for our souls.

Teach us to rest transparently on the one who created us, because we have received living water. Amen.

Antiphon:

You who know God, rejoice, for the savior is coming.

Readings:

"And he said to me, 'Son of man, hast thou seen this?' Then he brought me, and caused me to return to the brink of the river. Now when I had returned, behold, at the bank of the river were very many trees, on the one side and on the other. . . . Then he said to me, 'These waters issue out toward the east country and go down into the desert, and go into the sea; which being brought into the sea, the waters shall be fresh. And it shall come to pass, that everything which lives, which moves, wherever the rivers shall come, shall live: and there shall be a great multitude of fish, because these waters shall come hither: for they shall be healed; and every thing shall live where the stream cometh.'" *Ez. 47:1–9 (KJV)*

"And he that sat upon the throne said, 'Behold I make all things new.' And he said unto me: 'Write, for these words are true and faithful.' And he said to me, 'It is done. I am the Alpha and Omega, the beginning and the end. I will give to them that are thirsty the fountain of the water of life freely.'" *Rev. 21:5–7 (KJV)*

"Whoever drinks of the water that I shall give him will never thirst." *Jn. 4:14 (NKJV)*

MARCH 21 Benedicta Cambiagio Frassinello

Benedicta was born in 1781 in Italy as Benedetta Cambiagio. She married Giovanni Frassinello, but they had no children. They cared for Benedetta's younger sister, who had cancer and who lived with them until her death. They then decided to join separate orders; and for a while, she was an Ursaline, taking the name Benedicta. Ill health caused her to return to her homeland where, with Giovanni's help, she founded several schools. Although Giovanni was a member of the Somashan Fathers, their work together was a source of gossip. To prevent a scandal, Benedicta moved and founded a new congregation of Benedictine Sisters of Providence, still devoted to teaching. Her life was characterized by several mystical experiences and deep prayer. She died of natural causes in 1858 and was canonized in 2002. Benedicta is a patron of cancer sufferers.

Prayer:

Beloved Holy Spirit of God, you were the source of inspiration for Benedicta, who was a great teacher of wisdom for many. She sought to bring young women under her wing, sharing with them the deep mystic riches of her joy in Christ Jesus. As she was a river of God for those around her, so inspire us to remember that the only way we can be filled with the Spirit's joy is to go to the river and drink. Amen.

Antiphon:

Praise and exalt God above all, forever.

Readings:

"One thing I have asked of you, for this will I seek, that I may dwell in your holy house all the days of my life, to behold the beauty of your countenance and the holiness of your temple. In your shelter will you hide me in the day of trouble; you will conceal me under the cover of your tent; you will set me high upon a rock." *Psalm 27:3–5 (PCB)*

"There are, it may be, so many kinds of languages in the world, and none of them is without significance. Therefore, if I do not know the meaning of the language, I shall be a foreigner to him who speaks, and he who speaks will be a foreigner to me. Even so you, since you are zealous for spiritual gifts, let it be for the edification of the church that you seek to excel." *1 Cor. 14:10–12 (NKJV)*

"[therefore] exercise yourself toward godliness. For bodily exercise profits a little, but godliness is profitable for all things, having promise of the life that now is and of that which is to come." *1 Tim. 4:7–8 (NKJV)*

MARCH 22 Sophia of Kiev

Sophia of Kiev is considered to be one of the new martyrs of Soviet Russia, and although she did not die in prison, she spent many of her later years there. Born in Moscow in the mid-nineteenth century, she became abbess-confessor at an early age, under the direction of the great St. John of Kronstadt. After founding a community that quickly grew to six hundred sisters, Sophia was transferred to one of Kiev's largest monasteries, housing twelve hundred nuns, where she was tonsured as a Great Schema, the highest order for a nun. In both convents, her daughters loved her and she was known for her wisdom. During the Revolution, when the Russian Orthodox Church was betrayed into the communists' hands, the true Orthodox Christians of the Kiev monastery revolted. When a new calendar bishop—who did not represent the teachings they had grown up believing—was sent to the Kiev monastery, all the sisters spat on his hand and refused to kiss it. Mother Sophia and her clergy opened up one of the first catacomb convents where icons were hung so divine services could be sung and were then removed at night. She was eventually imprisoned, exiled to an island in the Far East, then moved to a prison in the Eastern Bloc, where she was known to convert even atheists. After many years and much suffering, Sophia was released to die amidst her spiritual daughters, who—still preserving their faith underground—drew deep consolation from her during her last days.

Prayer:

O God, you raised up your wise woman, Sophia of Kiev, to be a staunch defender of the living Church, protecting it from assaults of the enemy. She suffered inhumane prison conditions, but continued to bring souls to you wherever she found them. Through everything, she remembered you, who carried her through the darkness of a persecuted era. Through her intercession, grant us the grace to be ever mindful of your deliverance and your mercy. Amen.

Antiphon:

You are near at hand, O God, and your ways are true.

Readings:

"Fools, when will you be wise? Can God, who made the ear, not hear? The one who formed the eye, not see? . . . God who imparts knowledge knows our thoughts. . . . Happy are they whom you chasten, whom you teach by means of your law to give them respite from days of trouble, until oppression is no more. You will not abandon your people, you will not forsake your heritage; for justice will return to the righteous, and the upright in heart will follow it." *Psalm 94:8–15 (PCB)*

"Three times I was beaten with rods; once I was stoned . . . in journeys often . . . in weariness and toil, in sleeplessness often, in hunger and thirst, in fastings often, in cold and nakedness—besides the other things, what comes upon me daily: my deep concern for all the churches." *2 Cor. 11:25–27 (NKJV)*

"Blessed are those servants, whom the Lord, when he comes, shall find watching; verily I say to you, that he shall gird himself, and make them to sit down to meat and will come forth to serve them." *Lk. 12:37 (KJV)*

MARCH 23 Rafka al Rayes

Born as Petronilla in 1832 in a small town in Lebanon, Rafka (Rebecca) al Rayes chose to take her mother's name when she became a contemplative nun. Initially, Rafka was a member of an active teaching order, but when it merged with the Order of the Sacred Heart, there was dissension among the sisters. Rafka had several dreams wherein St. Anthony and St. Simon appeared to her. She then joined an Eastern-rite Catholic order of Maronites called the Order of St. Anthony, which suited her contemplative nature. By age forty, she was nearly blind but had memorized the Divine Office and had spent many hours in mystical prayer. She was so filled with the Eucharistic Lord that she began to eat very little other food. Although she suffered much during the last years of her life, she was always a source of joy to her sisters. She asked for her sight back for one hour to see them before she died, and her wish was granted. Then she had a vision of heaven, which dwarfed anything earthly she could compare it to. Rafka was canonized on June 10, 2001, after many miracles were reported around her grave.

Intercessory Prayer:

O holy Rafka, you once wrote, "We must become blind to the world to be able to be united to God alone." You were not afraid of suffering and death because your spirit dwelt securely in your beloved Jesus. Pray for those who feel devastated by blindness late in life, that they may have the courage and patience to see behind all earthly things to the inner light of God's personal revelation for them. Intercede for all those who struggle with contemplative prayer, that our work may bear the fruit of God's Spirit. Amen.

Antiphon:
God is my light and my salvation.

Readings:
"Save us, we beseech you, O God! O God, grant us success. Blessed are those who enter in your holy name. . . . Let us go forward in procession with branches up to your holy altar. You are my God, and I thank you." *Psalm 118:26–29 (PCB)*

"And I will bring the blind by a way that they knew not; I will lead them in paths that they have not known; I will make darkness light before them, and crooked things straight. These things will I do to them, and I will not forsake them." *Isa. 42:16 (KJV)*

"The light of the body is the eye; therefore, when your eye is single, your whole body also is full of light." *Lk. 11:34 (KJV)*

"For judgment I have come into this world, that those who do not see may see, and that those who see may be made blind." *Jn. 9:39 (NKJV)*

MARCH 24 Catherine of Sweden

Catherine was born in 1330, the fourth daughter of St. Bridget of Sweden (see Daily Readings, July 23, Birgitta of Sweden). Commanded by her father, Ulf Gudmarsson, to marry at age fourteen, she and her husband devoted themselves to good works. When her father and her husband died, Bridget and Catherine moved to Rome, where Bridget founded a convent. They spent their days caring for the poor and sick, and writing. Although her mother's *Revelations* are quite popular, Catherine's work, called *Consolation of the Soul,* has not survived. After her mother died, Catherine took her mother's body back to Sweden and then became abbess of a Bridgettine congregation there, in Vadstena, promoting her mother's order. The order received papal approval in 1375, and Catherine returned to Rome to work for her mother's canonization, a process that Catherine did not live to see. Catherine died in 1381 of natural causes, and her cult was confirmed in 1484. In art she is often depicted holding a lily or dressing the wounds of the sick. Catherine's cell still survives at the convent at Vadstena.

Intercessory Prayer:

Beloved Catherine, you and your mother labored tirelessly for the children of the Church who lived on the streets of Rome. Devoted to the highest ideals of Christian charity and justice, you worked together to bring the light of Jesus to all who crossed your path. Intercede for us that we may live lives that exemplify Christ's love among us. We ask your prayers for harmony between all mothers and their daughters. Amen.

Antiphon:

From my mother's womb, you are my God.

Readings:

"And they shall dwell safely there, and shall build houses, and plant vineyards; they shall dwell with confidence . . . and they shall know that I am the Lord their God." *Ez. 28:26 (KJV)*

"I am the rose of Sharon and the lily of the valleys. As the lily among thorns, so is my love among the daughters." *Song of Songs 2:1–2 (KJV)*

"These are the ones who follow the Lamb wherever he goes. These were redeemed from among [men], being firstfruits to God and to the Lamb. And in their mouth was found no deceit, for they are without fault before the throne of God." *Rev. 14:4–5 (NKJV)*

MARCH 25 Blessed Virgin at the Annunciation

The feast of the Annunciation of the Blessed Virgin Mary is based primarily on the Gospel of Luke, and it originated in the early Church as a feast day in the early fifth century. The Annunciation represents the very beginning of Jesus' human nature. At the feast, we celebrate the singular event in human history by which Jesus Christ was manifested in Mary's womb and became man. St. Thomas Aquinas taught that this event shows that Mary's consent was foreseen from all eternity and was an essential element in God's design to send the Messiah to save humanity. The angel Gabriel delivered the news to Mary that she had been chosen to be the mother of the Redeemer, and she responded with her fiat—a total and unconditional "yes" to God. The angel assures Mary that her desire to remain a virgin will prevail and the child will come to be when the Holy Spirit overshadows her. Mary's consent, therefore, was truly essential to the Redemption. The story of the Annunciation is found also in the Islamic Koran and became firmly established early in the Byzantine liturgy, embellished with hymns that glorified Mary as "the woman whose faith made possible the incarnation of God and the deification of humankind."

Intercessory Prayer:

Dear Blessed Virgin Mary, please help us to emulate your total fiat to God by accepting his will within our own lives each day. Let us realize that we must say "yes" to God at all times, even if we do not understand what his purposes may be. As you trusted that the angel's words to you would be fulfilled, help us to also be inspired by the angel's promise that nothing is impossible with God. May we say "yes" to all those who approach us in need and see Christ in each of them. Amen.

Antiphon:

Fear not, for you have found favor with God.

Readings:

"Therefore the Lord himself shall give you a sign: Behold a virgin shall conceive and bear a son, and shall call his name Emmanuel. Butter and honey shall he eat, that he may know to refuse the evil, and choose the good." *Isa. 7:14–15 (KJV)*

"Then the angel said to her, "Do not be afraid, Mary, for you have found favor with God. And behold, you will conceive in your womb and bring forth a Son, and shall call His name JESUS. He will be great, and will be called the Son of the Highest." *Lk. 1:30–32 (NKJV)*

"He has shown strength with His arm; He has scattered the proud in the imagination of their hearts." *Lk. 1:51 (NKJV)*

MARCH 26 Harriet Monsell

Born into the Anglican Church in 1811, Harriet O'Brien married Charles Monsell, a priest in Oxford. Both were highly devoted to the Oxford movement and the Anglo-Catholic Church. This was during a period in the Anglican Church when a "High Church" evolved, which became less Protestant ("Low Church") and more Catholic in nature, with a strong emphasis on the sacraments. After her husband's death in 1850, Harriet felt drawn to the lot of unwed mothers, and she started a House of Mercy for single mothers and former prostitutes near Windsor. The girls at Mercy House grew to love Harriet, who nurtured them like a mother hen. In 1881, she founded an order of nuns called the Community of St. John the Baptist, which was devoted to caring for the sick and orphaned. Harriet died two years later, beloved by all who knew her.

Prayer:

Beloved Jesus, you said that you would not leave us orphans, but would come to us and comfort us. Through compassionate souls like Harriet Monsell, you consoled the orphans and unwanted of this world, took them under your wings and gave them new life. You are like a tender mother to us, nurturing us always with the seeds of hope. Keep us ever close to you and help us to nurture those in our lives who come to us broken and in need of love and strength. Amen.

Antiphon:

My sheep hear my voice, and I know them.

Readings:

"How excellent is your loving-kindness, O God! Therefore the children . . . put their trust under the shadow of your wings. They shall be abundantly satisfied with the fatness of your house; and you shall make them drink of the river of your pleasures. . . . O continue your loving-kindness to those who know you; and your righteousness to the upright in heart." *Psalm 36:7–8, 10 (KJV)*

"Then He turned to the woman and said to Simon, "Do you see this woman? I entered your house; you gave me no water for my feet, but she has washed My feet with her tears and wiped them with the hair of her head. You gave me no kiss, but this woman has not ceased to kiss my feet since the time I came in. You did not anoint my head with oil, but this woman has anointed my feet with fragrant oil. Therefore I say to you, her sins, which are many, are forgiven, for she loved much." *Lk. 7:44–47 (NKJV)*

"Listen to Me, O house of Jacob, . . . Who have been upheld by Me from birth, Who have been carried from the womb: Even to your old age . . . And even to gray hairs I will carry you! I have made, and I will bear; Even I will carry, and will deliver you." *Isa. 46:3–4 (NKJV)*

MARCH 27 Louisa Jacques

 Born in 1901 in South Africa, Louisa Jacques never knew her mother, who died during childbirth. A quiet introverted soul in childhood, Louisa went to live with relatives in Switzerland. She had her first visionary experience before she really understood the Church's mystical traditions, and it led her to search for a faith that could embrace her experience. At age twenty-seven, she was baptized into the Roman Catholic Church, and she began to look for a contemplative order to fulfill her call to a more religious life. Since she suffered from poor health and had no dowry, this call turned into a series of rejections. She briefly belonged to a teaching order, but she did not take final vows because her heart's desire to become totally immersed in Christ's love would only find fertile ground within a contemplative tradition. Undaunted, after two more attempts, she found her true home in the Carmelite Order at Jerusalem. Throughout her spiritual journey, Louisa—now Sr. Mary of the Holy Trinity—kept journals of her conversations with Christ. A rich mystical treatise of longing and love, her conversations were published in 1950 as *The Spiritual Legacy of Sr. Mary of the Holy Trinity.* She died in 1942.

Prayer:

O Jesus, beloved of our hearts, Sr. Mary felt your love as vast and incomprehensible and knew that nothing could fathom to this greatness. Yet, through your incarnation, you engulfed our human nature to meet us where we are. She was resolved to sacrifice anything in her desire to drown her mystic soul in your love. Help our hearts to attain the full growth of love because we also are resolved to hold nothing back from you. Amen.

His word was in my heart as a burning fire.

Readings:

"But you are in your holy temple. You, whose throne is in heaven. Your eyes look down on the world; Your gaze tests mortal flesh . . . the upright shall behold your face." *Psalm 11:47 (PCB)*

"Keep your heart with all diligence; for from it flow the springs of life." *Prov. 4:23 (RSV)*

"For now we see in a mirror, dimly, but then face to face. Now I know in part, but then I shall know just as I also am known. And now abide faith, hope, love, these three; but the greatest of these is love." *1 Cor. 13:12–13 (NKJV)*

MARCH 28 Mother Carmelita Manning

The modern Church has enjoyed the leadership of many devout and pious women, and Mother Carmelita Manning was one of them. Her life was one of total service in responding to the needs of others. Mother Carmelita, a Sister of Mercy, founded Mercy College of Detroit. In a thirteen-month period, she purchased the land, contracted, and built Mercy College, the Novitiate, and the Provincial House in Detroit. She also supervised the building of sixteen Catholic hospitals in Dubuque, Cincinnati, and Detroit. A woman of strength and character, she was never deterred by obstacles that crossed her path. She was often seen carrying blueprints, patrolling construction sites, and inspecting building materials. She would cook midnight steak dinners for the construction workers to inspire them to complete the work on the Provincial House chapel, and she was not afraid to stand up to insurance companies that threatened to lower hospital reimbursement rates in the Catholic hospitals she helped to found. When she died in 1962, Mother Carmelita left behind a treasury of establishments dedicated to the service of others.

Prayer:

Heavenly Father, thank you for blessing this country with great and courageous women like Mother Carmelita Manning. She faced many obstacles, but she always managed to accomplish your will in meeting the needs of others by establishing hospitals and educational facilities. Help her strength of commitment and character become an inspiration to us in our own daily lives. Let us know that we, too, can accomplish great things for God if we listen and respond to the Holy Spirit's inspirations within our lives. Amen.

Antiphon:

We are your people, the sheep of your pasture.

Readings:

"So teach us to number our days, that we may gain a heart of wisdom . . . And let the beauty of the LORD our God be upon us, And establish the work of our hands for us; Yes, establish the work of our hands." *Psalm 90:12, 17 (NKJV)*

"Now he who establishes us with you in Christ and anointed us is God, who also sealed us and gave us the Spirit in our hearts as a pledge . . . [and] we are workers with you for your joy; for in your faith you are standing firm." *2 Cor. 1:21, 22, 24 (NASB)*

"And I thank Christ Jesus our Lord who has enabled me, because he counted me faithful, putting me into the ministry." *1 Tim. 1:12 (NKJV)*

MARCH 29 Mother Mary Skobtsova

Elizabeth Pilenko was born a Russian autocrat in 1841. She was married before deciding to live alone and devote her life to Christian charity, so she became an "unorthodox" Orthodox nun, one who lived, tonsured, in the world. The name she chose was Mary. She had deep philosophical interests and became the first woman to study at a theological academy in Russia, where she mingled with great Russian thinkers like Sergi Bulgakov and Nikolai Berdayev. In Paris, she became close friends with Liv Gillet (who authored numerous books on the Jesus Prayer under the pen name "A Monk of the Eastern Church"). They worked together to open a soup kitchen for refugees, alcoholics, and other street people. Mary also founded a social service group called Orthodox Action, and eventually she became immersed in the Jewish Resistance Movement in Paris, hiding Jews in her home. She was eventually arrested after vocally denouncing the Nazis, and it is believed that she died in Ravensbruck, where she took the place of someone condemned to the gas chamber. Metropolitan Anthony of Sourouz, who called her a "saint for our day," explains her decision to live in the world as a monastic. It was the Spirit of truth, he stated, that led her to criticize that which was deficient in classical monasticism: a preoccupation with fasting and a lack of involvement with the social gospel. By living as a revolutionary nun in the world, Mary lived and died as a witness who stood radically unafraid of the evils of her day. She was glorified by the Church of Constantinople on January 16, 2004, along with her son George (Yuri) Skobtsov.

Prayer:

> *Beloved Lord, you promised to send us your Spirit and that the Spirit of truth would teach us everything. Seal us with the Spirit's gifts, which proceed from the Father, that we may be Spirit bearers in the world. Give us the naked trust we need to be witnesses like your beloved St. Mary Skobtsova. Help us to move fearlessly into new territory, as she did, guided by the true Spirit of the gospel. Amen.*

Antiphon:

Blessed are those who are persecuted for righteousness' sake.

Readings:

"I have seen the wicked in great power, And spreading himself like a native green tree. Yet he passed away, and behold, he *was* no *more*; Indeed I sought him, but he could not be found. . . . But the salvation of the righteous *is* from the LORD; He is their strength in the time of trouble." *Psalm 37:35, 36, 39 (NKJV)*

"And if I go and prepare a place for you, I will come again and re-ceive you to myself: that where I am, you may be also." *Jn. 14:3 (KJV)*

"Love suffers long *and* is kind; love does not envy; love does not parade itself, is not puffed up; does not behave rudely, does not seek its own, is not provoked, thinks no evil; does not rejoice in iniquity, but rejoices in the truth; bears all things, believes all things, hopes all things, endures all things." *1 Cor. 13:4–6 (NKJV)*

MARCH 30 Thea Bowman

When Thea Bowman spoke, it was with spellbinding charisma, and when she taught, it was with creative concern for all her students. The granddaughter of a slave, Thea was born in Mississippi in 1937. Before the age of twelve, she decided to join the Roman Catholic Church, and at age sixteen, she joined the Franciscan Sisters in La Crosse, Wisconsin. Her passion was teaching, especially black culture and spirituality. When once asked what it meant to be black and Catholic, she replied that it included bringing her history, including African-American song and dance, into her vocation of teaching and preaching. In a time that predated the charismatic renewal movement in the Church, Sister Thea often had young people and bishops alike clapping and singing gospel spirituals. In 1985, a year after she was diagnosed with breast cancer, Thea was granted the Harriet Tubman Award at the National Black Sisters Conference, and Viterbo College, where she taught, gave her the Pope John XXIII Award. The television program *60 Minutes* interviewed her two years later, and she was still enthusiastically proclaiming a black Catholic gospel. In 1989, a year before her death, she spoke at the annual meeting of American bishops, where she said, "God has called us to speak the word that is Christ. . . . If we speak that word in love and faith, with patience and prayer and perseverance, it will take root."

Prayer:

Beloved Lord Jesus, Thea Bowman was a fervent and joyous singer of your praises and ran her marathon with your name on her lips. Her black soul saw you as a liberator of her people; as a shield of protection when the daggers flew. Help us, like her, to risk all for you, so that when our own marathon is over, we find that we have run directly into your arms. Amen.

Antiphon:

I will proclaim the glory of the risen Lord.

Readings:

"Your power and righteousness, O God, reach the high heavens,
You who have done great things: Who is like unto you?
You who have made me see many sore troubles
Will revive me once again:
From the depths of the earth, you will raise me.

You will exalt and comfort me again.
So I will praise you with the harp for your faithfulness, O God.
I will sing praises to you with the lyre, O Holy One. . . .
My lips will shout for joy when I sing praises to you;
My soul also, which you have redeemed.
My tongue will tell of your justice all day long.
For evil is put to rest, and all that sought to harm me." *Psalm 71:19–24 (PCB)*

"What is the conclusion then? I will pray with the spirit, and I will also pray with the understanding. I will sing with the spirit, and I will also sing with the understanding." *1 Cor. 14:15 (NKJV)*

MARCH 31 Balbina and Jane of Toulouse

 We celebrate two very different women, who lived centuries apart, on March 31. St. Balbina was an early Christian martyr who died in the year 130. Records of her life and martyrdom are based on Roman martyrology accounts. She was the daughter of Quirinus, and it appears that the young virgin martyr died along with her holy father. The two of them were buried together along the Appian Way, and her relics were later enshrined in a church dedicated to her honor in Aventine.

Jane of Toulouse, France, lived in the late thirteenth century and received her calling to become a Carmelite directly from the great St. Simon Stock (to whom the devotion of the brown scapular had been revealed). She eventually founded the Carmelite Third Order and spent her life tirelessly serving the poor and ill, as well as working to train and educate young Carmelite friars. Jane was beatified in 1895 due to her exceptionally pious and dedicated life spent in total service to others.

Prayer:

Heavenly Father, thank you for all the holy women who work for the coming of your kingdom. St. Balbina served you through her brave example of love for the early Church, and she was willing to give her life for that cause. Blessed Jane served you through a life of charity and service to others, and in her efforts to further spread the dedicated lifestyle of the Carmelite Order. May their examples inspire us to look for ways to serve you today through every opportunity that you may place on our path. Amen.

Antiphon:

God is my comforter.

Readings:

"I removed your shoulder of the burden: your hands were freed from the pots.
In distress you called, and I delivered you; I answered you, concealed in the storm cloud." *Psalm 81:6–7 (PCB)*

"But a certain Samaritan, as he journeyed, came where he was. And when he saw him, he had compassion. So he went to him and bandaged his wounds, pouring on oil and wine; and he set him on his own animal, brought him to an inn, and took care of him." *Lk. 10:33–34 (NKJV)*

"And a servant of the Lord must not quarrel but be gentle to all, able to teach, patient, in humility correcting those who are in opposition, if God perhaps will grant them repentance, so that they may know the truth." *2 Tim. 2:24–25 (NKJV)*

"You also, as living stones, are being built up a spiritual house, a holy priesthood, to offer up spiritual sacrifices acceptable to God through Jesus Christ." *1 Pet. 2:5 (NKJV)*

APRIL 1 Mary of Egypt

The famous patriarch of Jerusalem, St. Sophronius, wrote the life of Mary the Egyptian. He tells the story of how a monk named Zosimus withdrew into the desert to fast during Lent and came upon a beautiful woman with long matted hair. She knew his name, which shocked him, and while conversing, she told him her life story. She had been a prostitute since the age of twelve in Alexandria, when one day she boarded a boat to Jerusalem. During the Feast of the Exaltation of the Cross, she moved with the throngs toward the church, but an invisible force prevented her from crossing the threshold. Frightened, she prayed to the Mother of God and was allowed entrance. While venerating the Cross, she heard a voice say, "If you cross over Jordan you will find real peace!" This she did and lived in the desert wilderness for the next forty-eight years. While praying together, Zosimus saw her levitate in the air, and he realized he was speaking with a saint. She asked him to come back the following year. When he did, he found her dead body at the very spot they had conversed, which he then proceeded to honor with a Christian burial. She is such an important saint in the Eastern churches that her feast is celebrated twice, on April 1 and on the fifth Sunday of Lent, when she is honored as a model of repentance. Mary died in 421.

Prayer:

Beloved Lord Jesus, in Mary of Egypt your healing light sprung forth like a beacon for all the ages, as she became a faithful image of your cross and redemption. Teach us also how to spurn all that is transitory for the joy of your presence in our lives. In you, her body was glorified and made lighter than air. Through her intercession, may we enter into a deeper understanding of how to make our bodies temples of the Spirit, even while we wander in a wasteland, searching for you. Amen.

Antiphon:

He dwells in her; she will not falter.

Readings:

"My soul is downcast within me, therefore I think of you. . . . Deep calls to deep, in the thunder of your waters; all your waves and billows have swept over me. By day you will send me your steadfast love; and at night your song is with me, a prayer to the God of my life." *Psalm 42:6–9 (PCB)*

"For this is he who was spoken of by the prophet Isaiah, saying: *"The voice of one crying in the wilderness: 'Prepare the way of the LORD; Make His paths straight.'"* Now John himself was clothed in camel's hair, with a leather belt around his waist; and his food was locusts and wild honey. Then Jerusalem, all Judea, and all the region around the Jordan went out to him and were baptized by him in the Jordan, confessing their sins." *Mt.3:3–6 (NKJV)*

APRIL 2 Burgundofara (Fare/Fara)

Burgundofara (Fare) was born near Meaux, France, the daughter of Count Agneric, a principal courtier to King Theodebert II. She developed a religious vocation at an early age after being blessed by St. Columbanus, an Irish evangelist traveling in Europe, who had a great influence over Frankish Europe's religious development. When her father tried to arrange an honorable marriage for Fare, she became deathly ill. A companion of Columbanus, St. Eustace and Fare's brother were returning from missionary activity with St. Columbanus. Eustace stayed with the family and cured Fare of her illness. He realized that it stemmed from her father's vehement opposition to her call to religious life. St. Eustace reconciled father and daughter and was instrumental in Fare becoming a nun in 614. A couple of years later, Burgundofara, with Eustace's help, had a double monastery built that practiced the Rule of Columbanus. She became the first abbess of Evoriacum in Brie, and the monastery later became known as Faremoutiers (Fare's monastery). Burgundofara was superior at the monastery for thirty-seven years, and she insisted on a stringent rule. Penitence was at the center of the community's life, and Eucharist was a special and rare event. Burgundofara trained several English nuns there, among them, Ethelburga of Faremoutiers, Ercongota, and Saethrith, all of whom became saints. When she died in 657, Fare left the majority of her property to the monastery. Her relics were enshrined in 695, and many miracles are attributed to her intercession.

Prayer:

> *Dear Lord, the fire that was lit in Burgundofara at an early age burned so steadily that she focused solely on her wish to serve you. She was single-minded in her pursuit and succeeded in leaving home and family to become the leader of her community. We pray that we may imitate her example of dedication and faith in following the path that you have prepared for us. Amen.*

Antiphon:

We will seek his face forevermore.

Readings:

"[I]n their illness you heal all their infirmities. As for me, I said, 'O, Lord, be gracious to me; heal me, for I have sinned against you.' . . . They think that a deadly thing has fastened on me, that I will not rise again from where I lie. . . . But you, O Lord, be gracious to me, and raise me up that I may repay them.'" *Psalm 41:3, 4, 8, 10, 12 (NRSV)*

"But Boaz answered for her, 'All that you have done for your mother-in-law since the death of your husband has been fully told

me, and how you left your father and mother and your native land
and came to a people that you did not know before.'" *Ruth 2:11*
(NRSV)

"And whoever does not bear his cross and come after Me cannot
be My disciple." *Lk. 14:27 (NKJV)*

APRIL 3 The *Life-Giving Spring* Icon

The *Life-Giving Spring* icon is often called the "Lourdes of
Greece," and it has become a popular devotion in the Ukraine.
The image depicts the Mother of God on top of an enormous
stone chalice from which people from diverse walks of life drink and
receive healing. She is holding in her arms the pre-eternal Infant, who
wears a crown. Originally from Constantinople, Emperor Leo Mar-
cellos honored the icon with a cathedral. As the story goes, during the
reign of Emperor Marcion, a pious warrior named Leo came upon a
blind man weak from exhaustion; wanting to help, Marcion went
searching for some water. He suddenly heard a loud voice from
heaven directing him to dig at a spot in the mud, and a spring gushed
forth, the waters of which healed the blind man's eyes. Half a century
later, and after numerous miracles at the site, a church was built to
the Theotokos, and later a monastery. Muslims closed down the
spring after the fall of Constantinople in the fifteenth century, but Ecumenical Patriarch Constantine rebuilt it in 1834. Christians and
Muslims alike now venerate the spring, calling the shrine the "waters
of Holy Mary." Miraculous copies of the *Life-Giving Spring* icon are
still found in various villages, towns, and cities in Ukraine.

Intercessory Prayer:

> *O most Blessed Theotokos, we honor you as a protector of the weak*
> *and as the rock that refreshes those who thirst for the life of your*
> *son. Since you brought forth he who is our benefactor, we trust in*
> *your intercession on our behalf. Preserve, O Mother of God, your*
> *servants from every danger, for you are the dear desire of every*
> *nation and the joy of every mother's heart. We know that you will*
> *guide us safely into the haven of holiness as we are healed by your*
> *wondrous love. Amen.*

Antiphon:
Holy, holy, holy is our God most high.

Readings:
"Who *is* this coming up from the wilderness,
Leaning upon her beloved?
I awakened you under the apple tree.
There your mother brought you forth;
There she *who* bore you brought *you* forth.
Set me as a seal upon your heart,
As a seal upon your arm;
For love is as strong as death . . .
Many waters cannot quench love,
Nor can the floods drown it." *Song of Songs 8:5–7 (NKJV)*

"Then the eyes of the blind shall be opened, and the ears of the deaf shall be unstopped. Then shall the lame man leap as an hart, and the tongues of the dumb sing: for, in the wilderness shall waters break out, and streams in the desert. And the parched ground shall become a pool, and the thirsty land springs of water: in the habitation of dragons, where each shall lay, shall be grass with reeds and rushes. And a highway shall be there, and a way, and it shall be called, The Way of Holiness." *Isa. 36:5–8 (KJV)*

APRIL 4 Maria Crescentia Hoss

Maria Crescentia Hoss was born into a very poor family in Bavaria in 1682, the seventh of eight children. Although her father, who worked sometimes as a weaver, was destitute most of the time, she aspired to enter the religious life. At that time, a dowry was necessary to enter most convents. Maria Crescentia was eventually admitted to a Franciscan convent as a tertiary, where the other nuns ridiculed her for her poverty. She won them over, however, with her humility and forbearance, and eventually she became superior of the convent. Maria Crescentia recommended observing silence, meditation, and reflective reading, especially the Gospels, for her growing flock of sisters' spiritual development. In his homily at her canonization, Pope John Paul II praised her for her creative contributions: she was a beautiful singer and an esteemed advisor. Both simple folk and the aristocracy came to her doorstep; princes, priests, and bishops came to her for counseling. She died on Easter in 1744 of natural causes. Maria Crescentia is the patron of Bavaria.

Prayer:

> *O Christ our God, you shepherd us all with your tender care, and gave us holy Maria Crescentia to show forth your rich fountain of mercy. She knew that your love was better that an ocean of jewels, and she discovered that if she could lose herself, she would find her treasure in you. Through her intercession, bind us with the poor and the oppressed together in your body of love. Amen.*

Antiphon:

It is my joy, O God, to praise you with song.

Readings:

"I will sing to the LORD, for he is highly exalted. . . . The LORD is my strength and my song; he has become my salvation. He is my God, and I will praise him." *Ex. 15:1–2 (NIV)*

"Unto you, O God, I lift up my soul, In you I trust, let me not be put to shame. Let not the wicked exult over me. Those who wait on you shall not be put to shame, But only those who wantonly break faith. . . . You, O God, are good and upright; you instruct sinners in your way. You lead the humble in the right path; you teach your way to the poor." *Psalm 25:1–3, 8–10 (PCB)*

"The elders who are among you I exhort, I who am a fellow elder and a witness of the sufferings of Christ, and also a partaker of the glory that will be revealed: Shepherd the flock of God which is among you, serving as overseers, not by compulsion but willingly, not for dishonest gain but eagerly; nor as being lords over those entrusted to you, but being examples to the flock; and when the Chief Shepherd appears, you will receive the crown of glory that does not fade away." *1 Pet. 5:1–4 (NKJV)*

APRIL 5 Mary Pandita Ramabai

Mary Pandita Ramabai was born in 1858 in India, the daughter of a Sanskrit scholar. Her father believed in educating women during a period in Indian history when it was rare to do so. It paid off. Mary Pandita became a renowned poet and scholar herself, and she went on to champion women's rights in

India for the rest of her life. She was deeply touched by the devoted work of some Anglican nuns she met in Poona, and her spiritual search eventually led her to a Christian conversion. Toward the latter half of her life, she was a fervent missionary in her own country, working on behalf of orphans and widows. Having lost her own husband at age twenty-two, she understood well the plight of many widows in India, who were without status or protection; she sought to remedy this unfortunate situation by making more education and marketable skills available to them. Mary Pandita was an avid opponent of the caste system, and in 1877 she wrote *The High-Caste Hindu Woman*. After learning Greek and Hebrew, she went on to translate the entire Bible into her native tongue, the only example of a complete translation of the Scriptures at that time done by a woman. She refused to westernize Christianity, however, and set many psalms to Hindu music. Mary Pandita died April 5, 1922, and the Church of England remembers her on this day.

Prayer:

> *O precious Lord and lover of all souls, we thank you for the gift of Mary Pandita to India and to the world. You called for an elimination of structures of domination and submission. She fought valiantly for the equality that you lived and taught in your own life. Through her, we gleam hope that your redeeming action is taking place now in our world. We bless you for that hope and for all those who work for its fruition. Amen.*

Antiphon:
I will not leave you orphanless.

Readings:
"Cast your burdens on our God, and you will be supported.
Never will God permit the just to falter.
But you, O God, will bring down to the pit of the grave
All that is wicked and evil; that oppresses the poor and needy."
  Psalm 55:22, 24 (PCB)

"Pure religion and undefiled before God and the Father is this; To visit the orphans and widows in their affliction, and to keep oneself unspotted before the world." *James 1:27 (KJV)*

"The [man] who enters by the gate is the shepherd of his sheep. The watchman opens the gate for him, and the sheep listen to his voice. He calls his own sheep by name and leads them out. When he has brought out all his own, he goes on ahead of them, and

APRIL 6 Juliana of Cornillon

Born in Belgium in 1192, St. Juliana was ophaned at the age of five and brought up by the nuns in the Convent of Mt. Cornillon. She joined the order at age thirteen, and she spent much time in prayer in front of the Blessed Sacrament. When she was sixteen, she experienced a vision that she did not understand: the moon hung brightly in the middle of the sky, but it was marred by a black spot in the center. She did not comprehend at first that it was a vision from God. Later, this young mystic experienced a vision of Jesus in which he explained the vision. The full beautiful moon represented the Church, and the black spot represented the lack of a feast day honoring Christ in the Blessed Sacrament. Jesus made it known that he wished for the Church to establish an official feast day to honor him in the holy Eucharist. Juliana eventually became Prioress of Mt. Cornillon, and she worked her entire life trying to officially establish this feast day. Her tireless efforts were not realized until several years after her death when Pope Urban IV published the Bull that established the feast known as "Corpus Christi."

Intercessory Prayer:

Dear St. Juliana, we wish to imitate your ardent love for our Lord in the most holy Eucharist. Jesus told you that he wished for a feast day to honor the Blessed Sacrament to strengthen the faithful on their road to a virtuous life. Allow our prayers to make reparation for all the abuses heaped upon our Lord's Eucharistic Presence. May we imitate you by loving Jesus in the Eucharist as our truest friend. Amen.

Antiphon:

You are near at hand, O God, and all your ways are true.

Readings:

Teach me Your way, O LORD; I will walk in Your truth;
Unite my heart to fear Your name. I will praise You, O Lord my God, with all my heart,

And I will glorify Your name forevermore. For great *is* Your mercy
toward me,
And You have delivered my soul from the depths of Sheol." *Psalm
86:11–13 (NKJV)*

"And Moses took the tabernacle, and pitched it without the camp,
afar off from the camp, and called it the Tabernacle of the congregation. And it came to pass, that every one which sought the Lord
went out unto the tabernacle of the congregation. . . . And it
came to pass, when Moses entered the tabernacle, the cloudy pillar descended, and stood at the door of the tabernacle, and the
Lord talked with Moses. And all the people saw the cloudy pillar
stand at the tabernacle door; and all the people rose up and worshipped." *Ex. 33:8–10 (KJV)*

"Just as the Father who has life sent me, and I have life because
of the Father, so the one who feeds on me will have life because
of me. This is the bread that came down from heaven. Unlike your
ancestors who ate and died nonetheless, those who feed on this
bread shall live forever." *John 6:57–58 (RSV)*

APRIL 7 Mary Assunta and Blessed Ursulina of Palma

Blessed Mary Assunta was born in Italy in 1878, the eldest
of five children. She was a very pious child who spent hours
every day in prayer. At age nineteen she entered the Franciscan Missionaries of Mary in Rome. She ardently desired to become a
saint through missionary work. In 1904 she asked the Mother Superior if she could join her fellow sisters attending to the lepers in
China, and was given permission. Within a year she and two other
nuns in her company fell ill with typhoid. Mary Assunta experienced
severe sufferings with this illness for one week, and then she died at
age twenty-seven in the odor of sanctity. Her body was exhumed
eight years later and found to be miraculously incorrupt.

This is also the feast day of Blessed Ursulina of Palma, a brave virgin and visionary who lived in the thirteenth century. God spoke to
the young fifteen-year-old maiden and requested that she journey to
Avignon, France, to encourage the reigning anti-pope to step down
and end the Western schism. The anti-pope did not heed her request,

so she made a mortifying pilgrimage to the Holy Land in hopes that her sacrifices might bring an end to this horrible conflict. It wasn't until years later, after Ursalina died, that the schism finally ended and the Western Church was reunited.

Prayer:

Dear Lord, you gave us Blessed Assunta and Blessed Ursulina as examples of women who followed your inspirations. Blessed Assunta asked for the grace to help the world know the purity of intention; she knew that this would make all that one does an act of love for you. Please help us to offer up every small act and duty, even the most ordinary things, with purity of intention. It is through such ordinary events that we may also become saints. Help us to never pass up anything that would profit our souls. Amen.

Antiphon:

The Spirit of the Lord is upon me, because he anointed me to preach good tidings to the poor.

Readings:

"He led them by a straight way to a city where they could settle. Let them give thanks to the LORD for his unfailing love and his wonderful deeds . . .

for he satisfies the thirsty and fills the hungry with good things." *Psalm 107:7–9 (NIV)*

"Blessed be the God and Father of our Lord Jesus Christ, who according to his abundant mercy has begotten us again to a living hope through the resurrection of Jesus Christ from the dead, to an inheritance incorruptible and undefiled and that does not fade away, reserved in heaven for you, who are kept by the power of God through faith for salvation ready to be revealed in the last time." *1 Pet. 1:3–5 (NKJV)*

"I am the good shepherd; and I know My sheep, and am known by My own. As the Father knows Me, even so I know the Father; and I lay down My life for the sheep." *Jn. 10:14–15 (NKJV)*

APRIL 8 Julie Billiart

Julia (Julie) Billiart was born a peasant girl in France in 1751. During childhood, she loved playing school, and when she was sixteen, she began teaching to help support her family. Her desire for knowledge was insatiable, especially regarding spiritual matters. As a child, she learned the catechism by heart, and throughout her life she was called to a vocation of sharing her knowledge of Christ with whomever she could. She fostered the art of "mental prayer" with her Lord, as a form of preparation before receiving the Eucharist. As an adult, she offered her home as a hiding place for priests, and she was active in the French Revolution. After her father was shot when she was sitting next to him, she became partially paralyzed from the shock, which lasted for twenty-two years. She was miraculously healed of this paralysis in 1804 and later that year, following a vision, she organized a fledgling group of companions dedicated to the education of young Christian women, particularly the poor. This order became the Sisters of Notre Dame de Namur. Her latter years were spent nursing the wounded and feeding the starving, who were ravished by war. Julia is a patron of women's education.

Intercessory Prayer:

St. Julia, through you, God has shown women of today that we can be valiant builders of the kingdom. You, whose motto was that "we do the most common things in an uncommon manner," pray for us that we may offer all of our mundane activities as prayers in the eyes of God. Help us to use the resources we have to help our deprived sisters and brothers retain their dignity and be whole participants with us in life, through Jesus Christ our Lord. Amen.

Antiphon:

My soul clings to you, O God; your hand upholds me.

Readings:

"How sweet are your words to my taste! Yea, sweeter than honey to my mouth." *Psalm 119:97–103 (Mem) (KJV)*

"Therefore set your desire on my words; long for them, and you will be instructed. Wisdom is radiant and unfading, and she is easily discerned by those who love her, and is found by those who seek her. She hastens to make herself known to those who desire her." *Wisdom 6:11–13 (RSV)*

"Now a certain man was there who had an infirmity thirty-eight years. When Jesus saw him lying there, and knew that he already had been in that condition a long time, He said to him, 'Do you want to be made well?' The sick man answered Him, 'Sir, I have no man to put me into the pool when the water is stirred up; but while I am coming, another steps down before me.' Jesus said to him, 'Rise, take up your bed and walk.'" *Jn. 5:5–8 (NKJV)*

APRIL 9 Mary of Cleophas

Mary, the wife of Cleophas, was the mother of both James the Lesser and the martyr Simeon, Disciple from the Seventy. She is mentioned only once by name, in John 19:25, where she is noted as the sister of Mary, the mother of Christ. In the Eastern churches, the tradition is that she is the daughter of Joseph, Mary's betrothed, from a former marriage. She was very young when she came to live with Joseph and Mary, and the two women became as sisters. Mary of Cleophas is also considered to be one of the myrrh bearers at Jesus' tomb. While Western tradition remembers her on April 9, the Greek Church celebrates her feast day on May 23 and again during holy Pascha (Easter) season, on the Sunday of the myrrh-bearing women. Her commitment to Jesus serves as a hallmark to women of all ages: she stayed with her Lord, endured with him to the end, and was one of the first witnesses of the Resurrection.

Prayer:

> *Beloved Jesus, Mary stood with your mother in enduring*
> *faithfulness at the foot of your cross. She followed your dead body*
> *to the tomb to anoint it with holy oil. She was willing to risk her*
> *own life and well-being by becoming a faithful witness for your*
> *name. Through her intercession, bless all women who put their own*
> *lives and reputations at risk in order to minister to you. Amen.*

Antiphon:

Place me like a seal over your heart.

Readings:

"Naked I came from my mother's womb and naked I shall return there." *Job 1:21 (NASB)*

"And when Joseph had taken the body, he wrapped it in a clean linen cloth. And laid it in his own new tomb, which he had hewn out in the rock: and he rolled a great stone to the door of the sepulcher, and departed. And there was Mary Magdalene and the other Mary, sitting over against the sepulcher." *Mt. 27:59–61 (KJV)*

"Now there stood by the cross of Jesus his mother, and his mother's sister, Mary, wife of Cleophas, and Mary Magdalene." *Jn. 19:25*

APRIL 10 Magdalene of Canossa

Often known as Magdalene the Educator, this vivacious woman was born at the end of the eighteenth century into an aristocratic family in Verona. When she was only five, her father died suddenly, and two years later her mother remarried, leaving Magdalene and her siblings with her uncle and the servants at the family estate. Magdalene had numerous illnesses in her teenage years, and she wanted to enter a convent, but returned after a year at Carmel. She then had a dream wherein the Blessed Mother appeared to her and gave her instruction about her future vocation, which was fostering an apostolate with needy young women. Magdalene opened her first school in 1805 and started the congregation known as the Canossian Daughters of Charity. Magdalene placed the utmost importance on knowing and respecting each young woman's personality, and she believed that she would succeed in being a good educator only if she understood her pupils sufficiently. She wrote that "education is the moulding of the heart," but she believed that education must be provided with great discretion and care for the soul. When Pope John Paul II canonized her, he said that "charity consumed her like a fever." Magdalene's feast day is celebrated on April 8, but she died on April 10, 1835, during Passion Week.

Prayer:

Heavenly God and comforter, your holy woman Magdalene was driven to the height of true charity toward those around her, and she imitated your comforting love as a mother looks after her brood of hens. Enable us to foster the gifts of true love and respect that you continually re-create in us when we are open to your inspiration. Through her intercession, help us to use our gifts for the well-being of all women and men we meet today, through Christ our Lord. Amen.

Antiphon:

Love bears all things, believes all things, hopes in all things, and endures all things.

Readings:

"For you, O God, are my hope, my trust, O God, from my youth.
Upon you, I have leaned from my birth, from my mother's womb you claimed me.
I praise you forever and ever. I have been a portent to many; but you are my strong refuge. My lips are filled with your praise, with your glory all the day long." *Psalm 71:5–8 (PCB)*

"Oh Jerusalem! Jerusalem . . . How often have I wanted to gather your children together, just as a mother hen gathers her brood under her wings. . . ." *Lk. 13:34 (NKJV)*

"In all wisdom and insight he made known to us the mystery of his will, according to his kind intention which he purposed in him with a view to an administration suitable to the fullness of the times, that is, the summing up of all things in Christ." *Eph. 1:8–10 (NASB)*

APRIL 11 Gemma Galgani

Gemma Galgani was born in 1878 in Italy. Her pious mother instilled in her a love and devotion to her Catholic faith, but she died when Gemma was only five. When she was eighteen Gemma's father also died, and she became responsible for her seven siblings. It was always her desire to become a Passionist nun, but this was not to be. She had a seriously disfiguring case of spinal tuberculosis when she was just twenty, but after praying fervently to St. Gabriel of Our Lady of Sorrows, she was miraculously cured. A year later she was given the gift of the stigmata and suffered the wounds of Christ every Thursday and Friday for the next two years. She also was blessed with encounters with her guardian angel on a regular basis. In 1902 she again fell ill and suffered for many months. She finally died in 1903 on Holy Saturday at age twenty-five. Church authorities began examining her cause for beatification immediately, and Gemma was canonized just thirty-seven years after her death.

Prayer:

Heavenly Father, you gave us St. Gemma as an example of true sanctity lived out in an ordinary life. St. Gemma shows us how we can become saints by achieving personal holiness through living out the simple tasks of everyday life. She accepted suffering and mortification as gifts from you, dear Lord. Please help us to view the daily crosses we must bear with acceptance to your will. Amen.

Antiphon:

Cast your burden upon the Lord and he shall sustain you.

Readings:

"For he shall give his angels charge over you, to keep you in all your ways.
In their hands they shall bear you up lest you dash your foot against a stone.
You shall tread upon the lion and the cobra;
The young lion and the serpent you shall trample under foot."
Psalm 91:11–13 (NKJV)

"God tested them and found them worthy of himself; like gold in the furnace he tried them, and like a sacrificial burnt offering he accepted them. In the time of their visitation they will shine forth, and will run like sparks through the stubble." *Wis. 3:5–7 (RSV)*

"For he inflicts pain, and gives relief; He wounds, and his hands also heal. From six troubles he will deliver you, Even in seven evil will not touch you. . . . For you will be in league with the stones of the field; and the beasts of the field will be at peace with you." *Job 5:18, 19, 23 (NASB)*

APRIL 12 Athanasia of Aegina

Athanasia of Aegina was born in the early ninth century to wealthy parents who, against her wishes, arranged her marriage twice. The first time, her young husband died sixteen days after their vows. Although forced to marry again, she persuaded her second husband to adopt the lifestyle of a monk. Once while weaving, Athanasia saw a star that gave off an abundant light, and she was led to understand from this that she was to join with other women and form a monastic community. She gained renown as a wonder-worker when she healed a blind man, and she received numerous visions, including one of the Transfiguration. She built several Byzantine churches, and after a dream wherein she saw the holy Theotokos beckoning to her, she retired to her cell to prepare for her death. She died during the feast of the Dormition (Assumption), but the translation of her relics is celebrated on April 12. The male hagiographer who wrote her life was an eyewitness to posthumous miracles at her tomb, and several of the nuns in her convent had a vision of her ascending to heaven with angels. The West honors Athanasia's feast day on August 14.

Intercessory Prayer:

O holy Athanasia, you who are one of heaven's pure lights, we honor the great miracles that God wrought in you, and we ask your intercession for those on earth who are in need of healing. May we joyfully give thanks with you to the one who pardons our souls. With every breath, may we testify to the love that is the eternal light of our paths. Amen.

Antiphon:

O my God, I have trusted in you; let me not be put to shame.

Readings:

"God, My heart is steadfast, I will sing and give praise, even with my glory.
Awake, lute and harp: I will awaken the dawn.
I will praise you, O Lord, among the peoples,
And I will sing praises to you among the nations,
For your mercy is great among the heavens,
And your truth reaches to the clouds." *Psalm 108:1–4 (NKJV)*

"For it came to pass when the flame went up toward heaven from off the altar, that the angel of the Lord ascended in the flame of the altar. And Manoah and his wife looked on it, and fell on their faces to the ground. . . . And Manoah said to his wife: 'We shall surely die, because we have seen God.'" *Judg. 13:20–22 (KJV)*

"And in the last days, it shall be, God declares, that I will pour out my Spirit upon all flesh; and your sons and daughters shall prophesy, and your young men shall see visions, and your old men shall dream dreams." *Acts 2:17 (RSV)*

APRIL 13 Margaret of Castello

In 1287, Margaret of Castello was born a blind hunchback, the daughter of Italian nobility. Living in a beautiful castle and desiring a perfect child, her parents were shocked that this should happen to their first daughter. Embarrassed by her presence at court, when she was six they walled her up in a small room near the chapel, where she stayed till she was a teenager. A family servant instructed her in the ways of the Lord, and Margaret eventually received her First Communion. Her hunger for the spiritual life grew, and the local priest soon discovered that she had a brilliant mind. When she was nineteen, the territory her father ruled was threatened with invasion, and they moved her close to the town of Castello, where it was rumored that miracles were occurring at the tomb of a holy friar. The family took her there, hoping for a cure, but none occurred. Her parents then abandoned her. Some sisters at a monastery adopted Margaret, but they too shut her out, seeing her as little more than a pious eccentric. She claimed that, although blind, she could see Christ at Mass. Undaunted, she became a Third Order Dominican, and began ministering to prisoners. One prisoner reportedly saw her levitate while praying. She died at age thirty-three, and two hundred years later her incorrupt body was exhumed and still resides at Castello. Margaret is a patron of the disabled.

Prayer:

> *O Creator God, Blessed Margaret is a shining symbol that the most unwanted on earth are very much wanted by you. Create your reign of unity now; knit together the whole and the broken, the slave of oppression and the free. Through the intercession of Blessed Margaret of Castello, help us to loose the cords of mistakes that bind us, as we release the temptation to denigrate those whose paths we do not understand. Through Christ our Lord. Amen.*

Antiphon:

I will bind up that which was broken, and strengthen that which was sick.

Readings:

"My soul lies down among lions, who greedily devour the peoples of the earth. Their teeth are spears and arrows, their tongues a sharpened sword. . . . They laid a snare for my steps, my soul was bowed down . . . [But] my heart is steadfast, O God, my heart is steadfast." *Psalm 57:4–7 (PCB)*

"He was despised and rejected of men; a man of sorrows, and acquainted with grief, and we hid, as it were, our faces from him; he was despised and we esteemed him not. Surely he has borne our griefs, and carried our sorrows: yet we did esteem him stricken, smitten of God, and afflicted." *Isa. 53:3–4 (KJV)*

"Come let us return to the Lord: for he has torn us, but he will heal us; he has wounded us, but he will bandage us. He will revive us after two days; he will raise us up on the third day, that we may live before him. So let us know, let us press on to know the Lord; his going forth is as certain as the dawn." *Hosea 6:1–3 (NASB)*

APRIL 14 Pica, Mother of St. Francis

Pica Bernardone, although never officially beatified, is held dear in the popular mind and in the Franciscan tradition, which celebrates her feast April 14. Born into a French family, her real name was Joan, but she was nicknamed Pica ("magpie"). She married a wealthy Italian cloth merchant, Peter Bernardone, and although they lived quite well she was deeply devoted to the poor. She must have instilled this trait in her son Francis at an early age. When Francis took cloth from the family business to sell to help finance the San Damiano Church's reconstruction, his father chained him in the cellar. The family feud must have been equally horrible for his mother, who was the one to finally release him after nearly a month. Pica must have also agonized over Francis when he spent a year as a prisoner of war. A statue of Peter and Pica stands in the Piazza at Assisi; in her hands Pica holds the chains that represent her husband's efforts to bind her son to the destiny his father had planned for him, which Francis so heartily rejected. When he began his famous order known for its poverty, Pica eventually joined him, wearing penitential garb and devoting her life to works of charity.

Prayer:

> O Lord, when you brought forth many great saints into the world, you gave them mothers to be their earliest teachers, and Pica was a source of inspiration to her son, as she is to us. She understood well that the way of downward mobility is often the way toward the knowledge of higher things. Through her intercession, help us to always keep in mind that although we are in the world, we do not belong to the world. Help us likewise to move toward a radical conversion from the values of our secular culture to those of the Gospel. Bless all mothers who suffer anxiety for their sons' well-being. Amen.

Antiphon:

Go, sell all you have, and follow me.

Readings:

"Blessed are those who walk not in the counsel of the wicked,
Nor stand in the way of sinners, nor sit with those who scoff;
But delight in your law, O God, pondering it day and night.
They are like a tree planted by streams of water,
That yields its fruit in due season, and whose leaves never fade.
May they prosper in all they do." *Psalm 1:13 (PCB)*

"Do not lay up for yourselves treasures on earth where moth and rust consume, and where thieves break in and steal, but lay up for yourselves treasures in heaven. . . . For where your treasure is, there will your heart be also." *Mt. 6:19–21 (RSV)*

"Most of the brethren in the Lord, having become confident by my chains, are much more bold to speak the word without fear." *Phil. 1:14 (NKJV)*

APRIL 15 Corrie ten Boom

Born April 15, 1892, in Amsterdam, Holland, Corrie ten Boom was the youngest of four siblings. The daughter of a watchmaker, she became the first woman watchmaker in Holland. But this was only one of her many distinctions. Carrie was part of the Dutch Reformed Church, and, after two years at Bible school, she passed the exam, which allowed her to teach catechism and lecture. After her mother's death, Corrie's family began taking orphaned children into their home. During the war, as Germany was invading Holland, they began hiding Jews in their attic and helping them to escape. The family was imprisoned and, after preaching to other prisoners about God's goodness, they were placed in solitary confinement. Her sister, Betsy, died there, but Corrie lived and returned home to open a rehabilitation center for those harmed in the war. In 1946, she returned to Germany and began many years of itinerant preaching that took her to over sixty countries. She wrote *The Hiding Place*, about her experiences with the Jews, and the state of Israel honored her by inviting her to plant a tree in a place called the Avenue of Righteous Gentiles at Jerusalem (Oskar Schindler is also recognized there). Corrie once said, "If God sends us stony paths, he provides strong shoes."

Prayer:

Holy God, through the merciful deeds of Corrie ten Boom, remind us of water and spirit, present everywhere in your limitless love, and like cool water, refresh our hurts and pain. She prayed for all those harmed by the war and the Holocaust, and she shone like a beacon for those suffering imprisonment. We thank you for your merciful work in her life and ask for the gift of understanding that she had. May we praise you with righteousness and goodness toward one another, in Jesus' name. Amen.

Antiphon:

O Lord, how good and gentle is your Spirit in us, alleluia.

Readings:

"Will you not restore us again, that your people may rejoice in you?
Show us your steadfast love, and grant us your salvation.
Let me hear what you have to say, for you will speak peace to your people,
To those who are near you and who turn to you in their hearts.
Your salvation is near to those who fear you,
That glory may dwell in our land." *Psalm 85:6–10 (PCB)*

"We then, as workers together with him, also plead with you not to receive the grace of God in vain. For he says, 'In an acceptable time I have heard you; on a day of salvation I have helped you.' Behold, now is the acceptable time; behold, now is the day of salvation. We give no offense in anything, that our ministry may not be blamed. But in all things we commend ourselves as ministers of God: in much patience, in tribulations, in needs, in distresses . . . in imprisonments, in tumults, in labors, in sleeplessness, in fastings . . . by longsuffering, by kindness, by the Holy Spirit, by sincere love." *2 Cor. 6:1–6 (NKJV)*

APRIL 16 Bernadette of Lourdes

Bernadette Soubirous was born to a poor French family in 1844. She was a shepherdess when she began receiving visions of Mary, Our Lady of Lourdes, in 1858. Appearing at the rock of Massabielle, the Virgin ordered that a church be built, and a miraculous spring developed there that has since become a place of worldwide pilgrimage. Although a simple girl, Bernadette had great veracity and courage when it came to defending her visions. The Virgin with whom Bernadette communicated, unlike many of the officials who interrogated her, treated her with great gentleness and dignity. Ill much of her life, Bernadette received the Last Sacraments three times. She bore all her sufferings with dignity, and she was noted for her great humility. She once said, "The Blessed Mother only chose me because I was ignorant." After her series of visions, she retired to a convent and died at age thirty-five. Bernadette's body lies incorrupt today in the St. Gildard's Convent at Nevers, France.

Prayer:

Gracious Jesus, you worked miracles of healing through the grace of your Holy Mother at Lourdes. You bound Blessed Bernadette's life with a diadem of incorruption as a sign of your desire to protect our bodies from destruction. Through her intercession, make us worthy vessels of your Spirit, so being made strong in soul and body, we may joyfully proclaim your everlasting compassion for us in songs of praise. Amen.

Antiphon:

You put down the mighty from their throne and lift up the lowly.

Readings:

"Let us go to the place of God's dwelling; let us worship at God's footstool. Go up, O God, to the place of your rest, you and the ark of your might. Let your priests be clothed with justice, and your faithful shout for joy." *Psalm 132:7–10 (PCB)*

"When they had crossed over, they came to the land of the Gennesaret and anchored there. And when they came out of the boat, immediately the people recognized him, ran through that whole surrounding region, and began to carry about on beds those who were sick to wherever they heard he was. Wherever he entered, into villages, cities, or the country, they laid the sick in the marketplaces, and begged him that they might just touch the hem of his garment. And as many as touched him were made well." *Mk. 6:53–56 (NKJV)*

APRIL 17 Anna Dengal and Isabella Gilmore

Mother Anna Dengal founded the community of the Medical Mission Sisters (MMS) in 1925 in response to a need in underdeveloped countries, which she saw as critical. She was an Austrian doctor working in India among Muslim women whose custom of *purdah* prevented them from being seen by male doctors. Since there were practically no women doctors in India then, Anna felt the need to organize an international religious community of women health care professionals to offer medical assistance to these destitute women. At the time, however, Roman Catholic canon law did not permit religious to practice medicine or attend childbirth, which were precisely the types of care Mother Dengal saw as most needed in India. She continued to persist, the canon law was changed, and eventually the community was founded. Medical Mission Sisters still serve women in the world's most underdeveloped countries.

Isabella Gilmore, born in London in 1842, trained as a nurse. The Anglican calendar celebrates her as a holy woman and deaconess. Together with the bishop of her diocese, she organized the first Order of Deaconesses, which was formulated along the same lines as an ordained ministry. Ordained in 1887, she served nineteen years in the

Anglican Church, training head deaconesses for seven other dioceses. She died in 1923, and it was noted at her memorial service that the order of deaconess, alive in the early Church for nearly eleven centuries, could trace its revival in the modern era to Isabella's dedicated service.

Prayer:

O Holy Spirit of light and life, you inspired these holy women, Anna and Isabella, to follow their vocations into a deeper service for Christ and the world. Shepherd us, O God, as we embrace our own visions of service, and empower us to unite our wills with yours as we seek to make this service fruitful. Come Spirit of Holiness and blow through us; help us to trust in our uncommon sight. Amen.

Antiphon:

He has not left me alone, because I always do what pleases him.

Readings:

"And he has put into my mouth a new song, praise to our God, Many shall see . . . and place their trust in you.
Happy are we who have placed our trust in you, O God." *Psalm 40:3–5 (PCB)*

"For the Lord your God is the God of gods . . . the great, the mighty, and the awesome God who does not show partiality, nor take a bribe. He executes justice for the orphan and the widow, and shows his love for the alien by giving him food and clothing. So show your love for the aliens, for you were [once] aliens. . . ." *Deut. 10:18–19 (NASB)*

"I commend to you Phoebe our sister, who is deaconess of the church which is at Cenchrea, that you receive her in the Lord, as befits the saints, and help her in whatever she may require from you." *Rom. 16:1–2 (RSV)*

APRIL 18 Marie of the Incarnation (Barbe Acarie)

Two saints who took the name Marie of the Incarnation are celebrated in April; the first is Barbe Acarie, born in France in 1566. She was victimized by an abusive mother, who once left her in an unheated room for punishment; she got so cold she lost a toe to frostbite. Barbe was a better mother herself. Married to an aristocratic lawyer, she had six children, all of whom she was determined to raise as saints. If her success can be measured by their vocations, she did quite well: her three daughters became Carmelites, and one of her sons became a priest. Her husband, Peter, became bankrupt and impoverished the family, but Barbe was instrumental in restoring his name at court. A deep contemplative, Madame Acarie received various visions, including one of St. Teresa of Avila, who was alive during part of her lifetime. Barbe was inspired to bring the Discalced Carmelites to France, and she joined the order as a lay sister after her husband's death, taking the name Marie of the Incarnation. She died on Easter, 1618.

Intecessory Prayer:

Blessed Marie of the Incarnation, you were gifted with the graces of both contemplative prayer and motherhood. You are an inspiration for women who want to deepen their spiritual lives while living a busy family life. Pray for us that we may be sustained in all our efforts to find God in the mundane, as well as in the joy of spiritual ecstasy. For all women who are mothers, we ask for your intercession, that we may serve our children by being living examples of God's unending love in the world. Amen.

Antiphon:

You are my helper and my deliverer.

Readings:

"The wise will hear, and will increase learning . . . to understand a proverb, and the interpretation; the words of the wise and their dark sayings. The fear of the Lord is the beginning of knowledge; but fools despise wisdom and instruction. My child, hear the instruction of your father; and forsake not the law of your mother."
Prov. 1:5–8 (KJV)

"Thou did make me hope when I was upon my mother's breast. I was cast upon you from the womb: you are my God from my mother's belly." *Psalm 22:9–10 (KJV)*

"Everyone who believes that Jesus is the Christ is a child of God, and everyone who loves the parent loves the child. By this we know that we love the children of God, when we love God and obey his commandments . . . And his commandments are not burdensome. For whatever is born of God overcomes the world; and this is the victory that overcomes the world: our faith." *1 Jn. 5:1–4 (RSV)*

APRIL 19 Cornelia Connelly

Cornelia Connelly founded the Society of the Holy Child Jesus in 1846, but not before experiencing much pain and sacrifice in her life. Born into the Church of England, she married an Episcopal priest named Pierce Connelly. After several children, Pierce felt decidedly drawn to Roman Catholicism, while still wanting to be a priest. Crushed and confused about what this meant for their marriage, Cornelia nonetheless followed her husband into the new faith. After losing two of her children, Cornelia became deeply devoted to Our Lady of Sorrows. While pregnant with their fifth child, she stayed behind when Pierce went to Rome to study the priesthood. She later rejoined him, but they decided to live celibate lives. After discovering her own vocation to the religious life, Rome granted her permission to take her children with her to England and establish a congregation devoted to the education of young women. But after only three years, Pierce decided to leave the Roman Church and wanted her back as his wife. Supervising a now-flourishing society, Cornelia felt it would be untrue to her calling to leave what she felt God had begun in her. Pierce kidnapped her children and left the country; she never saw them again. Through all her grief, she remained steadfast in her mission of founding schools for poor girls in England. Cornelia was declared Venerable in 1992.

Prayer:

Beloved Lord, model us on your Word, so that, as we come into your chamber, we recognize that you alone are worthy and deserving of our love. We long to become vessels of devotion in your honor, willing to sacrifice all for a closer walk with you. Despite our suffering and struggle in this life, through the intercession of Venerable Cornelia, help us to remember that, in the end, you stand before the open door and bid us to come in. Amen.

Antiphon:

Whoever thirsts will drink freely of life-giving water.

Readings:

"I was glad when they said to me, 'Let us go to the house of God!' And now our feet are standing within your gates, O Jerusalem. . . . Peace be within your walls, and security within your borders! For the love of my family and friends, I will say, 'Peace be within you!' For the sake of the house of our God, I seek your good." *Psalm 122:1–9 (PCB)*

"He has put my brethren far from me and my acquaintances are completely estranged from me. My relatives have failed, and my familiar friends have forgotten me. Those who live in my house and my servants consider me a stranger: I am a foreigner in their sight." *Job 19:13–15 (NAS)*

"Then they will answer saying, 'Lord, when did we see you hungry, or thirsty, or a stranger, or naked, or sick, or in prison, and did not take care of you?' Then he will answer them saying, 'Truly I say to you, to the extent that you did not do it to one of the least of these, you did not do it to me.'" *Mt. 25:44–45 (NAS)*

APRIL 20 Agnes of Montepulciano

Agnes of Montepulciano, Italy, was a pious child who began pestering her parents to join a convent from a very young age. Finally, at the age of nine, she was allowed to join a nunnery at Montepulciano, whose sisters were sometimes called the Sisters of the Sack. Miracles seemed to surround her there. Agnes often levitated off the ground during times of prayer, she had visions of the Blessed Mother, and she received Holy Communion from an angel. At age fifteen, the Pope asked her to be the abbess at the convent in Procena, where she promoted a life of austerity. She lived mainly on bread and water and slept on the ground. The story was told that, at the moment of her death on April 20, 1317, young children throughout the region began to suddenly speak of Agnes and her piety. Many miracles were reported at the site of her tomb, where her incorrupt body still lies. Pope Benedict XIII eventually canonized Agnes nearly three hundred years after her death.

Prayer:

Heavenly Father, you gave us St. Agnes as a shining reminder of the great things that can be accomplished when we work to follow your holy will. From a young age your miracles surrounded her as proof of her unusual sanctity. Let us remember to voluntarily offer our actions to you, that they may serve to sanctify us and bring us closer to your heavenly kingdom. Amen.

Antiphon:

To the pure all things are pure.

Readings:

"But as for me, when they were sick, my clothing was sackcloth; I humbled myself with fasting; and my prayer would return to my own heart. I paced about as though he were my friend or brother; I bowed down heavily, as one who mourns for his mother." *Psalm 35:13–14 (NKJV)*

"It has seemed good to me to declare the signs and wonders which the Most High God has done for me. How great are his signs, and how mighty are his wonders! His kingdom is an everlasting kingdom. And his dominion is from generation to generation." *Dan. 4:2–3 (NASB)*

"And it shall come to pass that whoever calls on the name of the Lord shall be saved. . . . Jesus of Nazareth, a man attested by God to you, by miracles, wonders and signs which God did through him in your midst . . . [was] delivered up by the determined purpose and foreknowledge of God." *Acts 2:21–22 (NKJV)*

APRIL 21 Hildegund

Hildegund was born in the town of Neuss near the Rhine River in the mid-twelfth century, the daughter of a knight. After her mother's death, she went with her father on a pilgrimage to the Holy Land. She was about twelve years old at the time, and, probably for reasons of safety, he dressed her in male attire and called her Joseph. After her father's death, Hildegund continued to cross-dress for the rest of her life. Falsely branded a thief and nearly hanged, she managed to escape when the rope was miraculously sliced. She then made her way to Germany, where she entered a Cistercian monastery. She lived her life as Brother Joseph but related her biography to the abbot before she died, revealing her true identity. He compiled her *vita*. Although her cult was never formalized, she became a famous local saint; in art, she is depicted with an angel on horseback at the moment of death when her gender was discovered. Hildegund is a patron of the falsely accused.

Prayer:

Righteous King and God, you are holy, and your servant
Hildegund spent her life deepening her devotion to your holiness.
Help us to live in the awareness that all that has happened in our
lives until this point in time belongs completely to you. We are at
your mercy, for you are the only one who gives our soul the
passion it longs for. Amen.

Antiphon:

My help comes from the Lord, who made heaven and earth.

Readings:

"And I said, 'Oh, that I had wings like a dove!
For then I would fly away, and be at rest.
Then would I wander far off, and remain in the wilderness, Selah.
I would hasten my escape from the windy storm and tempest.'"
 Psalm 55:6–8 (KJV)

"Through their faith, they subdued kingdoms, wrought righteousness, obtained promises, stopped the mouths of lions, quenched the violence of fire, escaped the edge of the sword, [and] out of weakness were made strong. . . ." *Heb. 11:33–34 (KJV)*

"And in the morning, rising up a great while before the day, he went out and departed into a solitary place, and there prayed." *Mk. 1:35 (KJV)*

APRIL 22 Maria Gabriella of Unity

Maria Gabrielle Sagheddu was born in Italy to a poor family of shepherds in 1914. Many described her as an obstinate and rebellious child, but her demeanor changed around age eighteen when she became a member of a Roman Catholic youth movement and truly discovered her Catholic faith. At age twenty-one she joined the Trappestine monastery, where all her sisters acknowledged her as a tireless worker and a model of daily Christian charity. The abbess who was head of the community had a deep ecumenical devotion and desired to pray for unity among all faiths. Soon Sr. Maria Gabriella also felt a call from Christ to devote her life to the cause of unity. When she offered her life to God for this special cause, the normally healthy young woman was struck with tuberculosis. After fifteen long months of suffering for the sake of unity, she finally passed away at the tender age of twenty-five. Eighteen years later her body was found to be incorrupt when her relics were moved to a chapel at the monastery of Vitorchiano. Pope John Paul II beatified and recognized her as Blessed Maria Gabriella of Unity in January 1983. Representatives from many denominations, including Orthodox, Anglican, and Lutheran, attended Maria Gabriella's beatification ceremony.

Prayer:

> Heavenly Father, you gave us Blessed Maria Gabriella of Unity as a model who devoted her short but fruitful life as an intercessor for the cause of unity within all faiths. Maria Gabriella surrendered her life to you with the motto, "Now do what you will." Help us to emulate this wonderful model of self-giving and, as Sr. Maria Gabriella said, "in simplicity of heart, gladly offer everything, O Lord." Amen.

Antiphon:

> [There is] one body, and one Spirit, one Lord, one faith, one baptism.

Readings:

> "Behold, how good and how pleasant it is for brethren to dwell together in unity!
> It is like the precious ointment upon the head, that ran down on the beard,
> Even Aaron's beard, that went down to the skirts of his garments,

As the dew of Hermon, and as the dew that descended upon the mountains of Zion,

For there the Lord commanded the blessing, even life forevermore." *Psalm 133 (KJV)*

"He that descended is the same also that ascended up far above the heavens, that he might fill all things. And he gave some, apostles; and some, prophets; and some, evangelists; and some, pastors and teachers; for the perfecting of the saints, for the work of the ministry, for the edifying of the body of Christ. Till we all come in the unity of the faith, and of the knowledge of the Son of God, unto perfection, unto the measure of the stature of the fullness of Christ." *Eph. 4:10–13 (KJV)*

APRIL 23 Mary Euphrasia Pelletier

Rose Virginie Pelletier was born during the turbulent years of the French Revolution. At age eighteen she felt a calling to minister to destitute women in crisis, and she entered the Refuge of Our Lady of Charity in Tours, where she eventually made her formal religious profession and took the name Mary Euphrasia. At age twenty-nine she was elected Superior, and within a year she had founded an order known as the Sisters of Magdalens. Mary Euphrasia was known for the pearls of wisdom that she shared with others, such as "One person is of more value than the whole world" and "The old stars burn out and die, look to new horizons and even beyond." Perhaps her most favorite and well-known saying was "It is human to fall, but angelic to rise again." Before her life ended by natural causes in 1868, Mary Euphrasia had established over 350 convents and homes of charity and caused thousands of vocations in five continents, which led to her recognition as a patron saint of travelers.

Prayer:

Dear Jesus, you gave us St. Mary Euphrasia Pelletier as a model of Christian love and charity. She saw the value of each unique soul and the precious nature of each and every human life. Help us to emulate her devotion to life as we pray for respect for all human life, from conception to death. St. Mary Euphrasia told us that if we love one another and uphold each other, we may be capable of

working wonders in your name. Help us to live such words of
wisdom in our daily endeavors. Amen.

Antiphon:

And this gospel of the kingdom shall be preached in the
whole world for a testimony unto all the nations.

Readings:

"The wise woman builds a house; but the foolish pluck it down
with [their] hands. . . . In the mouth of the foolish is a rod of
pride; but the lips of the wise shall preserve them. A scorner
seeks wisdom, and finds it not; but knowledge is easy to one who
has understanding." *Prov. 14:1, 3, 6 (KJV)*

"The days of the afflicted are bad; but a cheerful heart has a continual feast." *Prov. 15:15 (NASB)*

"We also rejoice in God through our Lord Jesus Christ, through
whom we have now received the reconciliation . . . the law entered that the offence might abound. But, where sin abounded,
grace abounded much more, so that . . . grace might reign
through righteousness to eternal life through Jesus Christ our
Lord." *Rom. 5:11, 20–21 (NKJV)*

APRIL 24 Elizabeth the Wonder-worker

Elizabeth the wonder-worker who lived in the fifth century in
the Thracian town of Heraklea became famous for slaying a
dragon. Although this part of her life was myth, it may have
been based, in part, on the legend of St. George the dragon slayer,
since she lived in the convent that bears his name and gained renown
there for her asceticism and miracles. The "dragon" was apparently a
poisonous serpent that inhabited the monastery grounds and terror-
ized the other nuns. The Orthodox tradition honors her as a wonder-
worker because of her ability to heal. She is most often prayed to for
help with menorrhagia (excessive menstrual flow), although a long
list of miracles is attributed to her. Elizabeth refused to look up at the
sky for three years, in an attempt to keep her mind interiorly focused
on God. She had a number of premonitions, including the cata-
strophic fire that devastated Constantinople in 465, and she also
dreamed about her upcoming death. She died of a fever following the

feast of St. George, and her relics were venerated as far away as Russia after their evangelization. Even the dust from Elizabeth's relics was said to cure blindness.

Intercessory Prayer:

O Blessed Elizabeth, you were a temple of the Holy Spirit, who poured forth miracles through you in an abundant stream of mercy. Your example teaches us to look beyond all the beauties of this physical world to the maker of all. Pray for us mortals, that we who suffer from physical illness may be purged of all that stands in the way of God's healing goodness. Amen.

Antiphon:

The Lord is the stronghold of my life; whom shall I fear?

Readings:

"I will praise you, O God, you have rescued me and have not let evil triumph over me. O God, I cried to you for help and you have healed me. You have raised my soul from the dead, restored me to life among those gone down to the grave. We sing praises to you, we your people, and give thanks to your holy name. For your anger lasts but a moment, your favors for a lifetime." *Psalm 30:1–4 (PBC)*

"And the serpent poured water like a river out of his mouth after the woman to sweep her away with the flood. But the earth came to the help of the woman, and the earth opened its mouth and swallowed the river which the dragon had poured forth from his mouth." *Rev. 12:15–16 (RSV)*

"And behold, a woman, who was diseased with an issue of blood twelve years, came behind him and touched the hem of his garment: For she said within herself, If I may but touch his garment, I shall be whole. But Jesus turned about, and when he saw her, he said, 'Daughter, be of good comfort, your faith has made thee whole.'" *Mt. 9:20–22 (KJV)*

APRIL 25 Isabella of Spain

Queen Isabella I, although never canonized, has evoked a special reverence from her people, both when she was alive and for centuries after her death. The daughter of King John II of Castile, and Isabella of Portugal, she was married to King Ferdinand of Sicily in 1469. Early in the marriage, she made an agreement with Ferdinand that they would rule the two countries—Spain and Portugal—with equal authority, and the couple's union was harmonious. Both Third Order Franciscans, they endeavored to preserve religious unity among their subjects, and together they fought the Moors—Isabella herself appearing at times on the battlefield—to maintain the Spanish monarchy's territorial unity. Isabella appreciated Christopher Columbus's genius, when others thought him quite mad. Not only was she Columbus's protectress, she also avidly protected the indigenous peoples of the Americas against the early colonists. Under her sovereignty, agriculture, navigation, and commerce flourished, and she attempted to foster a love of books in her children and in everyone with whom she came into contact. Isabella is the patron of Spain.

Prayer:

God the Most High, you are the eternal ruler of the universe and of our souls. Through your subject Isabella, you shone forth your light with a brilliant spirit. Through her virtues of magnanimity, tolerance, and caring protection, everyone within her sphere of influence came to appreciate and love her and the work she performed for your glory. Help us, likewise, to be filled with sympathy for those less fortunate than ourselves and to seek to establish egalitarian relationships with all whom we meet. Amen.

Antiphon:

You are a lamp unto our feet and a light unto our path.

Readings:

"Hear this, all ye people: give ear, all you inhabitants of the world, Both low and high, rich and poor together. My mouth shall speak of wisdom and the meditation of my heart shall be of understanding." *Psalm 49:1–3 (KJV)*

"So he set a royal crown on her head and made her queen instead of Vashti. And the king gave a great banquet, Esther's banquet, for all his nobles and officials. He proclaimed a holiday throughout the provinces and distributed gifts with royal liberality." *Esther 2:17–18 (NIV)*

"Then you will understand what is right and just and fair—every good path. For wisdom will enter your heart, and knowledge will be pleasant to your soul. Discretion will protect you, and understanding will guard you. Wisdom will save you from the ways of wicked men, from men whose words are perverse." *Prov. 2:9–12 (NIV)*

APRIL 26 Mary Bosanquet

One of the first Methodist preachers, Mary Bosanquet was born in Essex in 1739. She left her Roman Catholic roots and her family after one of her servant girls introduced her to Methodism. At that time Methodist meetings were still a part of the body of the larger Anglican Church. Mary's husband, John Fletcher, was an Anglican Evangelical who was John Wesley's designated successor. The concept of female preaching was highly controversial in Mary's generation in the Church of England, but Wesley encouraged and supported her. She went on to become one of the first Methodist deacons, and she continued to preach for thirty years after her husband's death. She transformed her large home into a school, orphanage, and halfway house for the destitute. Her witness persuaded many to accept a new life in Christ, as the Methodist transformation from a sect to a religion evolved. For over fifty years, she corresponded with Methodists of every social class and was instrumental in expanding women's role in the evangelical revival of the period. Mary died in 1815 and is remembered as one of Methodism's early founding mothers.

Prayer:

Beloved Lord and master of all hearts who are conformed to you, you heard Mary Bosanquet's earnest call to serve and rewarded her with a lifetime of evangelical renewal and dedication to others. All those within her circle of influence recognized her extraordinary call, as she sought you without ceasing in all her daily actions. Inspire us to respond to the still, small voice you put within each of us as we seek to transform our destiny into a mirror where you may become most beautifully reflected. Amen.

Antiphon:

For all things work for good for those who love God and are called according to his purpose.

Readings:

"You are my portion and my cup;
You are my fortune, my prize.
The lines have fallen for me in pleasant places; I have been given a welcome heritage.
I will bless you who give me counsel
In the night my heart instructs me." *Psalm 16:5–7 (PCB)*

"The LORD is my strength and my song; he has become my salvation." With joy you will draw water from the wells of salvation. In that day you will say: 'Give thanks to the LORD, call on his name; make known among the nations what he has done, and proclaim that his name is exalted. Sing to the LORD, for he has done glorious things; let this be known to all the world.'" *Isa. 12:2–5 (NIV)*

APRIL 27 Zita

Zita, one of the favorite saints of the Franciscan tradition, was born while Francis was still living. She was born to a poor Italian family and became a domestic servant at age twelve, an occupation she kept all her life. Known for giving away food and clothing to those poorer than she was, she sometimes brought grief upon herself when the goods belonged to the master of her household. When she incurred ill treatment, she overcame it by envisioning peace for those who wronged her. Eventually Zita was placed in charge of all the other servants. Still, she was often seen sleeping on the bare ground, having given her bed to a beggar. All those under her charge held Zita in high veneration, and her cult spread rapidly after miracles were reported at her tomb. She died at age sixty, having spent her whole life in service to her fellow humans, each of whom she saw as the face of God. She is often pictured in art as a serving woman with a bag and keys. Zita is a patron of homemakers.

Intercessory Prayer:

St. Zita, you developed such a sweetness of character for the love of Christ in all you met that all those around you eventually fell in love with your soul. Nothing could disturb your inward and abiding peace and your respect for other human beings. Your charity toward others was never exhausted, and you taught us that the simplest things done for the love of God open the door of salvation for many. Pray to God for us that, casting all of our cares upon him, we may live in conformity to his will in all things. Amen.

Antiphon:

She opens her mouth in wisdom, and on her tongue is kindly counsel.

Readings:

"She sets about her work vigorously; her arms are strong for her tasks. She sees that her trading is profitable, and her lamp does not go out at night. In her hand she holds the distaff and grasps the spindle with her fingers. She opens her arms to the poor and extends her hands to the needy." *Prov. 31:17–20 (NIV)*

"He looked up and saw the rich putting their gifts into the treasury; and he saw a poor widow put in two copper coins. And he said, 'Truly I tell you, this poor widow has put in more than all of them; for they all contributed out of their abundance, but she out of her poverty put in all the living that she had.'" *Lk. 21:1–4 (RSV)*

"Out of the most severe trial, their overflowing joy and their extreme poverty welled up in rich generosity. For I testify that they gave as much as they were able, and even beyond their ability. Entirely on their own, they urgently pleaded with us for the privilege of sharing in this service to the saints. . . . they gave themselves first to the Lord and then to us in keeping with God's will." *2 Cor. 8:2–5 (NIV)*

APRIL 28 Hadewijch of Brabant

Hadewijch of Brabant, also known as Hadewijch of Antwerp, was lost to oblivion until she became famous for her remarkable love poems, which were rediscovered in the nineteenth century. Most likely, she lived in the mid-thirteenth century as a Beguine, probably a mistress of a Beguine hermitage. Though she was the subject of much criticism and was separated from her community, Hadewijch continued to correspond with them through letters, some of which describe her visions. Her visions, which began when she was in her late teens, were highly symbolic and often corresponded to a liturgical season, especially Easter, Pentecost, and the feasts of the Blessed Mother. Some of her imagery included apocalyptical symbols, such as the lamb and the eagle and images from New Jerusalem. She once had a vision on Christmas wherein she saw the universe absorbed in an abyss that was the infant Jesus. Her writings reflect a woman of remarkable culture, both secular and theological. She demonstrates an extensive knowledge of Scripture and the early fathers. Her poems to Christ are considered a hallmark of Dutch lyrical poetry. In her ecstatic mysticism—in which majestic eagles often brought her to the Lord's throne—she was totally engulfed by God, and she came to understand that the tumultuous waves of life could not affect her unity with Christ. This immersion is reflected in one of Hadewijch's most famous sayings: "Gracious or merciless: to me it is all one."

Prayer:

O Lord, Hadewijch realized from her relationship with you that holding onto her vision was the only thing of importance. She held as most true the ideal that love holds the world together. In her ecstasy, she felt possessed of your Holy Spirit, that she was indeed "a mother of God." Help us to understand the depth of such mystical union with you, that we may be open doors for your majesty and faithful footstools of your presence in our world. Amen.

Antiphon:

I will bear you up on eagle's wings and bring you to myself.

Readings:

"And Moses said unto the Lord, 'See, you said to me, Bring up this people, and you have not let me know whom you will send with me.' Yet you have said, 'I know you by name, and you have found grace in my sight.' Now therefore, I pray to you, if I have found grace in your sight, show me now your way, that I may know you, that I may find grace in your sight: and consider that this nation is your people. And he said, 'My Presence shall go with you and give you rest.'" *Ex. 33:12–14 (KJV)*

"A poor [man] is shunned by all his relatives—how much more do his friends avoid him! Though he pursues them with pleading, they are nowhere to be found. He who gets wisdom loves his own soul; he who cherishes understanding prospers." *Prov. 19:7–8 (NIV)*

"But they that wait upon the Lord shall renew their strength; they shall mount up with wings like eagles; they shall run, and not be weary; and they shall walk, and not faint." *Isa. 40:31 (KJV)*

"And the disciples came and said to Him, "Why do You speak to them in parables?" He answered and said to them, "Because it has been given to you to know the mysteries of the kingdom of heaven, but to them it has not been given. . . . Therefore I speak to them in parables, because seeing they do not see, and hearing they do not hear, nor do they understand." *Mt. 13:10–13 (NKJV)*

APRIL 29 Catherine of Siena

One of the most influential figures of the fourteenth century, Catherine of Siena fought valiantly for the Pope's rights while fearlessly criticizing bishops and cardinals for not living the true gospel message. Born in 1347 on the feast of the Annunciation, Catherine's entire life seemed to shine as a herald for the Word of God. She had her first vision of Christ at age six, and, like her beloved Lord, she died at age thirty-three. During her short lifetime, she worked for peace among cities, labored for the sick and the poor during the Black Plague, dispatched letters to men and women of every aspect of life, was influential in reforming the administration of the Papal States, and prayed continually for the unity of Christendom. Perhaps her greatest contribution is her *Dialogue*, the book of her revelations, which guides the reader toward her mystical heights. Although Catherine supported the Crusades in her early life, she later wrote that the Muslims were "our brothers, redeemed by the blood of Christ, just as we are." During her last vision, an image of the Church as a ship seemed to crush her to the earth, and she offered herself as a victim for it. She then suffered a paralytic stroke, which she died from eight days later. Catherine is the patron of Siena and those who work for diplomatic relations.

Intercessory Prayer:

Most holy St. Catherine, your soul rose up with a tremendous desire for God's honor, and you lived your life in pursuit of that mission. You wrote that "the world is lost through silence," and as you worked courageously for what you believed to be the truth, you saw the world disintegrating around you in wars and in political upheavals in the Church. Pray that we may be removed from the great dangers we have created by our unhappy divisions. In the end, you realized that the soul can only find peace in God, as you prayed, "Let that fire burst the seed of my body . . . given for the love of your blood; and with the key of obedience, let me unlock heaven's gate." Amen.

Antiphon:

As the Father has sent me, even so I send you.

Readings:

"You brought us into the net; You laid affliction on our backs. . . . We went through fire and through water; But you brought us out to rich fulfillment. I will go into Your house with burnt offerings; I will pay you my vows, Which my lips have uttered, and my mouth has spoken when I was in trouble. . . . Come and hear, all you who fear God, And I will declare what He has done for my soul." *Psalm 66:11–16 (NKJV)*

"Therefore says the Lord God of hosts, 'Because you speak this word, behold, I will make my words in your mouth fire, and this people wood, and it shall devour them.'" *Jer. 5:14 (KJV)*

"These are they who have come out of the great tribulation; they have washed their robes and made them white in the blood of the Lamb." *Rev. 7:14 (RSV)*

APRIL 30 Marie of the Incarnation (Marie Guyart Martin)

Marie of the Incarnation, a valiant woman of courage and fortitude, was a missionary to Canada in 1672. In addition, her varied vocations included wife, mother, religious, and foundress. Born in France in 1599, one of seven children in a middle-class family of bakers, Marie Guyart had a dream of Christ beckoning her at age seven, but she did not understand for many years that this portended her mystical marriage to him. She married at age seventeen, had a son, and was widowed by age nineteen. She supported her son by managing a delivery business and doing embroidery. During this time, she was given the mystical insight that the divine Word was, truly, her soul's spouse. At age thirty-one, she entered the Ursulines, and commanded by another dream, she left to evangelize Native Americans in Canada, in unbearable conditions. Marie learned four Indian languages and wrote dictionaries for each. She was a profound mystic who, nonetheless, was practical enough to be Superior of the Canadian Ursulines and to document colonial life in her new environment through more than twelve thousand letters. She never lost contact with her son, who became a priest. They corresponded for many years, and after her death, he became her biographer. Marie is patron of the Canadian Ursulines, and she was made Blessed in 1980.

Intercessory Prayer:

Oh, Blessed Marie, in your spirit of unconditional trust and surrender, you left the bounds of the known to seek service to God in a foreign land. Through your many hardships, your constant prayer was, "In thee, O Lord, I put my trust; let me never be confounded." Pray for us that we may respond with a powerful "yes" to Christ's call in our lives. Help us to imitate your deepest desire and expectation: to show the Lord that we want neither joy, nor consolation, nor happiness except in him and as he sees fit. Amen.

Antiphon:

I have other sheep that are not of this fold; I must bring them also.

Readings:

"God you are our Sovereign; you are robed in majesty,
You are girded with strength. The world is made firm; it shall never be moved,
Your throne is established from of old, From all eternity, you are."
    Psalm 93:1–2 (PCB)

"Oh, the depth of the riches of the wisdom and knowledge of God! How unsearchable his judgments, and his paths beyond tracing out! Who has known the mind of the Lord? Or who has been his counselor? Who has ever given to God, that God should repay

him? For from him and through him and to him are all things."
Rom. 11:33–36 (NIV)

"I found the one my heart loves. I held him and would not let him
go." *Song of Songs 3:4 (NIV)*

MAY 1 Isadora

The famous Bishop Palladius, who wrote the *Lausaic History* documenting the lives of the spiritual Desert Fathers and Mothers, wrote Isadora's *vita* around 417. She may well have been the first saint to receive the title Fool for Christ, which became an appellation for nearly forty other Orthodox saints. She lived in Egypt with a community of nuns on the Nile River, part of a much larger community of about seven thousand monastics. She did not, however, wear a traditional habit, but always went about in rags and refused to wear shoes. The Cinderella of the convent, she did not eat with her community, and most of the other nuns shunned her. No one knew of her profound sanctity until a monk across the river had a vision of an angel, who told him that if he wanted to find the person designated as his spiritual mother, he should go to the convent where Isadora dwelled and look for the woman with a crown of rags on her head. Upon his arrival, the nuns there laughed and told the pious monk that Isadora was touched in the head. When he saw her, however, he fell down on his knees and said, "Bless me, holy Mother." His praise of her caused the other nuns to change their constant caustic remarks to her to words of acclaim. Isadora found this to be unfitting to the vocation she had chosen, and, blessing the nuns, she left the convent to become a wandering mendicant.

Prayer:

Lord Jesus, you are the lover of all. Forgive us for the times we have failed to recognize you in the faces of those whom we think are far removed from you. Throughout your most precious life you always said: come, there is room enough for all of you. Through Blessed Isadora's intercession, may we recognize you in the vagabonds of the world and remember that you live on the street as well as in the sanctuary. Amen.

We will find our glory in the power of the cross.

Readings:

"You will not abandon your people,
You will not forsake your heritage,
For justice will return to the righteous,
And the upright in heart will follow it." *Psalm 94:14–15 (PCB)*

"We are made a spectacle to the world, and to angels, and to men. We are fools for Christ's sake; but you are wise in Christ. We are weak, but you are strong; you are held in honor, but we in disrepute. To the present hour, we hunger and thirst, we are ill-clad and buffeted and homeless. . . . When reviled, we bless; when persecuted, we endure." *1 Cor. 4:9–12 (RSV)*

"[He] said to his servant, 'Go out quickly into the streets and lanes of the city, and bring in here *the* poor and *the* maimed and *the* lame and *the* blind.' And the servant said, 'Master, it is done as you commanded, and still there is room.' Then the master said to the servant, 'Go out into the highways and hedges, and compel *them* to come in, that my house may be filled." *Lk. 14:21–24 (NKJV)*

MAY 2 Angela of the Cross

Angela of the Cross was born of a destitute family in 1846 in Seville, Spain. From early youth she wanted to join the Carmelites, but her lack of funds and poor health did not permit it. Because she had great devotion to the crucified Christ, she found a spiritual director, nonetheless. Together they worked out a plan whereby she lived at home, practiced a Rule, did charitable works, and yearly renewed her vows. Others joined her, and the Congregation of the Cross was born. It is a tertiary order that lives off of alms, protecting the homeless and sick around them. Angela was beatified in 1982 in the place of her birth.

Intercessory Prayer:

Dear holy Angela, you were fervent in your desire to follow a life completely devoted to Christ, despite all obstacles. Intercede for us that we may place others before ourselves, advancing the cause of Christ who said, "What you do to the least of my brethren, you do to Me." You who went out to meet Christ with your lamp lit brightly, pray for us that we may consecrate our daily lives to our Lord with utmost vigilance. Amen.

Antiphon:

With courageous heart she followed the lamb, who was crucified for love of us.

Readings:

"Bless the Lord, O my soul, all that is within me bless his holy Name.

Bless the Lord, O my soul, and forget not all his benefits.

Who forgives all your iniquities; who heals all your diseases

Who redeems your life from destruction; who crowns you with loving-kindness and tender mercies." *Psalm 103:14 (KJV)*

"Let us give thanks to God for having made us worthy to share the inheritance of the saints in light. God has delivered us from the power of darkness and transferred us into the kingdom of God's beloved Son, Jesus, in whom we have redemption; the forgiveness of our sins." *Col. 1:12–14 (PCB)*

"But the wise took oil in their vessels with their lamps. While the bridegroom tarried, they all slumbered and slept. And at midnight, there was a cry made, 'Behold the bridegroom comes, go out to meet him.' Then all those virgins arose, and trimmed their lamps." *Mt. 25:4–13 (KJV)*

MAY 3 Cunegund

St. Cunegund was born into royalty, the daughter of Siegfried and Hedwig in Luxembourg. She married Duke Henry of Bavaria, who was also later canonized as a saint. Cunegund's career as an empress was a difficult one. She was accused of adultery and slander, which caused her husband to doubt her. She voluntarily walked through red-hot coals barefoot to prove her innocence. Henry repented, and they lived the rest of their lives together promoting good works. After Henry's death, and partly because she had given away nearly all her own personal wealth to the bishops and to found monasteries, Cunegund retired to a life of holy poverty and took the veil of sisterhood. She then refused to be acknowledged as a former queen and performed the most menial of tasks in the monastery. She spent the last fifteen years of her life in quiet prayer. Perceiving that her death was near, she commanded that her burial clothes be her simple habit instead of the gold befitting a queen. After her death, her body was laid beside her husband's at Bamberg. She was canonized in 1200. Cunegund is a patron of philanthropists.

Prayer:

Holy God and lover of simplicity, Cunegund teaches us that detachment of mind is the surest path to your heart, and the world's power should always be subordinate to the power found in prayer and dedication to you. Through Cunegund's intercession, bless all of this world's rulers, that they may seek first your council and not their own profit. Help us to remain steadfast in trials that affect our good name, holding ever to the gift that your regard for us is all that really matters. Amen.

Antiphon:

You set us free, O God, from the chains that bind us.

Readings:

"Did You not . . . clothe me with skin and flesh, and knit me together with bones and sinews? You have granted me life and favor, And Your care has preserved my spirit." *Job 10:11–12 (NIV)*

"They said to him, Master, this woman was taken in adultery, in the very act. Now Moses in the law commanded us, that such should be stoned, but what do you say? This they said, tempting him, that they might have to accuse him. But Jesus stooped down, and with his finger wrote on the ground, as though he heard them not. So when they continued asking him, he lifted himself up, and said to them, 'He that is without sin among you, let him cast the first stone at her.'" *Jn. 8:4–7 (KJV)*

"I have come as a light into the world, that whoever believes in me shall not abide in darkness." *Jn. 12:46 (KJV)*

MAY 4 Pelagia of Tarsus

Sometimes confused with Pelagia the harlot and transvestite monk (see Daily Readings, October 8, Pelagia), this Pelagia was born of pagan parents in Tarsus during the era of the persecutor Diocletian. The story goes that the Emperor's son fell in love with Pelagia and desired her in marriage, but she refused, claiming that she was betrothed to Christ. She was baptized, which infuriated her mother, who betrayed her to Emperor Diocletian. Pelagia was calm in her refusal to abide by her family's wishes, and she was sent for trial. Unfaltering in her new faith, she was condemned to be burned in a metal box, where she melted like wax and was borne heavenward by her beloved. The Bishop (Linus) who converted her sought and found her remaining bones, and a church was later erected in her honor. Pelagia of Tarsus is celebrated in the old Byzantine calendar on May 4 and in the new calendar on May 17.

Prayer:

O sweet Jesus, lover of all hearts devoted to you, Pelagia was inflamed with love for you and became a Christian in her soul before she was even baptized. She abandoned the ignorance of philosophy for the newfound knowledge of a faith that is rooted in trust in you. Through Pelagia's intercession, grant grace to all modern martyrs who suffer for their belief. Grant us steadfastness in our struggles and deliver us in the time of trial. May we always trust in you, the rock of our salvation. Amen.

Antiphon:

The reign of God is at hand.

Readings:

"No enemy will subject [him] to tribute. [or] oppress him. I will crush his foes before him and strike down his adversaries. My faithful love will be with him. . . . He will call out to me . . . My God, the rock, my Savior." *Psalm 89:22–24, 26 (NIV)*

"With her two daughters-in-law she left the place where she had been living and set out on the road that would take them back to the land of Judah. Then Naomi said to her two daughters-in-law, 'Go back, each of you, to your mother's home.' . . . But Ruth replied, 'Don't urge me to leave you or to turn back from you. Where you go I will go, and where you stay I will stay. Your people will be my people and your God my God.'" *Ruth 1:7, 8, 16 (NIV)*

"Blessed is the one who reads the words of this prophecy, and blessed are those who hear it and take to heart what is written in it, because the time is near." *Rev. 1:3 (NIV)*

MAY 5 Irene of Thessalonika

St. Irene was born Penelope, the daughter of a pagan governor in Persia. From the time an angel of the Lord appeared to her in a dream at a young age, she seemed destined to do great deeds for the cause of spreading Christianity. St. Timothy, St. Paul's apostle, baptized her, which caused her pagan father to demand her execution. She was miraculously spared, and her father was mortally wounded instead. Irene prayed over him and he was healed, and he converted to Christianity. Various pagan kings subjected Irene to many unbelievable tortures, including attempts to drown her and saw her in half. Tradition imparts to us that she was spared from death each time by angels, and these miraculous occurrences caused thousands to convert to Christianity. Finally, she lay down in a grave and ordered her gravestone to be sealed. Four days later the grave was opened, and she was not there. The belief is that she was glorified by God and raised straightaway into heaven. Because she was such a great preacher, in the East Irene is given the title Equal to the Apostles.

Prayer:

> *Dear Lord, you gave us St. Irene as a living example of your power over evil. Through countless tortures she survived by your good graces and designs. Her ability to miraculously survive caused thousands to convert to the faith. Allow us to discern and follow your will in our lives so that we can serve you by also bringing others to know and love you. Like good St. Irene, let us feel the powerful presence of our heavenly companion, our guardian angel, each day of our lives on this earthly journey. Amen.*

Antiphon:

I send an angel before you.

Readings:

"Your angel, O God, is encamped around those who revere you, to deliver them.
Taste and see that God is good!
Happy are they who take refuge in you.
May all the saints revere you, O God.
Those who revere you have no want!
Young lions suffer want and hunger;
But those who seek you lack no blessing." *Psalm 34:7–10 (PCB)*

"And on my servants and on my handmaidens, I will pour out in those days my Spirit, and they shall prophesy. And I will show wonders in heaven above, and signs in the earth beneath." *Acts 2:18–19 (KJV)*

"Behold, I send an Angel before you, to keep you in the way, and to bring you into the place which I have prepared." *Ex. 23:20 (KJV)*

MAY 6 Margaret Cusack

Margaret Cusack was a nineteenth-century nun and social reformer who began her life in the Anglican Church, became Roman Catholic, and then returned to the church of her roots before she died. Inspired by the Oxford movement to leave an Anglican order of nuns, she initially joined the Poor Clares and became known as Sr. Frances Clare. Moved by the terrible poverty in Ireland, the land of her birth, she was active in land reform and famine relief. Sr. Frances was a prolific writer, authoring more than three dozen books on women's rights, education for women and the oppressed, public health, histories of Ireland, and biographies of the saints. Known as the "Mad Nun from Kenmore," she became a symbol for liberation and justice wherever her work found her. She established her own order, known as the Sisters of St. Joseph of Peace, in 1884, and she started *St. Joseph's Messenger,* a newsletter still in print today. Her fledgling congregation moved to New York and New Jersey and began organizing houses and orphanages to help immigrant Irish women and children. Her radical approach to reform found disapproval with several U.S. archbishops, and, to preserve her order, she left it and returned to the Church of England. Her educational theories, innovative for her day, are widely practiced now. A small sect, the Moorish Orthodox Church, has canonized her, and made May 6, the day of her birth, her feast day. The Carmelites of Indianapolis celebrate Margaret in their translation of the Breviary (*People's Companion to the Breviary*) on June 5, the day of her death.

Prayer:

> *Almighty God and liberator, Sr. Frances Clare fought fiercely for women's and children's fundamental rights and dedicated her life to reforms based on education for the oppressed. She felt led by your Spirit to draw together people of divergent faiths into a new vision of unity, based on the conviction that peace must be grounded in justice for all. Help her order, the Sisters of St. Joseph of Peace, to continue to carry her mission into the world. Comfort those who have been wrongfully censured, and whose only hope resides in you. Bless all those who work to bring the gospel message of freedom to those in destitute circumstances, in the name of Jesus, the way, the truth, and the life. Amen.*

Antiphon:

He has cast down the mighty from their thrones and lifted up the lowly.

Readings:

"For the work of the Lord is upright, and all his work is done in faithfulness.
He loves righteousness and justice,
The earth is full of the steadfast love of the Lord." *Psalm 33:4–5 (RSV)*

Until the Spirit is poured upon us from on high, And the wilderness becomes a fruitful field, And the fruitful field is counted as a forest. Then justice will dwell in the wilderness, And righteousness remain in the fruitful field. The work of righteousness will be peace, And the effect of righteousness, quietness and assurance forever." *Isa. 32:15–17 (NKJV)*

MAY 7 Rose Venerini

Born the daughter of a physician in Viterbo, Italy, Rose Venerini was a lively young woman. Happily engaged, she lost her fiancé before they were married. She initially took this as a sign to enter the convent, but this was not to be her vocation, as her father died shortly afterward and she returned home to care for her mother. Uncertain about her calling, Rose prayed fervently and soon organized a small prayer group in her home with other women. Through her prayer and spiritual direction, she eventually became convinced that the Lord was calling her to a teaching vocation in her city, where general education was not available to girls. In 1685, the Bishop of Viterbo, impressed by her organizational skills and the flourishing school she had started, established a diocesan teaching order, which today is known as the Venerini Sisters. Lucia Filippini (see Daily Readings, May 10, Solange and Lucia Filippini) was Rose's friend and an early coworker. Rose went on to found schools in many parts of Italy, and Cardinal Marcantonio Barbarigo eventually placed her in his diocese to oversee the training and administration of his faculty there. Although she met with much opposition, Rose was undaunted in carrying out the tasks set before her. The Venerini Sisters continue to work with Italian immigrants in the United States. Rose was beatified in 1952.

Prayer:

Almighty God, your divine providence has always placed women at the cradle of Christian learning, and in your grace you numbered Blessed Rose as a great teacher in the land where she labored. She called on you repeatedly to discover her true work in the world, and you revealed it as you poured graces upon her in her mission. Inspire us to listen to your voice when our best-laid plans dissolve and we are pointed to a different path. Help us to remember that we can serve you best in the situation wherein we find ourselves. Amen.

Antiphon:

May the grace and strength of our Lord Jesus Christ be with you and keep you blameless till he comes.

Readings:

"To perceive the words of understanding
To receive the instruction of wisdom, justice and judgment, and
    equity
O hear . . . your father's instruction; and reject not your mother's
    teaching." *Prov. 1:3, 8 (KJV)*

"Now to each one the manifestation of the Spirit is given for the
common good. To one there is given through the Spirit the message of wisdom, to another the message of knowledge by means
of the same Spirit, to another faith by the same Spirit, to another
gifts of healing by that one Spirit." *1 Cor. 12:7–9 (NIV)*

MAY 8 Julian of Norwich

We know little about Julian of Norwich except what comes
from her own pen. In her writings, she reveals that she experienced a life-altering series of visions as she lay deathly ill in
1373, when she was thirty years old. At the time, she was living as an
anchoress in Norwich. She was literate, and she knew the Bible well,
along with the spiritual classics of her era. From behind her curtain,
she counseled those seeking spiritual direction. She lived during the
period of the Plague, which was widespread and devastating, and
which caused her to meditate considerably on the reasons for human
suffering. After her visions, or "showings," she documented her conversations with Christ, who answered her questions about evil, suffering, salvation, and God's love. One of her central realizations was
that Christ experienced no human comfort in the midst of his painful
death—he was reduced to nothing and perhaps even felt abandoned
by God. She was led to understand Jesus as "mother." Christ's birthing
body was a result of the wound in his side. For Julian, the blood and
water flowing from Christ's side was a sign of his endlessly nurturing
love. She continued to reflect upon and make meaning of her near-
death visionary experience for the rest of her life. Her message has
great appeal to women today, who continue to find in her work a
deep mystical love for, and a boundless faith in, the goodness of
humanity.

Prayer:

Beloved Lord Jesus, Julian often called you mother, who suckles us with the food of life. From her, we learn how central faithfulness and love are to healing and to spiritual growth. Help us to face our pain honestly, as she did, and remind us, as you reminded her, that "all manner of things will be well." As we run into your open heart, may we never idle in the fears that separate us from you. Amen.

Antiphon:

I will trust and not be afraid, for God is my strength and my song.

Readings:

"There is no want to those who fear Him . . . those who seek the LORD shall not lack any good thing." *Psalm 34:9–10 (NKJV)*

"Blessed is the [one] who trusts in the LORD, And whose hope is the LORD. For [he] shall be like a tree planted by the waters, Which spreads out its roots by the river, And will not fear when heat comes; But its leaf will be green, And will not be anxious in the year of drought, Nor . . . cease from yielding fruit." *Jer 17:7–8 (NKJV)*

"Which of you, if his son asks for bread, will give him a stone? Or if he asks for a fish, will give him a snake? If you, then, though you are evil, know how to give good gifts to your children, how much more will your Father in heaven give good gifts to those who ask him!" *Mt. 7:9–11 (NIV)*

MAY 9 Theresa of Jesus Gerhardinger

Caroline Gerhardinger was born into a working-class family in Germany in 1797. In early adulthood she became convinced that family life would only improve if women were better educated. The Spirit led her to found the School Sisters of Notre Dame, where she took the name Theresa of Jesus in 1833. She struggled with church hierarchy for many years in her attempts to begin a new congregation. Perhaps reflecting on this difficult period of her life, she once wrote, "One Ave Maria is a thousand times better than talking politics." She was the first woman in the Roman

Catholic Church to lead a religious order without a male director's assistance. When her Rule was finally approved, it spread quickly. Mother Theresa of Jesus was particularly devoted to Mary and reflected much on Mary's role in salvation history, often referring to her as the mediatrix of divine graces. Theresa of Jesus died on May 9, 1877, and was beatified in 1985.

Intercessory Prayer:

Blessed Theresa of Jesus, your call was difficult, but you endured and became a witness of courage and a beacon of hope for the many women in your life. You once wrote that all God's works proceed slowly and in pain, but afterward, "their roots are sturdier and their flowering the lovelier." Pray for us when we are impatient for our spiritual gardens to grow, so that we may bring forth good fruit. Intercede for all women who want to imitate your vision of educating other women, and help us to find creative ways to dialogue with all who cross our path. Pray to the Mother of God for us. Amen.

Antiphon:

Make every effort to supplement your faith with virtue, and virtue with knowledge.

Readings:

"He established them forever; he gave them a duty which shall not pass away." *Psalm 148:6 (NAB)*

"Let them praise the name of the LORD, for he commanded and they were created. He set them in place for ever and ever; he gave a decree that will never pass away." *Psalm 146:5–6 (NIV)*

"Others, like seed sown on good soil, hear the word, accept it, and produce a crop—thirty, sixty or even a hundred times what was sown." *Mk. 4:20 (NIV)*

"So do not throw away your confidence; it will be richly rewarded. You need to persevere so that when you have done the will of God, you will receive what he has promised. . . . We are not of those who shrink back and are destroyed, but of those who believe and are saved." *Heb. 10:35–36, 39 (NIV)*

MAY 10 Solange and Lucia Filippini

Today we celebrate two little-known saints: St. Solange, who lived in the ninth century, and St. Lucia Filippini, who lived in the 1700s. Aside from sharing the same feast day, these two women have very little in common, though both lived amazing lives of total dedication to God. Solange was a shepherd girl who had vowed her virginity to Christ. Legend says that a star over her head accompanied the devout young woman when she was deep in prayer. When the local count's son made advances toward her, she refused him and he beheaded her on the spot. Legend further states that she miraculously carried her head into the nearest church before expiring! A cemetery at the Church of St. Martin-du-Cros had an altar built in her honor.

The life of St. Lucia is a little less dramatic, but one demonstrating exemplary service in answering Christ's call to catechize young, poor girls in the Catholic faith. Pope Clement IX asked her to begin an order of religious educators known as Maestre Pie Filippini. There are currently nearly 150 schools and educational centers worldwide established through her efforts. She suffered a long bout of painful cancer before dying on the date she had predicted in the year 1732. Lucia's incorrupt body remains under an altar in the Cathedral of Montefiascone.

Prayer:

Dear Lord, you have given us countless examples of love and service through so many of your chosen saints through the centuries. We uphold the courage and martyrdom of St. Solange and all who suffer for the sake of virtue. We wish to emulate St. Lucia Filippini's strength and stamina in striving to catechize a world that does not know you. May St. Solange and St. Lucia Filippini be sources of our inspiration today. Amen.

Antiphon:

With my mouth I will make known thy faithfulness to all generations.

Readings:

"I love the Lord because he has heard my voice and my supplication.

He has inclined his ear to me; therefore I will call upon him as long
as I live.
The sorrows of death encompassed me; and the pains of hell got
hold of me,
I found trouble and sorrow. Then I called upon the name of the
Lord,
O Lord I beseech you, deliver my soul.
Gracious is the Lord, and righteous; yes, our God is merciful."
Psalm 116:1–5 (KJV)

"I will feed my flock, and I will cause them to lie down, says the
Lord God. I will seek that which was lost, and bring again that
which was driven away, and will bind up that which was broken,
and will strengthen that which was sick." Ez. 35:15–16 (KJV)

MAY 11 Rictrude

Rictrude was born to a distinguished Gascon family in 612. Gascony was a turbulent area in the Pryenees that never fully fell under Frankish rule. Rictrude fell in love and married a Frankish nobleman, St. Adalbald of Ostrevant. Many in her family were opposed to the Frankish intrusion into Gascony, and as a result, opposed her marriage. Rictrude and Adalbald had four children, all of whom became saints: Maurontius, Eusebia, Clotsindis, and Adalsindis. After sixteen years of marriage, relatives of Rictrude's who were still displeased with her marriage to a Frank had Adalbald killed. Rictrude refused to remarry, disposed of all her worldly goods, and entered the Benedectine monastery at Marchiennes in Flanders, Belgium, which she and Adalbald had built. Her daughters, Adalsindis and Clotsindis, joined her, also choosing to dedicate their lives to Christ. Adalsindis died there while still in her childhood. Rictrude, now abbess of the monastery, continued her duties while mourning her daughter's death in the privacy of her cell. Her remaining son, Maurontius, became a priest and later was made an abbot. Rictrude lived into her seventies and was abbess at Marchiennes for forty years. Her daughter, Clotsendis, became abbess after Rictrude's death.

Prayer:

O Holy Spirit and Comforter, you sustained holy Rictrude during all her trials and afflictions; and when all opposed and deserted her, you upheld her with your merciful graces. Giving all back to you, including her children, she was tried in the refiner's fire and found worthy to enter your communion of saints. Through Rictrude's intercession, bless all those who suffer family discord and help us to each follow the path of perfection shown to us in our Lord, Jesus Christ. Amen.

Antiphon:

The one who abides in me will bear much fruit.

Readings:

"To you I lift up my eyes, you who are enthroned in the heavens! Behold like the eyes of servants look to the hand of their master, Like the eyes of the maid look to the hand of her mistress, So our eyes look to you, O God, till you have mercy on us." *Psalm 123:1–3 (PCB)*

"I will ransom them from the power of the grave; I will redeem them from death: O death, I will be your plague; O grave, I will be your destruction." *Hos. 13:14 (KJV)*

"Again he asked, What shall I compare the kingdom of God to? It is like yeast that a woman took and mixed into a large amount of flour until it worked all through the dough.'" *Lk. 13:20–21 (NIV)*

MAY 12 Imelda Lambertini

Imelda Lambertini came from a prominent family in Bologna. From an early age, she was recognized as an extremely devout and pious child. At age nine, she entered a Dominican convent, where a number of extraordinary experiences occurred. She had visions of St. Agnes of Rome, and the other nuns recognized her for her sanctity. Imelda's greatest desire was to receive Jesus in the Eucharist, but the required age at the time was twelve, so she was not yet able to fulfill this ardent wish. When she was eleven years old, on the feast day of the Ascension, a bright light enveloped her and a host miraculously appeared in the air and hovered over her.

The priest took this as a sign that she should be allowed to receive Holy Communion and promptly administered the Eucharistic host to her. She instantly fell into ecstasy and died. Her body remains miraculously incorrupt to this day in the Church of San Sigismondo near the University of Bologna. Imelda is the patron of first communicants.

Intercessory Prayer:

O dear Blessed Imelda, you wanted nothing more in life than to receive Jesus in Holy Communion. When this ardent desire was fulfilled, you died of pure joy. Inspire us with a like spirit of desire to love and receive our Blessed Lord in the most holy Eucharist whenever we can. May we imitate your childlike confidence in our Eucharistic Lord and strive to make him known, loved, and adored by all. Amen.

Antiphon:

Anyone who receives you, receives me, and anyone who receives me receives the one who sent me.

Readings:

"Blessed are they whose way is blameless, who follow your law, O God!
Blessed are they who do your will, who seek you with all their hearts.
Who never do anything wrong, But walk in your ways." *Psalm 119:1–4, 9 (PCB)*

Behold, you *are* fair, my love! Behold, you *are* fair! You *have* dove's eyes behind your veil. Your hair *is* like a flock of goats, Going down from Mount Gilead." *Song of Songs 4:1 (NKJV)*

"I sought you and you answered me, and delivered me from all my fears." *Psalm 34:4 (PCB)*

"So will it be with the resurrection of the dead. The body that is sown is perishable, it is raised imperishable . . . it is sown a natural body, it is raised a spiritual body." *1 Cor. 15:42, 44 (NIV)*

MAY 13 Our Lady of Fatima

In the year 1916, the Blessed Mother of Jesus appeared to three young shepherd children over the course of six months in a remote village in Fatima, Portugal. She made requests, which involved: making reparation to God for outrages committed against him, reciting the daily Rosary, adoring the Lord in the most Blessed Sacrament, wearing the brown scapular. She also revealed a new devotion—the Five First Saturdays of Reparation, which consists of going to receive the holy Eucharist on the first Saturday for five months. Mary promised that if the world would be consecrated to her Immaculate Heart, a period of peace would result for the entire world. During her last apparition, she also revealed an astonishing miracle for the thousands who witnessed it: the Miracle of the Spinning Sun. Two of the three saintly visionaries, Jacinta and Francisco Marto, died soon after the apparitions ceased, and they have since been canonized. The third visionary, Sr. Lucia, became a cloistered nun, and she continued to spread the messages of Our Lady of Fatima until her death in 2006.

Intercessory Prayer:

Dear Blessed Mother of Fatima, Our Lady of Mt. Carmel, please enliven our spirits to live the messages you revealed to the world nearly a century ago. Remind us to devote ourselves to the holy Eucharist, as we strive to live the message of Fatima today and to pass this message onto our children. May we pray to God, with the angel of Fatima, "I offer you the most precious body and blood, soul and divinity of our Lord Jesus Christ, present in all the tabernacles of the world, in reparation for all the outrages, sacrileges, and indifferences by which he is offended. By the infinite merits of his most Sacred Heart and through the intercession of the Immaculate Heart of Mary, I pray for the conversion of poor sinners." Amen.

Antiphon:

Depart from evil, and do good; seek peace, and pursue it.

Readings:

"O send her out of thy holy heavens, and from the throne of thy glory, that being present she may labour with me, that I may know what is pleasing unto thee. For she knows and understands all things, and she shall lead me soberly in my doings, and preserve me in her power." Wis. 9:10–12 (RSV)

"A great and wondrous sign appeared in heaven: a woman clothed with the sun, with the moon under her feet and a crown of twelve stars on her head. . . . Then I heard a loud voice in heaven say: 'Now have come the salvation and the power and the kingdom of our God, and the authority of his Christ.'" Rev. 12:1, 10 (NIV)

"I am the living bread which came down from heaven; if any one eats of this bread, he will live forever; and the bread which I shall give for the life of the world is my flesh. . . . For my flesh is food indeed, and my blood is drink indeed. He who eats my flesh and drinks my blood abides in me, and I in him." Jn. 6:51, 54–56 (RSV)

MAY 14 Maria Mazzarello

Maria Mazzarello was born in 1837 of deeply religious parents, the oldest of ten children. Her family worked the fields for a living, and they bonded tightly through their daily work and prayer life together. Their house was a shelter for the sick, and Maria devoted all her spare moments to this ministry. While still in her youth, she was recognized as an excellent teacher at her local parish where she gave catechism classes. At age twenty-three she nearly lost her life to typhus, and although she recovered, she never regained her former strength. To bring in extra money for her family's growing ministry, Maria started a tailor trade, and she began teaching older children in her community how to sew. She eventually opened a girls' boarding school, which supported itself through sewing. Under John Bosco's spiritual direction, she cofounded the Daughters of Mary Auxiliary. She became the first Salesian sister and the growing congregation's superior. In 1877 she traveled to France to open more schools and homes for poor children. By the time of her death in 1881, Maria had opened twenty-six houses in Italy and France, and she left 166 nuns to care for them.

Prayer:

Gracious Lord and lover of the needy, Maria Mazzarello responded to the call in your Beatitudes early in her childhood, and she spent her lifetime devoted to your service. Through Maria's intercession, who was able to hear your still small voice above the roar of the world, teach us to listen in the depths of our hearts for the sound of your call to serve needy women in our own circle of influence. Help us to remember that strong, self-supporting women make a better, safer world. Bless all who seek to make their work their service. Amen.

Antiphon:

Save us, O God, by your name; in your might, defend our cause.

Readings:

"Give justice to your Anointed, O God, and righteousness to those Chosen!
That your people may be judged in righteousness, and your poor with justice.
Let the mountains bring forth peace for the people, and the hills, justice.
May your Anointed defend the cause of the poor, give deliverance to the needy, and punish the oppressor! May your Anointed endure like the sun, and as long as the moon,
Through all ages, like rain that falls on the mown grass, like showers that water the earth.
In that day justice shall flourish, and peace till the moon be no more!" *Psalm 72:1–11 (PCB)*

"She makes linen garments and sells them, and supplies the merchants with sashes. She is clothed with strength and dignity; she can laugh at the days to come. She speaks with wisdom, and faithful instruction is on her tongue. She watches over the affairs of her household and does not eat the bread of idleness. Her children arise and call her blessed." *Prov. 31:24–28 (NIV)*

"Brethren, I do not count myself to have apprehended; but one thing *I do,* forgetting those things which are behind and reaching forward to those things which are ahead." *Phil. 3:13 (NKJV)*

MAY 15 Dymphna

Roman Catholic tradition relates the story of St. Dymphna as having occurred around the year 620, although the earliest accounts of formal veneration of this saint date to the thirteenth century. St. Dymphna was the daughter of a pagan Irish leader named Damon. When Dymphna's mother died, her father was driven insane with grief. Because the beautiful, young Dymphna so closely resembled her mother, Damon desired to take her as his wife. A saintly priest named St. Gerebernus helped her flee from her father and escape to Belgium. Her crazed father scoured the countryside and finally discovered where Dymphna and St. Gerebernus were hiding. In a fit of rage, he beheaded both of them. Dymphna's body was buried in a church nearby in Gheel, Belgium, and this holy ground of burial soon became known for miraculous cures and healings, especially for those suffering from mental problems and insanity. Dymphna has become a very popular Irish saint, and her patronage has expanded to include victims of incest and those suffering from depression and Alzheimer's disease.

Intercessory Prayer:

Dear St. Dymphna, patroness of those who suffer from mental anxieties of all sorts, please intercede for all those who suffer from depression, Alzheimer's disease, neurological disorders, and nervous disorders of all types. Bring peace and comfort to those who suffer and to their families. Protect us in all anxious moments with the knowledge that our heavenly Father will give us grace through Christ Jesus to handle all the day's worries. Amen.

Antiphon:

Have no anxiety about anything, but in everything let your requests be made known to God.

Readings:

"When anxiety was great within me, your consolation brought joy to my soul. Can a corrupt throne be allied with you—one that brings on misery by its decrees? They band together against the righteous and condemn the innocent to death. But the LORD has become my fortress, and my God the rock in whom I take refuge." *Psalm 94:19–22 (NIV)*

"Anxiety in the heart . . . causes depression, But a good word makes it glad." *Prov. 12:25 (NKJV)*

"But everyone that has forsaken houses or brethren, or sisters, or father, or mother, or wife, or children, or lands, for my Name's sake, shall receive a hundredfold, and shall inherit everlasting life." *Mt. 19:29 (KJV)*

MAY 16 Heloise

Heloise was never made a saint. After the tragedy of her affair with the great religious philosopher, Abelard, he continued to gain renown, while Heloise slipped into obscurity. Born in 1100 and raised by her uncle Fulbert, Heloise was seventeen when Abelard (who had studied under Anslem and was already a famous figure himself) was hired as her tutor. Abelard was twenty years her senior and, taken by her intelligence and beauty, he seduced her. She bore a son from the union, which was the scandal of Paris. Although Abelard secretly married her, when Fulbert discovered what had happened, he had Abelard forcibly castrated late one night. Following his agony and humiliation, Abelard placed Heloise in a convent and retired to a monastery, where he wrote many famous treatises. They did not see each other for ten years. Heloise wrote also, and rising above the scandal, eventually she became an abbess who was revered for her wisdom and charity. The couple continued to correspond by letter for many years, and through her letters we learn about the monastic Rule she developed, which was innovative for her day. We also learn much about Heloise herself, who, although traumatized by the events of her youth, demonstrates depth of character and brilliance as a scholar as she matured. It is unfortunate that the period managed to preserve Abelard's work, but so little of Heloise's. When she died, Heloise was buried next to her husband at the cloister, Benedictine House of the Paraclete, which Abelard had founded.

Prayer:

Dear Holy Spirit of God, you inspire those who feel called to express their souls through speaking and writing. As her deepest

*inspiration and comforter, only you knew the dreams and struggles
of Heloise, who sought to understand her trauma much of her life,
and whose soul poured out through her writing. Bless all women
who feel that part of their purpose is to respond to your inner call
to write. Direct us in your truth and empower our words to glorify
you as they find their way to souls who resonate to their love and
longing. Amen.*

Antiphon:

Let the words of my mouth and the meditation of my heart
be acceptable in your sight, O God.

Readings:

"Your law, O God, is perfect, reviving the soul. Your testimony is
to be trusted, making the simple wise. . . . God's ordinances are
true, and all of them just. More to be desired are they than gold,
more than the purest gold, and sweeter are they than honey. . . .
Let the words of my mouth, the thoughts of my heart, be acceptable in your sight, O God, my rock and my redeemer." *Psalm
19:8–14 (PCB)*

"If only you were to me like a brother, who was nursed at my
mother's breasts! Then, if I found you outside, I would kiss you,
and no one would despise me." *Song of Songs 8:1 (NIV)*

"If any one of you is without sin, let him be the first to throw a
stone." *John 8:7 (NIV)*

MAY 17 Josephina Bakhita

Josephina Bakhita was the first person from the Sudan to
be beatified by the Roman Catholic Church, an honor
given to her by Pope John Paul II in 1992. Like many children growing up in the turbulent Sudan region, she was sold into
slavery as a child. Through the years, she belonged to various owners.
Finally an Italian family took Josephine to Italy. It was there she
gained her freedom, was educated in the Catholic faith, and eventually was baptized. She recalled later that God's calling had always
been within her heart, but she fully understood it only at the moment
of her baptism. She joined the Sisters of Charity and dedicated herself
to educating the poor and to working in hospitals. For fifty years, she

served the poorest of the poor and became known for her tremendous sanctity. She recorded her fascinating life story as a child slave in her personal memoirs, which were published in 1930. She died in 1947, with the name of the Blessed Virgin Mary on her lips. Pope John Paul II returned Blessed Josephina's relics to Africa during a pilgrimage in 1993.

Intercessory Prayer:

Dear Blessed Josephina, you lived your life in the same example as Mother Teresa, serving Christ by serving the poorest of the poor. You lived out your interior life in a modest manner by fulfilling the humblest of daily duties with charity. Help us to emulate your way of life by striving to fulfill every daily chore, no matter how mundane, with charity and faith, that we may achieve our sanctity through our own destiny. May our path to heaven be paved by activities performed well and always for the love of Christ. Amen.

Antiphon:

But the aim of our charge is love that issues from a pure heart and a good conscience.

Readings:

"I will give you thanks, for you answered me; you have become my salvation. The stone the builders rejected has become the capstone; the LORD has done this, and it is marvelous in our eyes." *Psalm 118:21–23 (NIV)*

"If there is among you a poor [man] of your brethren, within any of the gates in your land which the LORD your God is giving you, you shall not harden your heart nor shut your hand . . . but you shall open your hand wide . . . and willingly lend him sufficient for his need, whatever he needs." *Deut. 15:7–8 (NKJV)*

"The spirit of the Lord is upon me, because he has anointed me to preach the gospel to the poor; he has sent me to heal the brokenhearted, to preach deliverance to the captives, and recovering of sight to the blind, to set at liberty them that are bruised." *Lk. 4:18 (RSV)*

MAY 18 Florence Nightingale

Born into aristocracy in England in an era that did not sanction single upper-class women working outside the home, Florence Nightingale had many battles to wage before seeing her vision take form in the world. At seventeen, she heard God speak to her, calling her to a life of service. She determined at that time not to marry. She joined the Anglican Church, but she struggled with its patriarchal notions about women much of her life. When she was thirty, she again heard the Lord tell her, "Give five minutes of every hour to the thought of me," which began her life of mystical contemplation. She was inspired to study nursing with a Lutheran order of deaconesses in a hospital in Germany. When she returned to England she became supervisor of a hospital there, which she completely transformed, mainly by reforming its poor hygiene habits. She was a close colleague with Cardinal Edward Manning, working with the London poor. Florence then organized a group of nurses and Anglican nuns to minister to soldiers in the Crimean War, where far more men were dying of infections than from wounds. She once again thoroughly reformed medical procedures, against much resistance from male doctors, many of whom believed she should be home crocheting. She became known as the "Lady with the Lamp" because she ministered so late at night at the soldiers' bedsides. Her writings include an anthology of the mysticism of the Middle Ages. Florence died on August 13, 1910, and the Lutheran calendar celebrates her feast on that date.

Prayer:

O Holy Spirit of God, you were the sustaining voice for Florence Nightingale's journey. As long as she was alive, she was a witness to your voice and Jesus' compassionate nature. You were the stronghold of her life, reminding her always to return to you. She wrote that the night is given to us to breathe deeply and to pray for the coming day. With every breath we take, may we be reminded to release your Spirit into the world, giving thanks for all things. Amen.

Antiphon:

You bring us springs of water; you wipe away the tears from our eyes.

Readings:

"I will abundantly bless her provision: I will satisfy her poor with bread. . . .
I have ordained a lamp for my anointed." *Psalm 132:15, 17 (KJV)*

"You are my lamp, O LORD; the LORD turns my darkness into light. With your help I can advance against a troop, with my God I can scale a wall. As for God, his way is perfect; the word of the LORD is flawless.
He is a shield for all who take refuge in him." *2 Sam. 22:29–31 (NIV)*

"No one lights a lamp and hides it in a jar or puts it under a bed. Instead, he puts it on a stand, so that those who come in can see the light." *Lk. 8:16 (NIV)*

MAY 19 Monesan of Britain (Monessa)

Monesan, a young British woman of the fifth century, was ardent in her pursuit of God. Born of high status, her parents beat her in an attempt to make her marry. Enlightened by the Holy Spirit, Monesan declared that she would never do so. She had a thirst for knowledge and longed to have the questions that dogged her answered: Who made the sun? What lay beyond the creation? Monesan was convinced that something greater lay behind the physical reality of the world surrounding her. According to her biographer, Muirchu, Monesan's parents relented, and they allowed her to leave Britain and go to Ireland in search of a man named Patrick, who was intimate with God. In 456, at the instant that St. Patrick baptized her, she died in a state of grace. She was buried on the spot where she died. Some twenty years later, Monesan's body was removed to a neighboring oratory where her relics were venerated for many years.

Prayer:

Beloved Holy Spirit and Comforter, you are the answer to every sincere question and the author of the silent voice within each of us who yearns to know the mystery of God and nature. You filled Monesan with a deep desire to still the roar of all other voices and find her truth in the life and deeds of our Lord Jesus. Teach us to listen in the depths of our hearts for the sound of your penetrating love and mercy, and to find daily consolation and strength in the living word he left us. Amen.

Antiphon:

Every good and perfect gift must come from you, God.

Readings:

"You . . . still the noise of the seas, The noise of their waves, and the tumult of the peoples." *Psalm 65:7 (NKJV)*

"Counsel is mine, and sound wisdom: I am understanding; I have strength.
By me kings reign, and princes decree justice.
By me princes rule, and nobles, even all the judges of the earth.
I love them that love me; and those that seek me early shall find me." *Prov. 8:14–17 (KJV)*

"For I gave them the words you gave me and they accepted them. They knew with certainty that I came from you, and they believed that you sent me." *Jn. 17:8 (NIV)*

MAY 20 Antoinette Blackwell

Born to preach, Antoinette Brown Blackwell struggled through many hardships and overcame many obstacles before she could realize her mission. She began her public speaking career when she was nine years old at her local church. After graduating from college, she yearned to study theology but was barred by the faculty at Oberlin College from participating in class discussions. Although she could attend classes, she was not granted a degree. Nonetheless, her faith and her Bible sustained her and she preached whenever and wherever she had the opportunity. Antoinette was active in the abolitionist movement and was an avid suffragette and writer, authoring eight books. In 1853, Antoinette became the first ordained minister of a mainstream congregation in the U.S.—the Congregational Church. She married, raised five daughters, and continued to preach until she was ninety years old. Oberlin College finally awarded Antoinette an honorary degree in theology.

Prayer:

Righteous God, you raised up the holy woman Antoinette to be a Moses in the wilderness, preaching in the desert until she arrived at the land of promise. You fulfilled her mission and her promise to speak your word, and thus opened the door for women everywhere to realize their own voices in serving you. She is a model of perseverance for so many of us. Help us to realize that no season is too late to respond to your deepest calling in our own hearts. Amen.

Antiphon:

The Lord has anointed me to preach good tidings to the afflicted.

Readings:

"I am like a pelican of the wilderness: I am like an owl of the desert.
I watch, and am as a sparrow alone upon the house top.
My enemies reproach me all the day; and they that are mad against me are sworn against me. For I have eaten ashes like bread, and mingled my drink with weeping. . . . But you, O Lord, shall endure forever; and your remembrance to all generations." *Psalm 102:6–8, 12 (KJV)*

"And he was there in the wilderness forty days, tempted by Satan; and was with the wild beasts; and the angels ministered to him. Now after John was put in prison, Jesus came to Galilee, preaching the Gospel of the Kingdom of God." *Mk. 1:13–14 (KJV)*

"How, then, can they call on the one they have not believed in? And how can they believe in the one of whom they have not heard? And how can they hear without someone preaching to them? And how can they preach unless they are sent? As it is written, 'How beautiful are the feet of those who bring good news!'" *Rom. 10:14–15 (NIV)*

MAY 21 Helen and the Holy Cross

In the Eastern calendar, May 21 commemorates St. Helen's discovery of the cross in Jerusalem during the reign of her son, Constantine. According to the story, Helen, whom we know little else about, undertook a voyage to the Holy Land, and in the course of excavating the foundation for Constantine's Basilica of the Holy Sepulchre, she found three crosses that she believed had been at Mt. Calvary. After approaching Patriarch Macarius concerning a method for determining the true cross, she was told to take all three crosses to a sick man to see which would heal him. A miracle occurred with one of the crosses. During the same excavation, Helen also found the inscription that had been fixed to Christ's cross, which she sent to Rome; it was unearthed again in 1492. There is an accompanying legend that, once she found the cross, Helen ordered a large fire to be built on a mountain; seeing it, a fire was lit on the next mountain, and so on, and in this manner the news of the discovery of the True Cross reached the capital, Constantinople. Helen's feast was also celebrated on August 18 in the West, but the Vatican suppressed it in 1969. In the Eastern Church Helen's titles are Empress and Equal to the Apostles.

Prayer:

Christ our true God, by your own free volition you chose to become one of us and suffer death by your elevation on the cross. Through her deep devotion to you, St. Helen was led to find the holy relic of the sacred wood, and she joyfully gave to the world the feast that commemorates your sacrifice. In your power of love, gladden our hearts and strengthen us in every good deed, so your cross may be for us a sign of real peace in the world. Amen.

Antiphon:

By your cross you have redeemed the world.

Readings:

"In the beginning you laid the foundations of the earth, and the heavens are the work of your hands. They will perish, but you remain; they will all wear out like a garment. Like clothing you will change them and they will be discarded. But you remain the same, and your years will never end." *Psalm 102:25–27 (NIV)*

"For the preaching of the cross is to them that perish foolishness; but unto us who are saved it is the power of God." *1 Cor. 1:18 (KJV)*

"And He, bearing His cross, went out to a place called *the Place* of a Skull, which is called in Hebrew, Golgotha, where they crucified Him, and two others with Him, one on either side, and Jesus in the center. Now Pilate wrote a title and put *it* on the cross. And the writing was: JESUS OF NAZARETH, THE KING OF THE JEWS." *Jn. 19:17–22 (NKJV)*

WomenSaints

Rita of Cascia

Rita Lotti was born in 1381 in Italy and was known from an early age for her devout life and prayerful disposition. Despite the fact that she wished to become a nun, her parents arranged a marriage for her, and she accepted this as an offering to God's will. She married Paolo Mancini and had two sons. Paolo was murdered, and her two sons wished nothing more than to extract vengeance on his murderer. Rita prayed that this desire for revenge on the part of her two sons would be removed from them. Soon after, both sons died. After many trials and rejections, Rita was finally accepted into the Augustinian Nuns of Cascia. She had long desired to share in Christ's physical sufferings, and one day as she knelt in prayer, her forehead was pierced with a wound from Jesus' Crown of Thorns. She carried this mysterious stigmatic wound until the day she died. Meanwhile, she devoted herself to the care of other sick nuns in her order. Her body remains incorrupt and is still venerated today in a shrine next to the convent in Cascia, Italy. Rita is the saint of impossible causes.

Intercessory Prayer:

O dear St. Rita, wife, mother, and widow, you experienced many aspects of life. Through your faith and desire to be spiritually united with Jesus, you were led to a path of prayerful suffering. Help us to accept the sufferings of life that the Lord places into our path. You are the Saint of Impossible Causes, and so we place into your patronage all the petitions of our present need, especially those cases that are most hopeless. Let us offer up our daily crosses, no matter how small and insignificant, as an act of reparation and abandonment to God's will. Amen.

Antiphon:

For we, through this severe suffering and endurance, shall have the prize of virtue.

Readings:

"I cry aloud to you, my God, cry aloud that you may hear me. In the day of my trouble I seek you, in the night I stretch out my hand without tiring; my soul refuses to be consoled. I remember you and I moan; I ponder and my spirit faints. You hold my eyelids from closing; I am so troubled, I cannot speak. . . . I converse with my heart in the night, I ponder and search my spirit." *Psalm 77:1–6 (PCB)*

"More than that, we rejoice in our sufferings, knowing that suffering produces endurance, and endurance, virtue, and virtue, hope. And this hope will not leave us disappointed, because the love of God has been poured into our hearts through the Holy Spirit who has been given to us." *Rom. 5:3–5 (NASB)*

"Father, I will that they also, whom thou has given me, be with me where I am; that they may behold my glory, which thou has given me." *Jn. 17:24 (KJV)*

MAY 23 Jane Antide Thouret

Jane (also called Joan or Jeanne) Antide Thouret was born during the tumultuous period of the French Revolution. She lost her mother as a young teenager and helped her father raise her siblings until she joined the Sisters of Charity of St. Vincent de Paul in 1787. Her mission was hospital work, but her order was suppressed in Paris, and she escaped to Switzerland, where she continued to minister to the sick. Still persecuted, Jane managed to open a school and a hospital there in the face of fierce opposition. She called the sisters who worked with her the Daughters of St. Vincent de Paul, and her order was approved in 1819. The Daughters continue to work in hospitals and prisons. Jane died of natural causes in 1828 and was canonized in 1934.

Prayer:

> *Grant, O God, that rejoicing in the feast of Blessed Jane, your holy woman, we may imitate her example and follow her fervent aspirations. With the fruit of her hands she planted a vineyard for you, and it has brought forth rich mercy in the lives of many who lived after her. Through Jane's intercession, may all who minister to the sick be fed by you, the great healer of our souls and bodies. Amen.*

Antiphon:

I will praise the most high for as long as I live.

Readings:

"See how my enemies have increased and how fiercely they hate me! Guard my life and rescue me; let me not be put to shame, for I take refuge in you. May integrity and uprightness protect me, because my hope is in you." *Psalm 25:19–21 (NIV)*

"If you have understanding, hear this; listen to what I say. Can he who hates justice govern? Will you condemn the just and mighty One . . . who shows no partiality . . . and does not favor the rich over the poor, for they are all the work of his hands?" *Job 34:16–19 (NIV)*

"The miracles I do in my Father's name speak for me." *Jn. 10:25 (NIV)*

MAY 24 Joanna the Myrrh Bearer and Judith of Prussia

Today we celebrate the feast day of two wonderful and saintly women who lived centuries apart: Joanna the Myrrh Bearer and St. Judith of Prussia. Joanna is mentioned in Scripture (Luke 8:3) as the wife of Chusa, who was a steward to King Herod Antipas. Joanna was one of a company of holy women who accompanied Jesus and the apostles, providing for them as Jesus performed his public ministry. The Eastern churches have a tradition that Joanna was responsible for giving John the Baptist's head a proper burial. She is also mentioned in Luke 24:10 as one of a company of women who went to Jesus' tomb to anoint his body after the Crucifixion. Thus she is called one of the myrrh bearers.

Jutta (Judith) of Prussia lived in the thirteenth century in central Germany. She was a wife and mother who nurtured her family, teaching them how to live humbly, despite their material wealth. Her husband died on a quest to the Holy Land. Jutta raised her children, and then followed a desire long held within her heart—to live a life of austerity and prayerful intercession for others. She gave away all her material possessions and lived her life as a hermit in a simple hut, where she ministered to others and prayed especially for the conversion of nonbelievers. Witnesses from the village often reported seeing

St. Jutta levitating while in prayer, and the local people believed that angels held her aloft.

Prayer:

Heavenly Father, thank you for the examples of St. Joanna the Myrrh Bearer and St. Judith of Prussia. As holy women who lived a life of charity and service to others, help us to remember that service to our own families and those in our environment can be a path to personal sanctity. May their lives of holiness inspire us, for we are your people and the sheep of your pasture. Amen.

Antiphon:

You shall love God with all your heart, and with all your soul, and with all your mind.

Readings:

"Lord, you have been our dwelling place throughout all generations. Before the mountains were born or you brought forth the earth and the world, from everlasting to everlasting you are God." *Psalm 90:1–3 (NIV)*

"And they remembered his words. And returned from the sepulchre, and told all these things unto the eleven, and to all the rest. It was Mary Magdalene, and Joanna, and Mary, the mother of James, and the other women that were with them. . . ." *Lk. 24:8–10 (KJV)*

"God also testified to it by signs, wonders and various miracles, and gifts of the Holy Spirit distributed according to his will. It is not to angels that he has subjected the world to come, about which we are speaking . . . [for God] made [him] a little lower than the angels, [and] crowned him with glory and honor, and put everything under his feet." *Heb. 2:4–7 (NIV)*

MAY 25 Madeleine Sophie Barat

Called Sophie as a girl, Madeleine Sophie Barat was destined for a good education because her older brother, who was also her godfather, recognized her special gifts when she was only ten. A deacon at the university at Sens, her brother taught her himself until he was forced to flee prosecution during the Reign of Terror under Louis XVI. During the French Revolution, the Society of Jesus was suppressed; in 1800, Sophie helped to open an educational school for girls and a convent dedicated to the Sacred Heart. Father Varin, superior of the reorganized Jesuit Order, appointed her as the abbess of the convent when she was only twenty-three years old. Battling numerous difficulties, including personal illness, she spent the next sixty-three years training novices and traveling extensively to propagate the order and a renewed devotion to the Sacred Heart of Jesus. The Society of the Sacred Heart was approved in 1826. Her daughters were established in twelve countries, including North America. Madeleine died on the feast of the Ascension in 1865.

Intercessory Prayer:

O holy mother, St. Madeleine, your apostolic zeal and devotion to the Heart of Jesus sparked a growing fever in the Church to find renewal through the heart of love. Although devotion was instilled in your daughters, you wrote to them to place duty before devotion, conforming both their will and emotions to God. May your advice to be lovable "with that lovability which is both energetic and thoughtful of others which you will find in the strong and sweet Heart of Jesus" find fertile soil in our minds and hearts also. Amen.

Antiphon:

Where your treasure is, your heart will be also.

Readings:

"Rejoice and be glad with all the heart, O daughter of Jerusalem. The Lord has taken away your judgments and cast out your enemy; . . . you shall not see evil any more." *Zeph. 3:14–15 (KJV)*

"There is no God like you in heaven above or on earth below—you who keep your covenant of love with your servants who continue wholeheartedly in your way." *1 Kgs 8:23 (NIV)*

"And God who knows the heart, bears them witness, giving them the Holy Spirit, even as he did to us." *Acts 15:8 (KJV)*

MAY 26 Mary Magdelene Pazzi

St. Mary Magdelene of Pazzi was born in Italy in 1566. She was especially devoted to the holy Eucharist, and she vowed her life and virginity to Christ at age ten, when she celebrated her First Communion. At age sixteen she became a Discalced Carmelite and took the name of her favorite saint, Mary Magdelene. She was known and loved by all in the convent for her religious fervor and charity, and she held various positions of authority. Mary Magdelene regularly experienced the hallmark of great mystic saints—raptures and ecstasies in prayer. She was also outwardly and visibly attacked and tempted by demonic apparitions on many occasions. Often she would utter words during such ecstasies that were so profound that her sisters would record them. These maxims became known as "The Maxims of Divine Love" and have been quoted through the centuries. After a long and painful illness, which she accepted with an open heart on behalf of sinners, Mary Magdelene died at age forty-one.

Intercessory Prayer:

Dear St. Mary Magdelene de Pazzi, please pray to God for us sinners, and for all people throughout the world. You said that if you had a voice loud enough and strong enough, you would make your voice heard in every part of the world so that all would know and love God. In Jesus' name, we pray especially today for all those who do not know the most holy Trinity, that they will receive the graces necessary for conversion and life everlasting. Amen.

Antiphon:

And whatever you ask in prayer, you will receive, if you have faith.

Readings:

"Though you probe my heart and examine me at night, though you test me, you will find nothing; I have resolved that my mouth will not sin . . . by the word of your lips I have kept myself from the ways of the violent. My steps have held to your paths; my feet have not slipped. I call on you, O God, for you will answer me; give ear to me and hear my prayer. Show the wonder of your great love." *Psalm 17:2–7 (NIV)*

"If you forgive anyone, I also forgive him. And what I have for-given—if there was anything to forgive—I have forgiven in the sight of Christ for your sake." *2 Cor. 2:10 (NIV)*

"Watch and pray, lest you enter into temptation. The spirit truly is ready, but the flesh is weak." *Mk. 14:38 (KJV)*

MAY 27 Melangell (Monacella)

Melangell, a Welsh solitary who later became the abbess of a community of nuns, epitomizes the harmony with nature found in the Celtic tradition. She is said to have had royal an-cestry, born the daughter of an Irish chieftain. At a young age, Melan-gell renounced her royal status to pursue a life of prayer and solitude. She fled Ireland when her parents ordered her to marry and settled in a secluded valley in the little kingdom of Powys in central Wales. In 604, after living there in solitude for fifteen years, Melangell had an encounter with Brochwel Ysgythrog, a prince of Powys. Out hunting one day, Brochwel's hounds were pursuing a hare that escaped into a thicket. Upon entering the thicket, Brochwel discovered Malangell praying. The hare had taken refuge in her garments. Brochwel or-dered the hounds to continue their pursuit of the hare, but they with-drew in the presence of the saint's strength and holiness. Brochwel was intrigued by this and sought to learn who this woman was and how she came to be there. Upon hearing her story and recognizing her dedication to God and a life of prayer, Brochwel honored her by making the valley a sanctuary. A community of nuns gathered around Melangell. They were semi-hermits who lived in huts around a church, nurtured the land, and grew herbs to heal the local people. Melangell is reputed to have lived another thirty-seven years after her encounter with Brochwel, providing a safe refuge for both animals and people who were in need. Brochwel is a patron of animal lovers.

Prayer:

Gracious God, you provide us with refuge when we are fearful and worn like the hare that leapt into Melangell's lap. Melangell lived in solitude, recognizing the gifts that you continually bestow upon us through the earth's abundance. Lead us to nurture the same faith and to live in harmony with, and gratitude for, the riches of this earth. Amen.

Antiphon:

You are robed in majesty.

Readings:

"God said, 'See, I have given you every plant yielding seed that is upon the face of all the earth, and every tree with seed in its fruit; you shall have them for food. And to every beast of the earth, and to every bird of the air, and to everything that creeps on the earth, everything that has the breath of life, I have given every green plant for food.' And so it was. God saw everything that he had made, and indeed, it was very good. And there was evening and there was morning, the sixth day." Gen. 1:29–31 (NRSV)

"And even those of Israel, if they do not persist in unbelief, will be grafted in, for God has the power to graft them in again. For if you have been cut from what is by nature a wild olive tree and grafted, contrary to nature, into a cultivated olive tree, how much more will these natural branches be grafted back into their own olive tree." Rom. 11:23–24 (NRSV)

MAY 28 Mary Ann of Jesus of Pardes

St. Mary Ann was born in 1614 in Ecuador, which had been under Spanish conquest for nearly a hundred years, the youngest of eight children. She became a Franciscan tertiary, taking the name Mary of Jesus of Pardes, initially living a life of prayer and simplicity in her own home after her parents died. She was devoted to ministering to the Native Indian and African-Americans through charitable works; and she opened a clinic and school in Quito. She had the mystical gift of being able to heal many people by sprinkling them with holy water, and she is credited with raising a dead woman to life. When plague broke out, Mary Ann nursed as many as she could before catching the disease herself. She died at age thirty-one, and because a lily sprouted at her grave, she has been known as the Lily of Quito. Mary Ann was canonized in 1950.

Intercessory Prayer:

Dear St. Mary Ann of Jesus of Pardes, your beloved mentor and father, St. Francis, believed that if self-denial and penance did not lead to charity, it was of little avail. He overcame his own fears of the sick by kissing a man with leprosy. You strove with little thought for yourself, to care for those stigmatized with plague, filled with zeal for those afflicted by a disease most people would shun. You were a lily among thorns, selflessly offering up everything for Jesus. Intercede for us that we may be made oblivious to self and fearless in our love of God and our neighbor. Amen.

Antiphon:

You free us from bondage and restore us to life.

Readings:

"The chariots of God are twenty thousand, even thousands of angels:
The Lord is among them, as in Sinai, in the holy place. . . .
You did ascend to the high mount, leading captives in your train.
. . .
Blessed be the Lord, who daily bears us up,
God is our salvation.
Our God is a God of salvation, and to God, the Lord
Belongs escape from death." *Psalm 68:17–20 (RSV)*

"O Lord, by these things [men] live; And in all these things is the life of my spirit; So You will restore me and make me live." *Isa. 38:16 (NKJV)*

"Truly, truly I say to you: Unless a grain of wheat falls into the earth and dies, it remains alone; but if it dies, it bears much fruit." *Jn. 12:24 (RSV)*

MAY 29 Mechtildis of Edelstetten and Theodosia of Constantinople

Mechtildis of Edelstetten was born of German nobilty and placed in a convent as a child oblate when she was five. When she was only twenty-eight, the Bishop of Augsberg asked her to assume leadership of a convent that was in need of reform. She was shy to accept the position, but when she did, she quickly created an environment wherein the cloister was protected from earlier scandal and gossip. It became again a place of silence, which Mechtildis herself practiced faithfully. Although she rarely spoke in her later years, it is reported that when she did, only words of wisdom fell from her lips. Mechtildis was also a renowned healer.

This is also the feast day of Theodosia, known as the "daughter of Constantinople." She was a martyr in the eighth century. Theodosia is known as the first Orthodox Christian to be murdered for defending icons during the iconoclastic controversy.

Prayer:

> *Holy Spirit, living love of God, you inspired both Mechtildis and Theodosia to give their whole lives for the sake of your call. They adored you, who covers yourself with light as with a garment, but who deigned to make known to us the powerful love of God through the divine image made flesh in Jesus. Teach us to know the joy of your life-giving Spirit, which permeates all of creation. Amen.*

Antiphon:

God's love has been poured into our hearts by the Holy Spirit.

Readings:

"I will sing to the LORD all my life; I will sing praise to my God as long as I live. May my meditation be pleasing to him, as I rejoice in the LORD." *Psalm 104:33–34 (NIV)*

"[They] listened to me expectantly, waiting in silence for my counsel. After I had spoken, they spoke no more; my words fell gently on their ears. They waited for me as for showers and drank in my words as the spring rain. When I smiled at them, they scarcely believed it; the light of my face was precious to them." *Job 29:21–24 (NIV)*

"He is the image of the invisible God, the firstborn over all creation" *Col. 1:15 (NIV)*

"[But] in these last days he has spoken to us by his Son, whom he appointed heir of all things, and through whom he made the universe. The Son is the radiance of God's glory and the exact representation of his being, sustaining all things by his powerful word." *Heb. 1:2–3 (NIV)*

MAY 30 Joan of Arc and Petronilla

Joan of Arc was a simple French peasant girl of the fifteenth century who knew all her Catholic prayers by heart, but could not read or write. As a young teen she began receiving heavenly advice from St. Michael the Archangel, St. Catherine, and St. Margaret. They all exhorted her to convince King Charles VII to rise up against the British and liberate France. After convincing King Charles of her divine mission, she donned the armor necessary to protect her innocence from the brutish soldiers and marched into battle with her banner bearing the names "JESUS, MARY." The first battle helped the French to gain the upper hand in the war, and Joan was dubbed "The Maid of Orleans." As time went by, the king did not continue to support her, leading to her eventual capture by the English. They brought false charges against her, including heresy. Joan was martyred by being burned at the stake. The young girl's heroic acceptance of death was a source of conversion for the crowd who witnessed her execution. Some present even commented that the English had most certainly murdered a saint. Pope Benedict XV canonized her in 1920. St. Joan is a patron of soldiers.

Joan shares this feast day with St. Petronilla, a virgin martyr of the early Christian Church and a follower and spiritual daughter of St. Peter. Little is known about Petronilla except that she was martyred and her remains were eventually transferred to St. Peter's Cathedral and are especially venerated by French monarchs, who have a special devotion to her.

Prayer:

Heavenly Father, you gave us St. Joan of Arc and St. Petronilla as models of courage and determination in accomplishing your will. Let these courageous women be an example for us on our life's journey, as we contemplate and strive to fulfill what you truly desire of us. Let their heroic virtue be an inspiration to us and may our motto be "All for Jesus and Mary." Amen.

Antiphon:

Be of good courage and he shall strengthen your heart, all you that hope in the Lord.

Readings:

"In you, O God, I take refuge, let me never be put to shame! In your justice, deliver and rescue me; Incline your ear to me and save me. Be for me a rock of refuge, A stronghold to save me. For you are my rock and my stronghold." *Psalm 71:1–3 (PCB)*

"Though He slay me, yet will I trust Him. Even so, I will defend my own ways before Him. He also *shall* be my salvation." *Job 13:15–16 (NKJV)*

"Set me as a seal upon your heart, As a seal upon your arm; For love *is as* strong as death." *Song of Songs 8:6 (NKJV)*

MAY 31 Queenship of Mary

The role of the Blessed Virgin Mary as queen has been well established throughout the Catholic Church's history. The faithful have sung her titles of Queen of Angels, Queen of Saints, Queen of Patriarchs, Queen of Apostles, and Queen of Martyrs through anitphons and prayerful supplications for centuries. In 1954 Pope Pius XII issued an encyclical in which he established the Church's official feast day to specifically honor Mary as queen on May 31. He declared that Jesus himself had constituted the Blessed Mother as the Queen of Heaven and Earth, and she should be honored as such above all the choirs of angels and saints in heaven, as well as above the faithful on earth. We honor Mary as queen of all on this day, acknowledging the many royal titles attributed to this lovely and fairest of mothers. The Anglican Church celebrates the feast of the Visitation of Mary on May 31 (see Daily Readings, St. Elizabeth, the cousin of Mary). Following Vatican II, the feast of the Queenship of Mary was moved to August 22, on the octave of the Assumption. In the old Roman calendar, that date was reserved for the Immaculate Heart of Mary.

In the East, the Russian Church commemorates the feast of Mary's queenship with the *Reigning Icon*, which made its miraculous appearance in 1917, the same year as Czar Nicholas's abdication. The icon was discovered after a dream wherein the Theotokos appeared to a peasant girl and told her where to dig to unearth it. The Russian Orthodox people revere the icon as a special symbol of their dedication to Mary through the stormy period of their country's communist history. In the icon, Mary wears a scarlet mantle, symbol of the Russian martyrs, and holds a regal scepter and orb. The *Reigning Icon* was kept in the convent of Grand Duchess Elizabeth (see Daily Readings, July 18, Elizabeth Feodorovna) and later became a miracle worker. The faithful in Russia believe that, at the moment of their country's greatest fall, the holy Theotokos took upon herself the Russian Empire's succession of authority, when the Czar, later canonized, was martyred.

Intercessory Prayer:

Heavenly Mother, Queen of All Christians, Queen of Heaven and Earth, we honor you today and give praise to Jesus Christ for giving us so lovely a mother to intercede for us at the throne of grace. With the angels and saints in heaven, we acknowledge you at the right hand of your son, Jesus Christ, and with heartfelt gratitude we thank you for the powerful intercession and maternal prayers you offer to God on our behalf. May all the world recognize and honor you in your queenship. Amen.

Antiphon:

She has come forth from a royal race and is crowned with glory.

Readings:

"She is more precious than rubies; nothing you desire can compare with her. Long life is in her right hand; in her left hand are riches and honor. Her ways are pleasant ways, and all her paths are peace. She is a tree of life to those who embrace her; those who lay hold of her will be blessed." *Prov. 3:15–18 (NIV)*

"To [him] who overcomes, I will give the right to sit with me on my throne, just as I overcame and sat down with my Father on his throne. He who has an ear, let him hear what the Spirit says to the churches." *Rev. 3:21 (NIV)*

JUNE 1 Marguerite of Porete

Little is known of Marguerite of Porete (also known as Marguerite of Hainaut), except that she was a Beguine mystic who authored the book *The Mirror of Simple Annihilated Souls*. Well educated, Marguerite's mysticism was most likely influenced by the early Platonic Greek Fathers. One of the first women mystics to be executed during the Inquisition, Marguerite quietly insisted on the truth of her revelations until she died. Her serenity in the face of a death by burning converted many souls who witnessed it, and her book continued to grow in popularity for several centuries, although Inquisitional authorities regularly confiscated it. Highly metaphorical, her book became very popular with a group of mystics attached to St. Catherine of Genoa, who used her book as a spiritual guide. The book's central tenet is that the soul's liberation is attained by annihilating oneself in God, thus being transformed into his very essence. The heresy accusations apparently stem from a misunderstanding of the text: where she speaks of union with God, they read an identification with God; when she speaks of inward peace and of knowing God only in spirit and in truth, they understood a sacrilegious denial of Christian institutions. Like Meister Eckhart, her contemporary, Marguerite's visions indicated to her that God is one who cannot be known perfectly; it is only through love, not by knowledge, that God can be known. She refused to defend her book during her trial, saying only that the soul's demands are "beyond the frontiers of all countries where a creature can have access to knowledge."

Intercessory Prayer:

O holy Marguerite, your life was a testimony that nothing can disturb the soul's deep contemplation of God. You wrote that the soul who trusts in God is strong and great, entirely free and disencumbered of everything, for God sanctifies her. Help us to find strength in times when all those around us doubt us, and pray for us on our spiritual journey to the fullness of the kingdom. Amen.

Antiphon:

When your word goes forth it gives light.

Readings:

"But the souls of the righteous are in the hand of God,
and no torment will ever touch them. In the eyes of the foolish
    they seemed to have died, . . . but they are at peace.
For though in the sight of [men] they were punished,
their hope is full of immortality. . . . God tested them and found
    them worthy. . . ." *Wis. 3:1–5 (RSV)*

"For God has not destined us for wrath, but to obtain salvation
    through our Lord Jesus Christ." *1 Thess. 5:9 (RSV)*

JUNE 2 Sojourner Truth

Sojourner Truth was born a slave in Ulster County, New
York, in 1797 and named Isabella. Most of her brothers and
sisters were sold when Isabella was young, as was she, when
she was old enough to do farm work. She married another slave and
had five children. After severe treatment, including some bloody
beatings from her master, she took her youngest child, Sophia, and
ran away. Isabella went to reclaim her oldest son, who had been sold
into slavery in Alabama, and won him back in an unprecedented court
case. In 1828 her freedom was secured because the state of New York
abolished slavery that year, and she moved there to join a group of
evangelists in the African Methodist Episcopal Church. She began a
street ministry with the poor, supporting herself as a household servant. Isabella soon discovered that she loved to preach, and recognizing that this was her true calling, she devoted the rest of her life to
teaching and preaching. In 1843, she moved to Massachusetts and became active in the abolitionist movement. At that time, she took the
name Sojourner Truth, believing this to be the inspiration of the Holy
Spirit. In 1846, she published her memoirs to help turn the tide
against slavery in the north. Recalling her days of bondage, Isabella
said that she had poured out her sufferings to God and the Lord had
told her she would someday be free. Committed to her activism, as
well as to the social gospel, she joined the women's rights movement,
insisting that if black men got their rights, and not black women, they
would still be slaves to their men. She helped free slaves through the
Underground Railroad, and she travelled to twenty states, preaching

emancipation and ministering to the poor. When she died, Sojourner said that she was unworried, for she knew she was going home like a shooting star.

Prayer:

> *Gracious Lord and liberator, Sojourner Truth labored to free her people and cared for the homeless everywhere. By adopting the name Sojourner Truth, she affirmed that her ministry was dedicated to fighting for truth and freedom wherever her travels took her. She once said that what we give to the poor, we lend to you, Lord. We thank you for giving us such a powerful role model for women and men today, for her journey to freedom has inspired us and brought us a little closer to the gospel message that if we know the truth, the truth will set us free. Amen.*

Antiphon:

The Lord knows the days of the upright, and their inheritance shall live forever.

Readings:

"Hear my prayer, O Lord, and give ear to my cry,
Hold not your peace at my tears! For I am your passing guest,
A sojourner, like all my fathers were. O spare me, that I may re-
    cover strength
Before I go hence, and be no more." *Psalm 39:12–13 (KJV)*

"As the truth of Christ is in me, this boast of mine will not be si-
lenced." *2 Cor. 11:10 (RSV)*

"And I will pray the Father, and he will give you another Counselor, to be with you for ever, even the Spirit of truth, whom the
world cannot receive, because it neither sees him nor knows
him; you know him, for he dwells with you, and will be in you."
Jn. 14:16–17 (RSV)

JUNE 3 Clothilde of France

St. Clothilde was born in France in the late fifth century, the daughter of the king of Burgundy. The beautiful princess soon won the heart of Clovis, the king of the Salian Franks. Her biography is mainly credited to St. Gregory of Tours, and from it we learn that Clothilde and Clovis had a happy marriage, although Clothilde tried to convince her pagan husband to embrace Christianity. When King Clovis won an important battle and attributed it to praying to "Clothilde's God," he converted. The couple had five children together, and after Clovis's death, Clothilde spent her life trying to bring peace to her warring family. Her life was fraught with trauma, as her sons and nephews were continually wrestling over control of the empire, massacring family members in the process. Eventually Clothilde retired to the shrine of her favorite saint, St. Martin at Tours, to spend the remainder of her life praying for peace within her family and country. In art, she is often pictured praying at the shrine of St. Martin. She died in the year 535, and it was reported that a miraculous and dazzling light filled the room at her passing. Clothilde's relics remain to this day at the Church of Saint-Leu in Paris.

Intercessory Prayer:

Dear St. Clothilde, you spent your life working to bring peace to your family and holding up the lamp of the Christian faith. Help us to be inspired by your example as we strive to find ways to bring peace to our own families. As you shared the wealth with which God blessed you, help us to find ways to share our talents and gifts to further the kingdom of God. Amen.

Antiphon:

The people of God will be blessed with peace.

Readings:

"Depart from evil, and do good; seek peace, and pursue it. The eyes of the LORD are toward the righteous, and his ears toward their cry. The face of the LORD is against evildoers, to cut off the remembrance of them from the earth. When the righteous cry for help, the LORD hears, and delivers them out of all their troubles. The LORD is near to the brokenhearted, and saves the crushed in spirit." *Psalm 34:14–18 (RSV)*

"Peace I leave with you; my peace I give to you; not as the world gives do I give to you. Let not your hearts be troubled, neither let them be afraid." *Jn. 14:27 (RSV)*

"If possible, so far as it depends upon you, live peaceably with all. . . . Now, 'if your enemy is hungry, feed him; if he is thirsty, give him drink; for by so doing you will heap burning coals upon his

head.' Do not be overcome by evil, but overcome evil with good."
Rom. 12:18, 20–21 (RSV)

JUNE 4 Martha and Mary (Orthodox Date)

Jesus was apparently good friends with Martha, Mary, and their brother, Lazarus, as the Bible records three visits to them (Luke 10:38, John 11:1, and John 12:1). Whereas Mary's goal was to listen to his Word, Martha's major goal seemed to center on serving Jesus. Because of her firm act of faith ("I believe you are the Messiah, the Son of God, coming into the world") in John's passage, Jesus reveals to Martha the mystery of the resurrection of the dead. Martha's deep understanding of who Jesus was parallels a similar confession of faith found in the Apostle Peter. Jesus' theological conversation with Martha concerning the resurrection illustrates the noble status that women occupied in his mind. Jesus mourned their brother's death with Martha and Mary, and the sisters were among the few to witness Jesus shedding tears. Jesus' final visit with Martha and Mary in John 12:1–8 is the one wherein Mary poured ointment over his feet, an act that he saw as an anointing in preparation for his burial. The Roman and Episcopal churches celebrate the feast of these two important women on July 29.

Intercessory Prayer:

> *In the town of Bethany, you once lived near our beloved master, O Blessed Martha and Mary. How special it must have been to minister to him and to wait in expectation for the appearance of his beautiful face. You were both strong in faith and loved him with an ardent longing; and now you dwell in heaven where you may continually behold his shining countenance. Pray for us, O holy ones, that we may be graced to see the sweet lover of our souls. In Jesus' name we pray, Amen.*

Antiphon:

Yes, Lord, I believe that you are the Christ.

Readings:

"Jesus said, 'Let her alone, let her keep it for the day of my burial. The poor you always have with you, but you do not always have me.'" *Jn. 12:7–8 (RSV)*

"As you have sent me into the world, even so have I also sent them into the world. And for their sakes I sanctify myself, that they also might be sanctified through the truth." *Jn.17:18–19 (KJV)*

JUNE 5 Sophia of Ainos

Sophia of Ainos was born during a turbulent time in Byzantine history. Constantinople and the surrounding country were continually being devastated by attacks from the Bulgarians, and the destroying armies left many people starving. Sophia was born to pious Orthodox parents, and she wed a man she dearly loved. Although they struggled with poor harvests through an economic depression, they had six children and a blessed family life. Then the plague struck, and Sophia's entire family perished. During her period of grief, she questioned why God had deprived her in such a manner when she had tried her whole life to serve him. The answer came one day when she was reflecting that so many of her neighbors had perished, leaving homeless children. Since she had a home of her own, she adopted several orphans; the word spread, and her children eventually numbered more than a hundred. It was said of her hospitality that her pitcher never ran dry; indeed, a legend circulated that angels refreshed it nightly. A year before she died in 950, Sophia decided to become a tonsured nun. After her death, the Orthodox Church bestowed on her the title *Orphantrophos* (literally, "one who cares for orphans"), which was a title generally reserved for bishops. The title indicates Sophia's special favor with God.

Prayer:

Gracious God, to you do we look for nurturing; you give us food in due season and you are near to all who call upon you. Through saints like Sophia of Ainos, you fed and nurtured the homeless children who were robbed of their parents by war and plague.

Help us to always remember that during hard times, it is our
hearts that serve as the center for your loving-kindness. Amen.

Antiphon:

You have searched me out and known me.

Readings:

"Remember, O LORD, what has befallen us;
behold, and see our disgrace! Our inheritance has been turned
     over to strangers,
our homes to aliens. We have become orphans, fatherless;
our mothers are like widows." *Lam. 5:1–3 (RSV)*

"And when he came to the gate of the city, behold, a widow was
there gathering sticks; and he called to her and said, 'Bring me a
little water in a vessel, that I may drink.' . . . And she said, 'As the
LORD your God lives, I have nothing baked, only a handful of meal
in a jar. . . .' And Eli'jah said to her, 'Fear not. . . . For thus says the
LORD the God of Israel, 'The jar of meal shall not be spent, and
the cruse of oil shall not fail, until the day that the LORD sends
rain upon the earth." And she went and did as Eli'jah said; and
she, and he, and her household ate for many days. The jar of
meal was not spent, neither did the cruse of oil fail. . . ." *1 Kings
17:10–16 (RSV)*

"If we live, we live to the Lord, and if we die, we die to the Lord; so
then, whether we live or whether we die, we are the Lord's." *Rom.
14:8 (RSV)*

JUNE 6 Miriam

Miriam is a heroine of the Old Testament who stands out as an independent and valiant leader. Miriam's verse honoring God's saving power is the finale of the Red Sea narrative. She is the first person in the Hebrew Torah to be given the title of prophet. Many women's studies researchers and authors believe that Miriam was a major female influence on the Israelites in the wilderness. Her conflict with her brother Moses about his marriage to a Cushite woman indicates that she believed that she and her brother Aaron also had prophetic and priestly authority; she believed that God spoke through her. Although the text indicates that God punishes her through seven days of isolation for challenging Moses, her people show their loyalty to her by not setting out on the march again until she returns. There appears to be a recognition of a leadership trinity in which Miriam was an equal with Aaron and Moses; later in the Micah text it says, "For I brought you up from the land of Egypt, and redeemed you from the house of slavery; and I sent before you Moses, Aaron and Miriam" (Micah 6:4). From the few sketches of her in the Torah, Miriam emerges as a cultic figure, prophetess, musician, and beloved leader.

Prayer:

Eternal Lord God, you have drawn us together with the saints of the Old Testament in a wonderful way to know you better. Enrich us evermore with your heavenly grace so that we may always remember that wisdom is treasure without end, and that those who attain to it are your friends. Through Christ our Lord. Amen.

Antiphon:

Sing to the Lord a new song.

Readings:

"Hide not your face from me in the day when I am in trouble; incline your ear to me. In the day that I call, answer me speedily." *Psalm 102:1–2 (KJV)*

"And Miriam the prophetess, the sister of Aaron, took a timbrel in her hand; and all the women went out after her with timbrels and with dances. And Miriam answered them, 'Sing to the Lord, for he has triumphed gloriously; the horse and his rider he has thrown into the sea.'" *Ex. 15:20–21 (KJV)*

JUNE 7 Anne of St. Bartholomew

Born in the seventeenth century, Anne of St. Bartholomew was a poor and uneducated peasant girl, the daughter of village laborers. She felt the calling to become a Carmelite nun and was one of the first to follow the great St. Teresa of Avila. She became St. Teresa's constant companion, and many miraculous events surrounded her holy life. When the prince of Orange seized the city of Antwerp, Anne led a prayer vigil to thwart the siege by praying through the night. Miraculously, the siege ended and Antwerp was spared. Anne, who did not know how to read or write, experienced "the gift of letters." She miraculously and instantly learned to read and write so that she could be St. Teresa's secretary. Teresa died in the arms of Anne, her beloved companion, and Anne wrote a memoir of the saint's passing. Anne is also credited with helping to found other houses of the Carmelite Order. She died in 1626, after following her superior's direction to write her own autobiography. Anne is a patron of Antwerp.

Prayer:

Dear Holy Spirit of God, you gifted Blessed Anne of St. Bartholomew with the miraculous ability to read and write so she could fulfill the earthly duties for which you had destined her. Her writings serve an important purpose in the history of the Church and the Carmelite Order. Help us to follow your inspirations within our own lives, for all of our fresh springs are in you. Amen.

Antiphon:

And the Lord said, Write the vision, make it plain upon the tablet.

Readings:

"You send forth your Spirit and they are created; and you renew the face of the earth. May the glory of the Lord endure forever." *Psalm 104:30–31 (NKJV)*

"And now, go, write it before them on a tablet, and inscribe it in a book, that it may be for the time to come as a witness for ever." *Isa. 30:8 (RSV)*

"Follow the pattern of the sound words which you have heard from me, in the faith and love which are in Christ Jesus; guard the truth that has been entrusted to you by the Holy Spirit who dwells within us." *2 Tim. 1:13–14 (RSV)*

"Do not be anxious beforehand what you are to say; but say whatever is given you in that hour, for it is not you who speak, but the Holy Spirit." *Mark 13:11 (RSV)*

JUNE 8 Melania the Elder

Melania the Elder, celebrated as a saint in the Greek Church, was one of the early Roman mothers who followed the ascetic path of the desert, which Jerome brought to Rome. Born into great wealth, she was married at age fourteen and had three children. At age twenty-two she lost her entire family, with the exception of one son, to an illness. She raised her surviving son until he was ten years old, when she left for Alexandria to join the monks and learn about the ascetic life. She remained devoted to the Eastern monastic tradition for the rest of her life. Melania was instrumental in drawing Evagrius, an early father of the Eastern Church, into the monastic life, and she supported him while he wrote his famous treatises on prayer and the mystical life. Jerome tells us that Melania was such an example of virtue that she received the name Thekla (Thekla of Iconium was a great model for women in the early Church; see Daily Readings, September 24, Thekla). Her son fathered a saint, Melania the Younger, whom the Roman Church celebrates on December 31. Melania the Elder formed a close relationship with her granddaughter. Melania was a contemporary of St. Paula (see Daily Readings, January 26, Paula of Rome) and like her, she funded the building of monasteries in the Holy Land. Paula's and Jerome's double monastery was in Bethlehem, and Melania supported Jerome's closest friend, Rufinus, in Jerusalem, on the Mount of Olives. Jerome and Rufinus were busy translating biblical texts and the early Church Fathers when they had a serious falling out over an interpretation of Origen's works. The monks at Bethlehem became alienated from the church at Jerusalem for some time. In the year 400, Melania went to Africa to visit Augustine, who was attempting to mediate the dispute between Rufinus and Jerome. Rufinus died shortly afterward, and Melania returned to spend her remaining years at her hermitage on the Mount of Olives.

Prayer:

O Blessed Jesus, holy woman Melania was one of the first mothers of the Church, setting an ideal for the religious and mystical life that was influential for centuries. Enlighten us by the divine rays of your holy Word, so that we may take it to heart as she did. As you, O God, unique and invisible, have taken flesh so that we may follow your holy precepts, make us also participate in your nature by becoming spirited vessels of your holy divinity. Amen.

Antiphon:

In your light may we see light.

Readings:

"Give thanks to the LORD, call on his name; make known among the nations what he has done. . . . Look to the LORD and his strength; seek his face always. Remember the wonders he has done, his miracles, and the judgments he pronounced." *Psalm 105:1, 4–5 (NIV)*

"For where your treasure is, there will your heart be also. The light of the body is the eye: if therefore, your eye be single, your whole body will be filled with light." *Mt. 6:21–22 (KJV)*

"And the light shines in the darkness, and the darkness did not comprehend it . . . That was the true Light which gives light to every man coming into the world." *Jn. 1:5, 9 (NKJV)*

JUNE 9 Anne Marie Taigi

Anne Marie Taigi was born Anne Gianetti in the city of Sienna in 1769. Her parents lived as servants within a palace, a job she eventually also assumed. At age twenty she met a porter who often came to the palace, Domenico Taigi, and they were soon married. After the birth of their first child, Anne Marie joined the Order of the Trinity as a tertiary. Although the marriage was sometimes a struggle for her, Anne Marie loved her husband and strove to lead a life of sanctity as his wife and as mother to the couple's seven children. Miracles surrounded her—most notably, a miraculous orb in which she could see future events, as well as the state of individual souls and the fate of the departed. Anne Marie also experienced the gift of the odor of sin, the ability to smell a horrible stench around individuals who were in a state of serious sin. She was so well known for her gifts of prophecy that numerous famous individuals of the era consulted her, including two popes. Anne Marie was beatified in 1920, after numerous people testified on behalf of her holiness, including her ninety-two-year-old husband.

Intercessory Prayer:

> Dear Blessed Anne Marie Taigi, the Church has recognized you as a model for wives and mothers everywhere. You lived a life of courage and holiness, amid the daily demands of ministering to your large family. Help us to imitate your love in serving others, especially those closest to us, within our own families. May we see that through serving our loved ones, we carry out a great act of charity and achieve our own personal sanctity through all tasks done with love of God as our motivation. Amen.

Antiphon:

Learn from me, for I am gentle and lowly in heart.

Readings:

> "O satisfy us in the morning with your steadfast love, that we may rejoice and be glad all of our days.
> Make us glad as many days as you have afflicted us.
> And as many years as we have seen evil.
> Let your work be manifest to your servants, and your glorious power to their children.
> Let the favor of the Lord our God be upon us, and establish the work of our hands upon us." *Psalm 90:14–17 (KJV)*

> "Your mother was like a vine in a vineyard, transplanted by the water, fruitful and full of branches by reason of abundant water. Its strongest stem became a ruler's scepter; it towered aloft among the thick boughs; it was seen in its height with the mass of its branches." *Ez. 19:10–11 (RSV)*

> "And having gifts that differ according to the grace given to us, let us use them; if prophecy, in proportion to our faith; if service, then in our serving." *Rom. 12:6–7 (RSV)*

JUNE 10 Marianne of Molokai

Marianne of Molokai was born in Germany in 1838 and named after her mother, Barbara. She acquired her new name when she went to Hawaii in her 20s to work there after it had been annexed to the United States. She joined an order of the Sisters of St. Francis and was inspired to teach. Marianne became a superior of St. Josepheus Hospital in Syracuse, New York, and then moved back to Maui to open a hospital there. This was during a period when leprosy was a greatly feared plague on all the islands. That only sparked Mother Marianne's boundless generosity. Robert Louis Stevenson immortalized her compassion for those who were made outcasts in a celebrated poem. She lived with the lepers on the island of Molokai for thirty years, and the Hawaiian government dedicated a royal award to her in thanksgiving. Like Florence Nightingale (see Daily Readings, May 18, Florence Nightingale), Mother Marianne made a significant contribution to reducing disease by teaching cleanliness. She was fond of buying bright-colored scarves for the colony's women, a loving gesture to improve their self-esteem. She died, with the people she loved, in 1918. Marianne is a patron of those suffering from skin diseases.

Prayer:

Beloved Lord Jesus, you granted your gifts of compassion to your most unwanted outcasts through Mother Marianne's love and care. She dedicated her life to making those rejected souls feel welcome for the sake of your kingdom, which is open to everyone. Help us to examine where in our own lives we may reject souls that you lovingly accept, and allow the gifts of acceptance and compassion to flower in our souls. Amen.

Antiphon:

You are my refuge and portion in the land of the living.

Readings:

"I cry out with my voice to you, O God, with my voice I make supplication to you. I pour out my complaints before you, before you I place all my troubles. When my spirit is faint, you, O God, know my way! In the path where I walk hidden traps surround me. I look to the right and watch, but no one takes notice of me . . . no one cares for my soul." *Psalm 142:1–4 (PCB)*

"He grew up before him like a tender shoot, and like a root out of dry ground. He had no beauty or majesty to attract us to him, nothing in his appearance that we should desire him. He was despised and rejected by men, a man of sorrows, and familiar with suffering. Like one from whom men hide their faces he was despised, and we esteemed him not. Surely he took up our infirmities and carried our sorrows, yet we considered him stricken by God, smitten by him, and afflicted." *Isa. 53:2–4 (NIV)*

"But first he must suffer many things and be rejected by this generation." *Lk. 17:25 (NIV)*

JUNE 11 Queen Margaret of Scotland

Born in Hungry in 1047, Queen Margaret is a Celtic saint who received universal, not merely local recognition. Margaret, the daughter of the Saxon heir to the English throne and a German princess, was reared and educated in the Benedictine tradition. Her family moved to England when Margaret was between ten and twelve years old, but they were forced to flee. They found refuge at the court of Malcolm III of Scotland. Malcolm was smitten with Margaret, and they were married in 1070. Although she was an outsider, Margaret transformed Malcolm and his court, changing it from a place of wild drunkenness to a place where knights remained after meals to say grace and ladies were treated with the utmost respect. Margaret was devoted to the poor. She brought them into the castle where she and Malcolm served them meals, and she was generous with alms. She strove for peace in a tumultuous time, ransoming Norman captives and returning them to England. With a hand in church administration, Margaret founded the Holy Trinity Abbey in Dunfermline and rebuilt Iona, the first stronghold of Christianity in Scotland. Margaret and Malcolm had eight children: three sons became rulers of Scotland, and a daughter married Henry I of England. Margaret died in 1093, four days after hearing of the death of her husband and a son in a battle to secure her brother's holdings. Through the beauty of her nature, compassion, and charitable works, she endeared herself to the people of Scotland. Margaret is the second patron saint of Scotland.

Prayer:

Beloved Jesus, St. Margaret sought to serve you in the true spirit of the Gospel, knowing that each soul was your face in disguise. A lover of peace and concord, we need her intercession in our troubled age of war and its discontents. Through her love of those in her care, both in her own family and in her country, may we find the model of perfect service to your holy name. May our lives give grace and glory to you in each and every soul we meet. Protect us and our families in times of danger. Amen.

Antiphon:

You will find me when you shall search for me with all of your heart.

"And I will be found of you, says the Lord, and I will turn away your captivity, and I will gather you from all the nations and from all the places whither I have driven you." *Jer. 29:13–14 (KJV)*

"People will come from east and west and north and south, and will take their places at the feast in the kingdom of God. Indeed there are those who are last who will be first, and first who will be last." *Lk. 13:29–30 (NIV)*

"Anyone who claims to be in the light but hates his [brother] is still in the darkness. Whoever loves his brother lives in the light, and there is nothing in [him] to make him stumble." *1 Jn. 2:9–10 (NIV)*

JUNE 12 Paula Frassinetti

Paula Frassinetti lived in the early nineteenth century in Genoa, Italy, the only girl in a family with four older brothers. Her devout Catholic home raised all the boys to become priests, but tragedy struck when Paula's mother died when she was six years old. By age nine, Paula was managing the family's household. At age twenty, she suffered poor health due to bronchial problems, so she went to live with one of her brother priests in a coastal village near Genoa. Working as the parish housekeeper, she realized the need to properly instruct the poor children in Catechism and other academics. Paula founded a school for the parish children, and soon other women wished to join her in her efforts to educate poor children. Eventually, Paula founded an order of holy women dedicated to this cause, the Sisters of St. Dorothy in Genoa. She spent her days in work, and many of her nights she prayed in front of the tabernacle. Her sisters continued to spread their educational efforts and established schools throughout Europe, Portugal, and Brazil. Paula died in Rome in 1882, and her remains were enshrined at the Dorothean motherhouse there. Her body was found to be incorrupt in 1906, and Pope John Paul II canonized Paula in 1984.

Intercessory Prayer:

Dear St. Paula, through your life of trials and obstacles, you realized the Holy Spirit's inspiration, spreading the kingdom of

God through educating the poorest of the poor. God blessed your
efforts, which spread throughout many regions of the world,
bringing the light and knowledge of Christ to countless children.
Help us to follow your example and to realize that the path to
our own destiny must embrace God's will and Christ's cross. Amen.

Antiphon:

Let the children come to me, for such is the kingdom of
heaven.

Readings:

"Teach me, O Lord, the way of your statutes, and I will observe it
to the end. Give me understanding, that I may keep your law and
observe it with my whole heart. Lead me in the path of your commandments, for I delight in it." *Psalm 119:33–35 (NRSV)*

"Then the king will say to those at his right hand, 'Come, you that
are blessed by my Father, inherit the kingdom prepared for you
from the foundation of the world; for I was hungry and you gave
me food, I was thirsty and you gave me something to drink, I was
a stranger and you welcomed me, I was naked and you gave me
clothing, I was sick and you took care of me, I was in prison and
you visited me.'" *Mt. 25:34–36 (NRSV)*

"By contrast, the fruit of the Spirit is love, joy, peace, patience,
kindness, generosity, faithfulness. . . ." *Gal. 5:22 (NRSV)*

JUNE 13 Barbara Heck and Aquilina

Barbara von Ruckle was born in Limerick, Ireland, of German parents fleeing from persecution in southern Germany
in 1709. However, the Reformers were no more welcome
in Ireland than they had been in Germany. Deprived of land and afflicted with unpayable taxes, her family emigrated to America, where
Barbara married Paul Heck. When she was eighteen, Barbara had met
John Wesley, and she was stirred by his intense devotion and
charisma. When she got to the new world, she initiated the building
of the first Methodist church there, in New York City. It was thronged
every Sunday, and many other Methodists from Ireland (where they
were known as the *Palatines*) soon joined her. When the Revolutionary
War broke out, the patriots arrested her husband, but he escaped. The

couple then moved to Canada. Barbara was as diligent in organizing a Methodist society there as she had been in New York. She is often referred to as the Mother of Canadian Methodism. Her guiding scriptural passage was Hosea 10:12, "Break up your fallow ground, for it is time to seek the Lord."

This is also the feast day of the holy martyr Aquilina, a virgin who suffered martyrdom under Diocletian in 293.

Prayer:

O Lord Jesus, you have called all of us into your kingdom, and you have promised us unfathomable blessings. Thank you for brave pioneers like Barbara Heck and Aquilina, who dedicated their lives to you. May we grow in knowledge of your Spirit and perceive your direction in our life and work, that our deeds may show the world that we have been sent by you. Help us to remember that faith is the substance of things hoped for. Amen.

Antiphon:

We are a priestly people, let us rejoice, allelulia.

Readings:

"Blessings crown the head of the righteous, but violence overwhelms the mouth of the wicked." *Prov. 10:6–7 (NIV)*

"Sow for yourselves righteousness, reap the fruit of unfailing love, and break up your unplowed ground; for it is time to seek the LORD, until he comes and showers righteousness on you." *Hos. 10:12 (NIV)*

"He will defend the afflicted among the people and save the children of the needy; he will crush the oppressor. He will endure as long as the sun, as long as the moon, through all generations." *Psalm 72:4–5 (NIV)*

"For the very work that the Father has given me to finish, and which I am doing, testifies that the Father has sent me. And the Father who sent me has himself testified concerning me." *Jn. 5:36–37 (NIV)*

JUNE 14 Edburga of Bicester

Edburga of Bicester was a Saxon princess, the daughter of Penda, king of Mercia. Her father gave her and her sister, St. Edith of Aylesbury, some land in Aylesbury, where they built a small monastery. There they educated their niece, St. Osith. Osith's marriage to Sighere, king of the Saxons, helped to establish Christianity in Essex. Osith was martyred when pirates ransacked Chich, where she had established a nunnery. Edburga served as Abbess of Aylesbury until her death in 650. Her relics, translated to Bicester Priory, became a popular medieval pilgrimage site. The base of Edburga's shrine, established in 1320, is still visible at the Church of Stanton Harcourt.

Prayer:

Dear God, Edburga of Bicester used her position in a way that best served you. She created a monastery and educated her niece, Osith, in your ways. Her success in doing so helped spread Christianity to new areas of England. Help us not to be consumed by the zeal we have for our daily concerns; but to appreciate what we have in this world by using it in a way that best serves you. Amen.

Antiphon:

For where your treasure is, there your heart shall be also.

Readings:

"Arise, shine, for your light has come, and the glory of the LORD rises upon you. See, darkness covers the earth and thick darkness is over the peoples, but the LORD rises upon you and his glory appears over you. Nations will come to your light, and kings to the brightness of your dawn. Lift up your eyes and look about you: All assemble and come to you; your sons come from afar, and your daughters are carried on the arm. . . . No longer will violence be heard in your land, nor ruin or destruction within your borders, but you will call your walls Salvation and your gates Praise." *Isa. 60:1–4, 18 (NIV)*

"But as for [the seed that fell] in the good soil, these are the ones who, when they hear the word, hold it fast in an honest and good heart, and bear fruit with patient endurance." *Lk. 8:15 (NRSV)*

"When I came to you, brothers and sisters, I did not come proclaiming the mystery of God to you in lofty words or wisdom. For I decided to know nothing among you except Jesus Christ, and him crucified. . . . Yet among the mature we do speak wisdom, though it is not a wisdom of this age or of the rulers of this age. . . . But we speak God's wisdom, secret and hidden, which God decreed before the ages for our glory." *1 Cor. 2:1–2, 6–7 (NRSV)*

JUNE 15 Germaine Cousin and Cresentia

St. Germaine Cousin was born in France in 1579. Her mother died when she was very small, and her father remarried. Germaine's stepmother despised her because of the infirmity that she was born with—a withered hand. Because of this and other conditions (possibly tuberculosis), her stepmother banished Germaine to sleep outside, under the steps or in the barn. When Germaine was old enough, she was sent into the fields to tend the sheep. She never complained about the ill treatment by her stepmother or many of the unkind townsfolk; instead, she offered her sufferings for their conversions. A story was told that when she wanted to attend Mass, she would summon her guardian angel to keep watch over the sheep, and she never lost a single sheep in her absences. Another legend is that Germaine parted the waters of a raging stream in her attempts to get to Mass. Many miracles surrounded her both before and after her death. She died at age twenty-two from an unknown cause, and her saintly life converted the hearts of many, including her cruel stepmother.

This is also the feast of St. Cresentia, who was a martyr in the time of Diocletian. She was St. Vitas's nursemaid. Cresentia was murdered with her husband, Modestos, and their cult was strong in Rome, where legend has it that angels transported their bodies.

Prayer:

Heavenly Father, you gave us good St. Germaine and Cresentia as living examples of how to live in the face of cruelty, prejudice, and banishment. You heard their prayers and showed your favor toward them by causing the conversion of many hearts. Let their example of love and acceptance be an inspiration for us as we pray the prayer of St. Germaine:"Oh Lord, I am not worthy of you. Come into my heart and soul and mind, guide my every thought, word, and deed."Amen.

Antiphon:

But I say unto you, love your enemies, and pray for them that persecute you.

Readings:

"You are worthy, our Lord and God, to receive glory and honor and power, for you created all things, and by your will they were created and have their being. . . . You are worthy to take the scroll and to open its seals, because you were slain, and with your blood you purchased [men] for God from every tribe and language and people and nation. You have made them to be a kingdom and priests to serve our God, and they will reign on the earth." Rev. 4:11; 5:9–10 (NIV)

"For your faithfulness is like a morning cloud, And like the early dew it goes away. Therefore I have hewn *them* by the prophets, I have slain them by the words of My mouth; and your judgments *are like* light *that* goes forth. For I desire mercy and not sacrifice, And the knowledge of God more than burnt offerings." Hos. 6:4–6 (NKJV)

'[He] lavished on us . . . all wisdom and understanding. And he made known to us the mystery of his will according to his good pleasure, which he purposed in Christ, to be put into effect when the times will have reached their fulfillment—to bring all things in heaven and on earth together under one head, even Christ." Eph. 1:8–10 (NIV)

JUNE 16 Evelyn Underhill

Evelyn Underhill was a major figure in the Anglican Church who introduced many modern Christians into the riches of the mystical life. She taught that the contemplative tradition can be integrated into the everyday lives of those willing to embrace it. Born in 1875, she studied history in college, where she supported herself as a bookbinder. She began her writing career at age sixteen and published for the rest of her life. She married her childhood sweetheart, Herbert Stuart Moore, and devoted her quiet life to prayer, writing, and giving spiritual direction. During World War I, she joined the Anglican Pacifist Fellowship and remained active in spiritual politics. Evelyn compiled some of the most exhaustive volumes of the twentieth century on critical studies of the mystics, clearly outlining the distinctions between apophatic and kataphatic mysticism, and demonstrating the schema of degrees of progress in the contemplative life that culminate in mystical union. She was deeply interested in the Greek Orthodox Church and joined the Fellowship of St. Alban and St. Sergios, an ecumenical group devoted to Anglican-Orthodox relations. All who knew her testified to her great wisdom and personal holiness, and she gained great renown as a spiritual advisor and retreat leader. Evelyn's personal notebooks reveal a depth of sanctity, as well as a number of mystical experiences she herself had but rarely spoke about. She was most fond of Teresa of Avila's saying that, to give the most perfect service to God, Martha and Mary must combine.

Prayer:

Beloved Lord, your name is the breath we breathe, and your Word is our daily bread, the substance within which we live and move and have our being. Evelyn Underhill was a faithful servant who strove to know your name and your Word in all she taught and in all she did. She once wrote, "God alone matters, God alone is, creation only matters because of God." Help us, through her steadfast faith and the work she left us, deepen in our awareness that you alone reside at the core of our being. Amen.

Antiphon:

You stand at the open door and bid us, come.

Readings:

"He made the storm be still and the waves of the sea were hushed. Then they were glad because they had quiet, And he brought them to their desired haven. Let them thank the Lord for his steadfast love." *Psalm 107:29–31 (RSV)*

"I will surely save you out of a distant place, your descendants from the land of their exile. . . . 'I am with you and will save you,' declares the LORD." *Jer. 30:10–11 (NIV)*

"Your beauty should not come from outward adornment, such as braided hair and the wearing of gold jewelry and fine clothes. Instead, it should be that of your inner self, the unfading beauty of a gentle and quiet spirit, which is of great worth in God's sight." *1 Pet. 3:3–4 (NIV)*

JUNE 17 Emily de Vialar

Emily de Vialar was born in the late eighteenth century to a prominent French family. Her father was a nobleman and a baron who lost his wife when Emily was just fifteen. A demanding character, he required Emily to take over most of the duties related to running the household. Emily experienced a profound vision of Jesus in the Passion, which forever changed her heart; henceforth, she felt that God meant for her to pursue a religious vocation. Her father did not support this idea, but eventually, after his death twenty years later, Emily was able to fulfill her desire to found a new religious community, the Sisters of St. Joseph of the Apparition. The Apparition refers to Joseph's vision of the angel Gabriel. The considerable amount of money that her father had left Emily allowed her to fund many of the congregation's missionary and educational endeavors. Despite great odds and personal physical ailments, Emily's order spread throughout the globe, including northern Africa, Malta, the Balkans, Burma, Australia, and even into the Holy Land. Her motto was "I have plenty of trials, but God is always there to support me." Emily died at age fifty-nine in 1856, and Pope Pius XII canonized her in 1951.

Prayer:

Heavenly Father, thank you for blessing our faith with great and holy women leaders like St. Emily. You called her at an early age, and she knew that she would be fulfilling a destiny that would help people throughout the globe. May her example of a life lived totally for Christ inspire us to find ways to sanctify our own lives and spread the Gospel. Amen.

Antiphon:

I have given you as a light to the nations.

Readings:

"The Lord is my portion; I promise to keep your words. I implore your favor with all my heart; be gracious to me according to your promise. When I think of your ways, I turn my feet to your decrees; I hurry and do not delay to keep your commandments. . . . At midnight I rise to praise you, because of your righteous ordinances. I am a companion of all who fear you, of those who keep your precepts. The earth, O Lord, is full of your steadfast love; teach me your statutes." *Psalm 119:57–60, 62–66 (NRSV)*

". . . to aspire to live quietly, to mind your own affairs, and to work with your hands, as directed you, so that you may behave properly toward outsiders and be dependent on no one." *1 Thess. 4:11–12 (NRSV)*

"But just when he had resolved to do this, an angel of the Lord appeared to him in a dream and said, 'Joseph, son of David, do not be afraid to take Mary as your wife, for the child conceived in her is from the Holy Spirit.'" *Mt. 1:20 (NRSV)*

JUNE 18 Elizabeth of Schonau

Elizabeth of Schonau was born in 1129 in Germany and entered a Benedictine monastery when she was just twelve years old. She was professed when she was eighteen. From a young age, she piously followed the Rule of St. Benedict, made great acts of charity and self-mortification, and experienced profound visions and ecstasies. These extraordinary spiritual events often occurred on holy days, when Elizabeth was in Mass, or on Sundays. She received revelations about future events and prophesies from Jesus, Mary, and many of the saints. She was also shown visions of such events in the life of Christ as the Passion, the Resurrection, and the Ascension. Under the spiritual direction of her brother Egbert, a monk in the Benedictine monastery, Elizabeth recorded these visions in several books. These spiritual writings were published with her named as "St. Elizabeth" after her death; however, she was never formally canonized. Her name was eventually added to the list of Roman martyrology and remains there. Because she frequently experienced diabolical encounters from the devil during her visions, Elizabeth is often invoked against diabolical temptations.

Prayer:

Dear Lord, you gave us holy women like St. Elizabeth of Schonau to inspire us through revelations on hidden events in Christ's life. Her extraordinary visions help us to see your continued presence with us throughout human history. You are a God who continues to reveal yourself to us today. Let us be inspired by St. Elizabeth to grow closer to you, and to be edified by the writings of the saints through history. May their lives and their writings grace us with a better knowledge of you and a deeper understanding of our faith. Amen.

Antiphon:
Blessed is the one who endures temptation.

Readings:
"One day the heavenly beings came to present themselves before the Lord, and Satan also came among them to present himself before the Lord. The Lord said to Satan, 'Where have you come from?' Satan answered the Lord, 'From going to and fro on the earth, and from walking up and down on it.' The Lord said to Satan, 'Have you considered my servant Job? There is no one like him on the earth, a blameless and upright man who fears God and turns away from evil. He still persists in his integrity, although you incited me against him, to destroy him for no reason.' Then Satan answered the Lord, 'Skin for skin! All that people have they will give to save their lives. But stretch out your hand now and touch his bone and flesh, and he will curse you to your face.' The Lord said to Satan, 'Very well, he is in your power; only spare his life.'" *Job 2:1–6 (NRSV)*

"But if I drive out demons by the Spirit of God, then the kingdom of God has come upon you." *Mt. 12:28 (NIV)*

"Blessed is anyone who endures temptation. Such a one has stood the test and will receive the crown of life that the Lord has promised to those who love him." *James 1:12 (NRSV)*

JUNE 19 Juliana Falconieri

Born in 1270 to a noble family in Florence, Juliana Falconieri was truly an answer to a prayer. Her elderly parents, who had given up hope of having a child, rejoiced at the miracle of her arrival. From a young age, she was a devout and pious girl considerably influenced by her uncle, Blessed Alexius, who was a founder of the Servite Order. At age fifteen, Juliana decided that she would never marry, and she was invested as a tertiary in the Servites. After her parents died, she joined other women in the Servite Order, wrote their constitution, and became the first official foundress of the

Order of Servite nuns. She ministered to the poor and lived a life of exemplary holiness, marked by acts of profound personal mortification. Her extensive periods of fasting may have led to a fatal stomach condition that prevented her from taking food in any form, including the holy Eucharist. This distressed her greatly, and on her deathbed she begged the priest to bring in the consecrated Host and place it upon a veil over her heart. She instantly fell into an ecstasy and died, and the Host disappeared, much to the amazement of numerous witnesses. Upon examining Juliana's body in preparation for burial, the form of a crucifix was found stamped upon her chest.

Intercessory Prayer:

Dear St. Juliana, you lived a life of personal love for Jesus in the holy Eucharist. This love empowered you to do many things for God's greater honor and glory. Help us to emulate your love for Jesus in Holy Communion, so the image of our Eucharistic Lord may be invited into our own souls and stamped indelibly upon our hearts. Amen.

Antiphon:

Blessed are those who are pure of heart.

Readings:

"O God, your strength gives joy to your people; how your saving help makes them glad!
You have granted them the desire of their hearts, you have not refused the prayer of their lips. You came to meet them with goodly blessings;
You have set blessings upon their heads." *Psalm 21:2–4 (PCB)*

"Moreover, when you fast, be not as the hypocrites, with a sad countenance. . . . But when you fast, anoint your head and wash your face; that you appear not to men to fast, but to your Father, which is in secret; and your Father, which sees in secret, shall reward you openly." *Mt. 6:16–18 (KJV)*

"The cup of blessing which we bless, is it not the communion of the blood of Christ? The bread which we break, is it not the communion of the body of Christ? For we, *though* many, are one bread *and* one body; for we all partake of that one bread." *1 Cor. 10:16–17 (NKJV)*

"My covenant in your flesh is to be an everlasting covenant." *Gen. 17:13 (NIV)*

JUNE 20 Margaret Ebner

The first beatification of Pope John Paul II's pontificate was the German mystic Margaret Ebner. Born in 1291 into a wealthy family, Margaret was well educated in the classics. She joined the Dominicans at Maria-Medigen in 1306, but was sent home several years later when she was overcome with a severe, mysterious illness that lasted for more than a decade. During this time she received many of her revelations and prophecies. Her devotional writings draw repeatedly from the paradigm of courtly love, characteristic of the mystics of her period. Her trance states included intense communications with the dead, and she shares details in her autobiography about her need to intervene for them to be released from Purgatory, or, alternately, her difficulty in praying for some whom she identified as "stray souls." Her physical and spiritual sufferings were balanced by a growing peace in Christ as she matured. At the request of her spiritual director, Henry of Nordlingen, she recorded her inner visions and her life. She died in 1351. Margaret's major works, *Revelations*, have recently been collected and published.

Prayer:

> *Good Jesus, beloved of our souls, your servant Blessed Margaret discovered that, through the unexpected and difficult events of life, one could be opened to your Spirit in unforeseen ways. Her experience of you as the love transcending love reminds us that, although you shared our human nature, the love you have for us is beyond all human intelligence. As a soul wishing to serve her Lord, she struggled with her trials, transforming all her sufferings into redemptive love for other souls. Through her intercession and example, teach us to drink deeply of the inebriating cup that is your unending life poured out for us. Amen.*

Antiphon:

For the Spirit searches everything, even the depths of God.

Readings:

"Keep me safe, O God, for in you I take refuge. I said to the LORD, 'You are my Lord; apart from you I have no good thing.' As for the saints who are in the land, they are the glorious ones in whom is all my delight. LORD, you have assigned me my portion and my cup; you have made my lot secure." *Psalm 16:1–5 (NIV)*

"But will God really dwell on earth? The heavens, even the highest heaven, cannot contain you. How much less this temple I have built! Yet give attention to your servant's prayer and his plea for mercy, O LORD my God. Hear the cry and the prayer that your servant is praying in your presence this day." *1 Kings 8:27–28 (NIV)*

"Eye has not seen, nor ear heard, Nor have entered into the heart of [man] the things which God has prepared for those who love Him." *1 Cor. 2:9 (NKJV)*

JUNE 21 Osanna of Mantua

Osanna of Mantua was marked by her first mystical ecstasy when she was only five, and her reputation for sanctity followed her all of her life. At age fourteen, she donned a Dominican habit, but she continued to live at home as a tertiary. Her routine consisted of prayer, penance, and charitable works, as well as caring for her large family. She had been born into wealth, and when her parents died, Osanna spent her fortune in the service of the poor. She miraculously learned to read, after having seen the names of Jesus and Mary printed on a piece of paper. She had great devotion for the Dominican reformer, Girolamo Savonarola, who denounced the decadence of Pope Alexander VII and was later burned at the stake. Osanna likewise predicted punishment for Italy because of the corruption in Rome. She is reported to have said that all of her pleadings for Alexander fell upon God's deaf ears. She died of natural causes in 1505. In art, Osanna is often pictured with a broken heart, enclosing a crucifix.

Prayer:

Dear Holy Spirit of God, you are a fire of everlasting love, but your Spirit may also emerge as the righteous fires of chastisement. Blessed Osanna suffered greatly for the sins of her fellow Christians and for the Church. Have mercy on us in our failure to live exemplary Christian lives. Support your Church during its dark hours. Inspire us all with the fire of your holy wisdom. Amen.

Antiphon:

I know my transgressions, and my sin is ever before me.

Readings:

"Rescue the weak and the needy; deliver them from the hand of the wicked. They have neither knowledge nor understanding, they walk around in darkness; all the foundations of the earth are shaken. I say, 'You are gods, children of the Most High, all of you; nevertheless, you shall die like mortals, and fall like any prince.' Rise up, O God, judge the earth; for all the nations belong to you!" *Psalm 82:4–8 (NRSV)*

"One who is often reproved, yet remains stubborn, will suddenly be broken beyond healing. When the righteous are in authority, the people rejoice." *Prov. 29:1–2 (NRSV)*

"Then Jeremiah spoke to all the officials and all the people saying, 'It is the Lord who sent me to prophesy against this house and this city all the words you have heard. Now therefore amend your ways and your doings, and obey the voice of the Lord your God, and the Lord will change his mind about the disaster that he has pronounced against you.'" *Jer. 26:12–13 (NRSV)*

"And they took offense at him. But Jesus said to them, 'Prophets are not without honor except in their own country and in their own house.'" *Mt. 13:57 (NRSV)*

JUNE 22 Marie d'Oignies

A Belgian mystic, Marie d'Oignies is often called the originator of the Beguine movement. She was married at fourteen, but she persuaded her husband to live chastely and they devoted their lives to good works. They opened a leper hospital and distributed their considerable wealth to the poor. Favored early with supernatural gifts and great charisma, Marie prophesied the Albinguensian crusade and was the first woman to receive the stigmata. Her *vita,* written within two years of her death by Cardinal Jacques de Vitry, served as a tool of official recognition for the holy Flemish women called the Beguines, who surrounded her, as well as a documentary of her life. Like St. Francis (who lived during the same era), she had visions of the seraphim, who represent the pure fire of God's love, which consumed her. She experienced many raptures when the Eucharist was present, and often even the sight of a crucifix would cause her to faint. She eventually became an anchoress in the priory at Oignies, which became famous after her death—both because of the circulation of her *vita* and because de Vitry brought back many relics from the Holy Land and enshrined them there. In art, Marie is often depicted with an angel at her side.

Prayer:

> *Beloved Lord Jesus, Blessed Marie was an ardent lover of your*
> *Passion, and when her soul entered the darkness of your suffering,*
> *she emerged like a silkworm from a cocoon, a glowing butterfly*
> *that radiated hope, joy, and inspiration to all in her circle of*
> *influence. Bless us with your Spirit so that we may encounter the*
> *flames of love that you hold out to us. Bless all modern Beguine*
> *women, who seek to serve you in the support of small communities*
> *throughout the world. Amen.*

Antiphon:

You make your angels spirits and your ministers a flame of fire.

Readings:

"Then one of the seraphs flew to me, holding a live coal that had been taken from the altar with a pair of tongs. The seraph touched my mouth with it and said, 'Now that this has touched your lips, your guilt has departed and your sin is blotted out.'" Isa. 6:6–7 (NRSV)

"And the smoke of the incense, with the prayers of the saints, rose before God from the hand of the angel. Then the angel took the censer and filled it with fire from the altar and threw it on the earth; and there were peals of thunder, rumblings, flashes of lightning and an earthquake." Rev. 8:4–5 (NRSV)

"Are not all angels spirits in the divine service, sent to serve for the sake of those who are to inherit salvation?" Heb. 1:14 (NRSV)

JUNE 23 Our Lady of Vladimir Icon

Our Lady of Vladimir was, like many of the oldest icons, attributed by tradition to St. Luke the Evangelist. In 450, the icon was taken from Jerusalem to Constantinople; in the early 1100s it was moved to Kiev, and then to Vladimir. The current classic Vladimir icon is considered to be an eleventh-century Byzantine work brought to Russia as a present from the Patriarch of Constantinople. Exposed to nomadic attacks in the twelfth century, *Our Lady of Vladimir* was repeatedly invoked by its Russian defenders. When Mongols sacked the Assumption Cathedral in the thirteenth century, the icon was miraculously saved. *Our Lady of Vladimir* is also popular in the West, and it has been used as a focal point for unity among Christians. Richard Cardinal Cushing wrote a prayer dedicated to the icon for world peace. The Virgin's image of empathy is powerful: her eyes seem to reflect the world's sorrows. The young Jesus presses his cheek to his mother's, wrapping his left arm around her neck. All replicas called *The Lady of Tenderness* are based on the Vladimir icon. One of the most beloved icons in the East, she is also called *The Lady Who Saves Russia*. Every Orthodox Church in the world has this image represented somewhere. This author was privileged to witness one of the miracle-working Vladimir icons that shed tears in the early 1990s in a monastery in Texas.

Intercessory Prayer:

Holy Virgin of Vladimir, Christ in his tenderness willed to be born as a child from your womb. With the bodiless angels and all the powers from on high, O Virgin Mother, please pray for us still struggling in a world of terror. We need your motherly care and protection. You who are the mountain overshadowed by divine grace, save us who cling to you. Amen.

Antiphon:

"O Holy Mother of inexpressible light, intercede with Christ for our souls." (Akathist)

Readings:

"Hail, holy Lady most holy Queen, Mary, Mother of God, ever Virgin; chosen by the most holy Father in heaven, consecrated by him, with his most Beloved Son and the Holy Spirit, the Comforter: on you descended and in you still remains all the fullness of grace and every good. Hail, his Palace, hail, his Tabernacle, hail, his Robe, hail, his Handmaid; hail, his Mother; and hail, all holy Virtues who, by the grace and inspiration of the Holy Spirit, are poured into the hearts of the faithful. So that, faithless no longer, they may be made faithful servants of God through you." —*(Traditional, Franciscan Office) Francis of Assisi*

"[For] your voice is sweet, and your face is lovely." *Song of Songs 2:14 (NIV)*

JUNE 24 Etheldreda Ely (Audrey)

Etheldreda Ely, known as Audrey in England, was at one time the most popular of the Anglo-Saxon women saints. Etheldreda was a princess, the daughter of King Anna of East Anglia. She was married twice for political reasons, yet she managed to remain chaste during both of her marriages. In 672, she was able to pursue her call to the religious life and took the veil at Coldingham under St. Ebbe. This community of highborn women became more secular and deteriorated after Ebbe's death. Etheldreda left Coldingham and established a double monastery on the Isle of Ely, where she lived a life of austerity. Several of her sisters and nieces joined her Rule there. Etheldreda died in 679 of a neck tumor, which she attributed to divine punishment for vanity, due to her fondness for necklaces in her youth. Her death was, in fact, due to the plague, which claimed the lives of several of the nuns in her community. Seventeen years after her burial, it was discovered that Etheldreda's body was incorrupt. Even the tumor was healed. Her sister, Sexburga, translated her body to a stone sarcophagus in 695, and it became a popular pilgrimage site. The word "tawdry" is a derivative of St. Audrey's name. Cheap lace and silk necklaces were sold at St. Audrey's fairs, which were held in late June. They became known as "tawdry lace."

Prayer:

Dear Etheldreda, you remind us that no one is beyond God's healing presence. He healed you as you slept in your grave. When we are ill, great fears can arise in us. During the times we are troubled, help us to remember that Christ is with us, so that, being free from anxiety, we may live our lives in joyful trust in him. May we remain ever mindful that his recovery and healing are part of the abundance he promised. Amen.

Antiphon:

> The Lord forgives all your iniquities and heals all your
> diseases.

Readings:

> "You cleared the ground for it; it took deep root and filled the land.
> The mountains were covered with its shade, the mighty cedars
> with its branches; it sent out its branches to the sea, and its
> shoots to the River." *Psalm 80:9–11 (NRSV)*

> "I am going to bring it recovery and healing; I will heal them and
> reveal to them abundance of prosperity and security." *Jer. 33:6
> (NRSV)*

> "When Jesus became aware of this, he departed. Many crowds fol-
> lowed him, and he cured all of them." *Mt. 12:15 (NRSV)*

JUNE 25 Febronia of Nisbis

In 303, Diocletian began the last and bloodiest of the early Christian persecutions. Born during this era, Febronia of Nisbis entered a convent as a child oblate at age two under the charge of her aunt, who was abbess and deaconess there. All the monasteries in Nisbis were attacked when she was twenty years old, and Febronia was seized. At her trial, Diocletian himself intervened in order to win her for his nephew, because of her exceptional beauty. When she refused to pay tribute to the gods, he stripped her naked. She replied that she would tolerate her nakedness because she was confident of winning the contest with the devil, his father. She was then slowly dismembered, as Diocletian was furious and wanted to torture her as much as possible. Her body parts were collected and the relics sent back to the convent. Afterward, Febronia began appearing at regular intervals to sing the Divine Office with her sisters. Six years later, the bishop had a large church built in her honor, and he desired to transfer the relics there. When the reliquary was opened, it was impossible to touch her relics because of the great heat and light that emanated from her casket. All present agreed that Febronia did not wish to be moved. Her relics remained in the convent until 363, when they were translated to Constantinople, where they continued to work many miracles. A sister at the convent in Nisbis, who later served as abbess there, wrote Febronia's biography.

Intercessory Prayer:

O holy martyr Febronia, the early Church celebrated you as a valiant warrior who won her crown of victory after a fierce and bloody struggle. The heavenly bridegroom himself bestowed upon you his gift of immortality. Intercede for all martyrs today, that they may walk their path home to the Lord without faltering. As you trampled on the serpent's head by your unwavering trust in Christ, pray that we may also be sustained in our darkest hours, as we call upon Jesus, our rock and our deliverer. Amen.

Antiphon:

Who will separate us from the love of Christ?

Readings:

"Clouds and thick darkness are round about you; righteousness and justice are the foundation of your throne. Fire goes before you, burning up all that is evil. Your lightenings lighten the world; the earth sees and trembles. . . . All who pay homage to idols . . . are put to shame. All gods bow before you." *Psalm 97:2–7 (PCB)*

"Who shall separate us from the love of Christ? Shall trouble or hardship or persecution or famine or nakedness or danger or sword? . . . No, in all these things we are more than conquerors through him who loved us." *Rom. 8:35–37 (NIV)*

"They will rejoice in the bounty of the LORD—the grain, the new wine and the oil, the young of the flocks and herds. They will be like a well-watered garden, and they will sorrow no more. Then maidens will dance and be glad. . . . I will turn their mourning into gladness; I will give them comfort and joy instead of sorrow." *Jer. 31:12–13 (NIV)*

JUNE 26 *Tikhvin Icon of the Mother of God*

The *Tikhvin* icon, an icon of the Theotokos, is one of the most revered in Russia. It was said to have been venerated in Constantinople as early as the fifth century, but it disappeared in 1383, only to reappear unexpectedly in Russia later that century. Many saw its image in the sky over Novgorod. It is believed that the holy Theotokos has taken Russia under her protection, with the *Pochaev* icon guarding Russia in the west, the *Kazan* icon in the east, and the *Iveron* icon in the south. The *Tikhvin* icon protects and blesses Russia's northern limits. The icon was on pilgrimage numerous times, healing the infirm and comforting those who sorrow. A noted miracle worker, an interesting characteristic of the icon is that an unusual warmth issued from the hands of the Theotokos for many years. The icon is a variant of the Hodigitria type, which "shows the way"; that is, Mary is seen "showing" us her Son. Mary's hand is raised toward her breast as a sign of silent worship of him. A famous copy resides in Chicago, where, like the copy at Mt. Athos, it has been known to flow with myrrh tears. It is the only iconographic image on which the Virgin's tear ducts can be seen. (This author was blessed to venerate a myrrh-streaming icon of the Tikhvin type while it was on tour, even managing to capture it on film.)

Intercessory Prayer:

O Blessed Mother, you are the fervent advocate of the faithful and a sheltering retreat for the whole world. Intercede for us during these times when the whole world is in such peril; enlighten us with your son's precepts, and by the power of your mighty intercession, bestow your peace upon us all. Amen.

Antiphon:

Help us, save us, have mercy on us, O God, by your grace.

Readings:

"Because You have been my help, therefore in the shadow of your wings I will rejoice. My soul follows close behind you; Your right hand upholds me." *Psalm 63:7–8 (NKJV)*

"Peace be with you! As the Father has sent me, I am sending you." And with that he breathed on them and said, "Receive the Holy Spirit." *Jn. 20:21–22 (NIV)*

"Thee who without corruption gave birth to God the Word; the very Theotokos, thee do we magnify." *Traditional, Orthodox Liturgy*

JUNE 27 Our Lady of Perpetual Help

The title of the Blessed Virgin Mary as *Our Lady of Perpetual Help* is one of the more popular devotions in the West, in the iconic style. According to history, the parchment paper bearing this very stunning Byzantine-style image of the Blessed Virgin holding the child Jesus against a stark gold background comes from the sixteenth century. This image is rich in symbolism; tiny angels are seen flying in the background bearing the various elements that will be used in Christ's crucifixion. For the past two centuries, the icon has been under the care of the Redemptorists. Those who pray to the Virgin Mary under the title of Our Lady of Perpetual Help or "Mother of Perpetual Help," a title promoted by Pope Pius IX, have attributed many miracles to the icon. Our Lady, Mother of Perpetual Help is a fitting title for Mary, who never ceased interceding for those who asked for her assistance, beginning with the Wedding at Cana and throughout the centuries. In the East, this icon is called *Our Lady of the Passion*.

Intercessory Prayer:

Dear Blessed Mother of Perpetual Help, from the beginning of Jesus' public ministry at the miracle of the wedding at Cana, you were present, offering your assistance to those who implored your help. We come to you today and ask you to remember all those intentions we hold deep within our hearts and the intentions of others who have asked us to pray for them. We place all of these intentions, great and small, into the abode of your tender, motherly heart. Our Lady, Mother of Perpetual Help, pray for us! Amen.

Antiphon:

His mother said to the servants, "Do whatever he tells you."

Readings:

"They will come and bind themselves to the LORD in an everlasting covenant that will not be forgotten." *Jer. 50:5 (NIV)*

"I have heard the prayer and supplication that you have made before me; I have hallowed this house, which you have built, to put my Name there forever; and my eyes and my heart shall be there perpetually." *1 Kings 9:3 (KJV)*

"And you child, will be called the prophet of the Most High; for you will go before the Lord to prepare his ways, to give knowledge of salvation to his people in the forgiveness of their sins, through the tender mercy of our God, when the day shall dawn upon us from on high to give light to those who sit in darkness and in the shadow of death, to guide our feet into the way of peace." *Lk. 1:76–79 (RSV)*

"And they said to him, 'Every man at the beginning sets out good wine, and when men have drunk freely, then the poor wine; but you have kept the good wine until now.'" *Jn. 2:10 (RSV)*

JUNE 28 Madeleine Fontaine

Madeleine Fontaine, sometimes called Marie-Madeleine, lived in France during the turbulent years when the Church was persecuted, known as "The Great Terror." Madeleine was born into a poor family and was instructed in a school run by the Daughters of Charity. She became a member of the order in 1748. Madeleine was a nurse and tended to the poor and destitute throughout the city slums for over forty years. During the year 1793–1794, Robespierre's government officially abolished religion, and nuns and priests were summarily rounded up throughout the city and executed. Madeleine and three other nuns from her order were arrested, falsely charged, and sentenced to the guillotine. The nuns went bravely to their deaths, singing "Ave Maria Stella." Many witnesses testified that Madeleine made a public prophecy before she died assuring everyone that the persecution would soon come to an end and Jesus' altars would rise again in victory. Her prophecy came about just a few months later when Robespierre was executed, and his reign of terror came to an end. The nuns were beatified in 1920.

Prayer:

Heavenly Father, you gave us Madeleine Fontaine in a time when holy martyrs nourished the Church's seeds with their blood freely given. Allow Madeleine's heroic life of virtue and self-giving to inspire us as we strive to live our daily lives in a virtuous way. May her daily acts of charity be a shining example to us and help us to reach out to others whom you place within our paths. Amen.

Antiphon:

Greater love hath no man than this, that he lay down his life for his friends.

Readings:

"The Anointed delivers the needy when they call, the poor and those who are helpless.
Having pity on the weak and the needy, saving the lives of the poor.
From oppression and violence they are redeemed
And precious is their blood." *Psalm 72:13–14 (PCB)*

"Come, my people, enter your chambers, and shut your doors behind you; hide yourselves for a little while, until the wrath is past. For behold, the Lord is coming forth out of his place to punish the inhabitants of the earth for their iniquity; and the earth will disclose the blood shed upon her; and will no more cover her slain [ones]. . . . [L]et them lay hold of my protection, let them make peace with me, let them make peace with me." *Isa. 26:20–21; 27:5 (RSV)*

"Finally, brethren . . . Become complete. Be of good comfort, be of one mind, live in peace; and the God of love and peace will be with you. Greet one another with a holy kiss. All the saints greet you. The grace of the Lord Jesus Christ, and the love of God, and the communion of the Holy Spirit *be* with you all." *2 Cor. 13:11–12 (NKJV)*

JUNE 29 Mary Francis Bachmann

Mary Francis Bachmann was destined for family and religious life, combining them both in a unique way. Born Mary Ann Boll in 1824 in Bavaria, she married Anthony Bachmann, and they emigrated to the United States to start their family. He was killed in a construction accident when she was twenty-seven and pregnant with their fourth child. When her sister, Barbara Boll, moved into the Bachmann home to help, they opened a boarding home; one of the borders was a Third Order Franciscan. The three women began to think about incorporating religious life with their other endeavors. Just when they consulted Bishop John Newmann about their plans to form some kind of community, Pope Pius IX, himself a Franciscan tertiary, advised Bishop Newmann to establish a congregation of Franciscan sisters in Philadelphia. The three women were overjoyed, and together they founded the Sisters of St. Francis of the Third Order Regular, with Mary as director. Mother Mary continued to mother her own children, and two of her girls eventually joined the order. They opened a mission for orphans and the aged in several other cities, and Mary's spiritual daughters numbered over four thousand. On June 30, 1863, Mother Mary Francis died of tuberculosis. She is remembered in the Franciscan calendar on June 29.

Prayer:

Beloved Lord Jesus, Mother Mary Francis once wrote that all her hopes were centered in you and that one who stands in need of no friend but you will be most effective to serve you. She lived what she wrote, and because she depended on you for her sole support, she had many who loved and supported her in the world. Teach us this radical confidence, so that nothing can ever shake us, for we stand firmly on you, our rock and our salvation. Amen.

Antiphon:

You, my God, make my darkness bright.

Readings:

"We ponder your steadfast love, O God, in the midst of your temple. Your name, O God, like your praise, reaches to the ends of the earth. Your right hand is filled with victory. Let Mount Zion be glad, let the towns of Judah rejoice because of your judgments." *Psalm 48:9–11 (NRSV)*

"The Lord has established his throne in the heavens, and his kingdom rules over all. Bless the Lord, O you his angels, you mighty ones who do his bidding, obedient to his spoken word. Bless the Lord, all his hosts, his ministers that do his will." *Psalm 103:19–22 (NRSV)*

"Here am I, and the children God has given me." *Heb. 2:13 (NKJV)*

JUNE 30 Anne Frank

Anne Frank became known to the world for the diary in which she poured forth her soul for two years, gazing out of a small warehouse window while hiding from the Nazis. She and her Jewish family had taken shelter in her father's office in Amsterdam when she was thirteen. Anne recorded her thoughts and prayers in her journal. Her extraordinary gifts as a writer are overshadowed only by the goodness reflected in her personality. Despite the trials of living in cramped quarters with almost no light, no company, and no nature—which Anne dearly loved—and with the constant anxiety of being caught, she still managed to give thanks to God every night for all that is good and beautiful. Discovered in 1944 and sent to a prison camp, Anne died the next year of typhus. Her journal, first published by her father, was translated into thirty languages. *The Diary of Anne Frank* is a lasting testimony of hope.

Prayer:

> *Beloved Spirit of God, you were present to your people in the form of a fiery cloud that led them through the wilderness. You likewise comforted Holocaust martyr Anne Frank by beckoning her toward your light and your most tender goodness in the midst of great trial and loneliness. She wrote that, because of you, there would always be comfort for every sorrow. Be our comforter in times of despair, and enable us to use the example of Anne to remember that the small still flame that hides behind the darkness can never be extinguished. Amen.*

Antiphon:

Let my prayer come before you like incense, the lifting of my hands as the evening sacrifice.

Readings:

"Happy are those whose strength is in you, in whose heart are the highways to Zion. As they go through the valley of Baca they make it a place of springs; the early rain also covers it with pools. They go from strength to strength; the God of gods will be seen in Zion." Psalm 84:5–7 (NRSV)

"God said, 'This is the sign of the covenant that I make between me and you and every living creature that is with you, for all future generations. I have set my bow in the clouds, and it shall be a sign of the covenant between me and the earth.'" *Gen. 9:12–14 (NRSV)*

". . . who goes before you on the way to seek out a place for you to camp, in fire by night and in the cloud by day, to show you the route you should take." *Deut. 1:33 (NRSV)*

"And we speak of these things in words not taught by human wisdom but taught by the Spirit, interpreting spiritual things to those who are spiritual." *1 Cor. 2:13 (NRSV)*

JULY 1 Elizabeth Lange

Sometimes one chooses a mission in life and sometimes it is chosen for us. Born in Haiti in 1784, Elizabeth Lange came to the United States in her late twenties with one intention: to offer education to children of color. A Silesian priest named Fr. Joubert, whose parish in Baltimore included a number of African-Americans, was impressed with her work and invited her to found a religious community. In a city still rigidly segregated, where whites and blacks did not even pray the same Mass together, securing the archbishop's support seemed providential. Elizabeth agreed, and with three other women of color, she established the first religious order of black women in the United States, called the Oblate Sisters of Providence. During this time, which was prior to the Emancipation Proclamation, they endured many insults and threats; even Baltimore Catholics were angered that black women were wearing habits. The sisters almost did not make it through their formative years, as a number of ecclesiastical authorities thought they should disband and go back to being servants. They were always lacking in funds. However, before her death in 1879, Mother Mary Elizabeth received the public support and recognition from the Church and her community that she had wanted most of her life. She died peacefully, knowing that her order would continue to implement her dream and that the day when African-American Catholics had a voice in the Church had arrived. The process of her canonization is under way.

Prayer:

O mysterious Holy Spirit, you instilled the destiny of being a beacon of hope for all people of color in Elizabeth Lange's heart, and she responded to your call with every fiber of her being. Her perseverance as a champion of God's justice calls us to resist prejudice and poverty wherever it still lurks in our world and to work for healing and hope for all people. Inspire us when we struggle with our own visions, and allow your holy fire to instill in us the blessed wisdom we yearn for when the vision begins to fade. Through Jesus' holy name, may we always trust in your inspiration and providence. Amen.

Antiphon:

You restore my soul in your living waters.

Readings:

"How can young people keep their way pure? By guarding it according to your word. With my whole heart I seek you; do not let me stray from your commandments. I treasure your word in my heart, so that I may not sin against you. Blessed are you, O Lord; teach me your statutes." *Psalm 119:9–14 (NRSV)*

"Listen to advice and accept instruction, that you may gain wisdom for the future." *Prov. 19:20 (NRSV)*

"Even if I am to be poured as a libation upon the sacrificial offering of your faith, I am glad and rejoice with you all. Likewise you also should be glad and rejoice with me." *Phil. 2:17–18 (RSV)*

JULY 2 Monegund (Monegundis)

Monegund was born in Chartres, where she married and had two daughters. When both of her daughters were stricken with fever and died, she mourned them deeply and turned to holy Scripture for solace. After a period of discernment, Monegund was inspired to turn to a life of asceticism. She left her household in Chartres and traveled to Tours to St. Martin's Basilica, where she became an anchorite, practicing rituals of vigil keeping, prayer, and fasting. According to her biographer, Gregory of Tours, God repeatedly worked miracles through her. Monegund healed through prayer and through the use of herbs, oils, blessing water, and the sign of the cross. Her charismatic devotion to God and prayer attracted a group of female disciples to her. They formed a prayer community, supporting themselves by weaving mats and baking bread. Monegund died in 570 among her disciples and was buried in her cell. Her burial site became a focal point for pilgrims. According to Gregory of Tours, many were healed at Monegund's tomb.

Prayer:

Beloved Lord, you raised up Monegund to be a woman of great sanctity devoted to healing others. In your name she ventured into the darkness of unknowing, responding to the call to renew her life and the lives of those whom she served. Through her intercession, help us to experience all of creation as part of your beautiful body. Teach us to remain true to our ideals of serving you with courage and love. Amen.

Antiphon:

Balance with joy our days of affliction.

Readings:

"LORD, thou hast been our dwelling place in all generations. Before the mountains were brought forth, or ever thou hadst formed the earth and the world, from everlasting to everlasting thou art God. Thou turnest man back to the dust. . . . For a thousand years in thy sight are but as yesterday when it is past, or as a watch in the night. Thou dost sweep men away; they are like a dream, like grass which is renewed in the morning: in the morning it flourishes and is renewed; in the evening it fades and withers. . . . The years of our life are threescore and ten, or even by reason of strength fourscore; yet their span is but toil and trouble; they are soon gone, and we fly away. . . . So teach us to number our days that we may get a heart of wisdom. *Psalm 90:1–6, 10–12 (RSV)*

"For land which has drunk the rain that often falls upon it, and brings forth vegetation useful to those for whose sake it is cultivated, receives a blessing from God." *Heb 6:7 (RSV)*

JULY 3 Non of Wales

St. Non of Wales (also Nonna or Nonnita) was the mother of St. David, the patron saint of Wales. During her education at Ty Gwyn in Wales, a local chieftain violated Non and she became pregnant. During her pregnancy, a traveling preacher, Gildas, came to the church at Ty Gwyn. Non hid to hear his sermon. Gildas, unable to speak, could not give the sermon. He called Non out of hiding and when she came forth, he declared that the child in her womb would be greater than he was, and that was why he couldn't preach: "the lesser cannot preach before the greater." David was born among the standing stones on the Bryn y Garn cliff top during a thunderstorm. The stone on which Non lay split at the time of her delivery (in empathy for her), and a spring sprang forth on the spot. According to legend, the stone also became soft, and the imprint of Non's hand remained forever on the stone. St. David was born dead. St. Ailbe, who was present at the birth, resuscitated the baby and baptized him in the spring that had appeared. David was then given to a bishop to be fostered and educated, and he became one of the greatest churchmen in Wales. Non later journeyed to Cornwall to join her sister Gwen. The two established a community and church at Altarnon in Cornwall. From there, Non continued her missionary work in Brittany. St. Non died in Brittany in 550 and was buried there. In some places, her feast is celebrated on June 24.

Prayer:
> Dear Lord, Non of Wales nurtured the life within her with the conviction that her child would serve you. Please, help us to nurture the life within us with an open heart like St. Non. Give us the strength to bring forth that which you deem fit to have us birth into this world. We pray that our hearts beat in service to your tender love, which nurtures all and constantly births new life. Amen.

Antiphon:
When your word goes forth it gives light.

Readings:
"'Come now, let us make a covenant, you and I; and let it be a wit-

ness between you and me.' So Jacob took a stone, and set it up as a pillar." *Gen 31:44–45 (RSV)*

"By his knowledge the deeps broke forth,
and the clouds drop down the dew. My son, keep sound wisdom and discretion;
let them not escape from your sight, and they will be life for your soul
and adornment for your neck." *Prov. 3:20–22 (RSV)*

"Lo! I tell you a mystery. We shall not all sleep, but we shall all be changed, in a moment, in the twinkling of an eye . . . the trumpet will sound, and the dead will be raised imperishable, and we shall be changed." *1 Cor. 15:51–52 (RSV)*

JULY 4 Elizabeth of Portugal

Like her saintly great aunt for whom she was named, St. Elizabeth of Hungary, this saintly Elizabeth lived during the thirteenth century. The daughter of a king, she was betrothed at a young age, and she eventually married King Denis of Portugal. Surrounded by the court's majesty, she never forgot the staple of her life: her Catholic faith. Amid her many duties as queen, she was able to incorporate Mass, fasting, her pious works, and other acts of charity and mortification into her daily life. Her husband was not a faithful spouse, but she grew to love his illegitimate children. She had two children herself, and she was able to help ease a conflict between her husband and their son, Alonso, thus earning her the title of "the Peacemaker." Elizabeth spent her years founding religious houses, hospitals, and orphanages, and she was beloved by her people. Her patience and prayers eventually caused her husband's conversion, and he lived the remainder of his life as a truly Christian king, before dying of an illness that lasted for over a year. After his death, Elizabeth became a Franciscan tertiary in a convent that she had helped to found. Numerous miracles were attributed to Elizabeth, both before and after her death at age sixty-five.

Prayer:

Heavenly Father, you gave us wonderful saints like St. Elizabeth of Portugal so we would have examples of how to live for you within every walk of life. Even though she was a queen, she made her faith the center of her life and brought that faith to others through her numerous acts of love and charity. Help us follow her example to incorporate acts of charity in our own lives. May we use our gifts to further Christ's kingdom. Amen.

Antiphon:

Blessed be the Lord, for he has shown a marvelous kindness.

Readings:

"Ascribe to the Lord, O heavenly beings, ascribe the Lord glory and strength. Ascribe to the Lord the glory of his name; worship the Lord in holy splendor. . . . May the Lord give strength to his people! May the Lord bless his people with peace!" *Psalm 29:1–2, 11 (NRSV)*

"I the Lord have called thee in righteousness, and will hold thine hand, and will keep thee, and give thee for a covenant of the people, for a light to the Gentiles; To open the blind eyes, to bring out the prisoners from the prison, and them that sit in darkness out of the prison house." *Is. 46:6–7 (KJV)*

"I will make a covenant of peace with them; it shall be an everlasting covenant with them; and I will bless them and multiply them, and will set my sanctuary in the midst of them for evermore." *Ez. 37:26 (RSV)*

"But the wisdom from above is first pure, then peaceable, gentle, open to reason, full of mercy and good fruits, without uncertainty or insincerity. And the harvest of righteousness is sown in peace by those who make peace." *James 3:17–18 (RSV)*

JULY 5 Morwenna

Morwenna was an early Celtic saint (480 C.E.), one of many daughters of the Welsh king, Brychan. Morwenstow, the northernmost parish in Cornwall, which was named after her, is located on high, rocky cliffs overlooking the Atlantic Ocean. Legend has it that Morwenna carried a large stone upon her head from the beach to the cliff top to establish a church for the local people. When she stopped to rest and laid the stone down, a holy well sprang up at the site where the stone lay. Seeing this as divine guidance, the local people built a church on that spot. The spring is still visible to the west of the church. In the church at Morwenstow an image believed to depict Morwenna shows a woman clasping a scroll or volume to her breast with her left hand and blessing a monk with her right hand. Morwenna is also shown teaching children to read. In the nineteenth century, Morwenstow was home to poet and vicar Robert Stephen Hawkes, known as "pastor to the shipwrecked." She is the patron saint of Morwenstow.

Prayer:

Beloved Lord Jesus, you are the savior of the shipwrecked and the solace of the despairing. Through Blessed Morwenna's intercession, help us to carry the rock of your strength and hope to all in need. May the wilderness around us sprout and be made fruitful in your blessed name. Amen.

Antiphon:

When you send forth your Spirit, you renew the face of the earth.

Readings:

"From your lofty abode you water the mountains; the earth is satisfied with the fruit of your work. You cause the grass to grow for the cattle, and plants for the people to use, to bring forth food from the earth, and wine to gladden the human heart, oil to make the face shine, and bread to strengthen the human heart. The trees of the Lord are watered abundantly, the cedars of Lebanon that he planted. In them the birds build their nests; the stork has its home in the fir trees. The high mountains are for the wild goats; the rocks are a refuge for the coneys. You have made the moon to mark the seasons; the sun knows its time for setting." *Psalm 104:13–19 (NRSV)*

"To each is given the manifestation of the Spirit for the common good. To one is given through the Spirit the utterance of wisdom, and to another the utterance of knowledge according to the same Spirit, to another faith by the same Spirit, to another gifts of healing by the one Spirit, to another the working of miracles, to another prophecy, to another the ability to distinguish between spirits. . . ." *1 Cor. 12:7–10 (RSV)*

JULY 6 Maria Goretti and Ursula Ledochowska

Today we celebrate the lives of two very different women who lived a century apart. St. Maria Goretti lived in the late 1800s in the Italian countryside. Her family was extremely poor and worked as tenant farmers. As a young girl, Maria was pious and devout and valued her purity. One day a young man who shared their tenant farmer's flat tried to rape her. Maria, although only twelve, resisted in an effort to preserve her chastity. The man stabbed her fourteen times. Maria died soon after, but not before she forgave her attacker. He was sentenced to thirty years, during which time he received a heavenly vision of the young martyred saint, which caused his conversion. He was even present at St. Maria Goretti's canonization. She is a model of purity for youth.

A century later, Ursula Ledochowska was born to a pious family in Poland. She followed her heart's inspirations and became a religious, eventually founding the Order of Ursulines of the Sacred Heart (often referred to as The Grey Ursulines). Her convents helped to establish many Catholic institutions, and Pope John Paul II beatified her in 1983 as an outstanding example of Christian witness and charity.

Prayer:

Holy God, throughout history you have given us holy women to inspire us with their lives of virtue and purity. St. Maria Goretti was a martyr for the cause of purity and chastity. Give your grace to the youth of today that they may be inspired by her witness. Blessed Ursula was an example of loving charity through serving others. Help us to understand how we can emulate her goodness in responding to your call to further Christ's kingdom on earth. Amen.

Antiphon:

Blessed are the pure in heart, for they shall see God.

Readings:

"[He] who loves purity of heart, and whose speech is gracious, will have the king as his friend" *Prov. 22:11 (RSV)*

"'He delivers the innocent man; you will be delivered through the cleanness of your hands.'" *Job 22:30 (RSV)*

"Steadfast love and faithfulness will meet; righteousness and peace will kiss each other. Faithfulness will spring up from the ground, and righteousness will look down from the sky. Yea, the LORD will give what is good. . . ." *Psalm 85:10–12 (RSV)*

"Blessed are the pure in heart, for they shall see God." *Mt. 5:8 (RSV)*

JULY 7 Ethelburga of Faremoutier

Ethelburga of Faremoutier, known as St. Aubierge in France, was an illegitimate daughter of Anna, King of East Anglia. Her half-sisters included Sexburga, Etheldreda, Withburga, and Saethrith. Ethelburga longed to be a nun. There were few monasteries established at that time in England, so Ethelburga was sent to the monastery of Faremoutier in France with Saethrith to be educated. She succeeded Saethrith as abbess of Faremoutier, and she was known to be a wise and just ruler. When she became abbess, Ethelburga began to build a church to honor all twelve apostles. She died in 664, prior to the church's completion and was buried in the unfinished building. Building of the church ceased when she died, and seven years later, when it was determined that there was not enough money to complete the church, her body was translated to the Church of St. Stephen the Martyr. Her body was found to be fresh and incorrupt. St. Ethelburga is depicted in art as an abbess carrying the instruments of the Passion. Ethelburga is invoked to cure rheumatism.

Prayer:

Holy Spirit, you guide us lovingly in so many ways. Ethelburga, who knew her vocation was to be a nun, was allowed the education that provided her with the ability to be a wise and just abbess. May we open our hearts to your guidance so that whatever our endeavors in the world, we can approach them in wise and just ways that pay tribute to the glory of the triune God. Amen.

Antiphon:

Countless are your works, O God.

Readings:

"If she is a wall, we will build upon her a battlement of silver; but if she is a door, we will enclose her with boards of cedar. I was a wall, and my breasts were like towers; then I was in his eyes as one who brings peace." *Song of Solomon 8:9–10 (NRSV)*

"For we know that if the earthly tent we live in is destroyed, we have a building from God, a house not made with hands, eternal in the heavens. For in this tent we groan, longing to be clothed with our heavenly dwelling." *2 Cor. 5:1–2 (NRSV)*

"So is it with the resurrection of the dead. What is sown is perishable, what is raised is imperishable. . . . It is sown a physical body, it is raised a spiritual body." *1 Cor. 15:42, 44 (RSV)*

JULY 8 *Kazan Icon of the Mother of God*

The *Kazan* icon of the Theotokos was considered one of the holiest of imperial Russia. The icon made its appearance in 1579 when a ten-year-old girl, Matryona, had a dream wherein the image appeared to her and told her to look for the icon resting under ashes in the ruins of a Kazan house. When uncovered, the icon shone like it had just been painted, and it became an instant miracle worker. The *Kazan* icon became a national sacred treasure and a symbol of Russia's historical destiny. During the war with the Poles in 1612, a three-day fast was undertaken by the entire country in honor of the *Virgin of Kazan* for intervention. With the expulsion of the Polish troops from Moscow, prince Dimitrious Pozharsky had the *Kazan* icon installed in the cathedral at Moscow. Her intercession was invoked again during the war with the French. It is believed that during the Napoleonic War of 1812, the original icon was moved to St. Petersburg, where one of the most magnificent cathedrals to Mary was built in 1821. After its installation, it was adorned with diamonds, emeralds, and a gold riza plate, and it became one of the treasured icons of the Romanov dynasty. At the dawn of the Bolshevik Revolution, it is believed that the original icon was smuggled out before the communists could destroy it. It then mysteriously made its way to Fatima, where it remained for many years; then it was presented to Pope John Paul II to keep in his private chambers. The icon was restored to the Russian people in August 2004, to their great rejoicing. The two major feasts of the *Kazan* icon are October 22, in celebration of Russia's 1612 deliverance from the Poles, and July 8, in honor of its initial appearance. Copies of the *Kazan* icon are used to bless couples when they marry, and it is famous for healing the blind. *Our Lady of Soufanieh* in Damascus, which also has become a famous myrrh-streaming icon and which has come to signify unity between the churches, is a Western copy of the *Kazan* icon.

Intercessory Prayer:

Blessed Theotokos, whose womb was made holy in order to receive the son of God, we earnestly beseech you to intercede for us who claim you as our mother. We long to join you in an embrace of motherly love that tenderly flows out to all your children equally. Help us to overcome the blind thinking that separates us from God's pure love and from one another. We await the day when the New Jerusalem stands together as one Church and one body, and we offer our prayers for the intention of unity, which would bring so much joy to your infinitely beautiful heart. Amen.

Antiphon:

Hail, O pre-eternal good-will of the Holy Sprit, which has no beginning of days! (Akathist)

Readings:

"Moreover you shall make the tabernacle with ten curtains of fine twined linen and blue and purple and scarlet stuff; with cherubim skilfully worked shall you make them." *Ex. 26:1 (RSV)*

"And he was afraid, and said, 'How awesome is this place! This is none other than the house of God, and this is the gate of heaven.'" *Gen. 28:17 (RSV)*

"More than the tabernacle of Moses, which was fashioned according to a heavenly plan, did God hallow thee wholly with the Holy Spirit, O Theotokos; and having dwelt wholly within thee, He has given life to all. A great and all-glorious mountain art thou, O Theotokos, surpassing Mt. Sinai. For, unable to bear the descent of the glory of God in types and shadows, it caught on fire; and thunder and lightning struck it; but thou, being all divine light, bore the Word of God in your womb without being consumed . . . Wherefore thine icon has been filled with the grace of God more than the ark of Aaron, and pours forth sanctification upon our souls." *Great Vespers, Kazan*

JULY 9 Withburga

St. Withburga was the youngest daughter of King Anna of East Anglia, and the half-sister of St. Ethelburga (see Daily Readings, July 7, Ethelburga of Faremoutier). She lived a solitary life in Holkham in Norfolk as a young girl. After her father's death, she moved to East Dereham and began construction of a nunnery there. Money was very scarce for this project, and the workmen as well as the nuns were desperate for food. Withburga appealed to the Virgin Mary for help, who directed her to send sisters down to the stream. At the stream, two does appeared and allowed themselves to be milked. The milk provided the means to make butter and cheese for the community. Withburga did not live to see the nunnery's completion. She died in 743 and was buried in the churchyard at Dereham. Her body was exhumed fifty years later so it could be translated into the completed church. When her body was found to be incorrupt, her gravesite became a popular pilgrimage site. In 974, the Abbot of Ely was given permission to translate Withburga's body to the Abbey at Ely so she could rest with her sisters Etheldreda and Sexburga. The abbot and the monks provided a feast for the townspeople of Dereham, then proceeded to carry off the body. The people in the town were dismayed, and they pursued the monks but failed to recover Withburga's body. Upon returning home, they found that a spring of clear water with curative powers gushed from the saint's original burial place. They felt that this was compensation for their loss. The spring still exists today and is known as St. Withburga's well. Withburga's Well is in East Dereham and is a popular tourist site today.

Prayer:

Precious Spirit, you provided Withburga and her community with food in their time of need. Help us to remember that as God provides for the birds of the air, so will our needs also be met if we trust in God's providence. May we open our hearts to your loving care, knowing that you bring us ever closer to the knowledge that God is the sure foundation of our lives. Amen.

Antiphon:

You restore my soul to life.

Readings:

"Should your springs be scattered abroad, streams of water in the streets?" *Prov. 5:16 (NRSV)*

"Then he looked up at his disciples and said: 'Blessed are you who are poor, for yours is the kingdom of God. Blessed are you who are hungry now, for you will be filled. Blessed are you who weep now, for you will laugh.'" *Lk. 6:20–21 (NRSV)*

"The woman said to him, 'Sir, you have no bucket, and the well is deep. Where do you get that living water? Are you greater than our ancestor Jacob, who gave us the well, and with his sons and his flocks drank from it?' Jesus said to her, 'Everyone who drinks of the water that I will give them will never be thirsty. The water that I give will become in them a spring of water gushing up to eternal life.'" *Jn. 4:11–14 (NRSV)*

JULY 10 Secunda and Rufina, and Veronica Giuliani

Sts. Secunda and Rufina were sisters who lived in the time of the early Church, around the third century. The two girls were privileged members of a prominent Roman family who were strong Christians. When the girls refused to accept the offer of marriage from two pagan suitors, they were scourged and beheaded. The relics of the two virgin-martyrs, Secunda and Rufina, were eventually transferred to the Lateran Basilica.

St. Veronica Giuliani lived much later, during the seventeenth century. From her infancy, profound miracles surrounded the holy child. At just three years old, she had her first mystical encounter with God, who encouraged her to work for the poor. In 1677, she joined the Order of the Capuchin Poor Clares and took the name of Veronica. She suffered the mystical experience of stigmata in the form of a cross impressed on her heart and a crown of thorns. The wounds from these stigmata were clearly visible, but she continued to serve thirty-four years as the Mistress of Novices within her order. She was eventually elected abbess and served in that capacity until her death in 1727. Pope Gregory XVI canonized Veronica in 1839. She is usually depicted in art wearing a crown of thorns and embracing the cross.

Prayer:

Dear Lord, you blessed your Church with many courageous women through the centuries, such as Sts. Secunda and Rufina, and St. Veronica Giuliani. These holy and devout women served you and spread the word of your Church through their self-sacrifice. Help us to learn from their example to accept the sufferings in our own lives. Let us always remember that inconveniences, trials, heartaches, and even the most mundane tasks of daily life may also serve to sanctify and purify us. Amen.

Antiphon:

Trust in the Lord, who is your help and your shield.

Readings:

"Thus says the LORD of hosts: Peoples shall yet come, even the inhabitants of many cities; the inhabitants of one city shall go to another, saying, 'Let us go at once to entreat the favor of the LORD, and to seek the LORD of hosts; I am going.' Many peoples and strong nations shall come to seek the LORD of hosts in Jerusalem, and to entreat the favor of the LORD . . . saying, 'Let us go with you, for we have heard that God is with you.'" *Zech. 8:20–23 (RSV)*

"Nathan'a-el said to him, 'How do you know me?' Jesus answered him, 'Before Philip called you, when you were under the fig tree, I saw you.' Nathan'a-el answered him, 'Rabbi, you are the Son of God! You are the King of Israel!'" *Jn. 1:48 (RSV)*

JULY 11 Olga of Russia

Called the "star of the East," Olga (also called Helga) was born in Pskov, Russia, in 879. She married Igor, prince of Kiev, in 903. Olga visited Constantinople several times and, influenced by the patriarch there, she converted to Christianity. The saint's name she chose was Helena of the Cross. Olga prayed for her son's conversion, but he died in a Viking war unconverted. The *Chronicle* of her life tells us that it was Olga's influence that led her grandson, Vladimir, to receive Christian training. There were no mass conversions in Russia (called "Rus") until after Olga died. Some time after her death, her tomb was opened and her relics found to be incorrupt, the first miracle of its kind in the history of the Russian Orthodox Church, which undoubtedly helped the cult of the "new religion" take root on Russian soil. Orthodox Russia is often believed to be the legacy of St. Vladimir, who married princess Anne of Constantinople and consolidated the Byzantine and Russian empires. But without an Olga, there would have been no initial conversion, no seeds planted in a future Kievan prince by a wise and determined grandmother.

Intercessory Prayer:

O Blessed Olga, you were more devoted to God than to country, and you followed the calling of your heart into the darkness of unknowing. Trusting implicitly in your faith in God, you spent your life praying for the cause of your beloved Rus. You who strove always to do good works, storing up treasures in heaven, intercede for us so that, when Christ comes for us, we may also appear with him in glory. Amen.

Antiphon:

You have shed upon us the new light of your incarnate Word.

Readings:

"How beautiful upon the mountains are the feet of him who brings good tidings, who publishes peace, who brings good tidings of good, who publishes salvation, who says to Zion, 'Your God reigns.'" *Isa. 52:7 (RSV)*

"I mean that the heir, as long as [he] is a child, is no better than a slave, though [he] is the owner of all the estate; but [he] is under guardians and trustees until the date set by the father. So with us; when we were children, we were slaves to the elemental spirits of the universe. But when the time had fully come, God sent forth his Son, born of woman, born under the law, to redeem those who were under the law, so that we might receive adoption as [sons]. . . . So through God you are no longer a slave but a [son], and if a [son] then an heir." *Gal. 4:1–5, 7 (RSV)*

JULY 12 Euphemia

St. Euphemia's fame was ascribed to her more than a century after she died. Little is known about her life, and the Eastern Church glorified her as a saint only when her postmortem deeds became so outstanding that it was decided such miracles could only be divine. It appears that she was born in Chalcedon and burned at the stake as a martyr. Entombed within the walls of a chapel, healings were attributed to pilgrimages to her tomb. The Synod of Chalcedon was convened in 451, and great conflict arose concerning Christ's dual nature (human and divine). One of the patriarchs proposed calling upon Euphemia's intercession—her tomb was nearby—and a period of discernment followed. There is a legend that when her casket was opened, a miracle scroll appeared in her hand, signifying that the single-nature proposal was heresy. The dual nature of Christ was made dogma, and through the centuries, the Byzantine churches have honored St. Euphemia for her intercession and patronage.

Prayer:

Beloved Lord Jesus, we thank you for guiding your Church toward the understanding that you were fully human as well as fully divine. We know you send forth your Spirit in mysterious ways, and that the Spirit is the source of unity and truth. We give honor and glory to you in all your saints, who deepen and widen our vision of your presence among us. Amen.

Antiphon:

Let us bless the living God, revealed in his glory.

Readings

"He has shown his people the power of his works, in giving them the heritage of the nations. The works of his hands are faithful and just; all his precepts are trustworthy. They are established forever and ever, to be performed with faithfulness and uprightness. He sent redemption to his people; he has commanded his covenant forever. Holy and awesome is his name." *Psalm 111:6–10 (NRSV)*

"By which he has granted to us his precious and very great promises, that through these you may escape from the corruption that is in the world because of passion, and become partakers of the divine nature." *2 Pet. 1:4 (RSV)*

"And he said to me, 'These words are trustworthy and true. And the Lord, the God of the spirits of the prophets, has sent his angel to show his servants what must soon take place.'" *Rev. 22:6 (RSV)*

JULY 13 Terese of the Andes

St. Terese of the Andes was born Juanita Fernandez Solar on July 13, 1900. Even from a young age, the beautiful young girl from Chile excelled in her love for Christ. At age nineteen, she felt the inner calling to totally devote her life to Jesus, so she entered the Discalced Carmelite Nuns at Los Andes, where she took the name Terese of Jesus. Her spiritual writings and letters stand as a testament to her amazing wisdom and unique theological observations, which far surpassed her years. Many of her writings were an example to her fellow Carmelites in achieving true sanctity. Her teachings also apply to everyone who strives to lead a virtuous life and purify their daily intentions for the glory of God. After being in the convent for less than a year, Terese fell ill and died at age twenty. Pope John Paul II canonized Terese in March 1993, when he called her the "first fruit of holiness of the Teresian Carmel of Latin America," and he praised her as an example and model for young people everywhere.

Intercessory Prayer:
Dear St. Terese of Jesus, through your spiritual writings you encouraged everyone to live intimately united with God, since "the one who loves tends to be united with the one loved, and the fusing of two souls is done through love." Help us to follow your example of humble sacrifice and self-giving for the sake of the kingdom. May we emulate your unique intimacy with Jesus, especially when we are spiritually united to him through Holy Communion. We ask this in Jesus' name. Amen.

Antiphon:
If we love one another, God lives within us; alleluia!

Readings:
"May my heart be blameless in thy statutes. . . . My soul languishes for thy salvation; I hope in thy word." *Psalm 119:80–81 (RSV)*

"Rejoice and be glad for the sons of the righteous;
for they will be gathered together,
and will praise the Lord of the righteous.
How blessed are those who love you!
They will rejoice in your peace.
Blessed are those who grieved over all your afflictions;
for they will rejoice for you upon seeing all your glory,
and they will be made glad for ever.
Let my soul praise God the great King.
A bright light shall shine to all parts of the earth,
Many nations shall come to you from afar.
And the inhabitants of all the limits of the earth,
Drawn to you by the name of the Most High God,
Bearing in their hands gifts for the Almighty." *Tobit 13:13–15
(NAB)*

"Let us draw near with a true heart in full assurance of faith, with
our hearts sprinkled clean from an evil conscience and our bodies
washed with pure water. Let us hold fast the confession of our
hope without wavering, for he who promised is faithful; and let us
consider how to stir up one another to love and good works." *Heb.
10:22–24 (RSV)*

JULY 14 Kateri Tekawitha

Kateri Tekawitha was born in 1656 in what is now Au-
riesville, New York. Her father was an Indian warrior chief,
and her mother was an Algonquin Indian who had converted
to Christianity through the influence of the Jesuits. Tekawitha's family
died when she was four years old when their village was overcome
with smallpox. This disease left her with a disfigured face, damaged
eyesight, and weakened legs. Her appearance isolated her from her
tribe, but joy entered her life when she converted to Christianity
through the French Jesuits, who arranged for her to be baptized and
take the name of Kateri (Catherine). She escaped to a Christian mission in Canada, where she was free to practice her Catholic faith by
attending Mass twice a day, often walking for miles barefoot in the
snow. Her inner beauty radiated to all who were privileged enough to
know her, as she ministered to the ill and taught children in St.
Lawrence. Kateri's death in 1679 at age twenty-four was followed by

numerous miracles and reported appearances, and Pope John Paul II beatified her in 1980.

Intercessory Prayer:

Dear Blessed Kateri, you taught us that physical beauty is not a prize we can take into Heaven, but that love for Christ and charity to others is what truly makes one beautiful. Help us not to become caught in the notions of society, which places so much stress on outer beauty, but rather to form our souls in Christ's image and likeness. Inspire young women in our society today to strive to make themselves beautiful from the inside out though a love for God and his Church. Amen.

Antiphon:

How beautiful are the feet of them that bring glad tidings of good things!

Readings:

"And I have other sheep, that are not of this fold; I must bring them also. . . ." *Jn. 10:16 (RSV)*

"Whoever gives you a cup of water to drink because you bear the name of Christ, will by no means lose his reward." *Mk. 9:41 (RSV)*

"He has made everything beautiful in its time. He has also set eternity in the hearts of [men]; yet they cannot fathom what God has done from beginning to end." *Eccl. 3:11 (NIV)*

JULY 15 Anne-Marie Javouhey

Anne-Marie Javouhey lived during the turbulent times of the French Revolution. Even as a young girl she worked to help persecuted priests, and she ministered to her village by teaching catechism when the parish priest had been removed. Through a vision, Anne-Marie felt called to begin a religious order of sisters. After much persuasion, her father finally agreed to help financially fund the order, and it became known as The Sisters of St. Joseph of Cluny. They became a teaching order, which soon spread to other areas of the globe, including South America. The community ministered to people of all races and all creeds through their schools and hospitals. Even King Louis-Philippe admired Anne-Marie for her courage and determination, and his army protected her during an uprising against the monarchy that occurred in 1848. Anne-Marie died at age seventy-two, and she was later declared Blessed for her life of dedication and service to others.

Prayer:

Dear Lord, you gave us dedicated women like Blessed Anne-Marie Javouhey to help in children's spiritual formation. She said that there was great resourcefulness in children, and they were most important in order for God's kingdom to spread. During a time of dangerous religious persecution, she bravely helped those most in need and ministered to help free persecuted peoples everywhere. Help us emulate her example of love and courage today. Amen.

Antiphon:

Be of good courage and he shall strengthen your heart, all you that hope in the Lord.

Readings:

"And he commanded us to preach to the people, and to testify that it is he which was ordained by God to be the judge of the quick and the dead. To him all the prophets bear witness, that through his name whosoever believes in him shall have remission of sin." Acts 10:42–43 (KJV)

"Behold, on the mountains the feet of him who brings good tidings, who proclaims peace!" Nahum 1:15 (RSV)

"Then he said to me, 'Go, for I will send you far away to the Gentiles.'" Acts 22:21 (NRSV)

"And we bring you the good news that what God promised to our ancestors he has fulfilled for us, their children, by raising Jesus; as also it is written in the second psalm, 'You are my Son; today I have begotten you.'" Acts 13:32–33 (NRSV)

JULY 16 *Our Lady of Mt. Carmel*

July 16 is a memorial feast day within the Catholic Church dedicated to *Our Lady of Mt. Carmel*. Mt. Carmel's location is mentioned a number of times in Old Testament Scripture. During the twelfth century, hermits gathered there to live together in a life of austerity and contemplative prayer. This community eventually became the Order of the Carmelites. The Rule of St. Albert was established for these contemplative hermits, and they were led to found their first chapel and prayer cells around the Blessed Virgin Mary, who was Jesus' first and most perfect disciple. Her title of *Our Lady of Mt. Carmel* came about as a result of this chapel devoted to her. She has also come to be known as Our Lady of the Brown Scapular, since it was *Our Lady of Mt. Carmel*'s image that appeared on the brown scapular that was revealed to St. Simon Stock. *Our Lady of Mt. Carmel* also appeared in a miraculous vision in the sky to the children visionaries at Fatima. Most agree that this apparition was a way to encourage the faithful to honor the devotion of the brown scapular.

Intercessory Prayer:

Dear Blessed Virgin Mary, Our Lady of Mt. Carmel, help us to be inspired to live a life of virtue and to strive daily to become true apostles of Jesus, your son. Help us to realize the graces we may receive through the use of devotional sacramentals like the brown scapular and be inspired to teach our children and others about such gifts. Amen.

Antiphon:

Surely the Lord's presence is in this place.

Readings:

"Make a joyful noise to the LORD, all the lands! Serve the LORD with gladness! Come into his presence with singing! Know that the LORD is God. It is he that made us, and we are his; we are his people, and the sheep of his pasture. . . . For the LORD is good; his steadfast love endures for ever, and his faithfulness to all generations." *Psalm 100:1–3, 5 (RSV)*

"So Ahab sent to all the Israelites and had the prophets assemble on Mount Carmel." *Kings 18:20 (RSV)*

"Your head crowns you like Mount Carmel, And the hair of your head is like purple; A king is held captive by your tresses." *Song 7:5 (NKJV)*

JULY 17 Mary Magdalen Postel

Mary Magdalen Postel lived in France during the turbulent era of the French Revolution. She was educated at a Benedictine convent and opened her own school for girls when she was just eighteen. Her schools were closed down at the onset of the French Revolution, and she worked to shelter fugitive priests in her home. After peace came to the region, she again returned to her dream of opening educational facilities for girls and founded the Sisters of the Christian Schools of Mercy. When she began the order, she took the name of Mary Magdalen. Her order of sisters focused on teaching and nursing, eventually spreading to over thirty-five houses throughout the region. She lived an amazingly long life of service and dedication and died in 1846 at age ninety-two. She was immediately acclaimed throughout the region for her outstanding holiness and miracles; Pope Pius XI canonized her in 1925. Mary Magdalen Postel is a patron of persecuted priests.

Prayer:

Almighty God, you blessed turbulent France with dedicated and courageous women like Mary Magdalen Postel to offer guidance and strength to a persecuted Church. Her desire was to fulfill the guidance you instilled in her to educate young girls and establish schools and religious houses. Despite many obstacles, she persevered in her efforts to teach the faithful and to expand your kingdom. May her pious and charitable life of self-giving be an inspiration to us in our daily walk with you. Amen.

Antiphon:

May the name of the Lord Jesus be glorified in you.

Readings

"O God, when you went out before your people, when you marched through the wilderness, the earth shook. . . . You sent a plentiful rain, O God, you showered abroad; you restored your heritage when it languished; your flock found a dwelling in it; in your goodness, O God, you provided for the needy. The Lord gives the command; great is the company of those who proclaim it." *Psalm 68:7, 9–11 (NRSV)*

"How often would I have gathered your children together as a hen gathers her brood under her wings . . ." *Mt. 23:37 (RSV)*

> "To do righteousness and justice is more acceptable to the LORD than sacrifice." *Prov. 21:3 (RSV)*

JULY 18 Elizabeth Feodorovna

Elizabeth Feodorovna was born a German Hessian princess to a strong Lutheran family. Against her parents' wishes, she converted to Orthodoxy when she married Sergei Alexandrovich, the brother of Czar Alexander III, the last czar of Russia before the Bolshevik Revolution. Confronted by the enormous contrast between the luxury of the court and the masses of the Russian poor, Elizabeth used her influence to found hospitals and orphanages. In 1905, with revolution gripping Moscow, Sergei was assassinated when a bomb was flung into his carriage. Elizabeth's response was to retrieve his body parts, sanctify them with a Christian burial, and visit her husband's imprisoned murderer to offer forgiveness. She then withdrew from public life and founded the Sisters of Love and Mercy to minister to the sick and orphaned. During that period, thousands of babies were abandoned every year in the major cities. When the Bolshevik's red flags were finally raised over the Orthodox cathedrals, she was arrested with the Czar and his family. The day after the deaths of the royal family, Elizabeth and her cell mates were thrown into an old mine shaft. As grenades were tossed down into the shaft, she was heard leading hymns of praise. Her body was later retrieved and found to be incorrupt. The Russian Church canonized her in 1991 as one of the New Martyrs of Russia. Until the time of her death, Elizabeth was confident that, although godlessness was sweeping across her country, the "gates of hell would not prevail" over the Holy Orthodox Church of Russia.

Intercessory Prayer:

O holy Elizabeth, although you did not understand why so much blood was spilled in your beloved Russia, you trusted implicitly in God's loving benevolence and held firm to your calm belief that you were journeying toward your true homeland. You wrote that in times of darkness, we must have an inner sun to guide us. Pray for us who live in times of great uncertainty, that we may be inspired by the true light of our souls to find inner peace in the midst of turmoil and compassionate love when it is most difficult. Amen.

Antiphon:

You have left everything to follow me; you will have it all returned one hundred fold and will inherit eternal life.

Readings:

"Hear my prayer, O LORD; give ear to my supplications! In thy faithfulness answer me, in thy righteousness! Enter not into judgment with thy servant; for no [man] living is righteous before thee. For the enemy has pursued me; he has crushed my life to the ground; he has made me sit in darkness like those long dead. . . . I stretch out my hands to thee; my soul thirsts for thee like a parched land." *Psalm 143:1–3, 6 (RSV)*

"Christ also suffered for you, leaving you an example, that you should follow in his steps. He committed no sin; no guile was found on his lips. When he was reviled, he did not revile in return; when he suffered, he did not threaten; but he trusted to him who judges justly." *1 Pet. 2:21–23 (RSV)*

"For each tree is known by its own fruit. For figs are not gathered from thorns, nor are grapes picked from a bramble bush." *Lk. 6:44 (RSV)*

JULY 19 Macrina

Born into a wealthy family in 324, Macrina chose the "secret" name of Thekla, the saint honored as the first woman martyr; and from an early age, she dedicated herself to God. St. Macrina is the spiritual mother of monastics in all Orthodox churches worldwide. Although her younger brother Basil is considered to be the founder of the first monastic order in community, Macrina was his inspiration for such a model. The other saint in the family, Gregory of Nyssa, wrote her *vita* and visited with her when she was dying. Macrina's philosophical conversations on the nature of God, life, and death became the basis of his greatest treatise, *De anima et resurrectione* ("On the Soul and the Resurrection"). The early women's community that Macrina organized included her widowed mother and her maidservants, whom she freed, and their first convent became a spiritual and philanthropic center. Throughout Gregory's last discourse with her, we see Macrina expounding the distinct Christian teaching as she understood it: that the human person does not give up its individuality during any part of the process of death, separation, body decay, or reconstitution. It does not cease its consciousness until the resurrection at the End-time (the older, Jewish belief). It does not melt into a monistic universal soul (the Platonic model). It does not become someone else through reincarnation, or fish or rocks through transmigration. She clearly rejected these prevalent alternative theories of her era. For Macrina, Christian salvation is always a salvation of the whole human person. It is not difficult to see why Gregory, himself a bishop, called her his greatest teacher.

Intercessory Prayer:

*O holy Mother Macrina, you were a living flame in the early
Church and a fervent source of inspiration to those around you.
With great willingness, you led the ascetic life for Christ into a
new era, and upon finishing the course, you were found worthy of
the heavenly bridal chamber. Pray for us on own journeys, that we
may find glory through confessing that Jesus Christ is Lord. Amen.*

Antiphon:

I came that you might have life and have it abundantly.

Readings:

"I will sing of thy steadfast love, O LORD, for ever; with my mouth I will proclaim thy faithfulness to all generations. For thy steadfast love was established for ever, thy faithfulness is firm as the heavens. Thou hast said, 'I have made a covenant with my chosen one.' . . . 'I will establish your descendants for ever, and build your throne for all generations.'" *Psalm 89:1–4 (RSV)*

"How shall we escape if we neglect such a great salvation? It was declared at first by the Lord, and it was attested to us by those who heard him." *Heb. 2:3 (RSV)*

"For mine eyes have seen thy salvation, which thou has prepared before the face of all people." *Lk. 2:30–31 (KJV)*

JULY 20 Harriet Tubman

❀ Harriet Tubman, a remarkable woman, was known as "Black Moses" to her people. Born into slavery in 1820 in Maryland, from an early age she heard in the slave master's Bible teaching, not the message of obedience, but the voice of liberation from bondage. Brutalized and abused as a child, she was once struck in the head by a rock that her master threw, and she was subject to trance states and narcolepsy the rest of her life. At twenty-five, Harriet planned her escape with her husband and two brothers. The men changed their minds and turned back, but Harriet made it to her promised land: the free state of Pennsylvania. Having achieved her freedom, she was not content. Subjecting her life to great danger, she sought to bring along as many other slaves as she could, including her parents, working with the Quakers in the Underground Railroad. Although a forty-thousand-dollar bounty was placed on her head (which would amount to several million dollars today), she was extraordinarily clever at making her pilgrimages furtively, and she never lost a slave. Believing firmly that she was guided by a pillar of fire, she freed more than three hundred people. Harriet once prayed for the death of a brutal slave owner. When he died, she was plagued with guilt for several years, after which she changed the way she prayed. She no longer asked for anything; her sole prayer was simply, "Use me, O Lord." When she was older, living in upstate New York, Harriet supported herself through her garden, and she started a home for needy and elderly African-Americans. She died peacefully on March 10, 1913. The Anglican remembrance of her feast is on July 20 with Sojourner Truth (see Daily Readings, June 2, Sojourner Truth).

Prayer:

O Holy Spirit of freedom and truth, you led the people of Moses by a pillar of fire through the desert, and likewise, the same image guided Harriet Tubman through the wilderness to liberation. She was willing to "wade in the waters and trouble the waters" (Negro spiritual) so she could achieve freedom for herself and her people. Through Harriet's inspiration, help us to examine what we are slaves to in our own lives and what we need to do to free ourselves. Help us, like her, to offer up everything to you in childlike simplicity, with only one prayer: "Use me, O Lord." Amen.

Antiphon:

He has scattered the proud in the conceit of their hearts.

Readings:

"Let thy steadfast love come to me, O LORD, thy salvation according to thy promise; then shall I have an answer for those who taunt me, for I trust in thy word. And take not the word of truth utterly out of my mouth, for my hope is in thy ordinances. I will keep thy law continually, for ever and ever; and I shall walk at liberty." *Psalm 119:41–45 (RSV)*

"And you shall hallow the fiftieth year, and proclaim liberty throughout the land to all its inhabitants; it shall be a jubilee for you, when each of you shall return to his property and each of you shall return to his family." *Lev. 25:10 (RSV)*

". . . because the creation itself will be set free from its bondage to decay and obtain the glorious liberty of the children of God. We know that the whole creation has been groaning in travail together until now." *Rom. 8:21–22 (RSV)*

JULY 21 Margaret of Antioch

Margaret of Antioch, known as Marina in the East, was an early virgin and martyr. She became one of the most popular saints in the West in the Middle Ages, when many *vitas* were written about her in various languages, including English. Margaret's mother died when she was an infant. A Christian woman nursed her and raised her. When her father, a pagan priest in Antioch, disowned her, her nurse adopted her. Margaret promised her life and her virginity to God. When she rejected the advances of a Roman prefect, he denounced her as a Christian, and she was brought to trial. Through prayer, she survived attempts to burn and boil her, which served as a source of conversion for many who witnessed the events. Legend has it that Satan took the form of a dragon and swallowed her. She escaped when the cross she wore irritated his throat, causing him to disgorge her. Margaret was finally put to death by beheading. Before her death, she prayed that women calling upon her in childbirth would be safely delivered. Margaret is one of the Fourteen Holy Helpers venerated for their response to prayers of intercession, and she is one of the saints who appeared to St. Joan of Arc.

Prayer:

Dear Lord, you heard Margaret of Antioch's prayers and spared her from death by burning, thus bringing many more to follow the teachings of your son, Jesus Christ. Strengthen us in our own time of trial. Help us to remember that we are written on the palm of your hand and thus held forever by you. Amen.

Antiphon:

The Lord is my rock and my salvation.

Readings:

"Can a woman forget her nursing child, or show no compassion for the child of her womb? Even these may forget, yet I will not forget you. See, I have inscribed you on the palms of my hands." *Isa. 49:15–16 (NRSV)*

"But all of you are kindlers of fire, lighters of firebrands. Walk in the flame of your fire, and among the brands that you have kindled!" *Isa. 50:11 (NRSV)*

"Blessed are you when people hate you, and defame you on account of the Son of Man." *Lk. 6:22 (NRSV)*

JULY 22 Mary Magdalene

Mary of Magdala was, for centuries, a maligned figure in the Western Church, where she was long believed to be a prostitute. Scripture scholars now believe that nothing in the Bible supports this. The "seven demons" that Jesus cast out from her are now interpreted to be a form of epilepsy or some other kind of mental illness. Greek hymnographers, from very early in the Church, hailed her as the first apostle ("apostle to the apostles") and evangelist, because she was the first witness to the Resurrection. Mary supported Jesus during his ministry, and she never abandoned him when the male apostles fled. Her name appears in all four Gospel accounts as leading the group of myrrh-bearing women who discovered Jesus' empty tomb. The account in John is one of the most touching stories concerning the personal relationship between Jesus and one of his disciples (Jn. 20:1–18). There is abundant literature today indicating that she was a well-known woman leader in earliest Christianity. In this generation, Mary Magdalene has emerged as one of the most in-spiring role models for twenty-first-century women disciples.

Prayer:

To the holy apostle Magdalene, O Lord, you gave the living Word, and you showed all through her that you are the inexhaustible stream of life and the abyss of great mercy. As the Holy Spirit illuminated her, show us also the Spirit of light and truth, that we may make you the foundation of our lives. The cornerstone rejected by many, she recognized you, Lord; teach us to do likewise. Amen.

Antiphon:

She turned around and saw Jesus standing there.

Readings:

"The wise woman builds her house." *Prov. 14:1 (NKJV)*

"Deal bountifully with thy servant, that I may live and observe thy word. Open my eyes, that I may behold wondrous things out of thy law. I am a sojourner on earth; hide not thy commandments from me! My soul is consumed with longing for thy ordinances at all times." *Psalm 119:17–20 (RSV)*

"But Mary stood weeping outside the tomb, and as she wept she stooped to look into the tomb; and she saw two angels in white. . . . They said to her, 'Woman, why are you weeping?' She said to them, 'Because they have taken away my Lord, and I do not know where they have laid him.' Saying this, she turned round and saw Jesus standing [there]. . . ." *Jn. 20:11–14 (RSV)*

JULY 23 Birgitta of Sweden

St. Birgitta (Bridget) of Sweden was born in the early four-teenth century to a prominent and devout family in Finsta, Swe-den. From a young age, she began receiving inspirational visions of Christ, and she desired to become a nun. However, accepting her parents' wishes, she instead married the prince of Ulf when she was fourteen. Their happy marriage resulted in eight children, one of whom (Catherine of Sweden) was also eventually canonized. St. Bir-gitta raised her children with a respect for the poor and taught them to engage in acts of charity for those less fortunate. When her husband died, Birgitta answered Christ's call to establish a monastery at Vadstena. Through her prophecy, she encouraged the exiled pope to return to Rome. Her visions of our Lord eventually became very popular devotions, which continue to have many followers today. "The Revelations of St. Bridget" are meditations that have powerful promises attached for those who read them in the form of a novena. She died at age seventy, and her daughter Catherine was a principal force behind her mother's canonization.

Intercessory Prayer:

Dear St. Bridget, you answered the call of God and spent your life ministering to others and sharing the wealth and gifts that God had bestowed upon you. You were not afraid to speak out against abortion and other moral issues of the day, and you drew many sinners back to the faith and into lives of virtue through your inspired words and holy lifestyle. Inspire us to speak out bravely, as you did, in a society that does not cherish life. Amen.

Antiphon:

Give light to those in darkness and in the shadow of death.

Readings:

"Give ear, O my people, to my teaching; incline your ears to the words of my mouth. I will open my mouth in a parable; I will utter dark sayings from of old, things that we have heard and known, that our ancestors have told us. We will not hide them from their children; we will tell to the coming generation the glorious deeds of the Lord, and his might; and the wonders that he has done." *Psalm 78:1–4 (NRSV)*

"Gentleness and self control, against such there is no law. And those who belong to Christ Jesus have crucified the flesh with its passions and desires. If we live by the Spirit, let us also walk by the Spirit." *Gal. 5:23–25 (RSV)*

"Now the word of the Lord came to me saying, 'Before I formed you in the womb I knew you, and before you were born I consecrated you; I appointed you a prophet to the nations.' Then I said, 'Ah, Lord God! Truly I do not know how to speak, for I am only a boy.' But the Lord said, 'Do not say, "I am only a boy": for you shall go to all to whom I send you, and you shall speak whatever I command you. Do not be afraid of them, for I am with you to deliver you,' says the Lord. Then the Lord put out his hand and touched my mouth; and the Lord said to me, 'Now I have put my word in your mouth.'" *Jer. 1:4–9 (NRSV)*

JULY 24 Susanna Wesley

Susanna Annesley Wesley was the daughter of a nonconformist Anglican minister in London, the youngest of twenty-five children. Those who knew her proclaimed her a matriarch and saint. She looked after her large family with the care of a devoted mother and the precision of a theological scholar, frequently debating her husband or her grown sons—John and Charles—on ecclesiastical questions. She home-schooled her children and spent one hour a day with them singing the psalms and studying Scripture. Her family experienced much financial hardship and two fires. In 1709, her son John, founder of the Methodist Church, was rescued from their rectory, which was in flames, and his deliverance was taken as a sign of special providence. Both John and Charles, who wrote more than six thousand hymns for the High Church, claim a deep indebtedness to their mother for their rich spiritual upbringing. Isaac Taylor has called her the "mother of Methodism." She died on July 23, 1742, and her son, John Wesley, conducted her funeral service.

Prayer:

Almighty God, you gave such grace to your daughter Susanna Wesley that she brought forth great disciples, called by your holy Word, into the world to tell the good news of your kingdom. Grant us your special grace in life that we too may accomplish with integrity and courage the task of multiplying your good works in the world. Through Jesus Christ our Lord. Amen.

Antiphon:

Sing praise to our God, all you servants, all you who worship him reverently, great and small.

Readings:

"Surely goodness and mercy shall follow me all the days of my life; and I shall dwell in the house of the LORD for ever." *Psalm 23:6 (RSV)*

"A Christian here her flesh laid down,
The cross exchanging for a crown.
True daughter of affliction, she,
Inured to pain and misery,
Mourn'd a long night of griefs and fears,
A legal night of seventy years.

The Father then revealed his Son,
Him in the broken bread made known;
She knew and felt her sins forgiven,
And found the earnest of her heaven.
Meet for the fellowship above,
She heard the call, 'Arise my love!'
'I come!' her dying looks replied,
And, lamb-like as her Lord, she died."
Charles Wesley, epitaph for his mother's gravestone

JULY 25 Olympia

St. Olympia was one of the great women deacons of the early church and a lifelong companion of St. John Chrysostom, who wrote the principal liturgy used in Orthodox churches throughout the world. We know much about Olympia through his letters to her while in exile (404–407) and from the historian Palladius, who wrote her *vita*. She was from a noble birth, orphaned young, and married into wealth at age eighteen. Soon afterward, her husband died and she refused to remarry, saying that God knew she could not make a husband happy and so he had freed her from a life of subjection to a man. Olympia was thus left with an enormous amount of wealth. Patriarch (St.) Nektarius ordained her into the diaconate, an office for women that survived in the East until the twelfth century. She became heiress of the great Hagia Sophia, which she enriched considerably. Olympia built a large convent to house visiting bishops, pilgrims, and the orphaned; and she invited all her slaves to live there, proclaiming them free and of equal nobility with herself. She suffered considerably during her separation from St. John, and because of her political endeavors to have him recalled from exile, she was eventually exiled herself. Although her community was dispersed, she continued her diaconal work wherever she was. Before he died, John sent her a comforting letter wherein he exhorts her to never abandon herself to sorrow, but to preserve her integrity because, he promises, their integrity will remain forever. And indeed it has.

Intercessory Prayer:

Dear St. Olympia, you knew that wealth was a treasure to be scorned, because we bring nothing into the world and take nothing from it when we leave. Rather, trusting in Christ who is the vehicle of love that accomplishes salvation, you strove to use your office of deaconess to open his floodgates to all those in your circle of influence. John wrote to you that the wrath of rulers are merely cobwebs; intercede for us who live in a world plagued by terror and injustice, that we may always hold onto the rock who is our deliverance. Amen.

Antiphon:

These sufferings that we now endure are nothing compared to the glory that shall be revealed.

Readings:

"Relieve the troubles of my heart, and bring me out of my distress. Consider my affliction and my trouble, and forgive all my sins. Consider how many are my foes, and with what violent hatred they hate me. O guard my life, and deliver me; compared to the glory do not let me be put to shame, for I take refuge in you. May integrity and uprightness preserve me, for I wait for you." *Psalm 25:17–21 (NRSV)*

"God answered Solomon, 'Because this was in your heart, and you have not asked for possessions, wealth, honor, or the life of those who hate you, and have not even asked for long life, but have asked for wisdom and knowledge for yourself that you may rule my people, . . . I have made you king. . . .'" *2 Chron. 1:11 (NRSV)*

". . . til I die I will not put away my integrity from me. I hold fast my righteousness; and will not let it go; my heart does not reproach me for any of my days." *Job 27:5–6 (RSV)*

JULY 26 Anne, Mother of Mary

The scant information we have about Anne and Joachim, the Blessed Virgin Mary's parents, comes mainly from second-century writings (apocryphal *Gospel of James*) and Church tradition. The apocryphal story relates that Anne was elderly and childless, but an angel appeared to her and announced that she would give birth to a very special child. This child was the Blessed Virgin Mary, and she was the joy of St. Anne's life. But at an early age Anne realized the need to allow her special little girl to fulfill her ultimate destiny and totally dedicate herself to God. Joachim and Anne presented the Virgin Mary in the temple, where she was consecrated and raised away from her family (see Daily Readings, November 21, Presentation of Mary). Justinian built a church in Anne's honor at Constantinople to house her relics. Later some of her relics were taken to Rome, and her feast was extended to the universal Church in 1584. Images of St. Anne in art have been popular since the eighth century; she is often represented as teaching the Virgin to read. Anne is a patron saint of Canada, where she enjoys special veneration.

Intercessory Prayer:

Good St. Anne, you struggled through much of your life as a childless mother. You were blessed with the joy of the Virgin Mary, but your joy as a mother was short-lived, as you humbly accepted God's will in consecrating her fully to him. Help us to discern and to accept God's will in all things. Please intercede for all mothers, especially those who are childless and suffer the pain of infertility. Amen.

Antiphon:

For he shows himself to them who have faith in him.

Readings:

"Blessed is every one who fears the LORD, who walks in his ways! You shall eat the fruit of the labor of your hands; you shall be happy, and it shall be well with you. Your wife will be like a fruitful vine within your house; your children will be like olive shoots around your table." *Psalm 128:1–3 (RSV)*

"The angel of the Lord said to her: 'I will so greatly multiply your descendants that they cannot be numbered for multitude.' And the angel of the Lord said to her, 'Behold, you are with child.'" *Gen. 16:10–11 (RSV)*

"For he has regarded the low estate of his handmaiden, for behold, henceforth, all generations shall call me blessed." *Lk. 1:48 (RSV)*

JULY 27 Mary Martinengo

Mary Martinengo lived in seventeenth-century Italy, born into a prominent family. Her mother died when she was only an infant, and from a very early age she showed unusual piety and a deep spirituality. She strove to follow the model of the lives of the saints in order to perfect her own personal sanctity. At age eighteen, she joined the Order of the Capuchinesses of Santa Maria. Mary held various positions of responsibility within the congregation, including Mistress of Novices and, eventually, Mother Superior of the convent. She spent hours in reflective and contemplative prayer, and her austere life was marked by many mystical experiences. Her particular devotion was to Jesus Crucified, and her own personal sanctity and profound advice led to the conversion of many hearts. Mary died at age fifty, and Pope Leo XIII beatified her.

Prayer:

Dear Lord Jesus, crucified savior, look down upon us this day and inspire us with a holy devotion to your sacred wounds, as professed by the good Mary Martinengo. May we always be aware of the sacrifice you made on our behalf on Calvary. May your precious blood cover and protect us from all evil. Amen.

Antiphon:

For by your cross you have redeemed the world.

Readings:

"LORD, why do You cast off my soul? Why do You hide Your face from me? I have been afflicted and ready to die from my youth; I suffer Your terrors; I am distraught. Your fierce wrath has gone over me; Your terrors have cut me off. . . . Loved one and friend You have put far from me, And my acquaintances into darkness." *Psalm 88:14–16, 18 (NKJV)*

"But he was wounded for our transgressions, he was bruised for our iniquities; upon him was the chastisement that made us whole, and with his stripes we are healed." *Isaiah 53:5 (RSV)*

"Pilate said to them, 'Then what shall I do with Jesus who is called Christ?' They all said, 'Let him be crucified.'" *Mt. 27:22 (RSV)*

JULY 28 Sancia

Sancia was born into royalty, daughter of the king of Majorca, and she became the wife of the king of Naples. She used her wealth for the sick and poor, and she was particularly devoted to the Franciscan Rule. Her two brothers joined the order, and a part of her yearned for the simple life of poverty. Queen Sancia built a Franciscan citadel, composed of two separate monasteries; and she was instrumental in procuring for the sons of St. Francis the guardianship of the Holy Sepulcher in Jerusalem in 1342. After her husband's death, she joined the Poor Clares, and she forbade any distinction to be made in her favor or any reference to be made regarding her nobility. Sancia died a year later, on July 28, 1343, in the odor of sanctity.

Prayer:

Beloved Lord, how sweetly you worked in the life of holy Sancia for the good of your Church and the growth of the Franciscan Order. Through Sancia, we learn that it is not so difficult for the rich to enter heaven, if the love one has for you is the guiding principle of our lives. Bind us also to the cord of Francis, that all of our highest ideals may find fruit in the gentle humility and gratitude of a simple life, lived well. Amen.

Antiphon:

Blessed are you, O God; you alone know our hearts.

Readings:

"May all who seek thee rejoice and be glad in thee! May those who love thy salvation say evermore, 'God is great!'" *Psalm 70:4 (RSV)*

"Turn to me and be saved, all the ends of the earth! For I am God, and there is no other." *Isa. 45:22 (RSV)*

"After this Joseph of Arimathe'a, who was a disciple of Jesus. . . . asked Pilate that he might take away the body of Jesus, and Pilate gave him leave. So he came and took away his body. Nicode'mus also, who had at first come to him by night, came bringing a mixture of myrrh and aloes, about a hundred pounds' weight. They took the body of Jesus, and bound it in linen cloths with the spices, as is the burial custom of the Jews. Now in the place where he was crucified there was a garden, and in the garden a new tomb where no one had ever been laid. So because of the

Jewish day of Preparation, as the tomb was close at hand, they laid Jesus there." *Jn. 19:38–42 (RSV)*

JULY 29 Irene of Cappadocia

Irene of Cappadocia lived in an era of political intrigue and religious upheaval. It was the ninth century; Patriarch Photius was preparing to defend the Nicene Creed (which eventually resulted in a split with Rome); and Emperor Michael III, who had placed Photius on the patriarchal throne, was preparing to receive a wife into the court. Of noble birth, Irene was a candidate to be Michael's wife. On the way to meet Michael, she stopped to receive spiritual direction from a renowned hermit who had the gift of foresight. He told her she was destined to shepherd the nuns at the convent of Chrysovalandov. Shocked, Irene detoured to the convent, and her sister continued on to the court to marry Bardas, Michael's principal adviser. In time, Irene was ordained a deaconess with a powerful gift of preaching, and she later became abbess of the convent. Many pilgrims, including senators and rulers, came to her door, for she also possessed the gift of discerning hearts. It was said that she already knew the sins of the nuns before she heard their weekly confession. Irene stayed up most nights keeping vigil, and one night a candle fell over, setting her habit on fire. She was so lost in prayer that when one of her sisters rushed in to put out the flames, Irene had not even noticed that she had been burned. A remarkable miracle was recorded about this event. The severe wounds on Irene's flesh resulting from the burns emitted a beautiful fragrance. Irene also made many predictions that came true. In 865, she advised her sister to leave the court because her husband was soon to die. She also predicted that Michael would lose his life and his kingdom. Basil of Macedonia murdered both Bardas and Michael, initiating the Macedonian dynasty in a bloody coup. Despite his ruthlessness, Basil proved to be a powerful leader, who consolidated the Bulgarian Church and made an effort to resume relations with Rome. Irene remained in the convent her whole life, and she predicted the day of her own death, when her body again gave off the odor of sanctity.

Prayer:

Almighty God, you raised up St. Irene to be a woman of fortitude and discernment, with the gift of seeing into souls. She abandoned fame and the riches of court life and renounced her nobility for the sake of your Church. Through Irene's intercession, help us to serve you with singleness of mind and heart. We pray with her for the unity of the Church, the body of Christ on earth. Amen.

Antiphon:

For if you would save your life you would lose it, and if you lose your life for my sake, you will find it.

Readings:

"Then these men were bound . . . and they were cast into the burning fiery furnace. Because the king's order was strict and the furnace very hot, the flame of the fire slew those men who took up Shadrach, Meshach, and Abed'nego. And these three men, Shadrach, Meshach, and Abed'nego, fell bound into the burning fiery furnace.

Then King Nebuchadnez'zar was astonished and rose up in haste. He said to his counselors, 'Did we not cast three men bound into the fire?' They answered the king, 'True, O king.' He answered, 'But I see four men loose, walking in the midst of the fire, and they are not hurt. . . .'" *Dan. 3:21–25 (RSV)*

"On the other hand, he who prophesies speaks to [men] for their upbuilding and encouragement and consolation. He who speaks in a tongue edifies himself, but he who prophesies edifies the church. Now I want you all to speak in tongues, but even more to prophesy." *1 Cor. 14:3–5 (RSV)*

JULY 30 Anthousa of Constantinople

St. Anthousa was the daughter of Emperor Constantine V, who was notorious during the iconoclastic controversy for smashing icons and persecuting monks and nuns. Since Anthousa grew up in the imperial palace surrounded by hedonists, she would frequently sneak away to Hagia Sophia (the Cathedral of Holy Wisdom) to pray. Although forbidden by her father to join the monastic life, she practiced a life of asceticism in the palace. When her father died, his first wife, who had given birth to the next heir Leo IV, claimed the throne.

Anthousa took her part of the inheritance and gave it to the poor. During Anthousa's lifetime, the last Ecumenical Council of the early Church was convened, which restored the veneration of sacred images. She joyfully became part of the movement to restore icons in monasteries and churches, and she peacefully passed her remaining days as abbess of the Convent at Omonia. Anthousa's feast day in the East is on April 12.

Prayer:

Beloved Lord and Savior, Anthousa was a cherished daughter who fought valiantly to preserve the dignity of monastics during a period when they suffered much persecution. She recognized that because the image of God was incarnate in your human and divine person, it was our right to faithfully create and venerate images in honor of your sacred memory. Help us to use all our holy images of you and your saints with consciousness and reverence. May we always be grateful for the action of your Holy Spirit in restoring icons to the faithful through the seventh Ecumenical Council, for our lives would be greatly impoverished without them. With St. Anthousa, we give honor and gratitude to you for all the sacred icons that you have given to us as windows into eternity. Amen.

Antiphon:

The grace of God is freely bestowed on us in the image of Christ our Lord.

Readings:

"My mouth will tell of thy righteous acts, of thy deeds of salvation all the day, for their number is past my knowledge. . . . O God, from my youth thou hast taught me, and I still proclaim thy wondrous deeds." *Psalm 71:15–17 (RSV)*

"For those whom he foreknew he also predestined to be conformed to the image of his Son, in order that he might be the first-born among many brethren. And those whom he predestined he also called; and those whom he called he also justified; and those whom he justified he also glorified." *Rom. 8:29–30 (RSV)*

"And the Word became flesh and dwelt among us, full of grace and truth; we have beheld his glory. . . ." *Jn. 1:14 (RSV)*

JULY 31 *Virgin Blachernitissa:* Dedication of the Temple at Blachernae

Blachernae was the site of a major shrine to the Mother of God in Constantinople. Empress Pulcheria (see Daily Readings, February 17, Empress Pulcheria of Constantinople) built the temple in 450; later a circular chapel was added that housed the Virgin Mary's robe, which was brought from Palestine in 473. The image of the *Our Lady of Blachernae*, often called the *Virgin Blachernitissa,* depicts the Theotokos portrayed full-length and facing front, her hands raised in prayer. An image of Christ giving a blessing is painted within a medallion on her breast. A veil that covered the Virgin's face was associated with miracles and was raised on special occasions. The veil has always been a symbol of the Theotokos as patron and protector of the Orthodox Church. When the Saracens besieged Constantinople, the greatly distressed people held an all-night vigil in the temple where the mantle was preserved, and the city was spared. From the time of Patriarch Timotheos (511), there was a procession each Friday from Blachernae to the church at the opposite end of the city near Hagia Sophia. During the iconoclastic controversy, the icon was hidden in the wall of the Church of Christ Pantocrator. In 834, the iconoclast movement collapsed, and the first Feast of Orthodoxy (now observed annually during Lent) was celebrated at the Blachernae church. Veneration of the protective mantle also developed early in the history of Rus-Ukraine and is celebrated on October 1.

Intercessory Prayer:

O immaculate Mother, you were chosen by the pre-eternal God to shelter the Savior of the world in your womb, and infinite power from heaven overshadows you. To you it is given that every petition you bring to your son shall be fulfilled. Therefore, most gracious Theotokos, make our prayer your own and shelter all those who take refuge under your most protective veil. Amen.

Antiphon:

"Hail our joy! Protect us from every ill by your precious veil." (Akathist)

Readings:

"Wisdom has built her house, she has hewn her seven pillars. . . . She has sent out her servant-girls, she calls from the highest places in the town: 'You that are simple, turn in here!'" *Prov. 9:1–3 (NRSV)*

"I will cause your name to be celebrated in all generations; therefore the peoples will praise you forever and ever." *Psalm 45:17 (NRSV)*

AUGUST 1 Nun Kassia

Nun Kassia was a magnificent hymn writer. Orthodox liturgy uses at least thirty of the fifty or more hymns that she wrote, and she also wrote free verse and maxims. Her most famous hymn is to Mary Magdelene, and it is part of Holy Week liturgy. We know little about her early life except that she was born in the early ninth century to an aristocratic family and she excelled in the Greek language. Nun Kassia became very active in supporting monks and icon painters during the iconoclastic controversy, when icons were forbidden. The Orthodox Church's hymns are intensely scriptural; therefore, for a woman of her period, she would have stood out as a Scripture scholar. Nun Kassia had a monastery built in Constantinople where she served as an abbess. Some of her maxims express her defiant personality; she also had a reputation for wit. "I hate silence," she wrote, "when it is time to speak." She likewise shows dislike for the "fool who acts like a philosopher." There is a legend that before entering the convent, her beauty had bewitched Emperor Theophilos, but he refused to marry her when she once sharply reproached him for a slur against the female sex. Her nuns were the first to sing her hymns, and the Church has, throughout the centuries, affectionately called her "Kassia the Melodos," or melodious.

Prayer:

O radiant Spirit of God, you are the source and inspiration of poets and philosophers everywhere. Nun Kassia's words were a mosaic of images in praise of you and your saints. Through her passionate hymns, thousands of Christians throughout the centuries have joined her soul in song. O holy vessel of purest joy, inspire us with a depth of feeling when we pray, and help us to deepen our awareness and concentration on God in all that we do, through the merits of Jesus, our Christ. Amen.

Antiphon:

For your voice is sweet, and you are lovely.

Readings:

"Sing for joy in the LORD, O you righteous ones; Praise is becoming to the upright. Give thanks to the LORD with the lyre; Sing praises to Him with a harp of ten strings. Sing to Him a new song; Play skillfully with a shout of joy." *Psalm 33:1–3 (NASB)*

"My heart is steadfast, O God, my heart is steadfast; I will sing, yes, I will sing praises! Awake, my glory! Awake, harp and lyre! I will awaken the dawn. I will give thanks to You, O Lord, among the peoples; I will sing praises to You among the nations. For Your lovingkindness is great to the heavens and Your truth to the clouds." *Psalm 57:7–10 (NASB)*

"And do not get drunk with wine, for that is dissipation, but be filled with the Spirit, speaking to one another in psalms and hymns and spiritual songs, singing and making melody with your heart to the Lord; always giving thanks for all things in the name of our Lord Jesus Christ. . . ." *Eph. 5:18–20 (NASB)*

AUGUST 2 Our Lady of the Angels at Portiuncula

The chapel of Our Lady of the Angels at Portiuncula ("Mary's Little Portion") in Assisi was the birthplace of the Franciscan Order. There, Francis heard a Bible reading call him to go out without gold or silver or traveling bag, and preach the good news of the kingdom (Mt. 10:7–12). On Palm Sunday eve, Lady Clare (see Daily Readings, August 11, Clare of Assisi) eagerly ran to the chapel so she could have her hair shorn and receive the religious garb from Francis that she was to wear for the rest of her life. Pope Honorius dedicated the chapel on August 2 in response to a plea from Francis, and in 1986, Pope John Paul II and many religious leaders from around the world initiated a Day of Prayer for World Peace in front of this tiny chapel. Interestingly, this same feast is kept in Costa Rica in honor of a Black Madonna that a native girl found some three hundred years ago. The legend is that whenever the Virgin's stone image was moved, it miraculously reappeared at the site where it was originally found. A church was later built there, the *Nuestra Senora de los Angeles.*

Intercessory Prayer:

Heavenly Mother of angels and saints, you gave us the king who brings life to all people. All Franciscan churches are dedicated to you, for through you, Christ has reconciled in himself the lowness of earth and the highness of heaven. Pray for your children everywhere, that God's mercy may prevail from generation to generation. With the angels we proclaim, "You are more honorable than the cherubim, for you gave us God the Word." Amen.

Antiphon:

He who is mighty has done great things for me.

Readings:

"In the daytime he led them with a cloud, and all the night with a firely light. He cleft rocks in the wilderness, and gave them drink abundantly as from the deep. . . . Yet he commanded the skies above, and opened the doors of heaven; and he rained down upon them manna to eat, and gave them the grain of heaven. Man ate the bread of the angels; he sent them food in abundance." *Psalm 78:14–15, 23–25 (RSV)*

"And again I lifted my eyes and saw, and behold, four chariots came out from between two mountains; and the mountains were mountains of bronze. The first chariot had red horses, the second black horses, the third white horses, and the fourth chariot, dappled gray horses. Then I said to the angel who talked with me, 'What are these, my lord?' And the angel answered me, 'These are going forth to the four winds of heaven, after presenting themselves before the Lord of all the earth.'" *Zech. 6:1–5 (RSV)*

"And coming in, he [Gabriel] said to her, "Greetings, favored one! The Lord is with you." *Lk 1:28 (NASB)*

AUGUST 3 Lydia

Lydia was the first European convert to the word of Christ. After listening to Paul's preaching, she and her whole household were baptized (Acts 16:1–5). She then insisted that Paul make her home his center while in Philippi. Philippi was named after Philip, the father of Alexander the Great, who Hellenized the name; Lydia, therefore, would have been Greek. Her house was a center of missionary activity and, most likely, early liturgical celebrations. She was a woman of considerable means and authority, a successful businesswoman who dealt in purple cloth, which was a luxury item worn by the wealthy. We know she supported Paul throughout his ministry; after Paul was released from prison, he went directly to her house (Acts 16:40). Paul spoke highly of her; his Epistles to the Philippians was written to the community started at her home. There is no mention of her having a husband, so it is believed that the center of Christianity in Philippi was organized, in large part, under her influence and effort. The modern women's movement holds up Lydia as a woman who modeled partnership and egalitarian church structure in its formative years. Her feast day in the East is celebrated on June 25.

Intercessory Prayer:

St. Lydia, you were such an inspiration to Paul that he longed to come back to your welcoming household; he saw in you a partner in spreading the word of the kingdom. In the heart of the Christian message you saw a radical renewal of your world wherein there was no longer Jew nor Greek, slave nor free, man nor woman, but all in Christ. Inspire women in Christ's Church today to be leaders and initiators. Paul judged you faithful, and you were a zealous witness for the Lord in your community. Intercede for women today who desire to be faithful to their own call to ministry. Amen.

Antiphon:

Your light will break forth as the morning.

Readings:

"Then your light will break out like the dawn, and your recovery will speedily spring forth. . . . Those from among you will rebuild the ancient ruins; You will raise up the age-old foundations." *Isa.58:8, 12*

"'This is My covenant with them' says the LORD: 'My Spirit which is upon you, and My words which I have put in your mouth . . .'" *Isa. 59:21 (NASB)*

"I thank my God always, making mention of you in my prayers, because I hear of your love and of the faith which you have toward the Lord Jesus and toward all the saints; and I pray that the fellowship of your faith may become effective through the knowledge of every good thing which is in you for Christ's sake. . . . The grace of the Lord Jesus Christ be with your spirit." *Philem 1:4–6, 25 (NASB)*

"If you have judged me to be faithful to the Lord, come into my house and stay." *Acts 16:15 (NASB)*

AUGUST 4 Mother Ann Lee

Ann Lee grew up in Manchester, England, during the early part of the Industrial Revolution. She was illiterate, but from her childhood, she was marked by charisms. Her parents joined a dissident society known then as the "Shaking Quakers"; soon Ann began to see visions. The fledgling society practiced no liturgical forms and recited no creeds, but they celebrated their gatherings in ecstatic dance and song. After a long period of religious persecution, in 1774 Ann had a revelation of Christ directing her to America. This vision was communicated to the Society of the Shakers, and a number of signs, spiritual presentations, and gifts from the Spirit confirmed it. Many members saw mysterious signs in the sky, and much of the Society left for America with their spiritual leader, whom they called Mother Ann. The Shaker movement grew in numbers when they reached the freedom shores that Mother Ann had seen in her vision. She predicted that the colonies would gain their independence and that liberty of conscience would be secured for all people. The Shaker Society still celebrates her memory on the first Sunday of August with song, dance, and a sharing of Mother Ann cake.

Prayer:

O Holy Spirit of God, Mother Ann asked that you lead her in all things. She felt that whatever path the Spirit may lead is acceptable to God, from whom the Spirit proceeds. When she had a vision of Jesus in his kingdom and glory, she felt that nothing on earth could compare to that moment, except endlessly singing God's praises. Teach us how to receive the gifts of your Spirit again, that we may be lifted up in joyful rapture in our worship, and show us how to grow in our understanding of you, so we may worship God in spirit and in truth. Amen.

Antiphon:

God has revealed this wisdom to us by the Spirit.

Readings:

"The voice of the LORD hews out flames of fire. The voice of the LORD shakes the wilderness." *Psalm 29:7–8 (NASB)*

"When thus it shall be in the midst of the land among the people, 'there shall be as the shaking of an olive tree, and as the gleaning of grapes when the vintage is done. They shall lift up their voice, they shall sing for the majesty of the Lord, they shall cry aloud from the sea. Wherefore glorify the Lord in the fires, even in the name of the Lord God of Israel in the isles of the sea." *Isa 24:13–15 (KJV)*

"So you shall know that I am the Lord your God, who dwell in Zion, my holy mountain. . . . And in that day the mountains shall drip new wine, and the hills shall flow with milk, and all the stream beds of Judah shall flow with water; and a fountain shall come forth from the house of the Lord and water the valley of Shit'tim." *Joel 3:17–18 (RSV)*

AUGUST 5 Nonna

St. Nonna was a deacon in the early Church and mother of the great Gregory the Theologian. We know little about her except what emerges from his writings. He had great love and respect for his mother, comparing her to Sarah of the Old Testament. He explains that his parents were equal in all things, "of one honor, of one mind." Nonna was not only her husband's partner, but even "his leader," drawing him deeper into the pursuit of excellence in all his actions. She was instrumental in his conversion, and later on he became a bishop. They had an active ministry together. Gregory writes that Nonna sought in all things to restore the divine image of the Godhead in all her children. She gave liberally to the poor and was a wise manager of their household. At Gregory's birth, she consecrated him to God, trusting completely in the Lord for his future. Throughout all her daily activities, Nonna never missed chanting the appointed psalms at evening vigil. She raised the future St. Gregory to be a thoughtful and sensitive man who loved the life of solitude, although the early Church needed him to publicly defend it against the heretical doctrine of Arius, a presbyter of Alexandria.

Intercessory Prayer:

> *Blessed Nonna, you diligently proclaimed the Christian faith to your family and all those in your ministry as deaconess. You were a source of spiritual encouragement to your son, a great father of the early Church, yet you knew from birth that he did not belong to you, but to God. Intercede for all mothers, that we may give back to the Lord the gifts he has given us in our children, molding them in righteousness and in truth as best as we can. Amen.*

Antiphon:

Her children will rise up and call her blessed.

Readings:

"Not unto us, O Lord, not unto us, But to your Name give glory; For the sake of your steadfast love, and for the sake of your truth." *Psalm 115:1 (KJV)*

"Come children, listen to me, I will teach you reverence for the Most High. Who among you longs for life . . . keep your tongue from speaking evil, your lips from speaking deceit. Turn aside from evil and do good. Seek peace and pursue it" *Psalm 34:11–13 (PCB)*

"Whatever Sarah tells you, listen to her. . . ." *Gen. 21:12 (NASB)*

"Yet Wisdom is justified by her children." *Mt. 11:19 (KJV)*

"The Spirit [Himself] testifies with our spirit that we are children of God, and if children, heirs also, heirs of God and fellow heirs with Christ. . . ." *Rom. 8:16–17 (NASB)*

AUGUST 6 Maria Francesca Rubatto and Potamia

Anna Maria Rubatto lived in the late nineteenth century near Turin, Italy. From an early age she felt an inner calling to devote herself and her chastity to Christ and decided she would never marry. A Capuchin priest encouraged her to enter a community of religious women, and eventually she professed her vows and took the name Sister Maria Francesca of Jesus. She became the Mother Superior of the sisters, later known as the Capuchin Sisters of Mother Rubatto. The sisters served as missionaries throughout regions of South America where many members of her order were martyred. Mother Rubatto escaped unharmed and eventually died while on a visit to the United States in 1904. She was buried at Montevideo, and Pope John Paul II beatified her in 1993. Mother Rubatto left behind a thriving religious community dedicated to serving the poor and destitute and a body of profoundly beautiful and instructive spiritual writings.

This is also the feast of Potamia the wonder-worker and virgin martyr (normally transferred to the next day, on account of the feast of Transfiguration). Potamia was strong in proclaiming the gospel and eventually was martyred in boiling pitch. Her calm strength during her ordeal converted the guard, who later became St. Basilides. Potamia appeared to him three nights in a row, consoling him for his part in her death.

Prayer:

Dear Lord Jesus, you blessed your Church with the strong character and spiritual strength evident in the saintly women, Blessed Mother Rubatto and St. Potamia. They answered your call to service and charity to others by devoting their lives to spreading the good news of the gospel to foreign lands. Help us to be inspired by their response to your call and to be mindful of your sustaining presence, which alone is sufficient for us. Amen.

Antiphon:

By faith, we sojourn in a land of promise.

Readings:

"You have enclosed me behind and before, and laid Your hand upon me." *Psalm 139:5 (NASB)*

"Where can I go from Your Spirit? Or where can I flee from Your presence? If I ascend to heaven, you are there; If I make my bed in Sheol, behold, you are there. If I take the wings of the dawn, if I dwell in the remotest part of the sea, even there Your hand will lead me, And Your right hand will lay hold of me." *Psalm 139:7–10 (NASB)*

". . . for he said, 'I have been a stranger in a foreign land.'" *Ex. 18:3 (NKJV)*

". . . for through Him we both have our access in one Spirit to the Father. So then you are no longer strangers and aliens, but you are fellow citizens with the saints, and are of God's household, having been built on the foundation of the apostles and prophets, Christ Jesus Himself being the corner stone. . . ." *Eph. 2:18–20 (NASB)*

AUGUST 7 Etheldritha

Born in the late eighth century, St. Etheldritha was the daughter of King Offa and Queen Quindreda of Mercia. King Ethelbert of East Angles sought her hand in marriage, but he was murdered as a result of the treachery of Etheldritha's father. Thereafter, Etheldritha gave her life entirely to God. She left her father's court and established herself in a small cell on Croyland Island in the marshes of Lincolnshire. She lived the remaining forty years of her life there as a recluse dedicating herself to prayer, austerities, and contemplation. Several miracles were attributed to her, but she was most famous for her prophecies. Etheldritha died in 834. Her tomb was among those arranged around the tomb of St. Guthlac, a hermit priest who retired to Croyland when he was inspired to follow the asceticism of the Desert Fathers. Etheldritha's relics were lost in 870 when the Danes destroyed the monastery at Croyland. Etheldritha is the patron of marsh dwellers.

Prayer:

Dear Lord thank you for the example of Etheldritha, who shows us that in the loss of a loved one we may find a deeper relationship with you. Your comfort, guidance, and love are apparent when we pray and reflect in solitude. Remind us to make time to search you out, the font of living water. Let gratitude burn in our hearts for the rich rewards of your love. Amen.

Antiphon:

Only in you, O Lord, will my soul find rest.

Readings:

"Blessed are those who trust in the Lord, whose trust is the Lord. They shall be like a tree planted by water, sending out its roots by the stream. It shall not fear when heat comes, and its leaves shall stay green; in the year of drought it is not anxious, and it does not cease to bear fruit." *Jer. 17:7–8 (NRSV)*

"Thus says the Lord; In a time of favor I have answered you, on a day of salvation I have helped you; I have kept you and given you as a covenant to the people, to establish the land, to allot the desolate heritages. . . ." *Isa. 49:8 (NRSV)*

"Behold I send you My messenger before your face, who will prepare your way before you." *Lk. 7:27 (NASB)*

AUGUST 8 Mary McKillop

Mary McKillop, outspoken and innovative for her time, was excommunicated before she was beatified. Born in 1842 in Scotland, she moved to Australia where she initiated a school for women and eventually an order: the Sisters of St. Joseph of the Sacred Heart. She was devoted to establishing a house that would be a refuge for women, and much of her energy during her early years was spent looking for funds to support her community. Misunderstood by the diocesan bishop—an alcoholic—he excommunicated her until an Apostolic Commission was set up to reinstate her as Superior. Waiting for her Rule to be approved was one of the more difficult periods of Mary's life; she had to abandon her fledgling community and wait in Rome for more than a year where, she writes, she had poor health, but "mental distress worst of all." Although the bishop of Queensland called her an obstinate and ambitious woman, Mary was known for her forbearance and simplicity among her sisters, who were willing to go begging to help the order survive when community funds were depleted. By the time of her death, 106 convents had been established; seventy-three priests attended her funeral. She was beatified in 1995.

Intercessory Prayer:

> *Dear Mother Mary McKillop, you were a pioneering woman for Christ, refusing to be deterred even in your darkest hour. You were committed to the poor and destitute, yet you wrote: "Poor garments are all exterior show if there is not a true spirit of poverty in our hearts." Pray that we too may imitate the path of inner poverty. Help us to remember that only by following unconditionally the Lord's inner call will we be found not wanting in the works to which we are called in the world. Amen.*

Antiphon:

The Lord will complete what was begun in you.

Readings:

"Do not say, 'Thus I shall do to him as he has done to me.'" *Prov. 24:29 (NASB)*

"Deliver me from my enemies, O my God; Set me securely on high away from those who rise up against me. Deliver me from those who do iniquity and save me from men of bloodshed. For behold, they have set an ambush for my life; Fierce men launch an attack against me, Not for my transgression nor for my sin, O LORD, For no guilt of mine. . . ." *Psalm 59:1–4 (NASB)*

"But if we are afflicted, it is for your comfort and salvation; or if we are comforted, it is for your comfort, which is effective in the patient enduring of the same sufferings which we also suffer." *2 Cor. 1:6 (NASB)*

AUGUST 9 Edith Stein

Edith Stein was born a Jew on Yom Kippur, and she died a Christian at Auschwitz. The youngest of eleven children, she was an introvert and a philosopher from early in her life. She did her doctoral work on the subject of empathy with Edmund Husserl, the great exponent of phenomenology. She became a widely known lecturer in Germany and Austria. Edith did not give much thought to Christianity until she read Teresa of Avila's *Autobiography*. Here she found that Teresa was also a mystic of Jewish descent, which resonated with Edith's experience. Edith decided she wanted to become Catholic and a Carmelite. She delayed her entrance into the Carmelite Order because of the shock her conversion had upon her mother. Instead, for eight years Edith taught with the Dominican Sisters at Speyer, during which time she wrote her famous treatise on women and spiritual direction. She finally followed her heart's desire and became a Carmelite in 1933, taking the name Teresa Benedicta of the Cross. While she was a novice, she continued to write philosophy, including her treatise on "Finite and Eternal Being." The year she was professed, she had to flee Nazi Germany to Holland, but she was traced there and taken into custody (for being of Jewish descent) in 1942. The Roman Catholic Church celebrates Edith as a martyr, and her life and death are a reverential testimony to her womanhood, her Jewishness, her Carmelite vocation, and her witness to Christ.

Intercessory Prayer:

Dear St. Edith, your life was one of patient listening and responding to God's call. You wrote that the modern woman must find a balance between her feminine vocation to nurture and her professional activity in the world, surrendering herself at all times to the Lord's call. You likewise felt that the redemptive order would restore a balanced relationship between the sexes. We suffer severely from disordered relationships in the modern world and need your continued prayers and guidance. As you were willing to risk all in your desire to honor the dignity of all oppressed peoples, intercede for us that we may respond to God by choosing to serve those still struggling to attain that dignity. Amen.

Antiphon:

I am with you, even to the end of the age.

Readings:

"Look upon my affliction and rescue me, For I do not forget Your law. Plead my cause and redeem me; Revive me according to Your word. Salvation is far from the wicked, for they do not seek Your statutes. . . . Many are my persecutors and my adversaries, Yet I do not turn aside from Your testimonies. . . . The sum of Your word is truth. And every one of Your righteous ordinances is everlasting." *Psalm 119:153–155, 157, 160 (NASB)*

"For the kingdom of heaven is as a man traveling into a far country, who called his own servants, and delivered unto them goods."
Mt. 25:14 (KJV)

AUGUST 10 Mary Sumner

Born in 1828, Mary Sumner grew up in a beautiful little town called Hope End, near Manchester, England. Her family was devout Anglican, with daily scripture study and prayers in the home. She fell in love with George Sumner, a bishop's son, when she was studying music in Rome, and they were married in 1848. It was not until Mary became a grandmother that she began to organize the program that later came to be known as the Mother's Union. She had realized from her own experience of motherhood how little preparation and support most women received for the vital role of child-rearing. Mary believed that motherhood involved much more than providing for a child's physical needs; she thus began developing mothers' groups of thirty or more women to meet regularly to support one another in creating home environments that would nurture children emotionally and spiritually. In 125 years, the Mother's Union has made a positive difference in the lives of hundreds of thousands of women and children worldwide. Prayer, support, and practical action are still at the root of what makes the Union so popular and successful. From a small diocesan organization to an international body, the Mother's Union is one of the most visible fruits of the Anglican communion. The Anglican Church celebrates Mary Sumner Day with a special prayer for the family in the Common Worship Lectionary on August 9.

Prayer:

Merciful God, you have knit together in one communion a family made in your image and likeness. Have mercy on us, we pray, when we fall out of communion with one another. Help mothers everywhere to discern a proper upbringing of their children that includes wisdom, reverence for life, and compassion for their fellow human beings. Through Mary Sumner's intercession, grant your fruitful blessings to the work of the Mother's Union throughout the world. Amen.

Antiphon:

Ascribe to the Lord, O families of the peoples, glory and strength!

Readings:

"He established a testimony in Jacob and appointed a law in Israel, Which He commanded our fathers that they should teach them to their children. That the generation to come might know, even the children yet to be born, That they may arise and tell them to their children, That they should put their confidence in God And not forget the works of God, But keep His commandments." *Psalm 78:5–7 (NASB)*

"And I will make you a great nation, and I will bless you . . . and I will bless those who bless you . . . and by you, all families of the earth will bless themselves." *Gen. 12:2–3 (RSV)*

"For you were formerly darkness, but now you are Light in the Lord; walk as children of Light (for the fruit of the Light consists in all goodness and righteousness and truth), trying to learn what is pleasing to the Lord." *Eph. 5:8–10 (NASB)*

"But Jesus said, 'Let the children come to me, and do not hinder them; for to such belongs the kingdom of heaven.'" *Mt. 19:14 (RSV)*

AUGUST 11 Clare of Assisi

St. Clare wrote one of the most remarkable Rules in women's history. Although little is known about her early life, we know Clare renounced her wealthy family and potential suitor after hearing a sermon by Francis of Assisi. Deciding to embrace the radical poverty of the friars, she ran away late one night and met Francis at the Portiuncula, the early Franciscan Order's mother church. There Francis shaved her hair, and she took his habit. She lived her entire life at San Damiano, and the women who joined her became known as the Poor Ladies of Assisi. Clare and Francis were deeply devoted to one another and shared a mutual commitment to the same vision of the gospel. It is generally believed that

Clare thought that her congregation would become itinerant caretakers of the poor, like the friars, but this was too innovative for her day, and it never happened. All the papal rules she was given before she wrote her own insisted on enclosure. Outliving Francis by twenty-seven years, it was only two days before her death that her own Rule found approval. Unlike the Benedictines, Clare's Rule adopts the first nonhierarchical structure in Western monastic life: the abbess does not have absolute authority, but is helped in decision making by a consensus of other sisters. In resisting material care by church authorities, she asserted—for the first time—that women had equal strength and ingenuity with men to support themselves with their hands. Clare's prayers were considered very powerful, and she is often depicted with a monstrance in her hands, recalling the story that when Saracen mercenaries were besieging the city, she appeared before them bearing the Blessed Sacrament, whereupon they fled.

Intercessory Prayer

Dear holy Mother Clare, your Rule for the sisters that you loved opened to them great freedom of spirit and blazed a trail for women to follow for many centuries to come. With your beloved Francis, you shared a dream that renewed and strengthened the Church and inspired future generations with reverence for God's creation. You challenge us to be guided by deep charity and inner wisdom, releasing everything that clutters our lives in a true spirit of poverty. We thank you for teaching us that freedom from attachment to material things is the key that opens our hearts to the depths of God's love for us. We ask that you continue to inspire women who live with your vision and all the Poor Clares throughout the world. Amen.

Antiphon:

They prevailed because they relied upon the Lord God.

Readings:

"Praise the Lord from the heavens; Praise Him in the heights! Praise Him, all His angels; Praise Him, all His hosts! Praise Him, sun and moon . . . all stars of light . . . highest heavens. . . . Let them praise the name of the LORD, For He commanded and they were created." *Psalm 148:1–5 (NASB)*

"Jesus said to them, 'The sons of this age marry and are given in marriage, but those who are considered worthy to attain to that age and the resurrection from the dead, neither marry nor are given in marriage; for they cannot even die anymore, because they are like angels. . . .' *Lk. 20:34–36 (NASB)*

"[For] their abundance of joy and their extreme poverty have overflowed in a wealth of liberality." *2 Cor. 8:2 (RSV)*

AUGUST 12 Attracta

St. Attracta, also known as St. Araght, lived in the late fifth century and was a contemporary of St. Patrick. According to legend she fled her home when her father refused to let her become a nun, and St. Patrick at Coolvin gave her her veil. She was an anchoress, and she later founded several churches in Galway and Sligo counties in Ireland. Her convents were known for their care of the sick, their aid to the poor, and serving as hospices for travelers. Most were built at crossroads. The most famous, a hospice founded at Lough Gara known as Killaraght (Cell Araght), lasted until 1539. Attracta was a noted healer and miracle worker. The O'Mochain family preserved her relics, her cross, and her cup through the Middle Ages. A healing well with her name survives in Clogher, Monasteraden, Ireland. Pope Pius IX personally authorized the Mass of St. Attracta for her feast day in Achonry diocese in 1829, demonstrating the longevity and influence of her veneration. Attracta is a patron saint of Achonry.

Prayer:

> *Beloved Lord, Attracta worked many healings in your name and founded homes for weary travelers. Rest is something the modern world is deeply in need of; we hurry from one thing to another while our souls suffer a hunger for quiet. Help us to take time to discover you in solitude, especially when we are at our own crossroads. May our rest on earth be a preparation for the eternal rest that you have promised. Amen.*

Antiphon:

The fruit of the Spirit is joy, peace, and patient endurance.

Readings:

"Oh, that I had in the wilderness a lodging place for travelers." *Jer. 9:2 (NKJV)*

"At that time Jesus declared, 'I thank thee Father, Lord of heaven and earth, that thou has hidden these things from the wise and clever and revealed them to the babes; yea, Father for such was thy gracious will. All things have been delivered to me by my Father, and no one knows the Father except the Son and any one to whom the Son chooses to reveal him. Come to me, all who labor and are heavy laden, and I will give you rest . . . your souls will find rest, for my yoke is easy and my burden light.'" *Mt. 11:25–28 (RSV)*

AUGUST 13 Athenas-Eudokia

A number of Eudokias were empresses in the Byzantine world; one of them became a saint. Called Athenas-Eudokia, she was a Greek maiden of exceptional beauty and intellect. Trained in the Greek classics and oratory, she was a powerful speaker. In 421, she was married to emperor Theodosios II and was baptized by the patriarch of Constantinople. She nonetheless never abandoned her Greek roots; it was said that seven philosophers accompanied her to the court. Under her patronage, a university was organized, and Eudokia herself authored a number of literary works, including commentaries on the Old Testament and poetic stories about Christ's life using the literary style of the Iliad. She made a pilgrimage to the Holy Land for a year, where she collected relics to bring back to Constantinople. Using her vast fortune for many charitable works, Eudokia later returned to the Holy Land, where she spent the last seventeen years of her life. Although she became fascinated with monophysite theology (which later became a heresy), the Orthodox Church canonized Eudokia for her kindness and philanthropy.

Prayer:

O Holy Spirit of love and truth, Blessed Eudokia was a fiery spirit, hungry for your word, who frequently used her philosophical training to combine the best fruits of her Greek culture with her newfound Christian faith. You are the lightning rod in our search for truth, always spurning us on to find more eloquent ways to express the Word made flesh in Jesus. Keep us attuned to your ever-present voice and always open to new expressions of your ever-expanding love. Amen.

Antiphon:

With my whole heart have I sought thee.

Readings:

"Know that the LORD Himself is God;
   It is He who has made us, and not we ourselves;
   We are His people and the sheep of His pasture.
Enter His gates with thanksgiving
   And His courts with praise
   Give thanks to Him, bless His name.

He has remembered his steadfast love and faithfulness to the house of Israel. All the ends of the earth have seen the victory of our God. Make a joyful noise to the Lord, all the earth; break forth into joyous song and sing praises." *Psalm 100:3-4 (NAB)*

"All the people who were in the court, and the elders, said, 'We are witnesses. May the LORD make the woman who is coming into your home like Rachel and Leah, both of whom built the house of Israel; and may you achieve wealth in Ephrathah and become famous in Bethlehem. Moreover, may your house be like the house of Perez whom Tamar bore to Judah, through the offspring which the LORD will give you by this young woman.'" *Ruth 4:11-12 (NASB)*

"When the Helper comes, whom I will send to you from the Father, that is the Spirit of truth who proceeds from the Father, He will testify about Me." *Jn. 15:26 (NASB)*

AUGUST 14 Radegund

St. Radegund—a queen, deaconess, foundress, scholar, hermit, and miracle worker—was one of the most beloved saints of France and England. Born around 520, the Franks abducted her in 531 and gave her as booty to the vicious King Clothar, son of Clovis. She was a reluctant queen but an able peacemaker and social servant, founding hospices and orphanages. When her brutal husband murdered her brother in her presence, she fled from the court and persuaded the bishop of Noyon to consecrate her as a deaconess. The nun Baudonivia, her biographer, tells us that Radegund then escaped her husband's territory and founded a monastery, Holy Cross at Poitiers. She lived in a small hermitage attached to the convent. Although she did not want to be abbess, Radegund did designate the Rule, which included that the sisters have an opportunity to study and copy manuscripts several hours a day. Radegund petitioned the Byzantine Emperor for relics from the Holy Land, including a fragment of the true cross, which ensured that the monastery would become a pilgrimage site. Rumors of miracles at the convent abounded at Poitiers, and Radegund was renowned for her kindness to pilgrims. When she died, Gregory of Tours came to perform the funeral rites; hundreds of nuns and townsfolk were beset with grief at losing her. Radegund was canonized in the ninth century, and numerous English parish churches are dedicated to her memory.

Intercessory Prayer:

Dear St. Radegund, you left a court of wealth and luxury to pursue a life of quiet scholarly study and contemplation with your sisters. Seeking no prestige of your own, you, a queen, washed the feet of pilgrims and served them at table. You insisted on creating serene personal space for all the sisters in your convent so they could pursue a life of meditation, and you used all of your royal resources to ensure the stability of their lifestyle. They loved you faithfully, for you were a tender and loving mother for all placed under your care. We ask your continued intercession, O holy one, for the sanctification of our own souls, and we thank you for modeling a role for us that is both heroic and humble. Amen.

Antiphon:

You will call your walls, salvation; and your gates, praise.

Readings:

"I will lift up my eyes to the hills, from whence comes my help. My help comes from the Lord, who has made heaven and earth. He will not suffer your foot to be moved; he that keeps you will not slumber." *Psalm 121:1–3 (KJV)*

"At that time, I will bring you home, at the time that I gather you together; I will make you renowned and praised among all people of the earth." *Zeph. 3:20 (RSV)*

"I am the vine, you are the branches; [he] who abides in Me and I in [him], [he] bears much fruit. . . ." *Jn. 15:5 (NASB)*

AUGUST 15 Assumption/Dormition

"Let the gates be opened wide, that the Gate of God may enter into abundant joy, she who asks without ceasing for great mercy on the world." Such is the praise sung during Vespers at the feast of the Dormition in the Eastern Church. The Dormition, or "falling asleep" (an interpretation by some early Church Fathers that Mary did not die), is celebrated on the same day as the feast of the Assumption. Both East and West base this feast day on apocryphal traditions and early liturgical hymns. The most widely accepted story is that the apostles had carried Mary's body to the burial site, when Thomas arrived late and begged to see her one more time. When the tomb was opened, it was empty. Without insisting on the literal truth of every element in this non-biblical material, the Orthodox tradition asserts clearly the same teaching as pronounced by Pope Pius XII in 1950: Mary was taken up into heaven, body and soul; thus she lives wholly in the age to come, prefiguring our own resurrection. Festivals commemorating the Assumption of the Mother of God were common from at least the fifth century onward. Although not recognized in most post-Reformation churches, Carl Jung saw the affirmation of Mary's Assumption as very significant teaching. It stresses the importance of the elevated feminine presence as well as the body; thus, it calls us to recollect that the whole person is what Christ came to save. Mary is now what we will be in due course: she is the first of the glorified saints.

Intercessory Prayer:

O beloved Theotokos, you are the hope that can never be put to shame for those who trust in you. Both the Eastern and Western churches rightly recognized that you are the Mother of Christ our God, for you have brought forth the never-setting light of our souls. In his great goodness, he carried your body and soul to the heavenly heights, the first fruit of our own resurrection. You who are the earth in blossom and the dove of heaven, be the perpetual helper of those who call on you. Amen.

Antiphon:

Death has been swallowed up in victory.

Readings:

"For as the Father has life in himself, so he has granted the Son also to have life in himself, and has given him authority to execute judgment, because he is the Son of man. Do not marvel at this; for the hour is coming when all who are in tombs will hear his voice and come forth, those who have done good to the resurrection of life. . . ." *Jn. 5:26–29 (RSV)*

"But if there is no resurrection of the dead, then Christ has not been raised; and if Christ has not been raised, then our preaching is in vain and your faith is in vain." *1 Cor 15:13–14 (RSV)*

"Blessed and holy are those who share the first resurrection! Over such the second death has no power, but they shall be priest of God and of Christ, and they shall reign with him a thousand years." *Rev. 20:6 (RSV)*

AUGUST 16 Matrona Popova

Matrona Naumouna Popova organized one of the first Russian monasteries to engage in charitable practices in addition to following the standard hermetic life of prayer and contemplation. Born into severe poverty in the eighteenth century, she was orphaned at an early age. In young adulthood, she met a woman hermit named Melaniia who was a *staritsa* (enlightened elder), whom she took as her spiritual director. Melaniia advised Matrona to make a spiritual pilgrimage, during which she had a profound mystical experience at St. Tikkon's gravesite in Russia. Matrona then lived on the streets as a "holy fool" for several years. She was finally offered housing near the Tikkon men's monastery; they recognized her as a prophet and holy woman. She immediately turned her new home into a homeless shelter for other wanderers while she herself slept on the ground. St. Tikkon appeared to her in a dream assuring her that a shelter would be built to house the growing number of pilgrims at the monastery, and the next day a stonemason appeared in order to build it on credit. The shelter grew and with it a women's community. It was called the Wayfarer's Home before it became an official women's monastery, devoted to nursing orphans and pilgrims like Matrona herself had been much of her life. After adopting a

Prayer Rule and gaining approval from the Synod, they became known as the Tikhonovskoe Sisters of Mercy. In 1851, Matrona drew her sisters to her bedside and, before dying, entrusted them to the Mercy of Christ and his holy mother.

Prayer:

Sweet Holy Spirit of God, Matrona was a sanctified soul who knew that at the core of every human life stood a longing for the vision of God. Inspired by you, she became possessed of a holy madness and a channel for your word to those around her. You counseled her continually by renewing her mind. We present ourselves before you this day. Be our guide and our counselor. Through Matrona's intercession, transform us by renewing our minds, so we may put off our old selves and put on the new image of Christ. Amen.

Antiphon:

Then your light will break forth and your holiness will go before you.

Readings:

"It is good to give thanks to the LORD And to sing praises to Your name, O Most High; To declare Your lovingkindness in the morning And Your faithfulness by night, With the ten-stringed lute and with the harp, With resounding music upon the lyre. For You, O LORD, have made me glad by what You have done, I will sing for joy at the works of Your hands." *Psalm 92:1–4 (NASB)*

"You also became imitators of us and of the Lord, having received the word in much tribulation with the joy of the Holy Spirit." *1 Thes. 1:6 (NASB)*

"Blessed be the God and Father of our Lord Jesus Christ, who according to His great mercy has caused us to be born again to a living hope through the resurrection of Jesus Christ from the dead, to obtain an inheritance which is imperishable and undefiled and will not fade away, reserved in heaven for you . . ." *1 Pet. 1:3–4 (NASB)*

"He has given help to Israel His servant, in remembrance of His mercy." *Lk. 1:54 (NASB)*

AUGUST 17 Jeanne Delanou

As a shopkeeper in seventeenth-century France, Jeanne Delanou was hardly the image or example of sainthood. She was miserly to the penny, turned away beggars from her shop, and kept it open on Sundays. To touch Jeanne's hardened heart, God brought an unusual old woman into her life named Frances Souchet. Jeanne agreed to give the old woman lodging. Soon they became friends, and Frances revealed to Jeanne the deeper, mystical side of her faith. Jeanne then had a vision wherein she saw in the poor, not an impoverished class of beggars, but Christ himself. It was a deep revelation for her. Jeanne began going to Mass regularly, and soon she felt called to open her own home to a desperate homeless family. This act of kindness became a regular occurrence, with the poor and destitute seeking assistance from a much kinder Jeanne. She eventually founded a religious order whose mission was to serve the sick and poor, the Sisters of St. Anne. When she died at age seventy, she left over four hundred sisters (now known as the Sisters of Jeanne Delanou) who continue to minister to the poor throughout France, Madagascar, and Sumatra. Jeanne died August 17, 1736, and Pope John Paul II canonized her in 1982.

Prayer:

> *Heavenly Father, through St. Jeanne Delanou's conversion, you showed us how the powerful witness of one Christian can affect the lives of many others. Her heart was touched when she became aware of your presence and providence, and she passed on her own newfound faith to many others through acts of love and charity toward those most in need. Let her example inspire us to truly live out our own faith on a daily basis and to be living witnesses to all around us. Amen.*

Antiphon:

I must do the works of him that sent me.

Readings:

"The bird also has found a house, and the swallow a nest for herself, where she may lay her young, even Your altars, O LORD of hosts, My King and my God. How blessed are those who dwell in Your house! They are ever praising You. Selah." *Psalm 84:3–4 (NASB)*

"Beyond all these things put on love, which is the perfect bond of unity. Let the peace of Christ rule in your hearts, to which indeed you were called in one body; and be thankful. Let the word of Christ richly dwell within you, with all wisdom teaching and admonishing one another with psalms and hymns and spiritual songs, singing with thankfulness in your hearts to God. Whatever you do in word or deed, do all in the name of the Lord Jesus. . . ." Col. 3:14–17 (NASB)

"For I was hungry, and you gave Me something to eat; I was thirsty, and you gave Me something to drink; I was a stranger, and you invited Me in." Mt. 25:35 (NASB)

AUGUST 18 Jane Frances de Chantal

Jane Frances de Chantal was born in France in 1572. When she was twenty, she was wed to Baron de Chantal, and they had a very happy marriage blessed with four children. Tragedy struck and put an end to their storybook life together after eight years of marriage, when the baron was killed in a hunting accident. Jane grieved for many months, but she did her best to restore a normal home life for her children's sake. What she most longed for was a spiritual director, and she prayed mightily that God might send her someone to give her the spiritual guidance necessary to endure her hardships and point the way toward her future. God answered in a powerful way, and soon St. Francis de Sales became Jane's closest spiritual friend and director. When her children were old enough, Jane and Francis began an order of contemplative nuns known as the Order of the Visitation, which eventually spread to over sixty-five houses of prayer throughout France. The order was specifically designed for older and infirm women, who were unable to bear the severity of established convents. Jane died in 1641 and was canonized in 1767. Jane's body was eventually buried near her dearest friend in life, St. Francis de Sales.

Intercessory Prayer:

Dear St. Jane, in your spiritual letters you advised us to be content to remain an empty vessel, simply receiving whatever holy charity the savior may wish to pour in. Help us to follow these

*words of wisdom and inspiration. Intercede for us so that we may
receive the grace to accept whatever path Christ may place us on
in order to accomplish his works on earth. May we always remain
empty vessels for God's greater honor and glory. Amen.*

Antiphon:

To him alone I pledge my trust; to him alone I give my
undivided love.

Readings:

"Establish my footsteps in Your word, and do not let any iniquity
have dominion over me." *Psalm 119:133 (NASB)*

"The mind of [man] plans his way, but the LORD directs his
steps." *Prov. 16:9 (NASB)*

"But the Lord is faithful, and He will strengthen and protect you
from the evil one. We have confidence in the Lord concerning
you, that you are doing and will continue to do what we command. May the Lord direct your hearts into the love of God and
into the steadfastness of Christ." *2 Thes. 3:3–5 (NASB)*

"A poor widow came and put in two small copper coins, which
amount to a cent. Calling His disciples to Him, He said to them,
'Truly I say to you, this poor widow put in more than all the con-
tributors to the treasury; for they all put in out of their surplus, but
she, out of her poverty, put in all she owned, all she had to live
on.'" *Mk. 12:42–44 (NASB)*

AUGUST 19 Mother Maria Maddalena Bentivoglio

Although Mother Maria Maddalena Bentivoglio was born in
Italy, she is celebrated as an American saint. Maria was born
to a large prominent family in the nineteenth century. She
was a creative, intelligent, and often mischievous child, but she was
also very devout and felt an early call to enter into religious life. She
became a Poor Clare in 1864 and took the name Maria Maddalena of
the Sacred Heart of Jesus. Eleven years later, Pope Pius IX sent
Mother Maria along with one of her sisters, who was also a Poor
Clare, to help establish the Poor Clares in the United States. This

mission was fraught with failures and frustrations. Not only did the sisters face a language barrier, they were unable to find a diocese that would support their efforts. Eventually, they ended up in Omaha, Nebraska, where a philanthropist named John Creighton generously assisted them in establishing the first Poor Clares Monastery in America. Two subsequent foundations were later established in New Orleans and one in Evansville, Indiana. This demonstrated that Americans could be attracted to the contemplative lifestyle and laid a foundation for future endeavors. Mother Maria died in Evansville when she was seventy-one years old. Before she died, she asked to be taken out of bed so she could die in the same place as her beloved father, Francis: on the floor. The Church declared Mother Maria venerable in 1932.

Intercessory Prayer:

Dear Mother Maria, you followed the Holy Spirit's inspirations to help found religious contemplative communities in the United States, despite many barriers in your path. You never lost the spirit and understanding of your mission. Help us to imitate your virtues of courage in the face of obstacles and intercede for us, that we may use our own unique gifts and talents for God's greater honor and glory. Amen.

Antiphon:

You will redeem us, O God, because of your love!

Readings:

"The LORD is for me; I will not fear; what can [man] do to me? The LORD is for me among those who help me; Therefore I will look with satisfaction on those who hate me. It is better to take refuge in the LORD than to trust in [man]. It is better to take refuge in the LORD. . . ." *Psalm 118:6–9 (NASB)*

". . . and are confident that you yourself are a guide to the blind, a light to those who are in darkness, a corrector of the foolish, a teacher of the immature, having in the Law the embodiment of knowledge and of the truth, you, therefore, who teach another, do you not teach yourself?" *Rom. 2:19–21 (NASB)*

"As for you, the anointing which you received from Him abides in you, and you have no need for anyone to teach you; but as His anointing teaches you about all things, and is true and is not a lie, and just as it has taught you, you abide in Him." *1 Jn. 2:27 (NASB)*

AUGUST 20 Austreberta

Austreberta's fate was sealed before she was conceived. Prior to her birth in 630, the Holy Spirit illuminated her mother, Framechilda, who learned that she would bear a girl child who would be a leader in the Lord's house and a pillar to the Christian people in the Frankish kingdom. Austreberta's calling was confirmed again, when at ten years old, she looked at her reflection in the water and saw a veil over her head. A serious and pious child, she took this vision to heart. When her father tried to arrange a marriage for her later on, she ran away to St. Omer, Bishop of Therouanne, to take the veil. Omer complied and escorted her home to ease the confrontation with her parents. He was successful, and her family consented to let Austreberta enter the monastery of Portus. Very observant and devout, Austreberta led by example and was the instrument of conversion for many others during her time there. After fourteen years, Austreberta was appointed abbess of Pavilly. Under her supervision, the monastery evolved into a thriving cultural center. Foreseeing her own death, she drew her community together and blessed them. Crowds thronged to her deathbed. At the time of Austreberta's death, she quieted the nuns who were chanting the psalms at her bedside to tell them the saints were already proceeding into the room to fetch her for her heavenward journey.

Prayer:

O Holy Spirit of God, St. Austreberta followed her early vision in life and found fulfillment in being a mother to many spiritual daughters. Help us to take responsibility for following our hearts' true calling, rather than worldly enticements, so our lives may yield the fruit of virtue and service. As a mother protects her children, let us cultivate a boundless nurturance for all the members of Christ's body. Amen.

Antiphon:

You chose disciples because they did not adhere to this world.

Readings:

"As face answers face reflected in the water, so one's heart answers another." *Prov. 27:19 (NEB)*

"Behold, I am standing by the spring of water, and the daughters of the men of the city are coming out to draw water." Gen. 24:13 (RSV)

"They said to Him, 'Where do You want us to prepare it?' And He said to them, 'When you have entered the city, a man will meet you carrying a pitcher of water; follow him into the house that he enters. And you shall say to the owner of the house, "The Teacher says to you, Where is the guest room in which I may eat the Passover with My disciples?" And he will show you a large, furnished upper room; prepare it there.' And they left and found everything just as He had told them; and they prepared the Passover." Lk. 22:9–13 (NASB)

AUGUST 21 Victoria Rasoamanarivo and Our Lady of Knock

Victoria Rasoamanarivo was a devout layperson who helped to evangelize the Church in Madagascar during the late nineteenth century. In 1864 she married the son of the island's prime minister. Her husband abused her horribly, but Victoria believed it was her responsibility to remain faithful to her marriage and to her position of ministry. She used the powers entrusted to her high office to help bring French Catholic missionaries to the island to develop a prospering Catholic community. She was an extremely devout woman who spent many hours a day in prayer in order to gain the strength she needed to fight for the Church in Madagascar and endure the trials in her personal life. When she died in 1894, the Church in Madagascar mourned her passing as a great protectoress. Pope John Paul II declared her Blessed in 1989, noting, "Victoria did not think that she could bring the Good News to her brothers and sisters without opening her whole being to the power of grace."

We also celebrate the apparition of Mary, under the title of Our Lady of Knock, in Ireland. In 1879, the Blessed Mother, along with St. Joseph, St. John the Baptist, and St. John the Evangelist, appeared in a vision that many people in County Mayo, Ireland, witnessed. An image of the Lamb with angels hovering overhead accompanied the three figures. The Blessed Mother did not speak, but the apparition site became

WomenSaints

noted as a place to recite the Rosary. Miraculous healings were reported soon afterward all throughout the region, and in 1954, Pope Pius XII blessed the "Knock" banner at St. Peters and gave permission to crown Our Lady of Knock. The Our Lady of Knock shrine has become a major site of pilgrimage for the faithful over the last century.

Intercessory Prayer:

Dear Blessed Virgin Mary, Our Lady of Knock, please intercede for us today. As you appeared to many faithful witnesses over a century ago to inspire the faithful in Ireland, please extend your loving care and protection to us. Blessed Victoria, we also entreat you today as a brave laywoman who devoted your life to spreading the faith and who loved Christ authentically by always remaining faithful to the Lord's Word. Inspire us to open up to the power of God's grace so we may serve as a vehicle for sanctifying others. Amen.

Antiphon:

Not unto us, O Lord, not unto us, but unto thy name give glory.

Readings:

"And every created thing which is in heaven and on the earth and under the earth and on the sea, and all things in them, I heard saying, 'To Him who sits on the throne, and to the Lamb, be blessing and honor and glory and dominion forever and ever.'" *Rev. 5:13 (NASB)*

"The name of the LORD is a strong tower; the righteous runs into it and is safe." *Prov. 18:10 (NASB)*

AUGUST 22 Immaculate Heart of Mary

Catholic devotion to the Immaculate Heart of Mary goes hand in hand with devotion and love toward the Sacred Heart of her divine son, Jesus. The history of Catholic devotion to the Immaculate Heart of Mary is based very much in Scripture. We first hear about the heart of Mary when Simeon's prophecy tells us that her heart will be pierced by a sword of sorrow for all she will endure as the mother of God. Luke tells us that Mary treasured all the early events of Christ's life in her heart. In later centuries, numerous saints—including St. Bernard, St. Anselm, St. Mechtilde, St. Bernadine, and St. Francis de Sales—have revealed an express devotion to the Immaculate Heart of Mary in various spiritual writings. However, it was not until the seventeenth century that St. Jean Eudes truly promulgated the devotion, working tirelessly to make this devotion public and to establish a feast day within the Church dedicated to the Immaculate Heart of Mary. The heart of Mary represents love, purity, and total and filial devotion to God. We should be inspired by the immaculate and purest heart of Mary. Images of the heart of Mary within our homes are one way to foster devotion and love for Mary, the Mother of God.

Intercessory Prayer:

> *Immaculate Heart of Mary, purest vessel of love and devotion, we come to you today and ask for your powerful intercession as we present all the needs of our lives totally to Jesus through you. Allow us to be inspired by the image of your purest and most loving heart, the heart that beat next to Jesus when you carried him within your virginal womb. Protect us always with your loving care and providence. Guide our youth and keep them sanctified and protected, in Jesus' name. Amen.*

Antiphon:

Singular vessel of devotion, pray for us! (Litany)

Readings:

"But of Zion it shall be said, 'This one and that one were born in her'; And the Most High Himself will establish her. The LORD will count when He registers the peoples, 'This one was born there.' Selah. Then those who sing as well as those who play the flutes shall say, 'All my springs of joy are in you.'" *Psalm 87:5–7 (NASB)*

"You shall love the LORD your God with all your heart and with all your soul and with all your might. These words, which I am commanding you today, shall be on your heart. You shall teach them diligently to your [sons] and shall talk of them when you sit in your house and when you walk by the way and when you lie down and when you rise up." *Deut. 6:5–8 (NASB)*

"And Simeon blessed them and said to Mary His mother, 'Behold, this Child is appointed for the fall and rise of many in Israel, and for a sign to be opposed—and a sword will pierce even your own soul—to the end that thoughts from many hearts may be re-vealed." *Lk. 2:34–35 (NASB)*

AUGUST 23 Rose of Lima

Patron of the Americas and the Philippines, Rose of Lima was named Isabel at birth. Some say her nurse nicknamed her Rose because she had such a devotion to flowers and animals; others say it was because of her beauty. It is told that she talked to birds and even insects, which did not bite her. When she was seven, her father was transferred to the Andes mountains in Peru, where Rose learned about the resentment many indigenous Indians had toward the Spanish for their imperialistic encroachment on their culture. In deep remorse for their suffering, she prayed for the Peruvian people for the rest of her life, for she had a strong sense of social as well as personal sin. Refusing to marry, Rose built her own cell close to her parents' home in Lima, where she helped to support her family through her needlework and gardening. She had both raptures and dark nights of the soul, and her visions were classically mystical, with descriptions of God, such as "ocean infinite," and "great light." As she began to attract disciples, theologians in the Church interrogated her, and she replied that she knew nothing of dogma except what God taught to her. Like many of the Beguine mystics of the Middle Ages, Rose's love poured into music and poetry. Rose is hailed as the patron of social workers in Peru because of her charitable activities, and herbalists honor her for her healing qualities.

Intercessory Prayer:

Dear St. Rose, you were the apple of your beloved's eye and wanted only to rest under the shadow of his wings. You reverenced all of nature as a reflection of God and radiated joy to all people and animals in God's creation. Intercede for all those whose lifestyle depends on tilling the soil and who care for the fruits of the earth. Lead us to the fullness you found in your Jesus, who alone is delectable and sweet, and the source of all good fruit. Amen.

Antiphon:

Nothing compares to the promise we have in you.

Readings:

"He changes rivers into a wilderness and springs of water into a thirsty ground; a fruitful land into a salt waste, because of the wickedness of those who dwell in it. He changes a wilderness into a pool of water and a dry land into springs of water." *Psalm 107:33–35 (NASB)*

"Awake, O north wind; and come O south; blow upon my garden, that the spices thereof may flow out. Let my beloved come into his garden, and eat his pleasant fruits." *Song 4:16 (KJV)*

"And God is able to provide you with every blessing in abundance, so that by always having enough of everything, you may share abundantly in every good work. . . . He who supplies seed to the sower and bread for food will supply and multiply your seed for sowing and increase the harvest of your righteousness." *2 Cor. 9:8, 10 (RSV)*

"So then, you will know them by their fruits." *Mt. 7:20 (NASB)*

AUGUST 24 Simone Weil

Simone Weil was born into a Jewish family in France in 1909, in a post-Industrial age wherein the gap between rich and poor was very great. She was a philosophical genius and a spiritually centered activist with an austere sense of the potential present in every human being. She spent her life in solidarity with the worker's plight, championing causes she saw as Christian ideals. When she was five, for example, Simone refused to eat sugar because the French soldiers in World War I had none. She was a close colleague with the Dominican Joseph Perrin, for whom she wrote her spiritual biography. In it, she explained her reasons for not being baptized. For her, baptism would have entailed a compromise with the deepest truth of her soul, which sought, above all else, to maintain intellectual purity free of dogma. Although she knew the mystics and she had several mystical experiences of Christ, she wrote that "we must have a saintliness demanded by the present moment . . . [which is] without precedent." While sick from tuberculosis, she hastened her death by refusing to eat more than the rations that workers in the French Resistance movement received. She was deeply in love with the Eucharistic Presence, and she attended Mass regularly, although she never received communion. Her book, *Waiting on God*, has become a classic describing the nature of the soul's mysticism.

Prayer:

> *Beloved Jesus, Simone Weil believed that you act through the soul if we wait for you to work in us and with us; that our lives should be devoted to attentively waiting for that call and responding to it. She reminded us that you come to us only when you will it and not because of our own efforts. She sought above all else to be the "marble under the sculptor's hands." An intellectual genius, she knew that reason would never uncover God's secret design, to which we must all submit in silence. Have mercy on us when we seek you impatiently. Reveal to us the holy abandonment that comes only from waiting for you. Amen.*

Antiphon:

From sunrise to sunset, my soul waits for you.

Readings:

"To You, O LORD, I lift up my soul. O my God, in You I trust. . . . none of those who wait for You will be ashamed. . . . Make me know Your ways, O LORD. Teach me Your paths. Lead me in Your truth. . . . For You I wait all the day." *Psalm 25:1–5 (NASB)*

"How blessed is [he] who keeps waiting. . . . [G]o your way to the end; then you will enter into rest and rise again for your allotted portion at the end of the age." *Dan. 12:12–13 (NASB)*

"Gathering them together, He commanded them not to leave Jerusalem, but to wait for what the Father had promised, 'Which,' He said, 'you heard of from Me; for John baptized with water, but you will be baptized with the Holy Spirit. . . .'" *Acts 1:4–5 (NASB)*

AUGUST 25 Glodesind (Transferred)

Glodesind's hagiographer calls her God's beloved and perpetual virgin. She lived around 600 C.E. and is one of the earliest women in Frankish society (Germany and France) to defy her family by insisting upon being a virgin for Christ. Born in a time when women and children were considered men's property, Glodesind spurned her father's attempt to have her marry. She fled to Metz to the Church of St. Stephen, where she took sanctuary. Glodesind remained in the church for six days and nights without food or water. On the seventh day, a stranger entered the church and laid the holy veil upon Glodesind. Upon hearing the story, her family recognized the stranger as an angel and were terrified. Her father begged for her pardon and sent her to Trier, a monastery where her aunt was abbess, for training. Following the completion of her training, Glodesind's parents generously set up a monastery for her in Metz where she ruled as abbess for six years. Glodesind died young, at about age thirty. Her body was buried at the Church of Holy Apostles because there was no cemetery at Subterius, her monastery. A cemetery was eventually established at Subterius, and Glodesind's body was transferred there twenty-five years later, at which time her body was found to be incorrupt. A myriad of miracles are attributed to St. Glodesind following her transference.

Prayer:

Beloved Lord Jesus, Glodesind provides an example of the benefits of the power of cleaving to you. She defied her father and the conventions of her time to become your bride and servant. You even sent an angel to support her. Help us to lead our lives in such a way that we demonstrate our love and allegiance to you, so we may be clothed in love, which binds everything together in perfect harmony. Amen.

Antiphon:

Teach me to follow in your footsteps.

Readings:

"Turn to me and be gracious to me, as you turn toward those who love your name. Keep steady my steps according to your promise, and let no iniquity get dominion over me. Redeem me from man's oppression that I may keep your precepts. Make your face shine upon your servant, and teach me your statutes." *Ps. 119:132–135 (RSV)*

"Beyond all these things put on love, which is the perfect bond of unity. Let the peace of Christ rule in your hearts, to which indeed you were called in one body; and be thankful." *Col. 3:14–15 (NASB)*

"But when the Comforter comes, whom I will send to you from the Father . . . the Spirit of truth, who proceeds from the Father . . . shall testify of me; and you also shall bear witness, because you have been with me from the beginning." *Jn. 15:26–27 (KJV)*

AUGUST 26 Mariam Bouardy

Mariam Bouardy lived in the mid-nineteenth century in Palestine. Her birth was the direct result of prayer, as her parents had twelve sons, all of whom died in infancy. Finally her mother made a pilgrimage to Bethlehem to pray to the Blessed Virgin for a daughter—Mariam was born soon after. Her parents died tragically, and she was raised by relatives. When she refused to wed, they disowned her. Mariam worked at menial jobs until she was finally able to realize her dream of becoming a religious, when she met a French woman who brought her back to France, where Mariam became a Sister of St. Joseph. She eventually joined the Carmelites and referred to herself as "a little nothing," basing this on the teachings of "the little way" of St. Therese, the Little Flower. Miracles and ecstasies abound in the story of Mariam's life. She had numerous visions of the Blessed Mother in which prophecy was revealed about the Church's future Church in the Holy Land. Eyewitnesses reported that she was able to levitate, and she also suffered Our Lord's supernatural wounds in the stigmata, and so she was known as Mary of Jesus Crucified. She was shown visions of heaven and hell, and like Jesus himself, she died at age thirty-three. Pope John Paul II beatified Mariam in 1983, when he invoked her prayers for peace in Palestine.

Prayer:

> *Dear Lord Jesus, you blessed good Mariam Bouardy with many spiritual gifts that were a testimony to your loving power. Despite the profound gifts you bestowed on her, she always remained humble in the eyes of the world. She referred to herself as "a little nothing" so she could emulate St. Therese's teachings. Teach us to incorporate Blessed Mariam's path into our daily lives and to do each task in a spirit of total charity and self-giving. May we never*

forget that even the most menial duties become great when we perform them with love for you. Amen.

Antiphon:

By a single offering God has perfected for all time those who are sanctified.

Readings:

"To You, O LORD, I lift up my soul. O my God, in You I trust, . . . none of those who wait for You will be ashamed. . . . Make me know Your ways, O LORD. Teach me Your paths. Lead me in Your truth. . . . For You I wait all the day." *Psalm 25:1–5 (NASB)*

"How blessed is [he] who keeps waiting . . . go your way to the end; then you will enter into rest and rise again for your allotted portion at the end of the age." *Dan. 12:12–13 (NASB)*

"Gathering them together, He commanded them not to leave Jerusalem, but to wait for what the Father had promised, 'Which,' He said, 'you heard of from Me; for John baptized with water, but you will be baptized with the Holy Spirit . . . '" *Acts 1:4–5 (NASB)*

AUGUST 27 Monica

St. Monica was given the title of Patron Saint of Mothers, and her life story makes it clear why such an important patronage is placed under her care. Monica was married to a pagan who was abusive and wayward, but her kind and prayerful manner prevented him from harming her, and he converted to Christianity just a year before his death. They had three children; Augustine was the wild youth that she worried about the most. For years she prayed incessantly for his conversion. After a heavenly vision, she accepted a local bishop's advice that God would not ignore her years of tearful prayers on Augustine's behalf. Augustine eventually did become a Christian, and much to Monica's joy, he decided to live a life of service to the Church. St. Augustine of Hippo was one of the Church's foremost doctors. Monica traveled with his company of theologians for a number of years. She is established as a model of wives and mothers, especially those who are praying for unbelieving spouses or children. St. Monica's relics are kept in the Church of St. Augustine in Rome.

Intercessory Prayer:

Dear St. Monica, you were a living example of never-ending and never-failing prayerful intercession for your family members. Your prayers for conversion were eventually answered, and your son became a great theologian of the Church. Help us to follow your example and continually lift up our loved ones to God in prayer. Please intercede for all mothers everywhere. Amen.

Antiphon:

Now with you is wisdom, who knows your works.

Readings:

"A foolish man despises his mother. Folly is a joy to him who has no sense, but a man of understanding walks aright. Without counsel, plans go wrong, but with many advisors, they succeed. . . . [T]he Lord tears down the house of the proud, but maintains the widow's boundaries." *Prov. 15:20–25 (RSV)*

"And God said to Abraham, As for Sarai, your wife, you shall not call her name Sarai, but Sarah shall be her name. And I will bless her, and she shall be a mother of nations; kings of people shall be of her." *Gen. 17:15–16 (KJV)*

"With thee is wisdom, who knows thy works and was present when thou didst make the world, and who understands what is pleasing in thy sight and what is right according to thy commandments." *Wisdom 9:9 (RSV)*

AUGUST 28 Jean Donovan

A modern martyr for Christ, Jean Donovan grew up in a supportive loving Roman Catholic family in the United States, and one of her earliest desires was to become an altar girl. She became involved with ministering to the poor in Ireland as an exchange student in college, and she decided to become a lay missionary with the Maryknolls in El Salvador in 1978. Jean was soon introduced into the fierce reality of murder and death squads in that revolutionary, war-torn country. Church workers there helped to manage refugee centers, health care, and food distribution programs. Influenced by leaders like Oscar Romero, she progressively understood about the injustices perpetrated upon the El Salvadoran people and the United States' passive role there. During this period, more than forty thousand civilians were murdered; when members of Jean's own team were shot, she refused to leave her mission with the refugees. She was sexually assaulted and shot with three other missionaries soon after Romero was gunned down while saying Mass. The film *Choices of the Heart* was made in 1983 commemorating Jean's life and death.

Prayer:

O suffering Savior, you are a friend of the oppressed. You knew Jean as a woman who found her strength in you and overcame all her fears through trust. Living the gospel message through simplicity in the midst of poverty, she worked tirelessly for the cause of your justice in the world. The blood of your martyrs in El Salvador is, as it was in times past, the seed of new faith in you. Bless those who put their lives at risk for the sake of your oppressed peoples everywhere and grant heroic strength and courage to those being tortured for the sake of your name. Amen.

Antiphon:

Guard me, O God, from the snares of darkness.

Readings:

"Rescue me, O LORD, from evil men;
Preserve me from violent men
Who devise evil things in their hearts;
They continually stir up wars.
They sharpen their tongues as a serpent;
Poison of a viper is under their lips. Selah.
I know that the LORD will maintain the cause of the afflicted
And justice for the poor.
Surely the righteous will give thanks to Your name;
The upright will dwell in Your presence." *Psalm 140:1–3, 12–13 (NASB)*

"Lift up your eyes to the heavens, and look upon the earth beneath: for the heavens shall vanish away like smoke, and the earth shall wax old like a garment; and they that dwell therein shall die in like manner: But my salvation shall be forever, and my righteousness shall not be abolished." *Isa. 51:6 (KJV)*

"Likewise also the chief priests mocking him, with the scribes and elders, said, 'He saved others, himself he cannot save. If he be King of Israel, let him now come down from the cross, and we will believe him.'" *Mt. 27:41–42 (KJV)*

AUGUST 29 Theodora of Thessaloniki

St. Theodora of Thessaloniki, who lived during the ninth century, was a simple soul who may not have been canonized a saint were it not for the prolific miracles at her tomb. Married, with three children, she lost two children and then begged her husband to consecrate their remaining daughter to God. The girl was taken to the convent of St. Luke as a young girl and named Theopiste. Several years later, Theodora's husband died, and she also entered this convent, which had an exceptionally strict abbess named Anna. Because of the stringent austerities, Theodora, who shared a cell with her daughter, was disturbed that Theopiste was made to subsist on too little food. When she approached Anna about it, the abbess angrily reminded her that the Scripture admonished one who is dedicated to God to take no thought for the body (Mt. 6:25). Seeing an attachment in Theodora that she did not like, Anna ordered mother and daughter not to speak to one another. For the next fifteen years they shared the same cell but never spoke. Theodora never performed miracles or feats of austerities, other than the austere afflictions she was made to bear at Anna's hands. When Anna retired, Theopiste was made abbess, and Theodora's daughter became her spiritual mother. When Theodora died, one of the most auspicious miracles in the Orthodox tradition occurred at her tomb. The oil lamp burning there exuded oil, gushing out in great quantities; then her relics themselves emitted an unearthly light and ran with oil for more than two years (during which time her *vita* was written). Finally a painter who had never met her, but had seen her in a dream, made an icon in her image. It too became a myrrh-streaming icon. For these reasons, it was deemed fitting that Theodora, the humble nun at Thessaloniki, should be glorified.

Intercessory Prayer:

Dear Blessed Theodora, you were an unassuming soul who led a simple life for Christ; yet the angels recorded your gracious deeds for your future glory and divinization. You lived many years in a convent where your daughter in the flesh became your own spiritual mother, whom you obeyed, as you would obey Christ himself. Your life was full of paradoxes, yet you demonstrated to the faithful that our God accomplishes great and miraculous deeds through those who love him. Intercede for us, that Christ's protective overshadowing mercy will be made manifest in our own lives. Amen.

Antiphon:

You anoint my head with oil; my cup overflows.

Readings

"Set a guard, O LORD, over my mouth; Keep watch over the door of my lips. . . . Let the righteous smite me in kindness and reprove me; It is oil upon the head; Do not let my head refuse it, for still my prayer is against their wicked deeds." *Psalm 141:3, 5 (NASB)*

"Afterward the [sons] of Israel . . . will come trembling to the LORD and to His goodness in the last days." *Hos. 3:5 (NASB)*

"Sitting down, He called the twelve and said to them, 'If anyone wants to be first, he shall be last of all and servant of all.'" *Mk. 9:35 (NASB)*

"You have loved righteousness and hated lawlessness; therefore God, your God, has anointed you with the oil of gladness above your companions." *Heb. 1:9 (NASB)*

AUGUST 30 Jeanne Jugan

Jeanne Jugan was born to a poor family in France in the late eighteenth century. Her father died when she was just a toddler, and her family struggled with desperate financial times during a politically turbulent era. Even in her own poverty, Jeanne felt called to assist those who were less fortunate than herself. Along with two companions, she founded the Little Sisters of the Poor, whose mission was to help the most destitute and needy in the region. With her gentle and personable personality, she became adept at fund-raising, and soon she was able to establish facilities and convent houses throughout the region. Unfortunately, Fr. Leo Pailler, the area priest, envied Jeanne's success, took control of her efforts, and banished her with orders to remain secluded within the motherhouse. Jeanne respectfully honored his request, and she worked with the postulants, who revered and loved her greatly for her words of wisdom and encouragement—most of them not realizing that Jeanne (who took the name Sr. Mary of the Cross) was the true foundress of their order. She lived to see Pope Leo XIII approve her order, which spread to over 2,400 sisters before she died in 1879. Pope John Paul II, aware of the true nature of all Jeanne had endured in humility and sanctity, beatified her in 1982.

Intercessory Prayer:

Dear Blessed Jeanne, you advised us to go and find Jesus when we feel spiritually exhausted and to tell him, as if we are speaking face to face with a best friend, exactly what is going on in our lives. Then we should go on with our day without worries, feeling secure in the knowledge that once we tell God our needs, he has heard us. Inspire us to have such a real and honest relationship with God. May we strive to always lift up our eyes to the hills, from whence comes our help. Amen.

Antiphon:

Into your hands, O God, I commend my spirit.

Readings:

O LORD, I love the habitation of Your house
    And the place where Your glory dwells.
Do not take my soul away along with sinners,
    Nor my life with men of bloodshed,
In whose hands is a wicked scheme,
    And whose right hand is full of bribes.
But as for me, I shall walk in my integrity;
    Redeem me, and be gracious to me.
My foot stands on a level place;
        In the congregations I shall bless the LORD." *Psalm 26:8–12 (NASB)*

"For not one of us lives for [himself], and not one dies for [himself]." *Rom. 14:7 (NASB)*

"He will not wrangle or cry aloud, nor will anyone hear his voice in the streets. He will not break a bruised reed or quench a smoldering wick until he brings justice to victory. And in his name the Gentiles will hope." *Mt. 12:19–21 (RSV)*

AUGUST 31 Cuthburga

Cuthburga was the sister of King Ina of Wessex. She married Aldfrid, King of Northumbria in 688. King Aldfrid was known for his learning and for his favors to the Church. He eventually allowed Cuthburga to renounce her wedding vows and become a nun at Barking under St. Hildelid's leadership. Around the year 705, Cuthburga established a double monastery at Wimbourne with her sister St. Queenburga. Cuthberga was the first abbess of Wimbourne. Several nuns who later evangelized Germany were educated at Wimbourne. The monastery consisted of a nunnery and an enclosed abbey, and a strict separation was enforced. Even the prelates were forbidden to enter the nun's quarters. Cuthburga communicated with the church fathers through a little hatch. She adhered to strict fasting and prayer for herself. According to her hagiographers, Cuthburga was "humble both to God and man, meek and tender to others, but always austere to herself."

Prayer:

> Almighty God, the protector of all who trust in you, Cuthburga initiated a new way of life for women and men to live through her double monastery in the British Isles. Through the intercession of all the saints who sought you behind convent doors, help us to pass through things temporal so that, despite the lifestyle we have chosen, we may never lose sight of things eternal. Through Christ our Lord. Amen.

Antiphon:

If anyone would serve me, let them follow me.

Readings:

"How precious also are Your thoughts to me, O God! How vast is the sum of them! If I should count them, they would outnumber the sand. When I awake, I am still with You." *Psalm 139:17–18* *(NASB)*

"Draw me after you, let us make haste. The king has brought me into his chambers. We will exult and rejoice in you; we will extol your love more than wine; rightly do they love you." *Song 1:4* *(RSV)*

"... For this I have been born, and for this I have come into the world, to testify to the truth. Everyone who is of the truth hears My voice." *Jn. 18:37 (NASB)*

SEPTEMBER 1 Beatrice da Silva

Beatrice da Silva was born in 1424 in Morocco, then under Portuguese rule. Related to the royal family of Portugal, she directly served the queen of Castile as a lady in waiting. She eventually left her position of prominence to pursue a life of quiet prayer and reflection in a Dominican convent for thirty-seven years. Although she never took vows as a Dominican, Beatrice eventually helped to establish a new order of women that was dedicated to the Immaculate Conception of Mary. The congregation was originally called the Congregation of the Immaculate Conception of the Blessed Virgin Mary, which Queen Isabella initially supported. Three years later, Pope Alexander VI gave the order the Rule of St. Clare and placed it under the jurisdiction of the Friars Minor. Now called the Conceptionist Poor Clares, the order has spread throughout Spain, Portugal, and Latin America. Beatrice was remembered in the old Franciscan calendar on this date for many years before her canonization in 1976. Beatrice was made a saint on the seven hundred and fiftieth anniversary of the death of St. Francis.

Prayer:

> *Heavenly Father, throughout time you have blessed the Church with inspirations from the Holy Spirit to begin new contemplative women's orders that give greater honor and glory to your kingdom. St. Beatrice brought many holy women to honor the Immaculate Conception and to serve the poor and destitute. Help us to follow her example in our daily lives by reaching out to anyone in need whom you may place within our path. In Jesus' name we pray. Amen.*

Antiphon:

For the needy shall not always be forgotten.

Readings:

> "O magnify the Lord with me, and let us exalt His name together. I sought the Lord, and He answered me, and delivered me from all my fears. They looked to Him and were radiant. . . ." *Psalm 34:3–6 (NASB)*

> "Many daughters have done nobly, but you excel them all. Charm is deceitful and beauty is vain; but a woman who fears the Lord, she shall be praised." *Prov. 31:29–31 (NASB)*

> "Now we who are strong ought to bear the weaknesses of those without strength and not just to please ourselves. Let each of us please [his] neighbor for [his] good, to his edification." *Rom. 15:1–2 (NASB)*

SEPTEMBER 2 Hermione

Holy Mother Hermione is honored as a saint in the East, and tradition tells us she was a prophet, an evangelist, and a martyr. She was the daughter of St. Phillip, mentioned in Acts 6, who was believed to have been born in Caesarea of Palestine in the first century. Hermione and her three sisters entered Christian history early: Paul met them on one of his missionary journeys while staying at Phillip's house on the coast of Palestine. They were his four prophesying daughters (Acts 21:7–9), and in the story in Acts Paul clearly acknowledges their authenticity and authority. The apocryphal story of Hermione tells us that after the Christians were driven out of Palestine, she traveled to Ephesus to seek out the Beloved Apostle John. By the time she got there, he was already deceased, but she and a sister stayed with Petronios, another disciple of Paul's. For many years Hermione was a well-known healer and preacher there, a woman filled with the Holy Spirit when she preached and prophesied. Her charisma eventually drew Emperor Trajan's attention, and she was arrested and ordered to be beheaded. The first time, however, it did not work: her executioners' hands became paralyzed. Her executioners were then converted, and Hermione healed them. The Orthodox tradition remembers Hermione as the founder of Christian "xenodolion," or hospital inn, where she healed many in Ephesus, both in body and in soul.

Prayer:

O fiery Holy Spirit, it was predicted by the prophet Joel that God would pour out the Spirit on all flesh (Acts 2:17) and that the sons and daughters would prophesy of things to come. Holy Mother Hermione caught your Spirit and fulfilled her destiny during a lifetime of preaching and healing in Jesus' name. She is a link in the chain of New Testament prophets tied to the great prophets of the Old Testament, who also were a channel for your Spirit in their own time. Help us to always remember that, as you proceed eternally from the Father, you are with all peoples at all times. We ask that you, everlasting God who lives and breathes in us, make us willing witnesses of your presence. Amen.

Antiphon:

You have not chosen me, but I have chosen you.

Readings:

"Let the redeemed of the Lord say so, whom He has redeemed from the hand of the adversary, and gathered in from the lands; from the east and from the west, And from the north and from the south. . . ." *Psalm 107:2–3 (NASB)*

"And on the next day we departed and came to Caesareà, and we entering the house of Phillip the evangelist, who was one of the seven, we stayed with him. Now this man had four virgin daughters who were prophetesses." *Acts 21:8–9 (NASB)*

"He who receives a prophet in the name of a prophet shall receive a prophet's reward; and he who receives a righteous man in the name of a righteous man shall receive a righteous man's reward. And whoever in the name of a disciple gives to one of these little ones even a cup of cold water to drink, truly I say to you he shall not lose his reward." *Mt. 10:41–42 (NASB)*

SEPTEMBER 3 Phoebe

The Eastern churches honor and celebrate the first deaconess, Phoebe, on September 3. She is mentioned in Romans 16:1–2, as Paul recommends her to the Christian congregation at Rome. He praises her for the assistance she had given to him and to many others. He requests that the community there assist her in whatever way she may need. When Origen, an early Church Father, wrote about Phoebe in a Pauline passage, he understood her to be officially ordained for the Church's ministry. Likewise, John Chrysostom praises her highly, and he notes that "in Christ Jesus, there is neither male nor female." Phoebe stands as a model for all women who aspire to ordained service because she represents the equalitarian model of ministry represented in the very early Church.

Prayer:

> Grant, O Lord, that we who celebrate the feast of St. Phoebe may find our perfect service for you in this life. You call us by name to be one with you and with one another. Help us to be faithful to our commitments, that we may be servants of your word and ministers to your needy. Through all that we say and do, make us witnesses of the good news to all of creation. Amen.

Antiphon:

You came to serve and not to be served.

Readings:

> "But not so with you; rather let the greatest among you become as the youngest, and the leader as one who serves. For which is the greater, one who sits at the table? But I am among you as one who serves." Lk. 22:26–27 (RSV)

> "Deacons likewise must be serious, not double-tongued, not addicted to much wine, not greedy for gain; they must hold the mystery of the faith with a clear conscience." 1 Tim. 3:8–9 (RSV)

> "I commend to you our sister Phoebe, who is a servant of the church which is Cenchrea; that you receive her in the Lord in a manner worthy of the saints, and that you help her in whatever matter she may have need of you; for she herself has also been a helper of many, and of myself as well." Rom. 16:1–2 (NASB)

SEPTEMBER 4 Rose of Viterbo

Rose lived in the Viterbo region of Italy during the thirteenth century. From the time she was a toddler, she exhibited amazing miracles, and tradition relates that she brought a person back from the dead when she was three. At ten, she began preaching in the streets and desired greatly to enter a convent; however, God had other plans for her. When she was fifteen, Rose became a Secular Franciscan and, blessed with the gift of prophecy, she began traveling and making predictions concerning the current political events. She was exiled because of these prophesies and left the city to reside at Soriano. From there, she announced the approaching death of Emperor Frederick II, after which she again returned to Viterbo. One legend concerning her fame relates that in a region where a sorceress had great influence, Rose caused the entire town's conversion by standing in a pyre of fire while miraculously remaining unharmed. She prophesied that she would be admitted to the Poor Clares after her own death. This occurred when she died at just seventeen, and Pope Alexander IV ordered that her body be put to rest in the convent of the Poor Clares. Her feast is celebrated on September 4, when her incorrupt body is still carried in procession through Viterbo, and on the date of her death, March 6. Rose is a patron of those rejected from religious orders and others in exile.

Intercessory Prayer:

Dear St. Rose, God blessed you with great miracles, which served as a testimony to bring souls to Christ. May your brave witness to the faith serve as an inspiration to us. May the genuineness of our faith, if tested by fire, result in Christ's glory and honor. We offer prayers especially on behalf of all those people in the world who are exiled from their homelands. May they be open to God's call within their lives and be nurtured by God's providential care. Amen.

Antiphon:

I have preached righteousness in the great congregation; I have not refrained my lips, O Lord.

Readings:

"Return to your place, and abide with the King, for you are a foreigner and also an exile." 2 Sam. 15:19 (NASB)

". . . And makes them wander in a pathless waste. But He sets the needy securely on high away from affliction, and makes *his* families like a flock. The upright see it, and are glad; But all unrighteousness shuts its mouth. Who is wise? Let [him] give heed to these things; And consider the lovingkindness of the Lord." Psalm 107:40–43 (NASB)

"Every day they wrest my words; all their thoughts are against me . . . they gather themselves together, they hide themselves, they mark my steps, when they wait for my soul. . . . You know my wanderings; put my tears in your bottle: are they not in your book? When I cry to you, then shall my enemies turn back: this I know for my God is for me." *Psalm 56:5–9 (KJV)*

SEPTEMBER 5 Mother Teresa

Mother Teresa was an Albanian Catholic born in 1910. At an early age she served as a Loreto Sister teaching children in India under the name of Sr. Agnes. When she was thirty-six, a calling from God inspired her to live a life devoted to serving the poorest of the poor. She received permission from her congregation to don a new habit, that of a simple white sari with a blue border. She went out into the streets of India and personally ministered to the sick and dying. She was soon joined by many of her former students and her order, the Missionaries of Charity, was officially recognized. She became the Mother Superior and took the name Mother Teresa. Mother Teresa established a home for the dying in Calcutta, where the dying could come and receive dignity and charity in their last days. Although she attempted to work in obscurity, the world soon recognized her outstanding accomplishments. She was awarded a Nobel Peace Prize in 1979 and was recognized everywhere as a living saint. Her motto was to inspire everyone to do great things by doing small things with great love. She left behind a body of beautiful and inspiring spiritual writings, and the world mourned when she died in 1997. Mother Teresa was beatified in October 2003 when thousands of devotees from India came out to celebrate her presence among them.

Intercessory Prayer:

Dear Mother Teresa, you lived a life of immense love and charity toward others. You inspired us with your words, such as "You can save only one at a time. We can love only one at a time." You truly believed that loving others, especially the most destitute, was the purpose for our existence and that God put each of us here on earth to do something beautiful for God. Inspire us to learn what particular mission God may have in mind for us in our own station of life. Amen.

Antiphon:

Christ yesterday, today, and forever. Allelulia.

Readings:

"Praise the Lord from the earth, you sea monsters and all deeps, fire and hail, snow and frost, stormy wind fulfilling his command! Mountains and all hills, fruit trees and all cedars! Wild animals and all cattle, creeping things and flying birds! Kings of the earth and all peoples, princes and all rulers of the earth! Young men and women alike, old and young together! Let them praise the name of the Lord, for his name alone is exalted; his glory is above earth and heaven." *Psalm 148:7–13 (NRSV)*

"And the King will answer and say to them, 'Truly I say to you, to the extent that you did it to one of these brothers of Mine, *even* the least of *them,* you did it to Me.'" *Mt. 25:40 (NASB)*

SEPTEMBER 6 Felicia Meda

A descendant of a wealthy and distinguished family, Felicia Meda was born in Milan in 1378. She lost both parents at an early age and became a very introverted child. At twelve, she went to live with the Poor Clares and was tormented much of her early life by demonic apparitions. Resorting to a constant repetition of the psalms, her visitations finally ended. Felicia was made abbess of her convent in 1425. News of her exemplary life reached the ears of Pope Eugene IV, who entrusted her to establish the Poor Clares at Pesaro. Felicia was known for her great humility, and she died in the odor of sanctity in 1444.

Prayer:

Dear Lord Jesus, Blessed Felicia Meda, when beset by temptations, overcame them by imitating your example of perfect concentration on God. She knew that her only help was in the name of the Lord, who made heaven and earth. Through her intercession, strengthen us also with the spirit of fortitude; and help us to never forget your promise to be with us till the end. In times of anxiety, may we recall this promise, for you alone are faithful. Amen.

Antiphon:

With outstretched arm, you lead us out of darkness.

Readings:

"He will deliver my soul in safety from the battle that I wage, for many are arrayed against me." *Psalm 55:18 (RSV)*

"I cry aloud with my voice to the Lord, make supplication with my voice to the Lord. I pour out my complaint before Him; I declare my trouble before Him. . . . I cried out to You, O Lord; I said, Thou art my refuge, my portion in the land of the living. Give heed to my cry; for I am brought very low." *Psalm 142:1–2, 5–6 (NASB)*

"And he said to her, 'For this saying you may go your way; the demon has left your daughter.' And she went home and found the child lying in bed, and the demon gone." *Mk. 7:29–30 (RSV)*

". . . discretion will watch over you; understanding will guard you; delivering you from the way of evil, from men of perverted speech, who forsake the paths of uprightness to walk in the way of darkness . . ." *Prov. 2:11–13 (RSV)*

SEPTEMBER 7 The *Theotokos of Pochaev* Icon (Vigil)

This is the vigil of the Pochaev Icon, which means that the Vespers service begins the feast day this evening, and September 8 is the day of the feast. The *Theotokos of Pochaev* Icon is enthroned in the Pochaev monastery. The story of the icon's appearance is as follows: In the year 1340, two (unnamed) monks had a vision of the Theotokos standing on a stone encircled in flames. After the apparition, an imprint of her right foot remained. Someone painted an account of the vision, and the wonder-working icon itself often emitted a radiance. In the sixteenth century, a noblewoman who possessed the icon gave it to the monks at Pochaev. The icon was placed in a church raised up in honor of Mary's Dormition (Assumption). Many miracles and legends were associated with the icon, such as curing of grave diseases, deliverance from sudden death, and showing the right way to those who err. The icon belongs to the Eleousa or Merciful type, with the Mother of God affectionately caressing her son's cheek, and him clinging to his mother's neck.

Intercessory Prayer:

Most holy Mother of God, you are the Burning Bush who preserves the world through your radiant love and constant care. By your glorious intercession, keep those who are devoted to you wrapped in your mantle of love until we inherit the bliss of paradise planned for all eternity by the one who made you his throne. Through the glorious miracle of the uniting of the Word with flesh in your sacred womb, save us who sing to you. Amen.

Antiphon:

You are the honor of our race; you are the joy of our people.

Readings:

"How lovely is your dwelling place, O God of hosts!
My soul longs and yearns for the courts of the Most High;
My heart and lips sing for joy to you, the Living God.
Even the sparrow finds a home
And the swallow a nest for its brood
Where it may lay its young at your altars,
O God of hosts!" *Psalm 83 (84):1–4 (PCB)*

"Power from on high overshadows those who run for refuge with faith and reverence to Thy precious protection: for to Thee alone, O all holy and all pure only Mother of God is it given that every petition of Thine be fulfilled. Therefore the faithful of all ages glorify Thee and Thy Son, crying: Alleluia!" *Kontakion 3, Akathist, To Our Lady of All Protection*

". . . give me the wisdom that sits by your throne, and do not reject me from among your servants. For I am your servant, the [son] of your servant-girl, a [man] who is weak and short-lived, with little understanding of judgement and laws; for even one who is perfect among human beings will be regarded as nothing without the wisdom that comes from you." *Wisdom 9:1–6 (NRSV)*

SEPTEMBER 8 Nativity of Mary and Feast of the Sophia Icon

We celebrate two distinct feast days September 8, both in honor of the Blessed Mother of God. The first celebrates the Virgin Mary's own birth, the Nativity of Mary. Because it was through Mary's creation and birth that God was able to manifest his presence in the world through the Word made flesh, Jesus, we highly venerate the day that the Blessed Virgin Mary was born. Her holy parents, St. Joachim and St. Anne, were elderly and had passed many years in grief longing for a child. Tradition relates that in their old age, the Archangel Gabriel visited them and told them that they would have a holy child who would become the mother of God. This day is so important that St. Andrew, Archbishop of Crete, declared the Nativity of the Theotokos to be the beginning of all feast days.

This is also the feast of the icon of *Sophia*, or holy Wisdom, perhaps the most archetypal of all the iconic images in the East. This Kiev icon at the cathedral of *Divine Sophia* pictures the Theotokos clothed in royal dress, with a crown and a medallion on her bosom containing the Emmanuel. In the icon which comes from the Novgorod school (a school of icon-painting in Novgorod, Russia), Divine Wisdom is shown as a fiery female angel. In her right hand is a cross, in her left is the scroll of the law. Sophia is seated on a throne of seven pillars, her feet on a crescent moon. This refers to the Wisdom text, "Wisdom has built up her House supported by seven pillars." All around is a star-studded sky, with the Savior in a gesture of blessing. The theme of Sophia, Divine Wisdom goes back to the time of the formation of Christian iconography. Already in the frescos of the catacomb in Alexandria we find the portrayal of an angel bearing the Greek inscription *Sophia*. In another variant of the Novgorod school, the Theotokos is enshrined in the image of a Burning Bush, and she is surrounded by Old Testament figures, who are witnesses to this manifestation of Wisdom.

Intercessory Prayer:

Dear Blessed Mother of God, we honor you on the feast day celebrating your birth. We thank God for the gift of your presence with us throughout the centuries and for the blessed fiat that helped to accomplish Christ's mission of salvation for all people. We ask for your continued heavenly intercession on behalf of the Church throughout the world, and we humbly seek your motherly protection, placing ourselves under the mantle of your care. Inspire us with the wisdom that, in the secret recesses of your heart, you shared with your Christ, Emmanuel. Amen.

Antiphon:

And I was daily his delight, rejoicing always before him.

Readings:

"And Mary said, Behold the bondslave of the Lord; be it done to me according to your word. And the angel departed from her." *Lk. 1:38 (NASB)*

". . . although He existed in the form of God, he did not regard equality with God a thing to be grasped, but he emptied Himself and took the form of a bond-servant, and being made in the likeness of men." *Phil. 2:6–7 (NASB)*

"O Mother of God, we have sought refuge in your tenderness: do not turn away from our supplication." Vespers, *Byzantine Daily Worship*

SEPTEMBER 9 Constance and Her Companions

Sister Constance was a member of the Anglican Community of St. Mary in England. She went, at her bishop's request, to Memphis, Tennessee, to found a girl's school. In 1876, an outbreak of yellow fever killed a quarter of the population there and brought the city to a standstill. The sky was filled with the smoke of thousands of burning mattresses of those who had died, and coffins lined the streets instead of cars. She and her staff of sisters worked zealously, ministering to the sick and taking in many children whose parents had died. In her last letter to Bishop Quintard, Constance said that as long as they had the daily celebration of the Eucharist, nothing depressed her. Three weeks later, she died of the fever herself.

Constance is remembered on this day in the Anglican calendar, with her religious companions.

Prayer:

O holy Jesus, your beloved sister Constance was a fierce protector of homeless children, whose families were torn apart by devastation. She put her life in danger to minister to you in those abandoned, and she lost her life in the process. Make us fearless in the face of death, as she was. Help us to always remember that it is you we serve and to you we shall return. Amen.

Antiphon:

Where there is despair, let us sow hope.

Readings:

"For your mercy is great above heavens; and your truth reaches to the clouds. Be exalted, O God, above the heavens: and your glory above all earth; that your beloved may be delivered: save with your right hand and answer me. God has spoken in his holinesss." *Psalm 108:4–7 (KJV)*

"Now it was not written for his sake alone, that it was imputed to him; But for us also, to whom it shall be imputed, if we believe on him that raised Jesus our Lord from the dead. Who was delivered for our offenses and was raised again for our justification." *Rom. 4:23–25 (KJV)*

"Beloved, think it not strange concerning the fiery trial which is to try you, as though some strange thing happened to you: But rejoice inasmuch as you are partakers of Christ's sufferings; that, when his glory shall be revealed, you may be glad also with exceeding joy." *1 Pet. 4:12–13 (KJV)*

SEPTEMBER 10 Margarita Tuchkova

Tolstoy's *War and Peace* is set during the tumultuous era in which Margarita Tuchkova was born. From an aristocratic family, she married a man whom she adored and they had a son, Nikolai. A general in the army against Napoleon, her husband was killed early in their marriage, a loss from which she never fully recovered. Investing all of her purpose in her son, she was devastated when he also died of scarlet fever at age fifteen. Margarita entered a deep period of spiritual desolation. Through a friendship with Metropolitan Filaret, she gradually took refuge in the Mercy of God, becoming attached to this devotion for the rest of her life. She began taking in abused women and widows and caring for them with the same devotion she once had for her own family. The community grew to forty, and all loved her as a mother. She allocated her pension for their support and created a Rule for them that included a perpetual reading of the Psalter for the Dead. On the twenty-fifth anniversary of the battle that took her husband's life, she sponsored a ceremony on the battlefield, which Czar Nicholas attended. Her new monastic Rule was approved, and Filaret, who advocated restoring the position of deaconess in the Church, consecrated her both as abbess and deaconess. Margarita is honored in Russia as organizing one of the first monasteries to minister to the homeless.

Prayer:

Almighty God, you drew the holy woman Margarita into your heart through her suffering and revealed to her your mercy, which she helped spread throughout your kingdom. The root of her passionate love for your people lay in her grieving heart, which when broken, was open to embrace the suffering of others. Keep us from falling into despair when we encounter our own losses, and empower us with the strength to transform our personal darkness into light for others who are struggling. Amen.

Antiphon:

Show us your mercy, O God.

Readings:

"Save me, O God, For the waters have threatened my life. I have sunk in deep mire, where there is no foothold; I have come into deep waters, and a flood overflows me." *Psalm 69:1–2 (NASB)*

"I will sing of your steadfast love, O Lord for ever; with my mouth I will proclaim your faithfulness to all generations. For your steadfast love was established for ever, your faithfulness is firm as the heavens." *Psalm 89:1–2 (RSV)*

"But you have come to Mount Zion and to the city of the living God, the heavenly Jerusalem, and to innumerable angels in festal gathering and to the assembly of the first-born who are enrolled in heaven, and to a judge who is God of all, and to the spirits of the just who were made perfect, and to Jesus, the mediator of a new covenant, and to the sprinkled blood that speaks more graciously than the blood of Abel." *Heb. 12:22–24 (RSV)*

SEPTEMBER 11 Mary of Agreda

A profoundly mystical woman, Mary of Agreda lived in seventeenth-century Spain. At age fifteen she became a Discalced Franciscan nun, and she was later chosen to be the abbess of her convent. She was favored with visions and locutions of Jesus, Mary, and the Saints, and when she was thirty-five, she received a vision of the Holy Spirit in which she was instructed to write down a detailed history of the mother of God. Mary obeyed, and soon this four-volume work, *The Mystical City of God*, was produced. Many popes have approved these private revelations regarding hidden aspects of the Virgin Mary's life, and the book has served through the centuries as inspirational reading for the faithful. Stories are told of Mary of Agreda's ability to miraculously bilocate, or be in two places at the same time. In some of her trances, she saw herself teaching in foreign lands. Mary died of natural causes in 1665, and her beatification is still pending.

Intercessory Prayer:

Dear blessed Mary of Agreda, the Blessed Mother of God revealed many great truths to you, which you shared with humanity through your written works. Let us follow the advice of our heavenly mother, and let us begin each day by placing ourselves in God's presence and giving him thanks and praise for his immutable being, his perfections, and his goodness in choosing to create each one of us. May we also place our spirit into God's hands each day and offer ourselves with humility to God's holy will. Amen.

Antiphon:

The heavens declare your glory, O Lord.

Readings:

"Believe me that I am in the Father and the Father in me; or else believe me for the sake of the works themselves. Truly, truly, I say to you, he who believes in me will also do the works that I do; and greater works than these, because I go to the Father. Whatever you ask in my name, I will do it, that the Father may be glorified in the Son." Jn. 14:11–13 (RSV)

"In Christ Jesus, then I have reason to be proud of my work for God. For I will not venture to speak of anything except what Christ has wrought through me to win obedience from the Gentiles, by word and deed, by the power of signs and wonders, by the power of the Holy Spirit, so that from Jerusalem and as far round as Illyricum I have fully preached the gospel of Christ." *Rom. 15:17–19 (RSV)*

SEPTEMBER 12 Raissa Maritain

 Raissa Oumansov was born a Russian Jew in 1883. She married the prominent Roman Catholic philosopher Jacques Maritain. Toying with atheism in her early adulthood, she chose to study science in her attempt to uncover a verifiable truth. She was converted to Christianity after reading *Salvation Comes from the Jews* by Leon Bloy. Both Raissa and her husband, also a convert, became Benedictine oblates, and she authored several books with him on contemplative prayer. She spent her mornings alone in quiet prayer and study and recorded a number of mystical experiences. In some of her writings she refers (like Julian of Norwich) to Jesus as her sweet and compassionate mother. She was a deeply philosophical mystic; fiercely honest and poignantly questioning, even of God. She once wrote, "Is not our confidence more meritorious for being able to spring up in uncertainty?" Having to flee war-torn Europe in 1940, Raissa experienced great anguish over the plight of the Jews during the Holocaust, and much of her philosophy centers on the meaning of suffering. Her writings, published by her husband after her death, have been a source of inspiration to Catholic intellectuals and to others who walk—as Raissa says—the philosophical path to "the true image and likeness of God." Thomas Merton has called her one of the great contemplatives of our modern age.

Prayer:

O Holy Spirit of God, Raissa suffered much both physically and philosophically in her search for the truth that resides in you. A diligent seeker, she is a light for many who seek to understand you with their minds. Sustain us during our most trying moments and help us to remember, as she did, that deep within our longing, the day is breaking. Amen.

Antiphon:

May God's love be with you, and may you stay blameless until he comes.

Readings:

"But Job answered and said, O that my grief were thoroughly weighed, and my calamity laid in the balances together! For now it would be heavier than the sand of the sea: therefore my words are swallowed up. For the arrows of the Almighty are within me . . . the terrors of God do set themselves in array against me." *Job 6:1–4 (KJV)*

"You must ask in faith never wavering, for the doubter is like the surf tossed and driven by the wind." *James 1:6 (KJV)*

"And they said to him, By what authority do you do these things? . . . And Jesus answered, I will also ask of you one question and if you answer me, I will tell you by what authority I do these things. The baptism of John, was it from heaven or of men? Answer me. And they reasoned with themselves, saying, we shall say, From heaven; he will say, Why then did you not believe him? But if we shall say, Of men; they feared the people: for all men counted John, that he was a prophet indeed. And they answered and said to Jesus, We cannot tell. In turn, Jesus said, neither do I tell you by what authority I do these things." *Mk. 11:28–33 (KJV)*

SEPTEMBER 13 Lucretia Mott

Lucretia Coffin was born a Quaker in Massachusetts in 1793. She married James Mott and became a Quaker minister in 1821. They were both active abolitionists and refused to use cotton, sugar, and other slave-produced goods. In 1840, she was selected as a delegate to the World's Anti-Slavery Convention in London. Lucretia later became a key organizer in the early conventions for women's rights. Her book, *Discourse on Women,* discussed the educational, economic, and political restrictions on women in America and Western Europe. She once said that the world had not yet seen a truly great and virtuous nation because, in degrading women, the very foundations of life were poisoned at their source. Lucretia was one of the most eloquent preachers and zealous activists of her era, and together with Elizabeth Cady Stanton, she helped to catapult the human rights movement into the next century.

Prayer:

O most holy Jesus, Lucretia Mott used her ministry to try to alleviate the injustices she encountered, and she raised the consciousness of her era. Have mercy on those who still suffer oppression throughout the world because of their sex, color, or religious affiliation. May they find strength in adversity and hope in times of despair. Inspire us with the justice with which you sought to restore the dignity of all human beings. Amen.

Antiphon:

The righteous shall shine like the sun in God's realm.

Readings:

"The strength of the King loves justice; You have established equity; You have executed justice and righteousness. . . ." *Psalm 99:4 (NASB)*

"Let the rivers clap their hands; Let the mountains sing together for joy before the Lord; for He is coming to judge the earth; He will judge the world with righteousness and the people with equity." *Psalm 98:8–9 (NASB)*

"Justice is turned back, and righteousness stands afar off; for truth has fallen in the public squares, and uprightness cannot enter. Truth is lacking, and he who departs from evil makes himself prey. The Lord saw it, and it displeased him that there was no justice. He saw that there was no one, and wondered that there was no one to intervene; so his own arm brought about the victory, and his righteousness upheld him." *Isa. 59:14–16 (RSV)*

". . . he will not break a bruised reed or quench a smoldering wick, till he brings justice to victory." *Mt. 12:20 (RSV)*

SEPTEMBER 14 Seven Sorrows/Seven Arrows of Mary (Vigil)

❀ The Feast of Our Lady of Sorrows dates to 1239, when the founders of the Servite Order took up the sorrows of the Heart of Mary as one of their principal devotions. The devotion, which grew throughout many places during the Middle Ages, honored seven crosses that Mary bore during her life: enduring

Simeon's prophecy of sorrow (Luke 9:23); fleeing with her babe into Egypt; experiencing the loss of her son at Jerusalem; meeting with him on the road to Calvary; standing beneath the cross; receiving his body into her arms; and placing Jesus into his tomb. The feast's significance as a feast is that, as her son's first disciple, Mary entered into his paschal mystery, and as her motherhood matured, she took up her cross to follow him. In Russia, there is a similar devotion, called the *Seven Arrow* icon, which made its appearance in the late eighteenth century. It depicts Mary, the Theotokos, clothed in bright red, with four arrows over her heart and three on her right side. In 1830, during the cholera epidemic at Vologda, the icon was glorified through many healings of the sick. Before the revolution of 1917, the icon was housed at St. John-Bogolyubsk Seven Arrow Church, near the town of Vologda. There is also an icon in the Georgian Orthodox Church called the Virgin with Seven Arrows, or the "Softener of Evil Hearts."

Intercessory Prayer:

O most holy Virgin of the Lord and Mother of all hearts who sorrow, bring our prayers to the throne of your Son and our God. Guide the lowly and downtrodden in finding mercy. Teach all oppressors the fear of God, and shelter those who are abused. Have pity on us, your weak and feeble children, and show compassion on us who suffer the pain of this temporal lifetime. You are the defender and consolation of those who come to you in faith. Commend us to our Lord, now and at the hour of our death. Amen.

Antiphon:

Your mercy is on those who fear you through all generations.

Readings:

"For the arrows of the Almighty are in me; their poison my spirit drinks; the terrors of God are arrayed against me. . . . O that my request might come to pass, and that God would grant my longing! Would that God were willing to crush me. . . . But it is still my consolation, and I rejoice in the unsparing pain, that I have not denied the words of the Holy One." Job 6:4, 8–10 (NASB)

"O Lord, rebuke me not in thy anger, nor chasten me in thy wrath! For thy arrows have sunk into me, and thy hand has come down on me. There is no soundness in my flesh because of thy indignation; there is no health in my bones because of my sin." *Psalm 38:1–3 (RSV)*

"Inspired with confidence we fly into thee, O Virgin of Virgins, Our Mother." *(Traditional)*

SEPTEMBER 15 Catherine of Genoa

Catherine of Genoa was one of the most famous mystics of the fifteenth century. She spent a good deal of her life in a very unhappy marriage that was childless, depressed much of the time because of her husband's callous and unfaithful lifestyle. Her life changed radically when she was infused with divine grace during confession. Her confession must have lasted a bit too long, because her biographer relates that her confessor left to attend to another matter and did not notice that she had been rendered nearly senseless until he returned. This was the first of a series of remarkable mystical experiences that she had. A few days later she had a vision of Christ carrying the cross, and it pierced her to her soul. Catherine felt that her conversion included an outreach to the poor and sick, and she worked principally in a hospital for lepers. She was a daily communicant at Mass, which was her greatest joy. Eventually her husband, on the verge of bankruptcy and other misfortunes, had a conversion also. They moved to a simple home, agreed to a life of continence, and devoted themselves to good works until he died. Catherine then began to draw a circle of disciples around her, while completing her famous text on Purgatory, which has become a classic. Catherine's Purgatory is not imagined as a state of pain and misery. It is a prelude to heaven, wherein the soul is prepared for the mystical fire of God's divine love. The soul's pain is separation from God, but it exists simultaneously with the absolute certainty that the soul's destiny is union with God.

Intercessory Prayer:

Beloved Catherine, you were the delight of Christ's heart, having experienced a union with him that was more intimate than anything else on earth. You wrote that God had locked himself inside you so firmly that you could not be occupied with anything else. Yet you lived a busy life in the world, endlessly caring for Christ in others. Intercede for us who desire to make God's understanding our own, as you were able to do. Work tirelessly for souls on earth, we pray, so that all may attain to the fruition of the eternal union that was the rapture of your soul. Amen.

Antiphon:

There is no limit, O God, to your love for us.

Readings:

"And the sight of the glory of the Lord was like a devouring fire upon the mountain." *Ex. 24:17 (KJV)*

"And call upon the name of your gods, and I will call upon the Name of the Lord, and the God that answers by fire, let him be God." *1 Kings 18:24 (KJV)*

"If any man's work shall be burned, he shall suffer loss, but he himself shall be saved, yet so as by fire." *1 Cor. 3:15 (KJV)*

SEPTEMBER 16 Edith of Wilton

St. Edith's birth was the scandal of the court: her father, King Edgar of England (934–975) had fallen in love with a young nun, Wulfthryth, and impregnated her. Edith was raised at the monastery in Wilton, where her mother returned after her birth. Edith was well-educated and a great artist of illuminated scripts and embroidery. Because she was the king's daughter, she was invited to the court and could have had an important position there, but three times she refused. Before her profession as a cloistered nun, Edgar tried to remove her from the convent, but her insistence was firm. She preferred to remain with her mother, who had, after her repentance, gone on to become abbess. Edith was devoted to the poor and noted for her familiarity with animals. She died when she was only twenty-three, but her sanctity had been established and miracles were reported at her tomb. Three churches were named in her honor; and her feast was celebrated in several ancient calendars. Edith's feast on this date was later translated to November 3.

Prayer:

Beloved Lord, bless all illegitimate children. May your loving presence dwell in them and help them not to become victimized by confusion or bitterness. Strengthen all who choose you, O God, and thus put worldly power to shame. In Jesus you demonstrated that the weak things of the world confound those who are strong. Therefore, grant that we who keep the feast of Blessed Edith may eternally claim you as our defender and savior. Amen.

Antiphon:

Under your wings we will find refuge.

Readings:

"Come now, let us reason together, says the Lord; though your sins be like scarlet, they shall be as white as snow; though they are red like crimson, they shall become like wool." *Isa. 1:18 (RSV)*

"I know your works, your love and faith and service and patient endurance, and that your latter works exceeded the first." *Rev. 2:19 (RSV)*

"You have not chosen me, but I have chosen you, and ordained you, that ye should go and bring forth fruit, and that your fruit should remain: that whatsoever you shall ask of the Father in my name, he may give it to you. These things I command you, that you love one another." *Jn. 15:16–17 (KJV)*

SEPTEMBER 17 Hildegard of Bingen

Called the "Sibyl of the Rhine," Hildegard of Bingen became the most famous mystic and prophet of her time. Her writings and music are still found in all major bookstores, and no woman saint is more popular in her native Germany. When she was eight, she was placed in a convent, where she later became abbess. She was a biblical exegete, visionary, preacher, composer, and herbalist, who corresponded with the major royalty and church leaders of her day, including four popes. Her greatest vision came when she was forty-two, which is recorded in her famous *Scivias*, or *Know the Ways of the Lord*, a treatise whose magnificence rivals William Blake's visionary work. Hildegard's spiritual writings found approval during her lifetime, and her lectures on the spiritual life drew crowds from all over Europe. She wrote prolifically, on topics as varied as history and drama, politics and liturgical poetry. Her monastery joyfully sang the praises she wrote. During the last year of her life, when she was eighty-one, she entered into a conflict with ecclesiastical authorities because she allowed a young man who had been excommunicated to be buried in her abbey cemetery, and her convent was placed under interdict. It is probable that, for this reason, Hildegard was never formally canonized, although she is found in all major saints' books and her cult was approved locally because of so many miracles reported at her tomb.

Intercessory Prayer:

Dear Hildegard, you are a major inspiration to all modern women who seek to capture God's beauty in writing. Your mind and heart were set ablaze by the Spirit's music and poetry, and your prayers to Mary are a testament of love for all who revere motherhood and the earth's goodness. Help us to be inflamed by the same fiery Spirit that you described as "not limited by space . . . and more brilliant than the radiance of the Sun."

Antiphon:

Who can compare with the beauty of the Lord?

Readings:

"And I have trusted in the Lord without wavering. . . .
I shall wash my hands in innocence, and I will go about Your altar,
    O Lord,
That I may proclaim with the voice of thanksgiving,
And declare all Your wonders.
O Lord, I love the habitation of Your house,
And the place where Your glory dwells." *Psalm 26:1, 6–8 (NASB)*

"In that day the Lord of hosts will become a beautiful crown and a glorious diadem to the remnant of His people." *Isa. 28:5 (NASB)*

"And David and all Israel were celebrating before God with all their might, even with songs and with lyres, harps, tambourines, cymbals and with trumpets." *1 Chron. 13:8 (NASB)*

SEPTEMBER 18 Sophia and Her Three Daughters

St. Sophia lived in Rome during the second century when Emperor Hadrian was slaying Christians as enemies of the state. The legend of her life is a sorrowful one. She was a widow with three daughters, whom she named Faith, Hope, and Charity. All were apprehended and brought before the Emperor, who perceived an opportunity to wrest a disavowal of Christ from the mother in exchange for her daughters' lives. The agonized Sophia was torn by her love of her children and pleaded for their release, begging that her life be taken instead. The magistrate was unmoved and ordered the oldest of her girls, a teenager, to be tortured and killed first. The horrified mother watched as each daughter, her own flesh and blood, was put to the sword, before she was martyred herself. The icon of Sophia and her three daughters is one of the most famous in the Orthodox Church, and it stands as a testimony that early Christianity transcended all aspects of human life to focus on the eternal message of Christ the deliverer. It is also an important archetypal icon, representing that the gifts of faith, hope, and charity are children of Mother Wisdom.

Prayer:

Gracious Lord, who waits with open arms for all martyrs, on this, the feast of Blessed Sophia and her children, have mercy on all those who suffer for their faith and on political prisoners everywhere. As wisdom and trust were her only clothing, help us, like Sophia, to know that all things of the world pass away, and only Christ's love remains. Through her intercession, help us to hold up the candle that never goes out in the midst of the darkness. Amen.

Antiphon:

When I awake, I shall be filled with the sight of your glory.

Readings:

"He will rescue their life from oppression and violence; and their blood will be precious in his sight." *Psalm 72:14 (NASB)*

"Remember not the former things, nor consider the things of old. Behold, I am doing a new thing; now it springs forth, do you not perceive it? I will make a way in the wilderness and rivers in the desert. . . . For I give water in the wilderness, rivers in the desert to give drink to my chosen people, the people whom I formed myself that they might declare my praise." *Isa. 43:18–21 (RSV)*

". . . my dove, my perfect one, is unique; She is her mother's only daughter; She is the pure child of the one who bore her." *Song of Songs 6:9 (NASB)*

"Therefore, since Christ suffered for us in the flesh, arm yourselves likewise with the same mind: for [he] who has suffered in the flesh has ceased from sin." *1 Pet. 4:1–2 (KJV)*

SEPTEMBER 19 Marjory Kempe

A contemporary of Julian of Norwich (see Daily Readings, May 8, Julian of Norwich), Marjory Kempe was born in 1373 to well-to-do parents in Norfolk. She married and had fourteen children before convincing her husband to practice mutual celibacy. Of extreme emotional temperament, Marjory frequently had the "gift of tears," especially when she was in church. Her autobiography, *The Book of Marjory Kempe* (which she dictated), provides a unique record of mysticism and lay spirituality in England during her era. She had many visions, including one wherein Christ assured her that she would spend eternity with him. She frequently had the mystical experience of Christ as lover. He once told her, "More pleasing to me than all your prayers, works, and penances is that you would believe I love you." Following one of her visions, Marjory undertook a pilgrimage to Rome and the Holy Land. Since its discovery in the twentieth century, Marjory's work has become one of the most widely read books in women's literature.

Antiphon:
For me, to live is Christ and to die is gain.

Prayer:
Beloved Lord and Beloved of our souls, Marjory was a penitent who wept often for the sins of the world, and she saw you as the only answer to the soul's deepest desire. So often we roam the

world in search of love. Make us one with you, so that we may radiate the love we want to attract. By the power of your unending love, help us to know you as the only source and center of our lives. Amen.

Readings:

"I will make with them an everlasting covenant that I will not turn away from doing good to them; and I will put the fear of me in their hearts, that they may not turn from me. I will rejoice in doing them good, and I will plant them in this land in faithfulness, with all my heart and all my soul." *Jer. 32:40–41 (RSV)*

"We shall know by this that we are of the truth, and shall assure our heart before Him, in whatever our heart condemns us; for God is greater than our heart, and knows all things." *1 Jn. 3:19–20 (NASB)*

"And this is the confidence that we have in him that, if we ask any thing according to his will, he hears us. And if we know that he hears us, whatsoever we ask, we know that we have the petitions that we desired of him." *1 Jn. 5:14–15 (KJV)*

SEPTEMBER 20 Christina of Markyate

Christina of Markyate was born Theodora, the eldest daughter of noble Anglo-Saxon parents in the late eleventh century. After visiting St. Albans, the famous hermitage, as a young girl, she made a private vow of virginity, which she hoped to fulfill by entering religious life at a later date. This decision led to complications with her parents, who had chosen an eligible nobleman for her, hoping her marriage would add to their prosperity. During this time, a bishop also assaulted her, attempting to seduce her. Another bishop, who initially came to her defense, later abandoned her. Under pressure, she finally consented to marrying the nobleman; then fled to take refuge with a hermit named Eadwin. He consulted with the archbishop of Canterbury, and the marriage, which had not been consummated, was annulled. She took the habit at St. Albans, where she also received the name Christina. Christina spent the remainder of her life in Markyate as an anchoress, where she gained renown as a visionary.

Prayer:

> *Beloved Lord Jesus, St. Christina wanted only to belong to you, living a life of simplicity and prayer. You alone were her sweetness, and you alone sustained her when her family and those whom she trusted in the Church abandoned and betrayed her. Have mercy on young women and men who suffer abuse at the hands of Church leaders, and preserve them when they sink into confusion or despair. Send them support and encouragement, we pray, in the form of significant others, who can help them regain a sense of self-esteem and human dignity. Through St. Christina's prayers, nurture their hearts with the seed of new hope. Amen.*

Antiphon:

> I cry aloud to God, who hears me.

Readings:

> "Many are rising against me, many are saying of me. Many are saying of my soul,
> 'There is no deliverance for [him] in God.'
> But You, O Lord, are a shield about me,
> My glory and the one who lifts my head." *Psalm 3:1–3 (NASB)*

> "Trust in the Lord with all your heart, and do not lean on your own understanding. In all your ways acknowledge Him, and He will make your paths straight." *Prov. 3:5–6 (NASB)*

> "Behold, I give you power to tread on serpents and scorpions; and over all the power of the enemy: and nothing shall by any means hurt you." *Lk. 10:19 (KJV)*

> "You belong to God, children, and you have conquered them, for the one who is in you is greater than the one who is in the world. . . . This is how we know the spirit of truth and the spirit of deceit." *1 Jn. 4:4–6 (KJV)*

SEPTEMBER 21 Columba Kim

Columba Kim was a devout Korean woman who lived during the era when the Church was persecuted in Korea. She is one of the martyrs of Korea, a title given to thousands of Christian missionaries whom the state government martyred during the years 1791–1867. Columba was arrested along with her sister, Agnes, in

1839. Her crime was that she was a Catholic and was striving to live her faith in a country that had banned any non-native religion. She was only twenty-six when she was sent to prison; the horrors that she and her sisters endured included being pierced with red hot instruments of torture and being stripped of all clothing and forced into a cell with male prisoners. Miraculously, the male prisoners left the holy women alone. Columba appealed to the Korean government about such treatment of women prisoners, and her objections were eventually acknowledged. However, she was sentenced to death by beheading and was killed along with her sister in Seoul on September 26, 1839. Columba was one of over eight thousand Korean Catholic men, women, and children—along with numerous priests and other foreign missionaries—that the Korean government executed.

Prayer:

Heavenly Father, throughout history you have given us brave martyrs who were called to make the ultimate sacrifice by laying down their own lives for the sake of their faith. Columba Kim was a model of bravery and faith in the midst of horrible persecution. Let us be inspired by the courage she manifested in her young life and through her death. The blood she shed helped to nourish the seeds of your Church in Korea. May we always remember the sacrifice such brave individuals have made for the faith throughout history. Amen.

Antiphon:

Precious in the sight of the Lord is the death of his saints.

Readings:

"They have poured out their blood like water round about Jerusalem, and there was none to bury them. We have become a taunt to our neighbors, mocked and derided by those round about us." *Psalm 79:3–4 (RSV)*

"Why should the nations say, Where is their God? Let the avenging of the outpoured blood of your servants be known among the nations before our eyes! Let the groans of the prisoners come before you; according to your great power preserve those doomed to die! . . . Then we your people, the flock of your pasture, will give thanks to you forever; from generation to generation we will recount your praise." *Psalm 79:10–13 (RSV)*

"Since therefore the children share in flesh and blood, he himself likewise partook of the same nature, that through death he might destroy him who has the power of death, that is, the devil, and deliver all those who through fear of death were subject to lifelong bondage. For surely it is not with angels that he is concerned but with the descendants of Abraham. Therefore he had to be made like his brethren in every respect, so that he might become a merciful and faithful high priest in the service of God, to make expiation for the sins of the people." *Heb. 2:14–17 (RSV)*

"And he said to him, 'Truly I say to you, today you will be with me in Paradise.'" *Lk. 23:43 (RSV)*

SEPTEMBER 22 Lucy of Caltagirone

Blessed Lucy of Caltagirone was born in Sicily and was marked, at the age of six, by a miraculous intervention. The story is told that while picking figs lightning struck the tree, and Lucy lay upon the ground as dead. But a rescuer carried her home and delivered her to her mother, saying she would survive and that he, St. Nicholas, was her special protector. She joined the Third Order Franciscans in her late teens and lived with a woman tertiary who trained her in daily spiritual disciplines. At her mentor's death, Lucy entered a convent at Salerno, where she became occupied with contemplating the Passion. She gained fame through her powerful intercession for others, and many thronged to see her. Miracles were reported at her tomb, and she is the patron of eye diseases. Lucy was remembered on this date in the old Franciscan calendar.

Prayer:

Beloved Spirit of God, we thank you for your presence among us always. Blessed Lucy was saved from the fire from heaven and destined to illuminate many hearts by her prayers. Pour out your Spirit upon all flesh, for we all share in the gifts you hold out for us, if we awaken to your presence in our lives. Give us eyes to see and ears to hear, and we will go joyfully into your courts with praise. Amen.

Antiphon:

If your eye be single, your whole body will be filled with light.

Readings:

"Bless the Lord, O my soul! O Lord my God, you are very great! You are clothed with honor and majesty . . . you make the winds your messengers, fire and flame your ministers." *Psalm 104:1, 4 (RSV)*

"May the glory of the Lord endure forever, may the Lord rejoice in his works, who looks on the earth and it trembles, who touches the mountains and they smoke! I will sing to the Lord as long as I live; I will sing praise to my God while I have being. May my meditation be pleasing to him, for I rejoice in the Lord." *Psalm 104:31–34 (RSV)*

"Is this not a brand plucked from the fire?" *Zech. 3:2 (NASB)*

"It is a fearful thing to fall into the hands of the living God. But recall the former days when, after you were enlightened, you endured a hard struggle with sufferings. . . . But we are not of those who shrink back and are destroyed, but of those who have faith and keep their souls." *Heb. 10:31–32, 39 (RSV)*.

SEPTEMBER 23 *Mirozh Sign* Icon of the Mother of God (Vigil)

The monastery of the Transfiguration of the Savior, established in 1156, is in Pslov, Russia, near the source of the Mirozh River. The monastery is the home of the miraculous *Mirozh Sign* icon, which depicts the Theotokos as standing full-length with small figures—the Prince of Pskov, Dovmont, and Princess Maria Dimitrievna—praying to her. The *Mirozh Sign,* or *Our Lady of the Sign,* is a type of icon that has many local cults. It pictures the Virgin facing the viewer, and an image of her Son encircled within her breast also faces out, giving a blessing. The *Mirozh Sign* icon was known for its miraculous flow of healing tears, especially during the Plague, which swept the region during the reign of Ivan IV. This icon of *Our Lady of the Sign* was glorified on September 24, 1567, and a service was composed. A copy of the *Mirozh Sign,* minus the Russian figures (painted by Fr. William McNichols), was made for Pope John Paul II as a gift to remember World Youth Day in Denver, Colorado, in 1993. It was named *Our Lady of the New Advent.*

Intercessory Prayer:

We thank you, most gracious and pure Virgin Mary for the bounties you shower upon the human race through the grace of your Son. Thank you for the great mercy shown through the appearance of your miraculous icons, which have been given for the sanctification of our lands. Grant all who ask for your intercession the grace beneficial for our souls. We pray that the spirit of forbearance may prevail among all nations and peoples. Amen.

Antiphon:

You are the glory of your people.

Readings:

"I will appoint you as a covenant of the people, as a light to the nations, to open blind eyes, to bring the prisoners out from dungeon. . . ." Isa. 42:6–7 (NASB)

"O God of my ancestors and Lord of mercy, who have made all things by your word . . . Send her forth from the holy heavens, and from the throne of your glory send her, that she may labour at my side. . . . For she knows and understands all things, and she will guide me wisely in my actions and guard me with her glory." Wis. 9:1, 10–11 (NRSV)

"More honorable than the Cherubim, and beyond compare more glorious than the Seraphim, thee who without corruption gave birth to God the Word, the very Theotokos, thee do we magnify." Vespers hymn to Theotokos

SEPTEMBER 24 Thekla

The Orthodox tradition honors a number of "transvestite" nuns, or women who dressed in male attire to hide their identity. St. Thekla is the prototype for this classification of women saints. Thekla is one of the favorite early saints in the East, and she was given the titles Proto-martyr and Equal to the Apostles. Apocryphal tradition (Acts of Paul and Thekla) tells us that she was from Iconium in Asia Minor and one of St. Paul's pupils. She met Paul while engaged to be married, and her betrothed saw Paul as an evil perpetrator who wanted to entice Thekla from her marriage plans.

The man had Paul thrown into prison, which upset Thekla greatly. She took all her jewelry to bribe the guard so that she might sit next to Paul and learn the gospel. This initial betrayal enraged her entire family, and although Paul was flogged and released, Thekla was imprisoned. Refusing to give up her new faith after receiving a vision of Christ, she was sentenced to be burned, but a downpour of rain extinguished the fire. Freed, when she found Paul preaching again, Thekla donned male dress so she could follow him without being discovered. She eventually withdrew to a cave and gained renown as a great healer, working miracles in Christ's name. A large church was built over her cave at Seleucia, and Emperor Justinian (527–565) had a cathedral dedicated to her honor. The Roman tradition considers Thekla's story legendary.

Intercessory Prayer:

O righteous St. Thekla, ardent follower of Christ, you abandoned everything in absolute surrender and trust to give your new life back to God. After hearing Paul preach the gospel, you were quick to hear God's Word and to follow it. As you became a passionate disciple once truth lay open before you, so intercede for us that we may do likewise and attain salvation by the same faith revealed to you nearly two thousand years ago. May all of God's people be gathered under the banner of the Prince of Peace. Amen.

Antiphon:

Behold, anyone in Christ is a new creation.

Readings:

"As a hart longs for flowing streams, so longs my soul for you, O God. My soul thirsts for God, for the living God. When shall I come and behold the face of God? My tears have been my food day and night, while men say to me continually, 'Where is your God?' These things I remember, as I pour out my soul: how I went with the throng, and led them in procession to the house of God, with glad shouts and songs of thanksgiving, a multitude keeping festival." *Psalm 42:1–4 (RSV)*

"For I will pour water on the thirsty land, and streams on the dry ground; I will pour my Spirit upon your descendants, and my blessings on your offspring." *Isa. 44:3 (RSV)*

"Such is the confidence that we have through Christ toward God . . . . who has qualified us to be ministers of a new covenant, not in a written code but in the spirit; for the written code kills, the Spirit gives life." *2 Cor. 3:4, 6 (RSV)*

"Now on the last day, the great day of the feast, Jesus stood and cried out, saying, 'If any man is thirsty, let him come to Me and drink. He who believes in Me, as the Scripture said, 'From his innermost being shall flow rivers of living water.'" *Jn. 7:37–38 (NASB)*

SEPTEMBER 25 Euphrosyne of Alexandria

Holy monk Euphrosyne was born in 410, of a noble family in Alexandria. When she was eighteen and engaged, she visited a monastery where a wise elder dwelled. After listening to him, she decided she much preferred to pursue a life of holiness in peace and silence than return to her decadent lifestyle. She secretly became tonsured, and then she tried to hide from her family. Euphrosyne reasoned that they would easily locate her in a convent, so she put on masculine attire and forsook her family and the man to whom she was betrothed. She then entered a male monastery under the name Smaragdos, pretending to be a palace eunuch. Her father, beset by grief, traveled from one palace to another in search of her, eventually coming to the monastery where she dwelt alone in an isolated cell. She had already gained renown for her godliness and her wisdom. Father and daughter met, but he did not recognize her. She offered him counsel, trying to explain that his daughter had left her mother and father for Christ, and had therefore chosen the better portion. He was comforted and left, after which she remained cloistered for thirty-eight years. Anticipating her death, she called for her father, and, revealing her true identity, she begged him to bestow her inheritance on the monastery. After Euphrosyne's death, miracles were attributed to her relics, and her father, widowed, moved into her cell and became a monk.

Intercessory Prayer:

O holy St. Euphrosyne, in search of perfection you chose to forsake family for the opportunity to live the angelic life of monkhood. Casting aside every possible persona, you put off your royal robes as well as your feminine nature. You sought only to dwell securely in the light of the one before whom there are no distinctions. We thank you for modeling a role for us that is free of all

*preconceptions, and we ask your intercession for those of us still
attached to role expectations we often define for ourselves. Help us
to always remember the one thing needful. Amen.*

Antiphon:
My soul has a desire and longing for the Lord's courts.

Readings:
"One thing is needful. Mary has chosen the good portion, which
shall not be taken from her." *Lk. 10:42 (RSV)*

"But now the righteousness of God has been manifested apart
from law, although the law and the prophets bear witness to it, the
righteousness of God through faith in Jesus Christ for all who believe. For there is no distinction; since all have sinned and fall
short of the glory of God, they are justified by his grace as a gift,
through the redemption which is in Christ Jesus." *Rom. 3:21–24
(RSV)*

SEPTEMBER 26 Marie Victoire Therese Couderc

When Marie Victoire Couderc was a young girl in
nineteenth-century France, she befriended a holy priest
named Fr. Terme. She felt a calling to enter the religious
life, and Fr. Terme eventually helped her to join the Order of the Sisters of St. Regis, where she took the name Therese. Many pilgrims
visited the mountain village and its shrine of St. Regis, so there was a
great need for a hostel for women pilgrims. Marie Therese eventually
helped to transform a new hostel from an inn-like atmosphere to a
spiritual center for retreats. The group of spiritual aspirants living
there became known as the Cenacle Sisters, and many women came
from across the country to study the Spiritual Exercises of St. Ignatius
at the prayerful hostel. St. Marie Therese wrote many beautiful and
simple spiritual maxims, such as "God always gives more than we ask"
and "I have just one desire—that God be glorified." She died at age
eighty, leaving behind a large body of beautiful spiritual writings that
continue to inspire us today. Pope Paul VI canonized Marie Therese in
1970.

Intercessory Prayer:

St. Marie Therese, you instruct your spiritual children to abandon our lives with our whole heart to God's will in order to achieve the greatest tranquility and peace. We must fully surrender ourselves, dying to everything and seeking ourselves in nothing. Help us to live by your words of wisdom, strength, and encouragement. May we become surrendered souls who will find our paradise on earth because we enjoy the sweet peace that belongs to those who have given their hearts, minds, and wills completely to God. Amen.

Antiphon:

The one who has a serene spirit possesses understanding.

Readings:

"O LORD, my heart is not proud, nor my eyes haughty; nor do I involve myself in great matters, or in things too difficult for me. Surely I have composed and quieted my soul; like a weaned child." *Psalm 131:1–2 (NASB)*

"He caused the storm to be still, so that the waves of the sea were hushed. Then they were glad because they were quiet; so He guided them to their desired haven." *Psalm 107:29–30 (NASB)*

"And such confidence we have through Christ toward God. Not that we are adequate in ourselves to consider anything as coming from ourselves, but our adequacy is from God, who also made us adequate as servants of the new covenant, not of the letter, but of the Spirit; for the letter kills, but the Spirit gives life." *2 Cor. 3:4–6 (NASB)*

SEPTEMBER 27 Theresa Hackelmeier and Thecla of England

Theresa Hackelmeier was born in Europe in 1827 and entered a convent in her early teens. Nine years later, she left her community in Austria and became a Franciscan missionary. She arrived in Oldenburg, Indiana, in 1851 and established a small community of Franciscans there. They staffed the town school and opened a girl's school and orphanage, and they still found time to spend in perpetual adoration in front of the Blessed Sacrament. Although her orphanage and school burned down in 1857, Mother Theresa was undaunted in her faith that her community would still prosper. At the hundredth anniversary of her death, on September 27, 1860, Theresa's order had grown to over six hundred sisters.

This is also the feast day of Thecla of England. She was a Benedictine nun and a relative of St. Lioba (see Daily Readings, September 28, Lioba), whom she served under until St. Boniface made her abbess of a monastery in Germany. Thecla and her sisters promoted the Benedictine Rule and influenced the Teuton women whom they were sent to evangelize. She was known for her gentleness, charity, and devotion. It is believed that she died around 790. Thecla's shrine stood at Ktizengen until it was destroyed during the Peasant's War of the sixteenth century.

Prayer:

Gracious Christ, giver of life and love, we thank you for Theresa and Thecla—missionaries, organizers, and builders of the faith. They knew that the world of action must be balanced by the inner world of contemplation, and their sisters spent their lives in prayer and service to you. Knit our wills together in your will and our spirits in your Spirit, so we may find the balance of working for you and knowing you in this life. Amen.

Antiphon:

May your salvation, O Lord, be with us always.

Readings:

"Let us join ourselves to the Lord in a perpetual covenant." *Jer. 50:5 (RSV)*

"Make a joyful noise to God, all the earth; sing the glory of his name; give to him glorious praise!" *Psalm 55:1–2 (RSV)*

"For no [man] can lay a foundation other than the one which is laid, which is Jesus Christ. Now if any [man] builds upon the foundation with gold, silver, precious stones, wood, hay, straw, each [man's] work will become evident; for the day will show it, because it is to be revealed with fire; and the fire itself will test the quality of each [man's] work. If any [man's] work which he has built upon remains, he shall receive a reward. . . . Do you not know that you are a temple of God, and that the Spirit of God dwells in you?" *1 Cor. 3:11–16 (NASB)*

SEPTEMBER 28 Lioba (Liobe)

Lioba was fortunate to live in a time when women had a significant role in Christian religious life in England—the eighth
century—including understanding the conversion process and
the education that accompanied it. Women and men were both literate. Lioba was a skilled classicist, well-versed in Scripture, the
Church Fathers, and canon law. It was said that she was never without
a book in her hand and never forgot what she read. Lioba was
schooled at Wimborne, and at St. Boniface's request, she and thirty of
her sisters joined him in his missionary work in Germany. Lioba was
the women's leader and abbess of Bischofsheim. She and her nuns established numerous Benedictine monasteries in Germany, and Lioba
ensured that her nuns were all well-educated and able to teach and
evangelize the young women under their care. Lioba's name means
"beloved." She combined beauty, charity, and common sense, and she
was a spiritual consultant to many, including Hildegard, Charle-
magne's wife. Lioba died in 776 and was buried close to Boniface in
Fulda. She is often depicted with a string of purple thread in her
hand. This symbol is related to a dream she had in which she pulled an
endless amount of thread from her mouth and wound it into a ball.
The dream was interpreted to signify Lioba's wise, heart-guided
counsel and the mystery and beauty of her teachings.

Prayer:

> O St. Lioba, the thread of your holy words bound all who met you
> to your heart, and through you, to Christ's heart. Bind us also to
> the holy heart of Jesus through our attempts to emulate your love
> of all those around you. May our lips speak no words that do not
> convey God's immeasurable love through Jesus Christ. Amen.

Antiphon:

You shall go out with joy and be led forth with peace.

Readings:

"You have dealt well with your servant, O Lord, according to your
word. Teach me good judgment and knowledge, for I believe in
your commandments. . . . The law of your mouth is better to me
than thousands of gold and silver pieces." *Psalm 119:65–66, 72
(RSV)*

"And your ears will hear a word behind you, 'This is the way, walk in it,' whenever you turn to the right or to the left." *Isa. 30:21 (NASB)*

"In the same way God, desiring even more to show to the heirs of the promise the unchangeableness of His purpose, interposed with an oath, in order that by two unchangeable things, in which it is impossible for God to lie, we may have strong encouragement, we who have fled for refuge in laying hold of the hope set before us. This hope we have as an anchor of the soul, a hope both sure and steadfast and one which enters within the veil." *Heb. 6:17–19 (NASB)*

SEPTEMBER 29 Margaret Fell

Margaret Fell Fox is often referred to as the Mother of Quakerism. Born in Lancashire, England, in 1614, she was married in her late teens to Thomas Fell, a member of Parliament. After he died, she met George Fox, an itinerant preacher, who convinced her of the Society of Friends' classic position: that God should be worshipped in spirit and in truth, rather than through the outward form of institutions. She married Fox and wrote extensively, despite hostile opposition and even imprisonment, pleading the rest of her life for religious freedom for the Friends. In 1660, she wrote *A Declaration and an Information from Us, the People Called Quakers* and submitted it to the king and both houses of Parliament, explaining the movement's principles. Many considered Margaret to be an early feminist, a premise based primarily on her treatise *Women's Speaking Justified, Proved, and Allowed by the Scriptures*, which highlights the differences between women under Old Testament law and women of the New Creation under Christ. Margaret died in 1702, at age eighty-eight, and she is remembered as one of the great leaders of the first generations of Friends.

Prayer:

Beloved Lord Jesus, Margaret Fell came to understand that the church is made of people, and a house of prayer is only its outward structure. She reminds us that it is important to trust in you and to return to the knowledge of you in the silence and simplicity of our hearts. Instill in us a new spirit, and enflame us with a love that burns deep and ignites other hearts with its spark of friendship. Help us to remain aware so when you, the one whom we seek, suddenly comes to his temple, our hearts will be an open door. Amen.

Antiphon:

For God alone, my soul in silence waits.

Readings:

"Therefore you will joyously draw water from the springs of salvation. And in that day you will say, 'Give thanks to the Lord, call on His name. Make known His deeds among the peoples'" *Isa. 12:3–4 (NASB)*

"A new heart also will I give you, and a new spirit will I put within you: and I will take away the stony heart out of your flesh, and I will give you a heart of flesh." *Ez. 36:26 (KJV)*

"And when you pray, you are not to be as the hypocrites; for they love to stand and pray in the synagogues and on the street corners, in order to be seen by men. Truly I say to you, they have their reward in full. But you, when you pray go into your inner room, and when you have shut your door, pray to your Father who is in secret, and your Father who sees in secret will repay you." *Mt. 6:5–6 (NASB)*

"Take heed, keep alert; for you do not know when the appointed time is." *Mk. 13:33 (NASB)*

SEPTEMBER 30 Waldetrude

St. Waldetrude, Abbess of Mons, came from a remarkable family in Belgium. She was the daughter of Waldeburt and Bertilla and the sister of Aldegund of Maubeuge, all of whom were celebrated as local saints. Waldetrude was married to a nobleman named Madelgarius, whom King Dogbert I sent to Ireland to bring back missionary monks. Eventually Madelgarius left to become a monk himself, and Waldetrude remained in her household raising their children, two sons and two daughters, all of whom entered the religious life. Waldetrude dedicated herself to caring for the sick, but she longed to withdraw from the world. Eventually she took the veil, becoming an anchorite under the supervision of her spiritual director, Gislenus. She later founded a monastery at Chateaulieu, and the town of Mons grew up around the monastery. Waldetrude was noted for her charity and miracles. She died in 688, and she is the patroness of Mons in Belgium.

Prayer:

Beloved Holy Spirit, it is only your love that gives meaning to the world. Through St. Waltrude's intercession, make us keepers of our inner temple, the meeting tent where we wait for Christ our Lord. She did not understand why she was left to raise her family on her own, but she surrendered her life and children completely to you. Help us to depend on God in all things, and to surrender what we do not understand to the God who is, was, and always remains with us. Amen.

Antiphon:

In the early morning, I will remember your steadfast love.

Readings:

"Lo, children are a heritage from the Lord, the fruit of the womb a reward. Like arrows in the hand of a warrior are the children of one's youth." *Psalm 127:3–4 (RSV)*

"'You know that the rulers of the Gentiles lord it over them, and their great men exercise authority over them. It is not so among you, but whoever wishes to become great among you shall be your servant, and whoever wishes to be first among you shall be your slave.'" *Mt. 20:25–27 (NASB)*

"Jesus said to them, 'If God were your Father, you would love Me; for I proceeded forth and have come from God, for I have not even come on my own initiative, but He sent Me.'" *Jn. 8:42 (NASB)*

OCTOBER 1 Theresa of Lisieux

Marie Theresa Martin, also known as Theresa of the Child Jesus, was born in France in 1873. Like several of her sisters, she entered the Carmelite Order at Lisieux, where she lived and practiced her "little way" until her untimely death at age twenty-four of tuberculosis. Her desire as a young girl was to become a martyr for Christ, but through studying the Scriptures, she eventually understood that the hinge of her vocation was to practice a simple love and, in doing so, to glorify God in all things. This she did beautifully, and had she not been instructed to write her short spiritual biography, we would probably know nothing about this unassuming young woman whose life was so simple and whose love was so great. After her death, Theresa became famous for sending roses as a sign of her continued work in heaven on behalf of those who call upon her intercession. Pope John Paul II declared Theresa a Church doctor, and she is the patron saint of missions.

Prayer:

O dear Theresa, you understood that the Lord promised his kingdom to those who became like little children and that spiritual freedom comes from realizing that we are loved as we are. You came to realize that without love, even martyrs would have shed their blood in vain, and you wrote that love sets the bounds of every vocation. Pray for us in striving to discern and accomplish our own vocations in this world, so that, whatever path we may walk, we behold that Christ is the lamp unto our feet and the culmination of our heart's desire. Amen.

Antiphon:

Blessed are the pure of heart, for they shall see God.

Readings:

"The wilderness and the solitary place shall be glad for them; and the desert shall rejoice, and blossom as the rose. It shall blossom abundantly and rejoice even with joy and singing."
Isa. 35:1–2 (KJV)

"Flowers appear on the earth; the season of singing has come, the cooing of doves heard in our land." *Song of Songs 2:12 (NIV)*

"Though I speak with the tongues of men and of angels, but have not love, I have become sounding brass or a clanging cymbal. And though I have the gift of prophecy, and understand all mysteries and all knowledge, and though I have all faith, so that I could remove mountains, but have not love, I am nothing." *1 Cor. 13:1–2 (NKJV)*

"May they be brought to complete unity to let the world know that you sent me and have loved them even as you have loved me." *Jn. 17:23 (NIV)*

OCTOBER 2 Protection of the Mother of God and the Holy Angels

The feast of the Protection of the Holy Mother was tradition-ally celebrated on October 1, and the feast of the Holy Guardian Angels was on October 2. Both feast days honor the protection of these heavenly intercessors. Mary is known as the Queen of Angels in the West (see Daily Readings, August 2, Our Lady of the Angels at Portiuncula). In the East, veneration of the Mother of God's protective mantle developed early in Rus'-Ukraine history (see Daily Readings, July 31, *Virgin Blachernitissa:* Dedication of the Temple at Blachernae). The Ukranians often drape embroidered cloth over their icons to symbolize this protection. In numerous apparitions, Mary has spread her holy mantle over cities and monasteries in the Ukraine during times of crisis.

Veneration of the guardian angels is long known in both East and West, although it was not officially added to the Roman calendar until 1608. Intercessory prayers and collects to the angels are found in Church liturgies as early as the seventh century. The first supplicatory canon to a guardian angel is attributed to John the Monk by the Greeks (early sixth century), demonstrating a clear belief that God endowed each human being with a special guardian for the whole of that soul's lifetime. Angelic messengers appear frequently in both the Old Testament and the Gospels, as well as in Acts and the Book of Revelation.

Prayer:

> *O holy Theotokos, you are queen of the angels, and your protective graces flow to us always because you were the chosen dwelling place of Christ and the Holy Spirit. You are the never-ceasing wonder of the angelic hosts on high, and your protective veil banishes the afflictions that assail us when we trust your gracious intercession. You comfort those who suffer; you mirror justice and bless homes and families. Angels chant your praises whenever you deign to appear on earth, and we join them in praising the beauty of your holy veil, which is spread over the whole world like a cloud. Pray for us who sing to you. Amen.*

Antiphon:

See, I am sending an angel before you, to guard you on the way.

Readings:

"O LORD my God, You are very great: You are clothed with honor and majesty, Who cover *Yourself* with light as *with* a garment, Who stretch out the heavens like a curtain. Who makes the clouds His chariot, Who walks on the wings of the wind, Who makes His angels spirits, His ministers a flame of fire. . . . *You* laid the foundations of the earth, So *that* it should not be moved forever." *Psalm 104:1–6 (NKJV)*

"And they reported to the angel of the LORD, who was standing among the myrtle trees, 'We have gone throughout the earth and found the whole world at rest and in peace.'" *Zech. 1:11 (NIV)*

"Then the high priest and all his associates, who were members of the party of the Sadducees, were filled with jealousy. They arrested the apostles and put them in the public jail. But during the night an angel of the Lord opened the doors of the jail and brought them out. 'Go, stand in the temple courts,' he said, 'and tell the people the full message of this new life.'" *Acts 5:17–20 (NIV)*

OCTOBER 3 Mother Theodore Guerin

Anne Teresa Guerin was educated by her mother, from whom she acquired a deep love of Scripture. When she was fifteen, Anne's father was murdered and she spent the next ten years caring for her family. At twenty-five, she joined the Sisters of Providence in France and took the name Theodore. She was soon asked to take a small band of sisters to America to found a motherhouse there. In 1850, the mission at Saint Mary of the Woods was established in Indiana, which became the sister college to the University of Notre Dame. Mother Theodore continued to open schools throughout Indiana and Illinois, teaching and evangelizing in the face of great difficulties. Her greatest challenge was the harassment caused by Monsignor Hailandiere, who took a dislike to her and thwarted her at every turn. He withheld approval of a large convent and boarding school, which the sisters needed to house their growing community. He finally demanded her resignation, but Mother Theodore was a faithful dissenter: her community had elected her. He then threatened to excommunicate all her sisters, who also defied him and demanded a new protector. The community's deliverance came when Hailandiere resigned. The Congregation of Bishops sent a replacement, with whom the Sisters of Providence developed a long and harmonious relationship. When she died a Celtic cross of stone was placed at her gravesite as her memorial. It reads, "I sleep, but my heart watches over this house which I have built." Mother Guerin was beatified in 1998.

Intercessory Prayer:

Dear Mother Theodore, you struggled with your crosses with an invincible fortitude and trust. Intercede for us, that we may have heroic faith and discernment in all the tests that we encounter. You wrote that we must be equally indifferent to everything, including reputation, health, and temptation, since all this we should leave sweetly to God's providence. May we learn to abandon our lives, our families, our hopes, and our futures to God alone. Amen.

Antiphon:

God, who is faithful, will not suffer you to be tempted beyond your strength.

Readings:

"Those who dwell at the earth's farthest bounds stand in awe at your wonders; you make the sunrise and sunset shout for joy. You care for the earth, give it water, you fill it with riches. Your river in heaven brims over to provide its grain." *Psalm 65:9–10 (PCB)*

"You intended to harm me, but God intended it for good to accomplish what is now being done, the saving of many lives. So then, don't be afraid. I will provide for you and your children." *Gen. 50:20–21 (NIV)*

"You all know that these hands of mine earned enough for the needs of myself and my companions. I showed you that it is our duty to help the weak in this way, by hard work, and that we should keep in mind the words of the Lord Jesus, who himself said, 'Happiness lies more in giving than in receiving.'" *Acts 20:34–35 (NEB)*

OCTOBER 4 Mary Frances of the Five Wounds

Anna Maria Gallo lived in the early seventeenth century in Naples, Italy. Her life was marked by trials inflicted by a brutal father, countered by a loving and pious mother. Her father, an arrogant and harsh man, nearly worked the poor child to death. She made her first Holy Communion at age seven, and she received our Eucharistic Lord nearly every day of her life after this great event. At least two saints, including St. John Joseph of the Cross, predicted her sainthood. When she became sixteen, her father attempted to force her to marry a wealthy young man from the village, and when she refused, he beat her and locked her in her room. Eventually, the cruel man relented and allowed her to become a Franciscan tertiary. She took the name Mary Frances of the Five Wounds, in honor both of St. Francis and the Passion of Our Lord. She suffered the stigmata like her patron, St. Francis, but her wounds were lessened and became invisible when she prayed. Her wounds intensified during the Fridays of Lent, when she suffered the Passion of Jesus. She became known in the region as a spiritual counselor, and many priests and laypeople sought her out for her advice and life-saving spiritual counsel. Mary Frances died in 1791, and Pope Pius IX canonized her in 1867.

Intercessory Prayer:

Dear St. Mary Frances of the Five Wounds, you suffered Christ's pains and united these sufferings with Jesus to save souls. You are an inspiration to us by your example to take up the cross and follow Christ. We offer our prayers along with your powerful intercession for all of the poor souls in Purgatory, especially those souls who are most forgotten and who have no one to pray for them. Help us to remember that "your inheritance is imperishable, undefiled, unfading, and kept in heaven for you" (1 Pet. 1:4). Amen.

Antiphon:

Far be it from me to glory save in the cross of our Lord Jesus Christ.

Readings:

"I am shut in so that I cannot escape; my eye grows dim through sorrow. Every day I call upon thee, O Lord; I spread out my hands to thee." *Psalm 88:9 (RSV)*

"O Lord God of hosts, hear my prayer; give ear, O God of Jacob! Behold our shield, O God; look upon the face of thine anointed! For a day in thy courts is better than a thousand elsewhere. I would rather be a doorkeeper in the house of my God than dwell in the tents of the wicked." *Psalm 84:8–10 (RSV)*

"And he called to him the multitude with his disciples, and said to them, 'If any man would come after me, let him deny himself and take up his cross and follow me. For whoever would save his life will lose it; and whoever loses his life for my sake and the gospel's will save it.'" *Mk. 8:34–35 (RSV)*

OCTOBER 5 Faustina Kowalska

The recently canonized St. Faustina was born into a peasant family in Poland on August 25, 1905. She experienced bright lights in prayer from an early age. After a vision of the suffering Christ when only a teenager, she announced to her parents her desire for the religious life and, after a number of setbacks, she entered the Sisters of Our Lady of Mercy in 1925. Faustina's visions were, like those of many visionaries of the Middle Ages, profoundly mystical. She rarely had visions of Christ's human life, and she felt her deepest union with God when her senses were "seemingly dead." Her experience was one of total immersion in God's ineffable lightness and mercy. Her life's principal vocation was to reveal to the world the new icon that the Lord requested her to have made: an image of the Sacred Heart of Jesus. It was not, however, depicted with blood and thorns. Rather, this heart radiates pink and white rays, which stream from it into the hearts of all humanity. He desired to have written at the bottom: "Jesus, I trust in you," and he stressed to her that she should make this image of Divine Mercy known throughout Poland. After her death at age thirty-three, devotion to the icon grew, and it has now been reproduced and enthroned in homes and churches throughout the world. Faustina died October 5, 1938, and Pope John Paul II canonized her on April 30, 2000. Faustina is the first female

Polish saint, and her spiritual diary has been translated into ten languages.

Prayer:

O St. Faustina, you were aware of the divine lover of your soul within you, around you, in all things, and in all circumstances. You made your own heart a garden for his dwelling-place, and you were permeated with the light of his presence in all your daily activities. You had a clear vision of the blood and water that poured forth from Christ's heart as a fountain of mercy for us, and you saw that this mercy is available to us always. As you became a transparent window through which Jesus' mercy shone, pray that we, too, may have God's consciousness in our own hearts and live in close intimacy with Christ there, now, and forevermore. Amen.

Antiphon:

My God stands by me; all my trust is in him.

Readings:

"And above the firmament over their heads *was* the likeness of a throne, in appearance like a sapphire stone; on the likeness of the throne *was* a likeness with the appearance of a man high above it. Also from the appearance of His waist and upward I saw, as it were, the color of amber with the appearance of fire all around within it; and from the appearance of His waist and downward I saw, as it were, the appearance of fire with brightness all around. Like the appearance of a rainbow in a cloud on a rainy day, so *was* the appearance of the brightness all around it. This *was* the appearance of the likeness of the glory of the LORD." *Ez. 1:26–28 (NKJV)*

"Place me like a seal over your heart, like a seal on your arm; for love . . . burns like blazing fire, like a mighty flame. . . . Many waters cannot quench love; rivers cannot wash it away. If one were to give all the wealth of his house for love, it would be utterly scorned." *Song of Songs, 8:6–7 (NIV)*

OCTOBER 6 Marie Rose Durocher

 Born Melanie Durocher in 1811 in Canada, this frail young girl suffered numerous hardships in her early life, including poor health and the loss of her mother. Educated by the Sisters of Notre Dame in Montreal, Melanie was a quick learner and felt drawn to the religious life. Refused by several communities because of her physical weaknesses, she lived for a while with her brother, who was a priest, and then founded her own order, the Sisters of the Holy Names of Jesus and Mary, and took the name Marie Rose. Her dream sprouted, and her order began to teach poor young women in rural areas who had no opportunity for education. The order soon became famous as a teaching congregation and spread to parts of the United States and South America. Marie Rose died of tuberculosis on October 6, 1849, her birthday. Pope John Paul II recognized her outstanding leadership and personal sanctity in 1982 when he beatified her. Marie Rose is the patron of those with weak constitutions.

Prayer:

Beloved Lord, the life of Blessed Marie Rose was one of passionate vision and conviction. Through her simple motto "Jesus and Mary, my strength and my glory," she sought to give you praise and honor in all her endeavors. Through her intercession, help us to embrace your call regardless of whether the world tells us that our heart's call is a vain one. Trusting in you alone for our strength, may we glorify you by following Marie Rose's example. Amen.

Antiphon:

I will instruct you and teach you in the way in which you should go.

Readings:

"You shall speak to him and put words in his mouth; I will help both of you speak and will teach you what to do. He will speak to the people for you, and it will be as if he were your mouth and as if you were God to him." *Ex. 4:15–16 (NIV)*

"Which of you shall have a friend, and go to him at midnight and say to him, 'Friend, lend me three loaves; for a friend of mine has come to me on his journey, and I have nothing to set before him'; and he will answer from within and say, 'Do not trouble me; the door is now shut, and my children are with me in bed; I cannot rise and give to you'? I say to you, though he will not rise and give to him because he is his friend, yet because of his persistence he will rise and give him as many as he needs. So I say to you, ask, and it will be given to you; seek, and you will find; knock, and it will be opened to you." *Lk. 11:5–10 (NKJV)*

"It is written in the prophets, 'And they shall all be taught by God.'" *Jn. 6:45 (NKJV)*

OCTOBER 7 Our Lady of the Rosary and *Tenderness* Icon of the Pskov-Caves

The Rosary has a long tradition among the faithful; it probably began as a method of replacing the 150 Psalms with 150 Our Fathers, and later with Hail Marys, using pebbles or berries strung on a cord as a counting device. Although legend ascribes the Rosary to St. Dominic, it was in use long before the twelfth century. The practice of introducing meditations on the events of Christ's life while reciting the Rosary is attributed to Dominic of Prussia, a Carthusian, and it became popular by the end of the fifteenth century. Pope Pius V established the feast in 1573 as thanksgiving for a battle the Christians won over the Turks through Mary's intercession.

Likewise, a corresponding feast in Russia, honoring the *Tenderness* Icon of the Pskov-Caves was instituted to commemorate Pskov's deliverance from the French invasion in 1812; the celebration included a procession about the city. The *Tenderness* icon, venerated at the Caves Monastery on October 7, is a popular icon throughout the East with a number of different feast days. The meaning of this *Tenderness* icon corresponds in many ways to the meaning of the Rosary: in the icon, the virgin offers the son to humanity, while the son is in a gesture of offering the mother.

Intercessory Prayer:

Holy Mother of God, as we meditate on the mysteries of your life with your Son, Jesus, help us to realize how we are crucifying him again in our own age by allowing our feelings of fear and self-protection to replace our trust in him. We have occupied our lives with our addictions and worldliness, which have pushed aside the true lover of our souls. Help us to surrender all to the son you brought forth into the world for us, that we may imitate your tender loving care for him always. Inspired by your confidence, we fly to you, O mother of all, and we seek to imitate your merciful love in all things. Amen.

Antiphon:

From this day, all generations shall call me blessed.

Readings:

"The angel went to her and said, 'Greetings, you who are highly favored! The Lord is with you.'" Lk. 1:28 (NIV)

"Truly fitting is it to sing your praises, O Theotokos!
The ever-blessed and completely sinless one,
And the Mother of our God.
You are more honorable than the cherubim
Beyond compare and more glorious than the seraphim!
Without stain you bore God the Word,
O Theotokos, we extol you!" Orthodox hymn at Vespers

OCTOBER 8 Pelagia

In his commentary on the Gospel of Matthew, John Chrysostom refers to the triumphal conversion of a brilliant and beautiful actress from Antioch. He was speaking of St. Pelagia, who began her adult life as a notorious actress, dancer, and harlot and ended it as a disguised monk living in a small cell on the side of a mountain at the Mount of Olives. She credited her conversion to another famous Byzantine saint, Bishop Nonnus, whom she happened to hear preaching. After her baptism, she gave all her riches to the bishop, who in turn asked her to distribute them to widows and orphans. Pelagia paid special attention to her own slave girls, giving each enough gold to be a freewoman in the world, but reminding them to free themselves also of attachment to the world. She then donned the bishop's tunic as her only clothing and went to live as an anchorite, where she gained the reputation of a miracle-working monk named Pelagius. It was believed that none of the surrounding monks or visitors to her cell knew Pelagia's real gender except Nonnus himself.

Prayer:

Almighty God, you knit together your elect in one communion and fellowship despite our gifts or our weaknesses. Give us the grace to follow holy Pelagia in renouncing all that is useless in the world so we may rejoice with her and all the saints in virtuous and fervent living for you alone. Grant that all who seek you, or a deeper understanding of you, may be found by you. Through Christ our Lord. Amen.

Antiphon:

You must know that your body is a temple of the Holy Spirit, who is within.

Readings:

"There is a time for everything, and a season for every activity under heaven: a time to be born and a time to die, a time to plant and a time to uproot, a time to kill and a time to heal, a time to tear down and a time to build, a time to weep and a time to laugh, a time to mourn and a time to dance." *Eccl. 3:1–6 (NIV)*

"Let Israel be glad in its Maker; let Zion's heirs exult in the Most High.
Let them praise God's name with dancing; and make music with timbrel and harp.
For you take delight in your people, O God;
You adorn the humble with victory." *Psalm 149:1–5 (PCB)*

"Do you not know that your body is the temple of the Holy Spirit *who is* in you, whom you have from God, and you are not your own? For you were bought at a price; therefore glorify God in your body." *1 Cor. 6:19–20 (NIV)*

OCTOBER 9 Mother Mollie Rogers

Mary Josephine Rogers ("Mother Mollie") lived from 1882 to 1955. She founded the Order of the Maryknoll Sisters, the first group of American Catholic women devoted to establishing foreign missions. Prior to this time, the American Catholic Church did not evangelize elsewhere, and the United States was itself still considered mission territory by the Vatican. Mother Mollie was inspired by her colleagues, Protestant students at Smith College, who had a passionate interest in evangelizing foreign nations, particularly China. When she initially sought support for her endeavor, she met with resistance from Vatican officials; at that time they did not think women were suited to the rugged demands of missionary work outside the confines of a convent. Mollie Rogers's intention was to mingle her sisters with the commonfolk, not to imitate traditional monastery living. Her project did eventually get approved, and her missions sprang up in China, the Philippines, and Korea. By the time of Mother Mollie's death, 1,100 Maryknoll Sisters were serving throughout the world.

Intercessory Prayer:

O holy Mother Mollie, you were an ardent lover of the fires of truth and charity. With joy you traveled an evangelical life to bring the beauty and wisdom of the gospel message to many foreign missions. You showed all who came into your orbit that, indeed, mercy reaches mightily from one end of the earth to the other. O holy sister and mother of many, pray for those who still suffer the difficulties of poverty and injustice. May we stand by the Lord's side until all injustice is placed under his feet. Amen.

Antiphon:

I shall know the fullness of joy when I see your face, O Lord.

Readings:

"And [God] confirmed it to Jacob for a statute, To Israel as an everlasting covenant, Saying, 'To you I will give the land of Canaan, As the allotment of your inheritance,' . . . When they went from one nation to another, From one kingdom to another people, He permitted no one to do them wrong; Yes, He rebuked kings for their sakes, Saying, 'Do not touch My anointed ones, And do My prophets no harm.'" *Psalm 105:10–15 (NKJV)*

"We were not looking for praise from [men], not from you or anyone else. As apostles of Christ we could have been a burden to you, but we were gentle among you, like a mother caring for her little children. We loved you so much that we were delighted to share with you not only the gospel of God but our lives as well, because you had become so dear to us. Surely you remember . . . our toil and hardship; we worked night and day in order not to be a burden to anyone while we preached the gospel of God to you." *1 Thess. 2:6–10 (NIV)*

OCTOBER 10 Mary Angela Truszkowska

Born Sophia Camille Truszkowska into a noble family in 1825 in Poland, this young woman was characterized early in life by a deep concern for others. Influenced by her father, a judge, she began a study of the causes of contemporary social problems. Realizing that growing family disintegration and lack of religious education were the root of many of the social ills of her day, she resolved to educate the poor and neglected. She took in as many of the downtrodden in her upstairs attic as she possibly could working initially as a Franciscan tertiary. Taking the name Mary Angela, she then started another Franciscan branch devoted to working with the exploited, the aged, and the homeless, called the Felician Sisters. She opened twenty-seven schools within four years, and then organized a contemplative branch of her foundation. The Felician Order became one of the first active-contemplative communities in Poland. During the Russian occupation in 1864, the Felician Sisters lost everything and took refuge in the Austrian sector of Poland. Passionately devoted to Our Lady of Czestochowa, Mother Angela spent many of her later years in prayer before the Blessed Sacrament, which is today exposed in every provincial house of her order. Mary Angela was beatified in 1993.

Prayer:

O God, who showed forth a testimony of service and inspiration in your daughter Mary Angela, awaken us to a genuine concern for others based on a deep interior life. Teach us that our prayers said in utmost confidence in you will never go unanswered. Bless all those who walk in the rule of a religious life, and make their lives a living fountain of your grace in the world. Through Christ our Lord. Amen.

Antiphon:

May the Lord build our house and guard our city.

Readings:

"Make me understand the way of your precepts; So shall I meditate on your wonderful works. My soul melts from heaviness; Strengthen me according to your word. Remove from me the way of lying, And grant me your law graciously. I have chosen the way of truth; Your judgments I have laid *before me." Psalm 119:27–30 (Daleth) (NKJV)*

"And we have the word of the prophets made more certain, and you will do well to pay attention to it, as to a light shining in a dark place, until the day dawns and the morning star rises in your hearts." *2 Pet. 1:19 (NIV)*

"At that time Jesus, full of joy through the Holy Spirit, said, 'I praise you, Father, Lord of heaven and earth, because you have hidden these things from the wise and learned, and revealed them to little children. Yes, Father, for this was your good pleasure.'" *Lk. 10:21 (NIV)*

OCTOBER 11 Ethelburga of Barking

Ethelburga of Barking was the sister of St. Erconwald, who established two monasteries—one for himself in Chertsey (Surrey) and a second for Ethelburga in Barking (Essex). Ethelburga became a great abbess, presiding over the double monastery at Barking. According to Bede, the historian, she showed herself in every way "worthy as her brother" in holiness of life and solicitude for those under her care. Ethelburga was said to have caused a storm at sea in order to encourage a monk to return a manuscript written by one of her nuns. Her sisters studied Scripture, the early Fathers, and the classics. A number of nuns at her monastery had visions and prophetic dreams. When the Plague ravaged the country, a heavenly light that appeared at midnight showed the nuns at Barking where the bodies should be laid to rest. When Ethelburga died, on October 11, 675, one of her nuns had a vision of her glorified body being drawn up to heaven by gold cords.

Prayer:

Merciful Jesus, you gave holy Mother Ethelburga to be a living flame in the cold north and a fervent source of inspiration to those around her. With great willingness, she led the ascetic life for you, and upon finishing the course, was found worthy of your pleasure and your glory. Teach us to be attached to nothing, so we may see everything as a gift from you. Through her intercession, may we also someday attain the heavenly bridal chamber. Amen.

Antiphon:

Come and fill our hearts with your love.

Readings:

"And I say, O that I had wings like a dove! I would fly away and be at rest;

I would lodge in the wilderness. I would haste to find me a shelter from the raging wind and tempest . . . But I will call upon God; and the Lord will save me.

Evening and morning and at noon I utter my complaint and moan, and he will hear my voice." *Psalm 55:6–7, 16–17 (RSV)*

"And it shall come to pass afterward, that I will pour out my spirit on all flesh; your sons and your daughters shall prophesy, your old men shall dream dreams and your young men shall see visions." *Joel 2:28 (RSV)*

"The disciples went and woke him, saying, 'Master, Master, we're going to drown!' He got up and rebuked the wind and the raging waters; the storm subsided, and all was calm. 'Where is your faith?'" *Lk. 8:24–25 (NIV)*

OCTOBER 12 Elizabeth Fry

Elizabeth Fry was a Quaker prison reformer who the Bank of England chose to appear on their five-pound notes. She was born in Norfolk in 1780 and suffered the death of her mother at an early age. She was a religious skeptic as a teenager but was transformed by a sermon by William Savery, an American Quaker. She then developed a profound Christian spirituality, and despite mothering eleven children, she found time in her busy marriage to minister to women prisoners and their children at Newgate prison. Women prisoners there lived in destitute conditions: hungry, cold, dirty, and without proper clothing, even for their babies. Elizabeth organized visiting committees, cleaned up the prison, and started the first prison school. Later in life, she traveled widely in the British Isles and Europe, stressing everywhere she went that prisoners were individuals who also had a right to decent living and self-respect.

Prayer:

Graciously hear us, O God, that rejoicing in the feast of Elizabeth Fry, your holy woman, we may imitate her example and follow her fervent aspirations. With the fruit of her hands she planted a vineyard for you, and it has brought forth rich mercy in the lives of many who lived after her. By her intercession, may we have the grace to treat each individual with dignity and respect despite their failures, knowing that you alone, O God, are the judge of each human life. Through Christ our Lord. Amen.

Antiphon:

As often as you did it for one of these, you did it for me.

Readings:

"We give thanks to you, Lord God Almighty, the One who is and who was, because you have taken your great power and have begun to reign. . . . [T]he time has come for judging the dead, and for rewarding your servants the prophets and your saints and those who reverence your name, both small and great—and for destroying those who destroy the earth." *Rev. 11:17–18 (NIV)*

"Therefore let it be known to you, brethren, that through this Man is preached to you the forgiveness of sins; and by Him everyone who believes is justified." *Acts 13:38–39 (NKJV)*

"Do not judge, or you too will be judged. For in the same way you judge others, you will be judged, and with the measure you use, it will be measured to you. Why do you look at the speck of sawdust in your brother's eye and pay no attention to the plank in your own eye?" *Mt. 7:1–4 (NIV)*

OCTOBER 13 Edith Cavell

The oldest of four children, Edith Cavell was born a vicar's daughter in Norwich, England, in 1865. She taught nursing at the Berkendael Institute, in Brussels, a nondenominational teaching facility based on the concepts of Florence Nightingale. When World War I started, she turned the institute into a Red Cross hospital, assisting soldiers of all nationalities. After the Germans took control of Belgium, Edith began an underground operation to help Allied staff and soldiers escape. She was arrested in August 1915 and convicted of treason. While awaiting death, she was allowed a visit by an English minister, who found her reading her Book of Common Prayer and the *Imitation of Christ* in her prison cell. Edith calmly went to her execution, and before she died said, "I know now that patriotism is not enough. I must have no hatred or bitterness toward anyone."

Intercessory Prayer:

O venerable Edith, you were a valiant woman in your ministry to Christ's sufferings in your fellow human beings. You risked your life and lost it for the sake of others, but your savior sustained you through all your difficulties. Intercede for us during our darkest hours. You who trusted in God with no doubts, pray that the imprisoned may be granted the fortitude and patience to suffer the trials of this life and to be a witness to the true gospel of love in the face of bitterness and even death. Amen.

Antiphon:

I will not leave you orphaned; I will come to you.

Readings:

"Pride has risen against me; corruption pursues my life, evil pays you no heed. But you are merciful and gracious, slow to anger, abounding in love. Turn to me and take pity; give strength to your servant, and save your handmaid's child. Show me a sign of your favor; let injustice be put to shame." *Psalm 86:14–17 (PCB)*

"For you yourselves know, brethren, that our coming to you was not in vain. But even after we had suffered before and were spitefully treated at Philippi, as you know, we were bold in our God to speak to you the gospel of God in much conflict." *1 Thess. 2:1–2 (NKJV)*

"If the world hates you, you know that it hated Me before it hated you. If you were of the world, the world would love its own. Yet because you are not of the world, but I chose you out of the world." *Jn. 15:18–20 (NKJV)*

OCTOBER 14 Paraskeva of Serbia

Although her relics ended up in Serbia, Paraskeva, also called Petka, was born near Constantinople. She was orphaned at an early age, and in her youth she found her way to a group of ascetics living outside the city. Eventually she made a pilgrimage to the Holy Land, where she decided to cross the Jordan River and live in the wilderness, eating little more than herbs and wild grasses. Legend tells us that an angel appeared to her toward the end of her life, instructing her to take her body back to Constantinople, where she was to part with it. This she did, and because no one knew who she was or where she came from, she was buried in an unmarked grave. In the Orthodox tradition, God often reveals the glory of a saint after her death, and sometimes not at all during her uneventful life. As the story goes, a grave digger had a dream in which Paraskeva appeared to him, announced who she was, and told him where to dig up her body. When he unearthed her body, it was uncorrupt and possessed a fragrant odor of sanctity. Her relics became famous for healings, especially of blindness. Her body was eventually transferred to the Moldavian capital of Jassey to preserve it during the Crusades, which later destroyed the Byzantine city of Constantinople.

Intercessory Prayer:

Blessed Paraskeva, you determined early in your life to dedicate yourself wholly to Christ. When you were alone in the wilderness, the angel called you from your desert wasteland to God's mansion in the heavens. In your desire to use your heavenly intercession on behalf of those in need of healing on earth, God manifested his glory in your body. Help us to remember that the wedding feast of the lamb has begun, if the bride has made herself ready. Amen.

Antiphon:

My spirit rejoices in God, my savior.

Readings:

"So will it be with the resurrection of the dead. The body that is sown is perishable, it is raised imperishable; it is sown in dishonor, it is raised in glory; it is sown in weakness, it is raised in power; it is sown a natural body, it is raised a spiritual body." *1 Cor. 15:42–44 (NIV)*

"Then Jesus, being filled with the Holy Spirit, returned from the Jordan and was led by the Spirit into the wilderness, being tempted for forty days by the devil. And in those days He ate nothing, and afterward, when they had ended, He was hungry. And the devil said to Him, 'If You are the Son of God, command this stone to become bread.' But Jesus answered him, saying, 'It is written, *Man shall not live by bread alone, but by every word of God.*'" Lk. 4:1–4 (NKJV)

"Then out of them shall proceed thanksgiving. . . . I will multiply them, and they shall not diminish [and] I will also glorify them." Jer. 30:19 (NKJV)

OCTOBER 15 Teresa of Avila

The first woman to be honored with the title "Doctor of the Church," Teresa of Avila struggled many years before her vocation became clear to her. In her youth, she was attracted to romances and fashion. After reading Jerome's letters, and fearing that her very soul might be lost forever, she joined the Carmelites at Avila, which, at the time, had fallen into a very relaxed Rule. For many years, Teresa practiced a form of mental prayer that was the subject of much of her writing, and in 1555, she experienced a breakthrough, or powerful conversion. There seems to be no phenomenon peculiar to the mystical state that she did not experience—including raptures, visions, even levitation—yet she remained an able administrator, a shrewd businesswoman, and a prolific author. She eventually reformed her order so that it reflected the contemplative lifestyle she believed was inspired by Christ's presence in her life. She was destined to generally wage an uphill battle with Church authorities, who often questioned her inner voices and visions. In order to clear herself of the charge of being part of the Illumanati movement (the current heresy), she was commanded to write her *Autobiography*. The document was a great blessing for her sisters and for us; for it is a magnificent record detailing the dynamic transformation of a mystical soul.

Intercessory Prayer:

Dear St. Teresa, you instructed us to let nothing disturb us and recall always that all things are passing and the only constant in our lives that we can truly depend upon is God. You believed that "death was ecstasy"—a vivid knowledge and understanding that only through dying to self can we enter truly into a full and complete life with God our creator. Pray that we do not allow life's daily troubles and worries to bring despair into our lives. Inspire us to always feel God's loving presence in the midst of the anxieties and vexations of daily living. Amen.

Antiphon:

Those who put their trust in the Lord cannot be shaken.

Readings:

"It shall come to pass in the day the LORD gives you rest from your sorrow, and from your fear and the hard bondage in which you were made to serve." *Isa. 14:3 (NKJV)*

"Therefore gird up your minds, be sober, set your hope fully upon the grace that is coming to you at the revelation of Jesus Christ. As obedient children, do not be conformed to the passions of your former ignorance, but as he who called you is holy, be holy yourselves in all your conduct; since it is written 'You shall be holy, for I am holy.'" *1 Pet. 1:13–16 (RSV)*

"Jesus said to her, 'I am the resurrection and the life; he who believes in me, though he die, yet shall he live, and whoever lives and believes in me shall never die.'" *Jn. 11:25–26 (RSV)*

OCTOBER 16 Hedwig of Poland

Hedwig was born the youngest daughter of Louis I, King of Hungary, who was heir to the throne of Poland through his uncle King Casimir. She fell in love with William, duke of Austria, but she had to marry the prince of Lithuania, Jagiello, in 1382 in order to form a political alliance between Lithuania and Poland. She saw the marriage as a sacrifice for the greater good. With a resigned heart, she went to the cathedral at Kracow to pray for her beloved William, covered in dark dress and veil; then she left her veil on the crucifix as a sign of her resignation. As was common during this period, her new alliance caused mass conversions in Lithuania, beginning with Jagiello. Hedwig became a compassionate queen known for her charity and care for the poor. She was instrumental in working for the cause of unification between the Roman and Orthodox churches. She died shortly after giving birth, together with her first-born daughter; and miracles were reported at her tomb. Her feast day is celebrated on October 16 in Poland. Hedwig was beatified in 1986. In the revised calendar, she is celebrated on July 17.

Intercessory Prayer:

O Blessed Hedwig, you sacrificed the love of your heart for the good of your people and worked selflessly to unify your country. In all things, you trusted your Lord to guide you in the right path, and when you left this world, your true bridegroom greeted you with love. Intercede for us, O good and holy queen, that we may discern God's will in our lives and be vigilant to God's voice in all things. Pray with us for unity of the faith. Amen.

Antiphon:

A heart that is broken and humbled, God will not despise.

Readings:

"Behold how good and pleasant it is when the brethren dwell in unity!" *Psalm 133:1 (RSV)*

"I therefore, a prisoner for the Lord, beg you to lead a life worthy of the calling to which you have been called, with all lowliness and meekness, with patience, forbearing one another in love, eager to maintain the unity of the Spirit in the bond of peace. . . . For the equipment of the saints, for the work of the ministry, for edifying the body of Christ, until we all attain to the unity of the faith and of the knowledge of the Son of God." *Eph. 4:1–3, 12–13 (RSV)*

"It was not through law that Abraham and his offspring received the promise that he would be heir of the world, but through the righteousness that comes by faith." *Rom. 4:13 (NIV)*

OCTOBER 17 Margaret-Mary Alacoque

Although many Christian saints venerated Christ's heart as the perfect symbol of the love God showed in Jesus, it was Margaret-Mary Alacoque who found that her mission was to institute an actual feast devoted to the Sacred Heart. Born in 1647, her life was one of great affliction, which she saw as participation in

Christ's suffering body. She spent her early teenage years—from eleven to fifteen—in bed nearly paralyzed; however, when she made a vow to consecrate herself to the religious life, she was healed. She entered the Visitation convent at Paray, where she received a series of private revelations, which she felt—against much opposition—commissioned to recommend to the world. In her vision, Christ told her that the sacred love of his heart needed to be more welcomed in people's lives. Margaret-Mary lived in an age characterized both by lack of religious sentiment and by Jansenism, a heresy that taught that Christ saved only the predestined. Margaret-Mary's revelations convinced her of Christ's passionate love for sinners and his desire to save them through the mercies of his Sacred Heart. Through her, the devotion spread, along with the practice—now common to Roman Catholics throughout the world—of receiving communion on the first Fridays of nine months in reparation for the sins committed against his Sacred Heart. In 1765, seventy-five years after Margaret-Mary's death, Pope Clement XIII approved the feast of the Sacred Heart as a liturgical observance.

Prayer:

Beloved Lord, who has graciously given St. Margaret-Mary to the world as a great star in a time of bleak darkness, give us also the grace to shine like a beacon in a world plagued by sin and injustice, fear and terror. She was a servant who spent her life attempting to render the most perfect service to you. Make us likewise models of fearlessness and give us the strength we need to follow our inner calling. Help us to respond to the warmth of your love and to offer reparation to you for the coldness of humankind. Show us that where we seek your Sacred Heart, there we may find our true treasure. Amen.

Antiphon:

Jesus, to thee be glory given, who from thy heart does grace outpour.

Readings:

"For this is what the Sovereign LORD says: 'I myself will search for my sheep and look after them. As a shepherd looks after his scattered flock when he is with them, so will I look after my sheep. I will rescue them from all the places where they were scattered on a day of clouds and darkness. I will bring them out from the nations and gather them from the countries, and I will bring them into their own land.'" *Ez. 34:11–13 (NIV)*

"Take my yoke upon you and learn from me, for I am gentle and lowly in heart, and you will find rest for your souls. For my yoke is easy and my burden is light." *Mt. 11:28–29 (NKJV)*

"God can testify how I long for all of you with the affection of Christ Jesus. And this is my prayer: that your love may abound more and more in knowledge and depth of insight, so that you may be able to discern what is best and may be pure and blameless until the day of Christ." *Phil. 1:8–10 (NIV)*

OCTOBER 18 Anna Nitschmann

Anna Nitschmann was a Moravian girl who, at age fourteen, was appointed a chief eldress of her community. Moravianism, also called United Brethren, was an offshoot of the Hussites in Bohemia. This religious sect, which mainly populated the region of Moravia in Eastern Europe, was considered to be pacifistic and "radically pious." Anna's charisma was evident to her Herrnhut Community, where a group of Moravians were experiencing a religious revival. The whole group experienced a profound spiritual awakening after a communion service on August 13, 1727. In response to God's call, Anna helped organize an around-the-clock prayer vigil, which started on that day and continued for over a hundred years. She later became part of the Pilgrim congregation, a group of spiritual missionaries who traveled to America. Anna's ministry helped to found Bethlehem and Nazareth, Pennsylvania. She is noted for her hymns, more than thirty of which were printed in the Moravian's German hymnal. It was said that when Anna spoke or sang or prayed, all hearts stood open to her.

Prayer:

Eternal God, creator and preserver of all people, you blessed Anna Nitschmann with a deep awakening, and you shone through her and all her work. We, too, want to be awakened and open our hearts so your Spirit may flood our souls with light and life. Grant that by the Holy Spirit's indwelling, we may be enlightened and strengthened for your service, and renewed by a God whose wonder can never be comprehended. Amen.

Antiphon:

Eye has not seen, nor ear heard . . . the things which God has prepared for those who love him.

Readings:

"LORD, I cry out to You; Make haste to me! Give ear to my voice when I cry out to You. Let my prayer be set before You as incense, The lifting up of my hands as the evening sacrifice. Set a guard, O LORD, over my mouth; Keep watch over the door of my lips." *Psalm 141:1–3 (NKJV)*

"Take the helmet of salvation and the sword of the Spirit, which is the word of God. And pray in the Spirit on all occasions with all kinds of prayers and requests. With this in mind, be alert and always keep on praying for all the saints." *Eph. 6:17–18 (NIV)*

"I tell you the truth, if anyone says to this mountain, 'Go, throw yourself into the sea,' and does not doubt in his heart but believes that what he says will happen, it will be done for him." *Mk. 11:23 (NIV)*

OCTOBER 19 Bertilla Boscardin

Bertilla Boscardin was not the kind of woman who became known for any extraordinary mysticism or theological reflection. In Orthodoxy, she might have belonged to the class of saints known as holy fools, since her life was characterized by its utter simplicity. Possessing below-average intelligence and often called "goose," she grew up in an alcoholic family and suffered poor health. At an early age, she dedicated herself to working at the children's ward of a hospital on the front lines during World War I. Soon she began caring for wounded Italian soldiers, dauntlessly exposing herself to danger. When she died of cancer at age thirty-nine the crowds who flocked to her tomb where miracles were reported, lauded her as an angel of mercy. Pope John XXIII canonized Bertilla during his short pontificate. She serves as a model of compassion and silent heroism attainable by anyone who faithfully walks, as she did, her own little path with conviction. Bertilla is a patron of war veterans.

Prayer:

Heavenly King and Comforter, you emptied yourself and took the form of a lowly servant to participate in our humanity. Bertilla strove to imitate you in humility, and through her simple ministry, she served you in each person she met. Help us to realize that our defining moment is when we choose to live our lives for you. Amen.

Antiphon:

The gate is the Lord's; the just shall enter it.

Readings:

"Therefore if there is any consolation in Christ, if any comfort of love, if any fellowship of the Spirit, if any affection and mercy, fulfill my joy by being like-minded, having the same love, being of one accord, of one mind. Let nothing be done through selfish ambition or conceit. . . . Let each of you look out not only for [his] own interests, but also for the interests of others." *Phil. 2:1–5 (NKJV)*

"Blessed are the poor in spirit, for theirs is the kingdom of heaven.
Blessed are those who mourn, for they will be comforted.
Blessed are the meek, for they will inherit the earth.
Blessed are those who hunger and thirst for righteousness, for they will be filled.
Blessed are the merciful, for they will be shown mercy." *Mt. 5:3–7 (NIV)*

"Not unto us, O Lord, not unto us, but to your name give glory, for your mercy, and for your truth's sake." *Psalm 115:1 (KJV)*

OCTOBER 20 Matrona of Chios

St. Matrona was born in the fourteenth century on an Aegean island near Chios, the youngest of seven daughters. She was called Maria. When she reached marriageable age, she ran away and hid in the mountains. When her family found the missing girl, she requested her dowry, which included numerous vineyards, but insisted she would not marry. Her parents finally agreed, and she joined a small convent at Chora, the island's capital. Since the sisters there were very poor, Sister Matrona, who took her religious name from an early church martyr, sold her properties and built a large church and monastery. Matrona grew in holiness, which won for her the grace of working miracles, including raising the dead on at least one occasion. The incident occurred when foreign invaders besieged the city and convent, and an invader died within the monastery walls. Although, in Greece, all foreigners were considered barbarians, Matrona prayed for this barbarian and brought him back to life. The invaders were so astonished, they left. Matrona died October 20, 1357, and she was buried in the church she had built. Non-Christians as well as Christians visited her tomb, which became famous for its healings. The Greek hymnographer, Nikiforos, wrote twenty-four hymns to Matrona for the Divine Liturgy celebrated on her feast day.

Intercessory Prayer:

O St. Matrona, you desired to spend your life in service to your sisters and to all who crossed your path. As a ray of light from the unwavering light which is Christ, you worked miracles of healing for Christians and non-Christians alike. May we learn that our Lord wishes to raise up all people, for there are no foreigners or aliens in God's country. Amen.

Antiphon:

Who is like the Lord our God? . . . Who raises up the lowly from the dust?

Readings:

"All my bones shall say, 'LORD, who is like You, Delivering the poor from him who is too strong for [him], Yes, the poor and the needy from him who plunders him?'" *Psalm 35:10 (NKJV)*

"There is neither Jew nor Greek, slave nor free, male nor female, for you are all one in Christ Jesus." *Gal. 3:28 (NIV)*

"And my God will meet all your needs according to his glorious riches in Christ Jesus. . . . All the saints send you greetings. . . . The grace of the Lord Jesus Christ be with your spirit." *Phil. 4:19, 21–23 (NIV)*

OCTOBER 21 Josephine Leroux

Blessed Josephine Leroux was a martyr and Poor Clare who lived during the French Revolution. She entered the convent at age twenty-two, and when the religious were singled out for persecution, she was returned to her family. After the convent of the Poor Clares at Vilenciennes was destroyed, she went to live with the Ursulines. She insisted, however, on publicly proclaiming herself a nun, which led to her arrest and death. When her captors came to arrest her, she was unperturbed and allowed herself to be taken to prison—after serving them refreshments. At the scaffold, she kissed the hand of her executioner before placing her head on the block. The old Franciscan calendar celebrated Josephine's feast on October 21, after Pope Benedict XV proclaimed her blessed.

Intercessory Prayer:

O Blessed Josephine, you proclaimed before your death that no one could fear to leave this place of exile if they understood the beauty of paradise. Pray for those who suffer imprisonment and martyrdom throughout the world, that they may be sustained by the grace of Christ's endurance and love. May the spirit of the cross sustain us during our darkest hours, through Jesus Christ our Lord. Amen.

Antiphon:

God arose in judgment to save the oppressed on earth.

Readings:

"Make haste, O God, to deliver me! Make haste to help me, O LORD! Let them be ashamed and confounded who seek my life; Let them be turned back and confused who desire my hurt. Let all those who seek You rejoice and be glad in You; And let those who love Your salvation say continually, 'Let God be magnified!'" *Psalm 70:1–4 (NKJV)*

"Then he said, 'Jesus, remember me when you come into your kingdom.' Jesus answered him, 'I tell you the truth, today you will be with me in paradise.'" *Lk. 23:42–43 (NIV)*

"[He] who has an ear, let him hear what the Spirit says to the churches. To [him] who overcomes I will give to eat from the tree of life, which is in the midst of the Paradise of God.'" *Rev. 2:7 (NKJV)*

OCTOBER 22 Ursula and Her Companions

The legend of Ursula and her companions was extremely popular throughout the medieval era, when it reached its final form in the *Golden Legend*. According to the story, the son of a great pagan king asked for Ursula in marriage. She was given three years of freedom, during which time she set sail with eleven thousand female companions. The eleven thousand were no doubt eleven (with their own servants and companions); the exaggeration was due to a misreading of Roman numerals and letters. Committed to her band of virgins, Ursula refused to return to the pagan king. Various interpretations of the story place her on a pilgrimage up the Rhine, or in Rome, where she met the pope. The women were all martyred in Cologne by the Huns. In 1155, a vast collection of bones found at Cologne was identified as the holy virgins' relics. Elizabeth of Schonau's revelations (see Daily Readings, June 18, Elizabeth of Schonau) gave support to the cult. In 1969, the feast was removed from the Roman calendar. Prior to that, Ursula was celebrated in various liturgical texts, calendars, and litanies; an order called the Ursulines was even named after her. Ursula is pictured in art with a bow and arrow, or else sheltering her maidens under her mantle.

Prayer:

Beloved Lord Jesus, the story of Ursula and her companions reminds us that some women feel the need to belong to no man because you are the center of their lives. Penetrate and possess us with your presence, so our lives may belong to you so perfectly that we are but a ray of your divine radiance. Your radiance is at the heart of the Christian mystery, and to that mystery we shall always return. Amen.

Antiphon:

Soul of Christ, sanctify me.

Readings:

"You O Lord, are the Most High over all the earth, exalted far above all gods. The Lord loves those who hate evil; you guard the lives of your saints; you deliver them from wickedness. Light dawns for the just and joy for the upright of heart." *Psalm 97:8–11 (PCB)*

"Scarcely had I passed them when I found the one my heart loves. . . . Daughters of Jerusalem, I charge you by the gazelles and by the does of the field: Do not arouse or awaken love until it so desires." *Song of Songs:3:4–5 (NIV)*

"I have set you an example that you should do as I have done for you." *Jn. 13:15 (NIV)*

OCTOBER 23 Mary Clotilde and Her Companions

Mother Mary Clotilde and a number of other Ursuline nuns lived during the dangerously turbulent era of the French Revolution. It was a time in history when the Catholic Church was particularly and brutally persecuted, especially those who had dedicated their lives to Christ through the religious life. Mary Clotilde and a group of over thirty Ursuline sisters were driven out of their convent and forced to seek refuge in Belgium. After returning to their convent in Valenciennes, the French reentered the town and the group was confined to stay within their convent walls, labeled as traitors and fanatics. While many of the sisters were eventually able to escape their persecutors, Mother Mary and nine other Ursuline sisters were arrested and put to death by the guillotine in 1794. The holy group of women who lost their lives that day is commemorated under the title of Blessed Mary Clotilde and Her Companions.

Prayer:

> *Dear Heavenly Father, you have granted that the seeds of the Church be nourished with the blood of holy martyrs throughout history. Blessed Mary Clotilde and Her Companions were a group of brave women who paid the ultimate price for loving and preaching the faith. As you bestowed immense glory upon these holy virgin martyrs through their death, allow their example to inspire us to live our own lives in a way worthy of being called a Christian. Amen.*

Antiphon:

And I thank him who has given me strength for this, Christ Jesus our Lord, because he judged me faithful.

Readings:

"For the righteous will never be moved; they will be remembered forever. They are not afraid of evil tidings; their heart is firm trusting in the Lord. . . . They will not be afraid. . . . The desire of the wicked man comes to nought." *Psalm 112:6–8, 10 (RSV)*

"May the God of peace himself sanctify you wholly; and may your spirit and soul and body be kept sound and blameless at the coming of our Lord Jesus Christ. He who calls you is faithful and he will do it." *1 Thess. 5:22–24 (RSV)*

"Rejoice in your hope, be patient in tribulation, be constant in prayer. Contribute to the needs of the saints, practice hospitality. Bless those who persecute you; bless and do not curse them." *Rom. 12:12–14 (RSV)*

OCTOBER 24 *Joy of All Who Sorrow Icon*

Joy of All Who Sorrow is a rare type of icon that originally depicted the Theotokos without Christ. A nineteenth-century icon of this type now includes Jesus in her arms. The *Joy of All Who Sorrow* type pictures Mary standing majestically over hundreds of mourners, the afflicted and homeless taking refuge beneath her sweeping bright red veil. Her dress is black. She extends a hand in blessing. The icon has been a miracle worker for numerous severe or incurable diseases in Russia since 1688, and it is particularly appealed to for strokes, tuberculosis, and muscle and throat disorders. In 1888, Mary was glorified in a special way in the image at St. Petersburg, when lightning struck the chapel where it was housed. Growing dark and obscure from centuries of candle soot and travels, the icon was nonetheless found lying face down on the floor after the lightning flash, and when it was turned over the colors were found to be restored, appearing new, clear, and bright. The icon's fame continued to spread, and it remains a favorite icon of the poor and oppressed in Russia today. The feast of *Joy of All Who Sorrow* is also celebrated on June 24.

Prayer:

Lord Jesus, through the prayers of your most holy mother, grant us mercy and hope in our lives, for she is the bush unconsumed who brought forth the freedom and salvation of our souls. The holy icon Joy of All Who Sorrow *reminds us that our lives, dark as they might sometimes seem, can shine with a new light when you send us her comforting presence. Through the power of Mary's intercession, may we be guided into rich mystical contemplation when we behold the images of you and your beloved mother. Amen.*

Antiphon:

The mother of God is exalted above the choirs of angels.

Readings:

"And the Angel of the LORD appeared to him in a flame of fire from the midst of a bush. So he looked, and behold, the bush was burning with fire, but the bush *was* not consumed. Then Moses said, 'I will now turn aside and see this great sight, why the bush does not burn.' So when the LORD saw that he turned aside to look, God called to him from the midst of the bush and said, 'Moses, Moses!' And he said, 'here I am.' Then He said, 'Do not draw near this place. Take your sandals off your feet, for the place where you stand *is* holy ground.'" *Ex. 3:2–6 (NKJV)*

"Who is like the LORD our God, Who dwells on high, Who humbles Himself to behold the things that are in the heavens and in the earth? Who raises the poor out of the dust, And lifts the needy out of the ash heap . . . [Who] grants the barren woman a home, Like a joyful mother of children." *Psalm 119:5–9 (NKJV)*

"For you who are mighty, have made me great.
Most holy is your Name.
Your mercy is upon those who fear you
Throughout all generations.
You have shown strength with your arm,
You have scattered the proud in their conceit.
You have put down the mighty from their seat
And have lifted up the powerless." *Lk. 1:49–52 (PCB)*

OCTOBER 25 Tabitha and Daria

On this day we commemorate two devout and holy women saints from the early Church. St. Tabitha is also referred to in sacred Scripture as Dorcas. We learn about Tabitha directly from the Acts of the Apostles. She is described as being a woman "full of good works and almsdeeds" (Acts 9:34–40), and so she is sometimes referred to as St. Tabitha, the Almsgiver. She died suddenly of an illness, and St. Peter, kneeling next to her body, prayed over it and spoke, "Tabitha, arise!" and she was raised from the dead. This miracle became known throughout the Joppa region and caused the conversion of many souls. In the Eastern churches, Tabitha is celebrated as a devoted disciple.

St. Daria lived in the late third century during the time that Romans persecuted Christians. Daria was originally a pagan priestess; however, when she married Chrysanthus, a devout Christian evangelizer, she converted to Christianity. The holy couple preached the Gospel fearlessly and converted many. They were finally arrested, suffered numerous tortures, and were martyred by being buried alive. In the East, Daria's feast day is on March 19.

Prayer:

Beloved Jesus, the holy women St. Tabitha and St. Daria both gave witness to your call to preach the Gospel fearlessly. St. Tabitha was given the priceless gift of being returned to life as an early testament and witness to the truth and authenticity of Christianity. St. Daria gave the ultimate price of her own life in order to accomplish this mission. Let us be inspired by the witness given by these two holy women so we can follow your call to evangelize within our own daily circle of friends, neighbors, and acquaintances. May we emulate their courage and bravery to live and preach Christ's Gospel. Amen.

Antiphon:

You are my hope, my trust from the days of my youth.

Readings:

"Why should the nations say, 'Where is their God?' Our God is in the heavens; he does whatever he pleases. Their idols are silver and gold, the work of men's hands. They have mouths, but do not speak; eyes, but do not see. . . . Those who make them are like them; so are all who trust in them." *Psalm 115:2–5, 8 (RSV)*

"Jesus said unto him, Thou shalt love the Lord thy God with all thy heart, and with all thy soul, and with all thy mind. This is the first and great commandment. And the second is like unto it, Thou shalt love thy neighbor as thyself. On these two commandments hang all the law and the prophets." *Mt. 22:37–40 (KJV)*

"I will pray my vows to the Lord in the courts of the house of the Lord, in your midst, O Jerusalem, Praise the Lord!" *Psalm 116:18–19 (RSV)*

OCTOBER 26 Mother Angelina

Born into Orthodox aristocracy in 1809, Aleksandra Shnakova married at an early age to a noble Baltic Russian who was a Lutheran. Although there were religious differences, they had a deep affection for one another and waited twenty-three years for their first child, Mariia. They lost her a year later, and Aleksandra, in deep grief, turned to a strict ascetic life. She ate only a bowl of porridge a day, which shocked even the servants. Eventually, her husband converted to Orthodoxy, taking the name Nikolai. They began a ministry dedicated to the poor and impoverished, and they purchased land for a monastery that would go to the partner left when one of them died. Nikolai died first and, at nearly fifty, Aleksandra built a women's religious community at Tvorozhkora. She was finally tonsured as Mother Angelina, and the community supported themselves by working the land, with an orphanage attached to the convent. Every night, in addition to the Daily Office, Mother Angelina recited the Akathists to Our Lord and the Mother of God, and she was once heard to say, "As the body demands food, so the soul can't live without prayer." Mother Angelina died revered by all her sisters and was known as a soul who transformed all who crossed her path.

Prayer:

Lord Jesus, you alone make us whole when we have been broken by the sufferings of this life. You blessed holy Angelina with two kinds of families, and she did her best to glorify you in her roles as wife, mother, and abbess. She only wanted to be molded into a deeper

image of you, and she mirrored you in her tenderness for others.
Teach us the hidden wisdom that is able to bear the scourges of
life and transform them into grace for others. Amen.

Antiphon:

If my delight had not been in your law, I would have
perished in my affliction.

Readings:

"[Man] born of woman is of few days and full of trouble. He springs
up like a flower and withers away; like a fleeting shadow, he does
not endure. . . . At least there is hope for a tree: if it is cut down,
it will sprout again, and its new shoots will not fail. Its roots may
grow old in the ground and its stump die in the soil . . . at the
scent of water it will bud and put forth shoots like a plant." *Job
14:1–2, 7–9 (NIV)*

"Do all things without complaining and disputing, that you may become blameless and harmless, children of God without fault in the
midst of a crooked and perverse generation, among whom you
shine as lights in the world." *Phil. 2:14–15 (NKJV)*

"But now I urge you to keep up your courage, because not one of
you will be lost." *Acts 27:22 (NIV)*

OCTOBER 27 Ruth

Ruth, the Old Testament heroine who was King David's
great-grandmother, is glorified as a saint in the Eastern
Church, much like Miriam and Sarah. Matriarchs in the
Torah each have a special place in the unfolding of God's plan. The
Book of Ruth narrates the story of two women (Ruth and her
mother-in-law, Naomi) and their steadfast love. It tells of their journey from Moab, after the deaths of their husbands, back to Naomi's
homeland, Bethlehem. A Moabite, Ruth presumably had her own culture and her own gods. Yet when they are both left widows and
Naomi decides to return to her own people, Ruth utters her famous
words of dedication, "Where you go, I will go. . . . Your people shall
be my people and your God my God" (Ruth 1:6). So Ruth goes forth,
foreign, childless, widowed, into a land whose inhabitants despise the
Moabites. Yet she was graced there: she was led to Boaz, who offered

the women support and then married Ruth. Ruth, like Hagar (see Daily Readings, January 22, Sarah and Hagar), is another heroine for the marginalized woman. The relationship between Ruth and Naomi demonstrates the strength, endurance, and faithfulness women can find—indeed, have always found—in one another.

Prayer:

Beloved Holy Spirit, Ruth felt the mystery of the Hebrew Yahweh calling her and, in responding, she found her pearl of great price. We thank you for your indwelling presence, which dissolves distinctions of race, color, or creed; and offers us a vision of your radiant light. Like our ancient ancestors, we glorify you because in your gracious mercy, you cause us to remember your wonderful works. Amen.

Antiphon:

Remember your covenant with us because we are your people and you are our God.

Readings:

"And she said, 'Look, your sister-in-law has gone back to her people and to her gods; return after your sister-in-law.' But Ruth said: 'Entreat me not to leave you, *Or to* turn back from following after you; For wherever you go, I will go; And wherever you lodge, I will lodge; Your people *shall be* my people, and your God, my God. Where you die, I will die, and there will I be buried. The LORD do so to me, and more also.'" *Ruth 1:15–17 (NKJV)*

"[My] dove, my perfect one, is unique, the only daughter of her mother, the favorite of the one who bore her. The maidens saw her and called her blessed." *Song of Songs 6:9 (NIV)*

"If you, being a Jew, live like the Gentiles and not like the Jews, how is it that you compel the Gentiles to live like Jews?" *Gal. 2:14 (NASB)*

OCTOBER 28 Frideswide

 St. Frideswide was born in the seventh century, the daughter of a Mercian prince. Her father owned extensive property, including the upper Thames area. Frideswide was brought up by a governess, and from an early age, she had a desire for the religious life. It was said that her motto from childhood was "Whatsoever is not God is nothing." Determined to remain a virgin, Frideswide fled the advances of Prince Alfgar, who insisted that she marry him. She hid herself for three years in a cell in Thornberry Wood near the site of a healing well. The legend is that because he made unwelcome advances toward her, Alfgar was temporarily blinded. Once he gave up his pursuit of Frideswide, his sight was restored. Frideswide eventually established a thriving double monastery, St. Mary Benedictine in the village of Binsey, which became the heart of the town of Oxford. She lived there until her death in 735, and her monastery became a prominent landmark in Oxford. The archbishop of Canterbury performed a great public ceremony in 1180 when Frideswide's remains were translated to another shrine. Her tomb was the site of many miracles and became one of the principal shrines in England. Frideswide was named the patroness of Oxford University in 1440. Oxford held feasts in her honor twice a year, when many came to venerate her relics. It was said that Henry II avoided visiting Oxford for fear of being blinded.

Prayer:

O Lord of all hopefulness, St. Frideswide knew that only in your voice could she know true contentment. May your presence be the healing balm of our lives, as we anticipate the precious growth of your love in our every action. Bless all those who are blind, that their inner eye may ever be turned on you. Amen.

Antiphon:

Lead me gently to thy wounded sacred feet.

Readings:

"The memory of the righteous will be a blessing, but the name of the wicked will rot." *Prov. 10:7 (NIV)*

"What goes into a man's mouth does not make him unclean, but what comes out of his mouth, that is what makes him unclean. . . . Every plant that my heavenly Father has not planted will be pulled up by the roots." *Mt. 15:11, 13 (NIV)*

"Do not love the world or the things in the world . . . for all that is in the world . . . is not of the Father . . . And the world is passing away . . . but he who does the will of God abides forever." *1 Jn. 2:16–17 (NKJV)*

OCTOBER 29 Amelia Bloomer

Amelia Bloomer was a revolutionary figure born in 1818 in Seneca Falls, New York. She spent her life working for the rights of women and blacks, campaigning for justice with a Bible in her hand. Instrumental in starting the first Episcopal Church in Council Bluffs, Iowa, she hosted many missionaries, including the famed Jackson Kemper. Working tirelessly for women's emancipation, she was never able to vote. Her writings include a critique of Paul's Letter to the Corinthians, wherein he admonishes women to keep silent in church (Cor. 14:34), and a reinterpretation of the Garden of Eden story, wherein Eve is no longer cast as carrying the principal blame for man's sins. Amelia published the first newspaper devoted to women's issues, called *The Lily*, which was also the first paper in this country that a woman owned.

Prayer:

Dear Lord, you planted the seeds of freedom in the heart of Amelia Bloomer when she wrote: ". . . the same Power that brought the slave out of bondage will, in his own good time and way, bring about the emancipation of woman and make her the equal in dominion that she was in the beginning." You treated women in your own life with radical equality and full discipleship. Help those who struggle in our world with the warring turbulence that still exists between the sexes, and lead us to true freedom in you. Amen.

Antiphon:

And you shall know the truth, and the truth shall set you free.

Readings:

"But I will deliver you on that day, says the Lord, and you shall not be given into the hands of the men of whom you are afraid." *Jer. 39:17 (RSV)*

"And the kingdom and the dominion and the greatness of the kingdoms under the whole heaven shall be given to the people of the saints of the Most High; their kingdom shall be an everlasting kingdom, and all dominions shall serve and obey them." *Dan. 7:27 (RSV)*

"Love the Lord, all you his saints! The Lord preserves the faithful, but abundantly requites him who acts haughtily. Be strong, and let your heart take courage, all you who wait for the Lord." *Psalm 31:23–24 (RSV)*

OCTOBER 30 Dorothy of Montau

 Born near Prussia, Germany, in 1347, Dorothy of Montau was never officially canonized, but she was highly venerated in much of Europe. She experienced many ecstasies and visions, most of which occurred in the latter part of her life. She married early and bore nine children, but she had an unhappy marriage, with hints of abuse. She made a pilgrimage to Rome at age forty-four, and her husband died in her absence. Dorothy then went to the Church of the Teutonic Knights and walled herself in as an anchoress, with an open window to the chapel where the Blessed Sacrament was exposed all day. Soon she developed a reputation as a spiritual director, including counseling her own confessor, who documented her visions and her life. Her name means "gift of God." She is often pictured with a lantern and rosary. Dorothy is the patron of Prussia.

Prayer:

Gracious Jesus, through Dorothy's intercession, help us to cut the chains that bind us to the suffering that springs from the inability to see the love you hold out to us continually. Like her, help us to find you at the source of everything that happens in our lives. All that our hearts desire, we seek to give to you. May we ever respond to your love with the declaration: Here I am, Lord. Amen.

Antiphon:

This is the day our God has made: Let us rejoice in praise!

Readings:

"O Lord, who shall visit your tent? Who shall dwell on your holy mountain?
They who walk blamelessly and do what is right:
Who speak the truth from their hearts, and do not slander with their tongues." *Psalm 15:1–3 (PCB)*

"The glory of Lebanon will come to you, the pine, the fir and the cypress together, to adorn the place of my sanctuary; and I will glorify the place of my feet." *Isa. 60:13 (NIV)*

"I have many things to say and to judge concerning you, but he who sent me is true; and I speak to the world those things which I heard from him." *Jn. 8:26 (NKJV)*

OCTOBER 31 Agneta Chang

Agneta Chang was a Korean-born nun who died a martyr in 1950. She was one of the first Koreans to join the Maryknoll Sisters to do missionary work in her own country. In her desire to aid her own people, she helped to develop the first Korean women's community, called the Sisters of Our Lady of Perpetual Help. After World War II ended, she was trapped north of the thirty-eighth parallel, where Soviet troops were arresting and murdering priests and nuns. She was last seen on October 4, 1950, when she was abducted by soldiers who later shot her. Her body and those of several of her sisters were subsequently found in a ditch. As she was being separated from her community, Agneta's last words were, "Lord have mercy on us."

Intercessory Prayer:

Agneta, holy virgin of God, your life was a testament to the goodness of a God who continually makes known to the world the power of perfect trust in him. Help us to grow in the holiness and devotion that were the foundation of your life, that we may receive mercy and strength in our lives. You who shone with the determination of your most deeply held principles, pray for us in following ours. Amen.

Antiphon:

Hope in God! For I shall again be thankful, in the presence of my savior and my God.

Readings:

"I will say to God my Rock, 'Why have You forgotten me? Why do I go mourning because of the oppression of the enemy?' As with a breaking of my bones, My enemies reproach me, While they say to me all day long, 'Where is your God?' Why are you cast down, O my soul? And why are you disquieted within me? Hope in God; For I shall yet praise Him, the help of my countenance and my God." *Psalm 42:9–12 (NKJV)*

"We ought always to thank God for you . . . and rightly so, because your faith is growing more and more, and the love every one of you has for each other is increasing. Therefore, among God's churches we boast about your perseverance and faith in all the persecutions and trials you are enduring. All this is evidence that God's judgment is right, and as a result you will be counted worthy of the kingdom of God, for which you are suffering." *2 Thess. 1:3–6 (NIV)*

"I know your deeds. See, I have placed before you an open door that no one can shut. I know that you have little strength, yet you have kept my word and have not denied my name." *Rev. 3:8 (NIV)*

NOVEMBER 1 Frances of the Redemption

Frances of the Redemption, a modern mystic soul, was born on November 1, 1947, in Germany during the French occupation. She was not raised in a particular religious tradition, but as a young teen, she became interested in religion classes, and a military chaplain baptized her later when she followed the French Army into Algeria. Frances became a world traveler, later studying different cultures in Australia and the Far East. While praying on an island near Hong Kong, she had her first mystical experience, where she felt God's presence within her so intensely that she wondered whether the temple of her body could contain such explosive power and love. Awed and somewhat overwhelmed by her experience, she decided to seek a contemplative lifestyle where she could better understand and deepen her mystical union with God. Frances entered a Carmelite convent in India, where she died a few years later at age thirty-two.

Prayer:

Beloved Jesus, when Sister Frances came to know you, she fell in love with you, and you captured her heart forever. Once she tasted you, she wanted only to find a solitary place where her soul could be engulfed in your secret abyss. Guide our feet to an ever closer walk with you. May we always be inspired to direct the arrow of our own will toward the love of your tender heart, and in the roaring fire of that passion, find our small selves consumed. Amen.

Antiphon:

Send forth your Spirit and enkindle in us the fire of your love.

Readings:

"You shall guide me with your counsel, and afterward receive me to glory.
Whom have I in heaven but you? And there is none upon earth that I desire but you.
My flesh and my heart fails; but God is the strength of my heart, and my portion forever. . . . It is good for me to draw near to God; I have put my trust in the Lord God." *Psalm 73:24–28 (KJV)*

"And after six days Jesus took with him Peter and James and John, and led them up into a high mountain apart by themselves and he was transfigured before them. And his raiment became shining, exceeding white as snow." *Mk. 9:2–3 (KJV)*

"Now the Lord is the Spirit, and where the Spirit of the Lord is, there is liberty. But we all, with unveiled face, beholding as in a mirror the glory of the Lord, are being transformed into the same image from glory to glory, just as from the Lord, the Spirit." *2 Cor. 3:17–18 (NASB)*

NOVEMBER 2 Ebbe

St. Ebbe was a friend and follower of St. Aidan. Ebbe's half-brother, King Oswald of Northumbria, requested a new abbot from the community at Iona to convert the Northumbrians; Oswald had converted to Christianity during his exile in Iona. Aidan replaced the previous abbot, Colman, who was disenchanted with the English, finding them barbaric and unable to obey his severe monastic rule. Aidan was well-received by the Northumbrians. Ebbe became a nun at the double monastery in Coldingham and eventually became its abbess. Over the years, the community of nuns at Coldingham, which consisted primarily of aristocratic women, had grown lax.

They wove fine garments for themselves and were said to befriend men, living the "high life" instead of a life of contemplation, prayer, and study. Ebbe attempted to remedy the situation, and it improved until her death in 683. In 686 the monastery burned to the ground. Ebbe was remembered as a wise and holy woman, and her name was given to various sites in Northumbria. The discovery of her relics in the late eleventh century led to a resurgence of interest and devotion to her in the following centuries. A church and a street in Oxford are named after Ebbe.

Prayer:

O God of all holiness and truth, St. Ebbe was a faithful servant of your Word who understood that your love was extravagant. Help us not to search for extravagance in worldly beauty, but to recall always that simplicity combined with an eager heart opens the door to the abundance of your love. Amen.

Antiphon:

Let us praise your name, O God, for only your name is exalted.

Readings:

"But I am afflicted and in pain; may Your salvation, O God, set me securely on high.
I will praise the name of God with song and magnify Him with thanksgiving.
And it will please the LORD better than an ox or a young bull with horns and hoofs. The humble have seen it and are glad; you who seek God, let your heart revive. For the LORD hears the needy and does not despise His who are prisoners. Let heaven and earth praise Him, the seas and everything that moves in them." *Psalm 69:30–35 (NASB)*

"Early in the morning He came again into the temple, and all the people were coming to Him; and He sat down and began to teach them." *Jn. 8:2 (NASB)*

"Grace and peace be multiplied unto you through the knowledge of God, and of Jesus Christ . . . whereby are given to us exceeding great and precious promises; that by these we might be partakers of the divine nature, having escaped the corruption that is in the world through lust." *2 Pet. 1:2, 4 (KJV)*

NOVEMBER 3 Fanny Crosby

Fanny Crosby is often called the "Queen of American Hymn Writers." Born into a Puritan family in 1820, she wrote more than nine thousand hymns during her lifetime. When she was very young, an eye infection caused her to go blind. Raised by her grandmother, Fanny learned about the world through her grandmother's eyes and was nourished by her spirit. Her grandmother's landlady helped Fanny, who had developed an astonishing memory, memorize the Bible. At age eight, she composed her first verse, and at age twelve, she went to the New York Institute for the Blind. She learned harp and piano and developed a beautiful soprano voice. Whenever Fanny wrote a hymn, she invoked God's grace and guidance. Much of her poetry was dedicated to the urban poor who were a focus of Fanny's speaking engagements and missionary work. Until her death in 1915, Fanny sought to witness, wherever she could, to the light of God's Word.

Prayer:

Beloved Lord of all hearts, you showed your love for your daughter, Fanny Crosby, by filling her soul with your joy. Although her eyes could not see your beautiful world, her soul merged, like a bird, with the bright air and flew heavenward with glorious songs of love. Help us, through her inspiration, remember to use all our senses in our worship of you and to lift our hearts and our voices in thanksgiving for your bountiful blessings in our lives. Amen.

Antiphon:

I will exalt you, O Lord, because you have lifted me up.

Readings:

"Is it not yet just a little while before Lebanon will be turned into a fertile field, and the fertile field will be considered as a forest? On that day the deaf will hear words of a book, and out of their gloom and darkness the eyes of the blind will see." *Isa. 29:17–18 (NASB)*

"I will sing of the lovingkindness of the LORD forever; to all generations I will make known Your faithfulness with my mouth. . . . The heavens will praise Your wonders, O LORD; Your faithfulness also in the assembly of the holy ones. . . . For who in the skies is comparable to the LORD? Who among the sons of the mighty is like the LORD?" *Psalm 89:1, 5, 6 (NASB)*

"Let the word of Christ richly dwell within you, with all wisdom teaching and admonishing one another with psalms and hymns and spiritual songs, singing with thankfulness in your hearts to God." Col. 3:16 (NASB)

NOVEMBER 4 Winefride

Winefride, or Gwenfrewi, was a Welsh saint who lived in the seventh century. Her father, Tefydd, was a local prince, and her mother, Gwenlo, was the sister of St. Bueno, who played a major role in Winefride's life. Winefride had a very strong attraction to the spiritual life at an early age, and she was sent to study with her uncle Bueno. Her family supported her decision not to marry, but Caradog, a local chieftain, pursued her relentlessly. Her legend relates that once, while attempting to flee from him, Caradog struck her with his sword, nearly beheading her in an angry fury. Through his healing hand and fervent prayers, her uncle Bueno nursed Winefride back to health. All that remained was a scar on her neck. In the place where her head was reputed to have fallen, a spring emerged with pebbles at the bottom stained red from her blood. The spring, Holywell, is one of the few sacred places in the British Isles that has been a continual pilgrimage site since the seventh century. Even the Protestant Reformation did not interrupt worship there. Winefride eventually established a double monastery at Gwytherin, some twenty miles from Holywell, under Bueno's direction. Winefride died in 650, after serving for fifteen years in her monastery, where she was well-loved and known for her great sanctity.

Prayer:

Holy God, we know that neither life nor death nor anything in this world can separate us from Christ's love. Winefride's story reflects the universal themes of wounding, healing, and resurrection, as important now as in the seventh century. We thank you for eternally saving us through the blood of Jesus, who delivers us from the powers of darkness, now and for all the ages to come. Amen.

Antiphon:

He is the beginning, the firstborn from the dead.

Readings:

"They will not hunger or thirst, nor will the scorching heat or sun strike them down; for He who has compassion on them will lead them and will guide them to springs of water." *Isa. 49:10 (NASB)*

"But whoever drinks of the water that I will give him shall never thirst; but the water that I will give him will become in him a well of water springing up to eternal life." *Jn. 4:14 (NASB)*

"And I saw thrones, and they sat upon them, and judgment was given to them: and I saw the souls of them that were beheaded for the witness of Jesus." *Rev. 20:4 (KJV)*

NOVEMBER 5 Elizabeth

The story of St. Elizabeth, the Blessed Virgin Mary's cousin, is chronicled in Luke. Elizabeth was married to Zachary, who was a priest at the temple. The two had remained barren for many years, until an angel of the Lord appeared to Zachary and informed him that Elizabeth would become pregnant and that the child she would bring forth would be a precursor to the Messiah. When the Blessed Virgin received word from the archangel Gabriel at the Annunciation that she would become the mother of the Messiah, she also was told of the news regarding Elizabeth's future prophet-child, and she made the trip to the hill country to be with her cousin. As Mary entered into Elizabeth's home, the baby within her womb "leapt for joy," and Elizabeth announced the words so often repeated in the Hail Mary, ". . . blessed art thou among women!" Luke records that Mary responded to Elizabeth's praises with her own beautiful prayer of praise to God—the Magnificat. St. Elizabeth is often invoked by women who are having difficulty achieving a pregnancy, and especially by older women who wish to have the blessing of children.

Intercessory Prayer:

Dear St. Elizabeth, you were the first to recognize the Messiah's presence and to sing praises to the Virgin Mary, the Mother of God. You suffered the anguish of infertility for many years, and you know the pain that results when a loving couple desires the blessings of children but are unable to achieve that dream. Please intercede for all infertile couples today as they struggle to accept their particular cross of Christ. May we be inspired to see the value of human life in the womb, just as your son, John the Baptist, recognized the Messiah from within his mother's blessed womb and leapt for joy. Amen.

Antiphon:

He who descended is the very one who ascended . . . that he might fill all with his gifts.

Readings:

"We give thanks to you, for you are good, and your steadfast love endures forever.

Let the descendants of Israel say: your steadfast love endures forever.

Let the descendants of Aaron say: your steadfast love endures forever.

Let those who fear you say: your steadfast love endures forever." *Psalm 118:1–5 (PCB)*

"So Boaz took Ruth, and she was his wife; and when he went to her, the Lord gave her a conception, and she bore a son. And the women said to Naomi, 'Blessed be the Lord, who has not left you this day without a kinsman, that his name shall be famous in Israel. And he shall be for you a restorer of your life, and a nourisher of your old age.'" *Ruth 4:13–15 (KJV)*

"And Hannah prayed and said, 'My heart rejoices in the Lord, my horn is exhaled in the Lord, my mouth is enlarged over my enemies, because I rejoice in your salvation. . . . He raises the poor out of the dust, and lifts the beggar from the dunghill to make them princes and to make them inherit the throne of glory.'" *1 Sam. 2:1–2, 8 (KJV)*

"For behold, when the sound of your greeting reached my ears, the baby leaped in my womb for joy." *Lk. 1:44 (NASB)*

NOVEMBER 6 Adrienne von Speyr

On November 6 we celebrate Adrienne von Speyr, a modern saintly woman who was a wife and mother, a doctor, a mystic, and a woman of profound theological writings. Adrienne was a Swiss Protestant who was born in 1902. After experiencing total rejection from her mother, she spent her childhood developing an intense relationship with God. She resisted the convention of her era and desired to become a doctor. Despite illnesses, she achieved her goal. She married a widowed history professor and lovingly accepted his children as her own. Adrienne was a compassionate doctor who cared for the poor without demanding pay, and she persuaded hundreds of pregnant women not to have abortions. Her life changed dramatically when she became friends with a prominent Swiss theologian priest named Fr. Hans Urs von Balthasar, and she converted to Catholicism. She began having mystical experiences, which resulted in rich theological writings and meditations, later edited by von Balthasar. Adrienne eventually founded a lay secular institute dedicated to the Blessed Virgin. She died at age sixty-five, leaving behind an amazing collection of spiritual works. Adrienne has been declared one of the most outstanding theological writers of our century.

Intercessory Prayer:

Heavenly Father, even in our own century you have blessed us with holy women who answer your call and serve our Church in profound and amazing ways. Adrienne instructed us to be pure, have a good disposition, and joyfully fulfill what God's service requires. Let us look for opportunities each day to live such simple words of virtue. Amen.

Antiphon:

The testimony of the Lord is sure, making wise the simple.

Readings:

"Thus says the LORD, the God of Israel, 'Write all the words which I have spoken to you in a book.'" *Jer. 30:2 (NASB)*

"As He spoke to me the Spirit entered me and set me on my feet; and I heard Him speaking to me . . . do not be rebellious like that rebellious house. Open your mouth and eat what I am giving you." *Ez. 2:2, 8 (NASB)*

"The Law of the Lord is perfect, converting the soul: the testimony of the Lord is sure, making wise the simple." *Psalm 19:7 (KJV)*

"I was in the Spirit on the Lord's day, and I heard behind me a loud voice like the sound of a trumpet, saying, 'Write in a book what you see, and send it to the seven churches.'" *Rev. 1:10–11 (NASB)*

NOVEMBER 7 Ann Worchester Robertson

Ann Eliza Worchester was born into a missionary family in Tennessee in 1826. Her family was Congregationalist, and her father was a minister. They worked principally with the Cherokees. She attended an academy in Vermont, then went to initiate missions in Oklahoma, where she met her husband, William Robertson, a Presbyterian minister. Ann and William taught school and began translating biblical texts into the language of the Creek Nation. They raised four children before William died tragically in a fire in 1880 at the school they had founded. Ann was destined to complete her mission in life and lived for another twenty-five years. She went to live with her daughter Alice Robertson, whom Ann had raised to be an independent woman with her own charisma; Alice was the second woman ever elected to the U.S. Congress. Ann continued her lifelong work of translating the Bible and was granted an honorary doctorate for her work, which she completed before her death in 1905.

Prayer:

> *Almighty God, in your expansive love, you raised up Ann Robertson to minister to Native Americans, which she did with wisdom, patience, and courage. She understood that our Lord came not to be ministered to, but to serve, and in his name, she came to serve the marginalized. Bless all who walk the path of teaching and ministering to others, that they may be enlightened by your Spirit and rejoice in the knowledge of your truth. Through Christ our Lord. Amen.*

Antiphon:

> I am the vine; you are the branches.

Readings:

"May there be abundance of grain in the earth on top of the mountains; its fruit will wave like the cedars of Lebanon; and may those from the city flourish like vegetation of the earth. May his name endure forever; may his name increase as long as the sun shines; and let men bless themselves by him; let all nations call him blessed." *Psalm 72:16–17 (NASB)*

"And concerning you, my brethren, I myself also am convinced that you yourselves are full of goodness, filled with all knowledge and able also to admonish one another. But I have written very boldly to you on some points so as to remind you again, because of the grace that was given me from God, to be a minister of Christ Jesus to the Gentiles, ministering as a priest the gospel of God, so that my offering of the Gentiles may become acceptable, sanctified by the Holy Spirit." *Rom. 15:14–16 (NASB)*

"If anyone hears My sayings and does not keep them, I do not judge him; for I did not come to judge the world, but to save the world." *Jn. 12:47 (NASB)*

NOVEMBER 8 Elizabeth of the Trinity

Blessed Elizabeth of the Trinity was one of the true mystics of the nineteenth century. Born in 1880 into a French military family, she was blessed at an early age with the gift of song. After her father's death, she was raised by a mother who wanted her well-educated but fought Elizabeth's desire to become a Carmelite. However, Elizabeth was certain that it was her destiny because, after receiving Communion when still a child, she had vividly heard the word "Carmel." At age twenty-two her mother relented, for by this time Elizabeth had already received mystical consolations. She had a desire to be "transformed into Christ Crucified" and asked for his crown of thorns. She then experienced violent headaches for two years, which disappeared at her spiritual director's command. Elizabeth's mysticism apparently ranged from Christ's humanity to the Trinity's indwelling. She devoutly referred to the Trinity as "my Three." Elizabeth felt there was very little difference between earth and heaven, for the Trinity dwelt inside her soul. Before her death, she wrote that her mission in heaven would be to draw souls to interior recollection: "I'll teach souls the necessity of a profound inner silence that will allow God to imprint Himself upon souls and transform them into Himself." She left behind a body of writings considered to be spiritual treasures for aspiring mystics. Elizabeth was beatified in 1984.

Prayer:

> *Blessed Trinity of the indwelling God, you taught Elizabeth that if she could become utterly forgetful of herself and establish her mind and soul on you, then she could penetrate the depths of your holy mystery, as though she dwelt already in eternity. Make our souls also your heaven, your dwelling place. May we always remember that God's kingdom is within us, and in remembering, establish that kingdom on earth. Amen.*

Antiphon:

Immerse yourself in me, that I may be immersed in you until I depart to contemplate in your light the abyss of your greatness. (Elizabeth of the Trinity)

Readings:

"It is no longer I who live, but Christ lives in me; and the life which I now live in the flesh I live by faith in the Son of God, who loved me and gave Himself up for me." *Gal. 2:20 (NASB)*

"Now when all the people were baptized, Jesus was also baptized, and while He was praying, heaven was opened, and the Holy Spirit descended upon Him in bodily form like a dove, and a voice came out of heaven, 'You are My beloved Son, in You I am well-pleased.'" *Lk. 3:21–22 (NASB)*

"For there are three that testify: the Spirit and the water and the blood; and the three are in agreement." *1 Jn. 5:7–8 (NASB)*

NOVEMBER 9 Matrona of Perge

Matrona lived in the early part of the sixth century in Perge, and later in Constantinople. Married at a young age, she had a daughter named Theodote. Matrona's marriage was not a happy one, and her *vita* hints that she was a victim of abuse. Theodote, whose name means "given to God," died as a baby, a portend that Matrona took to indicate that she should abandon everything and give her life to the Lord. Although there were injunctions against leaving a marriage partner without consent, she conspired to abandon him anyway. After a long prayer session with two of her closest women friends, including her teacher Eugenia, Matrona had a dream wherein her husband was pursuing her but monks kept her in a monastery. She told her friends that she interpreted this to mean she should disguise herself as a male monk so she could enter their monastery. Matrona shaved her head, and Eugenia took her to the monastery of Venerable Bassianos (later canonized a saint), who believed Matrona was a eunuch. She was later discovered, when one of the monks noticed that both of her ears were pierced. Terrified that she would be returned to her husband, she fled to Alexandria, where she became an anchorite in an old abandoned pagan temple. Many years later, she returned to Constantinople (her *vita* suggests that she found out her husband was now dead) and started a convent there. During the later years of her life, during a tumultuous period in the Church when there was a vehement disagreement over whether Christ was actually fully human, Matrona was active in defending the Council of Chalcedon during the monophysite controversy.

Intercessory Prayer:

O holy Matrona, wounded with divine love for Christ, you fled the bonds of earthly cares and a husband's desire. In a pagan temple, you found your heart's gladness, and you danced with the angels in your joy. Pray for those of us who love the king, our Jesus, and who want a closer walk with him here. Help us to find the intoxicating fragrance of his grace in our own secret places. Through Christ our Lord. Amen.

Antiphon:

You are the only one I need.

Readings:

"He made darkness His hiding place, His canopy around Him, darkness of waters, thick clouds of the skies. . . . He brought me forth also into a broad place; He rescued me, because He delighted in me. The LORD has rewarded me according to my righteousness; according to the cleanness of my hands He has recompensed me." Psalm 18:11, 19, 20 (NASB)

"In the same way God, desiring even more to show to the heirs of the promise the unchangeableness of His purpose, interposed with an oath, so that by two unchangeable things in which it is impossible for God to lie, we who have taken refuge would have strong encouragement to take hold of the hope set before us. This hope we have as an anchor of the soul, a hope both sure and steadfast and one which enters within the veil." *Heb. 6:17–19 (NASB)*

NOVEMBER 10 Hannah

Hannah is another Old Testament heroine who is a valuable model for modern women. Her short story appears in the first Book of Samuel, and numerous women scholars have analyzed it. The author tells us that before she gave birth to the prophet Samuel, Hannah had been sorely tried by barrenness, which was the worst possible destiny for a Hebrew woman of that period. Hannah's husband, Elkanah, had another wife, Peninnah, who derided Hannah and caused her deep grief and shame. From the depths of her heart, Hannah prayed that if God would grant her a son, she would dedicate him to God's service. When Hannah went up to the Lord's house to pray, however, Eli, the man in charge of maintaining order there, thought she was drunk. The reason he assumed this was because she was moving her lips but making her prayer in silence: she had lost herself in prayer because of her passionate longing. It is believed that Eli's confusion arose because the tabernacle, predecessor of the temple, was a place of high ritual and animal sacrifice, not a place of silent prayer. Hannah is a heroine of religious civilization because she originated inward prayer. She had the capacity to imagine that the Lord of history could listen to her still, small voice. And indeed, God did grace Hannah with her son, Samuel. When Hannah came to dedicate the newborn child to God, she sang the words that became the basis of the Magnificat: "My heart exults in the Lord, my strength is exalted in my God. I have swallowed up my enemies; I rejoice in my victory. There is no Holy One like the Lord. . . . He raises the needy from the dust. . . . To seat them with nobles and make a glorious throne their heritage . . ." (1 Sam. 2:1–8). Through her perseverance, Hannah's despair was changed into praise.

Prayer:

Almighty and everlasting God, Hannah was your daughter whom you found favor with because she could speak so frankly and personally to you. Her heart cried out to you, the living God, whose Spirit is the soul's fountain of water. Through her inspiration, help us to remember how steady and unchanging is your love. May we risk trusting all, knowing that anything is possible with God. Amen.

Antiphon:

My soul proclaims your greatness, O God, for your regard has blessed me.

Readings:

"As for Hannah, she was speaking in her heart, only her lips were moving, but her voice was not heard. So Eli thought she was drunk. Then Eli said to her, 'How long will you make yourself drunk? Put away your wine from you.' But Hannah replied, 'No, my lord, I am a woman oppressed in spirit; I have drunk neither wine nor strong drink, but I have poured out my soul before the LORD.'" *1 Sam. 1:13–15 (NASB)*

"Do all that is in your heart . . . here I am with you according to your desire." *1 Sam. 14:7 (NASB)*

"My mouth will speak wisdom, and the meditation of my heart will be understanding. I will incline my ear to a proverb; I will express my riddle on the harp." *Psalm 49:3–4 (NASB)*

NOVEMBER 11 Mother Ignatius Hayes and Catherine McAuley

Today we celebrate two foundresses, neither of them yet formally canonized. Mother Ignatius Hayes was born Elizabeth, the eighth child of an Anglican priest in England. As a young woman, she joined a convent whose sisters were dedicated to prayer and service, but, stirred by the Oxford movement, she converted to Roman Catholicism. She initially became a Third Order Franciscan, then left to do missionary work in America. In 1872 she founded the first Franciscan convent in Minnesota, followed by a boarding school.

Her order was called the Franciscan Sisters of the Immaculate Conception. In 1880, she established a community of her sisters in Rome. Mother Ignatius once wrote that the greatest miracle in her life was that she was a Franciscan.

Catherine McAuley was born in Dublin in 1778, where she grew up and went to school. Her father's deep love for the poor was no doubt a strong influence in her life, and as an adult Catherine opened up a house for destitute girls that became known as the House of Mercy. It was never Catherine's intention to form a religious order, but at the archbishop of Dublin's prompting, she founded the Order of the Sisters of Mercy in 1831. It quickly spread to England, America, and Australia. In Dublin they became known as *walking nuns* because they spent so much time ministering on the streets. Catherine died November 11, 1841, and has been declared venerable.

Prayer:

Beloved God our Comforter, by whose Spirit all the Church is governed and sanctified, we thank you for giving us Mother Ignatius and Catherine McAuley, who discovered their vocations in devotedly serving you. These were women with a mission who realized that you have made all the peoples of the earth of one blood; and thus they willingly ministered to you wherever they were planted. May you use us also as vehicles for your works of mercy, and may your merciful missions flourish throughout the world. Amen.

Antiphon:

Blessed are the merciful, for they shall obtain mercy.

Readings:

"Hear my cry, O God, listen to my prayer; from the end of the earth I call, when my heart is faint. Set me on the rock that is higher than I; for you are my refuge, my stronghold against evil. Let me dwell in your tent forever! Hide me in the shelter of your wings! For you, O God, have heard my vows, you have given me the heritage of those who love your Name." *Psalm 61:1–5 (PCB)*

"And therefore will the Lord wait, that he may be gracious to you, and therefore will God be exalted, that he may have mercy on you: for the Lord is a God of judgment: blessed are they that wait for God." *Isa. 30:18 (KJV)*

"And came to him and bandaged up his wounds, pouring oil and wine on them; and he put him on his own beast, and brought him to an inn and took care of him. . . . 'Which of these three do you think proved to be a neighbor to the man who fell into the robbers' hands?' And he said, 'The one who showed mercy toward him.' Then Jesus said to him, 'Go and do the same.'" *Lk. 10:34, 36, 37 (NASB)*

NOVEMBER 12 Elizabeth Cady Stanton

Elizabeth Cady Stanton was born November 12, 1815, to a Presbyterian family. At an early age, she lost her only brother; and after the shock and grief of his death, she resolved that she would become all that her brother never could be. She knew this meant getting a good education, so she persuaded her pastor to teach her Greek and Latin. Her early training served her well, as she later authored the first feminist commentary on Scripture, called *The Women's Bible*. Elizabeth was one of the first theologians to reason that equality with men, in the Christian tradition, was an impossibility without also changing the language we use to talk about God. In 1840, Elizabeth married Henry Stanton, who was active in promoting antislavery laws. At that time no college admitted women, so she went to a seminary called Troy Female Seminary. Afterward she traveled widely, preaching the gospel in the interpretative language of women's rights. Elizabeth worked with Amelia Bloomer (see Daily Readings, October 29, Amelia Bloomer) and Lucretia Mott (see Daily Readings, September 13, Lucretia Mott) in organizing conventions and petitions that eventually guaranteed property rights for women. Like many feminist theologians of today, Elizabeth spent much time reflecting on the different positions of woman in the two Creation stories in Genesis. In some places, the Anglican Communion celebrates Elizabeth's feast day on July 20, with Harriet Tubman.

Prayer:

> *O God, you are the inward tug that all women who love you have felt. Elizabeth Cady Stanton lived a life in service to you, attempting to respond to your call by insisting that the river of your justice runs deep and true, as does the river of your mercy. We are grateful for her gifts, for all women walk an easier path today because she refused to make peace with oppression. Help us to use*

our freedom in maintaining justice for all women whose rights are
suppressed throughout the world. Through Christ our Lord. Amen.

Antiphon:

God will come with justice for all people.

Readings:

"The north and the south, You have created them; Tabor and Hermon shout for joy at Your name. You have a strong arm; Your hand is mighty, Your right hand is exalted. Righteousness and justice are the foundation of Your throne; lovingkindness and truth go before You." *Psalm 89:12–14 (NASB)*

"You shall divide it for an inheritance, each one equally with the other; for I swore to give it to your forefathers, and this land shall fall to you as an inheritance." *Ez. 47:14 (NASB)*

"At this present time your abundance being a supply for their need, so that their abundance also may become a supply for your need, that there may be equality." *2 Cor. 8:14 (NASB)*

"They are like angels, and are sons of God." *Lk. 20:36 (NASB)*

NOVEMBER 13 Mother Frances Cabrini

Frances Cabrini was born in Italy in 1850, the youngest of thirteen children in a devout Catholic home. Although she desired to become a religious and serve in her own country, God had other plans for her. She discerned a call to initiate an order of sisters whose mission was to serve the poor in Italy, and this initiative so impressed Pope Leo XIII that he sent her and a small band of her order to minister to the numerous Italian immigrants who were living in America. They arrived in New York City in 1889, and her order, the Missionary Sisters of the Sacred Heart, began serving the local ethnic population in a number of apostolic projects. From providing catechetical instruction to Italian children to delivering meals to the poor, Frances's initiatives in ministering to the poor, abused, and neglected were a breath of the Spirit to countless individuals. She became a naturalized citizen of the United States in 1909 and died eleven years later, leaving behind more than fifteen thousand Missionary Sisters who continue to minister throughout the world.

Canonized in 1946, after over 150,000 miracles, healings, and answered prayers were attributed to her intercession, Frances became the first American saint.

Intercessory Prayer:

> *Dear Mother Cabrini, you answered God's call to evangelize by emigrating to America and serving Christ through ministering to those most desperately in need. Help all those who are in the process of emigrating in order to achieve religious and political freedom. Pray for the strength and guidance they need to find a life that will allow them to experience social, religious, and political freedom; and to always remain faithful and thankful to God for such privileges. Amen.*

Antiphon:

Let me hear in the morning of your steadfast love.

Readings:

"How blessed is he who considers the helpless; the LORD will deliver him in a day of trouble. The LORD will protect him and keep him alive, and he shall be called blessed upon the earth." *Psalm 41:1–2 (NASB)*

"The Spirit of the Lord is upon me, because he anointed me to preach the gospel to the poor . . . to proclaim the favorable year of the Lord." *Lk. 4:18–19 (NASB)*

"Paul said, 'John baptized with the baptism of repentance, telling the people to believe in Him who was coming after him, that is, in Jesus.' When they heard this, they were baptized in the name of the Lord Jesus." *Acts 19:4–5 (NASB)*

"For the promise is for you and your children and for all who are far off, as many as the Lord our God will call to Himself." *Acts 2:39 (NASB)*

NOVEMBER 14 Mary Hermina Grivot

Irma Grivot was born in 1866 to poor parents in Paris. In 1894 she realized her dream of a religious vocation and joined the Franciscan Missionaries of Mary, often dubbed the White Franciscans due to their distinguishing full, white habits.

She took the name Mary Hermina of Jesus, and she joined several other nuns and priests to run a missionary orphanage in the Shansi territory of China. She and the other nuns established an orderly and loving lifestyle for the orphans, most of whom were girls. The nuns saw to the orphans' every need, from medical attention to religious instruction. Less than two years later, anti-Christian political elements overtook their Franciscan house and orphanage. Hermina and her sister nuns were seized, and each suffered martyrdom at the hands of a hateful crowd. Two Chinese boys who witnessed Hermina's beheading were impacted significantly. Years later they attended the beatification of Hermina and the other martyrs of China, both of them wearing the habits of Franciscan friars. Hermina is the patron of Chinese missionaries.

Prayer

Heavenly Father, you gave us courageous witnesses to the faith through the lives and deaths of Blessed Hermina and the martyrs of China. Through their generous gift of charity and love of neighbor, they lived lives of total service to you. Allow their inspirational example to influence us positively today so we may look for even the smallest opportunity to serve others. Amen.

Antiphon:

Behold how they are numbered among the children of God, and their lot is among the saints.

Readings:

"Hear my prayer, O LORD! And let my cry for help come to You. Do not hide Your face from me in the day of my distress; incline Your ear to me; in the day when I call answer me quickly. For my days have been consumed in smoke, and my bones have been scorched like a hearth. My heart has been smitten like grass and has withered away, indeed, I forget to eat my bread . . . my days are like a lengthened shadow, and I wither away like grass. But You, O LORD, abide forever, and Your name to all generations." *Psalm 102:1–5, 11–12 (NASB)*

"It is a trustworthy statement: For if we died with Him, we will also live with Him; if we endure, we will also reign with Him." *2 Tim. 2:11–12 (NASB)*

"Make room for us in your hearts; we wronged no one, we corrupted no one, we took advantage of no one. I do not speak to condemn you, for I have said before that you are in our hearts to die together and to live together. Great is my confidence in you;

great is my boasting on your behalf. I am filled with comfort; I am overflowing with joy in all our affliction." *2 Cor. 7:2–4 (NASB)*

NOVEMBER 15 Mother Mary of the Passion and Jane of Signa

Helene Marie de Chappotin was born in France in the mid-nineteenth century. In 1864 at age twenty-five, she entered the religious order of women known as the Society of Marie Reparatrice and took the name Mary of the Passion. She became a missionary in India soon after, but in 1882 she was called to begin a new order named the Franciscan Missionaries of Mary. Mother Mary died in 1904, leaving a thriving community of over two thousand Franciscan Missionaries, as well as eighty community houses across the globe that continue to care for the sick and provide educational and social services to countless individuals. In 1900, seven sisters from her community were martyred in the Boxer Uprising. All were beatified in 1946. Pope John Paul II beatified Mother Mary in 2002 for her outstanding charity and her inspirational prayer life, which centered on the Eucharist.

This is also the feast, in the old Franciscan calendar, of Blessed Jane of Signa, an anchoress at Carmignano in Italy. She died in 1307, after a life of deep prayer and numerous miracles. It was said that at her death a mysterious ringing of bells attracted the townsfolk to her solitary hermitage. Her body was transferred to St. John the Baptist Church, where it remains incorrupt. Jane is the patron of epidemics and floods.

Prayer:

> Holy God, thank you for blessing humanity with strong and vibrant women of faith like Mother Mary of the Passion and Jane of Signa. Mary's response to your call to spread Christ's word to all ends of the earth was realized through the order she founded, which continues to serve countless individuals through acts of charity today. Jane was such a powerful person of prayer that the sick and the sorrowful flocked to her cell for many years. Please

give us opportunities to practice acts of charity in the world balanced with an interior life in which we deepen our relationship with you. Amen.

Antiphon:
O Christ, you are our light, the image of God.

Readings:
"You are my hiding place; You preserve me from trouble; You surround me with songs of deliverance. . . . I will instruct you and teach you in the way which you should go; I will counsel you with My eye upon you. . . . Be glad in the LORD and rejoice, you righteous ones; and shout for joy, all you who are upright in heart." *Psalm 32:7, 8, 11 (NASB)*

"Verily I say to you, He who receives whomever I shall send receives me; and he that receives me receives the One that sent me." *Jn. 13:20 (KJV)*

"Older women likewise are to be reverent in their behavior . . . so that the word of God will not be dishonored." *Titus 2:3–5 (NASB)*

NOVEMBER 16 Gertrude the Great

Gertrude was born in 1256, on Epiphany, the Feast of Lights. As a five-year-old oblate, she was left at a convent in Germany and began her monastic life of prayer and service to God. We know nothing about her family. St. Mary's monastery at Helfta was perhaps the most remarkable of the thirteenth-century convents. A spiritual oasis, it was also a center of distinguished artistic and literary activity. When Gertrude came as a young girl to Helfta, it was in its golden age of spiritual and artistic flowering. It was home to at least three great mystics of the period: Mechtild of Magdeburg (see Daily Readings, November 20, Mechtild of Magdeburg), Mechtild of Hackeborn (see Daily Readings, February 24, Mechtild of Hackeborn), and perhaps most famous, Gertrude herself, later called Gertrude the Great. The mystical treatises she left us were *Revelations of Divine Love* and a book called *Spiritual Exercises*. Long predating Margaret-Mary (see Daily Readings, October 17, Margaret-Mary Alacoque), Gertrude was one of the earliest saints to focus on the locus of the Sacred Heart of Jesus as the great transformation of the mystic soul. Unlike most of the other writers at Helfta, Gertrude was skilled in Latin, writing most of her works in Latin rather than her native German. Like Jerome, she translated many of the Scriptures, and her fame as a spiritual writer and counselor spread beyond her own convent walls to include an apostolate with both laity and clergy. Once, when unsure about approaching the Eucharist because she felt unworthy, the Lord appeared to her and said, "I will give you all the holiness of my divinity and my humanity, that you may be worthily prepared to come up to receive Holy Communion" (Leg 3:18).

Prayer:

O most Sacred Heart of Jesus, Gertrude was the delight of your soul, and she spent her life bringing other hungry hearts to you. She left us a priceless gift, in her poetic sojourn, through her journals. Through her intercession, guide our feet in walking in divine love with you. Your divine mercy is beyond our understanding. Help us not to exclude ourselves from your embrace by the choices we make. Amen.

Antiphon:

How much more delightful is your love than wine.

Readings:

"The law of Your mouth is better to me than thousands of gold and silver pieces. Your hands made me and fashioned me; give me understanding, that I may learn Your commandments." *Psalm 119:72–73 (NASB)*

"I am my beloved's, and his desire is for me. Come, my beloved, let us go out into the country, let us spend the night in the villages. Let us rise early and go to the vineyards; let us see whether the vine has budded and its blossoms have opened, and whether the pomegranates have bloomed. There I will give you my love. The mandrakes have given forth fragrance; and over our doors are all choice fruits, both new and old." *Song of Songs 7:10–13 (NASB)*

"He taught me also, and said, 'Let your heart retain my words.'" *Prov. 4:4 (KJV)*

"They said to one another, 'Were not our hearts burning within us while He was speaking to us on the road, while He was explaining the Scriptures to us?'" *Lk. 24:32 (NASB)*

NOVEMBER 17 Elizabeth of Hungary

The story of St. Elizabeth of Hungary and her husband, Louis, is an inspiration for married couples everywhere. Elizabeth was betrothed to Louis, and they wed when he was twenty-one and she was fourteen. They had a beautiful marriage marked with a deep sharing of their faith and an intense bond of holy love. Together they had three children, and Elizabeth's life was devoted to prayer and to sharing the temporal gifts of the wealthy court in which she lived. She is most remembered for sharing stores of grain during the country's terrible famine, building hospitals, and giving away food to hundreds of starving country folk who lined up outside her castle each day. Her husband died tragically of the plague. Elizabeth, deeply grieved, refused to remarry although she was only in her early twenties. She became a Franciscan tertiary in 1228 and spent the remainder of her life administering her funds to the poor and serving the most destitute through establishing various ministries. Her confessor was Conrad of Marburg, who was also an inquisitor of heretics, and Elizabeth is rumored to have suffered mental and physical abuse from him. Due to the severe asceticism under which she lived, she died at age twenty-four, and she was canonized just four years later. She is often pictured as a queen carrying a loaf of bread. Anglicans celebrate her feast on November 19. Elizabeth is the patron of Franciscan tertiaries and bakers.

Intercessory Prayer:

Dear St. Elizabeth of Hungary, your holy life and pious marriage are an inspiration to everyone. Let the example of your holy marriage be a reminder of the deep call to true commitment, which the sacrament of marriage exemplifies. Please inspire all engaged couples to be truly aware of this awesome sacrament and intercede that their marriages may be blessed and holy. We pray for all married couples everywhere, especially those who are struggling with difficult times or trying circumstances. May they be blessed through your intercession. Amen.

Antiphon:

Those who give to the poor will have treasure in heaven.

Readings:

> The LORD reigns, let the peoples tremble; He is enthroned above the cherubim, let the earth shake! The LORD is great in Zion, and He is exalted above all the peoples. Let them praise Your great and awesome name; holy is He. The strength of the King loves justice; You have established equity; You have executed justice and righteousness. . . . Exalt the LORD our God, and worship at His footstool; holy is He." *Psalm 99:1–5 (NASB)*

> "And you shall love the Lord your God with all your heart, and with all your soul, and with all your mind, and with all your strength . . . [and] you shall love your neighbor as yourself." *Mk. 12:30–31 (NASB)*

> ". . . from whom the whole body, being fitted and held together by what every joint supplies, according to the proper working of each individual part, causes the growth of the body for the building up of itself in love." *Eph. 4:16 (NASB)*

NOVEMBER 18 Philippine Duchesne

St. Philippine was born into a political family in 1769 and reared to be an educated lady; she was well versed in literature in order to make someone a good wife. When her parents resisted her urge to enter a convent, she responded by living as if the convent were in her home, refusing all social engagements. Deeply influenced by Marie of the Incarnation (see Daily Readings, April 30, Marie of the Incarnation), she was destined to follow in her path, both in contemplative prayer and in missionary work to the New World. Philippine's parents finally released her, and after a brief stay in a Visitation convent that was dispersed during the French Revolution, she came to North America to found houses for the Society of the Religious of the Sacred Heart. She devoted herself to agriculture with the Creole people and pioneer settlers. Because she found the English language difficult to learn, she preferred to occupy herself in manual labor. Even in her seventies, she was often the first to awaken in the morning and the last to make visitations at night. Philippine always found time for her beloved garden.

Prayer:

You, O God, have looked dearly on all that you have made and found it good. St. Philippine professed your gospel in a foreign land and built there a devoted new family and a beautiful garden. Keep our hearts and attitudes open to you at all times, and remind us always that the earth you gave to us, long nurtured and respected by Native American peoples, is ours only for stewardship. Amen.

Antiphon:

She opens her heart to the poor and reaches out her hand to the needy.

Readings:

"The LORD God planted a garden toward the east. . . . Out of the ground the LORD God caused to grow every tree that is pleasing to the sight and good for food; the tree of life also in the midst of the garden, and the tree of the knowledge of good and evil." *Gen. 2:8, 9 (NASB)*

"Indeed, the LORD will comfort Zion; He will comfort all her waste places and her wilderness He will make like Eden, and her desert like the garden of the LORD; joy and gladness will be found in her, thanksgiving and sound of a melody." *Isa. 51:3 (NASB)*

"In those days, when there was again a large crowd and they had nothing to eat, Jesus called His disciples and said to them, 'I feel compassion for the people.'" *Mk. 8:1–3 (NASB)*

NOVEMBER 19 Hilda of Whitby

Hilda, a Benedictine nun and abbess of Whitby, came from an aristocratic background with strong Celtic ties. King Edwin's niece, she was baptized and converted to Christianity with his household in 627 at age thirteen. She lived a secular life as a noblewoman until age thirty-three when she decided to become a nun. At Bishop Aidan's prompting, Hilda established a double monastery (which included both men and women) at Whitby in 657. Hilda proved to be an inspired educator and diplomat. The intellectual and spiritual environment at Whitby produced five bishops and Caedmon, the poet of vernacular English who produced the first holy writings in the English language. Because of Hilda's support for and encourage-ment of Caedmon, she is said to have mothered English literature. In 644, Hilda hosted a conference known as the Synod of Whitby, which focused on the differences between Celtic and Roman doctrine. Cen-tral to the discussion was the appropriate time to celebrate Easter. King Olwy, the abbey's benefactor, was convinced that the Roman tradition should be followed. Although Hilda's sympathies lay with the Celtic tradition, once the decision was made, she encouraged a peaceful acceptance of the change of the Easter date. Her diplomacy allowed her to focus on a united and universal Christian Church. Hilda died encouraging her community to preserve the evangelical peace that had been achieved during her lifetime.

Prayer:

Through Hilda's intercession, O Lord Jesus, strengthen us in the times when our faith is tested, that we may have the grace to persevere through the thorns of resistance and indecision. She found out that if the roots are consecrated, so will be all the branches. May we be worthy, like all the beloved holy women in your life, to contemplate the light of your countenance and to know that your infinitely loving presence is with us always. Amen.

Antiphon:

Sincere are all the words of my mouth, and right to those who aspire to wisdom.

Readings:

"All the utterances of my mouth are in righteousness. . . . They are all straightforward to him who understands, and right to those who find knowledge." *Prov. 8:8–9 (NASB)*

"And he gave some, apostles; and some, prophets; and some, evangelists; and some, pastors and teachers; For the perfecting of the saints, for the work of the ministry, for the edifying of the body of Christ." *Eph. 4:11–12 (KJV)*

"Therefore we have been buried with Him through baptism into death, so that as Christ was raised from the dead through the glory of the Father, so we too might walk in newness of life." *Rom. 6:4 (NASB)*

NOVEMBER 20 Mechthild of Magdeburg and Lydia Sellon

Mechthild of Magdeburg was born into a noble Saxon family in 1210, and she had her first spiritual experiences when still a child. She became a Beguine at Magdeburg, and she later joined the Helfta mystics (Gertrude the Great and Mechthild of Hackeborn). Her principal work, part autobiography and part theological and mystical reflection, is called *The Flowing Light of the Godhead*. Mechthild's visions were highly influenced by the language of the liturgy, as well as by the poetry of courtly love common to her era. Her main mysticism consisted of being submersed in the triune God. Mechthild strongly denounced abuses in the Church (calling her detractors "my pharisees"), and she was, for a time, persecuted. After taking refuge in Helfta, she dictated the seventh and last part of her book while going blind. She died with a reputation of holiness, but she was never canonized in the Roman Church. Mechthild is very popular in the Anglican Church, where her feast is kept on November 19. Her work became one of the most famous medieval poetic treatises on the love affair between God and the soul, and Mechtild's descriptions of the hereafter are thought by some to be the basis of Dante's *Divine Comedy*.

This is also the feast day of Lydia Sellon, who was instrumental in reinstating the religious life in the Church of England. Her order, known as the Sisters of Mercy, worked among the destitute in Plymouth. Lydia died in 1876.

Prayer:

Beloved God, Mechthild glorified you in her life and in her writing, seeing you always as the center of the soul's desire. Her passionate assertion, that she belonged to you by nature, serves to remind us that we too are deified by your mystical graces when we open our hearts to the springing fountain of your ineffable love. May our sisters Mechthild and Lydia intercede for us who still struggle with the mystical passion of the soul that is restless until it rests in you. Amen.

Antiphon:

God has enough of all things; only to touch the soul is never enough for God. (Mechthild)

Readings:

"'What kind of beloved is your beloved, O most beautiful among women? What kind of beloved is your beloved, that thus you adjure us?'

'My beloved is dazzling and ruddy, outstanding among ten thousand.

His head is like gold, pure gold; his locks are like clusters of dates and black as a raven.

His eyes are like doves beside streams of water.'" *Song of Songs 4:9–12 (NASB)*

"But to each one of us grace was given according to the measure of Christ's gift. Therefore it says,

'WHEN HE ASCENDED ON HIGH,
HE LED CAPTIVE A HOST OF CAPTIVES,
AND HE GAVE GIFTS TO MEN'

. . . He who descended is Himself also He who ascended far above all the heavens, so that He might fill all things." *Eph. 4:7–10 (NASB)*

NOVEMBER 21 Presentation of Mary

Today we celebrate the Presentation of the Blessed Virgin Mary, as well as the dedication of the Church of St. Mary in Jerusalem. Based principally on the apocryphal Gospel of James, the story is the source for missing information about Mary, including the names of her parents. The story was purportedly written by James, Jesus' brother (Mark 6:3), who claims to also be an eyewitness to Jesus' birth. When St. Joachim and St. Anne, the Virgin Mary's parents, received the news in their old age that they would be having a child who would be the mother of the Messiah, they chose to make the ultimate personal sacrifice: they presented Mary at the temple when the holy child was about three years old. At the temple, the holy ones instructed and raised Mary. Although modern scholarship affirms that the story is fiction (because the Jewish tradition had no place in the temple for girls to live or be educated) this feast day has a long tradition in both the Eastern and Western churches. In

Orthodoxy, it is one of the twelve great feasts, as important as Mary's Nativity or Dormition. The Presentation of Mary symbolizes Mary's wholehearted submission to God's will and serves as a reflection on the holy and honorable destiny of the Theotokos. Metaphorically, the feast's theme is that Mary, the Temple of the Living God, is offered to the Lord; thus the bond between Christ the Word and Mary the Virgin is forged for all eternity.

Intercessory Prayer:

Dear Blessed mother of God, today we celebrate the moment in history when you began to realize your mission as the Mother of God. When you were presented in the temple, your parents made a great personal sacrifice to release you from their loving care and entrust you to the future God had planned. Help us to realize that God sometimes calls us to make difficult choices in order to fulfill his divine will and the destiny best suited for our own lives. In meditating on your holy fiat to God's will in your life, may we also be open to the Holy Spirit in coming to understand how we may best serve God and further his kingdom on earth. Amen.

Antiphon:

Blessed art thou among women, and blessed is the fruit of thy womb.

Readings:

"Then I was beside [Him], as a master workman; and I was daily [His] delight, rejoicing always before [Him], rejoicing in the world, [His] earth. . . . Now therefore, O [children], listen to me, for blessed are they who keep my ways. Heed instruction and be wise, and do not neglect it." *Prov. 8:30–32 (NASB)*

"The most pure Temple of the Savior, the highly precious bridal chamber, the Virgin, the holy Treasury of the glory of God, is today led into the house of the Lord, and brings with her the grace which is the Divine Spirit. Of her, the angels of God sing—This is the heavenly Tabernacle!" *Orthodox Liturgy, November 21*

"O God, you willed that the Blessed Virgin Mary, the dwelling place of the Holy Spirit, should be presented in the Temple on this day. May we be worthy, through her intercession, to be presented in the temple of your Glory." *Roman Missal, November 21*

NOVEMBER 22 Cecilia

St. Cecilia's cult was well established by the fifth century, and she is a favorite early saint of both the Eastern and Western churches. She probably lived during the third century when Emperor Alexander Severus persecuted Christians. According to the legend, Cecilia was born of a patrician family and was betrothed to a pagan named Valerian. Valerian and his brother were converted by her example, and they devoted themselves to charity. They were brought to trial for refusing to offer pagan sacrifices. Cecilia was sentenced to be beheaded, but three blows failed to kill her and she lingered for three days. Pope Urban dedicated her house as a church. Cecilia is most famous as the patroness of musicians, and this is probably from a later medieval account that, on her wedding day, instead of listening to the festive music, she stood up and sang from her heart to the Lord. Raphael pictured her as playing an organ. She is the patron of a number of English churches, which also celebrate her feast on this day. Cecilia is also a patron of the Academy of Music in Rome.

Intercessory Prayer:

O St. Cecilia, your joyful voice resounds through history, and we honor you for opening up your praise to the Lord and bringing God into our everyday lives through song. When we sing our praises to our beloved we become, like you, angels in the flesh. Bless all musicians and singers everywhere, and likewise bless all modern martyrs, especially those who suffer the fate of beheading. Give them the peace of walking into the next life with faith and trust in God. Help us to eliminate acts of barbarism in our terror-filled world. Amen.

Antiphon:

And I will lift my voice to you, O God.

Readings:

"All the earth cries out to you with shouts of joy, O God; serving you with gladness; coming before you, singing for joy. You, Creator of all, are God. You made us, we belong to you; we are your people, the sheep of your pasture." *Psalm 100:1–2 (PCB)*

"Let the sea roar and all it contains, the world and those who dwell in it. Let the rivers clap their hands, let the mountains sing together for joy before the LORD, for He is coming to judge the earth; [He] will judge the world with righteousness and the peoples with equity." *Psalm 98:7–9 (NASB)*

"Behold, I am going to deal at that time with all your oppressors, I will save the lame and gather the outcast, and I will turn their shame into praise and renown in all the earth." *Zeph. 3:19 (NASB)*

NOVEMBER 23 Jeanne Fontbonne

Jeanne Fontbonne was born in France in the mid-eighteenth century. From an early age she felt a calling to devote herself totally to Christ, so she became a member of the Sisters of St. Joseph in 1778. When she became the superior of her community, she took the name Mother St. John. However, the turbulent times of the French Revolution caused her to be imprisoned and nearly to be executed. When she was freed after Robespierre's fall, she restored her order and made it her mission that her apostolates would spread to the United States. This dream eventually occurred; over two hundred new communities of her order spread throughout Europe and into the United States. Many believe that Europe would not have survived the chaotic time after the French Revolution without the charity of the good Sisters of St. Joseph. After years of struggle and toil to oversee the spread of her convents and their charitable works, Mother St. John died in France in 1843 at age eighty-four.

Intercessory Prayer:

Dear venerable Jeanne Fontbonne, your living witness to the faith was exemplified in a life of total service and dedication to helping others. You faced many obstacles in your efforts to spread Christ's Gospel and to administer kind works to those most in need. You never gave up, and God rewarded your efforts with an apostolate that caused the conversion of countless souls. May we be inspired to emulate your example of Gospel charity in our own daily lives. Amen.

Antiphon:

We are witnesses to those things and so is the Holy Spirit whom God has given us.

Readings:

"The just shall flourish like the palm tree and grow like a cedar in Lebanon. They are planted in your holy house, they flourish in your courts. They still bring forth fruit in old age, they are ever full of sap and green, to show that you, O God, are just; you are my rock; in you there is no injustice." *Psalm 92:12–15 (PCB)*

"But the goal of our instruction is love from a pure heart and a good conscience and a sincere faith." *1 Tim. 1:5 (NASB)*

"The LORD your God is in your midst, a victorious warrior [He] will exult over you with joy, [He] will be quiet in His love, [He] will re-joice over you with shouts of joy." *Zeph. 3:17 (NASB)*

NOVEMBER 24 *Iveron Mother of God Portaitissa Icon*

The original *Iveron Mother of God* icon is on Mt. Athos ("Holy Mountain"), which has come to be known as the center of Eastern monasticism. The story is that the *Portaitissa* image appeared to the monks at the monastery at Iveron in a pillar of fire in the ninth century, and the icon was given to one monk, Gabriel, with instructions that it be placed by the monks' gate. This image is there-fore also known as the Mother of God *Portaitissa* ("gatekeeper"), signi-fying her protection. In 1981, Jose Munoz, a convert to Orthodoxy from Montreal, went on a pilgrimage to Mt. Athos and painted a replica from the original, which he brought back to his home in Canada. Three weeks after his return, on November 24, 1982, Jose was sleeping when a powerful fragrance awakened him. When he ex-amined the icon, he saw that it was streaming myrrh. He took this icon to a local Orthodox church for inspection, and after much ex-amination, it was announced to be a miracle. The icon wept myrrh tears for fifteen years, except during Passion Week. The new icon traveled through America, Australia, and Western Europe. In Florida, the icon tears flowed upward, a most unusual miracle in the history of myrrh-streaming icons. On October 30, 1997, Jose was brutally killed in Athens, and the icon disappeared.

Intercessory Prayer:

> *Mary, Mother of God, if we could pause long enough to return the gaze of your holy face, perhaps we could learn what true wisdom really is. We know that all you ask of us through your miracle-working icons is an invitation to share in the immense love you have for your son. We know this love is overwhelmingly powerful, radical, merciful, and just. Through the signs and wonders with which you visit us in this age, teach us to follow you into the holy heart of that love. Amen.*

Antiphon:

Rejoice, Keeper of the Portal most gracious! (Akathist)

Readings:

"My tears have been my food day and night, these things I remember and I pour out my soul within me." *Psalm 42:3–4 (NASB)*

"You will say this word to them, let my eyes flow down with tears night and day, and let them not cease; for the virgin daughter of my people has been crushed with a mighty blow, with a sorely infected wound." *Jer. 14:17 (NASB)*

"She cries at the gates, at the entry of the city, at the coming in at the doors." *Prov. 8:3 (KJV)*

"In the daytime (for there will be no night there) its gates will never be closed; and they will bring the glory and the honor of the nations into it. . . ." *Rev. 21:25–26 (NASB)*

NOVEMBER 25 Catherine of Alexandria

The historian Eusebius tells us that when Maxentius was at Alexandria, he carried off the wives and daughters of numerous citizens, until his unbridled passion was defeated by the heroism of one woman: Catherine. Well educated, Catherine was reputed to have debated with him and fifty of his court's pagan philosophers over her Christian convictions. Legend has embellished the story of Catherine's relationship with Maxentius (who believed she was an incarnation of the goddess Athena), whom Catherine sought to convert. Eventually imprisoned, an angel visited her there. When she was sent to be executed, the wheel broke apart when she was laid upon it. Beheaded instead, milk flowed when her head was severed from her body. Eusebius believed her body, which disappeared after her death, was transported to Mt. Sinai, where one of the world's largest monasteries, St. Catherine's Monastery, remains today. It is one of Orthodoxy's most spectacular natural settings for priceless icons and illuminated manuscripts. Removed from the Roman calendar in 1969, Catherine remains one of the principal female saints in the Eastern traditions, as she synthesizes the knowledge of the ancient Roman and Greek platonic world with the New Era, represented by Christianity. Catherine is the patron of students and spinners.

Prayer:

Almighty God, by your spirit you raised up Catherine to reveal the glory of your Church and to show philosophers the way to perfection. May her inspired teaching serve to remind us that all people can be called to minister to your Word and show forth your glory. By her intercession and example, awaken in us a longing for true philosophy. Through Christ our Lord. Amen.

Antiphon:

She is clothed with strength and dignity, and she laughs at the days to come.

Readings:

"Strength and dignity are her clothing,
    And she smiles at the future.
She opens her mouth in wisdom,
    And the teaching of kindness is on her tongue.
She looks well to the ways of her household,
    And does not eat the bread of idleness.
Her children rise up and bless her." *Prov. 31:25–28 (NASB)*

"So Paul stood in the midst of the Areopagus and said, 'Men of Athens, I observe that you are very religious in all respects. For while I was passing through and examining the objects of your worship, I also found an altar with this inscription, "TO AN UN-KNOWN GOD." Therefore what you worship in ignorance, this I proclaim to you. The God who made the world and all things in it, since He is Lord of heaven and earth, does not dwell in temples made with hands; nor is He served by human hands, as though He needed anything, since He Himself gives to all people life and breath and all things.'" Acts 17:22–25 (NASB)

"Having been firmly rooted and now being built up in Him and established in your faith, just as you were instructed, and overflowing with gratitude. See to it that no one takes you captive through philosophy and empty deception, according to the tradition of men, according to the elementary principles of the world, rather than according to Christ." *Col. 2:7–8 (NASB)*

NOVEMBER 26 Kursk Root Icon of the Mother of God (Vigil)

The *Kursk Root* icon belongs to the type known as Our Lady of the Sign, whose principal feast day is celebrated on November 27. This is called the *Kursk Root* icon because it was first discovered and glorified at the root of a tree in Russia in 1295. A hunter stumbled upon it, and when he turned it over, a spring gushed forth. A small chapel was built there, and many healings occurred at the spring. When the icon was later moved to a larger church, it disappeared and found its way back to the original site. Tatars invaded the area and tried to burn the icon, but it refused to burn. In the seventeenth century, a monastery was built in honor of the Theotokos of the *Kursk Root*, and the icon was moved. Later, during an invasion, the church housing it was blown apart, but the icon remained untouched. After the revolution of 1917, the *Kursk Root* icon left Russia intact, traveling from place to place with the displaced faithful; for a while it resided in Serbia. During World War II, when Belgrade was bombed and much of the city was flattened, houses where the icon had visited were said to all be spared. Eventually the icon was moved to the Orthodox Cathedral of the Mother of God of the Sign in New York. Many of the faithful believe that it was this icon's presence that spared much of the surrounding area during the terrorist attacks on September 11, 2001. St. John the Wonder-worker died before this icon in 1966. At the cathedral, the *Kursk Root* is still a favorite pilgrimage site for the faithful, especially Russians abroad in the United States. The icon depicts many Old Testament prophets surrounding the Mother of God and her son, each holding a scroll indicating their prophecies, which were fulfilled when she gave birth to Christ, our prophet, priest, and king.

Intercessory Prayer:

Holy Mother of God, the star that rose out of Jacob was born from your womb. You have been proclaimed as the ark of the New Testament because you housed God in the tabernacle of your body. We plead that the hands with which you held our Lord now be extended to ask for pardon and grace in a world suffering from darkness and ignorance. Lead us back to the light of his glory, peace, and truth. Amen.

Antiphon:

"Rejoice! Indestructible Shield of the faithful!" (Akathist)

Readings:

"With the loyal, you show yourself loyal; with the blameless you show yourself blameless; with the pure you show yourself pure . . . For you deliver a humble people, but the haughty eyes you bring down." *Psalm 18:25–27 (NRSV)*

"I traverse the way of righteousness, in the midst of the paths of justice." *Prov. 8:20 (NKJV)*

"As shoes for your feet put on whatever will make you ready to proclaim the gospel of peace. With all of these, take the shield of faith, with which you will be able to quench all the flaming arrows of the evil one." *Eph. 6:15–16 (NRSV)*

NOVEMBER 27 Catherine Laboure

Catherine Laboure was born in the early nineteenth century in France. She was a devout child and felt a special calling to the religious life. She was allowed to realize this dream at age twenty-four, when she entered the religious order of the Sisters of Charity and joined their convent in Rue du Bac, Paris. All the sisters respected and loved her due to her unfailing charity to others in a variety of difficult tasks. Whether doing laundry or serving the poorest of the poor, Catherine lived a life of exemplary charity. She had a great devotion to the Blessed Virgin Mary, and perhaps this is why the Virgin chose Catherine to reveal a very special devotion. Catherine experienced a vision of the Blessed Virgin in which Our Lady revealed that all graces to humanity flow through Mary's hands. Our

Lady requested that Catherine have a medal struck that would depict this revelation. The medal reveals the Blessed Virgin with rays of graces flowing from her hands onto the globe. The prayer "Oh Mary, conceived without sin, pray for us who have recourse to you" encircles the image. The medal was made according to Our Lady's request, and soon the medal circulated throughout Europe and eventually the world. Due to the many miraculous cures and graces attributed to its possession, soon it became known as "the Miraculous Medal." St. Catherine died in 1845 and was canonized in 1947.

Intercessory Prayer:

Dear Blessed Mother of God, you revealed to the world that the rays on the Miraculous Medal represent the graces you distribute to all of humanity. You gave us this medal as a visible sign of your love for us and your desire to intercede before God's throne to obtain mercy and graces for everyone. You further promised that those who carry this medal would obtain indulgences and special protection from you, the Mother of God. Help us to cherish such outward visible signs as this medal and to use such sacramentals with love and reverence within our homes. Amen.

Antiphon:

Through you, the blind see, the lame walk, and the poor hear your good news.

Readings:

"My God, answer in time of trouble! May the name of our God protect us. Send your help, O God, from your sanctuary, and give your support from Zion. May you remember all our offerings and receive our sacrifice with favor. May you give us our heart's desire, and fulfill every one of our plans." *Psalm 20:1–6 (PCB)*

"But as you abound in everything—in faith, in speech, in knowledge, in all diligence, and in your love for us—see that you abound in this grace also." *2 Cor. 8:7 (NKJV)*

". . . [how] God anointed Jesus of Nazareth with the Holy Ghost and with power: who went about doing good, and healing all who were oppressed of the devil, for God was with him." *Acts 10:38 (KJV)*

NOVEMBER 28 Enfleda

Enfleda was the daughter of King Edwin of Northumbria and princess and saint Ethelburga of Kent (see Daily Readings, December 13, Ethelburga of Kent and Lucy) and the mother of St. Elfleda (see Daily Readings, February 8, Elfleda). Edwin wanted to evangelize his country to please his Christian wife, so he arranged for the first apostle to be sent to Northumbria—St. Paulinus of York. Paulinus, the bishop sent by Gregory the Great, eventually baptized Edwin and Enfleda together on Easter in 627 in a little wooden church at York. Enfleda's father died in battle when she was seven years old, and she and her mother returned to Kent. Enfleda married Oswiu of Bernicia; it was an arranged marriage to unify two separate sections of Northumbria. The major difference between Enfleda and her husband was their adherence to different calendars. Enfleda, who had had Roman-trained teachers, followed Rome's Easter calculation, and Oswiu followed the Northern Irish calendar. This dispute was not mediated until St. Hilda (see Daily Readings, November 19, Hilda of Whitby) called the Council of Whitby in 663. The dynastic struggles in Enfleda's family resulted in her husband murdering her brother Oswin. She persuaded her husband to build a monastery in reparation. After her husband's death, Enfleda took the veil at Whitby.

Prayer:

Almighty God, you bestow peace and love those who mediate conflict with love. Like us, Enfleda lived in troubling times when nations and even Christians were at war with each other. Instill in us trust and a willingness to find a way to clear the darkness that settles over family and church disputes, and guide all people to the openness and understanding so dear to your heart. Amen.

Antiphon:

Guide our feet unto the way of peace.

Readings:

"Great is the Lord, and greatly to be praised in the city of our God, in the mountain of his holiness. . . . As we have heard, so we have seen in the city of the Lord of Hosts, in the city of our God: God will establish it forever. We have thought of your lovingness,

O God in the midst of your temple. According to your name, so is your praise unto the ends of the earth." *Psalm 48:1, 8–10 (KJV)*

"For thus says the Lord: Behold I will extend peace to her like a river, and the glory of the Gentiles like a flowing stream. . . . And when you see this, your heart shall rejoice, and your bones shall flourish like an herb; and the hand of the Lord shall be known to his servants." *Isa. 66:12, 14 (KJV)*

"These things I have spoken to you, that in Me you may have peace. In the world you will have tribulation; but be of good cheer, I have overcome the world." *Jn. 16:33 (NKJV)*

NOVEMBER 29 Dorothy Day

Dorothy Day was born Episcopalian, experienced a "sweetness of faith" at a Methodist Sunday School, and converted to Roman Catholicism after living a bohemian lifestyle in New York, where she was a journalist. Her friends during the 1920s were socialists, intellectuals, and artists; an activist for justice and peace, she had many stays in jail. Dorothy's newfound faith caused her much ambivalence, and although she felt inspired by the lives of the saints, the burning question lingered in her mind: "Where were the saints to try to change the social order, not just to minister to the slaves, but to do away with slavery?" In 1933, she met Peter Maurin, and together they started the Catholic Worker movement and a penny newspaper that would become its trademark. They opened up houses of hospitality for the hungry and unemployed during the Depression. She continued to oversee the lay Catholic Worker movement as she raised her daughter, Tamar (born out of wedlock), and engaged in acts of civil disobedience that stemmed from her uncompromising commitment to nonviolence. Catholic Worker houses spread throughout the country and were active in strikes and protests to change wage and working conditions for the poor. Dorothy was passionately committed to the social gospel, and she was a prophetic voice for justice and equality and a ban on nuclear weapons. She died on November 29, 1980, with Tamar by her side. Dorothy challenges us to live simply "so that others can simply live."

Prayer:

Beloved Spirit of God, Dorothy Day is a reminder that you live within each individual soul, and your penetrating presence is everywhere. Because she saw you in rags, in prison, and starving on the streets, she was led to a radical vision that calls all followers of Christ's gospel to respond to the truth that we are our sisters' and brothers' keepers. A twentieth-century prophet who fought all kinds of exploitation, she was led to always try to discover common ground for dialogue. Bless us in our attempts to follow in her footsteps and open our hearts to find you in unexpected places. Amen.

Antiphon:

You will wipe away every tear from our eyes.

Readings:

"Do good, O LORD, to *those who are* good, and to *those who are* upright in their hearts." *Psalm 125:4 (NKJV)*

"[He] who continually goes forth weeping, bearing seed for sowing, shall doubtless come again with rejoicing, bringing [his] sheaves *with him*." *Psalm 126:6 (NKJV)*

"Behold! My Servant whom I have chosen, My Beloved in whom My soul is well pleased! I will put My Spirit upon Him, and He will declare justice to the Gentiles." *Mt. 12:18 (NKJV)*

"These *are* the things you shall do: Speak each man the truth to his neighbor; Give judgment in your gates for truth, justice, and peace; Let none of you think evil in your heart against your neighbor." *Zech. 8:16–17 (NKJV)*

NOVEMBER 30 Etty Hillesum

Etty Hillesum was a Dutch Jewish lawyer, considered by many to be a mystic, who lived in Amsterdam during World War II. Born of a Russian mother, she was much influenced by Dostoyevsky's Christianity. Through her dialogue with a Jungian therapist, she had learned to observe her own thoughts and feelings with a keen eye, and to use her journey of individuation to find the inner source, which is the center of every human life. She began a practice of meditation and discovered, in that "wide open space," a God who was her rest in the midst of great chaos. Her understanding of God granted her a radiant peace when she had a precognition of sudden death in a gas chamber. Etty wrote that she gained understanding of herself through suffering, and furthermore, only when one has rooted out every form of hatred toward fellow human beings of every race or nationality can one find peace within oneself. Incarcerated at Auschwitz, she faithfully kept a diary from 1941 until her death in 1943. Her acceptance of death was remarkable, especially since she was only twenty-nine when she died. A few months before her death, she wrote, "The only human thing that still remains in these times is: to kneel before you, O God." Her letters and journals, collected in the book *An Interrupted Life*, are a profound record of her ability to find meaning through the horror of the Nazi persecution and to remain true to her deepest ideal: compassion. Waiting for death gave Etta a sense of inevitability and made her feel always alive, always ready: "Every day I will put my papers in order and every day I will say farewell. And the real farewell, when it comes, will only be a small outward confirmation of what has been accomplished within me from day to day."

Prayer:

O God of wisdom and compassion, Etty Hillesum uncovered the despair and horror of a death camp and found you waiting there with a strength and goodness that restored a meaning to life. Have mercy on all those who have been given death sentences, and give them strength to sustain them during their final moments. May your hands be swift to welcome them and your compassion usher them into the place where angels sing. Through Christ our Lord. Amen.

Antiphon:

Sometimes the most important thing in a whole day is the rest we take between two breaths, or the turning inward in prayer for five short minutes. (*Journal of Etty Hillesum*)

Readings:

"Make haste, O God to deliver me; make haste to help me, O Lord. . . . Let all who seek you rejoice and be glad, and let such who love your salvation say continually: Let God be glorified. But I am poor and needy; make haste to help me, O God: you are my help and deliverer." *Psalm 70:1, 4–5 (KJV)*

"O God you have taught me from my youth; and hence I have declared your wondrous works. Now also when I am old and grey-headed, do not forsake me, O God, until I have showed your strength unto this generation, and your power to every one that is to come." *Psalm 71:4, 17–18 (KJV)*

"You have heard that it was said, '*An eye for an eye and a tooth for a tooth.*' But I tell you not to resist an evil person. But whoever slaps you on your right cheek, turn the other to him also." *Mt. 5:38–39 (NKJV)*

DECEMBER 1 Maria Clementine Anuarite Nengapete

The Church has been blessed by virgin martyrs through the centuries, including Maria Clementine Anuarite Nengapete in the twentieth century. Maria Clementine was born in Zaire in 1939, and her father introduced their family to the Christian faith after a visit to Palestine. Maria Clementine, her sisters, and her mother all took catechetical instruction at the local mission and were baptized in 1943. With her family's blessings, Maria Clementine joined the Holy Family Sisters in Bafwabaka when she was fifteen. She was especially devoted to the Blessed Virgin and Christ in the Eucharist, and her ministry included teaching in the girls' boarding school. When civil war broke out in the region in 1964, Maria Clementine and other nuns from her order were taken forcibly from their convent to be transported to rebel headquarters. One of the officers was attracted to Maria Clementine, but when she rebuked his advances, he stabbed her to death on the spot. She was martyred on December 1, 1964, at age twenty-three. Maria Clementine was instantly recognized throughout the region as a virgin martyr, and she was beatified in Zaire in 1985.

Intercessory Prayer:

Heavenly Father, we thank you for the witness of Maria Clementine, a modern virgin martyr. In remaining true to her vows, she served as a testament to countless individuals who were inspired by her holy life and her brave death. Her courage was an inspiration, especially to the Church in Zaire. Through her intercession, we pray for all individuals who have been forced to compromise their own purity through violent acts of rape and incest. May they be strengthened by Blessed Maria's life and given solace and peace. Amen.

Antiphon:

Blessed are the pure in heart, for they shall see God.

Readings:

"Lord, how they are increased that trouble me! Many are they that rise up against me. . . . But you O Lord are a shield for me, my glory and the lifter up of my head. I cried to the Lord with my voice, and he heard me out of his holy hill. I laid down and slept; I awakened, for the Lord sustained me. I will not be afraid of ten thousands of people, that have set themselves against me round about." *Psalm 3:1–6 (KJV)*

"But may the God of all grace, who called us to His eternal glory by Christ Jesus, after you have suffered awhile, perfect, establish, strengthen, and settle you." *1 Pet. 5:10 (NKJV)*

DECEMBER 2 Maria Angela Astorch and Myrope

Known as a mystic of the Divine Office, Maria Angela Astorch was born in Spain in 1592. Well educated, she was a lifelong student of theology and Christianity's sacred texts. Her left-brain approach to mysticism gave her critical insight into the Breviary, the daily liturgical schedule of prayers and readings sung in monasteries. Maria Angela entered the Poor Clare Capuchins at Barcelona and was soon made novice mistress and then abbess. She was a spiritual consultant to many, and she used her periods of deep contemplation to draw insight into understanding each person who came to her for spiritual direction. She died December 2, 1665, and was mourned by all the faithful of Spain. When Pope John Paul II beatified Maria Angela in 1982, he said, "She was able to respect the individuality of each person, helping the one concerned to keep in step with God."

In the East, December 2 is also the feast day of Myrope, a young woman martyr in the late third century. She was apprehended for attempting to retrieve the body of another martyred saint for a Christian burial. While in prison, in deep prayer, Myrope's body was reported to give off a sweet aroma, as angels began to surround her in preparation for her death, a miracle that caused her jailer's conversion.

Prayer:

Beloved Lord, we are filled with amazing grace when we realize how unique each individual soul is in your eyes. Through the intercession of Maria Angela and Myrope, help every woman find her path in life to best bring glory to your name. Wherever we find ourselves, make us ready to prepare a place for your kingdom. Amen.

Antiphon:

Joy and peace are your gifts to us.

Readings:

"Blessed is the man to whom the LORD does not impute iniquity, and in whose spirit there is no deceit. . . . I will instruct you and teach you in the way you should go; I will guide you with My eye. . . . Be glad in the LORD and rejoice, you righteous; and shout for joy, all you upright in heart!" *Psalm 32:2, 8, 11 (NKJV)*

"I thank my God, making mention of you always in my prayers, hearing of your love and faith which you have toward the Lord Jesus and toward all the saints that the sharing of your faith may become effective by the acknowledgment of every good thing which is in you in Christ Jesus. For we have great joy and consolation in your love, because the hearts of the saints have been refreshed by you, brother." *Philem. 4–7 (NKJV)*

"I know that you are as good in my sight as an angel of God." *1 Sam. 29:9 (NKJV)*

DECEMBER 3 Junia

St. John Chrysostom wrote about Junia, an early woman apostle whom Paul praises in Romans 16:7, "Oh how great is the devotion of this woman that she should be counted worthy of the appellation of apostle!" Like Paul, Junia suffered persecution and was put into prison for preaching the gospel. Junia is considered one of the first converts to the Christian faith, having accepted the Word even before Paul himself. Origen, Jerome, and Peter Abelard have written about her; and in Orthodoxy, she is known as Apostle to the Seventy, which may refer to the Pannonians near Moravia. Paul mentions her with Andronicus, who presumably was her husband. Early ministries included many missionary couples. In the thirteenth century, her name was redacted out of Romans, and the name "Junias" was inserted, implying that this early apostle was a man. However, subsequent scholarship has demonstrated that such a name never existed in ancient times, and later, the name of Junia was restored in the King James Version. Junia is celebrated May 17 in the Greek calendar.

Prayer:

Beloved Lord, you made Junia a brilliant star on the earth who spoke your Word bravely, enlightening all she met with the anointing of truth. Thank you, Lord, for the banquet of Christ's body, present in the early apostles, which so refreshed the Church and gave it life. Make us worthy also to be called your friends, with whom you share all good things. By holy Junia's intercession, give all women the strength to respond to the call of ministry they hear beckoning to them in their hearts. Amen.

Antiphon:

I lived among you as one who ministers to others.

Readings:

"[God] likewise predestined us through Christ Jesus to be his adopted children—such was his will and pleasure—that all might praise the glorious favor he has bestowed on us in his beloved. God has given us the wisdom to understand fully the mystery, the plan he was pleased to decree in Christ." *Eph. 1:4–9 (KJV)*

"And they continued steadfastly in the apostles' doctrine and fellowship, in the breaking of bread, and in prayers. Then fear came upon every soul, and many wonders and signs were done through the apostles. Now all who believed were together, and had all things in common, and sold their possessions and goods, and divided them among all, as anyone had need. So continuing daily with one accord in the temple, and breaking bread from house to house, they ate their food with gladness and simplicity of heart, praising God and having favor with all the people. And the Lord added to the church daily those who were being saved." Acts 2:42–47 (NKJV)

DECEMBER 4 Barbara

The tradition honoring St. Barbara goes back to the seventh century. The date of her legend is uncertain, but she is considered to have been a virgin and martyr in the third century. Barbara's heathen father, Dioscorus, wished to protect his beautiful daughter from outside forces, so he secluded her in a tower. Once, while he was gone on a journey, she requested baptism and became a Christian. She had a third window built into her tower to represent the Holy Trinity. It caught her father's attention when he returned. He became furious when he discovered that she had converted to Christianity, and he released her to the province's local prefect for trial. She suffered greatly in prison and was comforted by visions of Christ. When Barbara was stripped naked, angels came to clothe her. Her cruel father carried out the death sentence and beheaded her. He was then struck by lightning and completely consumed to ashes. The town that buried her became a famous locus of the cult of miracles attributed to her. Barbara's relics were later transferred to Constantinople, where the Emperor erected a church in her honor in the imperial palace.

Prayer:

Beloved Lord, Barbara valued her love for you above all things of this earth, and was comforted by your angels in prison. She is a model for all those who suffer abuse, especially from their parents. Strengthen and comfort all young people who strive to protect their purity and shun abuse in their lives, especially sexual abuse. Help us all to remember that although we may partake in Christ's suffering in this life, we will also participate in his glory in the next. Amen.

Antiphon:

I trusted, even when I said, I am sorely afflicted.

Readings:

"I believed, therefore I spoke,' I am greatly afflicted.' I said in my haste,' All men *are* liars.' What shall I render to the LORD *for* all His benefits toward me? I will take up the cup of salvation, and call upon the name of the LORD. I will pay my vows to the LORD now in the presence of all His people." *Psalm 116:10–14 (NKJV)*

"Even as the testimony of Christ was confirmed in you, so that you come short in no gift, eagerly waiting for the revelation of our Lord Jesus Christ." *1 Cor. 1:6–7 (NKJV)*

DECEMBER 5 Susanna

The Orthodox Church's liturgical calendar celebrates Susanna as a deacon and martyr of the fourth century. She was born in Palestine of a pagan father and a Jewish mother. Her mother brought her up to be a devout Jew, but died before Susanna reached her teens. Susanna was sent to live with a guardian, one of whose neighbors was a Christian presbyter who taught her about Jesus. After her father's death, Susanna became a Christian. She took her inheritance and distributed it to the poor. She then shaved her head, and, wearing men's clothing, sought admittance into a men's monastery. She called herself Ioannes (John). For twenty years, she lived a quiet contemplative life, until a scandal forced her to reveal that she was a female. A woman who went to the monastery for prayers had fallen in love with "Br. John," and when she failed to attract John's attention, she reported to the abbot that she had been seduced. When it was revealed that Susanna was an innocent woman, the abbot, who was astonished that she had surpassed many of the other monks in austerity and holiness, sent her to the bishop and suggested that she be ordained a deacon. She then became deaconess and abbess of a monastery in Eleutheropolis. Susanna died under Alexander's reign, after serving at the monastery for many years.

Prayer:

Beloved Jesus, lover of souls, your daughter Susanna demonstrated that women were not the "weaker vessel" (1 Pet. 3:7) and that a woman monk could attain the same degree of holiness as a man. Although she broke with convention, including the cultural injunction that a woman should not cut her hair, she knew that you inspired and protected her. As your Spirit called her to a life of service, so inspire us to respond to our inner calling, even if it violates man-made conventions. Help us to remember that listening to the still, small voice within can empower that voice to a powerful destiny. Amen.

Antiphon:

My vows to the Lord I will fulfill before all the people.

Readings:

"Who will bring me to the strong city? Who will lead me to Edom? . . . Give us help from trouble, for the help of man is useless. Through God we will do valiantly." Psalm 60:9, 11–12 (NKJV)

"For our boasting is this: the testimony of our conscience that we conducted ourselves in the world in simplicity and godly sincerity, not with fleshly wisdom but by the grace of God, and more abundantly toward you." 2 Cor. 1:12 (NKJV)

DECEMBER 6 Concepcion Cabrera de Armida

Concepcion (Conchita) Cabrera de Armida was one of the many inspirational women of the twentieth century, who touched countless souls through her vocation in the sacrament of marriage. Conchita was born in 1862 in Mexico. She was one of twelve children raised in a reverent Catholic home. When she married her beloved husband, Pancho, the devoted couple settled into a life filled with the blessing of many children. Conchita lived out her daily vocation quietly, but she had an intensely spiritual interior life, which she recorded in her journals. Her happy life was marked with events of intense suffering, including the death of one of her children, and later the death of her beloved husband after sixteen years of marriage. After Poncho's death, she befriended a priest who worked over the coming years to assist her in founding a number of apostolates. These missions included founding the Missionaries of the Holy Spirit, which was an order of priests, as well as an order of contemplative nuns, an order of catechetical sisters, and a variety of other lay apostolates. Her beautiful letters to her children and her spiritual diary were published after her death in 1937 and remain an inspiration to the faithful today. Concepcion's cause for canonization is under way.

Intercessory Prayer:

Heavenly Father, thank you for the gift of holy women like Concepcion de Armida who served your Church through living out the vocation of motherhood. Her life of service spread beyond the borders of her own immediate family, and she was inspirational in following your call and establishing many apostolates. Let her life be a living testament to the great things that can be accomplished when we openly respond to your divine call within our lives. Amen.

Antiphon:

You are my hope; my trust from the days of my youth.

Readings:

"Countless are the things you have made, O Lord, You have made all by your wisdom; and the earth is full of your creatures, beasts great and small; Here is the great immeasurable sea, in which move creatures beyond number. Here ships sail to and fro, here is Leviathan whom you have made your plaything. All of them look expectantly to you to give them food at the proper time; what you give them they gather up, When you open your hand, they eat their fill." *Psalm 104:24–28 (NEB)*

"Be sure, God will not spurn the blameless, nor grasp the hand of the wrongdoer. He will yet fill your mouth with laughter, and shouts of joy will be on your lips." *Job 8:20–21 (NEB)*

"Look to yourself, each of you; you may be tempted too. Help one another to carry these heavy loads, and in this way you will fulfill the law of Christ." *Gal. 6:2 (NEB)*

"For in the resurrection they neither marry nor are given in marriage, but are like angels of God in heaven." *Mt. 22:30 (NKJV)*

DECEMBER 7 Mary Joseph Rossello

Mary Joseph Rossello was born into a large Christian family in 1811 in the tiny seaport town of Albissola, Italy. Although she wanted to enter the convent, she had no dowry, and at age sixteen she became a Third Order Franciscan. She spent her early adult years as a household servant, while she simultaneously gathered about her young girls, whom she instructed in their Catholic faith. The Bishop of Savona was impressed with her self-initiated vocation, and eventually he purchased a house for her with two classrooms and living space for several other women. By the time she was twenty-six, Mary Joseph had organized her little institute into the Daughters of Mercy, whom she served as superior for the next forty years. She was sensitive to the problem of ardent young women being excluded because of a lack of dowry, and she abolished it as a requisite for her order. Mary Joseph was particularly loving to her older sisters as they aged, and she said that the sick were a vital part of her order because their patience, suffering, and prayers obtained great mercy and grace for the whole house. She also was keenly aware that idleness was a burden that must be avoided, and she was often heard to quote the maxim, "The hands should be at work, the heart with God." Mary Joseph died in 1880 and was canonized in 1949.

Prayer:

Blessed Jesus, St. Mary Joseph had a heart on fire to serve you, and she found ways to fulfill her vocation despite all obstacles in her way. She teaches us that personal ennoblement is not a given, but a task. Keep us from useless idleness, which so often causes us to become absorbed in the affairs and gossip of others' lives, rather than our own. Guide us with your Spirit, so that through all our weaknesses, we overcome all obstacles in our way and stay resolute in our desire to fulfill our own vocation. Amen.

Antiphon:

Blessed are those who delight in your work, O God.

Readings:

"Your word is a lamp to my feet
   And a light to my path.
I have sworn and confirmed
   That I will keep Your righteous judgments.

I am afflicted very much;
  Revive me, O LORD, according to Your word.
Accept, I pray, the freewill offerings of my mouth, O LORD,
  And teach me Your judgments.
The wicked have laid a snare for me,
  Yet I have not strayed from Your precepts.
Your testimonies I have taken as a heritage forever,
  For they are the rejoicing of my heart.
I have inclined my heart to perform Your statutes
  Forever, to the very end." *Psalm 119:105–112 (NKJV)*

"I tell you this: there is not a thoughtless word that comes from men's lips but they will have to account for it on the day of judgment. For out of your own mouth you will be acquitted; out of your own mouth you will be condemned." *Mt. 12:36–37 (NEB)*

"She watches over the ways of her household, and does not eat the bread of idleness." *Prov. 31:27 (NKJV)*

DECEMBER 8 Immaculate Conception/ Conception of Mary

The doctrine of the Immaculate Conception—a dogma found only in the Roman Catholic Church—states that the Blessed Virgin Mary's soul was preserved from original sin from the moment of her conception. The doctrine has a colorful history, although it is difficult to defend from either scriptural or apocryphal sources. Basil and John Chrysostom believed that Christ saved Mary, like everybody else. Yet some of the early Fathers, such as Irenaeus and Cyril of Jerusalem, believed she was the archetype of the New Eve, and therefore immaculate and incorrupt. Although the feast of the Conception of Mary was celebrated earlier in the East, the discussion of whether she was saved from all sin, including original sin, did not arise before the ninth century. The East and West church traditions agree that the purity of Mary's life is unquestioned; the disagreement is in the language of dogma and the understanding of original sin.

The East glorifies Mary with the highest crown because, despite impulses to temptation, she resisted and was therefore the perfect disciple: the West's "teaching of the grace-given sinlessness of the

Virgin Mary denies her victory over temptations . . . this makes her a blind instrument of God's Providence" (St. John Maximovitch). Orthodoxy, which believes in merit, asks: If Mary (like Jesus) could not sin, then for what did God glorify her? In the West, the controversy raged for several centuries, basically between the Dominicans, especially Thomas Aquinas who censured the dogma, and the Franciscans, particularly Duns Scotus who defended it. Aquinas's main difficulty was: how could Mary have been redeemed if she had no stain of sin (before the redemption)? Duns Scotus solved the problem by proposing that the Virgin Mother obtained redemption from her Son from the moment of her conception, because God's realm is timeless: God saw Mary's goodness from all eternity. The Roman Catholic position also rests on the concept of dogma's evolution; that is, through the action of the Holy Spirit more of the Church's doctrine is revealed over time. Roman scriptural foundation for the dogma is in Luke 1:28, where Mary is greeted by the angel Gabriel as "full of grace." Before the Annunciation, she is already a graced woman when the angel greets her. In this understanding, Mary already has received unmerited grace because the work of the Incarnation and Redemption belongs to God. The doctrine was brought to fruition in Pope Pius IX's Bull *Ineffabilis Deus* issued December 8, 1854, which declared that "by a singular privilege and grace granted by God, and in view of the merits of Jesus Christ" Mary was immune from original sin.

Intercessory Prayer:

> *O Immaculate Virgin Mother, to you are ascribed the most inscrutable mysteries of God. Yet, as the first and most perfect disciple, you—like us—pondered in your heart many things concerning Jesus, in order to extract their meaning. You never refused God's love, always carrying him in your heart. As your first beginning was holy and pure, pray for us that we may attain unity with our beloved Jesus for all eternity, being made pure in his sight by the fruit of his glorious Redemption. Amen.*

Antiphon:

You shall be a crown of beauty in the hand of the Lord.

Readings:

"Let me rejoice in the Lord with all my heart, let me exult in my God, for he has robed me in salvation as a garment and clothed me in integrity as a cloak; like a bridegroom with his priestly garland or a bride decked in her jewels. For, as the earth puts forth her blossom or bushes in the garden burst into flower, so shall the Lord God make righteousness and praise blossom before all the nations." *Isa. 61:10–11 (NEB)*

"Like a lily among thorns, so is my love among the daughters." *Song of Songs 2:2 (NKJV)*

"In Christ he chose us before the world was founded, to be dedicated, to be without blemish in his sight." *Eph. 1:4 (NEB)*

DECEMBER 9 Elizabeth the Good and Mary Frances Schervier

Blessed Elizabeth was called "Bona" (the Good) from an early age because of her utterly sweet disposition in all aspects of her life. She was born in Germany in 1386 to a poor family and became a Franciscan tertiary at age thirteen. She served as a weaver and servant girl to a household, and later in life she joined with a group of other tertiaries, where she worked in the kitchen. It was said that she lived such a life of innocence that it was difficult to find matter for absolutions in her confessions. Toward the end of her life she contracted leprosy, which she saw as a token of God's love. Elizabeth was a stigmatist on Fridays during Lent, and she died during Passion Week in 1420.

Mary Frances Schervier was born into a distinguished family in France in 1819. In 1844, she became a Secular Franciscan, but later she founded a religious community known as the Sisters of the Poor of St. Francis. She visited the United States in 1863, where she and her sisters nursed soldiers during the Civil War. Her order grew, and today they operate hospitals and homes for the aged. She had a commitment to extensive letter writing to her sisters, and she was most fond of reminding them of the words of St. Francis: "love lightens all difficulties and sweetens all bitterness." Mary Frances was beatified in 1974.

Prayer:

Loving God, make us to walk in your way, following the inspiration of holy women like Elizabeth and Mary Frances. By loving all whom you place in our path, may we partake of the blessing that you offer to all your children of continually growing in grace. Help us to always be motivated by the ideals nourished by your saints, so that we respect the God-given dignity of all persons we meet. Help us to remember the words of St. Francis that where there is love and wisdom, there is neither fear nor ignorance. Amen.

Antiphon:

I have given you as a light to the nations.

Readings:

"As smoke is driven away, so drive *them* away; as wax melts before the fire, *so* let the wicked perish at the presence of God. But let the righteous be glad; let them rejoice before God; yes, let them rejoice exceedingly. Sing to God, sing praises to His name . . . A father of the fatherless, a defender of widows." *Psalm 68:3–6 (NKJV)*

"He Himself took our infirmities and bore our sicknesses." *Mt. 8:17 (NKJV)*

"My sheep hear My voice, and I know them, and they follow Me. And I give them eternal life, and they shall never perish; neither shall anyone snatch them out of My hand." *Jn. 10:27–28 (NKJV)*

"These things I command you, that you love one another." *Jn. 15:17 (NKJV)*

DECEMBER 10 Alicia Domon

Alicia Domon was a Maryknoll missionary sister who served during the military reign of terror in Argentina from 1967 until her death in 1977. At the time, the dictatorship was waging a war against dissidents, especially advocates of human rights. Thousands of civilians were killed, and thousands more disappeared. Alicia served at the Toulouse Institute of the Sisters of Foreign Missions. Initially she worked with mentally retarded children, but by 1969, her community had moved out of their convent and into a city shanty-town. She became involved with the struggles of landless peasants and supported an organization of women known as the Mothers of the Disappeared. Each day they would courageously gather at the central plaza, dressed in black, and display photographs of their children who they believed the military had abducted. In 1977, Sister Alicia was preparing a Christmas retreat for the Mothers, but on December 8, the militia seized her, and she was never heard from again. Alicia's writings indicated that she knew she would die a martyr's death.

Prayer:

Beloved Jesus of Mercy, Sister Alicia courageously placed her life in danger in order to stand with the oppressed and resist evil where she saw it. May she serve as an inspiration to all modern martyrs who sacrifice their lives while proclaiming your justice and mercy. You, who spread out your arms on the cross, will receive them with the open arms of your infinite compassion. We thank you for giving us women of such courage and conviction and ask you to be with us during our own deaths. Amen.

Antiphon:

Christ Jesus, may we join you in your Passion.

Readings:

"They surrounded me, yes, they surrounded me; but in the name of the LORD I will destroy them. They surrounded me like bees; they were quenched like a fire of thorns. . . . You pushed me violently, that I might fall, but the LORD helped me. The LORD is my strength and song, and He has become my salvation. . . . I shall not die, but live, and declare the works of the LORD." *Psalm 118:10–14, 17 (NKJV)*

"Remember the prisoners as if chained with them—those who are mistreated—since you yourselves are in the body also." *Heb. 13:3 (NKJV)*

"I have glorified You on the earth. I have finished the work which You have given Me to do." *Jn. 17:4 (NKJV)*

DECEMBER 11 Henrietta Mears

Born in 1890 in Fargo, North Dakota, into a devout Presbyterian family, Henrietta Mears was soon on her way to becoming one of the most outstanding Christian educators of her time. Billy Graham once said no other woman had more influence in his life except his mother and his wife. As a child, doctors informed Henrietta's mother that she could well be blind before she reached adulthood. Undaunted, she decided to read everything she could before she lost her eyesight. After she graduated from college, she started her ministry in a church whose attendance grew quickly from four hundred to four thousand. Unsatisfied with the Christian education literature then used in her church, she wrote her own lesson material, which was more reflective of what actually happened in the Bible—including the miracle stories. She later established Gospel Light Publications, one of the first publishers in the Protestant Christian education field. She was famous for her powerful prayers, and she advised others to "dream big whenever God is involved." Her ministry drew her to the San Bernardino Mountains in California to found a retreat center, which became a place of conversion for many in the Los Angeles and Hollywood area. She had thousands of students during the course of her life, including Bill and Vonette Bright, who started the Campus Crusade for Christ. Henrietta died in 1963, her eyesight still intact.

Prayer:

Blessed Jesus, you caused your holy Scriptures to be written for our learning. Knowing you intimately and bringing the Christian message to others was the main objective in the life of your beloved daughter Henrietta Mears. Grant us also to hear your Word in ways that will cause us to inwardly digest it, holding fast to the hope of finding in it everlasting life through your grace. Amen.

Antiphon:

Come to us this day and set your people free.

Readings:

"Give the king Your judgments, O God, and Your righteousness to the king's Son.

He will judge Your people with righteousness, and Your poor with justice.
The mountains will bring peace to the people, and the little hills, by righteousness.
He will bring justice to the poor of the people; He will save the children of the needy,
and will break in pieces the oppressor." *Psalm 72:1–4 (NKJV)*

"But I make known to you, brethren, that the gospel which was preached by me is not according to man. For I neither received it from man, nor was I taught *it,* but *it came* through the revelation of Jesus Christ." *Gal. 1:11–12 (NKJV)*

"Every place that the sole of your foot will tread upon I have given you. . . ." *Josh. 1:3 (NKJV)*

DECEMBER 12 Our Lady of Guadalupe

Our Lady of Guadalupe, known as Our Lady of the Americas, is the most famous shrine of Our Lady in the Western hemisphere. Her legend dates from 1531, when she appeared to a fifty-five-year-old Indian named Juan Diego near Mexico City. She asked him, in his native tongue, Nahuatl, to deliver a message to the bishop that she wished a shrine to be built there. She told him that she was the mother of the true God. The bishop, not immediately believing the messenger, told Juan to ask the Lady for a sign. When Juan brought her the bishop's request, she told him to gather roses down by the rocks. Since it was winter and not a time for roses to be blooming, he doubted that he would find any, but they were profuse. He gathered them into his *tilma,* or cape, and returned to the bishop. When he opened his *tilma,* more than roses was exposed. An exquisite shining life-size icon of the Blessed Mother adorned the cape, to the astonishment of both Juan and the bishop. The Guadalupe shrine was built, and it has been the source of many miracle healings and is a famous place of pilgrimage. The coarsely woven *tilma,* which was made of vegetable fiber, did not deteriorate as expected after a century, and the color has remained vibrant since its initial appearance. Painters have not been able to explain the mysterious laying on of colors on the *tilma,* and scientists have not been able to determine the type of pigment from which the image was rendered. The Vatican officially recognized the miracle at Guadalupe in 1745.

Intercessory Prayer:

Bounteous Mother of God, we are all members of your family, bound as one people to our Lord Jesus. Endow us with your virtues, and help us to respect the lives of your children everywhere. Mother of the Americas, protect us from danger and keep families together in times of darkness. Through Christ our Lord. Amen.

Antiphon:

Great is your faithfulness.

Readings:

"'Sing, O barren, You *who* have not borne! Break forth into singing, and cry aloud, you *who* have not labored with child! For more *are* the children of the desolate than the children of the married woman,' says the LORD. . . . For your Maker *is* your husband, the LORD of hosts *is* His name; and your Redeemer *is* the Holy One of Israel; he is called the God of the whole earth." *Isa. 54:1, 5 (NKJV)*

"But God has chosen the foolish things of the world to put to shame the wise, and God has chosen the weak things of the world to put to shame the things which are mighty; and the base things of the world and the things which are despised God has chosen, and the things which are not, to bring to nothing the things that are." *1 Cor. 1:27–28 (NKJV)*

'We fly unto thee, O Virgin of Virgins, our Mother; despise not our petitions, but in thy mercy hear and answer us." *Traditional*

DECEMBER 13 Ethelburga of Kent and Lucy

Ethelburga of Kent was an early proponent of Christianity. She was influential in converting her husband, King Edwin, and she was the mother of St. Enfleda (see Daily Readings, November 28, Enfleda). Ethelburga and her family were Christians when she married Edwin, king of Northumbria. Her confessor, Paulinus, was sent to evangelize there. Initially Edwin, a pagan, resisted conversion, but later he relented and allowed his country to be evangelized. Following the king's conversion on Easter 627, most of the country converted as well. According to Bede, the historian, King Edwin's reign was one of peace and order until 633, when King Penda of Mercia, a pagan, killed him in battle. Ethelburga and her family fled to Kent, where her brother gave her land to establish a double monastery. She died in the monastery that she founded in 647 and was buried in the abbey. Ethelburga received the status of saint locally, and her abbey became a focal point for pilgrims.

St. Lucy was a young virgin martyr from the fourth century. Tradition tells us that, during her martyrdom, her eyes were torn out but were later miraculously restored. She is the patron of eye diseases. The name Lucy means "light."

Prayer:

> *Holy God, saints Ethelburga and Lucy were witnesses to your early Church and were instrumental in converting many souls. They truly reflected your blessed light wherever they found themselves. Lucy teaches us that seeing Christ's light is possible for those who believe, even without physical eyes. Help us to see your great goodness with the eyes of the soul and to joyfully spread that light to all we meet. Amen.*

Antiphon:

In your light shall we see light.

Readings:

"You send forth Your Spirit, they are created;
  And You renew the face of the earth.
May the glory of the LORD endure forever;
  May the LORD rejoice in His works." *Psalm 104:30–31 (NKJV)*

"When He had said these things, He spat on the ground and made clay with the saliva; and He anointed the eyes of the blind man with the clay. . . . Therefore they said to him, 'How were your eyes opened?' He answered and said, 'A Man called Jesus made clay and anointed my eyes and said to me, "Go to the pool of Siloam and wash." So I went and washed, and I received sight.'" *Jn. 9:6, 10–11 (NKJV)*

"Cast your burden on the LORD, And He shall sustain you; He shall never permit the righteous to be moved." *Psalm 55:22 (NKJV)*

DECEMBER 14 Mary di Rosa

Paula Frances Mary di Rosa lived in nineteenth-century Europe, born into a fairly wealthy Italian family. When Paula was just eleven years old, her mother died, and she eventually assumed the leadership role within her family of nine children, running the household at age seventeen. She lived at home into her late twenties and spent a good deal of her life finding ways to reach out to those less fortunate than herself. She arranged physical and spiritual care for young women working within her father's factory mill, and she was instrumental in greatly helping her entire village when a cholera epidemic struck in the mid-1800s. Paula was finally able to realize her life's dream by founding a new religious order of women whose mission was to care for the sick and run schools for the poor, including a school for deaf children. She became the superior of this new congregation known as the Handmaids of Charity and took the name Mary of the Crucified. The Pope approved her order in 1840, and she remained the superior until her death at age forty-two. Pope Pius XII canonized Mary in 1954.

Intercessory Prayer:

Heavenly Father, thank you for strong and vibrant women of faith like St. Mary di Rosa, whose lives were spent in total service to others and in responding in dramatic ways to your call. May St. Mary di Rosa inspire us to strive to respond to the Holy Spirit's inspirations each new day that we are blessed to receive from you. May we find new and simple ways to live the virtue of charity within our circle of family, friends, and neighbors. Amen.

Antiphon:

And above all things have fervent charity among yourselves.

Readings:

"This is the day the LORD has made;
   We will rejoice and be glad in it.
Save now, I pray, O LORD;
   O LORD, I pray, send now prosperity.
Blessed *is* he who comes in the name of the LORD!
   We have blessed you from the house of the LORD."
    Psalm 118:24–26 (NKJV)

"Then they brought to Him one who was deaf and had an impediment in his speech, and they begged Him to put His hand on him.
. . . Immediately his ears were opened, and the impediment of his
tongue was loosed, and he spoke plainly." *Mk. 7:32, 35 (NKJV)*

"In this is love, not that we loved God, but that He loved us and
sent His Son to be the propitiation for our sins. Beloved, if God so
loved us, we also ought to love one another. No one has seen
God at any time. If we love one another, God abides in us, and His
love has been perfected in us. By this we know that we abide in
Him, and He in us, because He has given us of His Spirit." *1 Jn.
4:10–13 (NKJV)*

DECEMBER 15 Catherine Doherty

Catherine Doherty was born into a Russian Orthodox family in 1896, and she was imbued with the elements of a
Russian culture that was saturated with Christian iconography and rich liturgical celebrations. Over her lifetime, she sought to
integrate the two great traditions of Orthodoxy and Roman Catholicism, which, to use the words of Pope John Paul II, she saw as the
"two lungs" of Christ's body. Catherine was educated from age six in
a Catholic school, and she was formally received into the Roman
Church in 1920. She married her cousin, an aristocrat named Boris
de Hueck, but the marriage was not a good one. During the Bolshevik Revolution, they escaped to Finland, and later they went to England. She ended her relationship with her abusive husband and left
with her small son to live with the poor in the slums of Toronto,
Canada. She became an activist in social reform and civil rights and
founded the first Friendship House in Canada. After her marriage was
annulled, she married Edward Doherty, a famous Chicago newspaper
reporter. Catherine discovered her own literary abilities, authoring
more than three hundred articles and books, including the famous
Poustinia (a Russian word that means "desert"), which has become a
classic of modern contemplative writing. Her mystical insight impressed Thomas Merton, who said that her sense of presence was so
powerful, it came directly from the Holy Spirit dwelling in her.
Throughout her life, Catherine prayed for the unity of the Russian
and Roman churches, feeling intensely that the Lord suffered from

the conflict between the two great traditions. Her lifelong passion was to "take Jesus off his cross" and bind up his wounds. She spent her life consoling him through the suffering and broken souls she served in her social ministries; she founded the Madonna House in 1947 to engage in rural mission work. Catherine is particularly loved in the Byzantine Catholic Church, and the cause of her canonization is under way.

Prayer:

Beloved Jesus, whose mercies cannot be numbered, bless the poor whose needs are served by the Friendship Houses founded by your daughter Catherine Doherty. Inspire us with the zeal she possessed to bring souls to you by serving them with graciousness and respect. Bless your Church throughout the world so that the divisions we have sown may dissipate and we may be one as you and your Father are one. Unite us mystically to your universal body as we strive to make your prayer of unity a reality in our world. Amen.

Antiphon:

Holy God, Holy and Mighty, Holy and Immortal, have mercy on us. *(Orthodox prayer)*

Readings:

"When I considered these things inwardly, and thought upon them in my mind, that in kinship with wisdom there is immortality, and in friendship with her, pure delight, and in the labors of her hands, unfailing wealth, and in the experience of her company, under-standing, and renown in sharing her words, I went about seeking how to get her for myself." *Wis. 8:17–18 (RSV)*

"Now I beseech you brethren, by the name of our Lord Jesus Christ, that you all speak the same thing, and that there be no di-visions among you; but that you be perfectly joined together in the same mind and in the same judgment." *1 Cor. 1:10 (KJV)*

DECEMBER 16 *Amy Carmichael*

Amy Carmichael was born in Northern Ireland on December 16, 1867, the oldest of seven children. Her father, who taught her to have a tomboy spirit, died when she was eighteen. Describing herself as a "wild-bird-child and in no wise tame," she never married. She had a mystical experience when still young, during which she felt a distinct calling from God to do missionary work. She went first to Japan, and after an illness there, she went to India. The Church of England's Zenana Missionary Society commissioned her to work in Dohnavur. During a period in India's history when young girls were "married to the gods" and sold into temple prostitution, Amy valiantly dedicated her life to saving more than a thousand children from a life of sexual abuse, including entering temples to take the children out physically. Despite numerous illnesses, once she got to India, Amy made it her home. She served there for fifty-six years. The Dohnavur Fellowship, which she founded, became, under her guidance, a place of sanctuary for children who would have otherwise had a very bleak future and for "temple babies," infants born from young prostitute temple girls. Her beloved adopted children called her "Amma" or "mother." A prolific author, Amy wrote more than three dozen devotional books.

Prayer:

Beloved Master, Amy Carmichael's life was devoted to making your love known to those children who suffered from the darkness of neglect and abuse. She is a model of utter abandonment to you. Help us to live, like her, with an ardent effort to dwell in your light and to follow wherever it may lead us. Have mercy on children around the world who are victims of child abuse and child labor. May we console them and help them to find a way to live out their childhood in wonder and in joy. Amen.

Antiphon:

And Jesus said, "Go and do the same."

Readings:

"Because of Your temple at Jerusalem, Kings will bring presents to You. Rebuke the beasts of the reeds. The herd of bulls with the calves of the peoples, *Till everyone* submits himself with pieces of silver. Scatter the peoples *who* delight in war. Envoys will come out of Egypt; Ethiopia will quickly stretch out her hands to God. . . . The Lord said, 'I will bring back from Bashan; I will bring *them* back from the depths of the sea.' *Psalm 68:29–31, 22 (NKJV)*

"For this reason I also suffer these things; nevertheless I am not ashamed, for I know whom I have believed and am persuaded that He is able to keep what I have committed to Him until that Day." *2 Tim: 1:12 (NKJV)*

"But when Jesus saw *it*, He was greatly displeased and said to them, 'Let the little children come to Me, and do not forbid them; for of such is the kingdom of God. Assuredly, I say to you, whoever does not receive the kingdom of God as a little child will by no means enter it.' And He took them up in His arms, laid *His* hands on them, and blessed them." *Mk. 10:14–16 (NKJV)*

DECEMBER 17 Adelaide and Mary Crucifixa

Adelaide was born a princess into a royal family in Burgundy during the tenth century. As was the custom, she was betrothed from a young age. Just three years after her marriage to the king of Italy, political enemies assassinated him. When Adelaide refused to wed a member of the warring party, she was imprisoned in a castle and held in solitary confinement. She was eventually rescued by a priest, and then Otto of Germany freed her and made her his wife. The couple had five children, and her son Otto III succeeded his father after his death. Adelaide was famous for her intellect, and she took part in affairs of the state. Eventually, Adelaide became the regent of Italy herself and was most known for her kindness, generosity to the poor, mass conversions, and establishment of monasteries. She died at age sixty-eight at one of the monasteries that she founded and was canonized the following century. Adelaide is the patron of those forced into exile.

December 17 is also the feast day of Mary Crucifixa Satellico, who was a Poor Clare in Venice in the eighteenth century. Pope John Paul II beatified Mary Crucifixa in 1993, declaring that she lived out her short life as a faithful daughter of St. Francis by conforming her life for love of the crucified Savior.

Intercessory Prayer:

Dear Lord, throughout history you have given us shining examples of saintly women who have served you in whatever station in life you have placed them. St. Adelaide was a princess and a regent who used the gifts you bestowed upon her to bring others to true faith. Help us to follow her example and use the gifts you have given to us to reach out to the poor and needy. Blessed Mary Crucifixa was devoted to you in the Eucharist and loved to sing for you in the choir. May we join her in praise of your endless wonders. Amen.

Antiphon:

My heart is steadfast, O God.

Readings:

"O God of my fathers and Lord of mercy, who hast made all things by thy word, and by thy wisdom hast formed man, to have dominion over the creatures thou hast made, and rule the world in holiness and righteousness, and pronounce judgment in uprightness of soul, give me the wisdom that sits by thy throne, and do not reject me from among thy servants." *Wis. 9:1–4 (RSV)*

"In that day you will ask in My name, and I do not say to you that I shall pray the Father for you; for the Father Himself loves you, because you have loved Me, and have believed that I came forth from God." *Jn. 16:26–27 (NKJV)*

"And above all things have fervent love for one another, for 'love will cover a multitude of sins.'" *1 Pet. 4:8 (NKJV)*

DECEMBER 18 Mother Alfred Moes and Virgin of Solitude Statue

Maria Catherine Moes lived during the nineteenth century in Luxembourg. In 1852 she met a bishop from Milwaukee. She moved to America in order to work with the Native Americans at the School of the Sisters of Notre Dame, where she took the name Alfred. She eventually helped to found a new community of women religious in Rochester, Minnesota, which was dedicated to Our Lady of Lourdes. Her order continues to serve through various ministries, including hospitals, schools, and homes for the aged. Mother Alfred was instrumental in helping to found the world-famous Mayo Clinic.

In Mexico, December 18 is also the feast day in honor of the Blessed Mother as Our Lady of Oaxaca. In 1620, a beautifully ornate statue of the Blessed Virgin appeared under miraculous circumstances in Oaxaca which became known as the *Virgin of Solitude*. The faithful built a chapel there in honor of the image. The statue was lost for centuries but was recovered in 1888. The *Virgin of Solitude* was restored with new robes and jewels, and it remains in a basilica that was erected where the image first inexplicably appeared centuries ago.

Intercessory Prayer:

Dear Blessed Mother of God, Virgin of Solitude, *bring solace and peace to our restless and fallen world through your intercession and grace. Inspire us to live our faith each day by looking for opportunities to bring others to come to know Christ's true love. May we also be inspired by Mother Alfred Moes, who lived her life in total service and charitable giving to others. Help us to enter into a deeper understanding of God's plan for us, that we may best serve his kingdom. Amen.*

Antiphon:

And the righteous shall flourish and have abundance of peace.

Readings:

"May your Anointed endure like the sun,
As long as the moon, through all ages,
Like rain that falls on the mown grass,
Like showers that water the earth.
In that day, justice shall flourish
And peace till the moon be no more." *Psalm 72:7 (PCB)*

"Shepherd Your people with Your staff, The flock of Your heritage, Who dwell solitarily in a woodland, In the midst of Carmel; Let them feed in Bashan and Gilead, As in days of old." *Micah 7:14 (NKJV)*

"Rising early the next morning, he went off to a lonely place in the desert; there he was absorbed in prayer." *Mk. 1:35 (NRSV)*

DECEMBER 19 Samthann

St. Samthann, also known as Safan, was a Celtic abbess in the eighth century. Samthann was the foster child of Cridan, king of Ireland. He married her to a nobleman; however, the marriage was never consummated. Samthann prayed ardently on her wedding night. Her legend narrates that her prayers were so powerful that a flame came from her mouth and caught the roof of the house on fire. Samthann hid and when Cridan found her, he decided to let her determine her own fate. Released from her marriage, she pursued her dream of becoming a religious. She became known as a famous "anam chara" or confessor and reader of souls. Several stories illustrate her wisdom and good counsel. The Holy Spirit's fire burned so fervently in Samthann that others sometimes perceived it as a burning flame. Funecha, founder of the monastery at Clonbrony, had a dream of Samthann in which she was a spark of fire that grew into a huge flame that burned the entire monastery. Funecha took this as a sign that Samthann was to become the monastery's next abbess, and that the monastery would grow in God's glory. Samthann was well-known for her generosity. She always shared what she had in the monastery with the poor outside its doors. Stories are told of her feeding great numbers of people during famine. She died in 739, and the night of her death, her friend Abbot Laserian had a dream of her coming to him in the form of a star to bid him good-bye.

Prayer:

O Holy Spirit of God, all who knew and loved Samthann recognized the fire that burned in her. She was a shining light, a radiant ray of your streaming grace. Through her intercession teach us to be loving flames of your love, remembering always that the Lord God is a consuming fire. Guide our wandering hearts to you, O God. May we give thanks to you always for your infinite grace and be ever indebted to your eternal love. Amen.

Antiphon:

Turn to me with all your hearts, says our God.

Readings:

"Now when Solomon had made an end of praying, the fire came down from heaven, and consumed the burnt offering and the sacrifices; and the glory of the Lord filled the house. And the priests could not enter into the house of the Lord, because the glory of the Lord had filled the Lord's house. And when all the children of Israel saw how the fire came down, and the glory of the Lord upon the house; they bowed themselves with their faces to the ground." *2 Chron. 7:1–3 (KJV)*

"Then the angel of the Lord put forth the end of the staff that was in his hand, and touched the flesh and the unleavened cakes; and there rose up fire out of the rock, and consumed the flesh and the unleavened cakes. Then the angel of the Lord departed out of his sight." *Judg. 6:21 (KJV)*

"I indeed baptize you with water unto repentance, but He who is coming after me is mightier than I, whose sandals I am not worthy to carry. He will baptize you with the Holy Spirit and fire." *Mt. 3:11 (NKJV)*

DECEMBER 20 Florence Allshorn

Florence Allshorn kept a series of notebooks, and she wrote on several occasions that holiness is an effect, not a cause. Because her tolerance and compassion were tested a number of times, she came to understand, as many holy souls do, that one's personal witness must never come from the self or be an end in itself; otherwise, "the thing breaks down." Born in 1887 in England and active in the Anglican Church during her youth, she found herself on a boat to Uganda when she was twenty-three years old, to do mission work at a girl's boarding school there. The woman in charge of the school had already gone through seven helpers, and she was so ill-tempered no one wanted to be around her. Florence was determined to find a way to love this woman, and she stayed on for eight years. In 1928, she contracted tuberculosis and was forced to return to Europe. Realizing that many other missionaries suffered both physically and emotionally from the strenuous labors they often engaged in, she began training other women missionaries, and in the 1940s she founded a house of refuge and rest for those returning from missionary work. It was known as St. Julian's House, and for the rest of her life Florence devoted her efforts to creating hospitality houses that would nurture those who nurtured others. Florence's philosophy was that our calling is not to become holy women, but to work for God, for "God can do nothing while my interest is in my own personal character—He will take care of this if I obey his call."

Prayer:

Almighty God, you raised up Florence Allshorn to be a minister to those who minister, refreshing them from their labors. You allowed her to see that love is a decision, and charity a costly virtue that must be practiced. She became determined to find a Christ-like way of living and loving, even with those she found difficult. As her charity united her to you and to those whom she served, so allow her inspiration to model for us a charity made perfect in Jesus Christ our Lord. Amen.

Antiphon:

Be merciful, as our God is merciful.

Readings:

"Praise the LORD!
    Oh, give thanks to the LORD, for *He is* good!
    For His mercy *endures* forever.
Who can utter the mighty acts of the LORD?
    Who can declare all His praise?
Blessed are those who keep justice,
    And he who does righteousness at all times!
Remember me, O LORD, with the favor You have toward Your people.
    Oh, visit me with Your salvation," *Psalm 106:1–4 (NKJV)*

"Pleasant words are like a honeycomb,
Sweetness to the soul and health to the bones." *Prov. 16:24 (NKJV)*

"But if you love those who love you, what credit is that to you? For even sinners love those who love them. And if you do good to those who do good to you, what credit is that to you? For even sinners do the same. . . . But love your enemies, do good, and lend, hoping for nothing in return; and your reward will be great, and you will be sons of the Most High. For He is kind to the unthankful and evil." *Lk. 6:32–35 (NKJV)*

DECEMBER 21 Hildelith and Cumania

Hildelith was a young English woman who took the veil at Faremoutier. Erconwald recalled her from France to train her sister, Ethelburga of Barking (see Daily Readings, October 11, Ethelburga of Barking) to be an abbess. Hildelith remained at Barking as a nun under Ethelburga, and in 675 she became the abbess of Barking. She had a reputation of being both a good administrator and a good confidante for her sisters, although she trained them in a strict Benedictine Rule. She had many relics translated into her church for veneration. Hildelith enlarged her monastery, and it grew to become a great cultural center. Aldhelm, abbot of Malmesbury, and Boniface, who evangelized Germany, personally knew and praised her. Aldhelm dedicated a treatise on virginity to her. Bede, the English historian, also held her in high regard. She lived to a very old age. The exact year of her death in uncertain, but it probably occurred around 721–727.

Very little is known about Cumania, an early Irish saint and sister of St. Columba of Iona. She founded monasteries in Ireland and on the island of Iona (Scotland). She was the mother of St. Caimin whose life of contemplation and austerity drew many to him. Cumania died in 597.

Prayer:

Almighty God, you have surrounded us with a cloud of witnesses to your saving love, and we give thanks for the many women who served you in the contemplative life. They serve us also, as models who attempted to be perfect, as Jesus encouraged us to attempt. Grant us, during our earthly pilgrimage, to abide in their fellowship and to grow in your grace. Amen.

Antiphon:

Our hearts are drawn to glorify you, O God.

Readings:

"With my whole heart I have sought You; Oh, let me not wander from Your commandments! Your word I have hidden in my heart, That I might not sin against You. Blessed are You, O LORD! Teach me Your statutes." *Psalm 119:10–12 (NKJV)*

". . . of which I became a minister according to the stewardship from God which was given to me for you, to fulfill the word of God,

the mystery which has been hidden from ages and from generations, but now has been revealed to His saints. To them God
willed to make known what are the riches of the glory of this mystery among the Gentiles: which is Christ in you, the hope of
glory." *Col. 1:25–27 (NKJV)*

"Jesus said to them, 'My food is to do the will of Him who sent Me,
and to finish His work.'" *Jn. 4:34 (NKJV)*

DECEMBER 22 Elizabeth of Austria

Elizabeth was born the daughter of Emperor Maximilian II
of Austria in 1554, and she married King Charles of France
when she was fifteen. She returned to Vienna four years
later, when Charles died, and vowed not to remarry. She joined the
Secular Franciscans, and, striving to avoid the public eye, she entered
into a period of seclusion and prayer. Elizabeth was later inspired to
serve the sick in hospitals and in their homes, bringing them medicine and words of hope. In remembrance of the Last Supper of Jesus,
she opened her table to the poor on Thursdays. Interested in education, she sponsored many young men into the priesthood, and she
used her fortune in the service of the Church. She often cooked for
the poor at the Poor Clare convent that she had founded, where she
derived satisfaction in simple menial work. When she died at age
thirty-eight, the citizens of Vienna and her beloved Franciscan brothers and sisters mourned her. Miracles were reported at her tomb. Although not officially sainted, Elizabeth is included in numerous books
that record lives of the saints as a servant of God.

Intercessory Prayer:

*O holy Elizabeth, you recognized that wealth and status cannot
purchase happiness, but those who come to God with clean hands
and a pure heart shall receive a blessing from the most high. Your
justice toward the weak shone like a radiance of hope, as you
invited them to the Lord's table. Pray with us for those who have
lost spouses and for the infirm; may they find their solace in the
one who bore all of our ills. Amen.*

Antiphon:

The earth is the Lord's and all that is in it.

Readings:

"You prepare a table before me in the presence of my enemies; You anoint my head with oil; My cup runs over. Surely goodness and mercy shall follow me. All the days of my life; And I will dwell in the house of the LORD Forever." *Psalm 23:5–6 (NKJV)*

"All the saints salute you. The grace of the Lord Jesus Christ and the love of God, and the communion of the Holy Ghost be with you all." *2 Cor. 13:14 (KJV)*

"By this we know love, that he laid down his life for us; and we ought to lay down our lives for the brethren. But if any one has the world's goods and sees his brother in need, yet closes his heart against him, how does God's love abide in him? Little children, let us not love in word or speech but in deed and in truth." *1 Jn. 3:16–18 (RSV)*

DECEMBER 23 Marguerite d'Youville

Born in eighteenth-century Quebec, Marguerite d'Youville was the eldest of six children. When her father passed away leaving them without income, she became the principal support for her siblings. At age twenty, life seemed to hold many promises as she was wed to a handsome and successful suitor named François. However, it soon became apparent that he was successful through a very dishonorable profession: trading liquor to the Indians for furs. Marguerite suffered the humiliation of a husband who was always on the road, drinking, gambling, and squandering the family's resources. She had several children, but lost one after another to various illnesses and tragedies. Two of her sons did survive, and it is a great tribute to Marguerite's influence and prayers that both eventually became priests. When Marguerite's husband died, she felt called to practice her faith by assisting the poorest and most neglected of society. Her charisma eventually attracted other women who also wished to assist homeless and mentally unstable women whom no one else wanted. They eventually were officially established as a congregation that became known as The Grey Nuns, which currently has thousands of members worldwide. Marguerite died at age seventy, and she was beatified in 1959.

Prayer:

Almighty God, you gave us Blessed Marguerite as a shining example of a woman called to minister to the poorest and most forgotten members of society. She was also a woman who suffered greatly in her personal life. Yet these personal tragedies opened the door of compassion in her heart so that she could assist those in society who were in greater need than herself. Give us grace to emulate her in seeing beyond the problems in our daily lives so we can also reach out to others in need. Amen.

Antiphon:

I desire mercy and not sacrifice; I did not come to call the virtuous.

Readings:

"Thus my heart was grieved, And I was vexed in my mind. I *was* so foolish and ignorant; I was *like* a beast before You. Nevertheless I *am* continually with You; You hold *me* by my right hand. You will guide me with Your counsel, And afterward receive me *to* glory. Whom have I in heaven *but You?* And *there is* none upon earth *that* I desire besides You. My flesh and my heart fail; *But* God *is* the strength of my heart and my portion forever." *Psalm 73:21–26 (NKJV)*

"I cried out to the LORD because of my affliction, And He answered me. Out of the belly of Sheol I cried, *And* You heard my voice. For You cast me into the deep, Into the heart of the seas, And the floods surrounded me; All Your billows and Your waves passed over me. Then I said, 'I have been cast out of Your sight; Yet I will look again toward Your holy temple.'" *Jon. 2:2–4 (NKJV)*

"For we, *though* many, are one bread *and* one body; for we all partake of that one bread." *1 Cor. 10:17 (NKJV)*

DECEMBER 24 Constance of Aragon
and Eugenia

Constance of Aragon is honored in the old Franciscan calendar on this, the eve of Our Lord's Nativity. Her father, Manfred, son of Emperor Frederick II, was a greedy nobleman who usurped the kingdom of Sicily against the Pope's wishes. Because of this and other serious disagreements, he was excommunicated. Constance, in fear for her father's soul, prayed and fasted for him continually. She married the King of Aragon, and one of her children, Elizabeth of Portugal (see Daily Readings, July 4, Elizabeth of Portugal), became a saint. When Charles of Anjou robbed her father of his throne and murdered him, she visited him in prison and forgave him. After her husband's death, Constance held the reins of government for eight years, after which she abdicated her throne and entered a Poor Clare convent. She spent the last sixteen years of her life there, where she was reputed to have lived a life of contemplation and prayer. Constance died in 1301.

In the East, this is also the feast day of St. Eugenia of Alexandria. She lived during the period of the early Church Father Origen, and she was converted by reading his works. She was persecuted for her faith and died in 257. Her legend narrates that she was thrown into a fiery furnace, but did not burn. Eugenia is reported to have died on the feast of the Nativity, after receiving a vision of Christ in her jail cell.

Prayer:

Dear Jesus, our Lord and Savior, both Constance and Eugenia were blessed with the great grace of your loving-kindness. You have honored them by making the eve of your blessed Nativity their feast day. Through their intercession, grant that we, who joyfully receive you as our redeemer, may be made your children by adoption, renewed and strengthened by your Spirit. Amen.

Antiphon:

We know that a person is not justified by works of law but by faith in Jesus Christ.

"Bless the LORD, O my soul, And forget not all His benefits: Who forgives all your iniquities, Who heals all your diseases, Who redeems your life from destruction, Who crowns you with lovingkindness and tender mercies, Who satisfies your mouth with good things, *So that* your youth is renewed like the eagle's. The LORD executes righteousness and justice for all who are oppressed." *Psalm 103:2–6 (NKJV)*

"But rise and stand on your feet; for I have appeared to you for this purpose, to make you a minister and a witness both of the things which you have seen and of the things which I will yet reveal to you . . . *to open their eyes, in order to turn them from darkness to light.*" *Acts 26:16–18 (NKJV)*

DECEMBER 25 Anastasia and the Nativity of Our Lord

St. Anastasia was an early Christian martyr in the second century who has the austere honor of celebrating her feast day on Jesus Christ's birthday. She was highly venerated in Rome from the earliest days of the Church, and the second Mass of Christmas Day is traditionally celebrated in her honor in Rome. Tradition tells us that she helped to hide Christians during the persecution. She was married to a pagan of nobility and often borrowed clothes from the servants to escape notice when she slipped out to visit fellow Christians in prison to bring them food and medicine. For her kindness, the Greeks called her "the healer" or "medicine woman." After her husband died, she was eventually arrested and jailed. Her legend tells us that during this time, Theodota, a friend who already had been martyred, appeared to her and fed her to keep her alive. Anastasia was later put on a ship that was to be released at sea and abandoned, but was miraculously saved when the ship came to shore. Finally, St. Anastasia followed the path of her saintly assistant, St. Theodota, and was burned alive in Palmaria. Both women are celebrated in the Eastern Church on December 22. Anastasia is patron of those lost at sea.

Prayer:

Almighty God, you gave us brave women like St. Anastasia to draw others to know Jesus Christ through their heroic lives of virtue. She paid the ultimate price for her love and defense of Christianity by winning the crown of martyrdom. Inspire us to imitate her life, especially helping to relieve others of their suffering. Help us in times of trial, for you alone give our suffering meaning. Amen.

Antiphon:

My God; save me from all who persecute me and deliver me.

Readings:

"Blessed is the man
    Who walks not in the counsel of the ungodly,
    Nor stands in the path of sinners,
    Nor sits in the seat of the scornful;
But his delight is in the law of the LORD,
    And in His law he meditates day and night.
He shall be like a tree
    Planted by the rivers of water,
    That brings forth its fruit in its season,
    Whose leaf also shall not wither;
    And whatever he does shall prosper." *Psalm 1:1–3 (NKJV)*

"O LORD my God, in You I put my trust; Save me from all those who persecute me; And deliver me." *Psalm 7:1 (NKJV)*

"Those who are well have no need of a physician, but those who are sick . . ." *Mt. 9:12 (NKJV)*

DECEMBER 26 *Kykkos Icon of the Theotokos*

The wonder-working icon of the Theotokos known as *Kykkos* or *Kikkiotissa* is an Eleousa (Merciful) type. Originally, the icon belonged to one of the earliest Christian communities in Egypt, and it has distinct Oriental features. Later *Kykkos* was brought to Constantinople, where it stayed until the time of Emperor Alexis Comneus (eleventh century), who transferred it to the island of Cyprus. Before this time, a desert-dweller named Isaiah had made a prediction that the icon would find its home in Cyprus, on the Kykkos mountain. When the prophecy was fulfilled, the icon became an instant miracle worker. A monastery and church were built for it, and the sick and infirm came from many miles to pray before it. Archbishop Makarios—president of Cyprus and head of the Church in Cyprus until his death in 1977—greatly revered the icon. The beautiful face of the Mother, intercessor of all who suffer, reveals that she offers the mercies that flow from her son. In the *Kykkos* icon, Christ does not sit on her lap facing his mother. Rather, they are both facing the same way, as they look out on the world with compassion toward those who invoke help and protection. Since the Ottoman rule, this particular Theotokos icon has been famous for drawing people of other faiths, including Muslim, to her side. *Kykko*'s feast days are also celebrated on November 12 and August 11.

Intercessory Prayer:

O Mother of God, Christ your Son has glorified you so that we could see the Church's unspoiled potential in you, his everlasting promise of mercy. Through you, grace bore its first fruits, bringing the beginning of joy for all the world. We pray that, as you would have gathered us together as a mother bird gathers her young, we will respond to your call by loving one another without judgment or condemnation. Weave us into God's family, so we may eternally sing the praises of your Son and our God, our Lord Jesus Christ. Amen.

Antiphon:

Comfort and heal all those who suffer.

Readings:

"I will praise You with my whole heart; Before the gods I will sing praises to You. I will worship toward Your holy temple, And praise Your name For Your lovingkindness and Your truth; For You have magnified Your word above all Your name. In the day when I cried out, You answered me, And made me bold with strength in my soul." *Psalm 138:1–3 (NKJV)*

"Today the Virgin is on her way to the cave where she will give birth in a manner beyond understanding to the Word who is in all eternity. Rejoice therefore, universe, when you hear it heralded." *—December Matins*

"For with God nothing will be impossible." *Lk. 1:37 (NKJV)*

DECEMBER 27 Christina Ebner

Christina Ebner was born in 1277 in Nuremberg, and she is one of the most popular mystics in Germany. Although she felt that one act of love was greater than all of her supernatural encounters, she certainly had a lifetime of mystical experiences. At age seven, she wanted to go to a monastery; her dream was realized several years later when she entered a Dominican convent at Engelthal, where she eventually became mother superior. A follower of the Eckhart school of German mysticism, she said that her teacher, John Tauler (a disciple of Eckhart's), had a fiery tongue, filled with the Holy Spirit. When she was twenty-four, she dreamed that she was pregnant with the Lord Jesus. She felt so full of his grace during periods of her life that she wrote once in her diary (later to become *Ecstatic Confessions*) that his love permeated every limb of her body. She reported that he said, "I will make you noble from my noble nature; I make you worthy from my nobility. I have bewedded you with the dew of divinity." She once asked him why he poured out his grace so abundantly on her, and he said, "The world is continually in unrest. Therefore wherever I find a restful heart, I am glad to be there." She was noted for her counseling; Charles IV came to her for advice. Christina died December 27, 1355, at her monastery.

Prayer:

> *Sweetest Jesus, you endowed your beloved Christina with such a mystical love, she was lost in you as a drop in the ocean. We know that by immersing ourselves in silence and being attentive, we learn to listen to your heavenly voice, and in that voice, we find ourselves engulfed in such happiness that no words can express it. May we, like Christina, find in you such a hidden fountain of joy that we truly understand that nothing in life or death can separate us from God's love. Amen.*

Antiphon:

God is in his temple; let all the earth keep silent.

Readings:

"You will keep *him* in perfect peace, *whose* mind *is* stayed *on You,* because he trusts in You. . . . For thus says the Lord GOD, the Holy One of Israel: 'In returning and rest you shall be saved; In quietness and confidence shall be your strength.' But you would not." *Isa. 26:3; 30:15 (NKJV)*

"For we do not preach ourselves, but Christ Jesus the Lord, and ourselves your bondservants for Jesus' sake. For it is the God who commanded light to shine out of darkness, who has shone in our hearts to *give* the light of the knowledge of the glory of God in the face of Jesus Christ." *2 Cor. 4:5–6 (NKJV)*

DECEMBER 28 Margaret Stadler and Mary Fontanella

Margaret Stadler is remembered in the old Franciscan calendar on December 28. Most of what we know of her is legend. Following the inspiration of her beloved spiritual father, Francis of Assisi, who was devoted to the infant Jesus, she spent many hours contemplating Christ's childhood. She lived in a convent at Sefflingen, where she worked in the kitchen. The story is told that once, when she was absorbed in meditation on God's lovableness in the infant child, she forgot about her cooking duties until well past supper. When she went down to the kitchen, she discovered that a beautiful little boy had prepared the meal, making the most delicious meal the sisters had ever been served. Margaret died in 1521, and she was remembered as a deeply caring soul, who treated everyone like they were an image of the Christ child.

Blessed Mary Fontanella was a Carmelite visionary who came from a noble family in Turin. Against her parents' wishes, she entered the convent at Turin, where she eventually served as mother superior. Her life was marked by numerous mystical experiences and by a long dark night of the soul when she felt abandoned by God and convinced of her worthlessness. She emerged from this trial into a state of peace, knowing a closer union with God. Mary died in 1661 and was beatified in 1865.

Prayer:

Christ our Savior, you took the form of a babe and came to show us your love and empathy by walking the same path and experiencing the same trials we do. You are our hope and our light; we need you more than the air that we breathe. Through the intercession of Margaret and Blessed Mary Fontanella, bring us also to your table so we may sing a song of love with the angels. Amen.

Antiphon:

We have come to know God's love for us.

Readings:

"For You *are* the God of my strength; why do You cast me off? Why do I go mourning because of the oppression of the enemy? Oh, send out Your light and Your truth! Let them lead me; let them bring me to your holy hill and to Your tabernacle. Then I will go to the altar of God, to God my exceeding joy; and on the harp I will praise You, O God, my God." *Psalm 43:2–4 (NKJV)*

"In that day the deaf shall hear the words of the book, and the eyes of the blind shall see out of obscurity and out of darkness. The humble also shall increase *their* joy in the LORD, and the poor among men shall rejoice in the Holy One of Israel." *Isa. 29:18–19 (NKJV)*

"Therefore I prayed, and understanding was given me; I called upon God, and the spirit of wisdom came to me. I preferred her to scepters and thrones, and I accounted wealth as nothing in comparison with her." *Wis. 7:7–8 (RSV)*

DECEMBER 29 Margaret Colonna

Margaret Colonna was born the daughter of Prince Odo Colonna of Palestrina, which was one of the most powerful princely houses of Rome. Orphaned at an early age, she was left to care for her two brothers, one of whom became her biographer after her death. When she was an adolescent, she refused several offers of marriage and withdrew alone to her country home on the outskirts of Palestrina. She later founded a Poor Clare convent there that was noted for its charity to the poor. She received many supernatural graces, including the foreknowledge of events. Her brother became cardinal of Colonna, and he was instrumental in helping her to found the Urbanist Poor Clares. During the last seven years of her life, Margaret suffered from cancer, which she concealed as long as she could. When he discovered it, her brother, then her spiritual director, ordered her to stop her voluntary austerities. Her brother's *vita* indicates that her tumor devoured much of her skin and flesh, yet she bore it with great magnanimity. Margaret died peacefully in 1284, and Pope Pius IX beatified her in 1847.

Prayer:

Almighty God, we are totally dependent on you for help to sustain us when we suffer. Through Blessed Margaret's inspiration, help us to bear our crosses with courage and hope in you. We are flowers quickly fading, we are vapors in the wind, O Immortal God, and we trust in you to sustain us. Although we live in a terror-filled world, the one thing we know is that you will never let us go. Help us to bear our own deaths with dignity. Amen.

Antiphon:

You give light to those who sit in darkness.

Readings:

"As far as the east is from the west, so far has He removed our transgressions from us. . . . But the mercy of the LORD is from everlasting to everlasting . . . His righteousness to children's children." *Psalm 103:12, 17 (NKJV)*

"My heart is severely pained within me, and the terrors of death have fallen upon me. Fearfulness and trembling have come upon me, and horror has overwhelmed me. So I said, 'Oh, that I had wings like a dove! I would fly away and be at rest. Indeed, I would wander far off, and remain in the wilderness.'" *Psalm 55:4–7 (NKJV)*

"Love has been perfected among us in this: that we may have boldness in the day of judgment; because as [Christ] is, so are we in this world. There is no fear in love; but perfect love casts out fear, because fear involves torment. But he who fears has not been made perfect in love." *1 Jn. 4:17–18 (NKJV)*

DECEMBER 30 Thomias of Lesbos

St. Thomias was born in the early tenth century on the island of Lesbos near Constantinople, and her life story was written shortly after her death. She is one of the few married women

of her era to be honored as a saint. Her parents had a happy life together, and the author of Thomias's *vita* referred to them as a "golden
team." Like other Byzantine women, she lived with her parents until
her marriage, which was tumultuous and tragic. A victim of abuse by
her husband, Stephen, she is hailed as a martyr in her *vita*. Passionately devoted to prayer and good works, Thomias spent her time at
church or else at home weaving clothes, which she then distributed to
the poor. On one occasion, she stripped herself of the only garment
she had on to give to a naked beggar on the street. After repeated
beatings, Stephen eventually forbade her to leave the house. Prohibit-
ing her from attending liturgical services was said to be the greatest
blow he dealt to Thomias. Her favorite place of prayer was the temple
at Blachernae (see Daily Readings, July 31, *Virgin Blachernitissa:
Dedication of the Temple at Blachernae*). Her first miracle happened when she took the sacred oil from the lamp in front of the
Virgin of Blachernae and cured a man possessed of demons. Many
other miracles are told about her life, but she was never able to ex-
orcise the demon in her own husband, at least during her lifetime.
After thirteen years of torturous beatings, she died at age thirty-
eight, childless. Her tomb became a locus of many healings and ex-
orcisms, including eventually Stephen's. Possessed by a demon that
caused him great torment, he finally found repentance and forgiveness at the tomb of his blessed wife, St. Thomias.

Intercessory Prayer:

*Dear holy Thomias, you knew that even in the midst of terrible
bitterness and abuse, the only real freedom was forgiveness. You
understood well the sinner, especially those who were obsessed, for
it is only when we know how far we have fallen that our love and
gratitude grow for him who was bitterly abused on the cross. Pray
for women who are victims of abuse today, that they may have the
courage to extricate themselves from danger and to forgive their
oppressors. May God grant them freedom from fear and the
courage to explore a new life in the joy of Christ Jesus. Amen.*

Antiphon:

Deliver us from evil.

Readings:

"I remembered God, and was troubled;
  I complained, and my spirit was overwhelmed. Selah

You hold my eyelids open;
    I am so troubled that I cannot speak.
I have considered the days of old,
    The years of ancient times.
I call to remembrance my song in the night;
    I meditate within my heart,
And my spirit makes diligent search." *Psalm 77:3–6 (NKJV)*

"So I said, 'Who are You, Lord?' And He said, 'I am Jesus, whom you are persecuting.'" *Acts 26:15 (NKJV)*

"We are hard-pressed on every side, yet not crushed; we are perplexed, but not in despair; persecuted, but not forsaken; struck down, but not destroyed." *2 Cor. 4:8–9 (NKJV)*

DECEMBER 31 Christina of Brusthem

St. Christiana of Brusthem, also known as Christina the Astonishing, was one of those marginal mystics who would have earned the title of Holy Fool if she had been canonized in one of the Eastern churches. Orphaned at an early age, she lived on the outskirts of Liege in the Low Countries, begging for alms. When she was twenty-two, she had a near-death experience that altered her life forever. Assumed dead, she sat up in her coffin during the funeral Mass and announced that she had visited heaven and hell. She exhibited erratic behavior for many years afterward, including climbing into dangerously high towers and trees, and into ovens, because she could not bear the smell of sinful humans. Christina often prayed while curled up into a contortionist ball. It was said that she could handle fire with impunity and could free herself when confined. Many thought she was crazy or possessed by the devil. Yet she was devoted to the Eucharist and once, when a priest who did not know her refused her Communion, she ran wildly away in grief and jumped into the river. Some Cistercian nuns eventually took her in, and her previous social marginalization became transformed. It was discovered that she could predict human events and was able to reprimand people for their secret sins, calling them to penance. She spent the remainder of her life in the convent of St. Catherine at Saint-Trond, where numerous famous people—including Count Louis of Looz and St. Lutgardis—sought her counsel. Christina died peacefully at age seventy-four.

Prayer:

Merciful and wondrous God, when Christina's body died to the world, her soul opened up to you in magnificent and strange new ways. Struggling to understand her inner voices, she revealed to many that your ways subvert the ways of the world, turning things upside down. Help us to be aware of times when we are critical of someone else's unconventional behavior, remembering always that the wisdom of the world may be quite foolish in your eyes. Give us the grace to see you behind the eyes of those who live on the streets. Amen.

Antiphon:

We are fools for Christ's sake, but we are wise in Christ.

Readings:

"But the humble in spirit will retain honor." *Prov. 29:23 (NKJV)*

"Let no one deceive himself. If anyone among you seems to be wise in this age, let him become a fool that he may become wise. For the wisdom of this world is foolishness with God. For it is written, 'He catches the wise in their own craftiness'; and again, 'The LORD knows the thoughts of the wise, that they are futile.'" *1 Cor. 3:18–20 (NKJV)*

"There are diversities of gifts, but the same Spirit. There are differences of ministries, but the same Lord." *1 Cor. 12:4–5 (NKJV)*

"Therefore tongues are for a sign, not to those who believe but to unbelievers; but prophesying is not for unbelievers but for those who believe." *1 Cor. 14:22 (NKJV)*

"For he who is the least among you all, is the one who is great." *Lk. 9:48 (RSV)*

Bibliography

Alacoque, Margaret Mary. *The Autobiography of Margaret Mary*. Translation of the French Text by the Sisters of the Visitation. Rockford, IL: Tan Books, 1986.

Attwater, Donald. *Penguin Dictionary of Saints*. Baltimore, MD: Penguin Books, 1965.

Atwell, Robert, and Christopher Webber, eds. *Celebrating the Saints: Devotional Readings for Saints' Days*. Harrisburg, PA: Morehouse Publishing, 2001.

Avila, Teresa of. *The Autobiography of St. Teresa of Avila, Including the Relations*. Translated by David Lewis. Rockford, IL: Tan Books, 1997.

Beasley-Topliffe, Keith, ed. *The Soul's Delight: Selected Writings of Evelyn Underhill*. Nashville, TN: Upper Room Books, 1998.

Bede. *A History of the English Church and People. Book 4*. Baltimore, MD: Penguin Books, 1968.

Bellis, Alice Ogden. *Helpmates, Harlots and Heroes: Women's Stories in the Hebrew Bible*. Louisville, KY: Westminister/John Knox Press, 1994.

Benedictine Monks of St. Augustine Abbey, Ramsgate. *The Book of Saints*. 5th ed. New York: Thomas Y. Crowell Company, 1966.

Bielecki, Tessa. *Holy Daring*. Shaftesbury, Dorset: Element Books, 1994.

Brown, Raymond, et al. *Mary in the New Testament*. New York: Paulist Press, 1978.

Brunn, Emilie Zum, and Georgette Epiney-Burgard. *Women Mystics in Medieval Europe*. Translated by Sheila Hughes. New York: Paragon House, 1989.

Bunson, Matthew, Margaret Bunson, and Stephen Bunson. *John Paul II's Book of Saints*. Huntington, IN: Our Sunday Visitor Publishing Division, 1999.

Byrne, Lavinia, ed. *The Hidden Tradition: Women's Spiritual Writings Revisited*. New York: Crossroad, 1991.

Carmelites of Indianapolis. *People's Companion to the Breviary, Volumes 1 and 2; The Liturgy of the Hours with Inclusive Language*. Indianapolis, IN: Carmelite Monastery, 1997.

Carmody, Denise Lardner. *Biblical Women: Contemporary Reflections on Scriptural Texts*. New York: Crossroad, 1989.

Catafygiotu-Topping, Eva. *Holy Mothers of Orthodoxy*. St. Louis Park, MN: Light and Life Publishing Co., 1987.

——. *Saints and Sisterhood: The Lives of Forty-Eight Holy Women*. St. Louis Park, MN: Light and Life Publishing Co., 1990.

Coon, Lyda L. *Sacred Fictions: Holy Women and Hagiography in Late Antiquity*. Philadelphia: University of Pennsylvania Press, 1997.

Corrigan, Kevin (trans., with introduction and notes) Gregory of Nyssa, Saint. *The Life of Saint Macrina*. Toronto, Ontario: Peregrina Publishing Co., 1995.

Cowan, Tom. *The Way of the Saints*. New York: Berkley Publishing Group, 1998.

Cunnees, Sally. *In Search of Mary: The Woman and the Symbol*. New York: Ballantine Books, 1996.

D'Alzon, Emmanuel. *Mary, Our Mother, Our Model, and Our Queen*. Brooklyn, NY: New City Press, 1988.

Davis, Courtney, and Elaine Gill. *The Book of Celtic Saints*. Blandford, UK: Sterling Publishing, 1995.

Delaney, John J. *Dictionary of Saints*. Abridged ed. Garden City, NY: Image Books, 1983.

De Sola Chervin, Ronda. *Prayers of the Women Mystics*. Ann Arbor, MI: Servant Publications, 1992.

——. *Treasury of Women Saints*. Ann Arbor, MI: Servant Publications. 1991.

Doyle, Brendan. *Meditations with Julian of Norwich*. Sante Fe, NM: Bear & Company, 1983.

Earle, Mary, and Sylvia Maddox. *Praying with the Celtic Saints*. Winona, MN: St. Mary's Press, 2000.

Ellsberg, Robert. *All Saints: Daily Reflections on Saints, Prophets, and Witnesses for Our Time*. New York: Crossroad, 2001.

Farley, Lawrence R. *A Daily Calendar of Saints*. St. Louis Park, MN: Light and Life Publishing Co., 1997.

Farmer, David Hugh. *The Oxford Dictionary of Saints*. 3rd ed. New York: Oxford University Press, 1992.

———. *Oxford Dictionary of Saints.* 4ᵗʰ ed. New York: Oxford University Press, 1997.

Fenn, Richard. *The Persistence of Purgatory.* Cambridge, MA, and New York: Cambridge University Press, 1995.

Flinders, Carol Lee. *Enduring Grace: Living Portraits of Seven Women Mystics.* San Francisco: HarperSanFrancisco, 1993.

Fox, Matthew. *Illuminations of Hildegard of Bingen.* Sante Fe, NM: Bear & Company, 1985.

Furlong, Monica. *Visions and Longings: Medieval Women Mystics.* Boston: Shambhala, 1996.

Gangloff, Sister Mary Francis, O.S.F. *Remarkable Women, Remarkable Wisdom.* Cincinnati, OH: Anthony Messenger Press, 2001.

Green, Deirdre. *Gold in the Crucible: Teresa of Avila and the Western Mystical Tradition.* Shaftesbury, Dorset: Element Books, 1989.

Harakas, Emily. *Through the Year with the Church Fathers.* St. Louis Park, MN: Light and Life Publishing Co., 1997.

Hildegard of Bingen. *Mystical Writings.* Edited and introduction by Fiona Bowie and Oliver Davies. With new translations by Robert Carver. New York: Crossroad, 1990.

Holy Apostles Convent. *The Lives of the Spiritual Mothers: An Orthodox Materikon of Women Monastics and Ascetics.* Translated and compiled from "The Great Synaxaristes of the Orthodox Church." Buena Vista, CO: Holy Apostles Convent, 1993.

Humphreys, Carolyn. *From Ash to Fire: A Contemporary Journey through the Interior Castle of Teresa of Avila.* New Rochelle, NY: New City Press, 1992.

Jones, Alison. *The Wordsworth Dictionary of Saints.* Ware, Hertfordshire: Wordsworth Editions, Ltd., 1994.

Jones, Kathleen. *Women Saints: Lives of Faith and Courage.* Maryknoll, NY: Orbis Books, 2000.

Joyce, Timothy. *Celtic Christianity: A Sacred Tradition, A Vision of Hope.* Maryknoll, NY: Orbis Books, 2001.

Kellion of St. Anthony the Great. *Wondrous Is God in His Saints.* Alamogordo, NM: St. Anthony the Great Orthodox Publications, 1985.

Liturgy of the Hours: Celebrating the Saints. New York: Pueblo Publishing Co., 1978.

Lord, Bob, and Penny Lord. *Saints and Other Powerful Women in the Church.* Westlake Village, CA: Journeys of Faith, 1989.

Luce, Clare Booth, ed. *Saints for Now.* New York: Sheed & Ward, 1952.

Massey, Lesly F. *Women and the New Testament.* Jefferson, NC, and London: McFarland and Co., Inc., 1989.

Maximovitch, Saint John. *The Orthodox Veneration of Mary, The Birthgiver of*

God. Translated and introduction by Fr. Seraphim Rose. Platina, CA: Saint Herman of Alaska Brotherhood, 1994.

McBrien, Richard P. *Lives of the Saints*. San Francisco: HarperSanFrancisco, 2001.

McCloskey, Pat, O.F.M. *Day by Day with Followers of Francis and Clare*. Cincinnati, OH: St. Anthony Messenger Press, 1999.

McEntire, Sandra J, ed. *Julian of Norwich: A Book of Essays*. New York: Garland Publishers, Inc., 1998.

McNamara, JoAnn, John E. Halborg, and Gordon Whatley. *Sainted Women of the Dark Ages*. Durham, NC, and London: Duke University Press, 1994.

Meehan, Bridget Mary. *Praying with Women of the Bible*. Liguori, MO: Liguori Publishing, 1998.

Meehan, Bridget Mary, and Regina Madonna Oliver. *Praying with Celtic Holy Women*. Liguori, MO: Ligouri/Triumph, 2003.

Metford, J.C.J. *Dictionary of Christian Lore and Legend*. London: Thames and Hudson, 1983.

Mitton, Michael. *The Soul of Celtic Christianity*. Mystic, CT: Twenty-third Publications, 1996.

Obbard, Elizabeth Ruth. *A Year with Mary*. Norwich, Norfolk: Canterbury Press, 1998.

Pennick, Nigel. *Celtic Saints; Passionate Wanderers*. New York: Thames & Hudson, 2000.

Pennington, Basil M. *Mary Today*. New York and London: Doubleday, 1989.

Raya, Rev. Joseph, and Baron Jose deVinck. *Byzantine Daily Worship: Byzantine Breviary, the Three Liturgies, Propers of the Day and Various Offices*. Philadelphia, PA: Alleluia Press, National Pub. Co., 1969.

Sawyers, June Skinner. *Praying with Celtic Saints: Prophets, Martyrs and Poets*. Franklin, WI: Sheed & Ward, 2001.

Schmemann, Alexander. *The Virgin Mary: Celebration of Faith*. Vol. 3, *Sermons*. Translated by John A. Jillions. Crestwood, NY: St. Vladimir's Seminary Press, 1995.

Sellner, Edward. *The Wisdom of the Celtic Saints*. Notre Dame, IN: Ave Maria Press, 1993.

Society of Saint Francis. *Devotional Companion, With Calendar and Liturgical Texts*. Third Order, Community of St. Francis, American Province, 2004.

Stein, Edith. *Essays on Woman*, Vol. 2. 2nd ed. Translated by Freda Mary Oben. Washington, DC: ICS Publication, 1996.

Thaisia of Leushino, Abbess. *The Autobiography of a Spiritual Daughter of St. John of Kronstadt*. Platina, CA: St. Herman of Alaska Brotherhood Press, 1989.

Thurston, Herbert, S.J., and Donald Attwater. *Butler's Lives of the Saints,*

Complete ed. Vol. 1, *January–March* and Vol. 4, *October–December*. New York: P.J. Kennedy & Sons, 1962.

Underhill, Evelyn. *Modern Guide to the Ancient Quest for the Holy*. Edited and introduction by Dana Greene. Albany: State University of New York Press, 1988.

———. *Mysticism: A Study in the Nature and Development of Man's Spiritual Consciousness*. New York: Signet, Mentor, Plume & Meridian Books, 1955.

Upson, Frieda. *Women of God*. Brookline, MA: Greek Orthodox Archdiocese of North and South America, 1978.

Walsh, Michael, ed. *Butler's Lives of the Saints*. San Francisco: HarperSanFrancisco, 1991.

Woods, Richard J. *Spirituality of the Celtic Saints*. Maryknoll, NY: Orbis Books, 2000.

Woodward, Kenneth L. *Making Saints: How the Catholic Church Determines Who Becomes a Saint, Who Doesn't, and Why*. New York: Simon & Schuster, 1990.

Zagano, Phyllis. *Woman to Woman: An Anthology of Women's Spiritualities*. Collegeville, MN: Liturgical Press, 1993.

THE
CROSSROAD
PUBLISHING
COMPANY

Robert Ellsberg
BLESSED AMONG ALL WOMEN
Women Saints, Prophets, and
Witnesses for Our time

Receive the Blessing!

From the bestselling author of *All Saints* comes this new collection of devotional meditations. The greatest women of *All Saints* join over 60 new women to share their unforgettable stories and draw us deeper into the mystery of the beatitudes—sanctity, the struggle for justice, poverty of spirit, and merciful love.

Among the dozens of women you meet are:

St. Mary Magdalene * St. Joan of Arc * Bd. Julian of Norwich * St. Therese of Lisieux * Bd. Mother Teresa * Sojourner Truth * Dorothy Day * Emily Dickinson * Anne Frank * Lady Godiva * St. Clare of Assisi * Hagar the Egyptian * St. Edith Stein * Mothers of the Disappeared * Sor Juana Ines de la Cruz * Flannery O'Connor * Mary

"A Stunning Achievement"

—JAMES MARTIN, S.J.,
author of *My Life with the Saints*

"Breathtakingly Beautiful."

—SISTER WENDY BECKETT,
host of Sister Wendy's Story of Painting

0-8245-2251-6, $19.95, hardcover

THE
CROSSROAD
PUBLISHING
COMPANY

Elizabeth Ficocelli
SHOWER OF HEAVENLY ROSES

Stories Of the Intercession of
St. Therese of Lisieux

Therese of Lisieux — Therese of the Little Flower — is universally recognized as one of the most influential saints of recent times. Since her death at an early age, countless miracles, healings, and life changes have been attributed to her inspiration and grace. In this book, Elizabeth Ficocelli, who herself experienced such a miracle, gathers together stories of Therese's grace, the "roses" she promised to send from heaven to the faithful. The book includes black and white art relating to Therese and photographs relating to the miracles.

0-8245-2256-7, $14.95, paperback

THE
CROSSROAD
PUBLISHING
COMPANY

Frederick Quinn
AFRICAN SAINTS

Saints, Martyrs, and Holy People
from the Continent of Africa

"The official calendar of the saints has long been
weighted toward the West. But in this era of the 'world
church' it is more important than ever to draw on the
inspiration and challenge of holy people from other
parts of the world. This important book reminds us of
the vital contributions of the African church, greatly
expanding that 'cloud of witnesses' who inspire and
challenge us on our path to holiness."
—ROBERT ELLSBERG, Editor-in-Chief of
Orbis Books, and author of *All Saints*

0-8245-1971-X, $22.95, paperback

Please support your local bookstore,
or call 1-800-707-0670 for Customer Service.
All prices subject to change.
For a free catalog, write to:
THE CROSSROAD PUBLISHING COMPNAY
16 Penn Plaza—481 Eighth Avenue, Suite 1550
New York, NY 10001
Visit our website at www.cpcbooks.com

THE
CROSSROAD
PUBLISHING
COMPANY